Final Report of the Thirty-seventh Antarctic Treaty Consultative Meeting

ANTARCTIC TREATY
CONSULTATIVE MEETING

Final Report
of the Thirty-seventh
Antarctic Treaty
Consultative Meeting

Brasilia, Brasil
28 April – 7 May 2014

Volume II

Secretariat of the Antarctic Treaty
Buenos Aires
2014

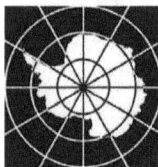

Published by:

Secretariat of the Antarctic Treaty
Secrétariat du Traité sur l' Antarctique
Секретариат Договора об Антарктике
Secretaría del Tratado Antártico

Maipú 757, Piso 4
C1006ACI Ciudad Autónoma
Buenos Aires - Argentina
Tel: +54 11 4320 4260
Fax: +54 11 4320 4253

This book is also available from: *www.ats.aq* (digital version)
and online-purchased copies.

ISSN 2346-9897
ISBN 978-987-1515-83-7

Contents

VOLUME I

Measure 11 (2014) Antarctic Specially Protected Area No 171 (Narębski Point, Barton Peninsula, King George Island): Revised Management Plan

Measure 12 (2014) Antarctic Specially Protected Area No 174 (Stornes, Larsemann Hills, Princess Elizabeth Land): Management Plan

Measure 13 (2014) Antarctic Specially Protected Area No 175 (High Altitude Geothermal Sites of the Ross Sea region): Management Plan

Measure 14 (2014) Antarctic Specially Managed Area No 1 (Admiralty Bay, King George Island): Revised Management Plan

Measure 15 (2014) Antarctic Specially Managed Area No 6 (Larsemann Hills, East Antarctica): Revised Management Plan

Measure 16 (2014) Antarctic Specially Protected Area No 114 (Northern Coronation Island, South Orkney Islands): Revoked Management Plan

2. Decisions

Decision 1 (2014) Measures on Operational Matters designated as no longer current
   Annex: Measures on Operational Matters designated as no longer current

Decision 2 (2014) Secretariat Report, Programme and Budget
   Annex 1: Audited Financial Report for 2012/2013
   Annex 2: Provisional Financial Report for 2013/14
   Annex 3: Secretariat Programme for 2014/15

Decision 3 (2014) Multi-year Strategic Work Plan for the Antarctic Treaty Consultative Meeting
   Annex: ATCM Multi-year Strategic Work Plan

3. Resolutions

Resolution 1 (2014) Fuel Storage and Handling

Resolution 2 (2014) Cooperation, Facilitation, and Exchange of Meteorological and Related Oceanographic and Cryospheric Environmental Information

Resolution 3 (2014) Supporting the Polar Code

Resolution 4 (2014) Site Guidelines for visitors
   Annex: List of Sites subject to Site Guidelines

Resolution 5 (2014) Strengthening Cooperation in Hydrographic Surveying and Charting of Antarctic Waters

Resolution 6 (2014) Toward a Risk-based Assessment of Tourism and Non-governmental Activities

Resolution 7 (2014) Entering into Force of Measure 4 (2004)

Heads of Delegation picture and picture diagram

VOLUME II

Acronyms and Abbreviations

ACAP	Agreement on the Conservation of Albatrosses and Petrels
ASMA	Antarctic Specially Managed Area
ASOC	Antarctic and Southern Ocean Coalition
ASPA	Antarctic Specially Protected Area
ATS	Antarctic Treaty System or Antarctic Treaty Secretariat
ATCM	Antarctic Treaty Consultative Meeting
ATME	Antarctic Treaty Meeting of Experts
BP	Background Paper
CCAMLR	Convention on the Conservation of Antarctic Marine Living Resources and/or Commission for the Conservation of Antarctic Living Resources
CCAS	Convention for the Conservation of Antarctic Seals
CEE	Comprehensive Environmental Evaluation
CEP	Committee for Environmental Protection
COMNAP	Council of Managers of National Antarctic Programs
DEM	Digital Elevation Model
EIA	Environmental Impact Assessment
EIES	Electronic Information Exchange System
HSM	Historic Site and Monument
IAATO	International Association of Antarctica Tour Operators
ICG	Intersessional Contact Group
IEE	Initial Environmental Evaluation
IHO	International Hydrographic Organization
IMO	International Maritime Organization
IOC	Intergovernmental Oceanographic Commission
IP	Information Paper
IPCC	Intergovernmental Panel on Climate Change
IUCN	International Union for Conservation of Nature
MPA	Marine Protected Area
RCC	Rescue Coordination Centre
SAR	Search and Rescue
SCAR	Scientific Committee on Antarctic Research
SC-CAMLR	Scientific Committee of CCAMLR
SGMP	Subsidiary Group on Management Plans

SOOS	Southern Ocean Observing System
SP	Secretariat Paper
TWG	Tourism Working Group
UAV	Unmanned Aerial Vehicle
UNEP	United Nations Environment Programme
UNFCCC	United Nations Framework Convention on Climate Change
WMO	World Meteorological Organization
WP	Working Paper
WTO	World Tourism Organization

PART II

Measures, Decisions and Resolutions (Cont.)

4. Management Plans

Management Plan for

Antarctic Specially Protected Area No. 113

LITCHFIELD ISLAND, ARTHUR HARBOR

ANVERS ISLAND, PALMER ARCHIPELAGO

Introduction

Litchfield Island lies within Arthur Harbor, SW Anvers Island, at 64°46' S, 64°06' W. Approximate area: 0.34 km². Designation on the grounds that Litchfield Island, together with its littoral zone, possesses an unusually high collection of marine and terrestrial life, is unique amongst the neighboring islands as a breeding place for six species of native birds and provides an outstanding example of the natural ecological system of the Antarctic Peninsula area. In addition, Litchfield Island possesses rich growths of vegetation and has the most varied topography and the greatest diversity of terrestrial habitats of the islands in Arthur Harbor.

The Area was originally designated as Specially Protected Area (SPA) No. 17 through Recommendation VIII-1 (1975) after a proposal by the United States of America. The site was renamed and renumbered as Antarctic Specially Protected Area (ASPA) No. 113 by Decision 1 (2002). The original Management Plan was adopted through Measure 2 (2004) and revised through Measure 4 (2009).

The Area is situated within Environment E – Antarctic Peninsula, Alexander and other islands based on the Environmental Domains Analysis for Antarctica and within Region 3 – Northwest Antarctic Peninsula based on the Antarctic Conservation Biogeographic Regions. Litchfield Island lies within Antarctic Specially Managed Area No.7 Southwest Anvers Island and Palmer Basin.

1. Description of values to be protected

Litchfield Island (Latitude 64°46' S, Longitude 64°06' W, 0.34 km²), Arthur Harbor, Anvers Island, Antarctic Peninsula was originally designated on the grounds that "Litchfield Island, together with its littoral, possesses an unusually high collection of marine and terrestrial life, is unique amongst the neighboring islands as a breeding place for six species of native birds and provides an outstanding example of the natural ecological system of the Antarctic Peninsula area".

The current management plan reaffirms the original reasons for designation associated with the bird communities. The island supports a diverse assemblage of bird species that is representative of the mid-western Antarctic Peninsula region. The number of bird species recorded as breeding on Litchfield Island is currently six, following the recent local extinction of Adélie penguins (*Pygoscelis adeliae*) on the island. Population decline has been attributed to the negative impact of increased snow accumulation and reduced sea ice extent on both food availability and survival of young (McClintock *et al.* 2008). The species continuing to breed on Litchfield Island are southern giant petrels (*Macronectes giganteus*), Wilson's storm petrels (*Oceanites oceanicus*), kelp gulls (*Larus dominicanus*), south polar skuas (*Stercorarius maccormicki*), brown skuas (*S. lonnbergi*), and Antarctic terns (*Sterna vittata*). The status of these bird colonies as being relatively undisturbed by human activities is also an important value of the Area.

In 1964 Litchfield Island supported one of the most extensive moss carpets known in the Antarctic Peninsula region, dominated by *Warnstorfia laculosa* which was then considered near its southern limit (Corner 1964a). *W. laculosa* is now known to occur at a number of sites further south, including Green Island (ASPA No. 108, in the Berthelot Islands) and Avian Island (ASPA No. 118, in Marguerite Bay). Accordingly, the value originally cited that this species is near its southern limit at Litchfield Island is no longer valid. Nevertheless, at the time Litchfield Island represented one of the best examples of maritime Antarctic vegetation off the western coast of Graham Land. Furthermore, several banks of *Chorisodontium aciphyllum* and *Polytrichum strictum* of up to 1.2 m in depth were described in 1982, which were considered to be some of the best examples of their kind in the Antarctic Peninsula area (Fenton and Lewis Smith 1982). In February 2001 it was observed that these values have been severely compromised by the impact of Antarctic fur seals (*Arctocephalus gazella*), which have damaged and destroyed large areas of vegetation on the lower accessible slopes of the island by trampling and nutrient enrichment. Southern elephant seals (*Mirounga leonina*) have also had a severe, although more localized, impact. Some areas previously richly carpeted by mosses have been completely destroyed, while others have suffered moderate-to-severe damage. Slopes of *Deschampsia antarctica* are more resilient and have persisted even where fur seals have been numerous, although here signs of damage are also obvious. However, on the steeper and higher parts of the island, and other areas that are inaccessible to seals, the vegetation remains undamaged. Furthermore, observations suggest that a recent local decline in Antarctic fur seal numbers has led to the recovery of previously damaged vegetation on Litchfield Island (Fraser and Patterson-Fraser pers. comms. 2014). While the vegetation is less extensive and some of the moss carpets have been compromised, the remaining vegetation continues to be of value and an important reason for special protection of the island. Litchfield Island also has the most varied topography and the greatest diversity of terrestrial habitats of the islands in Arthur Harbor.

The Antarctic Peninsula is currently experiencing regional warming at a rate that exceeds any other observed globally. The marine ecosystem surrounding Litchfield Island is undergoing substantial and rapid change in response to this climatic warming, which has included a decline in local Adélie penguin and Antarctic fur seal populations and changes in vegetation patterns. As such, maintenance of the relatively undisturbed state of Litchfield Island has potential value for long-term studies of this ecosystem.

Litchfield Island has been afforded special protection for most of the modern era of scientific activity in the region, with entry permits having been issued only for compelling scientific reasons. Litchfield Island has therefore never been subjected to intensive visitation, research or sampling and has value as a terrestrial area that has been relatively undisturbed by human activities. The Area is thus valuable as a reference site for some types of comparative studies with higher use areas, and where longer-term changes in the abundance of certain species and in the micro-climate can be monitored. The island is easily accessible by small boat from nearby Palmer Station (US), and Arthur Harbor is visited frequently by tourist ships. Continued special protection is therefore important to ensure the Area remains relatively undisturbed by human activities.

The designated Area is defined as including all of Litchfield Island above the low tide water level, excluding all offshore islets and rocks.

2. Aims and objectives

Management of Litchfield Island aims to:

- Avoid degradation of, or substantial risk to, the values of the Area by preventing unnecessary human disturbance and sampling in the Area;
- Allow scientific research on the ecosystem and physical environment in the Area provided it is for compelling reasons which cannot be served elsewhere and that will not compromise the values for which the Area is protected;
- Allow visits for educational and outreach purposes (such as documentary reporting (visual, audio or written) or the production of educational resources or services) provided such activities are for compelling reasons that cannot be served elsewhere and will not compromise the values for which the Area is protected;
- Minimize the possibility of introduction of alien plants, animals and microbes to the Area;
- Minimise the possibility of the introduction of pathogens that may cause disease in faunal populations within the Area; and
- Allow visits for management purposes in support of the aims of the management plan.

3. Management activities

The following management activities shall be undertaken to protect the values of the Area:

- Signs showing the location of the Area (stating the special restrictions that apply) shall be displayed prominently, and copies of this management plan, including maps of the Area, shall be made available at Palmer Station (US);

- Copies of this management plan shall be made available to all vessels and aircraft visiting the Area and/or operating in the vicinity of Palmer Station, and all personnel (national program staff, field expeditions, tourist expedition leaders, pilots and ship captains) operating in the vicinity of, accessing or flying over the Area, shall be informed by their national program, tour operator or appropriate national authority of the location, boundaries and restrictions applying to entry and overflight within the Area;

- National programs shall take steps to ensure the boundaries of the Area and the restrictions that apply within are marked on relevant maps and nautical / aeronautical charts;

- Markers, signs or other structures erected within the Area for scientific or management purposes shall be secured and maintained in good condition, and removed when no longer required;

- Visits shall be made as necessary (at least once every five years) to assess whether the Area continues to serve the purposes for which it was designated and to ensure management and maintenance measures are adequate.

4. Period of designation

Designated for an indefinite period.

5. Maps and photographs

Map 1: ASPA No. 113 Litchfield Island – Arthur Harbor, Anvers Island, showing the location of nearby stations (Palmer Station, US; Yelcho Station, Chile; Port Lockroy Historic Site and Monument No. 61, UK), the boundary of Antarctic Specially Managed Area No. 7 Southwest Anvers Island and Palmer Basin, and the location of nearby protected areas.
Projection: Lambert Conformal Conic; Central Meridian: 64° 00' W; Standard parallels: 64° 40' S, 65° 00' S; Latitude of Origin: 66° 00' S; Spheroid and horizontal datum: WGS84; Contour interval: Land – 250 m, Marine – 200 m.
Data sources: coastline & topography SCAR Antarctic Digital Database v4.1 (2005); Bathymetry: IBCSO v.1 (2013); Protected areas: ERA (Jul 2013); Stations: COMNAP (May 2013).
Inset: the location of Anvers Island and the Palmer Archipelago in relation to the Antarctic Peninsula.

Map 2: ASPA No. 113Litchfield Island: Physical features and selected wildlife.
Projection: Lambert Conformal Conic; Central Meridian: 64°06'W; Standard parallels: 64°46'S, 64°48'S; Latitude of Origin: 65°00'S; Spheroid and horizontal datum: WGS84; Vertical datum: mean sea level; Contour interval: Land – 5 m; Marine – 20 m; Coastline, topography, vegetation & southern elephant seal wallow derived from orthophoto (Feb 2009, ERA 2014) with a horizontal accuracy of ~ ± 2 m and a vertical accuracy of ~± 3 m; Bathymetry derived from Asper & Gallagher PRIMO survey (2004); Skuas: W. Fraser (2001-09); Former penguin colony: USGS Orthophoto (1998); Survey mark: USGS; Camp site, Boat landing site: RPSC; Protected area and zones: ERA (Jan 2014).

6. Description of the Area

6(i) Geographical coordinates, boundary markers and natural features

General description

Litchfield Island (64°46'15" S, 64°05'40" W, 0.34 km²) is situated in Arthur Harbor approximately 1500 m west of Palmer Station (US), Gamage Point, Anvers Island, in the region west of the Antarctic Peninsula known as the Palmer Archipelago (Map 1). Litchfield Island is one of the largest islands in Arthur Harbor, measuring approximately 1000 m northwest to southeast and 700 m from northeast to southwest. Litchfield Island has the most varied topography and the greatest diversity of terrestrial habitats of the islands in Arthur Harbor (Bonner and Lewis Smith 1985). Several hills rise to between 30-40 m, with the maximum elevation of 48 m being in the central western part of the island (Map 2). Rocky outcrops are common both on these slopes and on the coast. The island is predominantly ice-free in summer, apart from small snow patches occurring mainly on the southern slopes and in valleys. Cliffs of up to 10 m form the northeastern and southeastern coasts, with pebble beaches found in bays in the north and south.

The designated Area is defined as all of Litchfield Island above the low tide water level, excluding all offshore islets and rocks. The coast itself is a clearly defined and visually obvious boundary feature, so boundary markers have not been installed. Several signs drawing attention to the protected status of the island are in place and legible, although deteriorating (Fraser pers. comm. 2009).

Climate

Few meteorological data are available for Litchfield Island, although temperature data were collected at two north- and south-facing sites on Litchfield Island from January – March 1983 (Komárková 1983). The north-facing site was the warmer of the two, with January temperatures generally ranging between 2° to 9°C, February between -2° to 6°C, and March -2° to 4°C in 1983. A maximum temperature of 13°C and a minimum of -3°C were recorded at this site over this period. The south-facing site was generally about 2°C cooler, with January temperatures generally ranging between 2° to 6°C, February between -2° to 4°C, and March -3° to 2°C. A maximum temperature of 9°C and a minimum of -4.2°C were recorded at the south-facing site.

Longer-term data available for Palmer Station show regional temperatures to be relatively mild because of local oceanographic conditions and because of the frequent and persistent cloud cover in the Arthur Harbor region (Lowry 1975). Yearly air temperature averages recorded at Palmer Station during the period 1974 to 2012 show a distinct warming trend but also demonstrate significant inter-annual variability (Figure 1). The maximum temperature recorded during the period was 11.6° C in March 2010, whilst the minimum was −26° C in August 1995. Previous studies have identified August as the coldest month and January as the warmest (Baker 1996). Storms and precipitation at Palmer Station are frequent, with winds being persistent but generally light to moderate in strength, prevailing from the northeast.

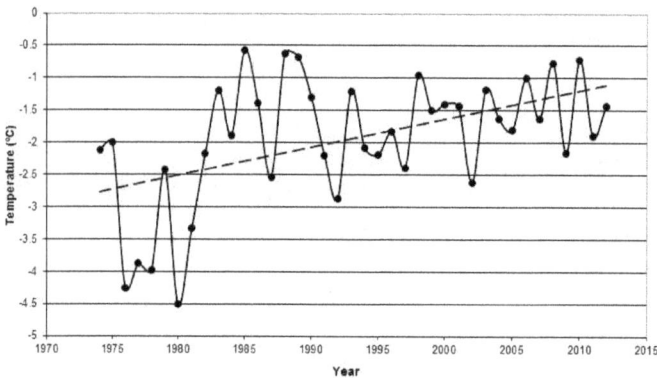

Figure 1. Mean annual surface air temperature at Palmer Station 1974 – 2012.
Data source: Palmer LTER (http://oceaninformatics.ucsd.edu/datazoo/data/pallter/datasets?action=summary&id=189).

Geology, geomorphology and soils

Litchfield Island is one of numerous small islands and rocky peninsulas along the southwestern coast of Anvers Island which are composed of an unusual assemblage of late Cretaceous to early Tertiary age rock types called the Altered Assemblage (Hooper 1962). The primary rock types of the Altered Assemblage are tonalite, a form of quartz diorite, and trondhjemite, a light-colored plutonic rock. Also common are granite and volcanic rocks rich in minerals such as plagioclase, biotite, quartz and hornblende. Litchfield Island is characterized by a central band of medium-dark gray, fine-grained diorites which separate the predominantly light gray medium-grained tonalites and trondhjemites of the east and west (Willan 1985). The eastern part is characterized by paler dykes up to 40 m across and trending north-south and east-west. Minor quartz, epidote, chlorite, pyrite and chalcopyrite veins of up to 8 cm thick strike SSE, cutting the tonalite. Dark gray fine-grained plagioclase-phyric dykes with traces of magnetite strike ENE to ESE. Numerous dark gray feldspar-phyric dykes are present in the west, up to 3 m thick and trending north-south and ESE. Some cut, or are cut by, sparse quartz, epidote, chlorite, pyrite, chalcopyrite and bornite veins of up to 20 cm thick.

The soils of Litchfield Island have not been described, although peaty soils of up to one meter in depth may be found in areas where there is, or once was, rich moss growth.

Freshwater habitat

There are a few small ponds on Litchfield Island: one small pond on a hill in the central, northeastern part of the island has been described as containing the algae *Heterohormogonium* sp. and *Oscillatoria brevis*. Another pond 50 m further south has been described as containing *Gonium* sp., *Prasiola crispa*, *P. tesselata* and *Navicula* sp (Parker *et al.* 1972).

Vegetation

The plant communities at Litchfield Island were surveyed in detail in 1964 (Corner 1964a). At that time, vegetation on Litchfield Island was well-developed and comprised several distinct communities with a diverse flora (Lewis Smith and Corner 1973; Lewis Smith 1982). Both species of Antarctic vascular plant, Antarctic hairgrass (*Deschampsia antarctica*) and Antarctic pearlwort (*Colobanthus quitensis*) were present on Litchfield Island (Corner 1964a; Greene and Holtom 1971; Lewis Smith and Corner 1973). Corner (1964a) noted that *D. antarctica* was common along the northern and northwestern coast of the island, with more localized patches growing further inland on ledges with deposits of mineral material and forms closed swards (Greene and Holtom 1971; Lewis Smith 1982). *C. quitensis* was present in two localities: a patch on the northeastern coast measuring approximately 9x2 m and a series of about six cushions scattered over a steep, flushed cliff above the northwestern coast. Commonly associated with the two vascular plants was a moss carpet assemblage comprising *Bryum pseudotriquetrum*, *Sanionia uncinata*, *Syntrichia princeps* and *Warnstorfia laculosa* (Corner 1964a). Factors controlling the distribution of *C. quitensis* and *D. antarctica* area include the availability of suitable substrate and air temperature (Komarkova et al. 1985). In conjunction with recent warming, existing populations of *C. quitensis* have expanded and new colonies have been established within the Arthur Harbor area, although this has not been studied specifically at Litchfield Island (Grobe *et al.* 1997; Lewis Smith 1994).

On well-drained rocky slopes, several banks of *Chorisodontium aciphyllum* and *Polytrichum strictum* were described in 1982 as up to 1.2 m in depth, and were considered to be some of the best examples of their kind in the Antarctic Peninsula area (Fenton and Lewis Smith 1982; Lewis Smith 1982). The more exposed areas of moss turf were covered by crustose lichens, species of *Cladonia* spp. and *Sphaerophorus globosus* and *Coelocaulon aculeatum*. In deep, sheltered gullies there was often a dense lichen cover comprising *Usnea antarctica*, *U. aurantiaco-atra* and *Umbilicaria antarctica*. Raised areas of *P. strictum* turf of approximately 0.5 m high occurred at the bottom of a narrow, east to west trending, valley. The hepatics *Barbilophozia hatcheri* and *Cephaloziella varians* were associated with the turf communities, particularly in frost heave channels and often occurred as stunted specimens on exposed humus.

There were a number of permanently wet areas on the island, an outstanding feature of which was one of the most extensive moss carpets known in the Antarctic Peninsula region, dominated by *W. laculosa* (Fenton and Lewis Smith 1982). Elsewhere, *S. uncinata* and *Brachythecium austro-salebrosum* formed smaller stands. *Pohlia nutans* lined the drier areas where the moss carpet communities merged with the moss turf communities.

Rock surfaces supported a variety of lichen-dominated communities in addition to the numerous epiphytic species that occurred on the moss banks. An open lichen and bryophyte community covered rocks and cliffs around the coast and in the center of the island. The southern coast of the island consisted of primarily crustose species of lichen, predominantly *Usnea antarctica* along with the mosses *Andreaea depressinervis* and *A. regularis*. The foliose alga *Prasiola crispa* forms small stands associated with the penguin colonies and other seabird habitats.

Other species recorded as present within the Area are: the hepatic *Lophozia excisa*; the lichens *Buellia* spp., *Caloplaca* spp., *Cetraria aculeata*, *Coelopogon epiphorellus*, *Lecanora* spp., *Lecidia* spp., *Lecidella* spp., *Lepraria* sp., *Mastodia tessellata*, *Ochrolechia frigida*, *Parmelia saxatilis*, *Physcia caesia*, *Rhizocarpon geographicum*, *Rhizocarpon* sp., *Stereocaulon glabrum*, *Umbilicaria decussata*, *Xanthoria candelaria* and *X. elegans*; and the mosses *Andreaea gainii* var. *gainii*, *Bartramia patens*, *Dicranoweisia grimmiacea*, *Pohlia cruda*, *Polytrichastrum alpinum*, *Sarconeurum glaciale* and *Schistidium antarctici* (BAS Plant Database 2009).

Previously, increasing populations of Antarctic fur seals (*Arctocephalus gazella*) have caused significant damage to the moss banks and carpets at lower elevations (Lewis Smith 1996; Harris 2001). However, observations suggest previously damaged vegetation is recovering at some sites following a recent decline in fur seal populations on Litchfield Island, although recent increases in southern elephant seals (*Mirounga leonina*) hauling out on the island has resulted in severe damage in their wallow locality (Map 2) and on access routes (Fraser and Patterson-Fraser, pers comms. 2014). South polar skuas (*Stercorarius maccormicki*) nest in the moss banks and cause some local damage.

Invertebrates, bacteria and fungi

The invertebrate fauna of Litchfield Island has not been studied in detail. Observations made in 1966 recorded the presence of large populations of invertebrates, particularly in areas colonised by plants, including *Cyrtolaelaps*, *Protereunetes*, *Stereotydeus*, *Rhagidia*, *Tydeus*, *Alaskozetes* and *Opisa*, in addition to *Cryptopygus*, *Parisotoma* and *Belgica*. Larvae of *Belgica* were numerous under grass and moss, numbering approximately 10,000 per m². Large numbers of *Nanorchestes* and some *Cryptopygus* were observed on the green algae *Pandorina*. The intertidal mite *Rhombognathus gressitti* was observed, although very scarce, on a rocky beach and mudflat of the island (Gressitt 1967). The tardigrades *Macrobiotus furciger*, *Hypsibius alpinus* and *H. pinguis* have been observed in moss patches, predominantly on north-facing slopes (Jennings 1976).

Breeding birds

Six bird species breed on Litchfield Island, making it one of the most diverse avifauna breeding habitats within the Arthur Harbor region. A small Adélie penguin (*Pygoscelis adeliae*) colony was previously situated on the eastern side of the island and has been censused regularly since 1971 (Table 1, Map 2). Following the substantial decline in the numbers of breeding pairs over a 30-year period, Adélie penguins are presently extinct on Litchfield Island (Fraser pers. comm. 2014). Population decline has been attributed to changes in both sea ice distribution and snow accumulation (McClintock *et al.* 2008). Adélie penguins are sensitive to changes in sea ice concentration, which has an influence on penguin access to feeding areas and on the abundance of Antarctic krill, which is their primary prey (Fraser and Hofmann 2003; Ducklow *et al.* 2007). The recent substantial extension of ice-free conditions within the Palmer LTER study area occurred concurrently with an 80 percent decrease in krill abundance along the northern half of the western Antarctic Peninsula and as a result may have significantly reduced the food supply of Adélie penguins inhabiting Litchfield Island (Fraser and Hofmann 2003; Forcada *et al.* 2008). In recent years, spring blizzards in the Arthur Harbor area have become more frequent and more intense, which coupled with widespread precipitation increases, is thought to have substantially increased mortality rates of Adélie chicks and eggs (McClintock *et al.* 2008; Patterson *et al.* 2003). The Litchfield Island colony receives the most snowfall of the seven penguin colonies studied in the Palmer area and has shown the most rapid decline, strongly implicating increased snowfall as a contributing factor in Adélie penguin losses (Fraser, in Stokstad 2007).

Table 1. Numbers of breeding Adélie penguins (*Pygoscelis adeliae*) on Litchfield Island 1971-2009

Year	BP	Count Type[1]	Source	Year	BP	Count Type[1]	Source	Year	BP Count Type[1]	Source
1971-72	890	N3	2	1986-87	577	N1	3	2000-01	274 N1	3

Year	BP	N	1	Year	BP	N	1	Year	BP	N	1
1972-73				1987-88	430	N1	3	2001-02	166	N1	3
1973-74				1988-89				2002-03	143	N1	3
1974-75	1000	N4	2	1989-90	606	N1	3	2003-04	52		4
1975-76	884	N1	3	1990-91	448	N1	3	2004-05	33		4
1977-78	650	N1	2	1991-92	497	N1	3	2005-06	15		4
1978-79	519	N1	2	1992-93	496	N1	3	2006-07	4		4
1979-80	564	N1	2	1993-94	485	N1	3	2007-08	0		4
1980-81	650	N1	2	1994-95	425	N1	3	2008-09	0		4
1981-82				1995-96	410	N1	3	2009-10	0		5
1982-83				1996-97	346	N1	3	2010-11	0		5
1983-84	635	N1	2	1997-98	365	N1	3	2011-12	0		5
1984-85	549	N1	2	1998-99	338	N1	3	2012-13	0		5
1985-86	586	N1	2	1999-2000	322	N1	3				

1. BP = Breeding pairs, N = Nest, C = Chick, A = Adults; 1 = < ± 5%, 2 = ± 5-10%, 3 = ± 10-15%, 4 = ± 25-50% (classification after Woehler, 1993)
2. Parmelee and Parmelee, 1987 (N1 and December counts are shown where several counts were made in one season).
3. W.R. Fraser data supplied February 2003, based on multiple published and unpublished sources.
4. W.R. Fraser data supplied January 2009.
5. W.R. Fraser data supplied February 2014.

Southern giant petrels (*Macronectes giganteus*) breed in small numbers on Litchfield Island. Approximately 20 pairs were recorded in 1978-79, including an incubating adult that had been banded in Australia (Bonner and Lewis Smith 1985). More recent data on numbers of breeding pairs are given in Table 2 and show a continuing upward trend in breeding pairs, followed by a stabilization in recent seasons. An increasing, and now stable, breeding population on Litchfield Island and in the vicinity of Palmer Station provide a notable exception to more widespread decline of southern giant petrels in the Antarctic Peninsula region, and have been attributed to the close proximity of prey-rich feeding grounds and the relatively low level of commercial fishing activity within the region (Patterson and Fraser 2003). In austral summer 2004, six southern giant petrel chicks from four colonies located close to the Palmer Station were found to have poxviral infection (Bochsler *et al.* 2008). While the reasons for the emergence of the virus and its potential impacts on southern giant petrel populations are currently unknown, it has been suggested that Adélie penguins may be equally vulnerable to infection.

Table 2. Numbers of breeding southern giant petrels (*Macronectes giganteus*) on Litchfield Island 1993-2012 (nest counts accurate < ± 5%)

Year	Breeding pairs	Year	Breeding pairs	Year	Breeding pairs
1993-94	26	2000-01	39	2007-08	45
1994-95	32	2001-02	46	2008-09	57
1995-96	37	2002-03	42	2009-10	52
1996-97	36	2003-04	47	2010-11	60
1997-98	20	2004-05	48	2011-12	54
1998-99	44	2005-06	43	2012-13	54
1999-2000	41	2006-07	50		

Source: Unpublished data supplied by W.R. Fraser, February 2003, January 2009, February 2014.

Wilson's storm petrels (*Oceanites oceanicus*) breed within the Area, although numbers have not been determined. Up to 50 pairs of south polar skuas (*Stercorarius maccormicki*) occur on the island, although the number of breeding pairs fluctuates widely from year to year. Brown skuas (*S. lonnbergi*) have in the past been closely associated with the Adélie penguin colony (Map 2), with the number of breeding pairs having ranged from two to eight. The low count of two pairs in 1980-81 followed an outbreak of fowl cholera, which killed many of the brown skuas on Litchfield Island in 1979. Hybrid breeding pairs also occur. Although 12-20 kelp gulls (*Larus dominicanus*) are seen regularly on the island, there are only two or three nests each season. A small number of Antarctic terns (*Sterna vittata*) regularly breed on Litchfield Island, usually less than a dozen pairs (approximately eight pairs in 2002-03) (Fraser pers. comm. 2003). They are most commonly found on the NE coast although their breeding sites change from year to year, and in 1964 they occupied a site on the NW coast (Corner 1964a). A recent visit to Litchfield Island indicates that the number of Wilson's storm petrels, south polar skuas, brown skuas, kelp gulls and Antarctic terns breeding on the island has undergone minimal change in recent years (Fraser pers. comm. 2009).

Among the non-breeding birds commonly seen around Litchfield Island, the Antarctic shag (*Phalacrocorax* [atriceps] *bransfieldensis*) breeds on Cormorant Island several kilometers to the east; chinstrap penguins (*Pygoscelis antarctica*) and gentoo penguins (*P. papua*) are both regular summer visitors in small numbers. Snow petrels (*Pagodroma nivea*), cape petrels (*Daption capense*), Antarctic petrels (*Thalassoica antarctica*) and southern fulmars (*Fulmarus glacialoides*), are irregular visitors in small numbers, while two gray-headed albatross (*Diomedea chrysotoma*) were sighted near the island in 1975 (Parmelee *et al.* 1977).

Marine mammals

Antarctic fur seals (*Arctocephalus gazella*) started to appear in Arthur Harbor in the mid-1970s and are now common on Litchfield Island from around February each year. Regular censuses conducted in February and March over the period 1988-2003 recorded on average 160 and 340 animals on the island in these months respectively (Fraser pers. comm. 2003), with a peak of 874 on 19 March 1994 (Fraser pers. comm. 2014). In recent years, however, Antarctic fur seal numbers have decreased within the Arthur Harbor area (Siniff *et al.* 2008). Population decline has been tentatively attributed to reduced Antarctic krill availability within the area, which represents a key component of the diet of Antarctic fur seals, particularly during pupping (Clarke *et al.* 2007; Siniff *et al.* 2008). Diminished Antarctic krill abundance is thought to be a result of reduced sea ice extent and persistence within the Arthur Harbor area (Fraser and Hoffman 2003; Atkinson *et al.* 2004).

Southern elephant seals (*Mirounga leonina*) haul out on accessible beaches from October to June, numbering on average 43 animals throughout these months since 1988 (Fraser pers. comm. 2003), with numbers remaining relatively stable or perhaps increasing slightly (Fraser and Patterson-Fraser, pers. comms. 2014). A group of a dozen or more is found on the northeastern side of the island, having moved in recent years from the low-lying valley to more elevated ground ~150 m northwest of the former haul-out site (Map 2). A few Weddell seals (*Leptonychotes weddellii*) occasionally haul out on beaches. Long term census data (1974–2005) indicate that elephant seal populations within the Arthur Harbor area have recently expanded, as larger ice-free areas have become available for breeding. In contrast, data indicate that Weddell seal numbers have declined as a consequence of reduced fast-ice extent, which is necessary for breeding (Siniff *et al.* 2008). Both crabeater seals (*Lobodon carcinophagus*) and leopard seals (*Hydrurga leptonyx*) may also commonly be seen on ice floes near Litchfield Island. Minke whales (*Balaenoptera acutorostrata*) have been sighted in the Arthur Harbor area during both the austral summer (Dec-Feb) and autumn (Mar-May) (Scheidat *et al.* 2008).

Littoral and benthic communities

Strong tidal currents occur between the islands within Arthur Harbor, although there are numerous sheltered coves along the coast (Richardson and Hedgpeth 1977). Subtidal rocky cliffs grade into soft substrate at an average depth of 15 m and numerous rock outcrops are found within the deeper soft substrate. Sediments in Arthur Harbor are generally poorly sorted and consist primarily of silt sized particles with an organic content of approximately 6.75 % (Troncoso *et al.* 2008). Significant areas of the seabed within Arthur Harbor are covered by macroalgae, including *Desmarestia anceps* and *D. menziesii*, and sessile invertebrates such as sponges and corals are also present (McClintock *et al.* 2008; Fairhead *et al.* 2006). The predominantly soft mud substrate approximately 200 m off the northeastern coast of Litchfield Island has been described as supporting a rich macrobenthic community, characterized by a high diversity and biomass of non-attached, deposit-feeding polychaetes, arthropods, molluscs and crustaceans (Lowry 1975). Analysis of molluscan assemblages within Arthur Harbor, conducted as part of an integrated study of the benthic ecosystem in the austral summers 2003 and 2006, indicates that species richness and abundance are relatively low (Troncoso *et al.* 2008). The fish species *Notothenia neglecta, N. nudifrons* and *Trematomus newnesi* have been recorded between 3 and 15 meters depth (De Witt and Hureau 1979; McDonald *et al.* 1995). The Antarctic limpet (*Nacella concinna*) is common in the marine area around Litchfield Island and is widespread within shallow water areas of the western Antarctic Peninsula (Kennicutt *et al.* 1992b; Clarke *et al.* 2004). Monitoring of zooplankton distribution within the marine area surrounding Litchfield Island indicates that the abundance of *Euphausia superba* and *Salpa thompsoni* decreased significantly between 1993 and 2004 (Ross *et al.* 2008).

Human activities and impact

In January 1989 the vessel *Bahia Paraiso* ran aground 750 m south of Litchfield Island, releasing more than 600,000 liters (150,000 gallons) of petroleum into the surrounding environment (Kennicutt 1990; Penhale *et al.* 1997). The intertidal communities were most affected, and hydrocarbon contaminants were found in both sediments and inter- and sub-tidal limpets (*Nacella concinna*), with an estimated mortality of up to 50% (Kennicutt *et al.* 1992a&b; Kennicutt and Sweet 1992; Penhale *et al.* 1997). However, numbers recovered soon after the spill (Kennicutt 1992a&b). Levels of petroleum contaminants found in intertidal sample sites on Litchfield Island were among some of the highest recorded (Kennicutt *et al.* 1992b; Kennicutt and Sweet 1992). It was estimated that 80% of Adélie penguins nesting in the vicinity of the spill were exposed to hydrocarbon pollution, and exposed colonies were estimated to have lost an additional 16% of their numbers in that season as a direct result (Penhale *et al.* 1997). However, few dead adult birds were observed. Samples collected in April 2002 detected hydrocarbons within the waters surrounding the *Bahia Paraiso* wreck, suggesting some leakage of Antarctic gas oil (Janiot *et al.* 2003) and fuel occasionally reaches beach areas on south-western Anvers Island (Fraser pers. comm. 2009). However, hydrocarbons were not found within sediment or biota samples collected in 2002 and high sea energy within the area is thought to significantly limit the impact of fuel leaks on local biota and the persistence of contaminants on beaches. In addition, marine debris, including fishing hooks, lines and floats are occasionally observed on Litchfield Island.

US permit records show that between 1978-92 only about 35 people visited Litchfield Island, with possibly around three visits being made per season (Fraser and Patterson 1997). This suggests a total of approximately 40 visits over this 12-year period, although given that a total of 24 landings were made at the island over two seasons in 1991-93 (Fraser and Patterson 1997), this would seem likely to represent an underestimate. Nevertheless, visitation at Litchfield Island was undoubtedly low over this period, and has remained at a minimal level. Visits have been primarily related to bird and seal censuses and work on terrestrial ecology.

Plant studies carried out on Litchfield Island in 1982 (Komárková 1983) used welding rods inserted into the soil to mark study sites. At nearby Biscoe Point (ASPA No. 139), where similar studies were conducted, numerous rods left *in situ* killed surrounding vegetation (Harris 2001). It is unknown how many of the rods were used to mark sites on Litchfield Island, or whether most were subsequently removed. However, one was found and removed from a vegetated site in a small valley approximately 100 m west of the summit of the island after a brief search in February 2001 (Harris 2001) and welding rods are still occasionally found (Fraser pers. comm. 2009). A more comprehensive search would be required to determine whether further welding rods remain within the Area. No other impacts on the terrestrial environment that could be attributed to human visitation were observed on 28 February 2001, although one of the two protected area signs was in poor condition and insecurely placed. The impact of human activities upon the terrestrial ecology, birds and seals on Litchfield Island from direct visits may thus be considered to have been minor (Bonner and Lewis Smith 1985; Fraser and Patterson 1997; Harris 2001).

6(ii) Access to the Area

The Area may be accessed over sea ice or by sea. Particular routes have not been designated for access to the Area, although the preferred small boat landing site is located in a small cove on the eastern coast of the island (Map 2). Overflight and aircraft landing restrictions apply within the Area, the specific conditions for which are set out in Section 7(ii) below.

6(iii) Location of structures within and adjacent to the Area

With the exception of a cairn on the summit of the island, there are no structures present within the Area. A permanent survey marker, consisting of a 5/8" stainless steel threaded rod, was installed on Litchfield Island by the USGS on 9 February 1999. The marker is located near the summit of the island at 64°46'13.97"S, 64°05'38.85"W at an elevation of 48 m, about 8 m west of the cairn (Map 2). The marker is set in bedrock and marked by a red plastic survey cap. A survival cache is located near the crest of a small hill overlooking the former Adélie penguin colony, approximately 100 m south of the small boat landing site.

6(iv) Location of other protected areas in the vicinity

Litchfield Island lies within Antarctic Specially Managed Area (ASMA) No.7 Southwest Anvers Island and Palmer Basin (Map 1). The nearest Antarctic Specially Protected Areas (ASPAs) to Litchfield Island are: Biscoe Point (ASPA No. 139) which is 16 km east of the Area adjacent to Anvers Island and South Bay (ASPA No. 146), which is approximately 27 km to the southeast at Doumer Island (Inset, Map 1).

7.   Permit conditions

7(i) General Permit conditions

Entry into the Area is prohibited except in accordance with a Permit issued by an appropriate national authority. Conditions for issuing a Permit to enter the Area are that:

- it is issued only for compelling scientific reasons that cannot be served elsewhere, and in particular for research on the terrestrial ecosystem or fauna in the Area;
- it is issued for compelling educational or outreach reasons that cannot be served elsewhere, or for reasons essential to the management of the Area;
- the actions permitted will not jeopardize the ecological or scientific values of the Area or the value of the Area as a terrestrial reference site;
- any management activities are in support of the objectives of the Management Plan;
- the actions permitted are in accordance with the Management Plan;
- the activities permitted will give due consideration via the environmental impact assessment process to the continued protection of the environmental and scientific values of the Area;
- the Permit shall be issued for a finite period;
- the Permit, or a copy, shall be carried when in the Area.

7(ii) Access to, movement within or over, the Area

Access to the Area shall be by small boat, or over sea ice by vehicle or on foot. Vehicles are prohibited and all movement within the Area shall be on foot. When access over sea ice is viable, there are no special restrictions on the locations where vehicle or foot access may be made, although vehicles are prohibited from being taken on land.

Foot access and movement within the Area

Persons on foot should at all times avoid disturbance to birds and seals, and damage to vegetation. Boat crew, or other people in boats or vehicles, are prohibited from moving on foot beyond the immediate vicinity of the landing site unless specifically authorised by Permit.

Pedestrians should maintain the following minimum approach distances from wildlife, unless it is necessary to approach closer for purposes allowed for by the permit:

- Southern giant petrels (*Macronectes giganteus*) – 50 m
- Antarctic fur seals (for personal safety) – 15 m
- other birds and seals – 5 m.

Visitors should move carefully so as to minimize disturbance to flora, fauna, and soils, and should walk on snow or rocky terrain if practical, but taking care not to damage lichens. Pedestrian traffic should be kept to the minimum consistent with the objectives of any permitted activities and every reasonable effort should be made to minimize effects.

Small boat access

The recommended landing site for small boats is on the beach in the small cove mid-way along the eastern coast of the island (Map 2). Access by small boat at other locations around the coast is allowed, provided this is consistent with the purposes for which a Permit has been granted.

Aircraft access and overflight

Landing by aircraft within the Area is prohibited and landings within 930 m (~1/2 nautical mile) of the Area should be avoided wherever possible. Overflight below 610 m (~2000 ft) Above Ground Level is prohibited except when operationally necessary for scientific purposes.

7(iii) Activities that may be conducted within the Area

- Scientific research that will not jeopardize the ecosystem values of the Area or the value of the Area as a reference site, and which cannot be served elsewhere;
- Activities with compelling educational and / or outreach purposes that cannot be served elsewhere;
- Essential management activities, including monitoring and inspection.

7(iv) Installation, modification or removal of structures

- No structures are to be erected within the Area except as specified in a permit and, with the exception of permanent survey markers and the existing cairn at the summit of the island, permanent structures or installations are prohibited;
- All structures, scientific equipment or markers installed in the Area must be authorized by permit and clearly identified by country, name of the principal investigator, year of installation and date of expected removal. All such items should be free of organisms, propagules (e.g. seeds, eggs) and non-sterile soil, and be made of materials that can withstand the environmental conditions and pose minimal risk of contamination or damage to the values of the Area;
- Installation (including site selection), maintenance, modification or removal of structures or equipment shall be undertaken in a manner that minimizes disturbance to flora and fauna.
- Removal of specific structures / equipment for which the permit has expired shall be the responsibility of the authority which granted the original Permit, and shall be a condition of the permit.

7(v) Location of field camps

Camping should be avoided within the Area. However, when necessary for essential purposes specified in the Permit, temporary camping is allowed at the designated site on the terrace above the former penguin colony. The campsite is located at the foot of a small hill (~35 m), on its eastern side, approximately 100 m south-west of the small boat landing beach (Map 2). Camping on surfaces with significant vegetation cover is prohibited.

7(vi) Restrictions on materials and organisms which may be brought into the Area

In addition to the requirements of the Protocol on Environmental Protection to the Antarctic Treaty, restrictions on materials and organisms which may be brought into the Area are:

- Deliberate introduction of animals, plant material, micro-organisms and non-sterile soil into the Area is prohibited. Precautions shall be taken to prevent the accidental introduction of animals, plant material, micro-organisms and non-sterile soil from other biologically distinct regions (within or beyond the Antarctic Treaty area);

- Visitors shall ensure that sampling equipment and markers brought into the Area are clean. To the maximum extent practicable, footwear and other equipment used or brought into the area (including backpacks, carry-bags and other equipment) shall be thoroughly cleaned at Palmer Station before entering the Area. Visitors should also consult and follow as appropriate recommendations contained in the Committee for Environmental Protection Non-native Species Manual (CEP 2011), and in the Environmental Code of Conduct for terrestrial scientific field research in Antarctica (SCAR 2009);

- All poultry brought into and not consumed or used within the Area, including all parts, products and / or wastes of poultry, shall be removed from the Area or disposed of by incineration or equivalent means that eliminates risks to native flora and fauna;

- No herbicides or pesticides shall be brought into the Area;

- Any other chemicals, including radio-nuclides or stable isotopes, which may be introduced for scientific or management purposes specified in the permit, shall be removed from the Area at or before the conclusion of the activity for which the permit was granted;

- Fuel, food, chemicals and other materials are not to be stored in the Area, unless specifically authorized by permit or are contained within an emergency cache authorized by an appropriate authority, and shall be stored and handled in a way that minimises the risk of their accidental introduction into the environment;

- All materials introduced shall be for a stated period only, shall be removed at or before the conclusion of that stated period, and shall be stored and handled so that risk of their introduction into the environment is minimized;

- If release occurs which is likely to compromise the values of the Area, removal is encouraged only where the impact of removal is not likely to be greater than that of leaving the material *in situ*.

7(vii) Taking of, or harmful interference with, native flora or fauna

Taking or harmful interference of native flora and fauna is prohibited, except in accordance with a permit issued under Article 3 of Annex II of the Protocol on Environmental Protection to the Antarctic Treaty. Where animal taking or harmful interference is involved, this should, as a minimum standard, be in accordance with the SCAR Code of Conduct for the Use of Animals for Scientific Purposes in Antarctica.

7(viii) Collection or removal of materials not brought into the Area by the Permit holder

- Material may be collected or removed from the Area only in accordance with a permit and should be limited to the minimum necessary to meet scientific or management needs. This includes biological samples and rock specimens.

- Material of human origin likely to compromise the values of the Area, which was not brought into the Area by the permit holder or otherwise authorized, may be removed from any part of the Area, unless the impact of removal is likely to be greater than leaving the material *in situ*. If this is the case the appropriate authority should be notified.

7(ix) Disposal of waste

All wastes shall be removed from the Area. Human wastes may be disposed of into the sea.

7(x) Measures that may be necessary to continue to meet the aims of the Management Plan

Permits may be granted to enter the Area to:

1) carry out monitoring and Area inspection activities, which may involve the collection of a small number of samples or data for analysis or review;
2) install or maintain signposts, markers, structures or scientific or essential logistic equipment;
3) carry out protective measures;
4) carry out research or management in a manner that avoids interference with long-term research and monitoring activities or possible duplication of effort. Persons planning new projects within the Area

should consult with established programs working within the Area, such as those of the US, before initiating the work.

7(xi) Requirements for reports

- The principal permit holder for each visit to the Area shall submit a report to the appropriate national authority as soon as practicable, and no later than six months after the visit has been completed.

- Such reports should include, as appropriate, the information identified in the visit report form contained in the Guide to the Preparation of Management Plans for Antarctic Specially Protected Areas. If appropriate, the national authority should also forward a copy of the visit report to the Parties that proposed the Management Plan, to assist in managing the Area and reviewing the Management Plan.

- Parties should, wherever possible, deposit originals or copies of such original visit reports in a publicly accessible archive to maintain a record of usage, for the purpose of any review of the Management Plan and in organising the scientific use of the Area.

- The appropriate authority should be notified of any activities/measures undertaken, and / or of any materials released and not removed, that were not included in the authorized permit.

References

Atkinson, A., Siegel, V., Pakhomov, E. & Rothery, P. 2004. Long-term decline in krill stock and increase in salps within the Southern Ocean. *Nature* **432**: 100–03.

Bonner, W.N. & Lewis Smith, R.I. (eds) 1985. *Conservation areas in the Antarctic*. SCAR, Cambridge: 73-84.

Baker, K.S. 1996. Palmer LTER: Palmer Station air temperature 1974 to 1996. *Antarctic Journal of the United States* **31** (2): 162-64.

Clarke, A., Murphy, E.J., Meredith, M.P., King, J.C., Peck, L.S., Barnes, D.K.A. & Smith, R.C. 2007. Climate change and the marine ecosystem of the western Antarctic Peninsula. *Philosophical Transactions of the Royal Society B* **362**: 149–166 [doi:10.1098/rstb.2006.1958]

Clarke, A., Prothero-Thomas, E. Beaumont, J.C., Chapman, A.L. & Brey, T. 2004. Growth in the limpet *Nacella concinna* from contrasting sites in Antarctica. *Polar Biology* **28**: 62–71. [doi 10.1007/s00300-004-0647-8]

Corner, R.W.M. 1964a. Notes on the vegetation of Litchfield Island, Arthur Harbour, Anvers Island. Unpublished report, British Antarctic Survey Archives Ref AD6/2F/1964/N3.

Corner, R.W.M. 1964b. Catalogue of bryophytes and lichens collected from Litchfield Island, West Graham Land, Antarctica. Unpublished report, British Antarctic Survey Archives Ref LS2/4/3/11.

Domack E., Amblàs, D., Gilbert, R., Brachfeld, S., Camerlenghi, A., Rebesco, M., Canals M. & Urgeles, R. 2006. Subglacial morphology and glacial evolution of the Palmer deep outlet system, Antarctic Peninsula. *Geomorphology* **75**(1-2): 125-42.

Ducklow, H.W., Baker, K., Martinson, D.G., Quentin, L.B., Ross, R.M., Smith, R.C. Stammerjohn, S.E. Vernet, M. & Fraser, W. 2007. Marine pelagic ecosystems: the West Antarctic Peninsula. *Philosophical Transactions of the Royal Society B* **362**: 67–94. [doi:10.1098/rstb.2006.1955]

Fairhead, V.A., Amsler, C.D. & McClintock, J.B. 2006. Lack of defense or phlorotannin induction by UV radiation or mesograzers in *Desmarestia anceps* and *D. menziesii* (phaeophyceae). *Journal of Phycology* **42**: 1174–83.

Fenton, J.H.C & Lewis Smith, R.I. 1982. Distribution, composition and general characteristics of the moss banks of the maritime Antarctic. *British Antarctic Survey Bulletin* **51**: 215-36.

Forcada, J. Trathan, P.N., Reid, K., Murphy, E.J. & Croxall, J.P. 2006. Contrasting population changes in sympatric penguin species in association with climate warming. *Global Change Biology* **12**: 411–23. [doi: 10.1111/j.1365-2486.2006.01108.x]

Fraser, W.R. in: Stokstad, 2007. Boom and bust in a polar hot zone. *Science* **315**: 1522–23.

Fraser, W.R. & Hofmann, E.E. 2003 A predator's perspective on causal links between climate change, physical forcing and ecosystem response. *Marine Ecological Progress Series* **265**: 1–15.

Fraser, W.R. & Patterson, D.L. 1997. Human disturbance and long-term changes in Adélie penguin populations: a natural experiement at Palmer Station, Antarctic Peninsula. In Battaglia, B. Valencia, J. & Walton, D.W.H. (eds) *Antarctic Communities: species, structure and survival*. Cambridge University Press, Cambridge: 445-52.

Greene, D.M. & Holtom, A. 1971. Studies in *Colobanthus quitensis* (Kunth) Bartl. and *Deschampsia antarctica* Desv.: III. Distribution, habitats and performance in the Antarctic botanical zone. *British Antarctic Survey Bulletin* **26**: 1-29.

Gressitt, J.L. 1967. Notes on Arthropod populations in the Antarctic Peninsula - South Shetland Islands - South Orkney Islands area. In *Entomology of Antarctica*, J.L. Gressitt (ed) Antarctic Research Series **10**. AGU, Washington DC.

Grobe, C.W., Ruhland, C.T. & Day, T.A. 1997. A new population of *Colobanthus quitensis* near Arthur Harbor, Antarctica: correlating recruitment with warmer summer temperatures. *Arctic and Alpine Research* **29**(2): 217-21.

Harris, C.M. 2001. Revision of management plans for Antarctic protected areas originally proposed by the United States of America and the United Kingdom: Field visit report. Internal report for the National Science Foundation, US, and the Foreign and Commonwealth Office, UK. Environmental Research & Assessment, Cambridge.

Holdgate, M.W. 1963. Observations of birds and seals at Anvers Island, Palmer Archipelago, in 1956-57. *British Antarctic Survey Bulletin* **2**: 45-51.

Hooper, P.R. 1958. Progress report on the geology of Anvers Island. Unpublished report, British Antarctic Survey Archives Ref AD6/2/1957/G3.

Hooper, P.R. 1962. The petrology of Anvers Island and adjacent islands. *FIDS Scientific Reports* **34**.

Janiot, L.J., Sericano, J.L. & Marcucci, O. 2003. Evidence of oil leakage from the *Bahia Paraiso* wreck in Arthur Harbour, Antarctica. *Marine Pollution Bulletin* **46**: 1615–29.

Jennings, P.G. 1976. Tardigrada from the Antarctic Peninsula and Scotia Ridge region. *BAS Bulletin* **44**: 77-95.

Kennicutt II, M.C. 1990. Oil spillage in Antarctica: initial report of the National Science Foundation-sponsored quick response team on the grounding of the *Bahia Paraiso*. *Environmental Science and Technology* **24**: 620-24.

Kennicutt II, M.C., McDonald, T.J., Denoux, G.J. & McDonald, S.J. 1992a. Hydrocarbon contamination on the Antarctic Peninsula I. Arthur Harbour – subtidal sediments. *Marine Pollution Bulletin* **24** (10): 499-506.

Kennicutt II, M.C., McDonald, T.J., Denoux, G.J. & McDonald, S.J. 1992b. Hydrocarbon contamination on the Antarctic Peninsula I. Arthur Harbour – inter- and subtidal limpets (*Nacella concinna*). *Marine Pollution Bulletin* **24** (10): 506-11.

Kennicutt II, M.C. & Sweet, S.T. 1992. Hydrocarbon contamination on the Antarctic Peninsula III. The *Bahia Paraiso* – two years after the spill. *Marine Pollution Bulletin* **25** (9-12): 303-06.

Komárková, V. 1983. Plant communities of the Antarctic Peninsula near Palmer Station. *Antarctic Journal of the United States* **18**: 216-18.

Komárková, V. 1984. Studies of plant communities of the Antarctic Peninsula near Palmer Station. *Antarctic Journal of the United States* **19**: 180-82.

Lewis Smith, R.I. 1982. Plant succession and re-exposed moss banks on a deglaciated headland in Arthur Harbour, Anvers Island. *British Antarctic Survey Bulletin* **51**: 193–99.

Lewis Smith, R.I. 1994. Vascular plants as bioindicators of regional warming in Antarctica. *Oecologia* **99**: 322-28.

Lewis Smith, R.I. 1996. Terrestrial and freshwater biotic components of the western Antarctic Peninsula. In Ross, R.M., Hofmann, E.E. and Quetin, L.B. (eds) *Foundations for ecological research west of the Antarctic Peninsula. Antarctic Research Series* **70**: 15-59.

Lewis Smith, R.I. & Corner, R.W.M. 1973. Vegetation of the Arthur Harbour – Argentine Islands region of the Antarctic Peninsula. *British Antarctic Survey Bulletin* **33 & 34**: 89-122.

Lowry, J.K. 1975. Soft bottom macrobenthic community of Arthur Harbor, Antarctica. In Pawson, D.L. (ed.). Biology of the Antarctic Seas V. *Antarctic Research Series* **23** (1): 1-19.

McClintock, J., Ducklow, H. & Fraser, W. 2008. Ecological responses to climate change on the Antarctic Peninsula. *American Scientist* **96**: 302.

McDonald, S.J., Kennicutt II, M.C., Liu, H. & Safe S.H. 1995. Assessing aromatic hydrocarbon exposure in Antarctic fish captured near Palmer and McMurdo Stations, Antarctica. *Archives of Environmental Contamination and Toxicology* **29**: 232-40.

Parker, B.C, Samsel, G.L. & Prescott, G.W. 1972. Freshwater algae of the Antarctic Peninsula. 1. Systematics and ecology in the U.S. Palmer Station area. In Llano, G.A. (ed) *Antarctic terrestrial biology. Antarctic Research Series* **20**: 69-81.

Parmelee, D.F, Fraser, W.R. & Neilson, D.R. 1977. Birds of the Palmer Station area. *Antarctic Journal of the United States* **12** (1-2): 15-21.

Parmelee, D.F. & Parmelee, J.M. 1987. Revised penguin numbers and distribution for Anvers Island, Antarctica. *British Antarctic Survey Bulletin* **76**: 65-73.

Patterson, D.L., Easter-Pilcher, A. & Fraser, W.R. 2003. The effects of human activity and environmental variability on long-termchanges in Adelie penguin populations at Palmer Station, Antarctica. In A. H. L. Huiskes, W. W. C. Gieskes, J. Rozema, R. M. L. Schorno, S. M. van der Vies & W. J. Wolff (eds) *Antarctic biology in a global context*. Backhuys, Leiden, The Netherlands: 301–07.

Patterson, D.L. & Fraser, W. 2003. *Satellite tracking southern giant petrels at Palmer Station, Antarctica*. Feature Article 8, Microwave Telemetry Inc.

Penhale, P.A., Coosen, J. & Marschoff, E.R. 1997. The *Bahia Paraiso*: a case study in environmental impact, remediation and monitoring. In Battaglia, B. Valencia, J. & Walton, D.W.H. (eds) *Antarctic Communities: species, structure and survival*. Cambridge University Press, Cambridge: 437-44.

Richardson, M.D. & Hedgpeth, J.W. 1977. Antarctic soft-bottom, macrobenthic community adaptations to a cold, stable, highly productive, glacially affected environment. In Llano, G.A. (ed.). *Adaptations within Antarctic ecosystems: proceedings of the third SCAR symposium on Antarctic biology*: 181-96.

Ross, R.M., Quetin, L.B., Martinson, D.G., Iannuzzi, R.A., Stammerjohn, S.E. & Smith, R.C. 2008. Palmer LTER: patterns of distribution of major zooplankton species west of the Antarctic Peninsula over a twelve year span. *Deep-Sea Research II* **55**: 2086–2105.

Sanchez, R. & Fraser, W. 2001. *Litchfield Island Orthobase*. Digital orthophotograph of Litchfield Island, 6 cm pixel resolution and horizontal / vertical accuracy of ± 2 m. Geoid heights, 3 m² DTM, derived contour interval: 5 m. Data on CD-ROM and accompanied by USGS Open File Report 99-402 "GPS and GIS-based data collection and image mapping in the Antarctic Peninsula". Science and Applications Center, Mapping Applications Center. USGS, Reston.

Scheidat, M., Bornemann, H., Burkhardt, E., Flores, H., Friedlaender, A. Kock, K.-H, Lehnert, L., van Franekar, J. & Williams, R. 2008. Antarctic sea ice habitat and minke whales. Annual Science Conference in Halifax, 2008.

Shearn-Bochsler, V. Green, D.E., Converse, K.A., Docherty, D.E., Thiel, T., Geisz, H. N., Fraser, W.R. & Patterson-Fraser, D.L. 2008. Cutaneous and diphtheritic avian poxvirus infection in a nestling Southern giant petrel (*Macronectes giganteus*) from Antarctica. *Polar Biology* **31**: 569–73. [doi 10.1007/s00300-007-0390-z]

Siniff, D.B., Garrot, R.A. & Rotella, J.J. 2008. Opinion: Projecting the effects of environmental change on Antarctic seals. *Antarctic Science* **20**: 425-35.

Stammerjohn, S.E., Martinson, D.G., Smith, R.C. & Iannuzzi, R.A. 2008. Sea ice in the Western Antarctic Peninsula region: spatio-temporal variability from ecological and climate change perspectives. *Deep-Sea Research II* **55**: 2041–58. [doi:10.1016/j.dsr2.2008.04.026]

Troncoso, J.S. & Aldea, C. 2008. Macrobenthic mollusc assemblages and diversity in the West Antarctica from the South Shetland Islands to the Bellingshausen Sea. *Polar Biology* **31**(10): 1253–65. [doi 10.1007/s00300-008-0464-6]

Vaughan, D.G., Marshall, G.J., Connolley, W.M., Parkinson, C., Mulvaney, R., Hodgson, D.A., King, J.C., Pudsey, C.J., & Turner, J. 2003. Recent rapid regional climate warming on the Antarctic Peninsula. *Climatic Change* **60**: 243–74.

Willan, R.C.R. 1985. Hydrothermal quartz+magnetite+pyrite+chalcopyrite and quartz+polymetallic veins in a tonalite-diorite complex, Arthur Harbour, Anvers Island and miscellaneous observations in the southwesternAnvers Island area. Unpublished report, British Antarctic Survey Archives Ref AD6/2R/1985/G14.

Woehler, E.J. (ed) 1993. *The distribution and abundance of Antarctic and sub-Antarctic penguins*. SCAR, Cambridge.

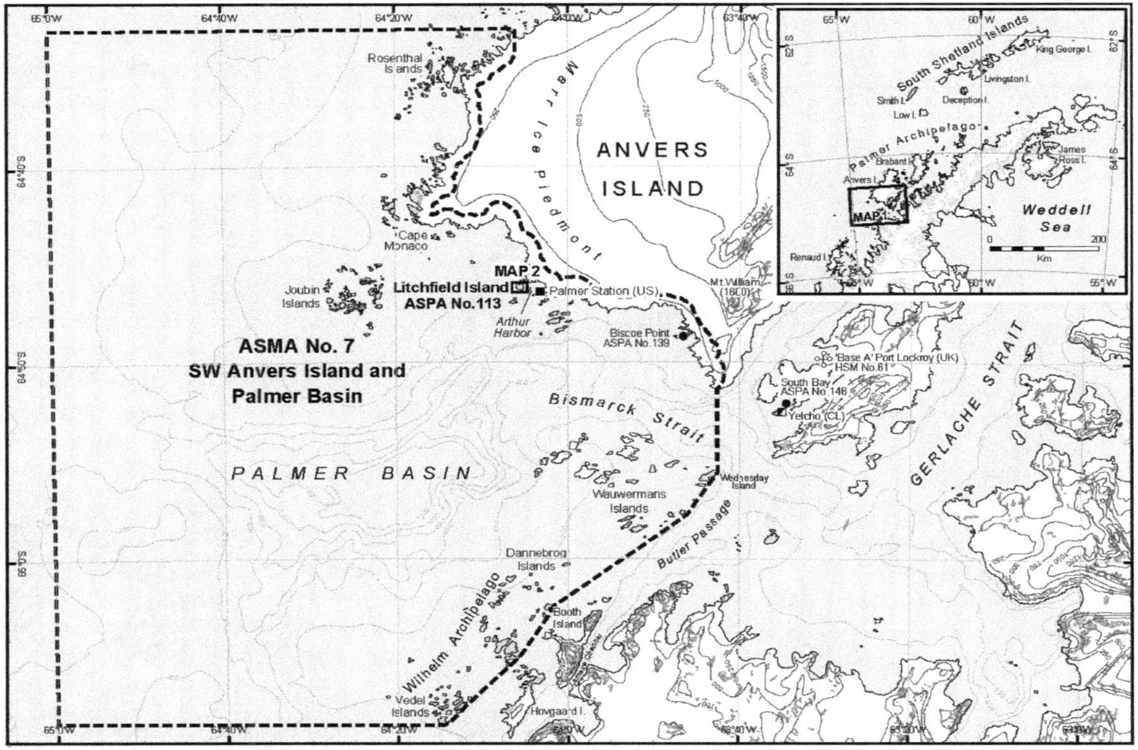

Map 1: ASPA No. 113 Litchfield Island - Arthur Harbor, Anvers Island

31

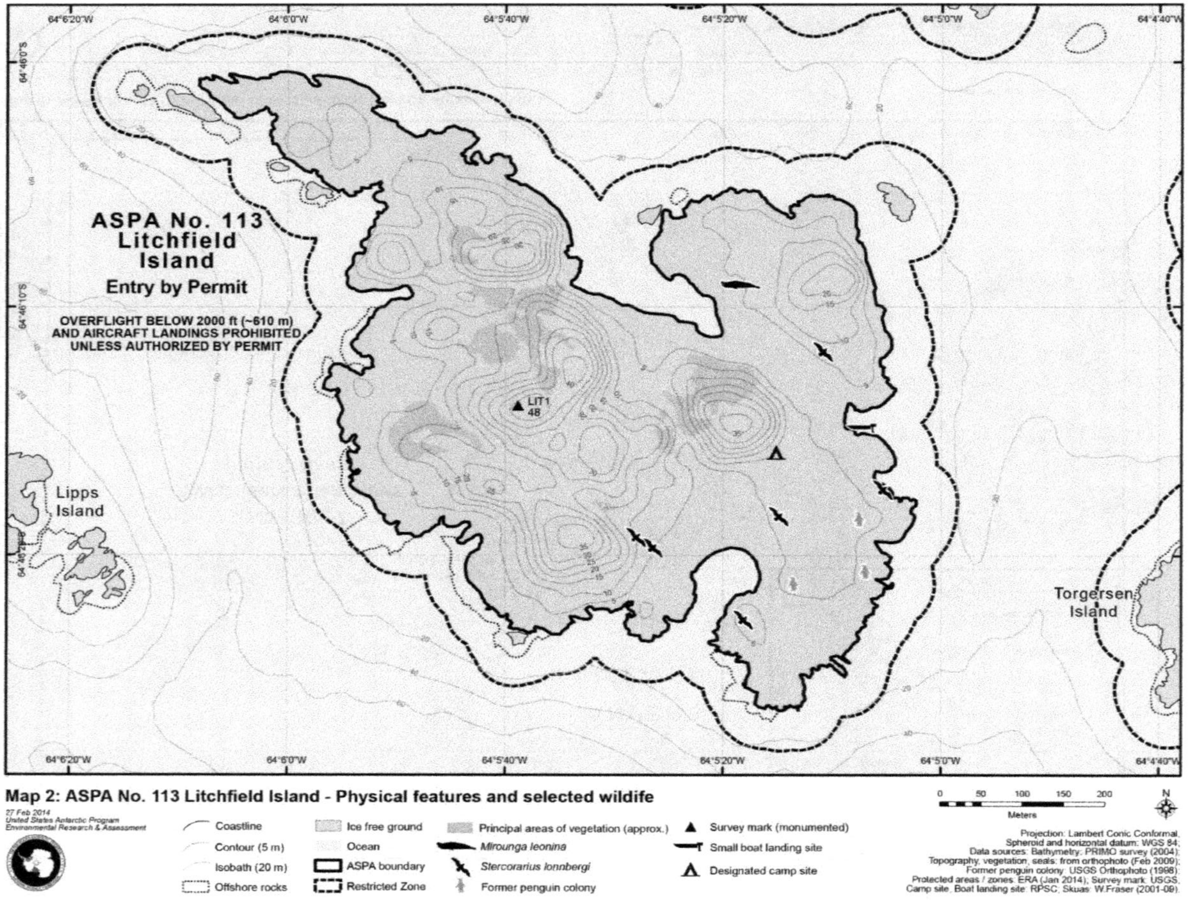

ASPA No. 113
Litchfield
Island

Entry by Permit

OVERFLIGHT BELOW 2000 ft (~610 m)
AND AIRCRAFT LANDINGS PROHIBITED
UNLESS AUTHORIZED BY PERMIT

Torgersen
Island

Lipps
Island

LIT1
48

Map 2: ASPA No. 113 Litchfield Island - Physical features and selected wildlife

27 Feb 2014
United States Antarctic Program
Environmental Research & Assessment

Coastline
Contour (5 m)
Isobath (20 m)
Offshore rocks

Ice free ground
Ocean
ASPA boundary
Restricted Zone

Principal areas of vegetation (approx.)
Mirounga leonina
Stercorarius lonnbergi
Former penguin colony

Survey mark (monumented)
Small boat landing site
Designated camp site

0   50   100   150   200
Meters

Projection: Lambert Conic Conformal
Spheroid and horizontal datum: WGS 84.
Data sources: Bathymetry: PRIMO survey (2004);
Topography, vegetation: steals from earthquake (Feb 2009);
Former penguin colony, USGS Ortleophoto (1998);
Protected areas / zones: ERA (Jan 2014); Survey mark: USGS
Camp site: Boat landing site: RPSC; Skuas: W.Fraser (2001-08)

64°46'0"S
64°46'10"S
64°46'20"S

64°4'40"W
64°4'50"W
64°4'50"W

Management Plan for

Antarctic Specially Protected Area (ASPA) No. 121

CAPE ROYDS, ROSS ISLAND

Introduction

Cape Royds lies at the western extremity of Ross Island, McMurdo Sound, at 166°09'56"E, 77°33'20"S. Approximate area: 0.66 km^2. The primary reasons for designation are on the grounds that the Area supports the most southerly established Adélie penguin (*Pygoscelis adeliae*) colony known, for which there exists a long time series of population data that is of unique and outstanding scientific value. In addition, the Area has important terrestrial and freshwater ecological values, including the most southerly observation of snow algae, the type locality for original descriptions of a number of species of algae, and the unusual presence of a form of Dissolved Organic Matter that is almost entirely microbially-derived.

The Area was originally designated as Site of Special Scientific Interest (SSSI) No. 1 in Recommendation VIII-4 (1975) after a proposal by the United States of America. The SSSI designation was extended through Recommendation X-6 (1979), Recommendation XII-5 (1983), Resolution 7 (1995) and Measure 2 (2000). A revision was adopted through Recommendation XIII-9 (1985). The site was renamed and renumbered as Antarctic Specially Protected Area (ASPA) No 121 by Decision 1 (2002). A revised management plan was adopted through Measure 1 (2002), and then through Measure 5 (2009) when the size of the marine component was reduced.

The Area is situated within Environment P – Ross and Ronne-Filchner based on the Environmental Domains Analysis for Antarctica and within Region 9 - South Victoria Land based on the Antarctic Conservation Biogeographic Regions.

1. Description of values to be protected

An area of about 300 m^2 at Cape Royds was originally designated in Recommendation VIII-4 (1975, SSSI No. 1) after a proposal by the United States of America on the grounds that it supports the most southerly established Adélie penguin (*Pygoscelis adeliae*) colony known. The Adélie penguin population at Cape Royds had declined from 1956 as a consequence of human interference during a period when heavy sea ice cover made the colony particularly susceptible to reduced recruitment. In 1963 United States and New Zealand authorities agreed to restrict activities and develop a management plan for the Area in order to protect the scientific values related to penguin research. The site was specially protected to allow the population to recover and protect on-going science programs. The population has recovered and now exceeds pre-1956 levels; since 1990 numbers have fluctuated between 2,500 and 4,500 pairs, primarily due to natural variation in local sea ice extent. The long time series of population data on the penguin colony at Cape Royds is of unique and outstanding scientific value, for it enables investigations into long-term biological interactions with and responses to environmental forcing factors. The colony remains of high scientific and ecological value and as such merits continued long-term special protection, especially in view of ongoing visits to Cape Royds from nearby stations and tourist groups.

The original Area was enlarged in 1985 as a result of a proposal by New Zealand (Recommendation XIII-9) to include a 500 m–wide coastal strip to protect the seaward access and nearshore feeding ground of the Adélie penguins, as well as projected research on the Cape Royds inshore marine ecosystem. This coastal area of Cape Royds was a site of studies on Nototheniid fish population structure and dynamics. More recently, research on foraging patterns of Adélie penguins from Cape Royds, conducted since this marine component of the Area was adopted, has shown that the marine area as it had been designated is not significant as a penguin feeding ground and that the birds forage more widely than had previously been known. In addition, projected research on the Cape Royds inshore marine ecosystem has not occurred to the extent that had been anticipated, and currently few studies are being carried out on the Nototheniid fish population at Cape Royds. In view of these factors, and because specific values related to the marine environment adjacent to Cape Royds remain undescribed, the marine boundary was redefined through Measure 5 (2009) to focus more particularly on the area immediately surrounding the Adélie penguin colony. The marine component immediately adjacent to the Cape Royds penguin colony has been retained because it includes the primary access route of the penguins to the colony, which could otherwise be subjected to unnecessary disturbance by both visitors and local helicopter activity in the vicinity.

Research carried out over the last several decades has also noted that the Area has important values related to freshwater and terrestrial ecology. Pony Lake is a type locality for original descriptions of a number of species of algae collected during Shackleton's British Antarctic Expedition of 1907-09. The most southerly observation of snow algae, dominated by *Chlamydomonas*, has been made within the Area. In addition, recent studies have shown fulvic acid Dissolved Organic Matter (DOM) present in Pony Lake is almost entirely microbially-derived, which is considered unusual. Because these substances are poorly understood, isolated reference samples are needed for research purposes: a sample collected from Pony Lake has made a valuable contribution as a reference for the International Humic Substances Society. Finally, it has been noted that the very low diversity of soil organisms at the site makes it valuable for comparisons with other, more favorable, habitats.

Shackleton's Hut (Historic Monument No. 15), located in ASPA No. 157 (Backdoor Bay), lies 170 meters to the northeast of the Adélie colony and, together with the colony, are attractions of high aesthetic and educational value to visitors. Regular and frequent visits to Cape Royds mean that the Area could easily be damaged by human impact if not provided with adequate protection. The scientific and ecological values of the Area require long-term protection from possible adverse impacts associated with these activities. However, in recognition of the value of the Adélie colony as the most accessible of any penguin species to the personnel of McMurdo Station (US) and Scott Base (NZ), provision has been made for controlled access to two viewing areas near to, but outside of, the boundaries in order to allow visitors to Cape Royds the opportunity to observe the colony without causing significant impact. Such visits are subject to Site Guidelines agreed through Resolution 4 (2009).

Relics from the time of Shackleton's voyages are present at the site of a small depot in an embayment on the west side of the penguin nesting area (166°09'35.2" E, 77°33'14.3"S: Map 2). The depot has historic value and should not be disturbed except by permit for conservation or management purposes.

The boundaries encompass the entire Adélie penguin colony, the southern part of Pony Lake, and the marine environment up to 500 meters from the shoreline surrounding Flagstaff Point, comprising a terrestrial component of 0.05 km^2 and a marine component of 0.61 km^2, giving a total area of 0.66 km^2.

2. Aims and objectives

Management at Cape Royds aims to:

- Avoid degradation of, or substantial risk to, the values of the Area by preventing unnecessary human disturbance and sampling in the Area;
- Allow scientific research on the ecosystem of the Area, in particular on the avifauna and terrestrial and freshwater ecology, provided it will not compromise the values for which the Area is protected;
- Allow other scientific research and visits for educational and outreach purposes (such as documentary reporting (visual, audio or written) or the production of educational resources or services) provided such activities are for compelling reasons that cannot be served elsewhere and will not compromise the values for which the Area is protected;
- Minimize the possibility of introduction of alien plants, animals and microbes to the Area;
- Minimise the possibility of the introduction of pathogens that may cause disease in faunal populations within the Area;

- Take into account the potential historic and heritage values of any artifacts before their removal and/or disposal, while allowing for appropriate clean-up and remediation if required;
- Allow visits for management purposes in support of the aims of the management plan.

3. Management activities

The following management activities shall be undertaken to protect the values of the Area:

- Brightly colored markers, which should be clearly visible from the air and pose no significant threat to the environment, should be placed to mark the helicopter landing pad adjacent to the protected area (Maps 1 and 2);
- Signs illustrating the location and boundaries with clear statements of entry restrictions shall be placed at appropriate locations at the boundaries of the Area to help avoid inadvertent entry. In addition, flags should be placed on the sea-ice in Backdoor Bay along the southeast boundary of the marine area (offshore from Derrick Point) on the first visit over sea-ice each season to indicate the restricted area so those travelling to Cape Royds over sea ice are aware of the marine boundary of the Area. Flags placed shall be removed immediately prior to closure of sea-ice travel each season;
- Signs showing the location of the Area (stating the special restrictions that apply) shall be displayed prominently, and a copy of this management plan shall be kept available, in all research hut facilities located at Cape Royds;
- Copies of this management plan shall be made available to all vessels and aircraft visiting and/or operating in the vicinity of Cape Royds, and all personnel (national program staff, field expeditions, tourist expedition leaders, pilots and ship captains) operating in the vicinity of, accessing or flying near the Area, shall be informed by their national program, tour operator or appropriate national authority of the location, boundaries and restrictions applying to entry and overflight within the Area;
- National programs shall take steps to ensure the boundaries of the Area and the restrictions that apply within are marked on relevant maps and nautical / aeronautical charts;
- Markers, signs or structures erected within the Area for scientific or management purposes shall be secured and maintained in good condition, and removed when no longer necessary;
- National Antarctic programs operating in the Area should maintain a record of all new markers, signs and structures erected within the Area;
- Visits shall be made as necessary (no less than once every five years) to assess whether the Area continues to serve the purposes for which it was designated and to ensure management and maintenance measures are adequate;
- National Antarctic Programs operating in the region shall consult together with a view to ensuring these steps are carried out.

4. Period of designation

Designated for an indefinite period.

5. Maps and photographs

Map 1: ASPA No. 121 Cape Royds - boundaries and topography.

Projection: Lambert Conformal Conic; Standard parallels: 1st 77° 33' 10" S; 2nd 77° 33' 30"S; Central Meridian: 166° 10' 00" E; Latitude of Origin: 78° 00' 00" S; Spheroid: WGS84.
Data sources:
The base map and contours are derived from an orthophotograph using aerial imagery acquired by USGS/DoSLI (SN7847) 16 November 1993 prepared at 1:2500 with a positional accuracy of ±1.25 m (horizontal) and ±2.5 m (vertical) and an on-ground pixel resolution of 0.4 m. Signposts: UNAVCO (Jan 2014). ASPA boundary: ERA (Jan 2014). Survey markers: LINZ (2011). Viewing areas and AWS (approx.): ERA (Jan 2014). Paths and anchorages from ASPA No. 157 Management Plan; approximate penguin nesting

area digitized from georeferenced aerial image acquired 19 Jan 2005 and supplied by P. Lyver, Landcare Research, Mar 2014. Contours (interval 10 m) and other infrastructure supplied by Gateway Antarctica (2009).

Inset 1: Ross Sea region, showing location of Inset 2.

Inset 2 Ross Island region, showing location of Map 1 and McMurdo Station (US) and Scott Base (NZ).

Map 2: ASPA No. 121 - access, facilities and wildlife. Map specifications as per Map 1, except the contour interval is 2 m.

6. Description of the Area

6(i) Geographical coordinates, boundary markers and natural features

General description

Cape Royds (166°09'56"E, 77°33'20"S) is situated at the western extremity of Ross Island, McMurdo Sound, on a coastal strip of ice-free land approximately 8 km wide, on the lower western slopes of Mount Erebus (Map 1, Insets). The Area comprises both a terrestrial and marine component.

The terrestrial component of the Area consists of ice-free land within approximately 350 m of Flagstaff Point (166°09'55"E, 77°33'21"S) that is seasonally occupied by a breeding Adélie penguin (*Pygoscelis adeliae*) colony. The boundary includes all of the area occupied by breeding penguins and the main southern route used by the penguins to access the sea. The marine component comprises an area of sea within 500 m of the Cape Royds coastline, which includes the main penguin access route to the colony.

Boundary

The northern boundary of the terrestrial component of the Area extends from a small embayment at the northwestern corner of the Area for 53 m in a straight line NE to a survey mark identified on earlier New Zealand maps as IT2 (166°09'33.8"E, 77°33'11.1"S), which is an iron tube embedded in the ground. The boundary thence extends 9 m east from IT2 to a signpost (166°09'35.2" E, 77°33'11.2" S), thence a further 30 m east-northeast to a signpost (166°09'39.4" E, 77°33'10.9" S) half way down the slope of a small hill. From this signpost the boundary extends in a SE direction for 133 m to a signpost (166°09'59.0", 77°33'11.8" S) east of Pony Lake. The boundary thence extends 42 m in a SSE direction to a signpost (166°10'01.9" E, 77°33'12.9" S), thence a further 74 m to a signpost (166°10'05.7" E, 77°33'15.2" S) at the southern end of the penguin viewing area. The boundary thence extends 18 m to the coast at Arrival Bay (166°10'06.6" E, 77°33'15.8" S). The northeastern boundary thence follows the coastline from Arrival Bay to Derrick Point. The boundary from Pony Lake (signpost at 166°09'59.0" E, 77°33'11.8" S) to Derrick Point is coincident with the southern boundary of ASPA No. 157 Backdoor Bay, which has been designated to protect Shackleton's historic hut and associated artefacts (Historic Site and Monument No. 15).

The marine component of the Area encompasses the area within 500 m of the mean high water coastline of Flagstaff Point, with the boundary extending 500 m southwest from Derrick Point in the east (166°10'22" E, 77°33'14.1" S), thence westward maintaining a distance of 500 m from the shore to 166°08'10" E, 77°33'11.8" S, thence due east 500 m to coast at the northwestern corner of the Area (166°9'25" E, 77°33'11.8" S).

Climate

An Automatic Weather Station (AWS) installed inside the Area near Shackleton's Hut (Map 2) has recorded summer data since 2007, with full-year records available for all 2012 and 2013. The maximum temperature recorded by this weather station was 7.5°C in December 2010 and the minimum -36.8°C in July 2012 (data from University of Wisconsin-Madison Automatic Weather Station Program, accessed http://uwamrc.ssec.wisc.edu/ 18 Feb 2014).

Air temperature data collected at nearby McMurdo Station, located approximately 35 km southeast of Cape Royds, during the period of 2004 – 2013 indicate hat December is the warmest month with a mean temperatire of -1.9 °C and that July is the coolest month with an average temperature of -25.7 °C (http://uwamrc.ssec.wisc.edu/ 21 Feb 2014). The minimum air temperature recorded during the period 2004 to 2013 was -47.8 °C recorded in July 2003, whilst the maximum temperature attained was 8.8 °C in January 2007. The wind at Cape Royds is predominantly from the southeast and deposits sea spray across the Area (Broady 1989a). Data from McMurdo Station over the period 1973–2004 showed average wind speeds of around 10 knots, whilst the maximum recorded reached 112.3 knots (Antarctic Meteorological Research Centre 2009).

Long term climate records indicate that during the 1960's air temperatures and wind speeds recorded at Scott Base were relatively low, which was followed by a period of warming in the early 1970's (Ainley *et al.* 2005). From the early 1980's a marked warming trend was observed across the McMurdo Sound area (Blackburn *et al.* 1991) and records from McMurdo Station suggest that air temperatures peaked in the late 1980's, before cooling once again in the early 1990's (Wilson *et al.* 2001).

Geology and soils

The terrestrial component of the Area comprises rocky terrain of irregular lava flows, volcanic gravels and dark reddish scoria, bounded on the seaward side by a low cliff of approximately 10-20 m in height. Mineral soils and sand are present together with encrusted salts and compacted ornithogenic soils associated with the Adélie penguin colony (Cowan and Casanueva 2007).

Breeding birds

The Area contains the world's most southerly established Adélie penguin (*Pygoscelis adeliae*) colony, with annual population numbers currently fluctuating between 2,500 and 4,500 breeding pairs during the approximate mid-October to mid-February occupation (Figure 1). The population size in 1959 was deemed to be equivalent to that in 1909 with no evidence that it had been larger in historical times (Ainley 2002), then declined to fewer than 1000 breeding pairs in 1963 as a result of severe ice conditions which made the colony more susceptible to disturbance by visitation and helicopter movements (Thompson 1977). Following visitor restrictions and relocation of the helicopter pad away from the colony, penguin populations gradually recovered during the 1970's, increasing at a mean annual rate of 15% between 1983 and 1987 and quadrupling the population (Ainley *et al.* 2005; Taylor and Wilson 1990). Following a peak in 1987, Adélie numbers at Cape Royds declined sharply in 1988 and 1989, before recovering once more to reach a population comparable to levels recorded during the late 1980's. By 1998, the Adélie population at Cape Royds had reached 4,000 breeding pairs, with numbers subsequently declining to 2,400 pairs by 2000 (Ainley *et al.* 2004).

Fluctuations in Adélie penguin populations at Cape Royds have been linked to changes in a range of climatic and environmental variables. Wilson *et al.* (2001) found a significant inverse correlation between Adélie numbers and winter sea ice extent, with more extensive (i.e. more northerly) sea ice coverage reducing sub-adult survival rates by restricting access to productive feeding areas. Consequently, total Adélie numbers at Cape Royds showed a 5-year lagged response to sea ice concentration variation. The influence of sea ice coverage on Adélie numbers within the Area was further highlighted following the grounding of a large iceberg (designated B15A, 175 x 54 km in size) on the shore of Ross Island prior to the 2000 nesting season (Arrigo *et al.* 2002; Ainley *et al.* 2003). The obstruction caused by the B-15 iceberg resulted in unusually extensive sea ice coverage in 2000, which in turn caused a 40 % reduction in primary productivity. While Adélie surveys carried out at Cape Royds in 2000 showed a significant change in penguin diet, the impact of increased sea ice coverage on chick production in that season was minimal (Ainley *et al.* 2003). In the years immediately following, the number of breeding pairs and the number of chicks fledged declined dramatically (Ainley 2014), with the number of breeding pairs showing a gradual recovery over 2001-2012 to reach a level similar to that which existed prior to the B-15 iceberg event (Figure 1).

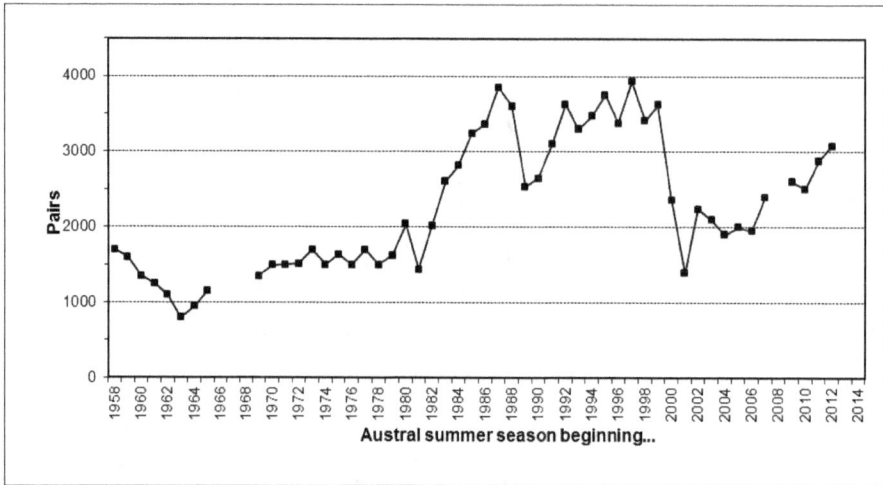

Fig ure 1. Number of breeding pairs of Adélie penguins at Cape Royds 1958-59 – 2012-13. (Sources: Stonehouse 1965; Taylor *et al.* 1990; Woehler 1993; Woehler pers. comm. 1999; Ainley *et al.* 2004; Lyver *et al.* in press; Ainley 2014)

In addition to specific influences of sea ice extent, Adélie population expansion at Cape Royds has been attributed to the broader effects of climatic warming within the McMurdo Sound area (Ainley *et al.* 2005; Blackburn *et al.* 1991), which began in the mid 1960's and became particularly pronounced in the 1980's (Taylor and Wilson 1990). Climatic amelioration is thought to have positively influenced Adélie populations by reducing sea ice extent and enlarging the Ross Sea polynya, increasing marine productivity and the availability of food, lowering winter mortality, and enhancing penguin breeding success (Taylor and Wilson 1990; Blackburn *et al.* 1991; Ainley *et al.* 2005). An alternative explanation for the rapid expansion of the Cape Royds colony in the 1980's may lie in a substantial decrease in numbers of Antarctic minke whale, *Balaenoptera bonaerensis*, removed from the Ross Sea during this decade (Ainley *et al.* 2007). The habitat and prey of the minke whale overlaps that of the Adélie penguin, suggesting that release from competition may have caused the population boom observed at Cape Royds and elsewhere on Ross Island.

The underlying causes of the Adélie population crash at Cape Royds in 1988 and 1989 have yet to be resolved, although a link has been made to changes in the Antarctic Oscillation (AAO), with resultant impacts on weather and sea ice conditions, which in turn may have increased Adélie mortality (Ainley *et al.* 2005). Subsequent to 1989, the Cape Royds colony grew rapidly, in contrast to trends at Cape Crozier, suggesting that changes in emigration patterns may have been responsible (Ainley, Ballard *et al.* unpublished data). In addition, continued oceanic warming within the region is likely to have significantly impacted upon sea ice persistence (Ainley *et al.* 2005) and may have contributed to colony growth.

The Area has been monitored regularly since 1957 and has been photographed from the air during the incubation phase of breeding annually since 1981.The annual assessment of Adélie penguin population size at colonies on Ross Island, Ross Sea, from 1959 to 1997 is one of the longest-running marine biological time series in the Antarctic (Taylor and Wilson 1990; Taylor *et al.* 1990; Wilson *et al.* 2001). The long history of scientific observations at Cape Royds thus provides rare opportunities to assess population trends over long periods, enabling assessment of the effects of changing ice regimes against the population dynamics of these bird colonies in the relatively pristine southern Ross Sea ecosystem (Ballard pers. comm. 2008).

Studies of Adélie foraging patterns during the austral summers 1997–98 to 2000–01 indicated the mean foraging distance from Cape Royds ranged between 9.70 km and 12.09 km (Ainley *et al.* 2004) and observations suggest that little foraging occurs within 200m of the coast (Ainley pers. comm. 2008). The foraging range of penguins belonging to the Cape Royds colony overlaps extensively (30–75%) with the ranges of birds originating from both Cape Bird and Beaufort Island (Ainley *et al.* 2004). Banded penguins from Cape Royds, Cape Bird and Beaufort Island are often seen within the other colonies (Ainley unpublished data, referenced in Ainley *et al.* 2003) and it has been suggested that immigration to Cape Royds from these locations was a major causal factor of population growth during the 1980's onwards (Ainley *et al.* 2004; Ainley pers. comm. 2008).

In addition to the Cape Royds Adélie penguin colony, a significant breeding population of south polar skuas (*Stercorarius maccormicki*) is located close to the ASPA boundary, which totalled 76 breeding pairs in 1981 (Ainley *et al.* 1986). The skuas have been observed to nest and forage for food within penguin rookeries at Cape Royds (Young 1962a). It was noted however, that preying of skuas on young penguins was limited and that only a portion of the skuas breeding at Cape Royds obtained food from within the Adélie colony (Young 1962b). Skua populations declined substantially following cessation of human refuse disposal at McMurdo Station, but are currently not thought to be under threat (Ainley pers. comm. 2008).

Marine biology and oceanography

The marine component of the Area has neither been intensively studied nor fully described. This region has not been subjected to the level of sampling that has occurred close to Hut Point further to the south on Ross Island. To 500 m west of the shore the sea floor generally drops off steeply down to several hundred meters, with some submarine cliffs. Sea floor samples collected several kilometers north of Cape Royds and approximately 100 m offshore consisted of coarse volcanic gravels and small to large boulders. Research on the Nototheniid fish population and structure in this vicinity between 1978–81 suggested that fish were abundant, with the most common species at that time being *Trematomus bernacchii*. The surveys also recorded the presence of *Trematomus hansoni, T. centronotus, T. nicolai* and *Gymnodraco acuticeps.* The surveys identified the presence of invertebrates such as echinoids, asteroids (e.g. *Odontaster validus*), ophiuroids, pycnogonids (e.g. *Pentanymphon antarcticum, Colossendeis robusta*), pteropods, copepods, amphipods, isopods, hirudinea, bryozoa, polycheates, ctenophores, mollusca, and medusae. More recent data describing the marine environment close to Cape Royds is not available.

Local ocean currents originate from the eastern Ross Sea continental shelf and flow westward along the Ross Ice Shelf past Cape Crozier, and then turns northward along the Victoria Land coast. The current divides at Beaufort Island, where a minor arm veers southward past Capes Bird and Royds (Jacobs et al. 1970; Barry 1988).

Terrestrial and freshwater ecology

Ponds within the Area, including Pony Lake, are nutrient-enriched and contain an abundant and diverse algal community adapted to high nutrients and salinity, dominated by phytoplankton, diatoms and oscillatorian benthic felts (Broady 1987). Some species of algae were first formally described from Pony Lake (West and West 1911), making the site a 'type locality'. Snow algae are present on small patches of snow on the coastal ice-foot adjacent to the penguin colony, dominated by species of *Chlamydomonas*, which is the most southerly record of snow algae (Broady 1989a).

Pony Lake has been identified as an important source of microbially derived Dissolved Organic Material (DOM) (Brown *et al.*2004). One type of DOM, fulvic acid, is derived from decaying plant matter and microbial activity. The fulvic acid present in Pony Lake has been identified as an important end-member as it is almostly entirely microbially-derived. Fulvic acids affect the chemistry, cycling and bioavailability of chemical elements in terrestrial and aquatic environments. Because these substances are poorly understood, isolated reference samples are needed for research purposes. A reference sample of Pony Lake fulvic acid was collected and made available to serve as a microbial end-member for distribution through the International Humic Substances Society. The lake's abundant levels of DOM and convenient location from McMurdo Station make it an ideal place to conduct such fieldwork.

Studies of terrestrial invertebrate (nematode) populations from the ornithogenic soils at Cape Royds have been carried out since 1990. In contrast to the greater invertebrate diversity in the Dry Valleys, only one species of nematode was observed at Cape Royds (*Panagrolaimus davidi*) (Porazinska *et al.* 2002). The very high-nutrient soils at Cape Royds lead to low biodiversity of soil organisms, making the Area susceptible to local and global human disturbance. Additionally, Cape Royds serves as a comparison for habitats under investigation in the McMurdo Dry Valleys.

There is little lichen growth within the Area, although different lichen growth forms (crustose, foliose and fruticose) are found in other parts of Cape Royds, distributed in three distinct zones believed to result from marine aerosol and snow accumulation patterns (Broady 1989a, 1989b).

Human activities and impact

Changes to the population of Adélie penguins at Cape Royds attributed at least in part to human visitation and helicopter movements is discussed in the section above on breeding birds.

Cape Royds is a popular destination for recreational visits from McMurdo Station (US) and Scott Base (NZ) to view Shackleton's Hut, particularly early in the season when travel to the site is possible by vehicle over sea ice. Visits are carefully controlled by national authorities, and entry to protected areas is strictly by permit. The number of station personnel visiting Cape Royds is recorded, and an average of 147 US and 78 NZ personnel visited Shackleton's Hut per season over the period 2008-09 – 2012-13. This compares with an average of 172 US and 143 NZ personnel visiting Shackleton's Hut in the previous 5-year period of 2003-04 – 2007-08.

Cape Royds is one of the most popular tourist sites in the Ross Sea (see Table 1), with Shackleton's Hut (Historic Site & Monument No.15 and ASPA No.157), located 170 m northeast of the colony, being the main attraction. The penguin viewing areas immediately to the north and east of the existing boundary, close to Pony Lake are also popular with visitors. Visitors are briefed and visits are supervised, and the boundaries of the Area are generally respected.

Table 1: Visitor overview

Season	Visitors all	Visitors landed	Tourists all	Tourists landed
2003-04	307	307	266	266
2004-05	586	586	502	502
2005-06	458	369	390	306
2006-07	456	456	377	377
2007-08	176	176	147	147
2008-09	284	282	236	236
2009-10	316	316	263	263
2010-11	328	328	283	283
2011-12	327	327	281	281
2012-13	358	247	300	206

Source: IAATO.

6(ii) Access to the Area

The Area may be accessed by traversing over land or sea ice, by sea or to nearby helicopter landing sites outside of the Area by air. Particular routes are recommended for access to the Area, and overflight and aircraft landing restrictions apply, the specific conditions for which are set out in Section 7(ii) below.

6(iii) Structures within and near the Area

Shackleton's Hut (ASPA No. 157 and Historic Site and Monument No. 15) (166°10'06.4" E, 77°33'10.7"S) is situated approximately 70 m from the NE boundary sign of the terrestrial component of the Area, 100 m northeast of which is a small research shelter (New Zealand) (166°10'10.6" E, 77°33'07.5"S) (Map 2). An Automatic Weather Station (AWS) was installed in January 2007 10 m inside the eastern boundary of the Area (Map 2), 80 m from Shackleton's Hut, and was present in January 2014. Two survey markers are present within the Area – marker IT2 is on the northern boundary of the terrestrial part of the Area and is described above, while marker IT3 (166°09'52.7" E, 77°33'19.7"S) (also an iron tube embedded in the ground) is 45 m NW of Flagstaff Point. Relics at the site of a small depot from the time of Shackleton's voyages are present in a small embayment on the west side of the penguin nesting area (166°09'35.2" E, 77°33'14.3"S: Map 2). The depot should not be disturbed except by permit for conservation or management purposes.

6(iv) Location of other protected areas within close proximity of the Area

The nearest protected areas to Cape Royds are Backdoor Bay (ASPA No.157 and HSM No.15) which is adjacent to and shares the northern boundary of the Area, Cape Evans (ASPA No.155) 10 km to the south, Tramway Ridge (ASPA No.130) close to the summit of Mount Erebus situated 20 km east, New College Valley (ASPA No.116) 35 km to the north at Cape Bird, and Arrival Heights (ASPA No.122) which is adjacent to McMurdo Station 35 km to the south. Cape Crozier (ASPA No.124) is 75 km to the east on Ross Island. Antarctic Specially Managed Area No. 2 McMurdo Dry Valleys is located approximately 70 km to the west of Cape Royds.

6(v) Special zones within the Area

There are no zones designated within the Area.

7. Permit conditions

7(i) General permit conditions

Entry into the Area is prohibited except in accordance with a Permit issued by an appropriate national authority. Conditions for issuing a Permit to enter the Area are that:

- It is issued for scientific research, and in particular for research on the avifauna in the Area, or for compelling scientific, educational or outreach reasons that cannot be served elsewhere, or for reasons essential to the management of the Area;
- The actions permitted are in accordance with this Management Plan;
- The activities permitted will give due consideration via the environmental impact assessment process to the continued protection of the environmental and scientific values of the Area;
- Approach distances to fauna must be respected, except when scientific needs may require otherwise and this is specified in the relevant permits;
- the Permit shall be issued for a finite period;
- the Permit, or a copy, shall be carried within the Area.

7(ii) Access to, and movement within, or over the Area

Within the terrestrial part of the Area access shall be on foot and vehicles are prohibited. Within the marine part of the Area, access should be by foot or vehicle when sea-ice is present, or by ship or small boat during open water periods. Foot access into the Area should be from the direction of the helicopter landing site, and if arriving over the sea ice or by boat, then access should first be to Backdoor Bay and thence on foot following the paths shown on Maps 1 and 2.

Foot access and movement within the Area

Movement on land within the Area shall be on foot. Pedestrians should maintain a minimum approach distance of 5 m from wildlife, unless it is necessary to approach closer for purposes allowed for by the permit. Visitors should move carefully so as to minimize disturbance to flora, fauna, soils, and water bodies. Pedestrians should walk around the penguin colonies and should not enter sub-groups of nesting penguins unless required for research or management purposes. Care should be taken to avoid trampling nests when moving through skua territories. Pedestrian traffic should be kept to the minimum consistent with the objectives of any permitted activities and every reasonable effort should be made to minimize effects.

Ship and small boat access

Ships and small boats are prohibited from entering the marine component of the Area except by Permit. Ships embarking passengers should remain at least 300 m from shore and visitor access either by small boat or over sea ice should be to the landing site on the NW shore of Backdoor Bay (Maps 1 and 2).

Aircraft access and overflight

Landing by aircraft within the Area is prohibited. Overflight below 610 m (~2000ft) Above Ground Level is prohibited except when operationally necessary for scientific purposes. Helicopters should land throughout the year at the Primary landing site (166°10.38'E, 77°33.06'S), 250 m northeast of the northern extent of Pony Lake (Map 2). A Secondary landing site is located at 166°10.24'E, 77°33.11'S, ~100 m SW of the Primary landing site, which should be avoided when the penguin colony is occupied (01 November through 01 March).

7(iii) Activities that may be conducted within the Area

- Scientific research that will not jeopardize the ecosystem or scientific values of the Area;
- Activities with educational and / or outreach purposes that cannot be served elsewhere;
- Activities with the aim of preserving or protecting historic resources within the Area;
- Essential management activities, including monitoring and inspection.

7(iv) Installation, modification or removal of structures / equipment

- No structures are to be erected within the Area except as specified in a permit and, with the exception of permanent survey markers and signs, permanent structures or installations are prohibited;
- All structures, scientific equipment or markers installed in the Area must be authorized by permit and clearly identified by country, name of the principal investigator, year of installation and date of expected removal. All such items should be free of organisms, propagules (e.g. seeds, eggs) and non-sterile soil, and be made of materials that can withstand the environmental conditions and pose minimal risk of contamination or damage to the values of the Area;
- Installation (including site selection), maintenance, modification or removal of structures or equipment shall be undertaken in a manner that minimizes disturbance to flora and fauna, preferably avoiding the main breeding season (01 Oct – 31 Mar);
- Removal of specific equipment for which the permit has expired shall be the responsibility of the authority which granted the original Permit, and shall be a condition of the permit.

7(v) Location of field camps

Camping within the terrestrial part of the Area is prohibited. A field campsite exists 175 m northeast of the Area adjacent to the New Zealand shelter (Map 2). Camping within the marine part of the Area when sea ice is present is allowed by permit. Such camps should avoid the penguin approach routes within 200 m of the breeding colony, but are otherwise not restricted to a particular location.

7(vi) Restrictions on materials and organisms which may be brought into the Area

In addition to the requirements of the Protocol on Environmental Protection to the Antarctic Treaty, restrictions on materials and organisms which may be brought into the Area are:

- Deliberate introduction of animals, plant material, micro-organisms and non-sterile soil into the Area is prohibited. Precautions shall be taken to prevent the accidental introduction of animals, plant material, micro-organisms and non-sterile soil from other biologically distinct regions (within or beyond the Antarctic Treaty area).
- Visitors shall ensure that sampling equipment and markers brought into the Area are clean. To the maximum extent practicable, footwear and other equipment used or brought into the Area (including backpacks, carry-bags and other equipment) shall be thoroughly cleaned before entering the Area. Visitors should also consult and follow as appropriate recommendations contained in the Committee for Environmental Protection Non-native Species Manual (CEP 2011), and in the Environmental Code of Conduct for terrestrial scientific field research in Antarctica (SCAR 2009);
- All poultry and poultry products, including products containing uncooked dried eggs, are prohibited from the Area. All poultry brought to and not consumed or used at nearby huts, facilities and / or camping sites, including all parts, products and / or wastes of poultry, should be removed or disposed of by incineration or equivalent means that eliminates risks to native flora and fauna;
- No herbicides or pesticides shall be brought into the Area;
- Any other chemicals, including radio-nuclides or stable isotopes, which may be introduced for scientific or management purposes specified in the permit, shall be removed from the Area at or before the conclusion of the activity for which the permit was granted;
- Fuel, food, chemicals, and other materials shall not be stored in the Area, unless specifically authorized by permit and shall be stored and handled in a way that minimises the risk of their accidental introduction into the environment;
- All materials introduced shall be for a stated period only, shall be removed at or before the conclusion of that stated period, and shall be stored and handled so that risk of their introduction into the environment is minimized;
- If release occurs which is likely to compromise the values of the Area, removal is encouraged only where the impact of removal is not likely to be greater than that of leaving the material *in situ*.

7(vii) Taking of, or harmful interference with, native flora or fauna

Taking or harmful interference with native flora and fauna is prohibited, except in accordance with a permit issued under Article 3 of Annex II of the Protocol on Environmental Protection to the Antarctic Treaty. Where animal taking or harmful interference is involved, this should, as a minimum standard, be in accordance with the SCAR Code of Conduct for the Use of Animals for Scientific Purposes in Antarctica.

7(viii) The collection or removal of materials not brought into the Area by the permit holder

- Material may be collected or removed from the Area only in accordance with a permit and should be limited to the minimum necessary to meet scientific or management needs. This includes biological samples, rock specimens, and historical items.
- Material of human origin likely to compromise the values of the Area, and which was not brought into the Area by the permit holder or otherwise authorized, may be removed from any part of the Area, unless the impact of removal is likely to be greater than leaving the material *in situ*. If this is the case the appropriate authority should be notified.
- Unless specifically authorized by permit, visitors are prohibited from interfering with or from handling, taking or damaging any historic artifacts found within the Area. Any new artifacts observed should be notified to the appropriate national authority. Relocation or removal of artifacts for the purposes of preservation, protection or to re-establish historical accuracy is allowable by permit.

7(ix) Disposal of waste

All wastes shall be removed from the Area.

7(x) Measures that may be necessary to continue to meet the aims of the Management Plan

Permits may be granted to enter the Area to:

1) Carry out biological monitoring and Area inspection activities, which may involve the collection of a small number of samples or data for analysis or review;
2) Install or maintain signposts, markers, structures or scientific or essential logistic equipment;
3) Carry out protective measures;
4) Carry out research or management in a manner that avoids interference with long-term research and monitoring activities or possible duplication of effort. Persons planning new projects within the Area should consult with established programs working within the Area, such as those of the US and New Zealand, before initiating the work.

7(xi) Requirements for reports

-   The principal permit holder for each visit to the Area shall submit a report to the appropriate national authority as soon as practicable, and no later than six months after the visit has been completed.
-   Such reports should include, as appropriate, the information identified in the visit report form contained in the Guide to the Preparation of Management Plans for Antarctic Specially Protected Areas. If appropriate, the national authority should also forward a copy of the visit report to the Parties that proposed the Management Plan, to assist in managing the Area and reviewing the Management Plan.
-   Parties should, wherever possible, deposit originals or copies of such original visit reports in a publicly accessible archive to maintain a record of usage, for the purpose of any review of the Management Plan and in organising the scientific use of the Area.
-   The appropriate authority should be notified of any activities/measures undertaken, and / or of any materials released and not removed, that were not included in the authorized permit.

References

Ainley, D.G. 2002. The Adélie penguin: bellwether of climate change. Columbia University Press, New York.

Ainley, D.G. 2014. Hatching eggs. Data from graph showing Adélie penguin breeding pairs at Cape Royds 1996-2007, accessed Feb 2014 at http://icestories.exploratorium.edu/dispatches/hatching-eggs/.

Ainley, D.G., Ballard, G., Ackley, S., Blight, L.K., Eastman, J.T., Emslie, S.D., Lescroël, A., Olmastroni, S., Townsend, S.E., Tynan, C.T., Wilson, P. & Woehler, E. 2007. Paradigm lost, or is top-down forcing no longer significant in the Antarctic marine ecosystem? *Antarctic Science* **19**(3): 283–290.

Ainley, D.G., Ballard, G., Barton, K.J. & Karl, B.J. 2003. Spatial and temporal variation of diet within a presumed metapopulation of Adélie penguins. *Condor* **105**: 95–106.

Ainley, D.G., Clarke, E.D., Arrigo, K., Fraser, W.R., Kato, A., Barton, K.J. & Wilson, P.R. 2005. Decadal-scale changes in the climate and biota of the Pacific sector of the Southern Ocean, 1950s to the 1990s. *Antarctic Science* **17**: 171–82.

Ainley, D.G., Morrell, S.H. & Wood R. C. 1986. South polar skua breeding colonies in the Ross Sea region, Antarctica. *Notornis* **33**(3): 155–63.

Ainley, D.G., Ribic, C.A., Ballard, G., Heath, S., Gaffney, I., Karl, B.J., Barton, K.J., Wilson, P.R. & Webb, S. 2004. Geographic structure of Adélie penguin populations: overlap in colony-specific foraging areas. *Ecological Monographs* **74**(1):159–78.

Arrigo, K. R., van Dijken, G.L., Ainley, D.G., Fahnestock, M.A. & Markus, T. 2002. Ecological impact of a large Antarctic iceberg. *Geophysical Research Letters* **29**(7): 1104.

Barry, J. 1988. Hydrographic patterns in McMurdo Sound, Antarctica and their relationship to local benthic communities. *Polar Biology* **8**: 377–91.

Blackburn, N., Taylor, R.H. & Wilson, P.R. 1991. An interpretation of the growth of the Adelie penguin rookery at Cape Royds, 1955-1990.New Zealand Journal of Ecology **15**(2): 117-21.

Broady PA 1987. Protection of terrestrial plants and animals in the Ross Sea regions, Antarctica. *New Zealand Antarctic Record* **8** (1): 18-41.

Broady PA 1989a. Broadscale patterns in the distribution of aquatic and terrestrial vegetation at three ice-free regions on Ross Island, Antarctica. In Vincent, W. & Ellis-Evans, C. (eds) *High latitude limnology*. Kluwer, Dordrecht. *Developments in Hydrobiology* **49**: 77-95.

Broady PA 1989b. The distribution of *Prasiola calophylla* (Carmich.)Menegh. (Chlorophyta) in Antarctic freshwater and terrestrial habitats. *Antarctic Science* **1** (2): 109-18.

Brown, A., McKnight, D.M., Chin, Y.P., Roberts, E.C. & Uhle, M. 2004. Chemical characterization of dissolved organic material in Pony Lake, a saline coastal pond in Antarctica. *Marine Chemistry* **89** (1-4): 327-37.

Cowan, D.A. & Casanueva, A. 2007. Stability of ATP in Antarctic mineral soils. *Polar Biology* **30** (12): 1599-1603.

Jacobs, S.S., Amos, A.F. &. Bruchhausen, P.M. 1970. Ross Sea oceanography and Antarctic bottom water formation. *Deep-Sea Research* **17**: 935–62.

Lyver, P.O'B., M. Barron, K.J. Barton, D.G. Ainley, A. Pollard, S. Gordon, S. McNeill, G. Ballard, and P.R. Wilson. [In Press]. Trends in the breeding population of Adélie penguins in the Ross Sea, 1981–2012: a coincidence of climate and resource extraction effects. Submitted to *PLoS One* 2014.

Martin, L. 1991. Cumulative environmental change: case study of Cape Royds, Antarctica. Unpublished M.Sc. thesis, University of Auckland.

Porazinska, D.L., Wall, D.H. &Virginia R.A. 2002. Invertebrates in ornithogenic soils on Ross Island, Antarctica. *Polar Biology* **25** (8): 569-74.

Sladen, W.J.L. & Leresche, R.E. 1970. New and developing techniques in Antarctic ornithology. In Holdgate, W.M. (ed) *Antarctic ecology I*. Academic Press, London: 585-96.

Stonehouse, B. 1963. Observations on Adélie penguins (*Pygoscelis adeliae*) at Cape Royds, Antarctica. *Proceedings XIIIth International Ornithological Congress, 1963*: 766-79.

Stonehouse, B. 1965. Counting Antarctic animals. *New Scientist* (July 29): 273-76.

Taylor, R.H. & Wilson, P.R. 1990. Recent increase and southern expansion of Adelie penguin populations in the Ross Sea, Antarctica, related to climatic warming. *New Zealand Journal of Ecology* **14**: 25-29.

Taylor, R.H., Wilson, P.R. & Thomas, B.W. 1990. Status and trends of Adélie penguin populations in the Ross Sea region. *Polar Record* **26** (159): 293-304.

Thomson, R.B. 1977. Effects of human disturbance on an Adélie penguin rookery and measures of control. In Llano, G.A. (ed) *Adaptations within Antarctic ecosystems. Proceedings of the Third SCAR Symposium on Antarctic Biology*. Smithsonian Institution, Washington, DC: 1177-80.

West, W. & West, G.S. 1911. Freshwater algae. *Reports on the scientific investigations: Biology, by the British Antarctic Expedition 1907-1909* **1**: 263-298; Plates 24-26.

Wilson, P.R., Ainley, D.G., Nur, N. Jacobs, S.S., Barton, K.J.., Ballard, G. & Comiso, J.C., 2001. Adélie penguin population change in the Pacific sector of Antarctica: relation to sea-ice extent and the Antarctic Circumpolar Current. *Marine Ecology Progress Series* **213**: 301-09.

Woehler, E.J. (ed) 1993. *The distribution and abundance of Antarctic and subantarctic penguins*. SCAR, Cambridge.

Young, E.C. 1962a. The breeding behaviour of the south polar skua *Catharacta maccormicki*. *Ibis* **105** (2): 203–33.

Young, E.C. 1962b. Feeding habits of the south polar skua *Catharacta maccormicki*. *Ibis* **105** (3): 301–18.

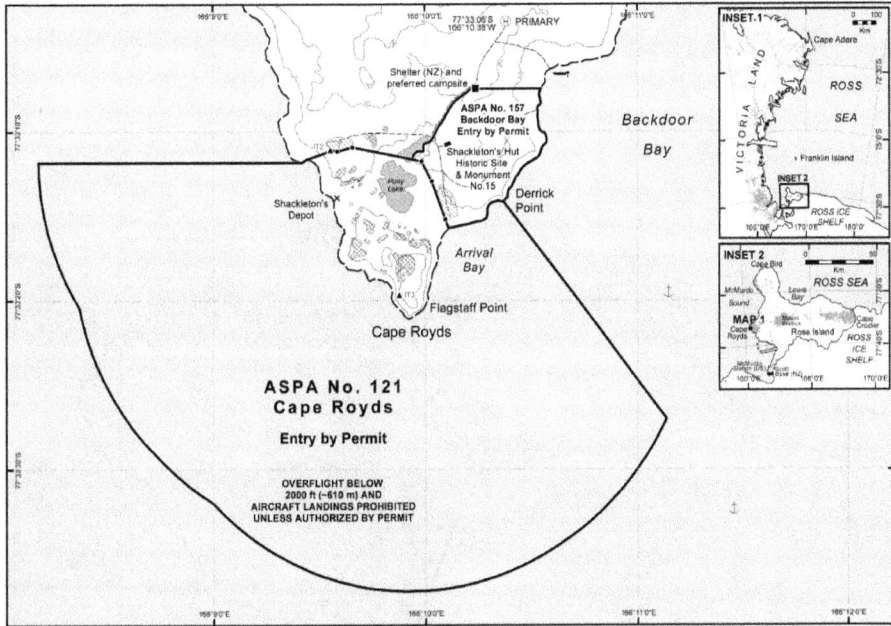

Map 1: ASPA No. 121 Cape Royds - boundaries and topography

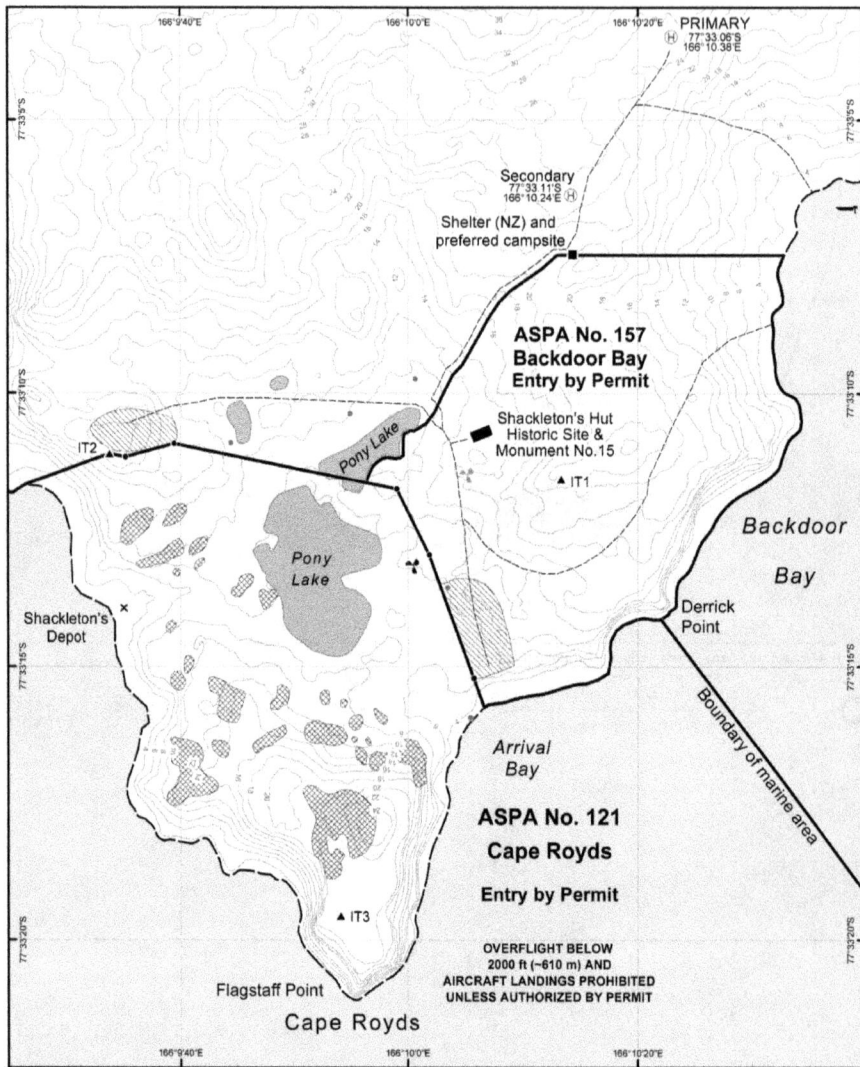

Map 2: ASPA No. 121 Cape Royds - access, facilities and wildlife

05 Mar 2014
United States Antarctic Program
Environmental Research & Assessment

Coastline (approx)	ASPA boundary
Contour (2 m)	Penguin nesting area (2005 approx.)
Ice free ground	Penguin viewing area
Ocean	Path
Lake / pond	Building
	Survey marker

Signpost / boundary point
Signpost
Helicopter landing site
Small boat landing site
Automatic Weather Station
Historic weather station

0   50   100
Meters

Projection: Lambert Conic Conformal.
Spheroid and horizontal datum: WGS 84
Data sources: ASPA boundary: ERA (Jan 2014).
Signposts: UNAVCO (Jan 2014).
Topography & infrastructure data supplied
by Gateway Antarctica (2009).
Penguins digitised by ERA from georeferenced aerial
image (2005) provided by Landcare Research.

Management Plan for

Antarctic Specially Protected Area (ASPA) No. 124

CAPE CROZIER, ROSS ISLAND

Introduction

The Cape Crozier Antarctic Specially Protected Area (ASPA) is located at the eastern extremity of Ross Island, Ross Sea. Approximate area and coordinates: ~70 km² (centered at 169° 19' 53" E, 77° 28' 54" S), of which ~43 km² (61%) is marine (including ice shelf) and ~27 km² is terrestrial (39%). The primary reasons for designation of the Area are its diverse avian and mammalian fauna, locally rich vegetation and historic values. The emperor penguin (*Aptenodytes forsteri*) colony at Cape Crozier is the most southerly known, and it also has the longest study records available. The Adélie penguin colony is one of the largest known. The Area is also one of the most southerly recorded locations of snow algae. The Area provides representation of relatively undisturbed terrestrial and aquatic habitats on Ross Island, including of mosses, lichens, algae, invertebrate and microbial communities.

The Area was originally designated as Specially Protected Area (SPA) No.6 through Recommendation IV-6 (1966) after a proposal by the United States of America on the grounds that the region supports a rich bird and mammal fauna as well as microfauna and microflora, and that the ecosystem depends on a substantial mixing of marine and terrestrial elements of outstanding scientific interest. With adoption of the Site of Special Scientific Interest (SSSI) category of protection in 1972, Cape Crozier's designation as an SPA was terminated by Recommendation VIII-2 (1975) and the site was re-designated as SSSI No. 4 by Recommendation VIII-4 (1975). The reason for designation of SSSI No. 4 was to protect long-term studies of the population dynamics and social behavior of emperor (*Aptenodytes forsteri*) and Adélie (*Pygoscelis adeliae*) penguin colonies in the region. Information gathered since designation of SSSI No. 4 supported the inclusion of skua populations and vegetation assemblages as important values to be protected at Cape Crozier. The SSSI was extended through Recommendation X-6 (1979), Recommendation XII-5 (1983), Recommendation XIII-7 (1985), Recommendation XVI-7 (1991), and Measure 3 (2001). The site was renamed and renumbered as Antarctic Specially Protected Area (ASPA) No. 124 by Decision 1 (2002). In Measure 1 (2002) the boundaries were extended south to include Igloo Spur and to protect the range of vegetation assemblages representative of the Cape Crozier region. In Measure 7 (2008) the western boundary of the Area was modified to follow a simple line of longitude because visitors found the previous boundary hard to follow. This boundary was further simplified in the current management plan, now following a line directly between the summits of Bomb Peak and Post Office Hill, and adjusted to exclude the Cape Crozier hut from the Area.

The Area comprises environments within two of the domains defined in the Environmental Domains Analysis for Antarctica: 'Environment P – Ross and Ronne-Filchner ice shelves' and 'Environment S - McMurdo - South Victoria Land geologic'. Under the Antarctic Conservation Biogeographic Regions classification the Area lies within 'ACBR9 – South Victoria Land'.

1. Description of values to be protected

The emperor penguin colony at Cape Crozier was first recorded by members of the British National Antarctic Expedition in 1902. The colony is the most southerly known and has the longest record of study on an emperor penguin population. The colony breeds on fast ice that forms between large cracks which develop in the Ross Ice Shelf where it abuts Cape Crozier. The positions of these cracks shift with movement of the ice shelf, and the colony itself is known to move around different parts of the cracks during the breeding season. The boundaries of the Area have been designed to include fast-ice areas consistently occupied by breeding birds.

Cape Crozier has a large Adélie penguin (*Pygoscelis adeliae*) population averaging around 150,000 breeding pairs, with just over 270,000 pairs in 2012, making it one of the largest Adélie colonies in Antarctica. The colony is divided into two main groups 1 km apart known as East and West Colonies (Maps 1 and 2). In addition, well-preserved ancient Adélie penguin remains found within the Area have particular scientific value for genetic studies. Associated with the penguin colonies is a large south polar skua (*Stercorarius maccormicki*) colony, estimated at 1000 breeding pairs.

Weddell seals (*Leptonychotes weddellii*) breed within the Area, while leopard seals (*Leptonyx hydrurga*) are frequent visitors and crabeater seals (*Lobodon carcinophagus*) are commonly seen at sea and on ice floes. Killer whales (*Orcinus orca)* are also frequently seen close off shore within the Area. While the mammal species recorded at Cape Crozier are neither unique to the Area nor known to be outstanding in this context, they form an integral and representative part of the local ecosystem.

There are moss, algae and lichen assemblages in the Area. Expanses of snow algae at Cape Crozier cover an area of more than 4 ha adjacent to the skua and penguin colonies. Growths as extensive as those at Cape Crozier have been noted only once before in the Continental Antarctic Zone, on the Wilkes Land Coast, and Cape Crozier has one of the most southerly records of snow algae. Lichens are also abundant, with large areas of bright orange crustose lichens on rocks and stones on the slopes above the Adélie colony, and rich growths of foliose and fruticose lichens in the vicinity of Wilson's Stone Igloo. Two lichen species (*Caloplaca erecta* and *C. soropelta*) observed within the Area have not previously been recorded in Antarctica. The Area therefore has value by providing representation of relatively extensive and pristine terrestrial and aquatic habitats on Ross Island that host a variety of moss, lichen, algal and microbial communities and an associated invertebrate fauna.

A message post from Scott's National Antarctic Expedition (1901-04) is situated in West Colony (169° 14' 37.5" E, 77° 27' 16.7" S) and was designated as Historic Site and Monument (HSM) No.69 through Measure 4 (1995). Wilson's Stone Igloo (169° 17' 56" E, 77° 31' 51" S), designated as HSM No.21 through Recommendation VII-9 (1972), is situated in the south of the Area. The rock shelter was constructed in July 1911 by members of the 1910-1913 British Antarctic Expedition during their winter journey to Cape Crozier to collect emperor penguin eggs.

The high scientific, ecological and historic values of this area along with its vulnerability to disturbance through trampling, sampling, pollution or alien introduction, are such that this Area requires long-term special protection.

2. Aims and objectives

Management at Cape Crozier aims to:

- Avoid degradation of, or substantial risk to, the values of the Area by preventing unnecessary human disturbance;
- Allow scientific research on the ecosystem of the Area, in particular on the avifauna, marine fauna and terrestrial ecology, while ensuring protection from oversampling or other possible scientific impacts;

- Allow other scientific research, scientific support activities and visits for educational and outreach purposes (such as documentary reporting (visual, audio or written) or the production of educational resources or services) provided that such activities are for compelling reasons that cannot be served elsewhere and will not jeopardize the values of the Area;
- Prevent or minimize the introduction of alien plants, animals and microbes into the Area;
- Prevent or minimize the introduction of pathogens that may cause disease in faunal populations within the Area;
- Allow visits to the historic sites under strict control by permit;
- Allow visits for management purposes in support of the aims of the management plan.

3. Management activities

The following management activities shall be undertaken to protect the values of the Area:

- Durable wind direction indicators should be erected close to the primary designated helicopter landing site whenever it is anticipated there will be a number of landings at the site in a given season. These should be replaced as needed and removed when no longer required;
- Brightly colored markers, which should be clearly visible from the air and pose no significant threat to the environment, should be placed to mark the primary and secondary designated helicopter landing sites adjacent to the field hut;
- Signs showing the location of the Area (stating the special restrictions that apply) shall be displayed prominently, and a copy of this management plan shall be kept available, in the research hut facility at Cape Crozier;
- National programs shall take steps to ensure the boundaries of the Area and the restrictions that apply within are marked on relevant maps and nautical / aeronautical charts;
- Markers, signs or structures erected within the Area for scientific or management purposes shall be secured and maintained in good condition, and removed when no longer necessary;
- National Antarctic programs operating in the Area should maintain a record of all new markers, signs and structures erected within the Area;
- Personnel (national program staff, field expeditions, and pilots) in the vicinity of, accessing or flying over the Area shall be specifically instructed by their national program or appropriate national authority to observe the provisions and contents of the Management Plan;
- Visits shall be made as necessary (no less than once every five years) to assess whether the Area continues to serve the purposes for which it was designated and to ensure management and maintenance measures are adequate;
- National Antarctic Programs operating in the region shall consult together for the purpose of ensuring that the above provisions are implemented.

4. Period of designation

Designated for an indefinite period.

5. Maps and photographs

Map 1: ASPA No.124 Cape Crozier - topography and boundary.

Projection: Lambert conformal conic; Standard parallels: 1st 77° 27' S; 2nd 77° 32' S; Central meridian: 169° 15' E; Latitude of Origin: 77° S; Spheroid and horizontal datum: WGS84.

Data sources:

Coastline, contours and bird data supplied by Gateway Antarctica; ASPA boundary: ERA (Feb 2014); Facilities: RPSC GPS survey (25 Dec 2007); Ice free ground, Emperor penguin colony: Quickbird imagery (09 Oct 2011); Ice shelf front 1993 estimated from orthorectified aerial imagery (DoSLI / USGS SN7848) and for 2002, 2007 and 2011 estimated from Quickbird imagery (Imagery © 2011 Digital Globe; NGA Commercial Imagery Program).

Inset 1: Ross Sea region, showing location of Inset 2.

Inset 2 Ross Island region, showing the location of Map 1 and McMurdo Station (US) and Scott Base (NZ).

Map 2: ASPA No. 124 Cape Crozier - access, facilities and wildlife.

Map specifications are the same as those for Map 1.

6. Description of the Area

6(i) Geographical co-ordinates, boundary markers and natural features

General description

Cape Crozier (169° 21' 30" E, 77° 30' 30" S) is at the eastern extremity of Ross Island, where an ice-free area comprises the lower eastern slopes of Mount Terror (Map 1). The designated Area is situated in the vicinity of Post Office Hill (407 m), Bomb Peak (740 m) and The Knoll (360 m), extending to encompass Gamble, Topping and Kyle Cones. Igloo Spur and the adjacent marine environment and an area of the Ross Ice Shelf where large cracks form as the shelf pushes against the land. These cracks are generally covered by fast-ice, which is occupied annually by breeding emperor penguins.

Boundaries and coordinates

The marine northern boundary of the Area extends 6.5 km along the 77° 26' 00" S line of latitude from 169° 12' 00" E to 169° 28' 00" E. The western boundary extends 1.68 km south from the northern boundary to the coast, thence south for a further 800 m to the edge of icefree ground before ascending to the summit of a low hill (~ 300 m) above and east of the field hut (Map 1). The boundary thence proceeds directly to the summit of Post Office Hill (407 m) at 169° 12' 40" E 77° 27' 55" S. The boundary thence follows a straight line southward direct to a point close to the summit of Bomb Peak (740 m) at 169° 11' 30" E 77° 31' 02" S. The boundary extends down the SE ridge of Bomb Peak to Igloo Spur at 169° 20' 00" E 77° 32' 00" S, from where it extends due east along latitude 77° 32' 00" S to the east boundary at 169° 28' 00" E.

Climate

The nearest Automatic Weather Station (AWS) to Cape Crozier is Laurie II, situated on the Ross Ice Shelf 35 km east of Cape Crozier. Air temperatures recorded at Laurie II between 2009-13 showed December as the warmest month over this period, with a mean temperature of -5.8 °C, and August as the coolest with a mean temperature of -33.1 °C (http://uwamrc.ssec.wisc.edu/ 06 Mar 2014). The minimum air temperature recorded at Laurie II during this period was -56.5 °C in July 2010, whilst the maximum was 5.9 °C in December 2011. The average wind speed over the period was ~ 6.3 m/s with the winds predominantly coming from the south to southwest. Conditions at Cape Crozier are likely to differ as a result of the local geography; for example, nearby Mount Terror probably influences local airflow and katabatic winds to affect the local climate, and Broady (1989) observed that prevailing winds in the ice-free region near Cape Crozier tend to be from the southeast.

Geology, geomorphology and soils

The ice-free ground at Cape Crozier is of volcanic origin, with numerous small cones and craters evident among gentle slopes of scoria and fine-grained basalt lava. Phonolite cones at Post Office Hill and The Knoll are 1.4 million years old, while other volcanic rocks in the area are less than 1 million years old (Cole *et al.* 1971; Wright & Kyle 1999). Several of these hills, including Post Office Hill, shelter the penguin colonies from southwesterly winds. On the surface are many volcanic bombs and other evidence of small-scale volcanic explosions. To the south of the Area coastal cliffs adjacent to the ice shelf are up to 150 m high. The cliff faces show bedded lava and brown palagonitic tuffs with several lenticular patches of columnar basalt towards the base. Large erratics of continental origin transported by the Ross Ice Shelf can be found on the northern side of Cape Crozier.

Breeding birds

The emperor penguin (*Aptenodytes forsteri*) colony at Cape Crozier was discovered in October 1902 by R.S. Skelton, a member of Scott's Discovery Expedition. The presence of the colony depends on fast-ice locked between cracks in the Ross Ice Shelf where it abuts Cape Crozier. The size of the colony is limited by the area and condition of the fast ice, which also affects the availability of breeding sites sheltered from the strong katabatic winds that descend from Mount Terror. The location of the colony varies from year to year (Map 2) and the colony moves within a breeding season, beginning the season near to shore and moving further offshore as fledging approaches. The breeding population has fluctuated widely since the turn of the century, for example with 400 adults recorded in 1902, 100 in 1911, and 1,300 in 1969. The number of chicks fledged and the fledging success of the colony has also been variable (Table 1). The mean number of chicks fledged at Cape Crozier is 514 over the years for which data are available (Table 1).

Table 1. Cape Crozier emperor penguin live chick counts 1983–2006 and adults 2007-12.

Year	Chicks	Year	Chicks	Year	Chicks	Year	Adults
1983	78	1995	623	2002	247	2007	537
1986	?	1996	859	2003	333 (a)	2008	623
1989	?	1997	821	2004	475	2009	303 (c)
1990	324	1998	1108	2005	0	2010	856
1992	374	1999	798	2006	339 (b)	2011	870
1993	?	2000	1201			2012	1189
1994	645	2001	0				

Sources: chick counts Barber-Meyer, Kooyman & Ponganis 2008. Adult counts: Kooyman pers. comm. 2014.
a) All chicks not counted due to rugged ice conditions and thus one chick assumed per adult counted.
b) G. Kooyman, *pers. comm.*, Nov. 2007.

c) Estimate from 2009 satellite imagery (Fretwell *et al*. 2012).

In 2000, a section of the Ross Ice Shelf calved to form an iceberg 295 km long and 40 km wide. A fragmented section of this iceberg, known as B15A, together with another iceberg (C16) lodged near Ross Island in 2001. These icebergs had a major effect on sea ice distribution and primary production, and impeded the arrival of emperor penguins. In 2001 and several subsequent years, icebergs C16 and B15A affected the breeding success and colony locations of emperor and Adélie penguins by blocking access to foraging areas and destroying nesting habitat. In 2005, the emperor colony remained well below its pre-2000 size, with no sign of breeding (Kooyman *et al*. 2007). However, in 2006 the colony had returned to its pre-iceberg location and 339 chicks were produced (G. Kooyman, *pers. comm.*, Nov. 2007; Table 1), and in recent years the number of adults has returned to levels similar to those last observed in the 1996-2000 period.

A comprehensive population study of Adélie penguins occurred at Cape Crozier from 1961-62 through the 1981-82 austral summers, with 2000 to 5000 chicks banded yearly. There are two Adélie penguin (*Pygoscelis adeliae*) colonies at Cape Crozier, known as East and West Colonies. These are about 1 km apart, separated by a 45-m high ridge and a sloping ice field across which the birds do not travel. A coastline of 1.6 km with three beaches separated by rock outcrops provides penguins with access to West Colony. By contrast, East Colony has one 50-m wide rocky beach and 550 m of sea cliffs. The population of the two colonies has increased substantially over the last 50 years, numbering 65,000 breeding pairs in 1958, 102,500 in 1966 and 177,083 in 1987. Numbers fell to 136,249 in 1989 and 106,184 in 1994. In 2000, the number of breeding pairs was estimated to be 118,772 (based on a projection from counts of selected subcolonies) (Ainley *et al*. 2004). The combined mean population of the East and West Colonies at Cape Crozier over a 28-year period was 153,632, and in 2012 there were 270,340 breeding pairs, making it one of the largest Adélie penguin colonies in Antarctica (Lyver *et al*. in press). The presence of the B15A and C16 icebergs from 2001 to 2005 in the foraging area had a significant effect on the Adélie penguin colony at Cape Crozier (Arrigo *et al*. 2002; Ballard *et al*. 2010; Dugger *et al*. 2010).

Approximately 1000 pairs of south polar skuas (*Stercorarius maccormicki*) breed on ice-free ground surrounding the Adélie penguin colony. A demographic study of this colony began in 1961-62 and was still continuing in 1996-97. Chinstrap penguins (*Pygoscelis antarctica*), Wilson's storm petrels (*Oceanites oceanicus*), snow petrels (*Pagadroma nivea*), Antarctic petrels (*Thalassoica antarctica*), southern fulmars (*Fulmaris glacialoides*), southern giant petrels (*Macronectes giganteus*), kelp gulls (*Larus dominicanus*), and south polar skuas from more northerly breeding sites, have been recorded as visitors to Cape Crozier.

Breeding mammals

Weddell seals (*Leptonychotes weddellii*) breed within the Area, with approximately 20 pups being recorded in recent years. Leopard seals (*Leptonyx hydrurga*) frequent the Area, with approximately 12 individuals recognized as regular visitors, while crabeater seals (*Lobodon carcinophagus*) are commonly seen at sea and on ice floes in the vicinity. Other mammals frequently observed within the Area include killer whales (*Orcinus orca*), of which several distinct types have been recognized. Regular killer whale observations were carried out at Cape Crozier between 2002-09 (Ainley *et al*. 2009), with the finding that sightings of killer whales of ecotype-C (also referred to as 'Ross Sea killer whales') appear to have been decreasing at Cape Crozier contemporaneously with an increase in Ross Sea commercial fishing, in particular for Antarctic toothfish (*Dissostichus mawsoni*). 'Ross Sea killer whales' appear to feed principally on fish, including Antarctic toothfish, so the authors suggest that changes to the foraging patterns of these whales in this region could be linked to decreased prey availability as a result of the fishery.

Terrestrial biology – aquatic and non-aquatic habitats

Algae can be found throughout the Area on large patches of snow and on soils and stones, often below the soil surface layer. Large areas of green snow algae, covering more than 4 ha, can be found in the north of the Area in snowfields around the periphery of the Adélie penguin colony and skua nesting areas (Broady 1989). Particularly large patches have been reported in the snow-filled valley between the two coastal hills at the northern end of the Adélie penguin colony, with green-tinted snow over at least one hectare. However, the extent of snow algae is not always obvious, with the green color often not revealed until a surface crust of white ice is broken away. Snow algae samples are dominated by a species of *Chlamydomonas*, and associated with occasional *Ulothrix*-like filaments and diatoms. Growth requires percolating meltwater during summer and nutrients derived from the bird colonies.

Prasiola crispa grows in slow water flows in the vicinity of the penguin colonies and ribbon-like growths of *P. calophylla* are found where water percolates over stones on the tallus slopes. Numerous small ponds are found throughout the Area, from small pools of ~1 m in diameter to a lake of ~150 m in diameter situated immediately south of The Knoll. The four ponds in the penguin colonies contain abundant phytoplankton populations of *Chlamydomonas* cf. *snowiae*, while ponds elsewhere support growths of red-brown to dark blue-green benthic mats dominated by Oscillatoriaceae. Occasional epilithic algae (dominated by *Gloeocapsa*, *Nostoc* and *Scytonema*) are found as blackish crusts coating rock surfaces where meltwater percolates.

Mosses are sparse and scattered in their distribution with most occurrences being of one or a small number of isolated cushions no larger than 10 cm in diameter. Richer growths than this occur up to 0.5 km NE of the hut on north and NW facing slopes and on slopes immediately above the coastal cliffs about 1 km south of the penguin colonies. The moss species occurring at Cape Crozier have yet to be identified.

Encrusting orange lichens are present in shallow hollows, on rock outcrops, boulders and encrusting bryophytes on the slopes above the penguin colonies. Also present adjacent to Wilson's Stone Igloo is the fruticose lichen *Usnea* and the foliose lichen *Umbilicaria*, both duller in color but structurally more complex. Green algal crusts are found throughout the Area. A survey conducted in 2010 near the Adélie colony identified 14 lichen species, of which two (*Caloplaca erecta* and *C. soropelta*) had not previously been recorded in Antarctica, and one (*Lecania nylanderiana*) had not previously been recorded in Victoria Land (Smylka *et al.* 2011). *Caloplaca soropelta* had not previously been recorded in the Southern Hemisphere, and is known as an Arctic species. The 11 other species, previously known in Antarctica, are *Buellia darbishirei*, *B. pallida*, *Caloplaca citrina C. saxicola*, *C. schofieldii*, *Lecanora expectans*, *L. mons-nivis*, *Lecidella siplei*, *Physcia dubia*, *Rhizoplaca melanophthalma*, and *Rinodina* sp.

Human activities and impact

Cape Crozier is relatively isolated and difficult to access, and the number of visitors to the Area each year is generally low, with only 30 permits for entry being issued by NZ and the US over the period 2009-14. Access is generally made by helicopter, and the designated landing site near the Cape Crozier hut requires careful approach to avoid inadvertent overflight of the Adélie penguin colony (Map 2). Pilots are briefed in advance to avoid the colonies when flying at low elevations.

Some materials such as nails, screws and hinges remain at the site of the old 'Jamesway' hut which has now been removed (Map 2). Vehicle tracks apparently made in the early 1970s remain evident in soils along the bench below Kyle, Topping and Gamble Cones (Ainley pers. comm. 2014).

6(ii) Access to the Area

The Area may be accessed by traversing over land or sea ice, by sea or by air. Particular routes have not been designated for access to the Area. Overflight and aircraft landing restrictions apply within the Area, the specific conditions for which are set out in Section 7(ii) below.

6(iii) Structures within and near the Area

The Cape Crozier hut (US) (169° 11' 13" E, 77° 27' 41" S) is situated on the NW side of a low peak ~ 675 m NW of Post Office Hill (Maps 1 and 2). A radio communications antenna is installed above the hut on a seasonal basis (Map 2). An observation hide installed during the period 1960–80 was located at the foot of the north side of Post Office Hill although no longer exists. An old 'Jamesway' hut was built on a small terrace approximately 1 km NE of the present hut (Map 2), although this was destroyed by fire and, with the exception of some small items such as nails etc., the hut debris has since been removed.

The historic Discovery's Message Post, designated as HSM No.69 through Measure 4 (1995), was erected on 22 January 1902, and is situated in the West Colony on the NE coast of the Area (169° 14' 37.5" E, 77° 27' 16.7" S). The post was used by the 1901–04 British National Antarctic Expedition to provide information to the expedition's relief ships. An historic rock hut known as Wilson's Stone Igloo (HSM No.21) (169° 17' 56" E, 77° 31' 51" S) is located on Igloo Spur (Map 1).

6(iv) Location of other protected areas within close proximity of the Area

The nearest protected areas to Cape Crozier are on Ross Island: Lewis Bay (ASPA No.156), the site of the 1979 DC-10 passenger aircraft crash is the closest and 45 km west; Tramway Ridge (ASPA No.130) near the summit of Mt. Erebus is 55 km west; Discovery Hut on the Hut Point Peninsula (ASPA No.158 and HSM No.18); Arrival Heights (ASPA No.122) is 70 km to the SW adjacent to McMurdo Station; Cape Royds (ASPA No.121), Backdoor Bay (ASPA No.157 and HSM No.15) and Cape Evans (ASPA No.155) are 75 km west; and New College Valley (ASPA No.116) are 75 km NW at Cape Bird.

6(v) Special zones within the Area

There are no zones designated within the Area.

7. Permit conditions

7(i) General permit conditions

Entry into the Area is prohibited except in accordance with a permit issued by an appropriate national authority. Conditions for issuing a permit to enter the Area are that:

- It is issued for scientific research, and in particular for research on the avifauna, marine or terrestrial ecosystems in the Area, or for compelling scientific, educational or outreach reasons that cannot be served elsewhere, or for reasons essential to the management of the Area;
- The actions permitted are in accordance with this management plan;
- The activities permitted will give due consideration via the environmental impact assessment process to the continued protection of the environmental, scientific and historic values of the Area;
- Approach distances to fauna must be respected, except when scientific needs may require otherwise and this is specified in the relevant permits;
- Visitors shall not enter Wilson's Stone Igloo (HSM No.21) or in any other way disturb this structure or the Discovery's Message Post (HSM No.69) unless specifically authorized to do so by the permit;

- The permit shall be issued for a finite period;
- The permit, or a copy, shall be carried when in the Area.

7(ii) Access to, and movement within, or over the Area

Access to the Area shall be by helicopter, by boat or on foot. Vehicles are prohibited on land within the Area.

Foot access and movement within the Area

Movement on land within the Area shall be on foot. All people in aircraft, boats, or vehicles are prohibited from moving on foot beyond the immediate vicinity of their landing or access site unless specifically authorised by Permit. Pedestrians should maintain a minimum approach distance of 5 m from wildlife, unless it is necessary to approach closer for purposes allowed for by the permit.

Visitors should move carefully so as to minimize disturbance to flora, fauna, soils, and water bodies. Pedestrians should walk on snow or rocky terrain if practical, but take care not to damage lichens. Particular care should be exercised when walking on rocky terrain in the vicinity of Wilson's Stone Igloo (HSM No.21) (169° 17' 56" E, 77° 31' 51" S) on Igloo Spur (Map 1), where fragile lichens are present on rocks. Wilson's Stone Igloo is itself fragile, and visitors should not enter or in any other way disturb the structure unless specifically authorized to do so by permit.

Pedestrians should walk around the penguin colonies and should not enter sub-groups of nesting penguins unless required for research or management purposes. Care should be taken to avoid trampling nests when moving through skua territories. Pedestrian traffic should be kept to the minimum consistent with the objectives of any permitted activities and every reasonable effort should be made to minimize effects.

Aircraft access and overflight

Aircraft may operate and land within the Area according to strict observance of the following conditions:

- Aircraft landings within the Area are prohibited unless authorized by permit for purposes allowed for by the Management Plan;
- Overflight of the Area below 2000 ft (~610 m) Above Ground Level is prohibited, unless authorized by permit for purposes allowed for by the Management Plan;
- Pilots should ensure aircraft maintain a horizontal separation distance of at least 2000 ft (~610 m) from the edges of the penguin colonies (Maps 1 & 2) when accessing the designated landing sites, or otherwise operating within the Area;
- Aircraft landings on sea ice within ½ nautical mile (~930 m) of the emperor colony are prohibited. Pilots should note that the emperor colony may shift from year to year, and move throughout the breeding season, and may be several kilometers from the nominal position shown in Map 1, and the colony may also comprise a number of smaller units within the Area;
- The primary helicopter landing site preferred for most access to the Area is located at 169° 11.19' E, 77° 27.64' S (elevation 240 m). This landing site is below and 150 m northwest of the Cape Crozier (US) field hut, and outside of the Area approximately 430 m west of the western ASPA boundary (Map 2). The site is marked by a circle of bright orange painted rocks. An alternative, secondary, landing site may be used when necessary, located at 169° 11.28' E, 77° 27.72' S. The landing site is 150 m above the hut and approximately 450 m west of the ASPA boundary;
- A third designated helicopter landing site is located above and 350 m northwest of Wilson's Stone Igloo at 169° 17.19' E, 77° 31.75' S (Map 1) in an area of relatively flat terrain;

- To minimize the risks of inadvertent overflight of bird colonies, helicopter pilots accessing the Area for the first time should be accompanied by another pilot with previous experience of flying into the Area;
- Use of helicopter smoke grenades is prohibited unless absolutely necessary for safety, and all grenades should be retrieved.

Ship or small boat access

Restrictions on ship and / or small boat operations apply during the period from 01 April through to 01 January inclusive, when ships and / or small boats shall operate within the Area according to strict observance of the following conditions:

- Ships and / or small boats are prohibited from the Area, including entering sea ice within the Area, unless authorized by permit for purposes allowed for by this Management Plan;
- There are no special restrictions on where access can be gained to the Area by small boat, although small boat landings should avoid areas where penguins are accessing the sea unless this is necessary for purposes for which the permit was granted.

7(iii) Activities that may be conducted within the Area

Activities that may be conducted within the Area include:

- Scientific research that will not jeopardize the values of the Area;
- Activities with educational and / or outreach aims that cannot be served elsewhere and will not jeopardize the values of the Area. Educational and outreach aims do not include tourism;
- Activities with the aim of documenting, preserving or protecting historic resources within the Area;
- Essential management activities within the Area, monitoring and inspection.

7(iv) Installation, modification or removal of structures / equipment

- No structures are to be erected within the Area except as specified in a permit and, with the exception of permanent survey markers and signs, permanent structures or installations are prohibited;;
- All structures, scientific equipment or markers installed in the Area must be authorized by permit and clearly identified by country, name of the principal investigator, year of installation and date of expected removal. All such items should be free of organisms, propagules (e.g. seeds, eggs) and non-sterile soil, and be made of materials that can withstand the environmental conditions and pose minimal risk of contamination or damage to the values of the Area;
- Installation (including site selection), maintenance, modification or removal of structures or equipment shall be undertaken in a manner that minimizes disturbance to values of the Area, preferably avoiding the main Adélie penguin and skua breeding season (01 Oct – 31 Mar);
- Removal of specific structures / equipment for which the permit has expired shall be the responsibility of the authority which granted the original Permit, and shall be a condition of the permit.

7(v) Location of field camps

Camping outside of the Area should be within a 100 m radius of the field hut (169° 11' 14" E, 77° 27' 39" S). When necessary for essential purposes specified in the Permit, camping is permitted within the Area to facilitate access to sites inaccessible from the hut. Such camping should preferably be at sites that have been previously used, are not vegetated or occupied by breeding birds, and should be on snow or ice-covered ground if available. Researchers should consult with the appropriate national authority to obtain up-to-date information on any sites where camping may be preferred.

7(vi) Restrictions on materials and organisms which may be brought into the Area

In addition to the requirements of the Protocol on Environmental Protection to the Antarctic Treaty, restrictions on materials and organisms which may be brought into the Area are:

- Deliberate introduction of animals, plant material, micro-organisms and non-sterile soil into the Area is prohibited. Precautions shall be taken to prevent the accidental introduction of animals, plant material, micro-organisms and non-sterile soil from other biologically distinct regions (within or beyond the Antarctic Treaty area);
- Visitors shall ensure that sampling equipment and markers brought into the Area are clean. To the maximum extent practicable, footwear and other equipment used or brought into the Area (including backpacks, carry-bags and other equipment) shall be thoroughly cleaned before entering the Area. Visitors should also consult and follow as appropriate recommendations contained in the Committee for Environmental Protection Non-native Species Manual (CEP 2011), and in the Environmental Code of Conduct for terrestrial scientific field research in Antarctica (SCAR 2009);
- All poultry brought into and not consumed or used within the Area (and / or at the nearby hut and camping site), including all parts, products and / or wastes of poultry, shall be removed from the Area (and / or from the nearby hut and camping site) or disposed of by incineration or equivalent means that eliminates risks to native flora and fauna;
- No herbicides or pesticides shall be brought into the Area;
- Any other chemicals, including radio-nuclides or stable isotopes, which may be introduced for scientific or management purposes specified in the permit, shall be removed from the Area at or before the conclusion of the activity for which the permit was granted;
- Fuel, food, chemicals and other materials are not to be stored in the Area, unless specifically authorized by permit, and shall be stored and handled in a way that minimises the risk of their accidental introduction into the environment;
- All materials introduced shall be for a stated period only, shall be removed at or before the conclusion of that stated period, and shall be stored and handled so that risk of their introduction into the environment is minimized;
- If release occurs which is likely to compromise the values of the Area, removal is encouraged only where the impact of removal is likely to be greater than that of leaving the material *in situ*.

7(vii) Taking of, or harmful interference with, native flora or fauna

Taking or harmful interference with native flora and fauna is prohibited, except in accordance with a permit issued under Article 3 of Annex II of the Protocol on Environmental Protection to the Antarctic Treaty. Where animal taking or harmful interference is involved, this should, as a minimum standard, be in accordance with the SCAR Code of Conduct for the Use of Animals for Scientific Purposes in Antarctica.

7(viii) The collection or removal of materials not brought into the Area by the permit holder

- Material may be collected or removed from the Area only in accordance with a permit and should be limited to the minimum necessary to meet scientific or management needs. This includes biological samples, rock specimens, and historical items.
- Material of human origin likely to compromise the values of the Area, and which was not brought into the Area by the permit holder or otherwise authorized, may be removed from any part of the Area, unless the impact of removal is likely to be greater than leaving the material *in situ*. If this is the case the appropriate authority should be notified.

- Unless specifically authorized by permit, visitors are prohibited from interfering with or attempting restoration of Wilson's Stone Igloo in any way, or from handling, taking or damaging any artifacts. Evidence of recent changes, damage or new artifacts observed should be notified to the appropriate national authority. Relocation or removal of artifacts for the purposes of preservation, protection, or to re-establish historical accuracy is allowable by permit.

7(ix) Disposal of waste

All wastes, including all human wastes, shall be removed from the Area.

7(x) Measures that may be necessary to continue to meet the aims of the Management Plan

Permits may be granted to enter the Area to:

1) Carry out monitoring and Area inspection activities, which may involve the collection of a small number of samples or data for analysis or review;
2) Install or maintain signposts, markers, structures or scientific or essential logistic equipment;
3) Carry out protective measures;
4) Carry out research or management in a manner that avoids interference with long-term research and monitoring activities or possible duplication of effort. Persons planning new projects within the Area should consult with established programs working within the Area, such as those of the US and New Zealand, before initiating the work.

7(xi) Requirements for reports

- The principal permit holder for each visit to the Area shall submit a report to the appropriate national authority as soon as practicable, and no later than six months after the visit has been completed.
- Such reports should include, as appropriate, the information identified in the visit report form contained in the Guide to the Preparation of Management Plans for Antarctic Specially Protected Areas. If appropriate, the national authority should also forward a copy of the visit report to the Parties that proposed the Management Plan, to assist in managing the Area and reviewing the Management Plan.
- Parties should, wherever possible, deposit originals or copies of such original visit reports in a publicly accessible archive to maintain a record of usage, for the purpose of any review of the Management Plan and in organising the scientific use of the Area.
- The appropriate authority should be notified of any activities/measures undertaken, and / or of any materials released and not removed, that were not included in the authorized permit.

8. Supporting documentation

Ainley, D.G., C.A. Ribic, G. Ballard, S. Heath, I. Gaffney, B.J. Karl, K.J. Barton, P.R. Wilson & S. Webb. 2004. Geographic structure of Adélie penguin populations: overlap in colony-specific foraging areas *Ecological Monographs* **74**(1):159–78.

Ainley, D.G., G. Ballard & S. Olmastroni. 2009. An apparent decrease in the prevalence of 'Ross Sea Killer Whales' in the southern Ross Sea. *Aquatic Mammals* **35**(3): 335-47.

Arrigo, K. R., G.L. van Dijken, D.G. Ainley, M.A. Fahnestock & T. Markus. 2002. Ecological impact of a large Antarctic iceberg. *Geophysical Research Letters* **29**(7): 1104.

Ballard, G., K.M. Dugger, N. Nur, & D.G. Ainley. 2010. Foraging strategies of Adélie penguins: adjusting body condition to cope with environmental variability. *Marine Ecology Progress Series* **405**: 287–302.

Barber-Meyer, S.M., G.L. Kooyman & P.J. Ponganis. 2008. Trends in western Ross Sea emperor penguin chick abundances and their relationships to climate. *Antarctic Science* **20** (1), 3–11.

Broady, P.A. 1989. Broadscale patterns in the distribution of aquatic and terrestrial vegetation at three ice-free regions on Ross Island, Antarctica. *Hydrobiologia* **172**: 77-95.

Cole, J.W., P.R. Kyle & V.E. Neall. 1971. Contribution to Quarternary geology of Cape Crozier, White Island and Hut Point Peninsula, McMurdo Sound region, Antarctica. *N.Z. Journal of Geology and Geophysics* **14**: 528-546.

Dugger, K.M., Ainley, D.G., Lyver, P., Barton, K. & Ballard, G. 2010. Survival differences and the effect of environmental instability on breeding dispersal in an Adélie penguin meta-population. *Proceedings of the National Academy of Sciences of USA* **107** (27): 12375–80.

Fretwell, P.T., M.A. LaRue, P. Morin, G.L. Kooyman, B. Wienecke, N. Ratcliffe, A.J. Fox, A.H. Fleming, C. Porter, & P.N. Trathan. 2012. An Emperor penguin population estimate: the first global, synoptic survey of a species from space. PLoS ONE **7**(4): e33751.

Kooyman, G.L. 1993. Breeding habitats of emperor penguins in the western Ross Sea. *Antarctic Science* **5**(2): 143-48.

Kooyman, G.L., D.G. Ainley, G. Ballard, & P.J. Ponganis. 2007. Effects of giant icebergs on two emperor penguin colonies in the Ross Sea, Antarctica. *Antarctic Science* **19**(1): 31-38.

Lyver, P.O'B., M. Barron, K.J. Barton, D.G. Ainley, A. Pollard, S. Gordon, S. McNeill, G. Ballard, and P.R. Wilson. [In Press]. Trends in the breeding population of Adélie penguins in the Ross Sea, 1981–2012: a coincidence of climate and resource extraction effects. Submitted to *PLoS One* 2014.

Smykla, J., B. Krzewicka, K. Wilk, S.D. Emslie & L. Ślima. 2011. Additions to the lichen flora of Victoria Land. *Polish Polar Research* **32**(2): 123-138.

Wright, A.C. & P.R. Kyle. 1990. A.16. Mount Terror. In: *Volcanoes of the Antarctic Plate and Southern Oceans* (Eds. W.E. LeMasurier, J.W. Thompson). Antarctic Research Series **48**, American Geophysical Union: 99-102.

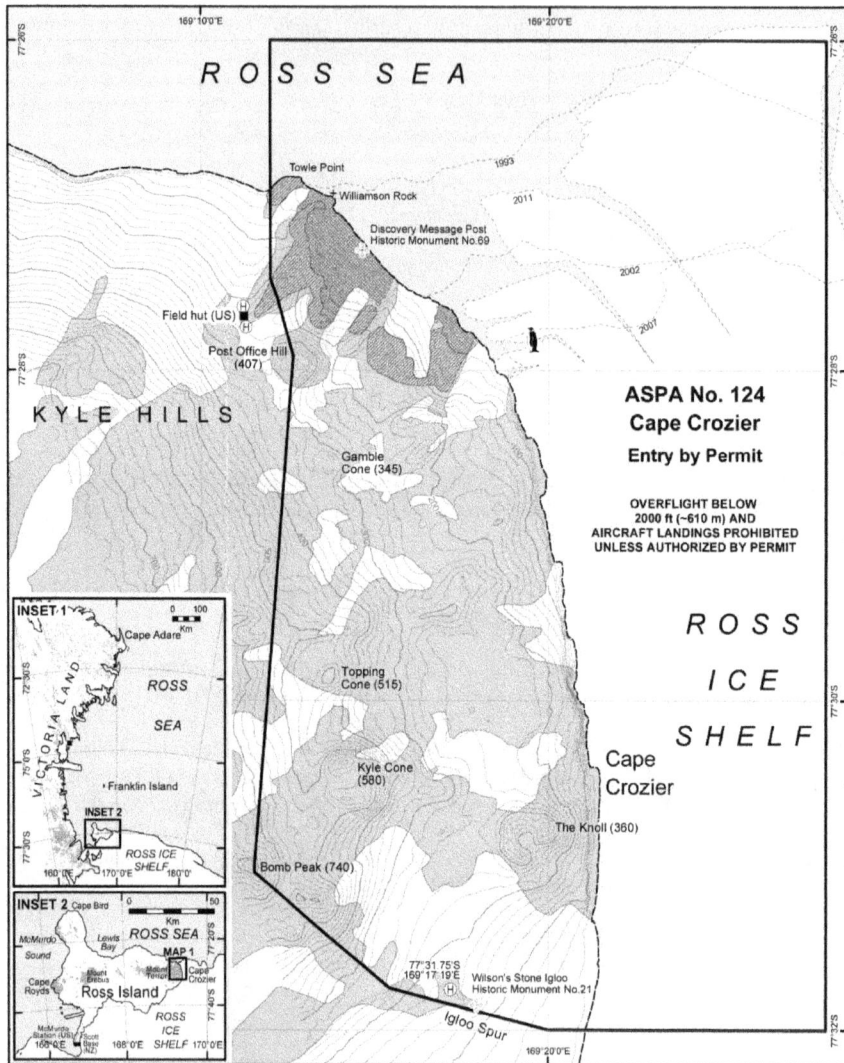

Map 1: ASPA No. 124 Cape Crozier - topography & boundary

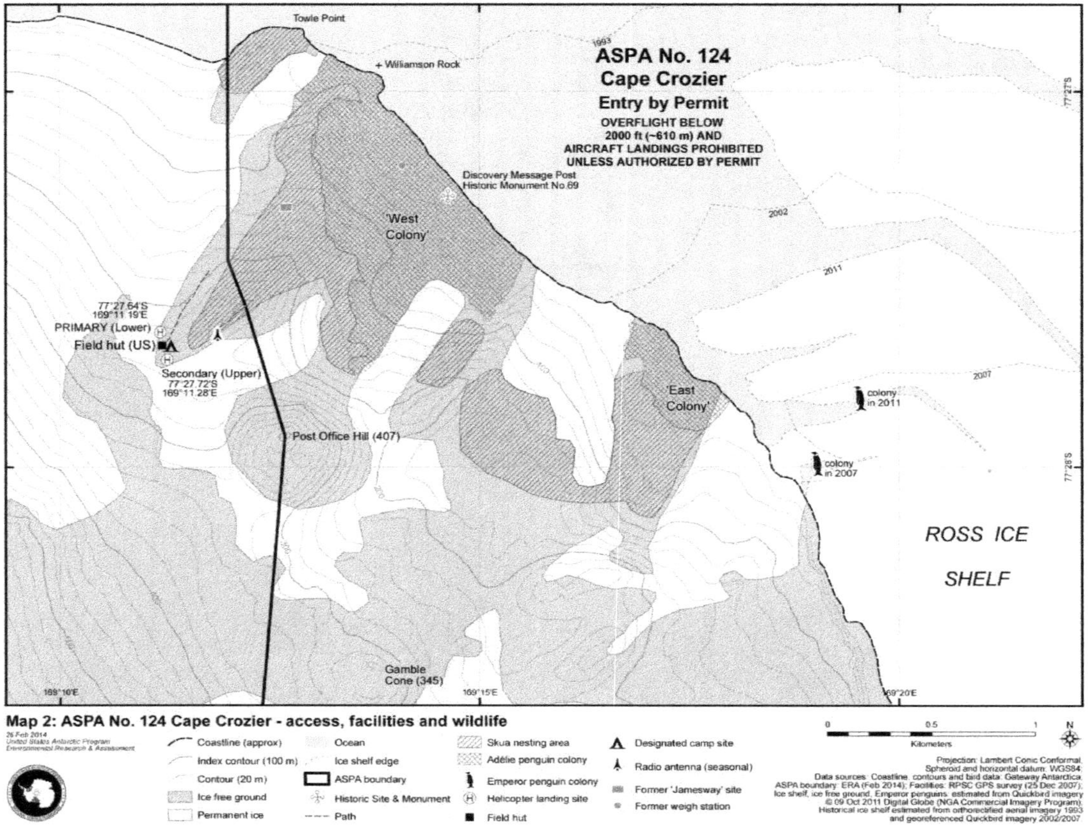

Towle Point
+ Williamson Rock
1993
ASPA No. 124
Cape Crozier
Entry by Permit
OVERFLIGHT BELOW
2000 ft (~610 m) AND
AIRCRAFT LANDINGS PROHIBITED
UNLESS AUTHORIZED BY PERMIT
Discovery Message Post
Historic Monument No.69
'West Colony'
'East Colony'
2002
2011
2007
colony in 2011
colony in 2007
77°27.64'S
169°11.19'E
PRIMARY (Lower)
Field hut (US)
Secondary (Upper)
77°27.72'S
169°11.28'E
Post Office Hill (407)
Gamble Cone (345)
ROSS ICE SHELF
169°10'E
169°15'E
169°20'E
77°27'S
77°28'S
Map 2: ASPA No. 124 Cape Crozier - access, facilities and wildlife
26 Feb 2014
United States Antarctic Program
Environmental Research & Assessment
Coastline (approx)
Index contour (100 m)
Contour (20 m)
Ice free ground
Permanent ice
Ocean
Ice shelf edge
ASPA boundary
Historic Site & Monument
Path
Skua nesting area
Adélie penguin colony
Emperor penguin colony
Helicopter landing site
Field hut
Designated camp site
Radio antenna (seasonal)
Former 'Jamesway' site
Former weigh station
0
0.5
1
Kilometers
N
Projection: Lambert Conic Conformal
Spheroid and horizontal datum: WGS84
Data sources: Coastline, contours and bird data: Gateway Antarctica
ASPA boundary: ERA (Feb 2014); Facilities: RPSC GPS survey (25 Dec 2007);
Ice shelf, ice free ground, Emperor penguins: estimated from Quickbird imagery
© 09 Oct 2011 Digital Globe (NGA Commercial Imagery Program);
Historical ice shelf estimated from orthorectified aerial imagery 1993
and georeferenced Quickbird imagery 2002/2007

Management Plan for
Antarctic Specially Protected Area No 128

WESTERN SHORE OF ADMIRALTY BAY, KING GEORGE ISLAND, SOUTH SHETLAND ISLANDS

Introduction

The Western Shore of Admiralty Bay is located on King George Island, South Shetland Islands, ~125 kilometers from the northern Antarctic Peninsula. Approximate area and coordinates: 16.8 km² (centered at 58° 27' 40" W, 62° 11' 50" S). The Area is wholly terrestrial, and the primary reasons for designation are its diverse avian and mammalian fauna and locally rich vegetation, providing a representative sample of the maritime Antarctic ecosystem. Long term scientific research has been conducted on the animals within the Area. The Area is relatively accessible to nearby research stations and tourist ships regularly visit Admiralty Bay, and the ecological and scientific values of the area need protection from potential disturbance.

The Area was originally designated as Site of Special Scientific Interest (SSSI) No. 8 in Recommendation X-5 (1979, SSSI No. 8) after a proposal by Poland. The SSSI designation was extended through Recommendation XII-5 (1983), Recommendation XIII-7 (1985) and Resolution 7 (1995). A revised Management Plan was adopted through Measure 1 (2000). The site was renamed and renumbered as Antarctic Specially Protected Area (ASPA) No 128 by Decision 1 (2002). The Area lies within Antarctic Specially Managed Area (ASMA) No. 1 Admiralty Bay, King George Island, South Shetland Islands, designated under Measure 2 (2006).

The biological and scientific values of the Area are vulnerable to human disturbance (e.g. oversampling, disturbance to wildlife, introduction of non-native species). Therefore, it is important that human activities in the Area are managed to minimize the risk of impacts. A small area of the introduced species *Poa annua* has been noted within the Area, and this is being given priority management attention. The Area is considered of sufficient size to protect the values for which special protection is required because it includes within the boundaries numerous examples of the features represented (e.g. plant and animal communities), which should ensure that the Area is able to withstand changes that could arise from local or regional pressures, particularly when considered in combination with other instruments that apply in the region such as Antarctic Specially Managed Area No.1 Admiralty Bay, the Convention on the Conservation of Antarctic Marine Living Resources (CCAMLR), and the Agreement on the Conservation of Albatrosses and Petrels (ACAP).

The Area comprises environments within three of the domains defined in the Environmental Domains Analysis for Antarctica: Environment A – Antarctic Peninsula northern geologic; Environment E – Antarctic Peninsula, Alexander and other islands; and Environment G – Antarctic Peninsula offshore islands. Under the Antarctic Conservation Biogeographic Regions classification the Area lies within ACBR3 – Northwest Antarctic Peninsula.

1. Description of values to be protected

The western shore of Admiralty Bay possesses a diverse avian and mammalian fauna and locally rich vegetation which is representative of the maritime Antarctic terrestrial ecosystem. The breeding colonies of Adélie (*Pygoscelis adeliae*) and gentoo penguin (*Pygoscelis papua*) within the Area are among the largest on King George Island, and the site is one of only a few protected areas where all three *Pygoscelid* penguins are found breeding together at the same location. Ten other birds breed within the Area, including chinstrap penguins (*Pygoscelis antarctica*), southern giant petrel (*Macronectes giganteus*), cape petrel (*Daption capense*), Wilson's storm petrel (*Oceanites oceanicus*), black-bellied storm petrel (*Fregetta tropica*), sheathbill (*Chionis alba*), south polar skua (*Stercorarius maccormicki*), brown skua (*Stercorarius lonnbergi*), Dominican gull (*Larus dominicanus*), and Antarctic tern (*Sterna vittata*).

Elephant seals (*Mirounga leonina*), Antarctic fur seals (*Arctocephalus gazella*), Weddell seals (*Leptonychotes weddellii*) rest and/or breed on a number of beaches within the Area. Leopard seals (*Hydrurga leptonyx*) and crabeater seals (*Lobodon carcinophagus*) frequent Admiralty Bay, and are occasionally present on beaches within the Area.

Rich terrestrial plant communities exist within the Area, including one of the most extensive areas colonized by the Antarctic hairgrass *Deschampsia* and the pearlwort *Colobanthus* in Antarctica. Extensive stands of moss from the families Andreaeaceae, Bryaceae, Polytrichaceae, Pottiaceae and Grimmiaceae are present, particularly near the coast up to 60 m a.s.l. Lichen assemblages are more dominant at higher elevations. Rich microbial communities are also represented, including algae (e.g *Prasiola*, *Phormidium*), mites (from the Orders / Suborders Prostigmata, Mesostigmata and Oribatida) and nematodes (e.g. *Plectus* and *Panagrolaimus*).

The values to be protected are those associated with the exceptionally diverse assemblage of plants and animals, which is a representative example of the Maritime Antarctic ecosystem, and the long-term scientific studies that have been undertaken within the Area, especially since 1976. In particular, scientific studies undertaken within the Area have been important in relation to documenting and interpreting large-scale regional shifts in pygoscelid penguin populations that have been observed on the Antarctic Peninsula and its offshore islands over recent decades.

Recent exposure of new areas of ice-free ground as a result of glacial recession offers opportunities for studies of colonisation processes, which represents an additional scientific value of the Area. The status of the non-native species *Poa annua* on the deglaciated moraines near Ecology Glacier is systematically monitored. The whole Area is also monitored for the presence of other unintentionally introduced species.

2. Aims and objectives

Management at the western shore of Admiralty Bay aims to:

- Avoid degradation of, or substantial risk to, the values of the Area by preventing unnecessary human disturbance;
- Allow scientific research on the ecosystem of the Area, in particular on the avifauna, pinnipeds and terrestrial ecology, while ensuring protection from oversampling or other possible scientific impacts;
- Allow other scientific research, scientific support activities and visits for educational and outreach purposes (such as documentary reporting (visual, audio or written) or the production of educational resources or services) provided that such activities are for compelling reasons that cannot be served elsewhere and will not jeopardise the natural ecological system in the Area;
- Minimize the possibility of introduction of additional alien plants, animals and microbes to the Area;
- Minimise the possibility of the introduction of pathogens that may cause disease in faunal populations within the Area;
- To prevent the spread of the non-native grass *Poa annua* present within the Area beyond its current limits of location and extent while further research is undertaken and management strategies for long-term control are developed, and to coordinate these strategies with those developed for the management of non-native species within ASMA No. 1 Admiralty Bay more generally; and
- Allow visits for management purposes in support of the aims of the management plan.

3. Management activities

The following management activities shall be undertaken to protect the values of the Area:

- Signs showing the location of the Area (stating the special restrictions that apply) shall be displayed prominently, and a copy of this management plan shall be kept available, in the research hut facilities within the Area and at all permanent scientific stations located within Admiralty Bay;
- Copies of this management plan shall be made available to all vessels and aircraft visiting the Area and/or operating in the vicinity of the adjacent stations, and all pilots and ship captains operating in the region shall be informed of the location, boundaries and restrictions applying to entry and overflight within the Area;

- National programs shall take steps to ensure the boundaries of the Area and the restrictions that apply within are marked on relevant maps and nautical / aeronautical charts;
- Markers, signs or structures erected within the Area for scientific or management purposes shall be secured and maintained in good condition, and removed when no longer required;
- National Antarctic programs operating in the Area should maintain a record of all new markers, signs and structures erected within the Area;
- The non-native species *Poa annua* present within the Area near Ecology Glacier should be monitored annually for changes in its extent and / or density, and policies on containment or eradication of the species within the Area be developed as a matter of urgency, then implemented and kept under review;
- Before an informed decision can be made on the likely success and benefits relative to the environmental damage of an eradication attempt, more information on the species distribution and current and likely future ecosystem impacts is needed, and further research to address these questions should be supported. However, should an appropriate authority approve it as necessary to protect the values of the Area, mechanical removal of non-native species by hand tools may be undertaken in accordance with procedures to be set out as part of an assessment of impacts in advance;
- Personnel (national program staff, field expeditions, tourist expedition leaders and pilots) in the vicinity of, accessing or flying over the Area shall be specifically instructed by their national program, tour operator or appropriate national authority to observe the provisions and contents of the Management Plan;
- Visits shall be made as necessary (no less than once every five years) to assess whether the Area continues to serve the purposes for which it was designated and to ensure management and maintenance measures are adequate;
- National Antarctic Programs operating in the region shall consult together with a view to ensuring that the above provisions are implemented.

4. Period of designation

Designated for an indefinite period.

5. Maps and photographs

Map 1. ASPA No. 128 Western Shore of Admiralty Bay, King George Island – Regional overview.

Inset: Location of King George Island, South Shetland Islands, Antarctic Peninsula.

Projection: Lambert Conformal Conic; Standard parallels: 1st 62°00' S; 2nd 62°15' S; Central Meridian: 58°15' W; Latitude of Origin 64°00 S; Spheroid and horizontal datum: WGS84. Topography and coastlines provided by Proantar, Brasil. Bathymetry: International Bathymetric Chart of the Southern Ocean (IBCSO) v1 (2013). Other data supplied by Environmental Research & Assessment.

Map 2. ASPA No. 128 Western Shore of Admiralty Bay: access, facilities & wildlife.

Map specifications: Projection: UTM Zone 21S; Spheroid and horizontal datum: WGS84. Topography and bathymetry provided by Proantar, Brasil. Coastline updated from WorldView-1 imagery (Mar 2008; imagery © Digital Globe courtesy of US NGA Commercial Imagery Program). Streams digitized from orthophoto map by Pudelko (1979). Location of *Poa annua*, small boat landing sites, marker and HSM No.51 supplied by Polish Antarctic Program. Other data supplied by Environmental Research & Assessment.

6. Description of the Area

6(i) Geographical co-ordinates, boundary markers and natural features

General description

The Area is situated on the western shore of Admiralty Bay on the south side of King George Island, which is the largest of the South Shetland Islands archipelago. Arctowski Station (Poland) is situated 0.5 km to the north. The Area comprises ice-free terrain including steep crags of up to 400 m in elevation with more gentle morainic slopes interspersed by several glaciers extending down to the coast. The shoreline consists of broad pebbly beaches interrupted by rocky headlands. The Area is ~17 km².

Boundaries and coordinates

The eastern boundary of the Area follows the coastline on the western shore of Admiralty Bay from the SE extremity of Halfmoon Cove (58°27'49"W, 62°09'44"S) for ~ 6 km SSE to Demay Point (Map 2). The boundary thence follows the coastline SW around Paradise Cove and Utchatka Point approximately 3.5 km to Telefon (Patelnia) Point (58°28'28"W, 62°14'03"S). From Telefon Point the boundary extends northward in a straight line for ~2.3 km to The Tower (367 m; 58°28'48"W, 62°12'55"S), a distinctive peak above Tower Glacier. The boundary continues in this direction a further 5.3 km to Jardine Peak (285 m; 58°29'54"W, 62°10'03"S). The boundary descends eastward in a straight line from Jardine Peak for ~1.7 km to the highest point on Penguin Ridge, ~ 550 m from Arctowski Station. The boundary thence extends NE for ~0.3 km to the SE coast of Halfmoon Cove. A marker is placed in Halfmoon Cove on the northern boundary of the Area at 58°27'48.7" W 62°09'43.7" S, ~500 m southeast of Arctowski station (Map 2).

Climate

The climate of the Area is typical of maritime Antarctica. Based on complementary data obtained at Arctowski Station (Poland) between 1977-2000 and from 2006 and at the Comandante Ferraz Station (Brazil) since 1984, the microclimate of Admiralty Bay is characterized by an average annual temperature of around -1.8 °C and an average annual wind speed of approximately 6.5 m s⁻¹. Annual average precipitation equals 508.5 mm, humidity is 82% and pressure 991 hPa. The waters of Admiralty Bay have an annual temperature range of -1.8° to +4°C, being well mixed by tides and strongly influenced by currents and coastal upwelling (from ASMA No.1 Admiralty Bay Management Plan).

The climate has recently been changing under the influence of unstable pressure systems such as the Southern Annular Mode (SAM) and the El Nino Southern Oscillation (ENSO) (Bers *et al.* 2012). Rapid regional warming of air temperature on the Western Antarctic Peninsula (WAP) observed over the last 50 years is exceptional and unprecedented in comparison with the record from ice core data over the past 500 years (Vaughan and Doake 1996). The most recent reconstructions show a warming trend between 1957 - 2006 of 0.12 °C per decade for the whole Antarctic continent, and of 0.17 °C per decade for West Antarctica (Steig *et al.* 2009). Schloss *et al.* (2012) show the 50-year warming trend has yielded an average increase of air temperature of about 2.0° C in summer and 2.4° C in winter at nearby Carlini Station (Map 1). Kejna *et al.* (2013), analysing data from all available meteorological sources on King George Island and on Deception Island, showed a 1.2 °C increase in annual average air temperature and a 2.3 hPa decrease in atmospheric pressure over a comparable time period.

Geology, geomorphology and soils

Geological investigations on King George Island prior to 1980 were performed by British, Argentinian, Russian and Chilean scientists, although the area within ASPA No. 128 was not described because it does not have any paternal lithostratigraphic rock sequences (for details see Birkenmajer 2003). The first geological map covering this area was presented by Birkenmajer (1980), republished with minor modifications in Birkenmajer (2003). The area of ASPA No.128 is included by Birkenmajer (2003) in the Warszawa tectonic block (terrane), that consists of Cretaceous, Paleocene, Eocene volcanic and pyroclastic rock with trace participation of sedimentary rocks. Volcanic rocks belong mainly to basal, basaltic andesite, andesite intercalated with tuffs, scoria and volcanic breccia. Sediments bearing plant remains occur only in the thin horizon (<1 m) of the upper part of Zamek sections. Moreover, dispersed petrified wood is present in agglomerates of the Tower, and abundant fossil flora was present in reworked clastics of the Błaszczyk moraine. A rich collection of dicotyledonous leaf, represented mainly by the genus *Nothofagus* and by laurophyllos plant frond impressions as well as conifer shoot imprints, was gathered and described from this site (Birkenmajer & Zastawniak 1989; Zastawniak 1994; Dutra & Batten 2000). Several hypabyssal intrusions (plug, dykes, sills) of diversified patrographic and geochemical composition cut stratiform volcanic complexes of Warszawa Terrane (Barbieri *et al.* 1987). Recently performed isotopic analyses (⁴⁰Ar-³⁹Ar of rock and U-Pb of zircons) gave Eocene ages for most of the rocks from the Area considered previously as Cretaceous, including the fossil flora bearing formations (Nawrocki *et al.* 2011).

Poor tundra soils occurring in the maritime Antarctic climate are difficult to describe according to criteria used in traditional soil classification systems. The first ecological and intuitive soil classification covering the maritime Antarctic, including ASPA No.128, was proposed by Everett (1976). Schaefer *et al.* (2007) identified 20 soil-scape units in the Arctowski Station vicinity and classified them according to their vulnerability in a geo-environmental map, partly comparable to that of more formal soil units proposed by Blume *et al.* (2002). Particular attention has been focused in this region on coastal soils around penguin colonies, since their fertile ecosystems are highly productive and biologically diverse. Ornithogenic soils were fully described and mapped (or indicated on air photographs) in papers by Tatur & Myrcha (1984); Tatur (1989) and Tatur (2002). Ornithogenic soils of the maritime Antarctic were subdivided into: organic soils of the rookery (with hydroxyapatite); soils of the phosphatized zone (with Al-Fe phosphates bearing K and NH4 ions) and soils accumulated from inactive reworked phosphates. Moreover, relic soils at the locations of abandoned penguin colonies were distinguished and are an important feature in the Area. The phosphatization was described as a soil forming process, investigated also in other papers (e.g. Simas *et al.* 2007). Blume *et al.* (1997) and Beyer *et al.* (1999) identified the phosphatization as a podzolization and, using the new version of the US Soil Taxonomy, summarised the dry permafrost-affected soils (which they identified as occurring within the Area) as Anhydrous soils and Gelisols, where pedogenetic processes like cryoturbation, brunification and podzolization occurred.

Glaciology, streams and lakes

The Area is shaped by valley glaciers draining the Warszawa icefield, which are constrained at the sides by exposed bedrock. Isolated rocky hills are covered by rock rubble, with glaciers and glacial deposits filling depressions among them. Prominent early Holocene cliffs may be observed in the coastal zone. Holocene raised beaches (up to 16 m a.s.l.) and more recent beaches are comprised of sand with pebbles and boulders.

Several glaciers descend into the Area, flowing eastward from the Warszawa Icefield (Map 2). These have been in continuous retreat for at least the last 30 years, with former tidal glacier fronts retreating up to 900 m inland between 1997–2007 (Battke *et al.* 2001; Pudełko 2007), which is consistent with a global warming trend and a local reduction in the size of floating glaciers in Admiralty Bay (Braun & Gossmann 2002) . The ice-free area of ASPA No128 has increased from 20% in 1979 to more than 50% in 1999 (Battke *et al.* 2001) and continues to increase. Retreating glaciers deposited bands of ridges formed by fresh lateral moraines and ground moraines on the flat areas at the front of glaciers, often with brackish water lagoons collecting glacial meltwaters mixed with seawater (Ecology, Baranowski, and Windy glaciers). Newly exposed land and new water bodies are colonized by biota that create a unique opportunity to study succession processes in the Antarctic environment (Olech & Massalski 2001) .

A number of small meltwater streams are present within the Area, mainly originating from the outlet glaciers flowing down from the Warszawa Icefield (Map 2).

Terrestrial ecology

Vegetation typical of the maritime Antarctic has partially colonised the ice-free terrain within the Area. Dry areas and rocks are colonised by lichens, with flowering plants such as *Deschampsia antarctica* and *Colobanthus quitensis* locally numerous and occupying fairly large areas particularly in the vicinity of Arctowski Station. This constitutes one of the largest areas covered by these species in the Antarctic. Bryophyta and flowering plants dominate the vegetation from 0 to 60 m a.s.l., while lichens are more dominant above this elevation. Mosses can be found from the families Andreaeaceae, Bryaceae, Polytrichaceae, Pottiaceae and Grimmiaceae. Around penguin colonies the species richness and diversity is lower due to the high nitrate and ammonia content of the soil (Olech 2002; Victoria, Pereira, and Pinheiro 2009).

One alien species of grass, *Poa annua*, was observed in 2008-09 within the Area on the deglaciated moraines of the Ecology Glacier (Olech & Chwedorzewska 2011) (approximate location 58° 27' 54"W 62° 10' 7"S, Map 2). This species was first recorded outside of the Area, at Arctowski Station, in summer 1985-86 (Olech 1996), first in places where the soil structure had been disturbed by human activities and later within native vegetation communities (Olech unpublished, after Chwedorzewska 2008)). High genetic variability suggests several separate immigration events from different sources, including Europe and South America (Chwedorzewska 2008).

Recently, propagules and pollen of the rush *Juncus bufonius* were found in one location within the Area (Cuba-Diaz *et al*. 2012).

Three different types of mite are present in the Area: Prostigmata, Mesostigmata and Oribatida. Prostigmata is the dominant community and Oribatida is only found in ice free areas that have been ice-free for more than 30 years (Gryziak 2009).

Glacial recession has exposed new ice-free areas that are being successively colonized by microbial and invertebrate communities including algae, mites and nematodes, as well as lichens, mosses and vascular plants. The pioneer species that appeared first were the moss *Bryum pseudotriquetrum*, and then the grass *Deschampsia antarctica*. In the second stage of succession the dominance of *Colobanthus quitensis* was marked. The first rock-inhabiting lichens (*Caloplaca johnstoni, C. sublobulata, Lecanora* spp.) appeared in the third stage of succession. The substantial influence of penguin colonies, which occur in the Telefon (Patelnia) Point region, was revealed in the fourth stage. On rocks the ornithocoprophilous communities of epilithic lichens dominated, while on soil the grass *Deschampsia antarctica* with the nitrophilous algae (*Prasiola crispa, Phormidium* spp.) and mosses (e.g. *Syntrichia magellanica*) were prominent (Olech & Massalski 2001). The abundance of nematodes increases with the age of the ice free area and common species present are *Plectus* and *Panagrolaimus* (Ilieva-Makulec & Gryziak 2009).

Breeding birds

Twelve bird species regularly breed within the Area, the most numerous of which are penguins. In 2012-13 there were 6017 breeding pairs of Adélie penguin (*Pygoscelis adeliae*), 984 breeding pairs of chinstrap penguin (*Pygoscelis antarctica*) and 5396 breeding pairs of gentoo penguin (*Pygoscelis papua*) (unpublished data US Antarctic Marine Living Resources (AMLR) program). Interannual variation in breeding pairs is large for all these species, with changes in some years in excess of 40% (Ciaputa & Sierakowski 1999). Significant decreases in average penguin breeding numbers were observed between the four-year periods of 1978-81 and 2009-12, when an average decrease of almost 69% was observed for Adélie penguins and over 83% for chinstrap penguins, while gentoo penguins have increased by 64%. These trends are consistent with those observed for these species at other nearby colonies on King George Island, in particular those at Lions Rump (Korczak-Abshire *et al*. 2013) and Stranger Point (Carlini *et al*. 2009). The regional trends and breeding data suggest differential over-winter survival between the species (Hinke *et al*. 2007, Carlini *et al*. 2009), which relates to influences remote from nesting sites within the Area. Therefore, the changes being observed in populations at breeding sites within the Area are not considered related to human pressures or impacts occurring within the Area.

Table 1: Four-year averages of numbers of penguin breeding pairs within ASPA 128 (based on data from Ciaputa & Sierakowski 1999, US AMLR program unpublished data).

Species	Location	Census Period			Average change (1978-81 to 2009-12)	Percent change (1978-81 to 2009-12)
		1978-81	1992-96	2009-2012		
Pygoscelis adeliae	Llano Point	10859	6073	2454	-8405	
	Point Thomas	11899	9886	4578	-7321	
	Total	*22758*	*15959*	*7032*	*-15726*	*-69.1%*
Pygoscelis antarctica	Telefon Point	2029	1511	604	-1425	
	Uchatka Point	1944	909	292	-1652	
	Demay Point	819	263	52	-767	

	Llano Point	347	8	2	-345	
	Point Thomas	541	1	0	-541	
	Total	*5681*	*2692*	*950*	*-4731*	*-83.3%*
Pygoscelis papua	Llano Point	2174	1765	4646	2472	
	Point Thomas	715	267	90	-625	
	Total	*2889*	*2032*	*4736*	*1847*	*+63.9%*

Nine other bird species breed within the Area: Southern giant petrel (*Macronectes giganteus*); cape petrel (*Daption capense*); Wilson's storm petrel (*Oceanites oceanicus*); black-bellied storm petrel (*Fregetta tropica*); American sheathbill (*Chionis alba*); Dominican gull (*Larus dominicanus*); Antarctic tern (*Sterna vittata*); south polar skua (*Stercorarius maccormicki*) and brown skua (*S. lonnbergi*) . Data for the latter two species show successful breeding was rare in the 2012-13 season (Table 2), when no south polar skua or mixed pairs bred. Despite the poor skua breeding performance in that season, numerous birds were present on territories (Hinke pers. comm. 2013, US AMLR program).

Table 2: Skua breeding pair census (Carneiro *et al.* 2009, US AMLR program unpublished data)

	Brown Skua			South Polar Skua			Mixed Skua			Total		
Location	2012-2013	2004-2005	1978-1979	2012-2013	2004-2005	1978-1979	2012-2013	2004-2005	1978-1979	2012-2013	2004-2005	1978-1979
Llano Point to Telefon Point	11	21	24	0	27	5	0	6	2	11	54	31
Point Thomas	7	21	23	0	45	7	0	10	7	7	76	38

Four other penguin species (king (*Aptenodytes patagonicus*), emperor (*Aptenodytes forsteri*), rockhopper (*Eudyptes chrysocome*) and Magellanic (*Spheniscus magellanicus*)) are occasionally observed within the Area. Other Antarctic bird species (e.g. snow petrel (*Pagodroma nivea*)) are also occasionally observed within the Area (Poland 2002).

Seven South American bird species have been observed within the Area as stray visitors that remained only temporarily: cattle egret (*Bubulcus ibis*), black-necked swan (*Cygnus melanocoryphus*), Chiloe wigeon (*Anas sibilatrix*), Yellow-billed pintail (*Anas georgica*), white-rumped sandpiper (*Calidris fuscicollis*), Wilson's phalarope (*Pharalopus tricolor*) and barn swallow (*Hirundo rustica*) (Poland 2002; Korczak-Abshire, Lees & Jojczyk 2011; Korczak-Abshire, Angiel & Wierzbicki 2011).

Breeding mammals

Elephant seals (*Mirounga leonina*), Antarctic fur seals (*Arctocephalus gazella*) and Weddell seals (*Leptonychotes weddellii*) are present on beaches at numerous sites, although only elephant seals breed within the Area. In 2009-10 six elephant seal harems with 238 pups were observed within the Area (Map 2), while in the same year the maximum number of fur seals exceeded 1290 individuals (Korczak-Abshire, pers. comm.). Annual seal censuses have been conducted by Poland year-round once every ten days since 1988 (Ciaputa

1996; Salwicka & Sierakowski 1998; Salwicka & Rakusa-Suszczewski 2002). A strong annual cycle in numbers is evident, with the number of elephant seals reaching a maximum from December to February and Antarctic fur seals showing a high peak around February and another lower peak around June. Leopard seals (*Hydrurga leptonyx*) and crabeater seals (*Lobodon carcinophagus*) are frequently seen on ice floes during the winter, although rarely come ashore (Salwicka & Rakusa-Suszczewski 2002).

Human activities / impacts

The permanent year-round station Henryk Arctowski (Poland) (58°28'15"W, 62°09'34"S) situated 0.5 km north of the Area (Map 1) has been occupied continuously since 1977 and can host up to 70 people during the summer, and 20 during winter. Several other permanent national program stations are located nearby within Admiralty Bay, including Ferraz (Brazil) (~9.5 km from the Area), Machu Picchu (Peru) (~7.6 km from the Area) and Vincente (Ecuador) (~5.2 km from the Area). Activities of national programs operating with the region are coordinated under the management plan for ASMA No. 1 Admiralty Bay.

A semi-permanent summer-only field camp (US) (58°26'49"W, 62°10'46"S) is situated within the Area south of Llano Point (Map 2). Known as 'Copacabana', the field camp, which has capacity for up to six people, has been occupied by ornithologists every summer season since it was established in 1985.

A small (16 m², 4 berth) wooden refuge (Poland) (58°26'32"W, 62°13'03"S) is situated ~300 m NW of Uchatka Point near the shore of Paradise Cove. The hut is used mostly by researchers who study the pinniped and penguin colonies located in the southern part of the Area. The refuge also serves as a base camp for glaciologists, geologists and botanists working on Baranowski and Windy Glaciers.

Admiralty Bay has been a perennial destination for tourism due to its location, historic and ecological values, and the interest provided by permanent scientific stations. Arctowski Station has been particularly popular (Chwedorzewska & Korczak 2010), with the number of visitors peaking in 2007-08 (Table 3). The principal activities conducted are station visits, with extended walks, kayaking and small boat cruises also being undertaken near to but outside of the Area.

Table 3: Number of tourist visits to Arctowski Station (Source: IAATO)

Season	Number of Tourists (landed and non landed)	Number of Tourists Landed only	Number of Vessels
2003-04	3284	3284	10
2004-05	2684	2684	8
2005-06	3178	3178	9
2006-07	3969	3969	12
2007-08	5772	5772	11
2008-09	1896	1896	6
2009-10	4022	1501	9
2010-11	387	387	4
2011-12	624	624	4
2012-13	1368	1350	7

The high level of visitation at Arctowski Station makes the Area relatively vulnerable to the introduction of non-native species. One such species, the grass *Poa annua*, has established a stable population at Arctowski Station (Olech 1996), and is present on a deglaciated moraine inside the Area (approximate location 58° 27'

54"W 62° 10' 7" S, Map 2). At this site in 2011 approximately 70 individuals were reported spread over an area of 100 m² (Olech and Chwedorzewska 2011). Poland is supporting further research on survival and dispersion of *Poa annua* in the region, which is expected to help inform decisions about management responses to the alien species within and nearby to the Area (Kidawa, pers. comm. 2013)

6(ii) Access to the Area

The Area may be accessed by traversing over land or sea ice, by sea or by air. Particular routes have not been designated for access to the Area. Small boat access, overflight and aircraft landing restrictions apply within the Area, the specific conditions for which are set out in Section 7(i) below.

6(iii) Location of structures within and adjacent to the Area

Two structures are located within the Area (Map 2): Copacabana Field Camp (US)(58° 26' 49.27" W 62° 10' 45.89" S), located ~500 m south of Llano Point and consisting of three wooden huts to accommodate up to six people. A four-berth wooden refuge (Poland) (58° 26' 32.27" W 62° 13' 2.9" S) is located in Paradise Cove ~1.2 km SW of Demay Point.

6(iv) Location of other protected areas in the vicinity

ASPA No.125, Fildes Peninsula, King George Island (25 de Mayo), and ASPA No 150, Ardley Island, Maxwell Bay, King George Island (25 de Mayo), lie ~27 km west of the Area (Map 1). ASPA No.132, Potter Peninsula, , and ASPA No.171 Narebski Point, Barton Peninsula, lie ~15 km and ~19 km to the west respectively on King George Island (25 de Mayo). ASPA No.151, Lion's Rump, King George Island, lies ~20 km to the east of the Area (Map 1). Historic Monument No.51, consisting of the grave of Wlodzimierz Puchalski surmounted by an iron cross, is situated ~80 m outside of the northern boundary of the Area (Map 2).

The Area lies within Antarctic Specially Managed Area (ASMA) No. 1 Admiralty Bay, King George Island, South Shetland Islands, designated under Measure 2 (2006) (Map 1).

6(v) Special zones within the Area

There are no zones designated within the Area.

7. Permit Conditions

7(i) General Permit conditions

Entry into the Area is prohibited except in accordance with a Permit issued by an appropriate national authority. Conditions for issuing a permit for the Area are that:

- It is issued for scientific research, and in particular for research on the avifauna in the Area, or for compelling scientific, educational or outreach reasons that cannot be served elsewhere, or for reasons essential to the management of the Area;
- The actions permitted are in accordance with this Management Plan;
- The activities permitted will give due consideration via the environmental impact assessment process to the continued protection of the environmental and scientific values of the Area;
- Approach distances to fauna must be respected, except when the scientific projects may require otherwise and this is specified in the relevant permits;
- The Permit shall be issued for a finite period;
- The Permit, or a copy, shall be carried when in the Area.

7(ii) Access to, movement within or over, the Area

Access into the Area is permitted on foot, by small boat or by aircraft. Vehicles are prohibited within the Area. Access to bird breeding areas during the breeding season (01 October to 31 March) is restricted to visitors conducting or supporting scientific research, carrying out educational or outreach activities consistent with the aims and objectives of the management plan, or undertaking essential management activities.

Foot access and movement within the Area

Persons on foot should at all times avoid disturbance to birds and seals, and damage to vegetation. Pedestrians entering the Area from the vicinity of nearby Arctowski Station should be particularly mindful of the potential to transfer plant material or seeds of the invasive non-native grass *Poa annua* and observe the precautions set out below in Section 7(v) to minimize the risk of further spread.

Pedestrians should maintain the following minimum approach distances from wildlife, unless it is necessary to exceed these for purposes allowed for by the permit:

- Southern giant petrels (*Macronectes giganteus*) – 50 m
- breeding/moulting other birds and seals – 15 m
- non-breeding birds and seals – 5 m.

Pilots, air, or boat crew, or other people in boats or aircraft are prohibited from moving on foot beyond the immediate vicinity of their landing site or the hut facilities unless specifically authorised by Permit. Visitors should move carefully so as to minimize disturbance to flora, fauna, and soils, and should walk on snow or rocky terrain where practical and avoid vegetated areas. Where possible avoid moist ground where foot traffic can easily damage sensitive soils, plant and algal communities, and degrade water quality. Pedestrian traffic should be kept to the minimum consistent with the objectives of any permitted activities and every reasonable effort should be made to minimize effects.

Small boat access

Access from the sea is permitted only by small boat. Access to the beach area between Llano Point and Sphinx Hill (Map 2) from the sea is prohibited in order to avoid interference with animal communities that are the subject of long-term and ongoing research, except for the purpose of visiting 'Copacabana' Field Camp for purposes allowed for by Permit, or in an emergency. The recommended landing sites for small boats are at the following locations (Map 2):

1) on the beaches at Halfmoon Cove or Arctowski Cove, both of which are outside of the Area where no permit for entry is required;
2) on the beach immediately in front of 'Copacabana' Field Camp (US); or
3) on the beach immediately in front of the refuge (PL) in Paradise Cove.

Access from the sea to any sites suitable for landing south of Sphinx Hill is allowed, provided this is consistent with the purposes for which a Permit has been granted. Visitors to the Area by small boat should inform Arctowski Station.

Aircraft access and overflight

Due to the widespread presence of seabirds and pinnipeds within the Area during the breeding season (01 October – 31 March), access to the Area by aircraft in this period is strongly discouraged. All restrictions on aircraft access and overflight apply between 01 October – 31 March inclusive, when aircraft shall operate and land within the Area according to strict observance of the following conditions:

1) Aircraft should maintain a horizontal and vertical separation distance 2000 ft (~610 m) from the coast generally, and from the breeding wildlife colonies in particular, as identified on Map 2, unless otherwise authorized by permit;
2) Weather with a low cloud ceiling often prevails over King George Island, particularly in the vicinity of the permanent ice caps such as the Warszawa Icefield, Aircraft should avoid the Area unless it is possible to maintain safely the minimum horizontal and vertical separation distance of 2000 ft (~610 m) given above;

3) Landing of helicopters within the Area is generally prohibited, except on permanent glaciers or in an emergency;

4) Helicopters operating in the region may land at the designated landing site located at Arctowski Station (58°58.849"W, 62°11.577"S), which should be approached from the NE over Admiralty Bay. Overflight of the northern boundary of Area where many birds and seals are present should be avoided;

5) Use of smoke grenades to indicate wind direction is prohibited within the Area unless absolutely necessary for safety, and any grenades used should be retrieved;

6) In circumstances not covered above pilots should, as a minimum standard, comply with the *Guidelines for the Operation of Aircraft near Concentrations of Birds* appended to Resolution 2 (2004);

7) These provisions do not apply to small unmanned aircraft which may be deployed for scientific or management purposes.

7(iii) Activities that may be conducted within the Area

- Scientific research that will not jeopardize the ecosystem or values of the Area;

- Activities with educational and / or outreach purposes that cannot be served elsewhere;

- Activities with the aim of preserving or protecting historic resources within the Area;

- Essential management activities, including management of non-native species within the Area, monitoring and inspection;

- Activities at the site within the Area known to be colonised by the invasive grass *Poa annua* (Map 2) are specifically restricted to research or management related to the non-native species, and other access to this site is prohibited unless access is necessary for other compelling scientific or management reason(s) that cannot be served elsewhere. Those accessing the site shall take precautions not to spread the grass further by thoroughly inspecting and cleaning footwear, equipment and clothing before moving to another location both within or outside of the Area.

7(iv) Installation, modification or removal of structures / equipment

- No structures are to be erected within the Area except as specified in a permit and, with the exception of permanent survey markers and signs, additional permanent structures or installations are prohibited;

- All structures, scientific equipment or markers installed in the Area must be authorized by permit and clearly identified by country, name of the principal investigator, year of installation and date of expected removal. All such items should be free of organisms, propagules (e.g. seeds, eggs) and non-sterile soil, and be made of materials that can withstand the environmental conditions and pose minimal risk of contamination or damage to the values of the Area;

- Installation (including site selection), maintenance, modification or removal of structures or equipment shall be undertaken in a manner that minimizes disturbance to values of the Area, preferably avoiding the main breeding season (01 Oct – 31 Mar);

- Removal of specific structures / equipment for which the permit has expired shall be the responsibility of the authority which granted the original permit, and shall be a condition of the permit.

7(v) Location of field camps

The facilities 'Copacabana' Field Camp (US) and refuge (Poland) at Paradise Cove (Map 2) provide limited accommodation for scientific use subject to the permission of the appropriate authority. Camping is prohibited elsewhere within the Area.

7(vi) Restrictions on materials and organisms which may be brought into the Area

In addition to the requirements of the Protocol on Environmental Protection to the Antarctic Treaty, restrictions on materials and organisms which may be brought into the area are:

- Deliberate introduction of animals, plant material, micro-organisms and non-sterile soil into the Area is prohibited. Precautions shall be taken to prevent the accidental introduction of animals, plant material, micro-organisms and non-sterile soil from other biologically distinct regions (within or beyond the Antarctic Treaty area).
- Visitors shall ensure that sampling equipment and markers brought into the Area are clean. To the maximum extent practicable, footwear and other equipment used or brought into the area (including backpacks, carry-bags and other equipment) shall be thoroughly cleaned before entering the Area. This is particularly important when travelling to the Area from nearby Arctowski Station where the invasive grass *Poa annua* has become established, and footwear and equipment that has potential to be contaminated should be cleaned before departing the station and not worn or used around the station before entering the Area. Visitors should also consult and follow as appropriate recommendations contained in the Committee for Environmental Protection Non-native Species Manual (CEP 2011), and in the Environmental Code of Conduct for terrestrial scientific field research in Antarctica (SCAR 2009);
- All poultry brought into and not consumed or used within the Area, including all parts, products and / or wastes of poultry, shall be removed from the Area or disposed of by incineration or equivalent means that eliminates risks to native flora and fauna;;
- No herbicides or pesticides shall be brought into the Area;
- Fuel, food, chemicals, and other materials shall not be stored in the Area, unless specifically authorized by permit and shall be stored and handled in a way that minimises the risk of their accidental introduction into the environment;
- All materials introduced shall be for a stated period only and shall be removed by the end of that stated period; and
- If release occurs which is likely to compromise the values of the Area, removal is encouraged only where the impact of removal is not likely to be greater than that of leaving the material *in situ*.

7(vii) Taking of, or harmful interference with, native flora or fauna

Taking or harmful interference with native flora and fauna is prohibited, except in accordance with a permit issued under Article 3 of Annex II of the Protocol on Environmental Protection to the Antarctic Treaty. Where animal taking or harmful interference is involved, this should, as a minimum standard, be in accordance with the SCAR Code of Conduct for the Use of Animals for Scientific Purposes in Antarctica.

7(viii) The collection or removal of materials not brought into the Area by the permit holder

- Material may be collected or removed from the Area only in accordance with a Permit and should be limited to the minimum necessary to meet scientific or management needs. This includes biological samples, rock specimens, whale bones, artefacts of the whaling industry, and any other historical item.
- Material of human origin likely to compromise the values of the Area, and which was not brought into the Area by the permit holder or otherwise authorized, may be removed from the Area, unless the impact of removal is likely to be greater than leaving the material *in situ*: if this is the case the appropriate authority must be notified and approval obtained.

7(ix) Disposal of waste

All wastes shall be removed from the Area, except human wastes and domestic liquid wastes, which may be removed from the Area or disposed of into the sea.

7(x) Measures that may be necessary to continue to meet the aims of the Management Plan

Permits may be granted to enter the Area to:

1) Carry out monitoring and Area inspection activities, which may involve the collection of a small number of samples or data for analysis or review;
2) Install or maintain signposts, markers, structures or scientific or essential logistic equipment;

3) Carry out protective measures, which may include mechanical removal of non-native species by hand tools;

4) Carry out research or management in a manner that avoids interference with long-term research and monitoring activities or possible duplication of effort. Persons planning new projects within the Area should consult with established programs working within the Area, such as those of Poland and the US, before initiating the work.

7(xi) Requirements for reports

• The principal permit holder for each visit to the Area shall submit a report to the appropriate national authority as soon as practicable, and no later than six months after the visit has been completed.

• Such reports should include, as appropriate, the information identified in the visit report form contained in the Guide to the Preparation of Management Plans for Antarctic Specially Protected Areas. If appropriate, the national authority should also forward a copy of the visit report to the Parties that proposed the Management Plan, to assist in managing the Area and reviewing the Management Plan.

• Parties should, wherever possible, deposit originals or copies of such original visit reports in a publicly accessible archive to maintain a record of usage, for the purpose of any review of the Management Plan and in organising the scientific use of the Area.

• The appropriate authority should be notified of any activities / measures undertaken, and / or of any materials released and not removed, that were not included in the authorized permit.

8. Supporting documentation

Barbieri, M, K Birkenmajer, MC Delitala, L Francalanci, W Narbski, M Nicoletti, A Peccerillo, A Petrucciniani, L Tolomeo, and C Trudu. 1987. Preliminary geological, geochemical and Sr isotopic investigations on Mesozoic to Cenozoic magmatism of King George Island, South Shetland Islands (West Antarctica). *Mineralogical and Petrological Acta (Bologna)* **37**: 37–49.

Battke, Z, A Marsz, and R Pudełko. 2001. Procesy deglacjacji na obszarze SSSI No. 8 i ich uwarunkowania klimatyczne oraz hydrologiczne (zatoka Admiralicji, Wyspa Króla Jerzego, Szetlandy Południowe). *Problemy Klimatologii Polarnej* **11**: 121–135.

Bers, AV, F Momo, IR Schloss, and D Abele. 2012. Analysis of trends and sudden changes in long-term environmental data from King George Island (Antarctica): relationships between global climatic oscillations and local system response. *Climatic Change*. doi:10.1007/s10584-012-0523-4.

Beyer, L, JG Bockheim, IB Campbell, and GGC Claridge. 1999. Genesis, properties and sensitivity of Antarctic Gelisols. *Antarctic Science* **11** (4): 387–398. doi:10.1017/S0954102099000498.

Birkenmajer, K. 1980. Geology of Admiralty Bay, King George Island (South Shetland Islands). An outline. *Polish Polar Research* **1**: 29–54.

———. 2003. Geological Results of Polish Antarctic Expeditions: Admiralty Bay, King George Island, South Shetland Islands West Antarctica. Geological map. *Studia Geologica Polonica* **120**: 1–73.

Birkenmajer, K, and E Zastawniak. 1989. Late Crataceous-Early Tertiary floras of King George Island, West Antarctica: their stratigraphic distribution and paleoclimatic significance. In *Origin and Evolution of Antarctic Biota. Geological Society of London, Special Publication,47*, edited by A J Crame, 227–240.

Blume, H-P, L Beyer, M Bölter, H Erlenkeuser, E Kalk, S Kneesch, U Pfisterer, and D Schneider. 1997. Pedogenic zonation in soils of southern circumpolar region. *Advances in GeoEcology* **30**: 69–90.

Blume, H-P, D Kuhn, and M Bölter. 2002. Soils and Soilscapes. In *Geoecology of Antarctic Ice–free Coastal Landscapes, Ecological Studies 154*, edited by L. Beyer and M Bölter, 91–113. Springer, Berlin.

Braun, M, and H Gossmann. 2002. Glacial changes in the areas of Admiralty Bay and Potter Cove, King George Island, maritime Antarctica. In *Geoecology and Antarctic Ice-Free Coastal Landscapes*, edited by L. Beyer and M Bölter, 75–89. Springer, Berlin.

Carlini, AR, NR Coria, MM Santos, J Negrete, M a. Juares, and G a. Daneri. 2009. Responses of *Pygoscelis adeliae* and *P. papua* populations to environmental changes at Isla 25 de Mayo (King George Island). *Polar Biology* **32** (10) (May 16): 1427–1433. doi:10.1007/s00300-009-0637-y. http://link.springer.com/10.1007/s00300-009-0637-y.

Carneiro, APB, MJ Polito, M Sander, and WZ Trivelpiece. 2009. Abundance and spatial distribution of sympatrically breeding *Catharacta* spp. (skuas) in Admiralty Bay, King George Island, Antarctica. *Polar Biology* **33** (5) (November 8): 673–682. doi:10.1007/s00300-009-0743-x. http://link.springer.com/10.1007/s00300-009-0743-x.

Chwedorzewska, KJ. 2008. *Poa annua* L. in Antarctic: searching for the source of introduction. *Polar Biology* **31**: 263–268. doi:10.1007/s00300-007-0353-4.

Chwedorzewska, KJ, and M Korczak. 2010. Human impact upon the environment in the vicinity of *Arctowski* Station, King George Island, Antarctica. *Polish Polar Research* **31** (1) (January 1): 45–60. doi:10.4202/ppres.2010.04. http://versita.metapress.com/openurl.asp?genre=article&id=doi:10.4202/ppres.2010.04.

Ciaputa, P. 1996. Numbers of pinnipeds during 1994 in Admiralty Bay, King George Island, South Shetland Islands. *Polish Polar Research* **17**: 239–244.

Ciaputa, P, and K Sierakowski. 1999. Long-term population changes of Adelie, chinstrap, and gentoo penguins in the regions of SSSI No. 8 and SSSI No. 34, King George Island, Antarctica. *Polish Polar Research* **20** (4): 355–365.

Cuba-Diaz, M, JM Troncoso, C Cordero, VL Finot, and M Rondanelli-Reyes. 2012. Juncus bufonius, a new non-native vascular plant in King George Island, South Shetland Islands. *Antarctic Science* **1** (1): 1–2.

Dutra, TL, and DJ Batten. 2000. Upper Cretaceous floras of King George Island, West Antarctica, and their palaeoenvironmental and phytogeographic implications. *Cretaceous Research* **21**: 181–209. doi:10.1006/cres.2000.0221. http://linkinghub.elsevier.com/retrieve/pii/S0195667100902210.

Everett, KR. 1976. A survey of soils in the region of the South Shetland Islands and adjacent parts of the Antarctica Peninsula. *Ohio State University Institute for Polar Studies Reports* **58**: 1–44.

Gryziak, G. 2009. Colonization by mites of glacier-free areas. *Pesquisa Agropecuária Brasileira* **44** (8): 891–895.

Hinke, JT, K Salwicka, SG Trivelpiece, GM Watters, and WZ Trivelpiece. 2007. Divergent responses of Pygoscelis penguins reveal a common environmental driver. *Oecologia* **153** (4) (October): 845–55. doi:10.1007/s00442-007-0781-4. http://www.ncbi.nlm.nih.gov/pubmed/17566778.

Ilieva-Makulec, K, and G Gryziak. 2009. Response of soil nematodes to climate-induced melting of Antarctic Glaciers. *Polish Journal of Ecology* **57** (4): 811–816.

Kejna, M, A Araźny, and I Sobota. 2013. Climatic change on King George Island in the years 1948 – 2011. *Polish Polar Research* **34** (2): 213–235. doi:10.2478/popore.

Korczak-Abshire, M, PJ Angiel, and G Wierzbicki. 2011. Records of white-rumped sandpiper (Calidris fuscicollis) on the South Shetland Islands. *Polar Record* **47** (3): 262–267.

Korczak-Abshire, M, AC Lees, and A Jojczyk. 2011. First documented record of barn swallow (Hirundo rustica) in the Antarctic. *Polish Journal of Ecology* **32** (4): 355–360. doi:10.2478/v10183.

Korczak-Abshire, M, M Węgrzyn, PJ Angiel, and M Lisowska. 2013. Pygoscelid penguins breeding distribution and population trends at Lions Rump rookery, King George Island. *Polish Polar Research* **34** (1): 87–99. doi:10.2478/popore.

Nawrocki, J, M Pańczyk, and IS Williams. 2011. Isotopic ages of selected magmatic rocks from King George Island (West Antarctica) controlled by magnetostratigraphy. *Geological Quarterly* **55** (4): 301–322.

Olech, M. 1996. Human impact on terrestrial ecosystems in West Antarctica. In *Proceedings of the NIPR Symposium on Polar Biology, 9*, 299–306.

———. 2002. Plant communities on King George Island. In *Geoecology of Antarctic Ice-Free Coastal Landscapes. Ecological Studies*, edited by L. Beyer and M Bölter, 215–231. Springer, Berlin.

Olech, M, and KJ Chwedorzewska. 2011. The first appearance and establishment of an alien vascular plant in natural habitats on the forefield of a retreating glacier in Antarctica. *Antarctic Science* **23** (2): 153–154.

Olech, M, and A Massalski. 2001. Plant colonization and community development on the Sphinx Glacier forefield. *Geographia* **25**: 111–119.

Poland, G of. 2002. The long-term monitoring of avifauna in Admiralty Bay in light of the changes in the sea-ice zone ecosystem (South Shetland Islands, Antarctica). In 25th ATCM Information Paper IP–001 Agenda Item CEP 5. 2002.

Pudełko, R. 2007. Orthophotomap Western Shore of Admiralty Bay, King George Island, South Shetland Islands. Warsaw, Poland: Dept. Antarctic Biology PAS.

Salwicka, K, and S Rakusa-Suszczewski. 2002. Long-term monitoring of Antarctic pinnipeds in Admiralty Bay. *Acta Theriologica* **47**: 443–457.

Salwicka, K, and K Sierakowski. 1998. Seasonal numbers of five species of seals in Admiralty Bay (South Shetland Islands, Antarctica). *Polish Polar Research* **3-4**: 235–247.

Schaefer, CEGR, RM Santana, FNB Simas, MR Francelino, EI Fernandes Filho, MA Albuquerque, and MI Calijuri. 2007. Geoenvironments from the vicinity of Arctowski Station, Admiralty Bay, King George Island, Antarctica: vulnerability and valuation assessment in Antarctica: A keystone in a changing wold. In *Online Proceedings of the ISAES, USGS Open–File Report 2007–1047, Short Research Paper 015*, edited by A K Cooper and C.R. Raymand, 1–4.

Schloss, IR, CA Michaud-Tremblay, and D Dumont. 2012. Modelling phytoplankton growth in polar coastal areas. International Polar Year (IPY) Conference "From knowledge to action". Montréal, Canada.

Simas, FNB, CEGR Schaefer, VF Melo, MR Albuquerque-Filho, RFM Michel, V V. Pereira, MRM Gomes, and LM da Costa. 2007. Ornithogenic cryosols from Maritime Antarctica: Phosphatization as a soil forming process. *Geoderma* **138** (3-4): 191–203. doi:10.1016/j.geoderma.2006.11.011.

Steig, EJ, DP Schneider, SD Rutherford, ME Mann, JC Comiso, and DT Shindell. 2009. Warming of the Antarctic ice-sheet surface since the 1957 International Geophysical Year. *Nature* **457**: 459–462. doi:10.1038/nature08286.

Tatur, A. 1989. Ornithogenic soils of the maritime Antarctic. *Polish Polar Research* **10** (4): 481–532.

———. 2002. Ornithogenic ecosystems in the Maritime Antarctic – Formation, development and disintegration. In *Geoecology of Antarctic Ice–free Coastal Landscapes. Ecological Studies 154*, edited by L. Beyer and M Bölter, 161–184. Springer, Berlin.

Tatur, A, and A Myrcha. 1984. Ornithogenic soils on King George Island, South Shetland Islands (Maritime Antarctic Zone). *Polish Journal of Ecology* **5** (1-2): 31–60.

Vaughan, DG, and CSM Doake. 1996. Recent atmospheric warming and retreat of ice shelves on the Antarctic Peninsula. *Nature* **379**: 328–331. doi:10.1038/379328a0.

Victoria, FDC, AB Pereira, and D Pinheiro. 2009. Composition and distribution of moss formations in the ice-free areas adjoining the Arctowski region, Admiralty Bay, King George Island, Antarctica. *Inheringia Botanical Series* **64** (1): 81–91.

Zastawniak, E. 1994. Upper Cretaceous leaf flora from Błaszczyk Moraine (Zamek Formation), King George Island, West Antarctica. *Acta Palaeobotanica* **34** (2): 119–163.

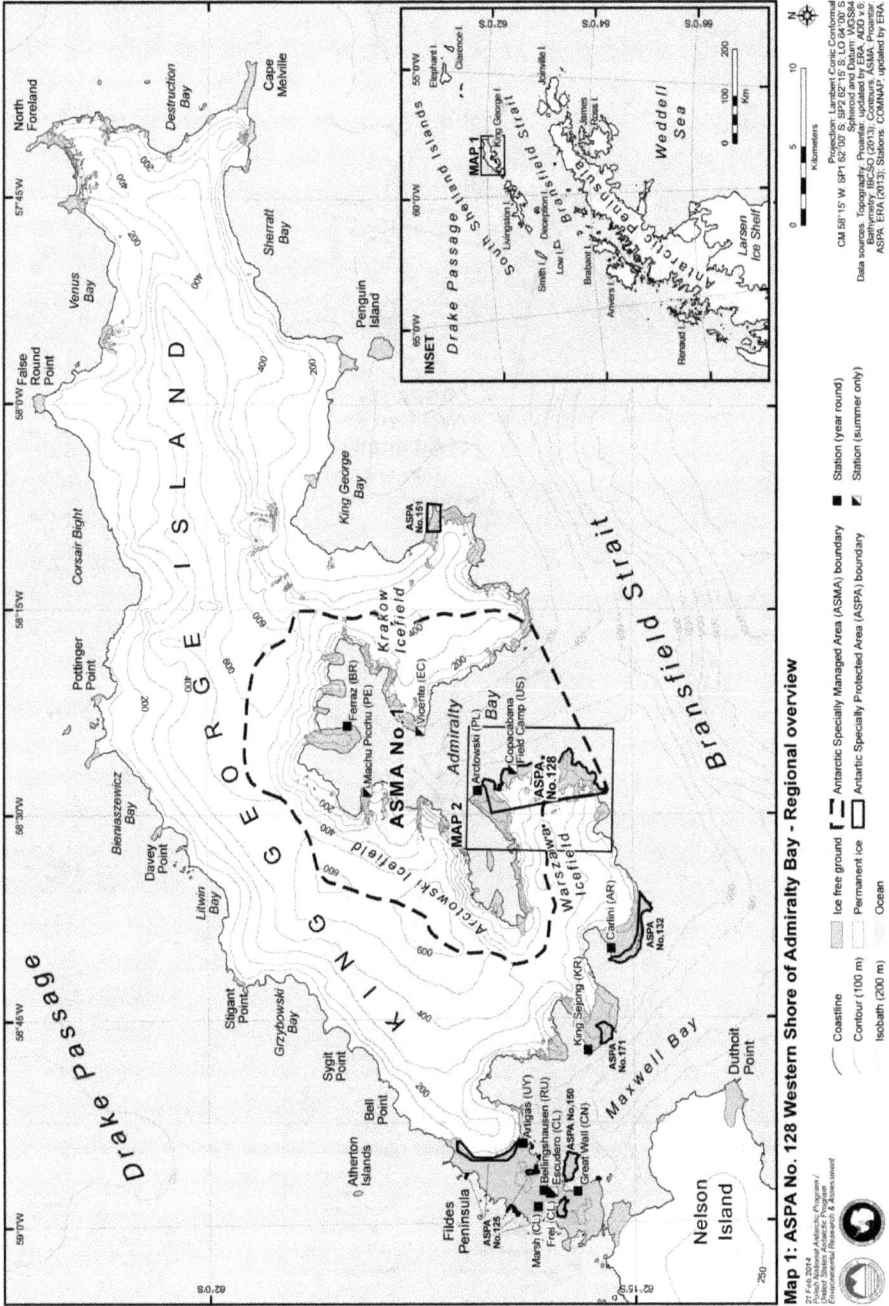

Map 1: ASPA No. 128 Western Shore of Admiralty Bay - Regional overview

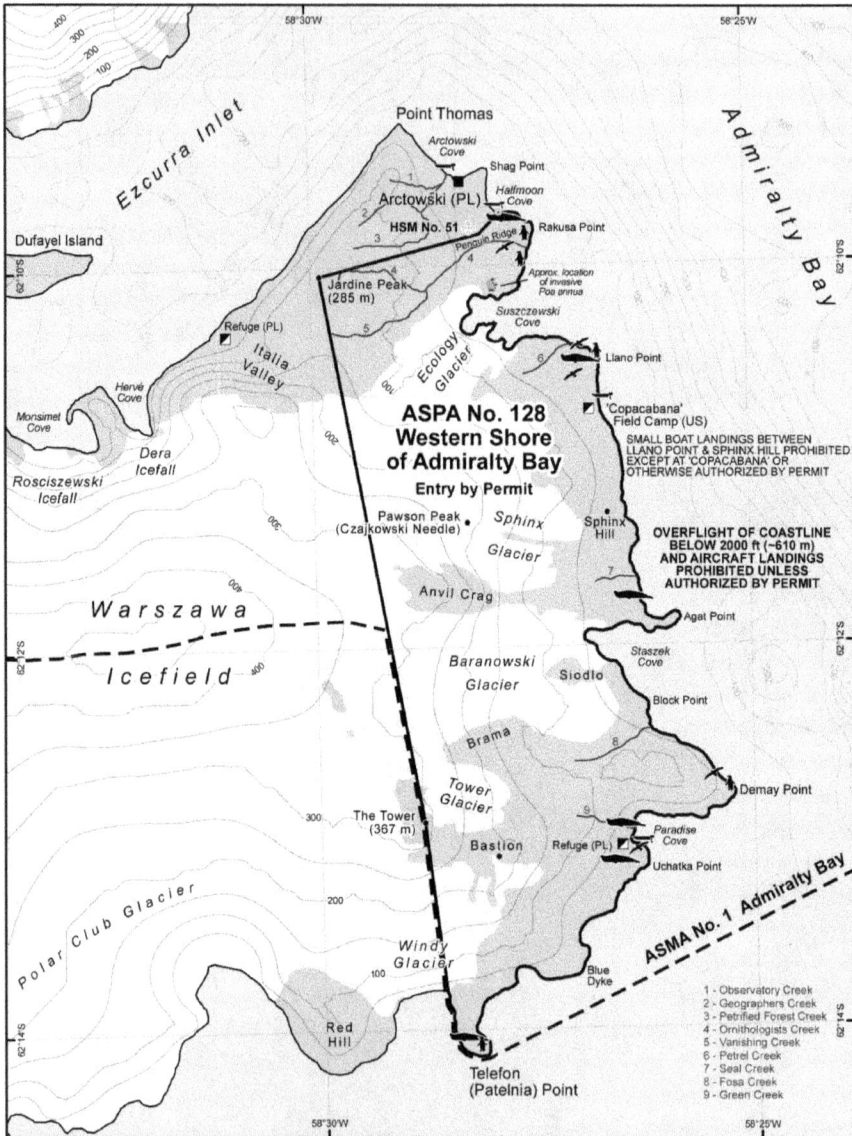

Map 2: ASPA No. 128 Western Shore of Admiralty Bay - access, facilities and wildlife

Management Plan for
Antarctic Specially Protected Area No. 136

CLARK PENINSULA, BUDD COAST, WILKES LAND, EAST ANTARCTICA

Introduction

Antarctic Specially Protected Area (ASPA) No. 136 is located on Clark Peninsula, Wilkes Land at 66°15'S, 110°36'E (see Map A).

The Clark Peninsula was originally designated as Site of Special Scientific Interest (SSSI) No. 17 under Recommendation XIII-8 (1985). A revised management plan for SSSI 17 was adopted under Measure 1 (2000). The area was redesignated and renumbered as ASPA 136 under Decision 1 (2002). Revised ASPA management plans were adopted under Measure 1 (2006) and Measure 7 (2009).

ASPA 136 is primarily designated to protect the Clark Peninsula's largely undisturbed terrestrial ecosystem. This ecosystem possesses one of the most extensive Antarctic flora communities outside of the Antarctic Peninsula and significant breeding populations of Adélie penguins (*Pygoscelis adeliae*) and south polar skuas (*Catharacta maccormicki*).

ASPA 136 is approximately 9.4 km² and is located approximately 5km north-west of Casey station. Scientific research within the Area has focused on plant communities and long term population studies of Adélie penguin colonies. The protection of this flora and fauna within the Area allows for valuable comparison with similar plant communities and penguin colonies closer to Casey station which are subject to greater levels of human disturbance.

1. Description of values to be protected

ASPA 136 is primarily designated to protect Clark Peninsula's largely undisturbed terrestrial ecosystem.

Clark Peninsula's ecosystem possesses one of the most extensive Antarctic flora communities outside of the Antarctic Peninsula. Its flora communities form a continuum of ecological variation along environmental gradients of soil moisture, soil chemistry and microclimate.

Clark Peninsula's ecosystem possesses intrinsic ecological value and scientific importance, particularly in the fields of botany, microbiology, soil science and glacial geomorphology. Ecosystem monitoring provides critical baseline data with which to analyse changes in Antarctic bryophyte, macrolichen and cryptogam communities. The cryptogam communities are also support studies into short-term microclimate fluctuations and long-term climate change in the region since deglaciation some 5000-8000 years ago.

Clark Peninsula possesses relatively undisturbed breeding populations of Adélie penguin (*Pygoscelis adeliae*) and South Polar skuas (*Catharacta maccormicki*). The significant populations of Adélie penguins at Whitney Point and Blakeney Point have been studied since 1959. These studies provide valuable comparative data for measuring human impacts upon the Adélie penguin colonies located near Casey Station. Breeding populations of Wilson's storm petrels (*Oceanites oceanicus*) and snow petrels (*Pagodroma nivea*) are present in most ice-free areas.

Clark Peninsula possesses intrinsic geological value. It provides a visible time sequence of the emergence of the Windmill Islands from the sea since the Holocene deglaciation.

The Area requires protection because of its ecological importance, its significant scientific value and the limited geographical extent of the plant communities. The Area is vulnerable to disturbance from trampling, scientific sampling, pollution and alien introductions, while being sufficiently distant from Casey station to avoid immediate impacts and disturbances from activities undertaken there. It is because of the scientific and ecological values, and the usage of the Area for long term monitoring, that it should continue to be protected.

2. Aims and objectives

Management at the Clark Peninsula aims to:

- avoid degradation of, or substantial risk to, the values of the Area by minimising human disturbance;
- protect the ecosystem as a reference area for the purpose of comparative studies and to assess direct and indirect effects of Casey station;
- prevent the introduction of non-native species to the Area; and
- prevent the introduction of pathogens which may cause disease in fauna populations within the Area.

3. Management activities

The following management activities shall be undertaken to protect the values of the Area:

- information about the Area (including its boundaries and the special restrictions that apply within it) and copies of the management plan shall be made available at: the abandoned Wilkes station; Wilkes Hilton refuge hut; Jack's Donga refuge hut; Casey station; and on ships that visit the region;
- signs shall be erected on the Area boundary to prevent inadvertent entry;
- markers, signs or structures erected within the Area for scientific or management purposes shall be secured and maintained in good condition and removed when no longer required;
- visits shall be made to the Area as necessary (where practicable, not less than once every five years) to assess whether the Area continues to serve the purposes for which it was designated and to ensure that management activities are adequate; and
- the management plan shall be reviewed at least every five years and updated as required.

4. Period of designation

Designated for an indefinite period.

5. Maps

- Map A: Antarctic Specially Protected Areas, Windmill Islands, East Antarctica
- Map B: Antarctic Specially Protected Area No. 136, Clark Peninsula, Windmill Islands, East Antarctica – Topography and distribution of birds
- Map C: Antarctic Specially Protected Area No. 136, Clark Peninsula, Windmill Islands, East Antarctica – Distribution of major vegetation types
- Map D: Antarctic Specially Protected Area No. 136, Clark Peninsula, Windmill Islands, East Antarctica – Geology

6. Description of the Area

6(i) Geographical co-ordinates, boundary markers and natural features

General description

Clark Peninsula (66°15'S 110°36'E) is located on the northern coastline of Newcomb Bay at the eastern end of Vincennes Bay on Budd Coast, Wilkes Land (see Map A). It is an area of permanent ice, snow fields and rocky exposures. It is approximately 3.5 km wide and 4.5 km long.

The ASPA itself covers an area of 9.4 km² and comprises all of the land on Clark Peninsula north of the southern boundary line connecting the east side of Powell Cove at 66°15'15" S 110°31'59" E, through 66°15'29"S 110°33'26"E, 66°15'21"S 110°34'00"E, 66°15'24"S 110°35'09"E, 66°15'37"S 110°34'40"E, 66°15'43"S 110°34'45"E to a point to the east-south-east on the Løken Moraines at 66°16'06"S 110°37'11"E. The eastern boundary is the westernmost limit of the Løken Moraines as far north as a point east of Blakeney Point at 66°14'15"S 110°38'46"E and thence to the coastline at 66°14'15"S 110°38'06"E, returning along the coast to the point of origin. The boundary of the ASPA is indicated on Maps A, B, C and D.

Geology

Clark Peninsula possesses intrinsic geological value. It provides a visible time sequence of the emergence of the Windmill Islands from the coastal sea since the Holocene deglaciation. It is comprised of low lying, rounded, ice-free rocky outcrops. Its intervening valleys are filled with permanent snow, ice or glacial moraine and exfoliated debris. It rises eastward to the Løken Moraines where it reaches an approximate altitude of 130 metres above sea level.

Outcrops of metapelitic rock and leucocratic granite gneiss predominate. The metapelitic rock is generally foliated, migmatized and fine to medium grained. Mineralogy of the metapelitic rock includes biotite-sillimanite and biotite-sillimanite±cordierite. The sillimanite is strongly lineated in the foliation and the cordierite is generally pinnitized.

The early granite gneiss is white, medium grained and foliated. It comprises two felsic intermediate intrusions which predate and/or are synchronous with the deformation in the Windmill Islands. The larger intrusion, which occupies most of central Clark Peninsula, is a quartz, K-feldspar, biotite, white mica and opaque-bearing granitic augen gneiss. Small outcrops of mafics and metapsammite occur. The rock beds lie in a south-west to north-east orientation. The surface geology of Clark Peninsula is depicted at Map D.

Islands of the Windmill Islands group are located offshore from the ASPA. The Windmill Islands represent one of the easternmost outcrops of a Mesoproterozoic low-pressure ganulite facies terrain that extends westward to the Bunger Hills and the Archaean complexes in Princess Elizabeth Land and eastward to Dumont D'Urville and Commonwealth Bay. The rocks of the Windmill Islands group comprise a series of migmatitic metapelites and metapsammites interlayered with mafic to ultramafic and felsic sequences with rare calc-silicates, large partial melt bodies (Windmill Island supacrustals), undeformed granite, charnockite, gabbro, pegmatite, aplites and late dolerite dykes.

Gravels and soils appear to be derived from marine sediments deposited in the Pleistocene. Subfossil penguin colonies are common at Whitney Point and Blakeney Point and along the central ridge. Around the abandoned penguin colonies the soils are pebbly and rich in organic matter derived from penguin guano. Small lakes, pools and melt streams are prevalent in summer. The distribution of lakes on Clark Peninsula is depicted at Map B.

Flora

Clark Peninsula's comparatively mild temperatures facilitated the development of a complex, diverse and stable vegetation cover. The ice-free rocky exposures support an extensive cover of lichen. Mosses predominate in lower lying areas. Factors responsible for the distribution of vegetation include wind exposure, the availability of water and the location of abandoned penguin colonies.

The broader Windmill Hills region possesses 4 species of bryophytes, 30 species of macrolichens, 44 species of cyanobacteria and 75 species of algae. Many of these taxa are known to inhabit Clark Peninsula. Well developed lichen communities of *Umbilicaria decussata*, *Pseudephebe minuscula*, *Usnea sphacelata* communities predominate in the northeast. Further inland *U. sphacelata* predominates and forms extensive carpets over the metamorphic rocks and gravel beds.

Bryophyte communities of *Bryum pseudotriquetrum*, *Schistidium antarctici* and *Ceratodon purpureus* predominate in moist, sheltered sites where they form closed stands up to 300mm in depth. The lichens

Xanthoria mawsonii, Candelariella flava and *Buellia frigidida* predominate around the Adélie penguin colonies of the north-western and western coasts. *Usnea. decussata* and *U. sphacelata* predominate around the abandoned penguin colonies of the southern coastal areas, and *U. decussata, P. minuscula, B. soredians* and *B. frigid* predominate in the centre of Clark Peninsula alongside smaller assemblages of *Pleopsidium chlorophanum*. Clark Peninsula's microflora includes algae (with *Botrydiopsis constricta* and *Chlorella conglomerata* predominating), bacteria, yeasts and filamentous fungi. Flora distributions on the Clark Peninsula are depicted at Map C.

Fauna

Adélie penguin (*Pygoscelis adeliae*) colonies are located on Whitney Point and Blakeney Point. In 2012-13 Whitney Point possessed approximately 11,000 occupied nests and Blakeney Point possessed approximately 4,000 occupied nests. The breeding populations of these two sites have increased since research commenced in 1959-60. The breeding population of Adélie penguins at nearby Shirley Island (located 3 km southwest of Casey station) has remained stable since 1968. Wilson's storm petrels (*Oceanites oceanicus*), South Polar skuas (*Catharacta maccormicki*) and Snow petrels (*Pagodroma nivea*) breed within the ASPA. Terrestrial invertebrate microfauna include protozoa, nematodes, mites, rotifers and tardigrades. The invertebrates are mainly confined to moss beds, lichen stands and moist soils. Fauna distributions on the Clark Peninsula are depicted on Map B.

Climate

Clark Peninsula and the Windmill Islands possess a dry, frigid Antarctic climate. Meteorological data collected at nearby Casey station indicates that the Clark Peninsula's mean temperature range is 0.3°C to -14.9°C. Temperature extremes of 9.2°C and -41°C have been recorded. Precipitation occurs as snow at approximately 195mm rainfall equivalent annually. Approximately 96 days of gale-force winds are experienced annually. These are predominantly easterly in direction and emanate from the polar icecap. Snow gathers in the lee of rocky exposures and in substratum depressions.

Environmental domains and Antarctic Conservation Biogeographic Regions

Based on the Environmental Domains Analysis for Antarctica (Resolution 3 (2008)), Clark Peninsula is located within Environment D *East Antarctic coastal geologic*. Based on the Antarctic Conservation Biogeographic Regions (Resolution 6 (2012)) the Frazier Islands are located within Biogeographic Region 7 *East Antarctica*.

6(ii)   Access to the Area

The Area may be accessed from Casey station by over-snow vehicle or small boat in accordance with section 7(ii) of this management plan.

6(iii)   Location of structures within and adjacent to the Area

A dilapidated wood and canvas hide known as "the Wannigan" is located on the Lower Snow Slope (unofficial place name) on the western facing slope of Whitney Point. It was constructed in 1959 by R. L. Penney to facilitate behavioural studies of Adélie penguins.

The Area possesses several survey markers and several boundary markers delineate the Area's southern boundary.

Three automated camera facilities are located within the Area. Their purpose is to monitor long term variations in the breeding parameters of Adélie penguins. They form part of an ongoing automated camera network across east Antarctica. They are located at Whitney Point (66°15'5.70"S 110°31'50.10"E and 66° 15' 3.20"S 110°32'2.60"E) and Blakeney Point (66° 14'32.20"S 110°34'53.20"E).

Several structures are also located adjacent to the Area. At its closest point, the Area's boundary is located approximately:

- 3.5 km northeast of Casey station (66°17' S 110°31' E);
- 1.0 km north of the former Wilkes station and 0.2 km north of Wilkes Hilton refuge hut (66°15'25.6"S 110°31'32.2"E);
- 1.5 km southwest of Jack's Donga refuge hut (66°13.7'S 110°39.2'E).

6(iv)   Location of other Protected Areas in the vicinity

Other protected areas within 50 km include (see Map A):

- Antarctic Specially Protected Area 135, Northeast Bailey Peninsula (66°17'S 110°33'E): located 2.5 km south-west of Clark Peninsula, across Newcomb Bay, adjacent to Australia's Casey station;
- Antarctic Specially Protected Area 103, Ardery Island (66°22'S, 110°27'E), and Odbert Island (66°22'S, 110°33'E) Budd Coast: located in Vincennes Bay, 13 km south of the former Wilkes station; and
- Antarctic Specially Protected Area 160, Frazier Islands (66°13'S 110°11'E): located approximately 16 km to the north-west in Vincennes Bay.

6(v)   Special zones within the Area

A Transit Zone is located north-east of a line that runs north-west from the ASPA boundary at 110°38'34"E, 66°14'47"S to 110°36'54"E, 66°14'31"S (see Map B). Over-snow vehicles may pass through the Transit Zone to undertake scientific or management activities at the edge of the sea ice. To prevent disturbance to vegetation and relic penguin colonies, over-snow vehicles must only travel on ice or snow covered ground. Use of the Transit Zone may be subject to specific permit conditions.

7. Terms and conditions for entry permits

7(i)   General permit conditions

Entry into the Area is prohibited except in accordance with a permit issued by an appropriate national authority. Conditions for issuing a permit to enter the Area are that:

- the permit is issued only for compelling scientific reasons that cannot be served elsewhere, in particular for the scientific study of the avifauna and ecosystem of the Area, or for essential management purposes consistent with the objectives of this management plan, such as inspection, management or review;
- the actions permitted will not jeopardise the values of the Area or other permitted activities;
- the actions permitted are in accordance with this Management Plan;
- the permit, or an authorised copy, shall be carried within the Area;
- a visit report will be supplied to the authority that approved the permit, as soon as practicable after the visit to the ASPA has been completed, but no later than six months after the visit has occurred;
- permits shall be issued for a finite period;
- permit holders shall notify the appropriate authority of any activities or measures undertaken that were not authorised by the permit; and
- all census and GPS data shall be made available to the permitting authority and to the Parties responsible for the development of the management plan.

7(ii)   Access to, and movement within or over, the Area

The Area should only be accessed via:

- Wilkes Hilton refuge hut in the south-west;
- Jack's Donga refuge hut in the north-east; or

- a descent of the western slope of Løken Moraines in the vicinity east of Stevenson Cove following a traverse from Casey station to Jack's Donga refuge hut.

The abandoned Wilkes station may be accessed from Casey station via a cane marked route to the south of the ASPA's southern boundary. On approaching the ASPA from Casey station, in the areas east and north-east of Noonan Cove, a section of the route is split providing two alternative routes (see Map B). The more southerly route should be used when ice conditions near Noonan Cove allow for safe access. When access via the more southerly route is not possible, the more northerly route should be used. As the Casey–Wilkes route is very close to the ASPA boundary, pedestrian and vehicular traffic should take care not to stray northward into the ASPA.

Wilkes Station may also be accessed via small boat from Casey station. A designated small boat landing site is located in Powell Cove at 110°31'29"E 66°15'22"S.

Access to the sea ice by over-snow vehicles is allowed within the Transit Zone that is located north-east of a line that runs north-west from the ASPA boundary at the Løken Moraines at 110°38'34"E 66°14'47"S to the coastline at 110°36'54"E 66°14'31"S. All vehicles must only travel on ice or snow covered ground to avoid disturbance to vegetation and relic penguin colonies.

Vehicles must not access the remainder of the ASPA except in emergencies. Access to the ASPA in all other circumstances should be made on foot. Pedestrian traffic in the ASPA should be kept to the minimum necessary to achieve the objectives of permitted activities. To prevent damage to sensitive soils, plant and algae communities and water quality, visitors must avoid walking on visible vegetation and moist ground.

Helicopters are not allowed to land within the ASPA, except in emergencies or for essential management activities. The operation of aircraft over the ASPA should be carried out in accordance with the Resolution 2 (2004) *Guidelines for the Operation of Aircraft Near Concentrations of Birds in Antarctica.*

7(iii)   Activities which may be conducted in the Area

The following activities may be conducted in the Area:

- compelling scientific research, which cannot be undertaken elsewhere and which will not jeopardise the avifauna or the ecosystem of the Area; and
- essential management activities, including monitoring.

7(iv)   Installation, modification, or removal of structures

Permanent structures and installations are prohibited in the Area. Temporary structures and installations may only be established in the Area for compelling scientific or management reasons as specified in a permit.

Any temporary structure established in the Area must be:

- clearly identified by country, name of the principal agency, date of installation and date of expected removal;
- first cleaned of organisms, propagules (e.g. seeds, eggs) and non-sterile soil;
- made of materials that can withstand Antarctic conditions and pose minimal contamination risk to the Area; and
- removed when they are no longer required, or before the expiry of the permit, whichever is earlier.

7(v)   Location of field camps

Camping is not allowed within the Area. Field parties should camp at either the Wilkes Hilton refuge hut or at Jack's Donga refuge hut (see Map A).

7(vi)   Restrictions on materials and organisms which may be brought into the Area

The following restrictions apply:

- no living animals, plant materials, microorganisms or non-sterile soils are to be deliberately introduced into the Area. Precautions must be taken to prevent the accidental introduction of living animals, plant materials, microorganisms or non-sterile soils into the Area;

- no herbicides are to be taken into the Area unless needed to mitigate any non-natives species incursions. Such chemicals must only be used as a last resort and controlled by permit conditions. Any other chemicals (including radionuclides or stable isotopes which may be introduced for scientific or management purposes specified in a permit) will be removed from the Area at or before the conclusion of the activity for which the permit was granted;

- fuel must not to be stored in the Area unless it is required for essential purposes connected with the activity for which the permit has been granted. All such fuel must be removed from the Area at or before the conclusion of the permitted activity. Permanent or semi-permanent fuel depots are not permitted;

- all material introduced to the Area shall be for a stated time period only and if left unattended, labelled with a country identifier. All material introduced to the Area must be removed at or before the conclusion of that stated time period, and must be stored and handled in a manner that will minimise the risk of environment impacts;

- no poultry products, including dried food containing egg powder, are to be taken into the Area; and

- no depots of food or other supplies are to be left within the Area beyond the time period for which they are required.

7(vii) Taking of, or harmful interference with, native flora and fauna

Taking of or harmful interference with native flora and fauna is prohibited except in accordance with a permit. Where taking or harmful interference with animals is involved this should, as a minimum standard, be in accordance with the *SCAR Code of Conduct for the Use of Animals for Scientific Purposes in Antarctica*.

7(viii) Collection or removal of materials not brought into the Area by the permit holder

Material may only be collected or removed from the Area as authorised under a permit and should be limited to the minimum necessary to meet scientific or management needs.

7(ix) Disposal of waste

All wastes, including human wastes, must be removed from the Area.

7(x) Measures that may be necessary to ensure that the aims and objectives of the management plan can continue to be met

Permits may be granted to allow monitoring and Area management and inspection activities which may involve:

- the collection of samples for analysis or review;
- the establishment or maintenance of scientific equipment, structures and signposts; and
- other protective measures.

Any specific sites of long-term monitoring shall be appropriately marked and GPS coordinates obtained for lodgement with the Antarctic Data Directory System through the appropriate national authority.

Ornithological research shall be limited to activities that, where practicable, are non-invasive and non-disruptive to the breeding birds present within the Area. Invasive and/or disruptive research activities shall only be authorised if they will have no effect or only a temporary and transient effect on the population.

Visitors shall take special precautions against the introduction of non-native species into the Area; this includes the transfer of species from other locations in Antarctica, particularly other Antarctic Conservation Biogeographic Regions. Of particular concern are pathogenic, microbial or vegetation introductions sourced from soils, flora or fauna at other Antarctic sites (including research stations). To minimise the risk of introductions, before entering the Area all visitors shall thoroughly clean their footwear, sampling equipment, markers etc.

7(xi)   Requirements for reports

Parties shall ensure that the principal permit holder for each permit issued submits, to the appropriate national authority, a report on activities undertaken.

Such reports shall include, as appropriate, the information identified in the visit report form contained in the *Guide to the Preparation of Management Plans for Antarctic Specially Protected Areas.*

Parties shall maintain a record of such activities.

In the Annual Exchange of Information, Parties shall provide summary descriptions of activities conducted by persons subject to their jurisdiction, in sufficient detail to allow an evaluation of the effectiveness of the management plan.

Parties shall, wherever possible, deposit original reports or copies of such in a publicly accessible archive to maintain a record of usage for the benefit of a review of the management plan and the organisation of science in the Area.

A copy of the report shall be forwarded to the Party responsible for the development of the management plan.

Additionally, visit reports shall provide detailed information on census data, locations of any new colonies or nests not previously recorded, a brief summary of research findings, and copies of photographs taken in the Area.

8. Supporting documentation

Adamson, E., and Seppelt, R. D., (1990) A Comparison of Airborne Alkaline Pollution Damage in Selected Lichens and Mosses at Casey Station, Wilkes Land, Antarctica. In: Kerry, K. R., and Hempel, G. (Eds.), *Antarctic Ecosystems: Ecological Change and Conservation*, Springer-Verlag, Berlin, pp. 347-353.

Azmi, O. R., and Seppelt, R. D., (1997) Fungi in the Windmill Islands, continental Antarctica. Effect of temperature, pH and culture media on the growth of selected microfungi. Polar Biology 18: 128-134.

Azmi, O. R., and Seppelt, R. D., (1998) The broad scale distribution of microfungi in the Windmill islands region, continental Antarctica. Polar Biology 19: 92-100.

Beyer, L. and Bölter, M., (2002) Geoecolgy of Antarctic Ice-Free Coastal Landscapes. Ecological Studies, Vol. 154. Springer-Verlag Berlin Heidelberg.

Beyer, L., Pingpank, K., Bolter, M. and Seppelt, R. D., (1998) Small-distance variation of carbon and nitrogen storage in mineral Antarctic Cryosols near Casey Station (Wilkes Land). Zeitschrift fur Pflanzenahrung Bodendunde 161: 211-220.

Bircher, P.K., Lucieer, A. and Woehler, E.J. (2008) Population trends of Adélie penguin (Pygoscelis adeliae) breeding colonies: a spatial analysis of the effects of snow accumulation and human activities, Polar Biology, 31:1397-1407.

Blight, D. F., (1975) The Metamorphic Geology of the Windmill Islands Antarctica, Volumes 1 and 2, PhD thesis, University of Adelaide.

Blight, D. F. and Oliver, R. L., (1997) The metamorphic geology of the Windmill Islands Antarctica: a preliminary account. Journal of the Geological Society of Australia, 24: 239-262.

Blight, D. F. and Oliver, R. L.,(1982) Aspects of the Geological history of the Windmill Islands, Antarctica. In: Craddock, C. (Ed.), *Antarctic Geoscience*, University of Wisconsin Press, Madison, WI, pp. 445-454.

Clarke, L.J., et al, (2012) Radiocarbon bomb spike reveals biological effects of Antarctic climate change, Global Change Biology 18, 301-310.

Cowan, A. N., (1979) Giant Petrels at Casey, Antarctica. Australian Bird Watcher 8: 66-67.

Cowan, A. N., (1981) Size variation in the Snow petrel (*Pagodroma nivea*). Notornis 28: 169-188.

Emslie, S. D., Woehler, E. J., (2005) A 9000 year record of Adélie penguin occupation and diet in the Windmill Islands, East Antarctica. Antarctic Science 17, 57-66.

Giese, M., (1998) Guidelines for people approaching breeding groups of Adélie penguins (*Pygoscelis adeliae*), Polar Record 34 (191): 287-292.

Goodwin, I. D., (1993) Holocene deglaciation, sea-level change, and the emergence of the Windmill Islands, Budd Coast, Antarctica, Quaternary Research, 40: 70-80.

Heatwole, H., et al. (1989) Biotic and chemical characteristics of some soils from Wilkes Land Antarctica, Antarctic Science 1: 225-234.

Hovenden, M. J., and Seppelt, R. D., (1995) Exposure and nutrients as delimiters of lichen communities in continental Antarctica, Lichenologist 27: 505-516.

Ling, H. U. and Seppelt, R. D. (1998) Non-marine algae and cyanobacteria of the Windmill Islands region, Antarctica with descriptions of two new species. Algological Studies 89, 49-62.

Martin, M. R., Johnstone, G. W. & Woehler, E. J. (1990) Increased numbers of Adélie Penguins *Pygoscelis adeliae* breeding near Casey, Wilkes Land, East Antarctica. Corella 14, 119-122.

Melick, D. R., Hovenden, M. J., & Seppelt, R. D., (1994) Phytogeography of bryophyte and lichen vegetation in the Windmill Islands, Wilkes land, Continental Antarctica, Vegetatio 111: 71-87.

Melick, D. R., and Seppelt, R. D., (1990) Vegetation patterns in Relation to climatic and endogenous changes in Wilkes Land, continental Antarctica, Journal of Ecology, 85: 43- 56.

Murray, M. D., and Luders, D. J., (1990) Faunistic studies at the Windmill Islands, Wilkes Land, east Antarctica, 1959-80. ANARE Research Notes 73, Antarctic Division, Kingston. ASPA 136: Clark Peninsula 9

Newbery, K.B. and Southwell, C. (2009). An automated camera system for remote monitoring in polar environments. Cold Region Science and Technology 55: 47-51.

Newsham, K.K. and Robinson, S.A. (2009) Responses of plants in polar regions to UVB exposure: a meta-analysis, Global Change Biology, 12, 2574-2589.

Olivier, F., Lee, A. V. and Woehler, E. J., (2004) Distribution and abundance of snow petrels *Pagodroma nivea* in the Windmill Islands, East Antarctica. Polar Biology 27, 257-265.

Orton, M. N., 1963. A Brief Survey of the fauna of the Windmill Islands, Wilkes Land, Antarctica. The Emu 63: 14-22.

Paul, E., Stüwe, K., Teasdale, J., and Worley, B., (1995) Structural and metamorpohic geology of the Windmill Islands, east Antarctica: field evidence for repeated tectonothermal activity. Australian Journal of Earth Sciences 42: 453-469.

Robinson SA, et al. (2000) Desiccation tolerance of three moss species from continental Antarctica. Australian Journal of Plant Physiology, 27, 379-388.

Robinson S.A., Wasley J. and Tobin A.K., (2003) Living on the edge – plants and global change in continental and maritime Antarctica. Global Change Biology, 9, 1681-1717.

Robinson S.A., Turnbull, J.D., Lovelock, C.E. (2005) Impact of changes in natural ultraviolet radiation on pigment composition, physiological and morphological characteristics of the Antarctic moss, Grimmia antarctici. Global Change Biology, 11, 476-489.

Roser, D. J., Melick, D. R. and Seppelt, R. D., (1992) Reductions in the polyhydric alcohol content of lichens as an indicator of environmental pollution. Antarctic Science 4: 185-189.

Roser, D. J., Melick, D. R., Ling, H. U. and Seppelt, R. D. (1992) Polyol and sugar content of terrestrial plants from continental Antarctica. Antarctic Science 4: 413- 420.

Roser, D. J., Seppelt, R. D. and Nordstrom(1994) Soluble carbohydrate and organic content of soils and associated microbiota from the Windmill Islands, Budd Coast, Antarctica. Antarctic Science 6: 53-59.

Selkirk, P.M. and Skotnicki, M.L., (2007) Measurement of moss growth in continental Antarctica, Polar Biology, 30:407-413.

Smith, R. I. L., (1980) Plant community dynamics in Wilkes Land, Antarctica, Proceedings NIPR Symposium of polar biology, 3: 229-224.

Smith, R. I. L., (1986) Plant ecological studies in the fellfield ecosystem near Casey Station, Australian Antarctic Territory, 1985-86. British Antarctic Survey Bulletin, 72: 81-91.

Smith, R. I.L., (1988) Classification and ordination of cryptogamic communities in Wilkes Land, Continental Antarctica. Vegetatio 76, 155-166.

Southwell, C. and Emmerson, L., (2013) Large-scale occupancy surveys in East Antarctica discover new Adélie penguin breeding sites and reveal an expanding breeding distribution, Antarctic Science 25(4), 531–535.

Turnbull, J.D. and Robertson, S.A. (2009) Accumulation of Accumulation of DNA damage in Antarctic mosses: correlations with ultraviolet-B radiation, temperature and turf water content vary among species, Global Change Biology, 15, 319-329.

Woehler, E. J. (1990) Two records of seabird entanglement at Casey, Antarctica. Marine Ornithology 18, 72-73.

Woehler, E. J. (1993) Antarctic seabirds: their status and conservation in the AAT. RAOU Conservation Statement 9, 8pp.

Woehler E. J., Riddle M. J. and Ribic C.A. (2003) Long-term population trends in southern giant petrels in East Antarctica. In: Huiskes AHL, Gieskes WWC, Rozema J, Schorno RML, van der Vies SM and Wolff W (eds) *Antarctic Biology in a global context*. Backhuys Publishers, Leiden, pp 290-295.

Woehler, E. J., Martin, M. R. & Johnstone, G. W. (1990) The status of Southern Giant-Petrels, *Macronectes giganteus*, at the Frazier Islands, Wilkes Land, East Antarctica. Corella 14, 101-106.

Woehler, E. J., Slip, D. J., Robertson, L. M., Fullagar, P. J. and Burton, H. R., (1991) The distribution, abundance and status of Adélie penguins *Pygoscelis adeliae* at the Windmill Islands, Wilkes Land, Antarctica, Marine Ornithology 19: 1-18.

Woehler, E. J., et al (1994) Impacts of human visitors on breeding success and long-term population trends in Adélie Penguins at Casey, Antarctica, Polar Biology 14: 269-274.

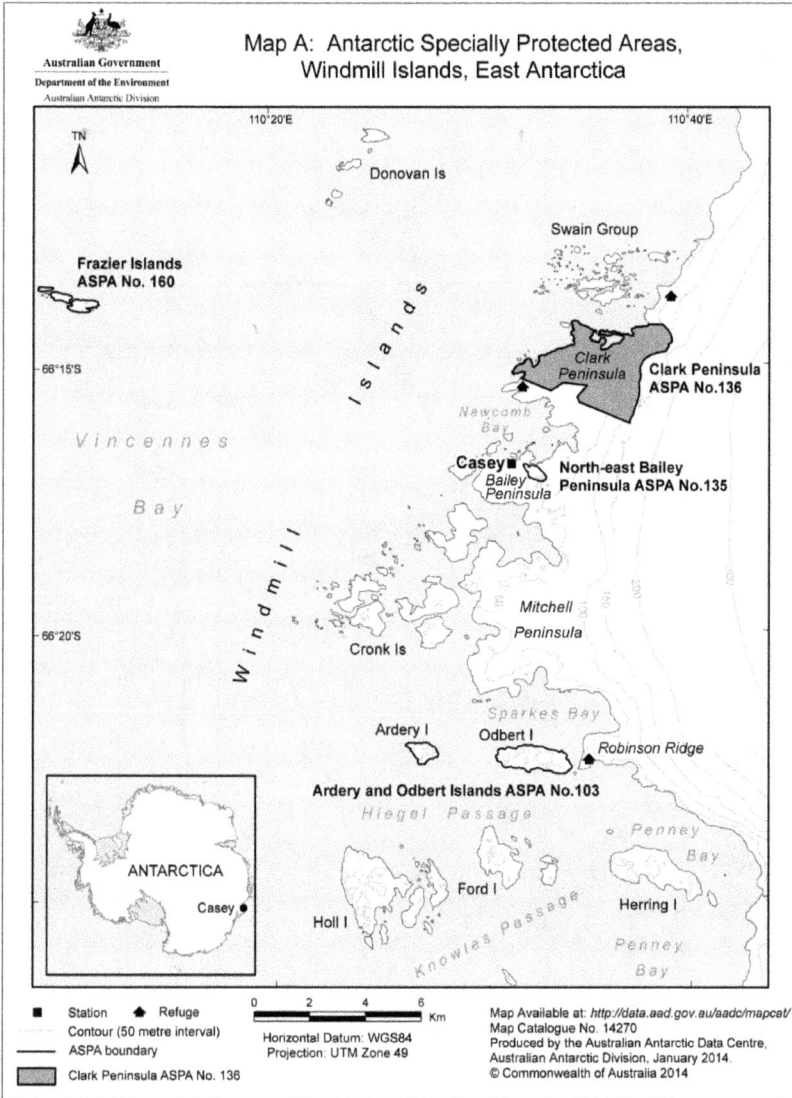

Map A: Antarctic Specially Protected Areas, Windmill Islands, East Antarctica

Map B: Antarctic Specially Protected Area No. 136, Clark Peninsula
Topography and Bird Distribution

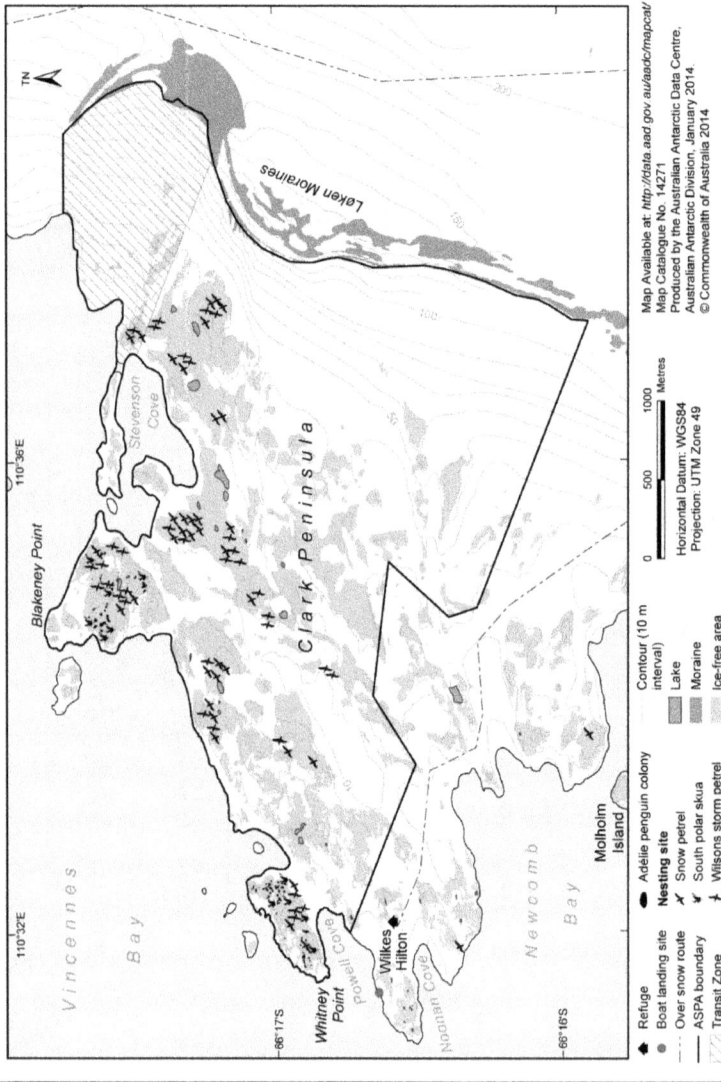

Australian Government

Department of the Environment

Australian Antarctic Division

Vincennes Bay

Whitney Point

Powell Cove

Wilkes

Hilton

Noonan Cove

Molholm Island

Newcomb Bay

Clark Peninsula

Blakeney Point

Stevenson Cove

Løken Moraines

TN

110°32'E

110°36'E

-66°17'S

-66°16'S

Refuge

Boat landing site

Over snow route

ASPA boundary

Transit Zone

Adélie penguin colony

Nesting site

Snow petrel

South polar skua

Wilsons storm petrel

Contour (10 m interval)

Lake

Moraine

Ice-free area

0   500   1000   Metres

Horizontal Datum: WGS84

Projection: UTM Zone 49

Map Available at: *http://data.aad.gov.au/aadc/mapcat/*

Map Catalogue No. 14271

Produced by the Australian Antarctic Data Centre,
Australian Antarctic Division, January 2014.
© Commonwealth of Australia 2014

94

Map C: Antarctic Specially Protected Area No. 136, Clark Peninsula
Vegetation

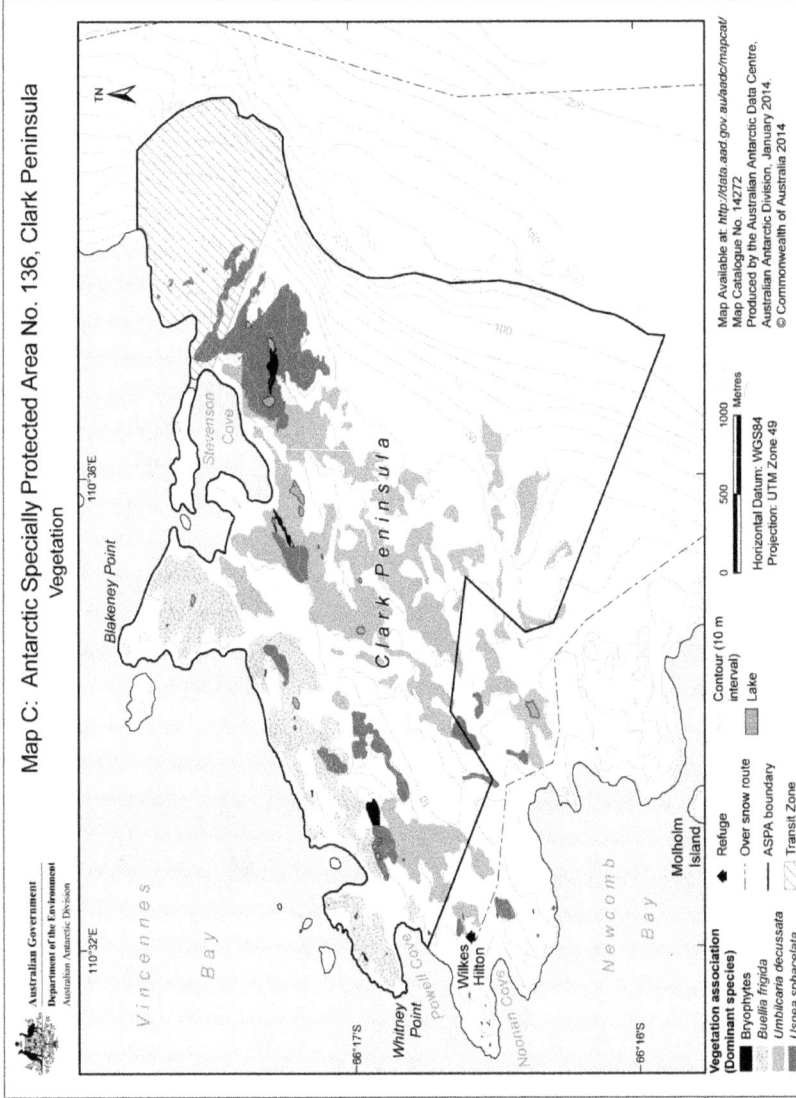

Map D: Antarctic Specially Protected Area No. 136, Clark Peninsula
Geology

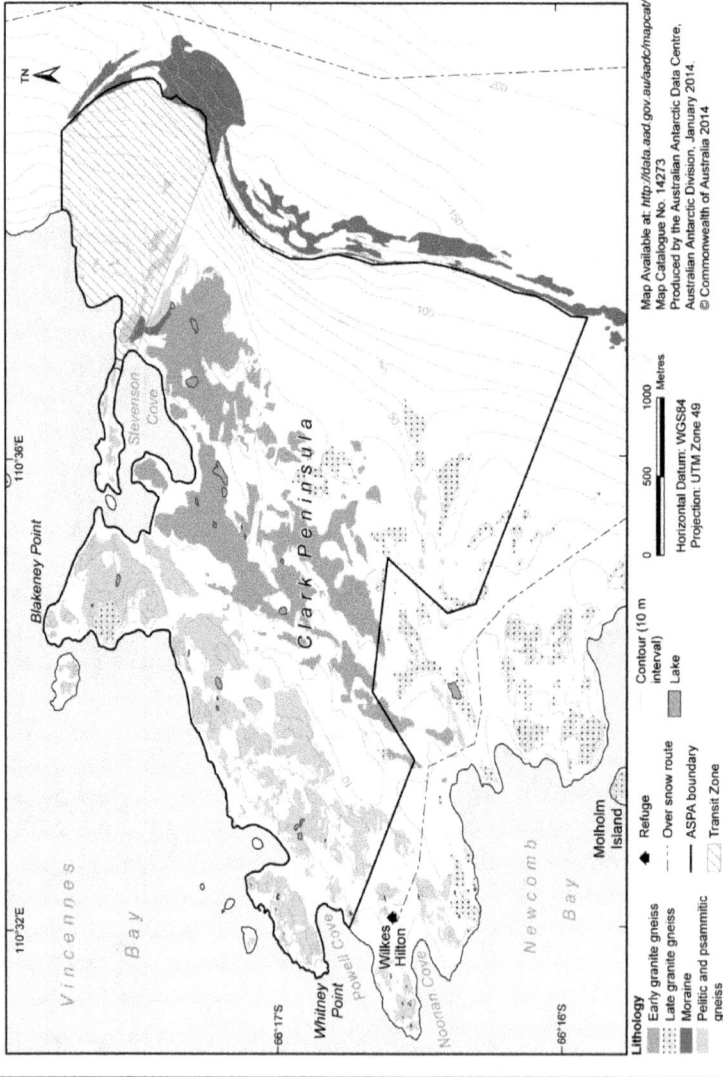

Management Plan for

Antarctic Specially Protected Area (ASPA) No. 139

BISCOE POINT, ANVERS ISLAND, PALMER ARCHIPELAGO

Introduction

The Biscoe Point Antarctic Specially Protected Area is located near the south-west coast of Anvers Island, in the Palmer Archipelago, Antarctic Peninsula, at 64°48'40"S, 63°46'27"W. Approximate area: 0.59 km². The primary reason for the designation of the Area is its extensive vegetation communities, soils and terrestrial ecology. The Area contains the most extensive stands of Antarctic hair grass (*Deschampsia antarctica*) and Antarctic pearlwort (*Colobanthus quitensis*) in the Anvers Island region, as well as numerous species of mosses and lichens. The Area is a breeding site for several bird species, including Adélie (*Pygoscelis adeliae*) and gentoo (*P. papua*) penguins, brown (*Stercorarius lonnbergi*), south polar (*S. maccormicki*) and hybrid skuas, which have been the subject of long-term monitoring and ecological research. Furthermore, the long history of protection of the Area makes it a valuable reference site for comparative studies and long-term monitoring.

The Area was proposed by the United States of America and adopted through Recommendation XII-8 [1985, Site of Special Scientific Interest (SSSI) No. 20]; date of expiry was extended by Resolution 3 (1996) and through Measure 2 (2000); and the Area was renamed and renumbered by Decision 1 (2002). The boundary of the Area was revised through Measure 2 (2004) to remove its marine component, and following the collapse of the ice ramp joining the island to Anvers Island. A revised Management Plan was adopted through Measure 7 (2010).

The Area is situated within Environment E – Antarctic Peninsula, Alexander and other islands based on the Environmental Domains Analysis for Antarctica and within Region 3 – Northwest Antarctic Peninsula based on the Antarctic Conservation Biogeographic Regions. Biscoe Point lies within Antarctic Specially Managed Area No.7 Southwest Anvers Island and Palmer Basin.

1. Description of values to be protected

Biscoe Point (64°48'47"S, 63°47'41"W, 0.59 km²), Anvers Island, Palmer Archipelago, Antarctic Peninsula, was designated on the grounds that the "Site contains a large (approximately 5000 m²) but discontinuous stand of the two native vascular plants, Antarctic hair grass (*Deschampsia antarctica*) and, less commonly, Antarctic pearlwort (*Colobanthus quitensis*). A relatively well developed loam occurs beneath closed swards of the grass and contains a rich biota, including the apterous midge *Belgica antarctica*. Long-term research programs could be jeopardised by interference from nearby Palmer Station and from tourist ships."

The present management plan reaffirms the exceptional ecological and scientific values associated with the rich flora and invertebrate fauna within the Area. In addition, it is noted that the first observation of *C. quitensis* growing south of 60°S was made at Biscoe Point, reported by Jean-Baptiste Charcot from the Expédition Antarctiques Française in 1903-05. The island on which Biscoe Point lies contains the most extensive communities of *D. antarctica* and *C. quitensis* in the Anvers Island vicinity, and they are of unusual abundance for this latitude. The abundance is much greater than previously described, with almost half of the island of Biscoe Point, and much of the ice-free area of the peninsula to the north, possessing significant stands of vegetation. The communities extend over a large proportion of the available ice-free ground, with a discontinuous cover of *D. antarctica*, *C. quitensis* and bryophytes and lichens of several species varying in density over an area of approximately 250,000 m². One stand of mosses in the prominent valley on the northern side of the main island extends almost continuously for 150 m along the valley floor, covering an area of approximately 6500 m². Individual, near-continuous stands of *D. antarctica* and *C. quitensis* reach a similar size, both on the main island and, to a lesser extent, on the promontory to the north.

Several plant community studies were in progress when the Area was designated in 1985. Although these studies were discontinued soon after site designation, botanical research at the site has continued. For example, *D. antarctica* and *C. quitensis* seeds have been collected from Biscoe Point for plant studies examining the influence of climate change and enhanced UV-B radiation (Day, pers. comm. 1999). Biscoe Point was valuable for these studies because of the amount and quality of seeds available within the Area. Cores containing plant material and soils have been collected within the Area to investigate carbon and nitrogen fluxes within the ecosystem and to evaluate the influence of increased temperature and precipitation on the ecosystem (Park *et al.*, 2007, Day *et al.*, 2009). In addition, Biscoe Point is one of the few low-lying vegetated sites that has not yet been substantially damaged by Antarctic fur seals, and as such the Area has been identified as a potential control site for assessing Antarctic fur seal impacts on vegetation and soils in this region. While recent expansion of the gentoo penguin colony has resulted in damage to and loss of some vegetation surrounding nest sites, these are relatively small compared to the overall vegetation cover at Biscoe Point, and the vegetation values of the Area are not considered to have been significantly compromised.

Biscoe Point is also valuable for ornithological research. Research into seabird ecology and long-term monitoring studies are being conducted on Adélie (*Pygoscelis adeliae*) and gentoo (*P. papua*) penguin colonies, as well as brown (*Stercorarius lonnbergi)* and hybrid skuas (Patterson-Fraser, pers. comm. 2010). The gentoo penguin colony became established at Biscoe Point around 1992 and, as a recently founded colony, is of particular value for monitoring long-term ecological changes to the local bird population structure and dynamics (Fraser, pers. comm., 1999). The Adélie penguin colony is valuable for long-term monitoring and comparison with other colonies in Arthur Harbor that are subjected to higher levels of human influence. In this respect, the fact that the Area has been protected from significant human use, and that use allowed has been regulated by permit, for such a long period of time is of particular value. The Adélie penguin colony is one of the oldest in the southern Anvers Island region (more than 700 years), and as such is valuable for paleoecological studies. The site is also the only site in the region where brown (*S. lonnbergi*), south polar (*S. maccormicki*) and hybrid skuas are known to occur annually.

Until recently, Biscoe Point was on a peninsula joined to Anvers Island by an ice ramp extending from the adjacent glacier. The ice ramp disappeared as the glacier retreated, and a narrow channel now separates Anvers Island from the island on which Biscoe Point lies. The original boundary of the Area was of geometric shape and extended to include a separate ice-free promontory 300 m to the north of this island, and also included the intervening marine environment. The Area is now defined to include all land above the low tide water level of the main island on which Biscoe Point is situated (0.48 km²), all offshore islets and rocks within 100 m of the shore of the main island, and most of the predominantly ice-free promontory 300 m to the north (0.1 km²). The marine component is now excluded from the Area because of the lack of information on its values. The Area in total is now approximately 0.59 km².

In summary, the Area at Biscoe Point therefore has high value for its outstanding:

- examples of vegetation communities, soils and associated terrestrial ecology;
- ornithological interest, with several of the resident breeding bird species and associated paleoecological features possessing unusual properties, and which are the subject of long-term studies; and
- utility as a reference site for comparative studies and monitoring.

In order to protect the values of the Area, it is important that visitation continues to remain low and be carefully managed.

2.   Aims and Objectives

Management at Biscoe Point aims to:

- Avoid degradation of, or substantial risk to, the values of the Area by preventing unnecessary human disturbance and sampling in the Area;

- Allow scientific research on the ecosystem and physical environment in the Area provided it is for compelling reasons which cannot be served elsewhere and that will not compromise the values for which the Area is protected;
- Allow visits for educational and outreach purposes (such as documentary reporting (visual, audio or written) or the production of educational resources or services) provided such activities are for compelling reasons that cannot be served elsewhere and will not compromise the values for which the Area is protected;
- Minimize the possibility of introduction of alien plants, animals and microbes to the Area;
- Minimize the possibility of the introduction of pathogens that may cause disease in faunal populations within the Area; and
- Allow visits for management purposes in support of the aims of the management plan.

3.   Management activities

The following management activities shall be undertaken to protect the values of the Area:

- Signs showing the location of the Area (stating the special restrictions that apply) shall be displayed prominently, and copies of this management plan, including maps of the Area, shall be made available at Palmer Station (US) on Anvers Island and at Yelcho Station (Chile) on Doumer Island;
- Copies of this management plan shall be made available to all vessels and aircraft visiting the Area and/or operating in the vicinity of Palmer Station, and all personnel (national program staff, field expeditions, tourist expedition leaders, pilots and ship captains) operating in the vicinity of, accessing or flying over the Area, shall be informed by their national program, tour operator or appropriate national authority of the location, boundaries and restrictions applying to entry and overflight within the Area;
- National programs shall take steps to ensure the boundaries of the Area and the restrictions that apply within are marked on relevant maps and nautical / aeronautical charts;
- Markers, signs or other structures erected within the Area for scientific or management purposes shall be secured and maintained in good condition, and removed when no longer required;
- National Antarctic programs operating in the Area should maintain a record of all new markers, signs and structures erected within the Area;
- Visits shall be made as necessary (at least once every five years) to assess whether the Area continues to serve the purposes for which it was designated and to ensure management and maintenance measures are adequate.

4.   Period of designation

Designated for an indefinite period.

5.   Maps and photographs

Map 1: ASPA No. 139 Biscoe Point, Arthur Harbor, Anvers Island, showing the location of nearby stations (Palmer Station, US; Yelcho Station, Chile; Port Lockroy Historic Site and Monument No. 61, UK), the boundary of Antarctic Specially Managed Area No. 7 Southwest Anvers Island and Palmer Basin, and the location of nearby protected areas.
Projection: Lambert Conformal Conic; Central Meridian: 64° 00' W; Standard parallels: 64° 40' S, 65° 00' S; Latitude of Origin: 66° 00' S; Spheroid and horizontal datum: WGS84; Contour interval: Land – 250 m, Marine – 200 m.
Data sources: coastline & topography SCAR Antarctic Digital Database v4.1 (2005); Bathymetry: IBCSO v.1 (2013); Protected areas: ERA (Jul 2013); Stations: COMNAP (May 2013).
Inset: the location of Anvers Island and the Palmer Archipelago in relation to the Antarctic Peninsula.

Map 2: ASPA No. 139 Biscoe Point – Physical features, boundaries and access guidelines.

Projection: Lambert Conformal Conic: Central Meridian: 63° 46' W; Standard parallels: 64° 48' S; 64° 50' S; Latitude of Origin: 65° 00' S; Spheroid and horizontal datum: WGS84; Vertical datum: mean sea level; Contour interval: 5 m. The coastline of the island on which Biscoe Point lies is digitized from an orthophoto (Nov 2009) estimated as accurate to ± 1 m (ERA, 2010). The peninsula to the north of Biscoe Point, several offshore islands and Anvers Island are also derived from the recent orthophoto and a georeferenced WorldView-2 image (16 Jan 2012) (Imagery © 2012 Digital Globe; NGA Commercial Imagery Program). Penguin colonies and other features: orthophoto (Nov 2009) and GPS survey (ERA 2001).

Map 3: ASPA No. 139 Biscoe Point – Penguin colonies, approximate vegetation extent, and known contaminated sites.
Map specifications as for Map 2. Contamination: partial survey (Feb 2001); Vegetation: estimated from air and ground photos.

6.   Description of the Area

6(i) Geographical coordinates, boundary markers and natural features

General description

Biscoe Point (64°48'47" S, 63°47'41" W) is at the western extremity of a small island (0.48 km²), located close to the southern coast of Anvers Island (2700 km²) about 6 km south of Mount William (1515 m), in the region west of the Antarctic Peninsula known as the Palmer Archipelago (Map 1). Until recently, this island was joined to Anvers Island by an ice ramp extending from the adjacent southward-flowing glacier, and many maps (now incorrectly) show Biscoe Point as lying on a peninsula. A narrow, permanent, marine channel of approximately 50 m in width now separates the island on which Biscoe Point lies from Anvers Island. This mostly ice-free island lies south-east of Biscoe Bay and to the north of Bismarck Strait. A smaller extent of mostly ice-free land about 300 m to the north remains joined as a peninsula to Anvers Island by an ice ramp.

The island on which Biscoe Point lies is approximately 1.8 km long in an east-west direction and of up to about 450 m in width (Map 2). Topography consists of a series of low-lying hills, with the main east-west oriented ridge rising to a maximum altitude of about 24 m. A small ice cap that previously rose to 12 m at the eastern end of the island no longer exists. The coastline is irregular and generally rocky, studded by offshore islets and rocks, and pitted by numerous bays. A number of the more sheltered bays harbor gentle and accessible gravel beaches. The unnamed promontory to the north is approximately 750 m in length (east-west) by 150 m wide and is of similar character, although of lower topography.

Palmer Station (US) is located 13.8 km north-west of the Area at Arthur Harbor, Yelcho Station (Chile) is located approximately 12 km to the southeast at Doumer Island, while 'Base A' (UK, Historic Site No. 61) is located at Port Lockroy, Goudier Island (off Wiencke Island) approximately 13 km to the east (Map 1).

Boundaries

The original boundary of the Area was of geometric shape to include the land associated with Biscoe Point, the separate ice-free promontory 300 m to the north, and also the intervening islands and marine environment. A recent detailed review revealed little information to substantiate special values associated with the local marine environment. The marine area is not the subject of current or planned scientific studies, nor is it being subjected to specific pressures or threats requiring management. For these reasons, the boundary was revised to exclude the marine environment. The Area is now defined to include all land above the low tide water level of the main island on which Biscoe Point is situated (0.48 km²), all offshore islets and rocks within 100 m of the shore of this main island, and most of the predominantly ice-free promontory 300 m to the north (0.1 km²) (Map 2). The landward (eastern) boundary on the northern promontory bisects the peninsula at the point where it protrudes from Anvers Island, distinguished by a small bay cutting into the glacier in the south and a similar, although less pronounced, coastline feature in the north. The total area including the main island and the northern promontory is approximately 0.59 km².

Climate

No meteorological data are available for Biscoe Point, although data are available for Palmer Station (US), where conditions are expected to be broadly similar. Longer-term data available for Palmer Station show regional temperatures to be relatively mild because of local oceanographic conditions and because of the frequent and persistent cloud cover in the Arthur Harbor region (Lowry 1975). Annual average air temperatures recorded at Palmer Station during the period 1974 to 2012 show a distinct warming trend, although also demonstrate significant inter-annual variability. The annual average temperature for the years 2010-12 was -1.34° C. The minimum annual average temperature recorded was -4.51° C in 1980. The minimum temperature recorded over that period was -26°C (Aug 1995) and the maximum is 11.6°C (Mar 2010).

Between 1990 and 2012 the average annual precipitation was 64 cm and snowfall averaged 342 cm. Storms and precipitation at Palmer Station are frequent, with winds being persistent but generally light to moderate in strength, prevailing from the north-east. Cloud cover is frequent and extensive, often with a ceiling of less than 300 m.

These patterns are expected to be broadly similar at Biscoe Point, although the Area will have minor climatic differences as a result of local geography.

Geology and soils

Specific descriptions are not available of the geology of island on which Biscoe Point lies, or of the peninsula to the north. However, the bedrock appears to be composed mainly of gabbros and adamellites of Late Cretaceous to Early Tertiary age belonging to the Andean Intrusive Suite, which dominate the composition of southeastern Anvers Island (Hooper, 1958). Gabbro is a dark, coarse-grained plutonic rock that is mineralogically similar to basalt, and which is composed mainly of calcium-rich plagioclase feldspar and pyroxene. Adamellite is a granitic rock composed of 10-50% quartz and which contains plagioclase feldspar. A fine mineral soil is present on the gentle terrain, although precise soil characteristics have yet to be described. A relatively well-developed, loamy soil is associated with the closed swards of *Deschampsia*. Cores extracted in the south of the island, close to the Adélie penguin colony, consisted of an organic horizon, overlying a sandy loam glacial drift or bedrock (Day *et al.* 2009).

Freshwater habitat

A number of small seasonal streams and ponds are present on the island on which Biscoe Point lies, although they have not been scientifically described. A small pond (perhaps the largest, at approximately 30 m x 8 m) and stream occur in a valley on the southern side of the principal ridge of the island, 50 m NE of the southern small boat landing site (Map 2). The presence of a long rubber hose suggests that at one time visitors may have collected fresh water from this site. The hose was removed in 2009-10 and disposed of at Palmer Station. Another freshwater pond of similar size (approximately 25 m x 6 m) is found in the prominent east-west trending valley on the northern side of the island. A small associated stream drains this pond to the west. A series of small ponds appear present in satellite imagery (mid-Jan 2012) at the eastern end of the island, nestled in depressions where a small ice cap previously existed. The freshwater environment has thus far escaped significant disturbance from seals. Some ponds near the gentoo penguin colony are frequented by washing / bathing penguins, and as a result have become locally enriched by nutrients (Patterson-Fraser pers. comm. 2014). Information on the hydrology of the separate promontory to the north is not available.

Vegetation

The most significant aspect of the vegetation at Biscoe Point is the abundance and reproductive success of the two native Antarctic flowering plants, the Antarctic hair grass *Deschampsia antarctica* and Antarctic pearlwort *Colobanthus quitensis*. The communities of *D. antarctica* and *C. quitensis* at Biscoe Point are the most extensive in the Anvers Island vicinity and are considered particularly abundant for such a southerly location (Greene and Holtom 1971; Komárková 1983, 1984; Komárková, Poncet and Poncet 1985). The first observation of *C. quitensis* growing south of 60°S was made near Biscoe Point, recorded (as *C. crassifolius*) by the biologist Turquet on Jean-Baptiste Charcot's Expédition Antarctiques Française (1903-05). More recently, seeds from both flowering plants within the Area have been collected for propagation in studies on the effects of climate change and UV-B exposure on these species being conducted out of Palmer Station (Day, pers. comm., 1999; Xiong, 2000). In January 2004, cores of plant material and soils were collected from Biscoe Point and were used in multi-year experiments into the tundra ecosystem. The cores were used in combination with precipitation and surface runoff samples to measure pools and fluxes of carbon and nitrogen within the Biscoe Point ecosystem and to evaluate the role of nitrogen inputs from the nearby penguin colony (Park *et al.*, 2007). Cores were also used in climate manipulation experiments at Palmer Station, which investigated the influence of increased temperature and precipitation on plant productivity and the abundance of the springtail *Cryptopygus* (Day *et al.*, 2009).

The abundance of *D. antarctica* and *C. quitensis* is much greater than previously described, and almost half of the island on which Biscoe Point lies, and much of the ice-free area of the peninsula to the north, possess significant stands of these species and a wide range of bryophytes and lichens. The approximate distribution of the most substantial stands of vegetation on the main island has been estimated from air and ground photography (Map 3). The distribution illustrated in Map 3 is intended as a general guide to the main areas of vegetation cover, rather than as a definitive description, and is not based on a precise ground survey. However, it does serve to indicate the scale of the vegetated communities, which comprise a discontinuous cover of varied composition and density over an area of approximately 250,000 m². Komárková (1983) noted a discontinuous stand of *D. antarctica* and *C. quitensis* reaching approximately 5000 m² on the main island. One particularly extensive stand of mosses in the principal valley on the northern side of the main island extends almost continuously for 240 m along the valley floor, occupying an area of approximately 8000 m² (Harris, 2001). Stands of lesser extent are present elsewhere on the island and on the separate promontory 300 m to the north. Colonization has been observed occurring on recently deglaciated material.

Mosses tend to dominate on valley floors, close to streams and ponds, and in moist depressions. Mosses specifically recorded at Biscoe Point include *Bryum pseudotriquetrum* and *Sanionia uncinata* (Park *et al.*, 2007). On valley sides, mixed communities of moss and *C. quitensis* are frequent on lower north-facing slopes, with an increasing prevalence of *D. antarctica* with elevation. Mixed *D. antarctica* and *C. quitensis* communities are particularly prolific on northern slopes between 10-20 m, while *D. antarctica* tends to be more frequent on the higher exposed sites above 20 m. Mosses and lichens are frequently co-dominants or subordinate taxa. In some habitats *C. quitensis* may occur in small patches alone. Plant communities are commonly found on snow-free benches below the ridgelines on which Adélie and gentoo penguins nest (Park and Day, 2007).Patches of dead vascular plants of up to 20 m² have been observed within the Area, believed to result from the effects of desiccation, flooding and frost during some summers (Komárková, Poncet and Poncet 1985).

Unlike many other low-lying coastal sites in the region, the vegetation at Biscoe Point does not appear to have been severely affected by the recent substantial increase in numbers of Antarctic fur seals (*Arctocephalus gazella*). As such, the Area has been identified as a potential control site for assessing Antarctic fur seal impacts on vegetation and soil (Day, pers. comm., 1999). Expansion of the gentoo penguin colony has resulted in local damage to areas of vegetation where the birds are concentrated and building nests (Patterson-Fraser pers. comm. 2014). These sites are relatively small compared to the overall area of vegetation cover at Biscoe Point, and the vegetation values of the Area are not considered to have been significantly compromised as a result.

Invertebrates, bacteria and fungi

The apterous midge *Belgica antarctica* has been observed associated with the well-developed loam and closed swards of grass. Cores collected at Biscoe Point contained several species of microarthropod, including several species or genera of Acari, one species of Diptera and three species of Collembola. The springtail *Cryptopygus antarcticus* was the most abundant microarthropod (Day *et al.*, 2009) No further information is available on the invertebrate assemblages in the Area, although in view of the well-developed plant communities a rich invertebrate fauna might be expected. There is no information available on local bacterial or fungal communities.

Breeding birds and mammals

At least six species of birds breed on the island on which Biscoe Point lies. An Adélie penguin (*Pygoscelis adeliae*) colony is located on the ridge of a promontory on the south side of the island, above a narrow cove on the southern coast (Map 3). Numbers at this colony have declined from around 3000 in the 1980s to around 500-600 in recent years (Table 1). A gentoo penguin (*Pygoscelis papua*) colony was discovered on slopes on the northern side of this cove, on the southern side of the main island ridge, in 1992-93 (Fraser, pers. comm., 1999) (Map 3) and gentoo numbers have increased significantly in recent years with 3197 breeding pairs in the 2012-13 season (Patterson-Fraser, pers. comm. 2010, 2014; Ducklow *et al.*, 2013) (Table 1).

Table 1. Numbers of breeding Adélie (*Pygoscelis adeliae*) and gentoo (*Pygoscelis papua*) penguins on the island on which Biscoe Point lies 1971-2012.

	Pygoscelis adeliae			*Pygoscelis papua*		
Year	Breeding pairs	Count type[1]	Source	Breeding pairs	Count type[1]	Source
1971-72	3020	N3	2	0	N3	2
1983-84	3440	C3	3	0	C3	3
1984-85	2754	N1	3	0	N1	3
1986-87	3000	N4	4			
...						
1994-95				14	N1	5
1995-96				33	N1	5
1996-97	1801	N1	5	45	N1	5
1997-98				56	N1	5
1998-99				26	N1	5
1999-2000	1665	N1	5	149	N1	5
2000-01	1335	N1	5	296	N1	5
2001-02	692	N1	5	288	N1	5
2002-03	1025	N1	5	639	N1	5
2009-10	594	N1	6	2401	N1	6
2010-11	539	N1	7	2404	N1	7
2011-12	567	N1	7	3081	N1	7
2012-13	522	N1	7	3197	N1	7

1. N = Nest, C = Chick, A = Adults; 1 = < ± 5%, 2 = ± 5-10%, 3 = ± 10-15%, 4 = ± 25-50% (classification after Woehler, 1993)
2. Müller-Schwarze and Müller-Schwarze, 1975
3. Parmelee and Parmelee, 1987
4. Poncet and Poncet 1987 (note: the number of 3500 given in Woehler (1993) appears to be in error).
5. Fraser data supplied February 2003, based on multiple published and unpublished sources.
6. Patterson-Fraser data supplied March 2010 based on census at time of peak egg presence.
7. Ducklow *et al.* 2013.

The Adélie penguin colonies are some of the oldest in the region (more than 700 years), and have been the subject of paleoecological studies (Emslie, 2001), while the gentoo penguin colony is considered particularly interesting because it has been recently established (Fraser, pers. comm., 1999). Long-term studies are being conducted on the population structure and dynamics of the penguin colonies within the Area, which make a useful comparison with other colonies in Arthur Harbor that are subjected to higher levels of human influence (Fraser, pers. comm., 1999). The pattern of a decline in the Adélie penguin breeding population at Biscoe Point and increasing gentoo penguin breeding population is consistent with recent observations of colonies at nearby Palmer Station (Ducklow *et al.* 2013) and elsewhere in the Antarctic Peninsula region (Hinke *et al.* 2007, Carlini *et al.* 2009).

South polar skuas (*Stercorarius maccormicki*) and brown skuas (*S. lonnbergi*) breed within the Area annually, and hybrids also occur. On the island on which Biscoe Point lies, 132 pairs of south polar skuas and one pair of brown skuas were counted on 26-27 February 2001 (Harris, 2001). Concurrently, 15 pairs of south polar skuas, usually with one or two chicks, were counted on the promontory 300 m to the north. Kelp gulls (*Larus dominicanus*) and Antarctic terns (*Sterna vittata*) breed within the Area (Fraser, pers. comm., 2000), although data on numbers are not available. Information on other bird species that breed within the Area, or that transiently visit, is not available.

Small numbers of non-breeding Antarctic fur seals (*Arctocephalus gazella*) (several counted on the island in late-February 2001 – Harris, 2001), Weddell seals (*Leptonychotes weddellii*) and southern elephant seals (*Mirounga leonina*) have been observed on beaches in summer. Despite the presence of beaches and terrain suitable for haul-out, relatively few seals are typically observed within the Area. This may be a result of the observed frequent persistence of dense brash ice originating from glaciers calving from nearby Anvers Island (Fraser, pers. comm., 1999). Further information on numbers and breeding status, or on other seal species, is not available. No information is available on the local marine environment.

Human activities and impact

Human activity within the Area appears to have been minimal, but few details have been recorded. The first documented human activity in the vicinity of Biscoe Point occurred over 150 years ago, when John Biscoe, Royal Navy, entered the bay now named after him on 21 February 1832. Biscoe recorded a landing on Anvers Island, probably near Biscoe Point, to take formal possession for the United Kingdom of what he believed to be part of the mainland of Antarctica (Hattersley-Smith, 1991). The next recorded visit to Biscoe Point was in 1903-05, when Turquet made observations of *C. quitensis* at the site on the Première Expédition Antarctiques Française led by Charcot.

More recently, formal plots for plant studies were established on the island near Biscoe Point in 1982 (Komárková, 1983), although the long-term research originally planned was discontinued soon thereafter. Komárková used welding rods inserted into the soil to mark study sites. A partial survey accurately mapped the positions (± 2 m) of 44 welding rods found in soils and vegetation during a systematic search made on the northeastern side of the island in February 2001 (Map 3) (Harris, 2001). The rods were located in an area of some of the richest vegetation on the island, and distributed over an area of at least 8000 m^2. In general, they had been inserted into soil or vegetation with chemically coated ends downwards. Contaminants from the rods appeared to kill all vegetation up to 20 cm from where the rods lay. Numerous rods have been found in previous seasons, possibly numbering in the hundreds (Fraser, Patterson, Day: pers. comms., 1999-2002). Additional welding rods were found on and near the beach during the 2009-10 season, which were collected and disposed of at Palmer Station (Patterson-Fraser, pers. comm., 2010). The Area is not considered suitable as a reference site for measuring chemical contamination, because there remains uncertainty over contaminant types and concentrations, which sites have been affected, and the extent to which contaminants may have moved through soil, water and biological systems.

Fraser (pers. comm., 2001) also reported markers made of lead present in the gentoo penguin colony. In addition, seaborne litter (mostly wood) may be found on beaches. A rubber hose (15 m long, ~15 cm diameter) was removed from a small valley near the southern small boat landing site in 2009-10.

Recent scientific studies within the Area have focused on monitoring the breeding status of penguins and skuas The Area has also been used for the collection of seeds of *Deschampsia* and *Colobanthus* and cores of soil and plant material for ecological research in the Palmer Station region. Permits have been required to visit the Area since the site was specially protected in 1985.

6(ii) Access to the Area

Access to the Area may be made by small boat, by aircraft or across sea ice by vehicle or on foot. Particular routes have not been designated for small boat access to the Area. Overflight, preferred helicopter access routes and aircraft landing restrictions apply within the Area, the specific conditions for which are set out in Section 7(ii) below. The designated Helicopter Access Zone that applies around the Area is described in Section 6(v) and 7(ii) below.

The seasonal cycle of sea ice formation in the Palmer area is highly variable, with sea ice formation beginning between March and May. For the period 1979 to 2004, the seasonal duration of sea ice in the Palmer area varied between five and 12 months (Stammerjohn *et al.*, 2008). Dense brash ice is frequently found in the vicinity of the island and originates from calving glaciers on Anvers Island, which may impede small boat access.

6(iii) Location of structures within and adjacent to the Area

No structures or instruments are known to be present within the Area. A permanent survey marker, consisting of a 5/8" stainless steel threaded rod, was installed on the island on which Biscoe Point lies by the USGS on 31 January 1999. The marker, named BIS1, is located at 64°48'40.12"S, 63°46'26.42"W at an elevation of 23 m (Maps 2 & 3). It is sited approximately midway along the principal ridgeline of the island, about 100 m north of the southern small boat landing site. The marker is set in bedrock and marked by a red plastic survey cap.

6(iv) Location of other protected areas within close proximity of the Area

The nearest protected areas to Biscoe Point are: Litchfield Island (ASPA No. 113) which is 16 km west of the Area in Arthur Harbor; South Bay (ASPA No. 146), which is approximately 12 km to the southeast at Doumer Island (Map 1).

6(v) Special zones within the Area

An Helicopter Access Zone (Maps 2 and 3) has been defined within the Management Plan for Antarctic Specially Managed Area No. 7, which applies to aircraft accessing the designated landing sites within the Area. The Helicopter Access Zone extends in northwesterly and northeasterly directions from the designated landing sites out to a distance of 2000 feet (610 m) from the edges of known bird colony breeding locations within the Area.

7.   Permit conditions

7(i) General permit conditions

Entry into the Area is prohibited except in accordance with a Permit issued by an appropriate national authority. Conditions for issuing a Permit to enter the Area are that:

- It is issued for scientific research, and in particular for research on the terrestrial ecosystem and fauna in the Area;
- It is issued for compelling educational or outreach reasons that cannot be served elsewhere, or for reasons essential to the management of the Area;
- the actions permitted will not jeopardize the ecological, scientific, or educational values of the Area;
- any management activities are in support of the objectives of the Management Plan;
- the actions permitted are in accordance with the Management Plan;
- the activities permitted will give due consideration via the environmental impact assessment process to the continued protection of the environmental and scientific values of the Area;
- the Permit shall be issued for a finite period;

- the Permit, or a copy, shall be carried when in the Area.

7(ii) Access to, and movement within, or over the Area

Access to the Area shall be by small boat, by aircraft, or over sea ice by vehicle or on foot. When access over sea ice is viable, there are no special restrictions on the locations where vehicle or foot access may be made, although vehicles are prohibited from being taken on land.

Foot access and movement within the Area

Movement on land within the Area shall be on foot. All people in aircraft, boats, or vehicles are prohibited from moving on foot beyond the immediate vicinity of their landing or access site unless specifically authorised by Permit.

Pedestrians should maintain the following minimum approach distances from wildlife, unless it is necessary to approach closer for purposes allowed for by the permit:

- Southern giant petrels (*Macronectes giganteus*) – 50 m
- Antarctic fur seals (for personal safety) – 15 m
- other birds and seals – 5 m.

Visitors should move carefully so as to minimize disturbance to flora, fauna, soils, and water bodies. Pedestrians should walk on snow or rocky terrain if practical, but taking care not to damage lichens. Pedestrians should walk around the penguin colonies and should not enter sub-groups of nesting penguins unless required for research or management purposes. Pedestrian traffic should be kept to the minimum consistent with the objectives of any permitted activities and every reasonable effort should be made to minimize effects.

Small boat access

The recommended landing sites for small boats are at either of the following locations (Maps 2 & 3):

1) on the beach on the northern shore of the elongated cove on the southern coast of the island, which is the site most likely to be free of sea ice;
2) on the beach in the small cove mid-way along the northern coast of the island, adjacent to the designated camp and helicopter landing sites.

Access by small boat at other locations around the coast is allowed, provided this is consistent with the purposes for which a Permit has been granted.

Aircraft access and overflight

Restrictions on aircraft operations apply during the period between 01 October and 15 April inclusive, when aircraft shall operate and land within the Area according to strict observance of the following conditions:

1) Overflight of the Area below 2000 ft (~610 m) is prohibited outside of the Helicopter Access Zone (Map 2), except when specifically permitted for purposes allowed for by the Management Plan. It is recommended that aircraft maintain a 2000 ft (~610 m) horizontal separation distance from the edges of bird colonies breeding within the Area as shown in Map 2, unless accessing the designated landing sites through the Helicopter Access Zone;
2) Helicopter landing is permitted at two designated sites (Map 2), the first (A) on the main island on which Biscoe Point lies, and the second (B) on the separate promontory 300 m further to the north. The landing sites with their coordinates are described as follows:
    (A) 64°48.59' S, 63°46.82' W – on beach gravels a few meters above sea level 35 m east of the beach on the eastern shore of a small cove on the northern coast of the island. A small tidal pool of about 25

        m in diameter is located 30 m east of the landing site; and

        (B) 64°48.37' S, 63°46.40' W – on the lower (western) slopes of a ridge, which may be snow-covered, extending from Anvers Island towards the northern promontory. Care should be exercised on snow slopes extending east and up-slope on Anvers Island, which are likely to be crevassed .

3) Aircraft landing within the Area should approach within the Helicopter Access Zone to the maximum extent practicable. The Helicopter Access Zone allows access from the north and west, from the region of Biscoe Bay, to landing site (A), and from the north and east to landing site (B) (Map 2). The Helicopter Access Zone extends over the open water between landing sites (A) and (B).

4) Use of smoke grenades to indicate wind direction is prohibited within the Area unless absolutely necessary for safety, and any grenades used should be retrieved.

7(iii) Activities that may be conducted within the Area

- Scientific research that will not jeopardize the ecosystem or values of the Area;

- Activities with educational and / or outreach purposes that cannot be served elsewhere;

- Essential management activities, including monitoring and inspection.

7(iv) Installation, modification or removal of structures / equipment

- No structures are to be erected within the Area except as specified in a permit and, with the exception of permanent survey markers and signs, permanent structures or installations are prohibited;

- All structures, scientific equipment or markers installed in the Area must be authorized by permit and clearly identified by country, name of the principal investigator, year of installation and date of expected removal. All such items should be free of organisms, propagules (e.g. seeds, eggs) and non-sterile soil, and be made of materials that can withstand the environmental conditions and pose minimal risk of contamination or damage to the values of the Area;

- Installation (including site selection), maintenance, modification or removal of structures or equipment shall be undertaken in a manner that minimizes disturbance to flora and fauna, preferably avoiding the main breeding season (01 Oct – 31 Mar);

- Removal of specific structures / equipment for which the permit has expired shall be the responsibility of the authority which granted the original Permit, and shall be a condition of the permit.

7(v) Location of field camps

Temporary camping is allowed within the Area at the designated site located approximately 50 m north-east of helicopter landing site (A), on the northern coast of the main island on which Biscoe Point lies. The camp site is located on beach gravels and rocky ground a few meters above sea level, immediately north of a transient tidal pool, and is separated from the sea further to the north by a low rocky ridge of about 8 m. When necessary for essential purposes specified in the Permit, temporary camping is allowed on the separate peninsula 300 m to the north, although a specific camping site has not been determined. Camping on surfaces with significant vegetation cover is prohibited.

7(vi) Restrictions on materials and organisms which may be brought into the Area

In addition to the requirements of the Protocol on Environmental Protection to the Antarctic Treaty, restrictions on materials and organisms which may be brought into the Area are:

- Deliberate introduction of animals, plant material, micro-organisms and non-sterile soil into the Area is prohibited. Precautions shall be taken to prevent the accidental introduction of animals, plant material, micro-organisms and non-sterile soil from other biologically distinct regions (within or beyond the Antarctic Treaty area);

- Visitors shall ensure that sampling equipment and markers brought into the Area are clean. To the maximum extent practicable, footwear and other equipment used or brought into the Area (including backpacks, carry-bags and other equipment) shall be thoroughly cleaned before entering the Area. Visitors should also consult and follow as appropriate recommendations contained in the Committee for Environmental Protection Non-native Species Manual (CEP 2011), and in the Environmental Code of Conduct for terrestrial scientific field research in Antarctica (SCAR 2009);

- All poultry brought into and not consumed or used within the Area, including all parts, products and / or wastes of poultry, shall be removed from the Area or disposed of by incineration or equivalent means that eliminates risks to native flora and fauna;

- No herbicides or pesticides shall be brought into the Area;

- Any other chemicals, including radio-nuclides or stable isotopes, which may be introduced for scientific or management purposes specified in the permit, shall be removed from the Area at or before the conclusion of the activity for which the permit was granted;

- Fuel, food, chemicals and other materials are not to be stored in the Area, unless specifically authorized by permit and shall be stored and handled in a way that minimizes the risk of their accidental introduction into the environment;

- All materials introduced shall be for a stated period only, shall be removed at or before the conclusion of that stated period, and shall be stored and handled so that risk of their introduction into the environment is minimized;

- If release occurs which is likely to compromise the values of the Area, removal is encouraged only where the impact of removal is not likely to be greater than that of leaving the material *in situ.*

7(vii) Taking of, or harmful interference with, native flora or fauna

Taking or harmful interference with native flora and fauna is prohibited, except in accordance with a permit issued under Article 3 of Annex II of the Protocol on Environmental Protection to the Antarctic Treaty. Where animal taking or harmful interference is involved, this should, as a minimum standard, be in accordance with the SCAR Code of Conduct for the Use of Animals for Scientific Purposes in Antarctica.

7(viii) Collection or removal of materials not brought into the Area by the permit holder

- Material may be collected or removed from the Area only in accordance with a permit and should be limited to the minimum necessary to meet scientific or management needs. This includes biological samples and rock specimens.

- Material of human origin likely to compromise the values of the Area, which was not brought into the Area by the permit holder or otherwise authorized, may be removed from any part of the Area, unless the impact of removal is likely to be greater than leaving the material *in situ.* If this is the case the appropriate authority should be notified.

- The appropriate national authority should be notified of any items removed from the Area that were not introduced by the permit holder.

7(ix) Disposal of waste

All wastes, including all human wastes, shall be removed from the Area.

7(x) Measures that may be necessary to continue to meet the aims of the Management Plan

Permits may be granted to enter the Area to:

1) carry out monitoring and Area inspection activities, which may involve the collection of a small number of samples or data for analysis or review;
2) install or maintain signposts, markers, structures or scientific or essential logistic equipment;

3) carry out protective measures;

4) carry out research or management in a manner that avoids interference with long-term research and monitoring activities or possible duplication of effort. Persons planning new projects within the Area should consult with established programs working within the Area, such as those of the US, before initiating the work.

7(xi) Requirements for reports

- The principal permit holder for each visit to the Area shall submit a report to the appropriate national authority as soon as practicable, and no later than six months after the visit has been completed.

- Such reports should include, as appropriate, the information identified in the visit report form contained in the Guide to the Preparation of Management Plans for Antarctic Specially Protected Areas. If appropriate, the national authority should also forward a copy of the visit report to the Parties that proposed the Management Plan, to assist in managing the Area and reviewing the Management Plan.

- Parties should, wherever possible, deposit originals or copies of such original visit reports in a publicly accessible archive to maintain a record of usage, for the purpose of any review of the Management Plan and in organising the scientific use of the Area.

- The appropriate authority should be notified of any activities/measures undertaken, and / or of any materials released and not removed, that were not included in the authorized permit.

8. Supporting documentation

Baker, K.S. 1996. Palmer LTER: Palmer Station air temperature 1974 to 1996. *Antarctic Journal of the United States* **31** (2): 162-64.

Carlini, AR, NR Coria, MM Santos, J Negrete, M a. Juares, and G a. Daneri. 2009. Responses of *Pygoscelis adeliae* and *P. papua* populations to environmental changes at Isla 25 de Mayo (King George Island). *Polar Biology* **32** (10) (May 16): 1427–33.

Day, T.A., Ruhland, C.T., Strauss, S., Park, J-H., Krieg, M.L., Krna, M.A., and Bryant, D.M. 2009. Response of plants and the dominatn microarthropod *Cryptopygus antarcticus*, to warming and contrasting precipitation regimes in Antarctic tundra. *Global Change Biology* **15**: 1640-1651.

Ducklow, H.W., W.R. Fraser, M.P. Meredith, S.E. Stammerjohn, S.C. Doney, D.G. Martinson, S.F. Sailley, O.M. Schofield, D.K. Steinberg, H.J. Venables, and Amsler, C.D. 2013. West Antarctic Peninsula: An ice-dependent coastal marine ecosystem in transition. *Oceanography* **26**(3):190–203.

Emslie, S.D., Fraser, W., Smith, R.C. and Walker, W. 1998. Abandoned penguin colonies and environmental change in the Palmer Station area, Anvers Island, Antarctic Peninsula. *Antarctic Science* **10**(3): 257-268.

Emslie, S.D. 2001. Radiocarbon dates from abandoned penguin colonies in the Antarctic Peninsula region. *Antarctic Science* **13**(3):289-295.

ERA. 2010. Biscoe Point Orthophoto 2010. Digital orthophotograph of Biscoe Point and adjacent areas of coast on Anvers Island. Ground pixel resolution 8 cm and horizontal / vertical accuracy of ± 1 m. MSL heights, 5 m² DTM. Aerial photography acquired by BAS on 29 Nov 2009 BAS/4/10. Unpublished data, Environmental Research & Assessment, Cambridge.

Greene, D.M. and Holtom, A. 1971. Studies in *Colobanthus quitensis* (Kunth) Bartl. and *Deschampsia antarctica* Desv.: III. Distribution, habitats and performance in the Antarctic botanical zone. *British Antarctic Survey Bulletin* **26**: 1-29.

Harris, C.M. 2001. Revision of management plans for Antarctic protected areas originally proposed by the United States of America and the United Kingdom: Field visit report. Internal report for the National Science Foundation, US, and the Foreign and Commonwealth Office, UK. Environmental Research & Assessment, Cambridge.

Hattersley-Smith, M.A. 1991. The history of place-names in the British Antarctic Territory. British Antarctic Survey Scientific Reports **113** (Part 1).

Hinke, JT, K Salwicka, SG Trivelpiece, GM Watters, and WZ Trivelpiece. 2007. Divergent responses of Pygoscelis penguins reveal a common environmental driver. *Oecologia* **153** (4) (October): 845–55.

Hooper, P.R. 1958. Progress report on the geology of Anvers Island . Unpublished report, British Antarctic Survey Archives Ref AD6/2/1957/G3.

Hooper, P.R. 1962. The petrology of Anvers Island and adjacent islands. *FIDS Scientific Reports* **34**.

Komárková, V. 1983. Plant communities of the Antarctic Peninsula near Palmer Station. *Antarctic Journal of the United States* **18**: 216-218.

Komárková, V. 1984. Studies of plant communities of the Antarctic Peninsula near Palmer Station. *Antarctic Journal of the United States* **19**: 180-182.

Komárková, V, Poncet, S and Poncet, J. 1985. Two native Antarctic vascular plants, *Deschampsia antarctica* and *Colobanthus quitensis*: a new southernmost locality and other localities in the Antarctic Peninsula area. *Arctic and Alpine Research* **17**(4): 401-416.

Müller-Schwarze, C. and Müller-Schwarze, D. 1975. A survey of twenty-four rookeries of pygoscelid penguins in the Antarctic Peninsula region. In *The biology of penguins*, Stonehouse, B. (ed). Macmillan Press, London.

National Science Foundation, Office of Polar Programs, 1999. Palmer Station. OPP World Wide Web site address http://www.nsf.gov/od/opp/support/palmerst.htm

Park, J-H. and Day, T.A. 2007. Temperature response of CO_2 exchange and dissolved organic carbon release in a maritime Antarctic tundra ecosystem. *Polar Biology* 30: 1535–1544. DOI 10.1007/s00300-007-0314-y.

Park, J-H., Day, T.A., Strauss, S., and Ruhland, C.T. 2007. Biogeochemical pools and fluxes of carbon and nitrogen in a maritime tundra near penguin colonies along the Antarctic Peninsula. *Polar Biology* **30**:199–207.

Parmelee, D.F. and Parmelee, J.M. 1987. Revised penguin numbers and distribution for Anvers Island, Antarctica. *British Antarctic Survey Bulletin* **76**: 65-73.

Poncet, S. and Poncet, J. 1987. Censuses of penguin populations of the Antarctic Peninsula, 1983-87. *British Antarctic Survey Bulletin* **77**: 109-129.

Rundle, A.S. 1968. Snow accumulation and ice movement on the Anvers Island ice cap, Antarctica: a study of mass balance. *Proceedings of the ISAGE Symposium, Hanover, USA, 3-7 September, 1968*: 377-390.

Sanchez, R. and Fraser, W. 2001. *Biscoe Point Orthobase*. Digital orthophotograph of island on which Biscoe Point lies, 6 cm pixel resolution and horizontal / vertical accuracy of ± 2 m. Geoid heights, 3 m² DTM, derived contour interval: 2 m. Data on CD-ROM and accompanied by USGS Open File Report 99-402 "GPS and GIS-based data collection and image mapping in the Antartcic Peninsula". Science and Applications Center, Mapping Applications Center. Reston, USGS.

Smith, R.I.L. 1996. Terrestrial and freshwater biotic components of the western Antarctic Peninsula. In Ross, R.M., Hofmann, E.E and Quetin, L.B. (eds). Foundations for ecological research west of the Antarctic Peninsula. *Antarctic Research Series* **70**: 15-59.

Smith, R.I.L. and Corner, R.W.M. 1973. Vegetation of the Arthur Harbour – Argentine Islands region of the Antarctic Peninsula. *British Antarctic Survey Bulletin* **33 & 34**: 89-122.

Stammerjohn, S.E., Martinson, D.G., Smith, R.C. and Iannuzzi, R.A. 2008.Sea ice in the western Antarctic Peninsula region: Spatio-temporal variabilityfrom ecological and climate change perspectives. *Deep-Sea Research II* **55**: 2041– 2058.

Woehler, E.J. (ed) 1993. *The distribution and abundance of Antarctic and sub-Antarctic penguins*. SCAR, Cambridge.

Xiong, F.S., Mueller, E.C. and Day, T.A. 2000. Photosynthetic and respiratory acclimation and growth response of Antarctic vascular plants to contrasting temperature regimes. *American Journal of Botany* **87**: 700-710.

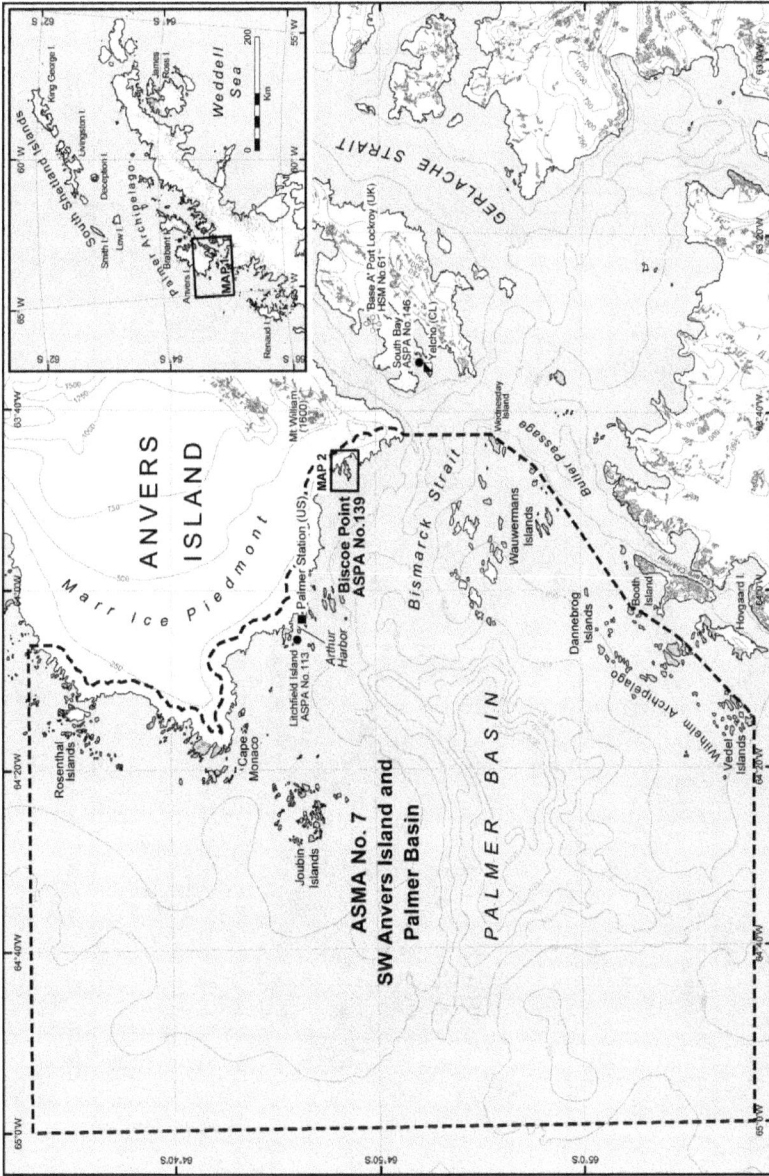

Map 1: ASPA No. 139 Biscoe Point, Anvers Island

111

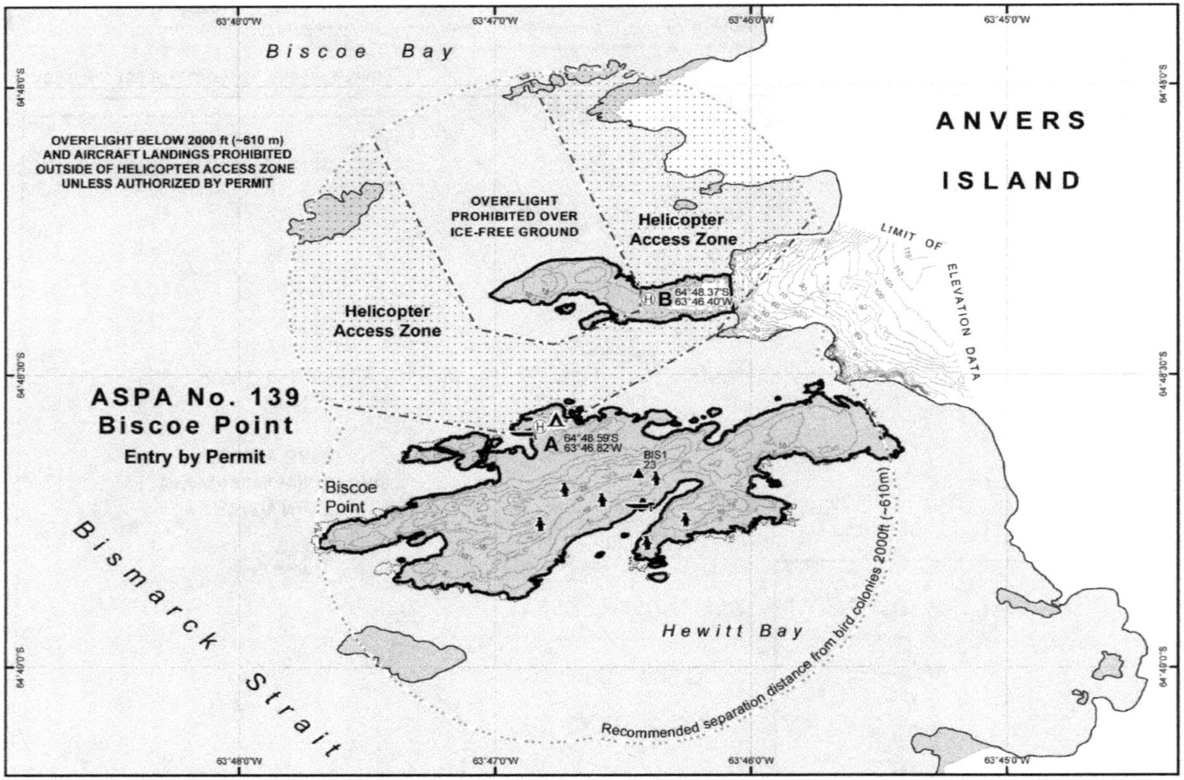

Map 2: ASPA No. 139 Biscoe Point - Physical features, boundaries and access guidelines

26 Feb 2014
United States Antarctic Program
Environmental Research & Assessment

Contour (5 m) · Coastline · Offshore rock · Ice free ground · Permenant ice · Ocean · ASPA boundary · Recommended separation distance · Penguin colony (approx.) · Helicopter Access Zone · Helicopter landing site · Small boat landing site · Designated camp site · Survey control (monumented)

0 100 200 300 400 500 Meters

Projection: Lambert Conic Conformal. Spheroid and horizontal datum: WGS 84. Data sources: Coastline: USGS orthophoto (2001), ERA orthophoto (Nov 2009) and georeferenced WV-2 image (© Jan 2012 Digital Globe; NGA Commercial Imagery Program). Penguin colonies & other features: Orthophoto (Nov 2009) & GPS survey (ERA 2001).

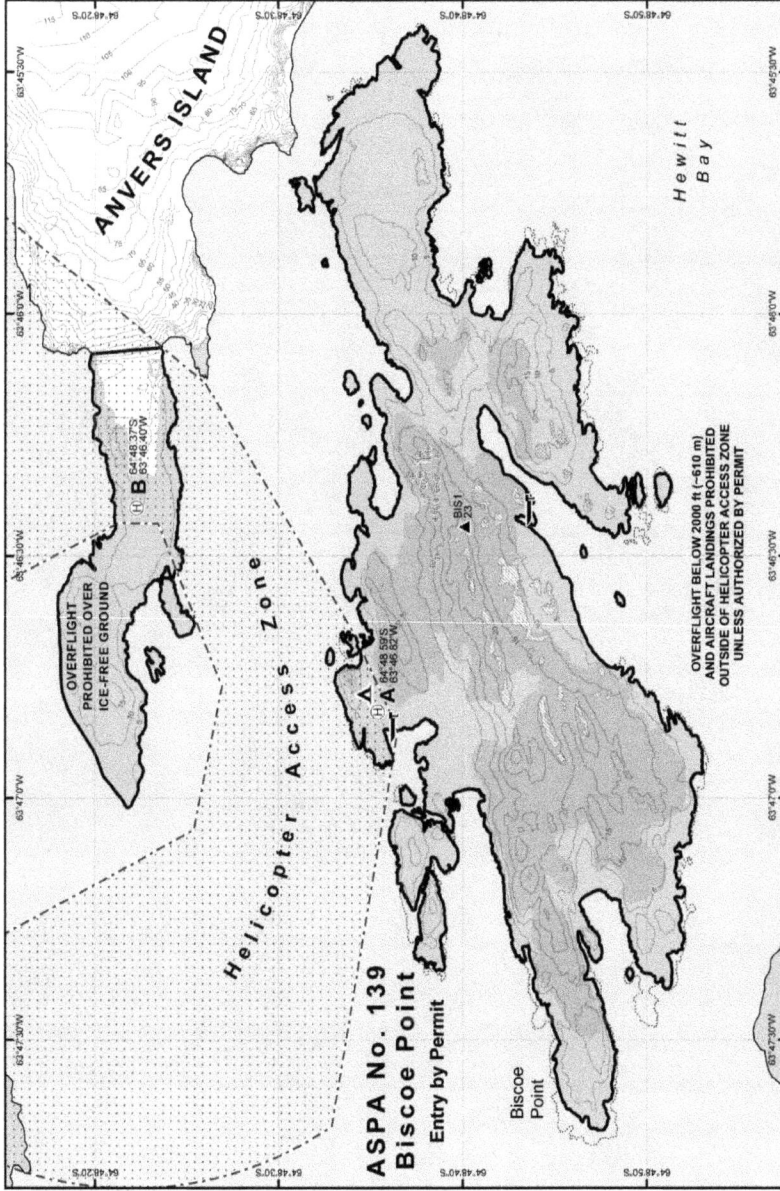

Map 3: ASPA No. 139 Biscoe Point - Penguin colonies, approximate vegetation extent and known contaminated sites

113

Management Plan for
Antarctic Specially Protected Area No. 141

YUKIDORI VALLEY, LANGHOVDE, LÜTZOW-HOLM BAY

Introduction

The Yukidori Valley (69°14'30"S, 39°46'00"E) is located in the middle part of Langhovde on the east coast of Lützow-Holm Bay, continental Antarctica, which is about 20 km south of the Japanese Syowa Station (69°00'22"S, 39°35'24"E) on the Ongul Islands (Map 1). The Valley is 2.0-2.5 km long from east to west, 1.8 km wide and contains a prominent melt stream and two lakes (Map 2).

The Area was originally designated in Recommendation XIV-5 (1987, SSSI No.22) after the proposal by Japan. A management plan for the Area was adopted under Recommendation XVI-7 (1991) and revised under Measure 1 (2000).

Based on the Environmental Domains Analysis for Antarctica (Resolution 3 (2008)) the Area lies within Environment D – East Antarctic coastal geologic. In accordance with the Antarctic Conservation Biogeographic Regions (ACBR) (Resolution6 (2012)), the Area lies within ACBR 5 Enderby Land. The Yukidori valley is designated as ASPA to protect a fragile, typical continental Antarctic fellfield ecosystem and its component species, some of which are endemic to Antarctica, from the human activity in Antarctica. Additionally, long-term monitoring programs have been conducted in this valuable site.

1. Description of values to be protected

A fragile, typical continental fellfield ecosystem has developed in the Yukidori Valley. Field surveys of geological and biological sciences have been carried out in Langhovde since 1957 of the IGY period and a long-term monitoring program started in the Yukidori Valley area in 1984. More intensive studies have been carried out after the Area was designated as SSSI No.22 in 1987. Since 1984, the long-term monitoring program has continued in this Area, in particular to monitor temporal and spatial changes in vegetation of mosses and lichens (Map 2).

The values to be protected are those associated with this fragile, typical continental Antarctic fellfield ecosystem under quite harsh Antarctic environment, and the long-term scientific studies that have been carried out since 1984. Permanent quadrats for monitoring lichen and moss vegetation have been established in this typical continental ecosystem in relation to long-term environmental change. The Area requires protection in order to ensure that this long-term scientific monitoring program is not compromised. Based on these reason, the Area was designated in Recommendation XIV-5 (1987, SSSI No.22) after the proposal by Japan, and the management plan for the Area was adopted under Recommendation XVI-7 (1991). The human activity in this area will easily destroy the fragile ecosystem under the harsh environment in continental Antarctica, and it will take so long period or absolutely impossible to recover. By designed as ASPA, this valuable fellfield ecosystem should be protected and the value for research on the ecosystem and environmental monitoring.

The Yukidori Valley is inhabited by several thousand snow petrels. Excrement of snow petrels is important as a major supply of nutrients for mosses and lichens.

By the continuous environmental monitoring study in the ASPA area, the effect of global environmental change in Antarctica will be detected and it will contribute as a sentinel system for the whole world.

2. Aims and objectives

Management at Yukidori Valley aims to:

- avoid degradation of, or substantial risk to, the values of the Area by preventing unnecessary human disturbance to the Area;
- allow a continuation of long-term monitoring programs;
- avoid major changes to the structure and composition of the terrestrial vegetation, in particular the moss and lichen banks;
- prevent unnecessary human disturbance to the snow petrels, as well as to the surrounding environment, and
- minimise the possibility of introduction of alien plants, animals and microbes into the Area, and
- Allow visits for management purposes in support of the aims of the Management Plan.

3. Management activities

The following management activities are to be undertaken to protect the values of the Area:

- Maps showing the location of the Area (stating the special restrictions that apply) shall be displayed prominently at "Biological research hut" located outside of the western boundary of the Area, where copies of this management plan shall also be made available.
- Signs showing the location and boundaries of the Area and listing entry restrictions should be placed at the entry point at the western boundary of the Area to help avoid inadvertent entry.
- Markers, signs or structures erected within the Area for scientific or management purposes shall be secured and maintained in good condition and removed when no longer necessary.
- Information about the ASPA, including copies of the Management Plan, should be made available at all facilities operating in the region
- Personnel (national programme staff, field expeditions, tourists and pilots) in the vicinity of, accessing or flying over the Area shall be specifically instructed, by their national program (or appropriate national authority) as to the provisions and contents of the Management Plan.
- All pilots operating in the region shall be informed of the location, boundaries and restrictions applying to entry and over-flight in the Area.

4. Period of designation

Designated for an indefinite period.

5. Maps

Map 1: Sôya Coast, Lützow-Holm Bay, East Antarctica.

Map 2: Yukidori Valley, Langhovde and the boundary of ASPA No. 141.

Map 3: The biological research hut and surroundings.

6. Description of the Area

6(i) Geographical co-ordinates, boundary markers and natural features

The Yukidori Valley (69°00'30"S, 39°46'00"E) is situated in the middle part of Langhovde, on the east coast of Lützow-Holm Bay, Continental Antarctica. The Area encompasses 2.0-2.5 km by 1.8 km, located between a tongue of the ice cap and sea at the western end of the Valley. The fellfield

116

ecosystem and long-term monitoring sites are contained entirely within Yukidori Valley, and the Area boundary is designed to afford protection to the entire valley/ catchment system. The Area does not include any marine area.

The location of the Area and its boundaries are shown on the attached maps (Map 2). It is described as all the land within the Area bounded by the following lines:

The eastern boundary of the Area follows a straight line from 69°14'00"S, 39°48'00"E due south to 69°14'00"S, 39°48'00"E.

The northern boundary of the Area follows a straight line from 69°14'00"S, 39°48'00"E due west to the coastline at 69°14'00"S, 39°44'20"E.

The southern boundary of the Area follows a straight line from 69°15'00"S, 39°48'00"E due west to the stream of Yatude Zawa at 69°15'00"S, 39°45'20"E (Map 2-G).

The western boundary of the Area between 69°14'00"S, 39°48'00"E(Map 2-A) and 69°15'00"S, 39°45'20"E (Map 2-G), is delineated by the highwater line of the coast, rope boundaries and stream of Yatude Valley.

Map 2-A (69°14'00"S, 39°44'.20"E) to Map 2-B (69°14'13"S, 39°43'23"E): Highwater line of the coast

Map 2-B (69°14'13"S, 39°43'23"E) to Map 2-C (69°14'17"S, 39°43'12"E): Rope boundaries

Map 2-C (69°14'17"S, 39°43'12"E) to Map 2-D (69°14'31"S, 39°42'57"E): Highwater line of the coast

Map 2-D (69°14'31"S, 39°42'57"E) to Map 2-F (69°14'32"S, 39°43.01"E): Rope boundaries

Map 2-F (69°14'38"S, 39°43.04"E) to Map 2-G (69°15'00"S, 39°45'20"E): Stream of Yatude Valley

Geology

The Yukidori Valley contains a prominent melt stream and two lakes. The stream flows from the ice cap towards the sea through V-shaped and U-shaped sectors of the Valley and enters Lake Yukidori, in the middle of the Valley, 125 m above sea level; it then flows from the south-west corner of the lake and runs through the lower valley formed by steep cliffs. Sorted stone circles with mean diameter of 1 m are situated on moraines near the northwestern part of Langhovde Glacier to the east of Lake Higasi-Yukidori, which is located at the head of the Valley, about 200 m above sea level abutting the edge of the ice cap. Poorly-developed stone circles are found on fluvioglacial deposits in the Yukidori Valley. Small talus aprons and talus cones are located around Lake Yukidori. In the lower reaches of the Yukidori Valley, at on altitude of about 20 m, fluvioglacial terraces 20 to 30 m wide stand 2 to 3 m high above the present channel bed. These flat terraces consist of rather fine sand and gravel. There is a dissected deltaic fan formed at the mouth of the stream. The Valley is underlain by well-layered sequences of late Proterozoic metamorphic rocks, consisting of garnet-biotite gneiss, biotite gneiss, pyroxee gneiss and hornblende gneiss with metabasite. The foliation of the gneisses strike N10°E and dips monoclinally to the east (Map 3).

Flora and fauna

Almost all of the plant species recorded from the Langhovde area occur within the Area. They include the mosses *Bryum pseudotriquetrum* (= *Bryum algens*), *Bryum argenteum*, *Bryum amblyodon*, *Ceratodon purpureus*, *Hennediella heimii*, *Pottia austrogeorgica*, *Grimmia lawiana* and lichens *Usnea sphacelata*, *Umbilicaria antarctica*, *Umbilicaria decussata*, *Pseudephebe minuscula*, and *Xanthoria elegans*. Four species of free living mites (*Nanorchestes antarcticus*, *Protereunetes minutus*, *Antarcticola meyeri*, *Tydeus erebus*), have been reported. There are over sixty species of microalgae, including species endemic to the Yukidori Valley, *Cosmarium yukidoriense* and a variety of *Cosmarium clepsydra*. Such vegetation is distributed all along the stream. Several pairs of the south polar skua (*Catharacta maccormicki*) and several thousand snow petrels (*Pagodroma nivea*; note "Yukidori" is Japanese for the snow petrel) breed at the cliff along the valley.

117

6(ii) Access to the area

Access to the Area is covered under section 7(ii) of this plan

6(iii) Location of structures within and adjacent to the Area

The biological research hut is located just outside the western boundary of the Area at (69°14'36"S, 39°42'59"E).The boundary of the Area near the hut is enclosed by ropes. It was constructed in 1986 near the beach at the mouth of the Valley so that there would be minimal impact on the flora, fauna, and terrain of the Area. There are three sites for microclimatic observations in the lower, middle and upper reaches of the stream within the Area. Microclimatic factors such as relative humidity and air temperatures at ground level, soil temperatures and temperatures at moss level are measured. Hexagon chambers made of acrylic fiber are installed at the vegetated area in the lower and middle reaches in order to assess vegetational and environmental changes. These sites are indicated in the attached maps.

6(iv) Location of other protected areas in the vicinity

None.

6(v) Special zones within the Area

There are no special zones within the Area.

7. Terms and conditions for entry permits

7(i) General permit conditions

Entry into the Area is prohibited except in accordance with a Permit issued by an appropriate national authority. Conditions for issuing a Permit to enter the Area are that:

- it is issued for compelling scientific or educational reasons that cannot be served elsewhere, or for essential management purposes consistent with plan objectives such as inspection, maintenance or review;
- the actions permitted will not jeopardize the ecological or scientific values of the Area;
- any management activities are in support of the aims and objectives of the management plan;
- the actions permitted are in accordance with this management plan;
- the Permit, or an authorized copy, shall be carried within the Area;
- a visit report shall be supplied to the authority named in the Permit;
- Permit shall be issued for a stated period.
- The appropriate authority should be notified of any activities/measures undertaken that weren't included in the authorized Permit.

7(ii) Access to, and movement within or over, the Area

- The area is situated about 20 km south from Syowa station. In winter, snow vehicle access route is settled on the frozen sea ice. In summer, helicopter is used to access from Syowa station and ice-breaker.
- Access route of snow vehicle and helicopter are shown in Map3. Heliport is located outside of the boundary at 69°14'37"S, 39°42'53"E .
- Vehicles are prohibited within the Area and helicopter should not land within the Area.
- Only those pedestrians with compelling research activities are allowed to enter at the entry point (Map 2-E).
- No pedestrian routes are designated within the Area, but persons on foot should at all times avoid walking on vegetated areas or disturbance to birds and natural features.

- The operation of aircraft over the Area should be carried out, as a minimum requirement, in compliance with the 'Guidelines for the Operation of Aircraft near Concentrations of Birds' contained in Resolution 2 (2004).

7(iii) Activities which may be conducted in the Area, including restrictions on time or place

- Compelling scientific research which cannot be undertaken elsewhere and which will not jeopardize the ecosystem of the Area
- Essential management activities, including monitoring;

7(iv) Installation, modification or removal of structures

- No structures are to be erected in the Area, or scientific equipment installed, except for essential scientific or management activities, as specified in the Permit.
- All markers, structures or scientific equipment installed in the Area must be clearly identified by country, name of the principal investigator or agency, year of installation and date of expected removal.
- All such items should be free of organisms, propagules (e.g. seeds, eggs) and non-sterile soil, and be made of materials that can withstand the environmental conditions and pose minimal risk of contamination of the Area.
- Installation (including site selection), maintenance, modification or removal of structures and equipment shall be undertaken in a manner that minimises disturbance to the values of the Area
- Structures and installations must be removed when they are no longer required, or on the expiry of the permit, whichever is the earlier.

7(v) Location of field camps

Camping is prohibited within the Area. All the visitors stay in the biology research hut (69°14'36"S, 39°42'59"E) just outside the western boundary of the Area, or tent settled around the hut.

7(vi) Restrictions on materials and organisms which may be brought into the Area

No living animals, plant material, microorganisms or soils shall be deliberately introduced into the Area and the precautions listed in 7(x) below shall be taken to prevent accidental introductions. Further guidance can be found in the CEP Non-native species manual(CEP,2011) and the Environmental code of conduct for terrestrial scientific field research in Antarctica(SCAR, 2009)In view of the presence of breeding bird colonies in the Area, no poultry products, including products containing uncooked dried eggs, shall be taken into the Area.

No herbicides or pesticides shall be brought into the Area. Any other chemicals, including radio-nuclides or stable isotopes, which may be introduced for scientific or management purposes specified in the Permit, shall be removed from the Area at or before the conclusion of the activity for which the Permit was granted. Fuel is not to be stored in the Area, unless specifically authorized by Permit for specific scientific or management purposes. Anything introduced shall be for a stated period only, shall be removed at or before the conclusion of that stated period, and shall be stored and handled so that risk of any introduction into the environment is minimized. If release occurs which is likely to compromise the values of the Area, removal is encouraged only where the impact of removal is not likely to be greater than that of leaving the material in situ. The appropriate authority should be notified of anything released and not removed that was not included in the authorized Permit.

7(vii) Taking of, or harmful interference with, native flora and fauna

Taking or harmful interference with native flora and fauna is prohibited, except by Permit issued in accordance with Annex II to the Protocol on Environmental Protection to the Antarctic Treaty. Where taking or harmful interference with animals is involved, the SCAR Code of Conduct for the Use of Animals for Scientific Purposes in Antarctica should be used as a minimum standard.

7(viii) The collection or removal of materials not brought into the Area by the permit holder

Collection or removal of anything not brought into the Area by the Permit holder shall only be in accordance with a Permit and should be limited to the minimum necessary to meet scientific or management needs. Permits shall not be granted in instances where it is proposed to take, remove or damage such quantities of soil, native flora or fauna that their distribution or abundance in the Area would be significantly affected. Anything of human origin likely to compromise the values of the Area, which was not brought into the Area by the Permit Holder or otherwise authorized, may be removed unless the impact of removal is likely to be greater than leaving the material in situ: if this is the case the appropriate authority should be notified.

7(ix) Disposal of waste

Liquid human wastes may be disposed of into the sea adjacent to the area. All other wastes should be removed from the Area. Solid human waste should not be disposed of to the sea, but shall be removed from the Area. No solid or liquid human waste shall be disposed of inland.

7(x) Measures that may be necessary to continue to meet the aims of the Management Plan

- Permits may be granted to enter the Area to carry out biological monitoring and area inspection activities, which may involve the collection of a small number of samples or data for analysis or review.

- Any specific sites of long-term monitoring shall be appropriately marked on site and on maps of the Area. To help maintain the ecological and scientific values of the Area, visitors shall take special precautions against introductions. Of particular concern are microbial, animal or vegetation introductions sourced from soils, from other Antarctic sites, including stations, or from regions outside Antarctica. To the maximum extent practicable, visitors should ensure that footwear, clothing and any equipment particularly camping and sampling equipnment· is thoroughly cleaned before entering the Area.

- To avoid interference with long-term research and monitoring activities or duplication of effort, persons planning new projects within the Area should consult with established programs and/or appropriate national authorities.

7 (xi) Requirements for reports

- The principal permit holder for each visit to the Area shall submit a report to the appropriate national authority as soon as practicable, and no later than six months after the visit has been completed.

- Such reports should include, as appropriate, the information identified in the visit report form contained in the Guide to the Preparation of Management Plans for Antarctic Specially Protected Areas.

- Parties should maintain a record of such activities and, in the Annual Exchange of Information, should provide summary descriptions of activities conducted by persons subject to their jurisdiction, which should be in sufficient detail to allow evaluation of the effectiveness of the management plan.

- Parties should, wherever possible, deposit originals or copies of such original reports in a publicly accessible archive to maintain a record of usage, to be used both in any review of the management plan and in organizing the scientific use of the Area.

8. Supporting documentation

Akiyama, M. 1985. Biogeographic distribution of freshwater algae in Antarctica, and special reference to the occurrence of an endemic species of *Oegonium*. Mem. Fac. Edu., Shimane Univ., 19, 1-15.

Hirano, M. 1979. Freshwater algae from Yukidori Zawa, near Syowa Station, Antarctica. Mem. Natl Inst. Polar Res., Spec. Issue 11: 1-25.

Inoue, M. 1989. Factors influencing the existence of lichens in the ice-free areas near Syowa Station, East Antarctica. Proc. NIPR Symp. Polar Biol., 2, 167-180.

Ino, Y. and Nakatsubo, T. 1986. Distribution of carbon, nitrogen and phosphorus in a moss community-soil system developed on a cold desert in Antarctica. Ecol. Res., 1:59-69.

Ino, Y. 1994. Field measurement of the photosynthesis of mosses with a portable CO_2 porometer at Langhovde, East Antarctica. Antarct. Rec., 38, 178-184.

Ishikawa, T., Tatsumi,T., Kizaki, K., Yanai, K., Yoshida, M., Ando, H., Kikuchi, T., Yoshida, Y. and Matsumoto, Y. 1976. Langhovde. Antarct. Geol. Map Ser., 5 (with explanatory text, 10 p.), Tokyo, Natl Inst. Polar Res.

Kanda, H. 1987. Moss vegetation in the Yukidori Valley, Langhovde, East Antarctica. Papers on Plant Ecology and Taxonomy to the Memory of Dr. Satoshi Nakanishi. Kobe Botanical Society, Kobe, 17-204.

Kanda, H. and Inoue, M. 1994. Ecological monitoring of moss and lichen vegetation in the Syowa Station area, Antarctica. Mem. NIPR Symp. Polar Biol., 7: 221-231.

Kanda, H. and Ohtani, S. 1991. Morphology of the aquatic mosses collected in lake Yukidori, Langhovde, Antarctica. Proc., NIPR Symp., Polar Biol., 4, 114-122.

Kanda, H., Inoue, M., Mochida, Y., Sugawara, H., Ino, Y., Ohtani, S. and Ohyama, Y. 1990. Biological studies on ecosystems in the Yukidori Valley., Langhovde, East Antarctica. Antarct. Rec., 34, 76-93.

Matsuda, T. 1968. Ecological study of the moss community and microorganisms in the vicinity of Syowa Station, Antarctica. JARE Sci. Rep., Ser. E. (Biol.), 29, 58p.

Nakanishi, S. 1977. Ecological studies of the moss and lichen communities in the ice-free areas near Syowa Station, Antarctica. Antarct. Rec. 59, 68-96.

Nakatsubo, T. and Ino, Y. 1986. Nitrogen cycling in an Antarctic ecosystem. I. Biological nitrogen fixation in the vicinity of Syowa Station. Mem. Natl Inst. Polar Res., Ser. E. 37:1-10.

Ohtani, S. 1986. Epiphytic algae on mosses in the vicinity of Syowa Station, Antarctica. Mem. Natl. Inst. Polar Res., Spec. Issue 44:209-219.

Ohtani, S., Akiyama, M. and Kanda, H. 1991. Analysis of Antarctic soil algae by the direct observation using the contact slide method. Antarctic. Rec. 35, 285-295.

Ohtani, S., Kanda, H. and Ino, Y. 1990. Microclimate data measured at the Yukidori Valley, Langhovde, Antarctica in 1988-1989. JARE Data Rep., 152 (Terrestrial Biol. 1), 216p.

Ohtani, S., Kanda, H., Ohyama, Y., Mochida, Y., Sugawara, H. and Ino, Y. 1992. Meteorological data measured at biological hut, the Yukidori Valley, Langhovde, Antarctica in the austral summer of 1987-1988 and 1988-1989. JARE Data Rep., 178 (Terrestrial Biol., 3), 64p.

Ohyama, Y. and Matsuda, T. 1977. Free-living prostigmatic mites found around Syowa Station, East Antarctica. Antarct. Rec., 21:172-176.

Ohyama, Y. and Sugawara, H. 1989. An occurrence of cryptostigmatic mite around Syowa Station area. Proc. Int. Symp. Antarct. Rec., pp.324-328. China, Ocean Press. Tianjin.

Sugawara, H., Ohyama, Y. and Higashi, S. 1995. Distribution and temperature tolerance of the

Antarctic free-living mire Antarcticola meyeri (Acari, Cryptostigmata). Polar Biol., 15: 1-8.

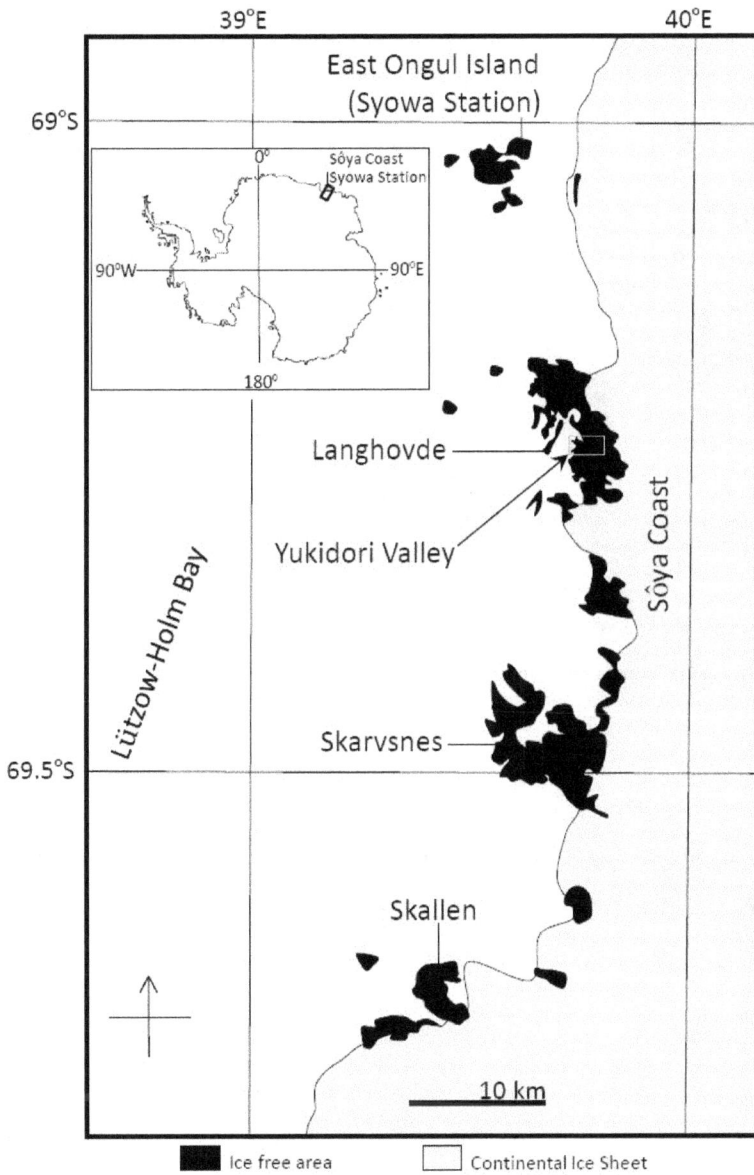

Map 1. The map of Soya Coast, Lutzow-Holm Bay, East Antarctica.
Universal Transverse Mercator projection. Spheroid and Datum: WGS84.

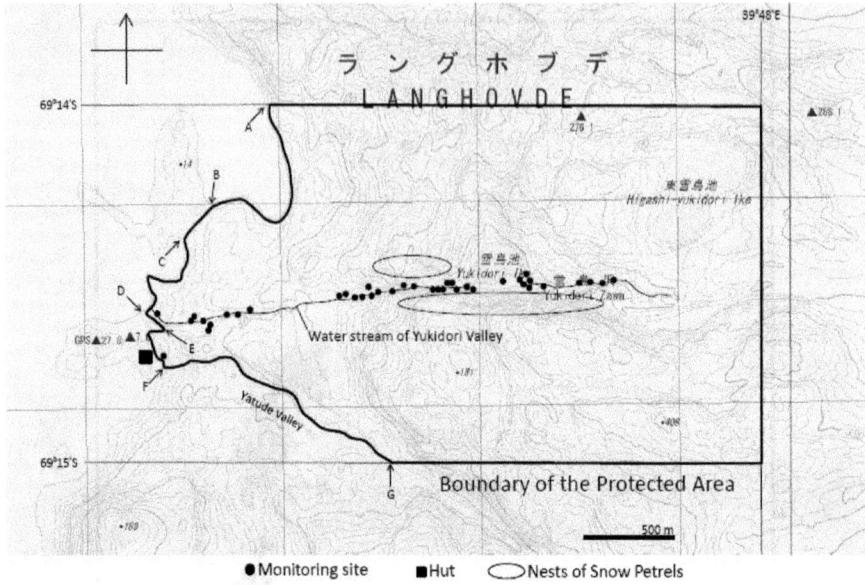

Map 2. Yukidori Zawa Valley, Langhovde and the boundary of the Protected Area. Universal Transverse Mercator projection. Spheroid and Datum: WGS84.

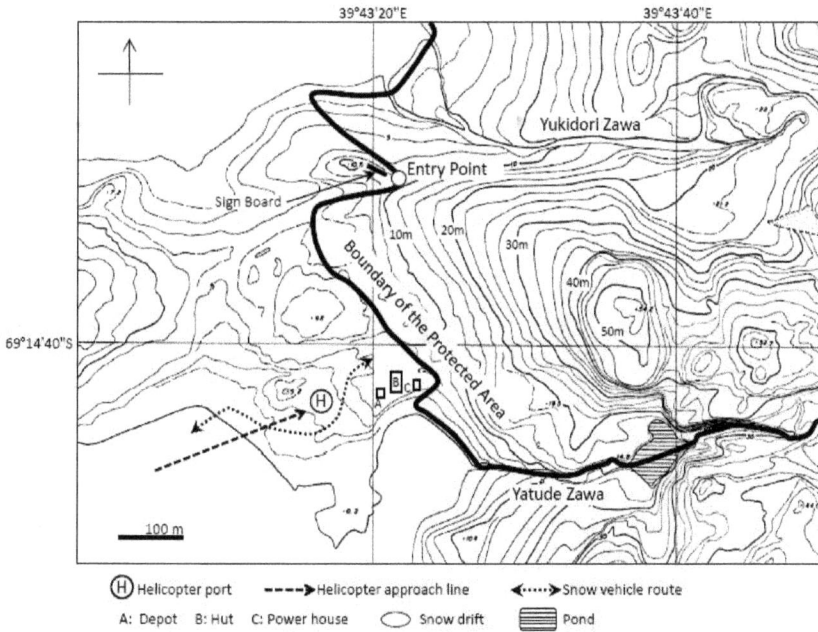

39°43'20"E   39°43'40"E

Yukidori Zawa

Entry Point

Sign Board

10m   20m   30m

40m

50m

69°14'40"S

Boundary of the Protected Area

H

B

Yatude Zawa

100 m

Ⓗ Helicopter port   ➤Helicopter approach line   ◀·····➤ Snow vehicle route

A: Depot   B: Hut   C: Power house   ◯ Snow drift   ▤ Pond

Map 3. The biological research hut and surroundings.
Universal Transverse Mercator projection. Spheroid and Datum: WGS84.

Management Plan for
Antarctic Specially Protected Area No. 142

SVARTHAMAREN

Introduction

Svarthamaren nunatak (71°53'16"S - 5°9'24"E to 71°56'10"S - 5°15'37"E) is part of the Mühlig-Hoffmanfjella in Dronning Maud Land, Antarctica. The ASPA area is approximately y 7.5 km² and consists of the ice-free areas of the Svarthamaren nunatak. Included are also the areas in immediate vicinity of the ice-free areas naturally belonging to the nunatak (i.e. rocks and boulders).

The nunatak has one unique characteristic as it holds the largest known seabird colony in the Antarctica. Between 110,000 and 180,000 pairs of Antarctic petrels (*Thalassoica antarctica*) are breeding annually here and about several hundred of thousands non-breeding of this species are present during breeding season. In addition colonies of more than 1000 pairs of snow petrel (*Pagodroma nivea*) and about 100 pairs of south polar skua (*Catharacta maccormicki*) are found here.

Primary purpose: To avoid human induced changes to the population structure, composition and size of the seabird colonies present at the site, to allow for undisturbed research on the adaptations of the Antarctic petrel, snow petrel and south polar skua to the inland conditions in Antarctica.

1. Description of values to be protected

The Area was originally designated in Recommendation XIV-5 (1987, SSSI No. 23) after a proposal by Norway based on the following factors, which still give relevant grounds for designation:

- the fact that the colony of Antarctic petrel (*Thalassoica antarctica*) is the largest known inland seabird colony on the Antarctic continent
- the fact that the colony constitutes a large proportion of the known world population of Antarctic petrel
- the fact that the colony is an exceptional "natural research laboratory" providing for research on the Antarctic petrel, snow petrel (*Pagodroma nivea*) and south polar skua (*Catharacta maccormicki*), and their adaptation to breeding in the inland/interior of Antarctica

2. Aim and objectives

The aim of managing Svarthamaren is to:

- avoid human induced changes to the population structure, composition and size of the seabird colonies present at the site
- prevent unnecessary disturbance to the seabird colonies, as well as to the surrounding environment
- allow for undisturbed research on the adaptations of the Antarctic petrel, snow petrel and south polar skua to the inland conditions in Antarctica (Primary Research)
- allow access for other scientific reasons where the investigations will not damage the objectives of the bird research

The focus of the *Primary Research* in Svarthamaren ASPA is as follows:
- Improve the understanding of how natural as well as anthropogenic changes in the environment affect the spatial and temporal distribution of animal populations, and, furthermore, how such changes affect the interaction between key species in the Antarctic ecosystem.

3. Management activities

Management activities at Svarthamaren shall:

- ensure that the seabird colonies are adequately monitored, to the maximum extent possible by non-invasive methods
- allow erection of signs/posters, border markers, etc. in connection to the site, and ensure that these are serviced and maintained in good condition
- include visits as necessary to assess whether the Area continues to serve the purposes for which it was designated and to ensure management and maintenance measures are adequate

Any direct intervention management activity in the area must be subject to an environmental impact assessment before any decision to proceed is taken.

4. Period of Designation

Designated for an indefinite period.

5. Maps and Illustrations

Map A: Map of ASPA 142 Svarthamaren in Dronning Maud Land (showing location of Map B 71°53'16"S - 5°9'24"E to 71°56'10"S - 5°15'37"E). Map specifications:

- Projection: Transverse Mercator, UTM zone 31S
- Spheroid: WGS 1984
- (EPSG code: 32731)
- Additionally, the map is rotated 2,5 degrees to the left

Map B:. Svarthamaren – ASPA 142. Boundaries and Main Seabird Concentrations (2014).Map specifications :

- Projection: Transverse Mercator, UTM zone 31S
- Spheroid: WGS 1984
- (EPSG code: 32731)
- Additionally, the map is rotated 2,1 degrees to the left

Map C: Aerial photo of Svarthamaren (1996, Norwegian Polar Institute)

6. Description of Area

6 (i) Geographic co-ordinates, boundary markers and natural features

The Svarthamaren ASPA is situated in Mühlig-Hoffmannfjella, Dronning Maud Land, stretching from approx. 71°53'16"S - 5°9'24"E to the north-east to approx. 71°56'10"S - 5°15'37"E in the south-east. The distance from the ice front is about 200 km. The Area covers approximately 7.5 km^2, and consists of the ice-free areas of the Svarthamaren nunatak, including the areas in the immediate vicinity of the ice-free areas naturally belonging to the nunatak (i.e. rocks). The Area is shown in Map B and C.

The Norwegian field station Tor is located in the Svarthamaren nunatak at lat. 71°53'22"S, 5°9'34"E. The station, including a 10-metre buffer zone around the station buildings, is excluded from the Svarthamaren Antarctic Specially Protected Area. Access to the station is by the shortest route from the ice.

The main rock types in the Area are coarse and medium grained charnockites with small amounts of xenoliths. Included in the charnockitoids are banded gneisses, amphibolites and granites of the amphibolite facies mineralogy. The slopes are covered by decomposed feldspathic sand. The north-eastern side of the Svarthamaren nunatak is dominated by scree slopes (slope 31°-34°), extending 240 metres upwards from the base of the mountain at about 1600 metres above sea level. The major features of this area are two rock amphitheatres inhabited by breeding Antarctic petrels. It is this area which makes up the core of the protected site.

No continuous weather observations have been carried through in the Area, but prevalent air temperature has been observed to range between -5° and -15°C in January, with somewhat lower minimum temperatures in February.

The flora and vegetation at Svarthamaren are sparse compared with other areas in Mühlig-Hofmannfjella and Gjelsvikfjella to the west of the site. The only plant species occurring in abundance, but peripherally to the most manured areas, is the foliose green alga, *Prasiola crispa*. There are a few lichen species on glacier-borne erratics 1-2 km away from the bird colonies: *Candelariella hallettensis* (= *C. antarctica*), *Rhizoplaca* (= *Lecanora*) *melanophthalma*, *Umbilicaria* spp. and *Xanthoria* spp. Areas covered with *Prasiola* are inhabited by collembola ASPA No. 142: Svarthamaren *Cryptopygus sverdrupi*) and a rich fauna of mites (*Eupodes anghardi, Tydeus erebus*) protozoan, nematodes and rotifers. A shallow pond measuring about 20 x 30 m, lying below the middle and largest bird sub-colony at Svarthamaren, is heavily polluted by petrel carcasses, and supports a strong growth of a yellowish-green unicellular algae, *Chlamydomonas*, sp. No aquatic invertebrates have yet been recorded.

The colonies of breeding seabirds are the most conspicuous biological element in the Area. The north-eastern slopes of Svarthamaren are occupied by a densely populated colony of Antarctic petrels (*Thalassoica antarctica*) divided into three separate sub-colonies.

The total number of breeding pairs is estimated to be approximately 100,000 and 200,000 pairs, with large inter-annual fluctuations. In addition, more than 1000 pairs of snow petrels (*Pagodroma nivea*) and approximately 100 pairs of south polar skuas (*Catharacta maccormicki*) breed in the area. The two main colonies of Antarctic petrels are situated in the two rocky amphitheatres. The main colonies of snow petrels are located in separate parts of the scree-slope that are characterised by larger rocks. The south polar skuas nest on the narrow strip of flat, snow-free ground below the scree-slopes.

The main concentrations of seabirds are indicated on Map B. Readers should, however, be aware that birds are also found in other areas than these densely populated areas.

Based on the Environmental Domains Analysis for Antarctica (2007, Morgan et al.) both Environments T-Inland continental geologic - and U- North Victoria Land geologic - are found to be represented at Svarthamaren (2009, Harry Keys, pers. comm.). Svarthamaren belongs to Antarctic Conservation Biogeographic Region 6 – Dronning Maud Land (ACBR 6) (2012, Aleks Terauds et al.).

6 (ii) Restricted zones within the Area

None

6 (iii) Location of structures within the Area

A weather station is located at the edge of the main petrel colony. During the austral winter only the mast (2 meters high) remains, while the station proper is installed during the summer season. The mast has not been permanently fixed into the ground and can easily be removed. With this exception there are no structures within the Area.

The Norwegian field station Tor is located on the Svarthamaren nunatak, at 71°53'22"S, 5°9'34"E. The station, including a 10 meter buffer zone around the station buildings, is excluded from the Area.

6 (iv) Location of other Protected Areas within close proximity

None

7. Permit Conditions

Permits may be issued only by appropriate national authorities as designated under Annex V, Article 7 of the Protocol on Environmental Protection to the Antarctic Treaty. Conditions for issuing a permit to enter the Area are that:

- the actions permitted are in accordance with this Management Plan
- the permit, or a copy, shall be carried within the area
- any permit issued shall be valid for a stated period
- a visit report is supplied to the authority named in the permit

7 (i) Access to and movement within the Area

Access to the area is restricted by the following conditions:

- No pedestrian routes are designated, but persons on foot shall at all times avoid disturbances to birds, and as far as possible also to the sparse vegetation cover in the Area.
- Vehicles should not enter the site.
- No flying of helicopters or other aircraft over the Area is allowed.
- Helicopter landings are not allowed within the boundaries of the ASPA. Landings associated with activities at the field station Tor should preferably take place at the north-eastern tip of the Svarthamaren nunatak (as marked on map C).

7 (ii) Activities that are or may be conducted within the Area, including restrictions on time and place

The following activities may be conducted within the Area in accordance with permit:

- Primary biological research programs for which the area was designated.
- Other research programs of a compelling scientific nature that will not interfere with the bird research in the Area.

7 (iii) Installation, modification or removal of structures

No structures are to be erected in the Area, or scientific equipment installed, except for equipment essential for scientific or management activities as specified in a permit, or for modification of the field station, also as specified in a permit.

7 (iv) Location of field camps

No field camps should be established within the Area. (Cf. 6 iii)

7 (v) Restrictions on materials and organisms which may be brought into the Area

- No living animals or plant material shall be deliberately introduced into the Area.
- No poultry products, including food products containing uncooked dried eggs, shall be taken into the Area.
- No herbicides or pesticides shall be brought into the Area. Any other chemicals (including fuel), which may be introduced for a compelling scientific purpose specified in the permit, shall be removed from the Area before or at the conclusion of the activity for which the permit was granted. (cf. 6 iii). Limited fuel storage at the field station Tor is acceptable, taking into account that the station and its immediate surroundings are not part of the Area.
- All materials introduced shall be for a stated period, shall be removed at or before the conclusion of that stated period, and shall be stored and handled so that risk of their introduction into the environment is minimized.

7 (vi) Taking or harmful interference with native flora and fauna

Taking or harmful interference with native flora and fauna is prohibited, except in accordance with a permit issued in accordance with Annex II to the Protocol of Environmental Protection to the Antarctic Treaty. Where taking or harmful interference with animals is involved, *SCAR Code of Conduct for Use of Animals for Scientific Purposes in Antarctica* should be used as a minimum standard.

It is recommended that those responsible for the primary research in the Area should be consulted before a permit is granted for taking of birds for purposes not associated with the primary research. Studies requiring taking of birds for other purposes should be planned and carried through in such a manner that it will not interfere with the objectives of the bird research in the Area. ASPA No. 142: Svarthamaren

7 (vii) Collection and removal of anything not brought into the Area by the Permit holder

Material may be collected or removed from the Area only in accordance with a permit, except that debris of man-made origin should be removed and that dead specimens of fauna may be removed for laboratory examination.

7 (viii) Disposal of waste

All wastes are to be removed from the area.

7 (ix) Measures that may be necessary to ensure that the aims and objectives of the Management Plan continue to be met

Permits may be granted to enter the Area to carry out biological monitoring and site inspection activities which may involve the collection of small amounts of plant material or small numbers of animals for analysis or audit, to erect or maintain notice boards, to maintain the field station, or to undertake protective measures.

7 (x) Requirements for reports

Parties should ensure that the principal holder of each permit issued submit to the appropriate authority a report describing the activities undertaken. Such reports should include, as appropriate, the information identified in the Visit Report form suggested by SCAR. Parties should maintain a record of such activities and, in the Annual Exchange of Information, should provide summary descriptions of activities conducted by persons subject to their jurisdiction, which should be in sufficient detail to allow evaluation of the effectiveness of the Management Plan. Parties should, wherever possible, deposit originals or copies of such original reports in a publicly accessible archive to maintain a record of usage, to be used both in any review of the management plan and in organizing the scientific use of the Area.

Bibliography

Amundsen, T. 1995. Egg size and early nestling growth in the snow petrel. *Condor* 97: 345-351.

Amundsen, T., Lorentsen, S.H. & Tveraa, T. 1996. Effects of egg size and parental quality on early nestling growth: An experiment with the Antarctic petrel. *Journal of Animal Ecology* 65: 545-555.

Andersen, R., Sæther, B.E. & Pedersen, H.C. 1995. Regulation of parental investment in the Antarctic petrel *Thalassoica antarctica*: An experiment. Polar Biology 15:65-68

Andersen, R., Sæther, B.-E. & Pedersen, H.C. 1993. Resource limitation in a long-lived seabird, the Antarctic petrel *Thalassoica antarctica*: a twinning experiment. Fauna Norwegica, Serie C 16:15-18

Bech, C., Mehlum, F. & Haftorn, S. 1988. Development of chicks during extreme cold conditions: the Antarctic petrel *Thalassioca antarctica*. Proceedings of the 19'th International Ornithological Congress:1447-1456

Brooke, M.D., Keith, D. & Røv, N. 1999. Exploitation of inland-breeding Antarctic petrels by south polar skuas. *OECOLOGIA* 121: 25-31

Fauchald, P. & Tveraa, T. 2003. Using first-passage time in the analysis of area restricted search and habitat selection. Ecology 84:282-288

Fauchald P. & Tveraa T. 2006. Hierarchical patch dynamics and animal movement pattern. *Oecologia*, 149, 383-395

Haftorn, S., Beck, C. & Mehlum, F. 1991. Aspects of the breeding biology of the Antartctic petrel (*Thalassoica antarctica*) and krill requirements of the chicks, at Svarthamaren in Mühlig-Hofmannfjella, Dronning Maud Land. Fauna Norwegica, Serie C. Sinclus 14:7-22

Haftorn, S,, Mehlum, F. & Bech, C. 1988. Navigation to nest site in the snow petrel (Pagodrom nivea). Condor 90:484-486

Lorentsen, S.H. & Røv, N. 1994. Sex determination of Antarctic petrels *Thalassoica antarctica* by discriminant analysis of morphometric characters. Polar Biology 14:143-145

Lorentsen, S.H. & Røv, N. 1995. Incubation and brooding performance of the Antarctic petrel (*Thalassoica antarctica*) at Svarthamaren, Dronning Maud Land. *Ibis* 137: 345-351.

Lorentsen, S.H., Klages, N. & Røv, N. 1998. Diet and prey consumption of Antarctic petrels *Thalassoica antarctica* at Svarthamaren, Dronning Maud Land, and at sea outside the colony. *Polar Biology* 19: 414-420.

Lorentsen, S.H. 2000. Molecular evidence for extra-pair paternity and female-female pairs in Antarctic petrels. Auk 117:1042-1047

Morgan, F., Barker, G., Briggs, C. Price, R., Keys, H. 2007. Environmental Domains of Antarctica, Landcare Research New Zealand Ltd

Nygård,T., Lie, E., Røv, N., *et al.* 2001. Metal dynamics in an Antarctic food chain. *Mar. Pollut. Bull.* 42: 598-602

Ohta, Y., Torudbakken, B.O. & Shiraishi, K. 1990. Geology of Gjelsvikfjella and Western Muhlig-Hofmannfjella, Dronning Maud Land, East Antarctica. *Polar Research* 8: 99-126.

Steele, W.K., Pilgrim, R.L.C. & Palma, R.L. 1997. Occurrence of the flea Glaciopsyllus antarcticus and avian lice in central Dronning Maud Land. *Polar Biology* 18: 292-294.

Sæther, B.E., Lorentsen, S.H., Tveraa, T. *et al.* 1997.Size-dependent variation in reproductive success of a long-lived seabird, the Antarctic petrel (*Thalassoica antarctica*). *AUK* 114 (3): 333-340.

Sæther, B.-E., Andersen, R. & Pedersen, H.C. 1993. Regulation of parental effort in a long-lived seabird: An experimental study of the costs of reproduction in the Antarctic petrel (*Thalassoica Antarctica)*. Behavioral Ecology and Sociobiology 33:147-150

Terauds, A., Chown, S. L., Morgan, F, Peat, H.J., Watts, D. J., Keys, H, Convey, P. , Bergstrom, D.M. 2012. Conservation biogeography of the Antarctic. Diversity and Distributions: 1–16.

Tveraa, T., Lorentsen, S.H. & Saether, B.E. 1997. Regulation of foraging trips and costs of incubation shifts in the Antarctic petrel (*Thalassoica antarctica*). *Behavioral Ecology* 8: 465-469.

Tveraa, T. & Christensen, G.N. 2002. Body condition and parental decisions in the Snow Petrel (*Pagodroma nivea*). *AUK* 119: 266-270.

Tveraa, T., Sæther, B.E., Aanes, R. & Erikstad, K.E. 1998. Regulation of food provisioning in the Antarctic petrel; the importance of parental body condition and chick body mass. *Journal of Animal Ecology* 67: 699-704.

Tveraa, T., Sæther, B.-E., Aanes, R. & Erikstad, K.E. 1998. Body mass and parental decisions in the Antarctic petrel *Thalassoica antarctica*: how long should the parents guard the chick? Behavioral Ecology and Sociobiology 43:73-79

Varpe, Ø., Tveraa, T. & Folstad, I. 2004. State-dependent parental care in the Antarctic petrel: responses to manipulated chick age during early chick rearing. Oikos, in press ASPA No. 142: Svarthamaren

MAP A: Map of ASPA 142 Svarthamaren in Dronning Maud Land

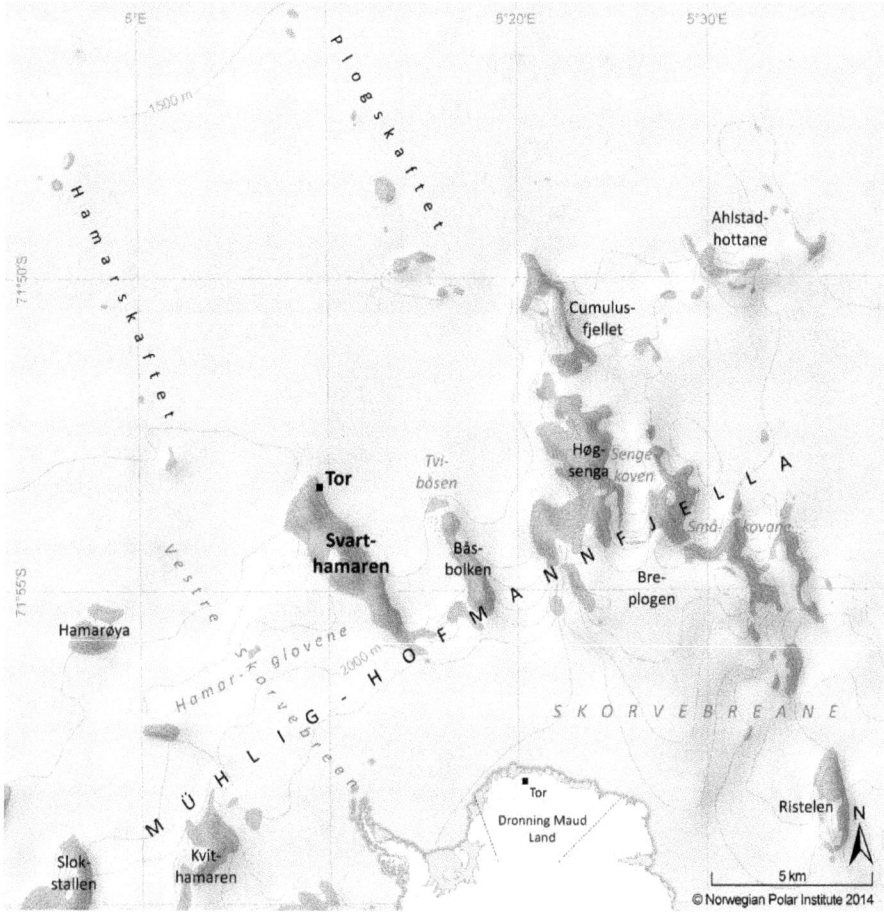

Map B: Svarthamaren – ASPA No. 142. Boundaries and Main Seabird Concentrations (2014).

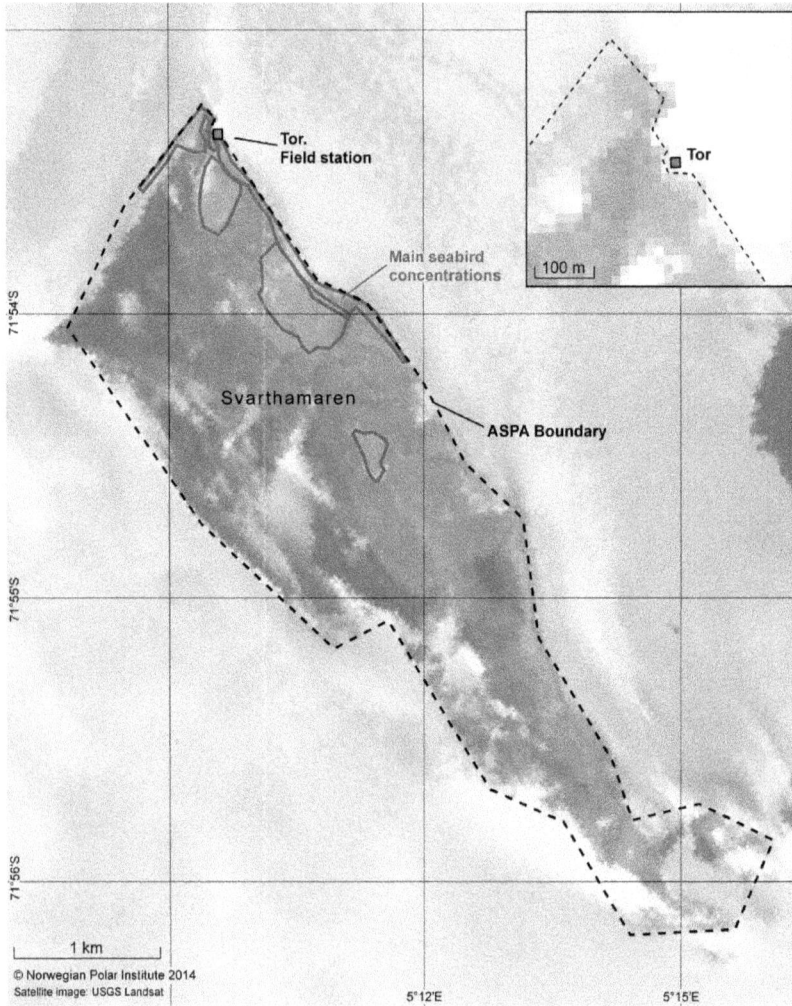

Map C: Aerial Photograph of Svarthamaren ASPA 142 (1996, Norwegian Polar Institute)

Management Plan for
Antarctic Specially Protected Area No. 162

MAWSON'S HUTS, CAPE DENISON, COMMONWEALTH BAY, GEORGE V LAND, EAST ANTARCTICA

Introduction

Cape Denison, Commonwealth Bay (67°00'31"S 142°40'43"E) is one of the principal sites of early human activity in Antarctica. It is the location of four timber huts, known as 'Mawson's Huts', which served as the base of the Australasian Antarctic Expedition (AAE) of 1911-14 organised and led by Dr (later Sir) Douglas Mawson. An important symbol of the 'heroic age' of Antarctic exploration (1895-1917), Cape Denison is one of only six hut sites remaining from this period. Cape Denison hosted some of the earliest comprehensive studies of Antarctic geology, geography, terrestrial magnetism, astronomy, meteorology, glaciology, oceanography, biology, zoology and botany. It was also the base of numerous explorations inland and features artefacts associated with these sledging parties, including food caches and equipment.

Cape Denison is characterised by four valleys aligned northwest/southeast. The majority of Australasian Antarctic Expedition artefacts, including Mawson's Huts and other structures, are concentrated in the westernmost valley and on the ridges on either side of the valley (see Map A).

In recognition of the rarity and richness of this social, cultural and scientific resource, the Mawson's Huts site (comprising the four huts and a 5 metre buffer around each hut) was designated under Measure 2 (2004) as Antarctic Specially Protected Area (ASPA) No. 162, to protect the important historical, technical, architectural and aesthetic value of the four AAE huts. The ASPA also contains the site designated under Measure 3 (2004) as Historic Site and Monument No. 77 Cape Denison, Commonwealth Bay, George V Land, and was originally embedded within Antarctic Specially Managed Area (ASMA) No. 3 Cape Denison, Commonwealth Bay, George V Land, designated under Measure 1 (2004).

Under Measure XX (2014), ASMA No. 3 was de-designated and the boundary of ASPA No. 162 was expanded to coincide with the previous ASMA boundary. This provides additional protection for the historic landscape and artefact scatters at Cape Denison, and simplifies the management arrangements for the site.

Cape Denison is subject to a relatively low level of human activity, but does receive periodic visits during summer months by small conservation works teams and commercial tour groups. Visitor Site Guidelines adopted under Resolution 4 (2011) are in place for the site.

1. Description of values to be protected

The ASPA is primarily designated to protect Mawson's Huts and the associated landscape which has considerable historic, archaeological, technical, social and aesthetic values. The building form of the huts themselves shows the functional and efficient planning that was undertaken in response to the site position and the elements endured by the expedition members. The weathering of the huts and the decay of the remains gives a feeling of time elapsed and exposure to the elements.

Historic value

Cape Denison provides the setting for the buildings, structures and relics of the Main Base of the Australasian Antarctic Expedition (AAE) of 1911–14, led by Dr Douglas Mawson. Mawson's Huts is one of a group of only six sites of 'heroic age' huts where pragmatic consideration of the need to provide permanent shelter in the Antarctic environment resulted in an expedition hut structure suitable for Polar Regions.

Mawson's prime focus was scientific research. Nevertheless, the expedition also had an exploratory agenda, with the aim of charting the entire Antarctic coastline immediately south of Australia. For this purpose at least five sledging expeditions were undertaken from Cape Denison from spring 1912, including the infamous Far-Eastern Sledging Party during which expeditioners Belgrave, Ninnis and Xavier Mertz perished, and Mawson himself barely survived. Overall, more than 6,500 km of coastline and hinterland was explored by sledging parties of the Expedition.

Cape Denison contains numerous relics relating to the work of Mawson's expedition, including Mawson's Huts and other significant and relatively untouched artefacts from the 'heroic age'. While the majority is concentrated in the westernmost valley and its immediate surrounds, the historical boundaries of the Main Base extend further. Artefacts and other evidence of occupation, such as food caches, extend across the entire Cape, forming a rich resource of material available for research and interpretation, and potentially yielding scientific data and information about aspects of expeditioner life not included in official written accounts.

Mawson's Huts were built in January, February and March 1912 and May 1913. In their surviving form and setting the huts illustrate the isolation and harsh environment of Cape Denison. They also demonstrate the cramped internal conditions endured by expedition members. The living quarters in the Main Hut, for example, a single space measuring 7.3m x 7.3m, provided sleeping and kitchen facilities for 18 men.

The external form and internal structure of the largest hut, known as the Main Hut (67°00'31"S, 142°39'39"E), are a simple but strong architectural concept: a square base topped by a pyramid roof (to prevent damage by blizzards), with skylights to provide natural lighting. Following the decision to combine two expedition bases into one, a hip-roofed accommodation hut measuring 5.5m x 4.9m was adjoined to the living quarters and equipped as a workshop. A 1.5m wide verandah surrounded the structure on three sides, under the same roof. The verandah was used as a storage space that also assisted in insulating the hut from the weather.

The two huts that form the Main Hut were built of Oregon timber frames clad with Baltic pine tongue-and-groove boards. They were prefabricated in Australia, and on-site construction was assisted by a branded letter code on framing members and coded colours painted on board ends. (None of the expedition party had any previous construction experience). The survival of the Main Hut at one of the windiest sites on Earth is testimony to the strength of its design and care of its construction.

Mawson's Huts contain numerous significant and relatively untouched artefacts from the 'heroic age', which form a rich resource of material available for research and interpretation, and potentially yielding information about aspects of expeditioner life not included in official written accounts.

The three other AAE huts are:

- The Absolute Magnetic Hut (67°00'23"S, 142°39'48"E), constructed during February 1912. It measured 1.8m x 1.8m in plan with a skillion roof and had an Oregon timber frame to which boards of remnant timber were fixed. The hut was used in association with, and as a reference point for, observations made in the Magnetograph House. Today it is considered to be a standing ruin.
- The Magnetograph House (67°00'21"S, 142°39'37"E) was erected in March 1912 to house equipment used to measure variations in the South Magnetic Pole. It measures 5.5m x 2m with a shallow pitched skillion roof and no windows. After the first building attempt was demolished by

high winds, large rocks were heaped against the new hut to provide a wind barrier. Sheepskin and hessian attached to the roof also assisted in keeping the internal temperature constant and in minimising the ingress of drift snow. These innovations may have contributed to the relatively intact condition of the hut today.

- Construction of the Transit Hut (67°00'30"S, 142°39'42"E) commenced in May 1913, with packing case timbers being affixed to an Oregon frame. The structure was also clad in sheepskin and canvas. Originally known as the Astronomical Observatory, the hut housed the theodolite used to take star sights to determine the exact longitude of Cape Denison. It is now considered to be a standing ruin.

Aesthetic values

The Area is designated to preserve not only the artefacts remaining in situ but also the cultural landscape of Cape Denison in which Mawson and his men lived and worked. Cape Denison is characterised by its almost incessant blizzard conditions, which severely limit access to the region and activities at the site. Katabatic winds pour down the plateau and funnel through the Cape's valleys; blasting the hut with gusts that in May 1912 reached 322 km/h. (The average wind speed for the month was 98 km/h). Cape Denison is not only the windiest place in Antarctica, but also the windiest place on Earth at sea level. The site thus demonstrates the physical and symbolic context of the extreme isolation and harsh conditions endured by the expedition members and, by association, all other 'heroic age' researchers and explorers. In designating the entire area as an ASPA, Cape Denison's unique 'sense of place' is protected, with Mawson's Huts and Boat Harbour as the focus of the visual catchment.

Educational values

Cape Denison's wildlife and undisturbed artefacts, framed against the dramatic backdrop of the Antarctic Plateau, represent significant educational values. The Area's isolation and extreme weather provide visitors with a unique insight into the conditions endured by 'heroic age' researchers and explorers, and a chance to form a deeper appreciation of their achievements.

Environmental values

The paucity of relatively ice-free areas in the immediate region means that Cape Denison represents an important assemblage of life forms (Appendix A). The closest ice-free areas of similar or greater size to Cape Denison are approximately 20 km to the east of Cape Denison (from the centre of the ASPA), and approximately 60 km to the west. A haul-out site for Weddell, leopard and elephant seals, the Cape is also an important breeding area for Adélie penguins, Wilson's storm-petrels, snow petrels and south polar skuas.

Flora at Cape Denison is represented by 13 lichen species distributed on boulders and other moraines throughout the peninsula. These species are listed at Appendix A to the management plan for ASPA 162. No bryophytes are evident. The lichens' distribution on rocks, which are subject to different patterns of snow ablation, makes them vulnerable to trampling and other interference by visitors, however infrequent visitation may be.

Cape Denison has 13 small lakes. These are associated with glacial action, are a permanent feature, and are frozen over for most of the year. Since such lakes are also susceptible to physical, chemical and biological modification within their catchment boundaries, a catchment-based approach to the management of human activities is required.

Scientific values

Mawson, a geologist, planned his expedition in order to examine the theories about continental connection and the processes of glaciation and climate. He also sought to study the South Magnetic Pole and magnetic charting for navigational purposes; to conduct biological studies, including the identification of new species; and to establish a weather station.

Cape Denison provides opportunities to repeat Mawson's experiments and conduct further research into magnetism, meteorology, biology, and other sciences. For example, although Antarctic lakes are generally recognised as valuable due to their relatively simple natural ecosystems, the lakes at Cape Denison have neither been sampled nor their biota studied. There are also numerous non-marine algae present; however, no surveys have been undertaken. The records from Mawson's expedition provide a dataset against which the results of modern research may be compared, and the site's isolation lends it considerable value for future use as a reference site for other areas that experience a greater level of human activities

2. Aims and objectives

The aim of the Management Plan is to provide protection for the Area so that the identified values can be preserved. Management of the Area aims to:

- maintain the historic values of the Area through planned conservation[1] and archaeological work programmes;
- allow management activities which support the protection of the values and features of the Area, its features and artefacts through managed access to the huts;
- allow activities in the Area for educational and outreach purposes (including tourism), provided that such activities are for compelling reasons which cannot be served elsewhere and which will not jeopardise the cultural values and natural ecological systems in the Area;
- allow scientific research; and
- avoid degradation of, or substantial risk to, the values of the Area by preventing unnecessary human disturbance to the Area, its features and artefacts by means of managed access to the four Australasian Antarctic Expedition huts and surrounding artefact scatters.

3. Management activities

The following management activities may be undertaken to protect the values of the Area:

- research and other activities essential or desirable for understanding, protecting and maintaining the values of the Area
- programmes of conservation and archaeological work and environmental monitoring work on Mawson's Huts and any artefacts contained within the huts and found in the Area;
- the removal of objects not related to the AAE of 1911–14 and/or the British Australian New Zealand Antarctic Research Expeditions (BANZARE) of 1929–31 and that compromise the historic and aesthetic values of the Area, provided that removal does not adversely impact on the values of the Area, and that the objects are appropriately documented prior to removal. Priority should be given to the removal of field infrastructure from the Visual Protection Zone, giving consideration to the needs (including those of safety) of conservation workers and the program of conservation works;

---

[1] In the context of this Management Plan the term *conservation* "means all the processes of looking after a place so as to retain its cultural significance", as defined in Article 1.4 , of The Burra Charter: The Australian ICOMOS Burra Charter, 1999.

- essential maintenance of other objects and infrastructure, including the Automatic Weather Station;
- visits made as necessary for management purposes;
- review of the Management Plan at least once every five (5) years, and update as required;
- consultation among national Antarctic programs operating in the region, or those with an interest or experience in Antarctic historic site management, with a view to ensuring the above provisions are implemented effectively.

4. Period of designation

This ASPA is designated for an indefinite period.

5. Maps

Map A: Mawson's Huts, Cape Denison.

The map shows the boundaries of the ASPA, the Historic Site, the Visual Protection Zone, and significant topographic features of the Area. The inset map indicates the location in relation to the Antarctic continent.

Map B: Cape Denison Visual Protection Zone.

The map shows the boundaries of the Visual Protection Zone and indicates the position of significant historic artefacts, including the four Australasian Antarctic Expedition huts, the Memorial Cross, and Anemometer Hill, the site of the BANZARE Proclamation Pole.

Map C: Cape Denison Flight Paths and Bird Colonies.

The map indicates the approaches, departures and landing site for helicopters, as well as the location of bird colonies in the vicinity.

Specification for all maps:

> Projection: UTM Zone 54
> Horizontal Datum: WGS84

6. Description of the Area

6(i) Geographical coordinates, boundary markers and natural features

Cape Denison (142°40'6"E—67°00'35"S) is located on the coast of Commonwealth Bay, a 60 km-wide stretch of coast in George V Land some 3,000 km south of Hobart, Australia. The Cape itself is a rugged, 1.5 km-wide tongue of ice, snow, rock and moraine projecting into Commonwealth Bay from the steeply rising wall of the ice cap of continental Antarctica. On the western side of the Cape is Boat Harbour, a 330m-long indentation in the coast.

The designated ASPA (Map A) extends from Land's End (67° 00' 47" S, 142° 39' 28" E) in the west, along the coastline to the northern tip of the western shore of Boat Harbour (67° 00' 21" S, 142° 39' 28" E), across the mouth of Boat Harbour (in a straight north-easterly diagonal) to the eastern shore of Boat Harbour (67° 00' 21" S, 142° 39' 27" E), south-west of Penguin Knob, and then along the coastline in a south-easterly direction down to John O'Groats (67° 00' 47" S, 142° 41' 27" E). The southern boundary extends in a straight line from Land's End to John O'Groats along latitude 67° 00' 47" S. With the exception of the boundary across the mouth of Boat Harbour, the northern coastal boundary extends to that land above the lowest tide.

The shoreline and the ice cliffs at both ends of the Cape (Land's End and John O'Groats) form a clearly defined boundary; as such, no boundary markers have been installed because the coast is a clearly defined boundary.

Environmental domains and biogeographic regions
Based on the Environmental Domains Analysis for Antarctica (Resolution 3 (2008)) the Area is located within Environment L Continental coastal-zone ice sheet. The Area is not classified in accordance with the Antarctic Conservation Biogeographic Regions identified in Resolution 6 (2012).

Natural features: Topography and geomorphology

The topography of Cape Denison is defined by a series of four rocky ridges, running south- southeast to north-northwest, and three valleys. The largest, most westerly of these valleys contains the AAE buildings. The basement rock of the Cape Denison area consists of partially migmatised, massive felsic orthogneiss intruded about 2350 million years ago (Ma) into an older metamorphosed sequence. Above the basement the area features a lower zone of relatively polished rock and a higher zone of relatively unpolished rock; the former being especially prominent below 12 metres above sea level and indicative of more recent uplift and exposure than the upper zone. Upper and lower moraines are apparent, with the upper moraine, closer to the edge of plateau, containing a diversity of angular boulders. The lower moraine is dominated by local rocks sorted into bands, perhaps the result of an 'ice push' from the sea rather than being genuine glacial moraine.

Water bodies

Cape Denison contains 13 small glacial lakes, which are generally oriented parallel to the foliation of the basement rocks. At the height of summer Cape Denison also features numerous melt streams which flow into Commonwealth Bay. It is not known whether the streams flow down established courses, or whether the streams are a feature of the regular freeze/thaw cycle.

Biological features

Cape Denison is the summer habitat for breeding Adélie penguins, Wilson's storm-petrels, snow petrels and the south polar skua (Map C). Other species sighted in the area include the Cape petrel, Antarctic petrel, southern giant petrel and emperor penguin. A full list of species and number of breeding pairs (where available) is attached as Appendix B. Weddell seals, southern elephant seals and leopard seals have been recorded as hauling out and, in the case of elephant seals, moulting at Cape Denison. However, the sporadic nature of visits to the Area means that monitoring has been inconsistent and the exact extent of the seal population uncertain. Some data is presented in Appendix B(ii).

The only flora evident at Cape Denison is lichens, for which a list of species is included at Appendix A and non-marine algae, which have yet to be studied.

6(ii) Access to the Area

Sea, land and air access to Mawson's Huts is difficult due to the rugged topography and climate of the area. Sea ice extent and uncharted bathymetry may constrain ship access up to 10nm or more from the coastline. Access can be gained either by small watercraft or by helicopter, although attempts to land are frequently hampered by heavy seas and prevailing north-westerly or katabatic winds. Boat landings can be made at Boat Harbour and due north of Sørensen Hut. The helicopter landing site (67°0'30"S, 142°39'19"E) and approach and departure flight paths are indicated on Map

C.

Travel within the ASPA is to be on foot, except where vehicle use is authorised for work parties, in accordance with the terms and conditions of entry described in Section 7(ii). Pedestrian access within the Area is unrestricted except in places where AAE buildings, artefacts, or bird or lichen colonies are present, and should be conducted in accordance with the terms and condition of entry. With the exception of a short boardwalk close to the Main Hut, there are no roads or other transportation infrastructure on shore. The boardwalk is frequently covered by snow and therefore unusable for all but a few weeks of the year.

Helicopter operations have the potential to disturb breeding and moulting wildlife. To minimise disturbance to seals and nesting birds at Cape Denison during the summer months, helicopters should only land at the site indicated on Map C and approach and depart in accordance with the flight paths indicated on the map. Departure paths have been selected to avoid wildlife concentrations as much as possible. Use of a single-engine helicopter is preferable; however twin-engine helicopters may be used with due regard for the potentially greater disturbance to wildlife. The presence of seals and the breeding cycle of birds nesting in the Area are charted at Appendices B(i) and B(ii); twin-engine helicopter operations should be avoided during weeks that birds are hatching eggs or raising chicks (late October to early March).

6(iii) Location of structures within and adjacent to the Area

Cape Denison is notable for being the location of four historic buildings (described in section 1) and a Memorial Cross (67°0'36"S, 142°39'48"E) constructed by the AAE of 1911-1914. The AAE also installed the survey markers and mast which are still present on top of Anemometer Hill, about 150 m east of Mawson's Main Hut. On 5 January 1931 members of the BANZARE party (including Douglas Mawson) visited Cape Denison to claim formal possession of George V Land on behalf of Great Britain, and used the mast to support the proclamation flag and canister containing the proclamation itself. A small timber plaque and proclamation, still attached to the mast, are the only 'formal' artefacts of that visit remaining in situ today. A time capsule was installed on 16 January 2012 at the base of the proclamation pole (142°39'51.9"E 67°0'33.3"S) to commemorate the centenary of the AAE. A plaque to commemorate this event was laid at the base of the proclamation pole next to the time capsule.

Cape Denison additionally features seven other structures: an automatic weather station (AWS); a tide gauge; a field shelter and conservation laboratory known as Sørensen Hut; a red fibreglass 'Apple' hut; a wooden platform on which tents may be pitched; a field shelter known as Granholm Hut, and a plaque near Mawson's Main Hut indicating that the hut is a Historic Monument.

The AWS is located at 67°00'33"S, 142°39'51"E on a rise near Round Lake and approximately 150m southeast of Mawson's Main Hut. It has been operating since 1990 as part of the Antarctic Automatic Weather Project of the University of Wisconsin—Madison, and is the property of that institution.

In 2008 French personnel installed a tide gauge in the Area. The gauge is bolted to a rock on the sea bed on the east side of Boat Harbour at 142°39'30"E, 67°0'25"S. A cable to the shore is to be installed, when the opportunity arises, to allow the streaming of data from the tide gauge remotely via Iridium satellite.

Sørensen Hut is located about 400m east of Mawson's Main Hut at 67°00'29"S, 142°40'12"E. It was constructed by the Australian Antarctic program in 1986 to provide temporary shelter for parties conducting conservation works on Mawson's Huts and contains some provisions and field equipment. Numerous items are also stored underneath and immediately adjacent to Sørensen Hut, and in the adjacent Apple hut. Access to Sørensen Hut is limited to those who are part of authorised work parties.

Granholm Hut is situated at 67°00'29"S, 142°39'26"E, some 160 m northwest of Mawson's Main Hut. It was constructed in 1978 to provide a temporary shelter and workshop for parties working on Mawson's Huts. It contains numerous building materials, some field equipment and limited provisions. The hut has been painted to blend into the rocky landscape to lessen its visual impact on the site.

Objects left by Mawson's expedition are scattered throughout the Area, and appear from year to year depending on snow cover. These include cairns; cached seal and penguin carcasses; timbers; and a large collection of disassembled penguin skeletons. It is believed that a significant number of artefacts exist under the snow and have yet to be uncovered. It is additionally possible that artefacts from the ice cave known as 'Aladdin's Cave', sledging depot excavated by Mawson's expedition in 1912, may also be present in the vicinity of the ASPA, if not within the ASPA itself. The cave was originally located on the plateau at 67°05'S, 142°38'E, some 8 km south of Mawson's Main Hut, but it may have been relocated (via the movement of ice) up to 4.5 km down-slope from the original 1912 location. Its exact location has yet to be determined.

6(iv) Location of other protected areas in the vicinity

There are no other ASPAs or ASMAs within 50 km of Cape Denison.

6(v) Special zones within the Area

The visual catchment of Mawson's Huts and the Memorial Cross is of particular importance within the Cape Denison cultural landscape. In order to protect the landscape setting and 'sense of place' of Mawson's Huts, a Visual Protection Zone is defined within the ASPA. To preserve these values, no new structures should be built within the Visual Protection Zone. The Visual Protection Zone is illustrated on Maps A and B and is generally defined as the area enclosed by the western and eastern ridge lines of the valley containing the historic structures. The boundary extends from the coastline (67°00'24.9"S, 142°39'14.3"E) and runs southeast along the western side of the westernmost ridge to the ice plateau (67°00'46.8"S, 142°39'37.2"E); northeast along the edge of the ice plateau to 67°00'43.9"S, 142°40'5.6"E; north- northwest between Round Lake and Long Lake to 67°00'33.7"S, 142°39'59.8" E; then as far as Magnetograph House (67°00'20.3" S, 142°39'46.6"E); and then northwest along the eastern side of the eastern ridge line to the sea (67°00'15.7"S, 142°39'28.2"E).

7. Terms and conditions for entry permits

Annex V of the Protocol on Environmental Protection to the Antarctic Treaty prohibits entry into an ASPA except in accordance with a Permit. Permits shall only be issued by appropriate national authorities and may contain general and specific conditions. A Permit may be issued by a national authority to cover a number of visits in a season by the same operator. Parties operating in the Commonwealth Bay area shall consult together and with non-government operators interested in visiting the Area to ensure that visitors are managed appropriately.

7(i) General permit conditions

Conditions for issuing a Permit to enter the Area are that:
- it is issued for compelling scientific, educational (such as tourism) or outreach reasons which cannot be served elsewhere, or for reasons essential to the management of the Area;
- activities related to conservation, inspection, maintenance, research and/or monitoring purposes, consistent with the aims and objectives of this Management Plan;
- the actions permitted are in accordance with this Management Plan;

- the activities permitted will give due consideration via the environmental impact assessment process to the continued protection of the historic values of the Area;
- the Permit shall be issued for a finite period; and
- the Permit shall be carried when in the Area.

A visit report must be supplied to the authority named in the Permit on or before the expiry date of the Permit.

7(ii) Access to and movement within or over the Area

All land vehicles are prohibited within the Area, with the exception of small all-terrain vehicles by authorised work parties which, due to the colonisation of rocky areas by lichens and seabirds, should be used on snow and ice surfaces only and with due consideration of the location of historic artefacts. Pedestrian access within the Area is unrestricted but artefact-rich areas (such as the scatter immediately to the north of the Main Hut), bird or lichen colonies, and penguin 'highways' (the established route of birds moving between their nest and the sea) should be avoided.

Authorised work parties, when undertaking conservation work on the huts, may use small all-terrain vehicles within the Area to assist with the transport of materials and equipment to and from the buildings.

Access to Sørensen Hut is limited to those who are part of authorised work parties.

Visitors may enter the Main Hut and Magnetograph House provided that:

- a person who has approved cultural heritage skills (to the satisfaction of the permitting Party) accompanies all visitors inside the huts;
- visitation of the interior of the huts is limited to up to four (4) persons (including the guide) at any one time inside the Main Hut, and up to three (3) persons (including the guide) in the Magnetograph House;
- artefacts, scientific and related conservation management equipment and the interior building fabric are not touched;
- briefings on this Management Plan and the values of the ASPA are conducted prior to visits and adequate site interpretation materials are made available to each visitor;
- visitors accessing the Area avoid sensitive historic artefacts, such as the artefacts scatter to the immediate north of the Main Hut, and other sensitive areas, such as lichen communities;
- visitors do not touch the exterior fabric of the buildings or any artefacts; and
- smoking in or near the huts is not permitted.

Authorised work parties undertaking approved conservation and/or archaeological work programmes are exempt from the provisions of this sub-section.

7(iii) Activities which may be conducted within the Area

Activities which may be conducted within the Area include:

- compelling scientific research which cannot be undertaken elsewhere;
- sampling, which should be the minimum required for approved research programs;
- conservation, inspection and maintenance;
- essential management activities, including monitoring;
- operational activities in support of scientific research or management within or beyond the Area, including visits to assess the effectiveness of the Management Plan and management activities;

and

- educational and/or recreational visits, including tourism.

7(iv) Installation, modification, or removal of structures

To preserve the historic, archaeological, social, aesthetic and environmental values of the ASPA, no new structures or equipment should be constructed, nor additional scientific equipment installed in the Area, except for the conservation, research or maintenance activities specified in Section 3 above.

All equipment and infrastructure left in the Area should be periodically reviewed for maintenance and potential removal.

Cape Denison is also designated as a Historic Site. In accordance with Annex V, Article 8 (4) of the Protocol, no historic structure or other artefact at Cape Denison (including Mawson's Huts) should be damaged, removed or destroyed except in accordance with an approved conservation and/or archaeological work programme. A historic artefact may only be removed from the Area for the purposes of conservation and/or preservation and then only in accordance with a Permit issued by a national authority in consultation with the Australian Antarctic program.

The repatriation of the artefact to its original location at Cape Denison is generally preferable unless further damage or deterioration may result from repatriation.

7(v) Location of field camps

- Only tents associated with authorised works parties should be pitched on the wooden platform adjacent to Sørensen Hut.
- Camping by other personnel is permitted within the Visual Protection Zone.
- Use of Mawson's Huts for accommodation is not permitted.
- If Sørensen Hut is used in an emergency, use of any supplies should be reported to the Australian Antarctic Division as soon as practicable to ensure the safety of other people who may be reliant upon known stores.
- Existing non-historic infrastructure should be used by parties undertaking activities in accordance with this Management Plan, in preference to establishing new infrastructure.

7(vi) Restrictions on materials and organisms that may be brought into the Area

- No living animals, plant material, micro-organisms or soils shall be deliberately introduced into the Area, and all reasonable precautions shall be taken to prevent accidental introductions.
- No poultry products, with the exception of sterilised egg powder, may be brought into the Area.
- No polystyrene packaging materials may be brought into the Area.
- No pesticides or herbicides may be brought into the Area, except those used for the purposes of conservation or preservation of historic structures or artefacts, which shall be allowed into the Area in accordance with a Permit, and then removed from the Area at or before the conclusion of the activity for which the Permit was granted.
- Fuel, food and other materials are not to be deposited in the Area, unless required for essential purposes connected with the activity for which the Permit has been granted.
- Use of combustion-type lanterns is not permitted inside the Area under any circumstances.

7(vii) Taking or harmful interference with native flora or fauna

Taking or harmful interference with native flora and fauna is prohibited, except in accordance with a separate Permit issued under Article 3 of Annex II (of the Protocol on Environmental Protection to the Antarctic Treaty) by the appropriate national authority specifically for that purpose.

Approach distances to wildlife should be consistent with those agreed within the Committee for Environmental Protection. Until guidelines are adopted by the Committee, Table 1 below provides guidance.

Visitors are prohibited from washing, swimming or diving into the lakes. These activities could contaminate the water body and disturb the water column, microbial communities, and sediments.

Table 1: Minimum distances to maintain when approaching wildlife on foot

Species	Phase of life	On foot (m)
Snow petrels	Nesting	15
Wilson's storm-petrels	Nesting	15
South polar skuas	Nesting	15
Adélie penguins	Summer: on ice or away from colony	5
	Summer: breeding birds in colonies	15
Breeding Weddell seals and pups (includes weaners)	All times	15
Mature seals on their own (all species)	All times	5

7(viii) The collection or removal of anything not brought into the Area by the permit holder

- No historic structure or other artefact in the Area may be handled, disturbed or removed from the Area unless for conservation, preservation or protection purposes, or for scientific reasons, and then only in accordance with a Permit issued by an appropriate national authority.

- The repatriation of the artefact to the location at Cape Denison from which it was removed is generally preferable unless further damage or deterioration may result from repatriation.

- If an artefact is to be removed, the Australian Antarctic program should be informed so that documentation regarding that program's archaeological research at Mawson's Huts may be amended accordingly.

- Material of human origin (excluding historic material) that is likely to compromise the values of the Area, and which was not brought into the Area by the Permit holder or otherwise authorised, may be removed unless the impact of removal is likely to be greater than leaving the material *in situ*. If material is to be removed, the appropriate Authority must be notified and approval obtained.

7(ix) Disposal of wastes

- All wastes, including human wastes, should be removed from the Area.

- Refuelling of vehicles, generators and other essential equipment should be conducted with due care for the surrounding environment. Refuelling activities should not be conducted in the catchment areas of lakes or melt streams, at the ice edge, or in other sensitive areas.

7(x) Measures that may be necessary to ensure aims of the Plan can continue to be met

- The provision of information for tourists and other visitors to the Area, including a briefing video and interpretative literature;

- a post-visit survey to assist in the formal monitoring of visitor impact (with primary regard to conservation requirements, rather than visitor access);

- off-site interpretation of the Area that maximises the use of available media, including the internet; and

- the development of skills and resources, particularly those related to the excavation of artefacts from ice, to assist in the protection of the Area's values.

7(xi) Requirements of reports

The principal permit holder for each visit to the Area shall submit a report to the appropriate national authority as soon as practicable, and no later than six months after the visit has been completed.

Such visit reports should include, as applicable, the information identified in the recommended visit report form contained in the *Guide to the Preparation of Management Plans for Antarctic Specially Protected Areas*, available from the website of the Secretariat of the Antarctic Treaty www.ats.aq.

If appropriate, the national authority should also forward a copy of the visit report to the Party that proposed the Management Plan, to assist in managing the Area and reviewing the Management Plan.

Parties should, wherever possible, deposit originals or copies of such original visit reports in a publicly accessible archive to maintain a record of usage, for the purpose of any review of the Management Plan and in organising further visitation and/or use of the Area.

8. Supporting documentation

Australian Antarctic Division 2013. *Mawson's Huts Historic Site Management Plan 2013-18*. Kingston, Tas.

Australia ICOMOS Inc. 2000. *The Burra Charter: The Australian ICOMOS Charter for Place of Cultural Significance,* 1999. Burwood: Australia ICOMOS Inc.: 2.

Ayres, P. 1999. *Mawson: a Life.* Melbourne: Melbourne University Press/Miegunyah Press: 68–69 passim.

Dodge, CW. 1948. *BANZARE Reports*, Series B, Vol. VII. British Australia New Zealand Antarctic Expedition.

Godden Mackay Logan 2001. *Mawson's Huts Historic Site, Cape Denison Commonwealth Bay Antarctica: Conservation Management Plan 2001*. Sydney: Godden Mackay Logan: 36, 41–43, 110, 146, 147, passim.

Godfrey, I. 2006. *Mawson's Huts Conservation Expedition 2006*. Mawson's Huts Foundation, Sydney

Hughes, J (2012). *Deterioration processes affecting historic sites in Antarctica and the conservation implications*. PhD Thesis, University of Canberra.
http://www.canberra.edu.au/researchrepository/items/e3d37990-6655-337a-f1e1-b317f04f1200/1/

Hughes, J. and B. Davis. "The Management of Tourism at Historic Sites and Monuments." In: Hall, C. M. and M.E. Johnston. 1995. *Polar Tourism: Tourism in the Arctic and Antarctic Regions.* London: John Wiley & Sons Ltd: 242, 245, 246.

Lazer, E. *"Recommendations for Future Archaeological and Conservation Work at the Site Associated with Mawson's Hut Commonwealth Bay Antarctica."* October 1985: 1, 9, 10, Map 3.

Hayes, J. Gordon 1928. *Antarctica: a treatise on the southern continent*. London: The Richards Press

Ltd.: 212.

McGregor, A. 1998. *Mawson's Huts: an Antarctic Expedition Journal*. Sydney: Hale and Iremonger: 7–15.

McIntyre, D, and M. McIntyre 1996. "Weddell seal survey in Boat Harbour". In: Australian Antarctic Division 1997. *Initial Environmental Evaluation: AAP Mawson's Huts Foundation Conservation Program 1997–98*: Attachment D.

Mawson, D. 1996 (reprint). *The Home of the Blizzard*. Adelaide: Wakefield Press: 53, 54, 62, 68.

Mawson's Huts Foundation 2005. *Mawson's Huts Conservation Expedition 2005*. Sydney

Mawson's Huts Foundation 2008. *Mawson's Huts Conservation Expedition 2007-08*. Sydney

Mawson's Huts Foundation 2009. *Mawson's Huts Conservation Expedition 2008-09*. Sydney

Mawson's Huts Foundation 2011. *Mawson's Huts Conservation Expedition 2010-11*. Sydney

Patterson, D. 2003. *Mawson's Huts Conservation Expedition 2002: Field Leader's Report.*

Secretariat of the Antarctic Treaty, *Environmental Protection, Protected Areas* http://www.ats.aq/e/ep_protected.htm (Accessed 5 July 2013).

Stillwell, F.L. 1918. *The metamorphic rocks of Adélie Land. Australasian Antarctic Expedition*, Scientific Reports, Series A, Vol. III part 1:15–22.

Appendix A

Flora recorded at Cape Denison, Commonwealth Bay

The following taxa were recorded at Cape Denison by the Australasian Antarctic Expedition (AAE) of 1911–14 and the British Australian New Zealand Antarctic Research Expedition (BANZARE) in 1929–31 and published by Carroll W. Dodge in BANZARE Reports, Series B, Vol. VII, July 1948.

LICHENS

Lecideaceae

Lecidea cancriformis Dodge & Baker
Toninia johnstoni Dodge

Umbilicaiaceae

U*mbilicaria decussata* (Vill.) Zahlbr.

Lecanoraceae

Rhizoplaca melanophthalma (Ram.) Leuck. & Poelt
Lecanora expectans Darb.
Pleopsidium chlorophanum (Wahlenb.) Zopf

Parmeliaceae

Physcia caesia (Hoffm.) Th. Fr.

Usnaeceae

Pseudephebe minuscula (Nyl. ex Arnold) Brodo & D. Hawksw.
Usnea antarctica Du Rietz

Blasteniaceae

Candelariella flava (C.W. Dodge & Baker) Castello & Nimis
Xanthoria elegans (Link) Th. Fr.
Xanthoria mawsonii Dodge

Buelliaceae

Buellia frigida Darb.

BRYOPHYTES

No bryophytes evident at Cape Denison.

There are numerous non-marine algae; however, no surveys have been undertaken.

Appendix B(i)

Breeding cycles of nesting seabirds at Cape Denison, Commonwealth Bay

Species breeding at Cape Denison	Number	Summer breeding cycle
Wilson's storm-petrel (*Oceanites oceanicus*)	Approximately 38 pairs; three small colonies	Before mid-December: adults; after mid-December: adults, eggs and chicks
Snow petrel (*Pagodroma nivea*)	Approximately 30; one small colony	Before late November: adults; after late November: adults, eggs and chicks
Adélie penguin (*Pygoscelis adeliae*)	Approximately 18,800 pairs; numerous colonies	Before November: adults; after November: adults, eggs and chicks
South polar skua (*Catharacta maccormicki*)	Approximately 8 pairs; scattered nests on fringes of penguin colonies	Before mid-December: adults; after mid-December adults and chicks

Appendix B(ii)

Breeding cycles of seals at Cape Denison, Commonwealth Bay

Species	Number	Summer breeding cycle
Weddell seal (*Leptonychotes weddellii*)	Exact number not known, no established colonies	Before November: no seals; between mid-November to end December, approx. 24 adults per day
Southern elephant seal (*Mirounga leonina*)	Exact number not known, no established colonies	Approx. 2 or more adults per day in December

Map A Mawson's Huts, Cape Denison

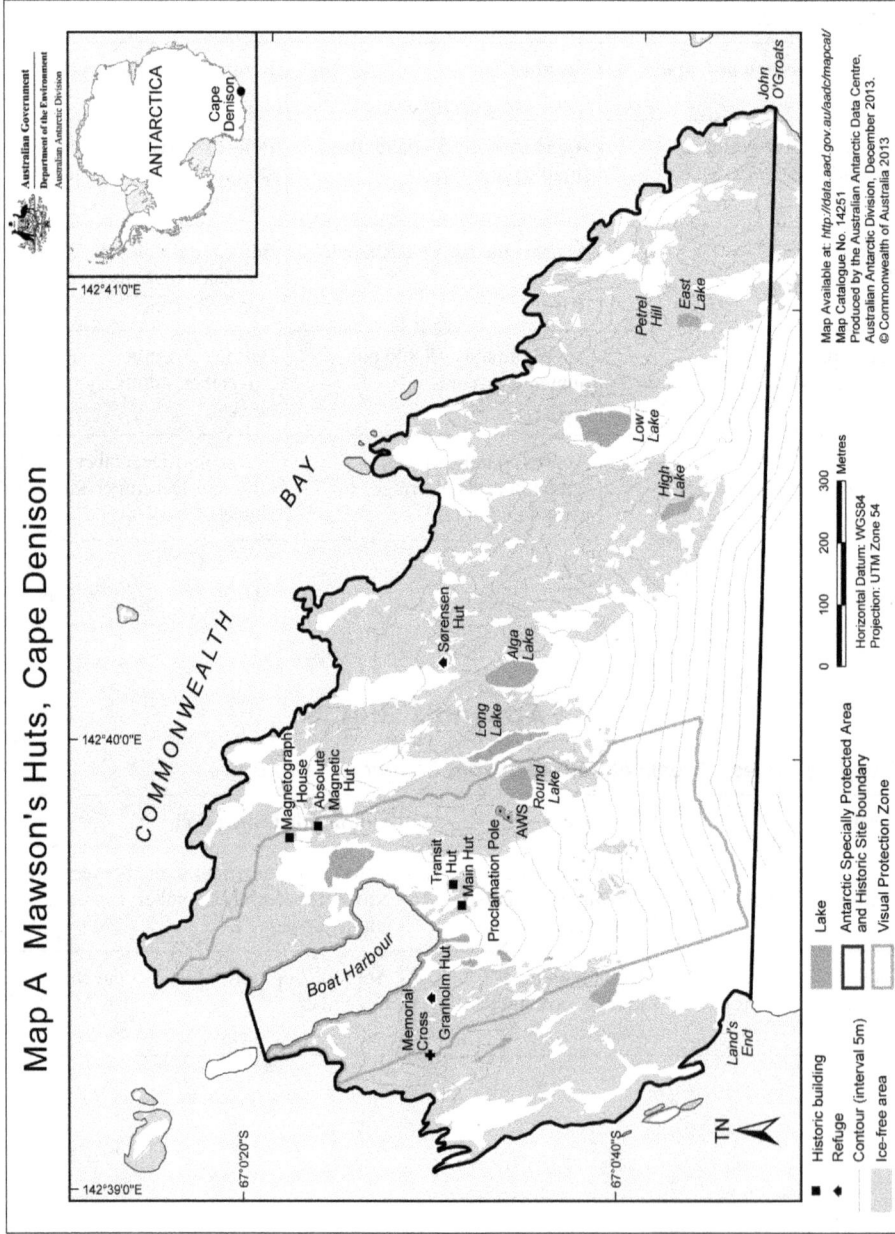

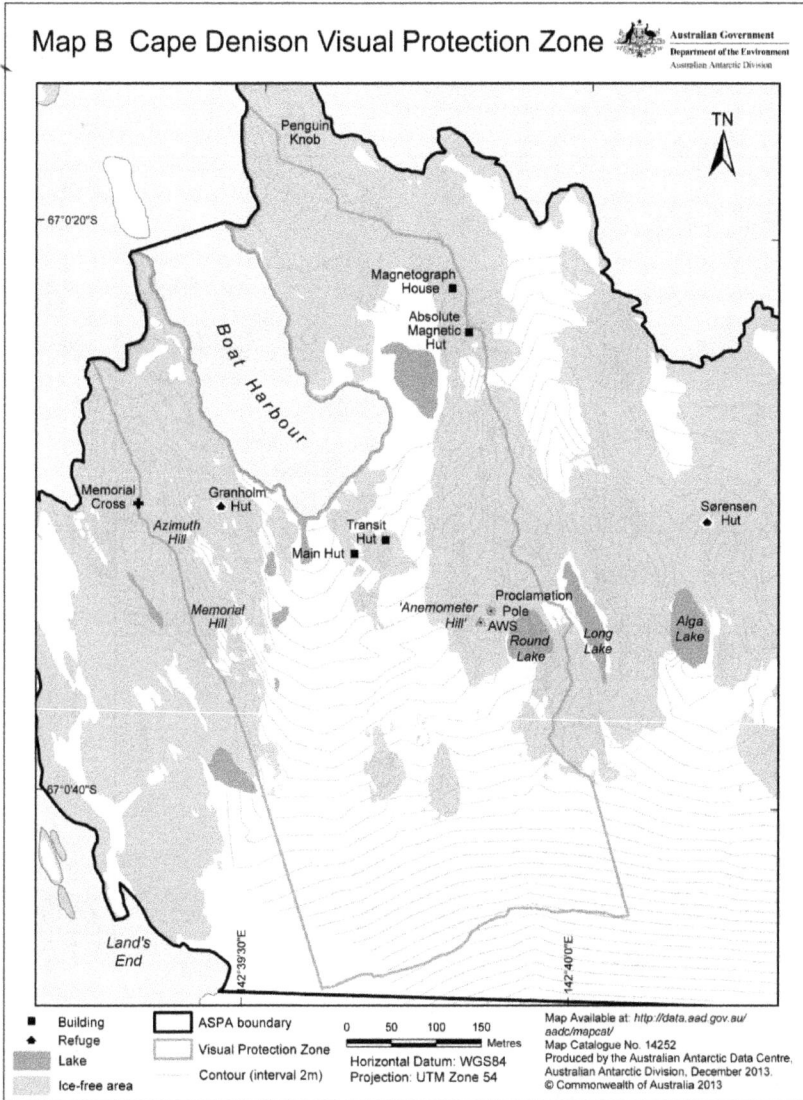

Map B Cape Denison Visual Protection Zone

Australian Government
Department of the Environment
Australian Antarctic Division

TN

Penguin Knob

67°0'20"S

Magnetograph House ■

Absolute Magnetic Hut ■

Boat Harbour

Memorial Cross ✚   Granholm ♦ Hut

Azimuth Hill

Transit Hut ■

Main Hut ■

Sørensen ♦ Hut

Memorial Hill

'Anemometer Hill'   Proclamation Pole ● AWS

Round Lake

Long Lake

Alga Lake

67°0'40"S

Land's End

42°39'30"E

142°40'0"E

Legend		
■ Building	▭ ASPA boundary	
♦ Refuge	▭ Visual Protection Zone	
▨ Lake	Contour (interval 2m)	
▨ Ice-free area		

0   50   100   150
Metres

Horizontal Datum: WGS84
Projection: UTM Zone 54

Map Available at: http://data.aad.gov.au/ aadc/mapcat/
Map Catalogue No. 14252
Produced by the Australian Antarctic Data Centre, Australian Antarctic Division, December 2013.
© Commonwealth of Australia 2013

153

Map C Cape Denison Flight Paths and Bird Colonies

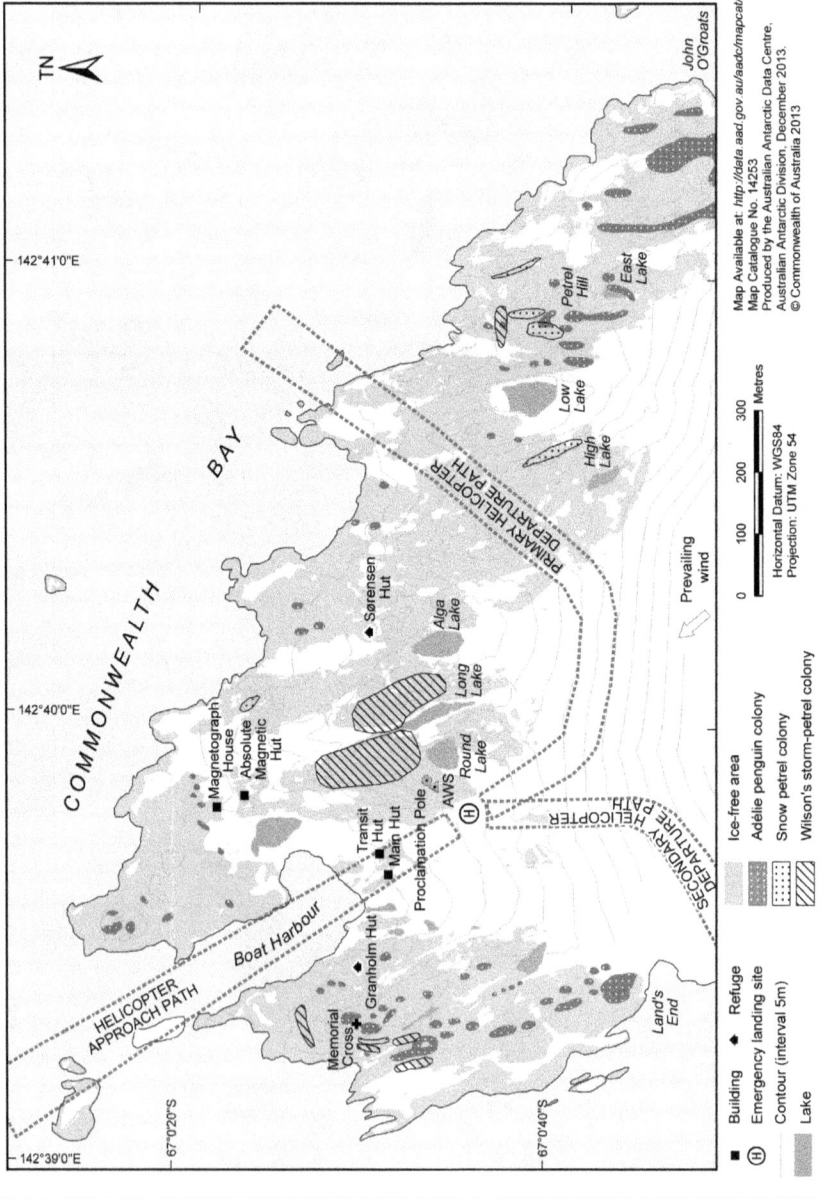

Management Plan for
Antarctic Specially Protected Area No. 169

AMANDA BAY, INGRID CHRISTENSEN COAST, PRINCESS ELIZABETH LAND, EAST ANTARCTICA

Introduction

The Amanda Bay Antarctic Specially Protected Area (ASPA) is located adjacent to Prydz Bay, on the Ingrid Christensen Coast of Princess Elizabeth Land, East Antarctica, at 69°15'S, 76°49'E (Map A). The ASPA was designated under Measure 3 (2008) following a proposal by China and Australia, primarily to protect the breeding colony of several thousand pairs of emperor penguins (*Aptenodytes forsteri*).

Only three other East Antarctic emperor penguin colonies are protected within ASPAs (ASPA 101 Taylor Glacier, ASPA 120 Point Géologie Archipelago and ASPA 167 Haswell Island). Being proximate to research stations in the Larsemann Hills and Vestfold Hills, Amanda Bay is among the most accessible emperor penguin colonies in East Antarctica. Its location facilitates the collection of valuable long-term population monitoring data and comparative studies with other East Antarctic emperor penguin colonies. Although advantageous for research purposes, Amanda Bay's proximity to research stations increases the potential for human disturbance of the emperor penguin colony.

Amanda Bay and its resident emperor penguin colony were discovered on 30 November 1956 during an aerial survey by expeditioners from the former Soviet Union. On 26 August 1957 an Australian surveying party observed an astro fix at the Larsemann Hills. During the return flight to Davis, the area was photographed and named Amanda Bay after the newly-born daughter of the pilot, RAAF Squadron Leader Peter Clemence. Since 1957 the colony has been visited by researchers from Australia, China, Russia and the former Soviet Union (see Appendix 1). A small number of tourist operators have also made visits.

1. Description of values to be protected

The Area is primarily designated to protect the breeding colony of emperor penguins. The colony possesses intrinsic and scientific values. The collection of long-term population monitoring data in the Area is valuable for comparative studies with other emperor penguin colonies in East Antarctica.

During winter, the emperor penguin colony is located on the fast ice in the south-west corner of Amanda Bay. As the breeding season progresses, the various parts of the colony move away from the wintering ground and cover most of the southern section of the ASPA. The colony comprises up to 11 000 pairs, however the number of birds attending the colony is highly variable (Wienecke and Pedersen 2009).

Emperor penguins live all year in Antarctic waters and have a circumpolar breeding distribution. There are currently 46 known breeding colonies (Fretwell *et al.* 2012). Many of these colonies have not been systematically counted.

The first estimate of the global population of emperor penguins drew upon satellite imagery and indicated that there may be some 238 000 breeding pairs (Fretwell *et al.* 2012).

Emperor penguin colonies are typically located on winter fast ice in areas where this ice forms early in the year and remains stable until early summer. Only two are located on land – one near Taylor Glacier, Mac.Robertson Land (ASPA 101, 67°28'S, 60°53'E) and one in the area of Richardson Lakes near Amundsen Bay in Enderby Land (66°45'S, 50°38'E). A small colony (less than 200 breeding pairs) existed on Dion Island in Marguerite Bay on the western Antarctic Peninsula (ASPA 107, 67°52'S, 68°43'W) but this is now deemed to be extinct (Trathan *et al.* 2011).

The Amanda Bay area also supports breeding colonies of other seabird species and is a haul-out area for Weddell seals.

2. Aims and objectives

Management at Amanda Bay aims to:

- avoid degradation of, or substantial risk to, the emperor penguin colony by preventing/minimising unnecessary human disturbance;
- provide for ongoing research and monitoring of the emperor penguin colony, and other compelling scientific activities which cannot be undertaken elsewhere;
- gather survey data on the population status of the emperor penguin colony on a regular basis; and
- minimise the possibility of the introduction of pathogens which may cause disease in fauna populations within the Area.

3. Management activities

The following management activities shall be undertaken to protect the values of the Area:

- information about the Area including its boundaries and the special restrictions that apply within it, plus copies of this management plan, shall be made available at research and field stations in the Vestfold Hills and Larsemann Hills, and to ships that visit the vicinity;
- pilots operating in the region shall be informed of the location, boundaries and restrictions applying to entry and over-flight in the Area;
- national program personnel undertaking activities in the vicinity of, accessing or flying over the Area, shall be specifically instructed by their national program as to the provisions and contents of the management plan;
- visits shall be made to the Area as necessary (where practicable, not less than once every five years) to assess whether the Area continues to serve the purposes for which it was designated and to ensure that management activities are adequate;
- the management plan shall be reviewed at least every five years and updated as required; and
- national Antarctic programs operating in the Area shall consult with a view to ensuring the above management activities are implemented.

4. Period of designation

Designated for an indefinite period.

5. Maps

- Map A: Amanda Bay Antarctic Specially Protected Area, Ingrid Christensen Coast, Princess Elizabeth Land, East Antarctica. Location Amanda Bay on Ingrid Christensen Coast. Map Specifications: Projection: Lambert Conical Conformal; Horizontal Datum: WGS84; Vertical Datum: Mean Sea Level.
- Map B: Amanda Bay Antarctic Specially Protected Area, Ingrid Christensen Coast, Princess Elizabeth Land, East Antarctica. Location of Emperor Penguin Colony and Physical Features. Map Specifications: Horizontal Datum: WGS84; Vertical Datum: Mean Sea Level.

6. Description of the Area

6(i) Geographical co-ordinates, boundary markers and natural features

General description

Amanda Bay (69°15'S, 76°49'E) lies south-west of the Brattstrand Cliffs, between the Vestfold Hills to the north-east and the Larsemann Hills to the south-west, on the Ingrid Christensen Coast, Princess Elizabeth Land, East Antarctica (see Map A). Amanda Bay is approximately 3 km wide and 6 km long and opens north-west into Prydz Bay. It is flanked by the Flatnes Ice Tongue and the Hovde Glacier on its south-west and south-east side respectively. Its southern side is bounded by continental ice cliffs and rock outcrops. There are small islets in the south-western section and several un-named islands a few kilometres offshore.

The ASPA comprises the rocks, islands and water (including fast ice) commencing at a point to the north-east of Hovde Island at the terminus of the Hovde Glacier, 76°53'54.48"E, 69°13'25.77"S; then south along the coastline at the base of the Hovde Glacier ice cliffs, to a point at 76°53'44.17"E, 69°16'22.72"S; then west along the coastline at the base of a series of ice-free bluffs to a point 76°49'37.47"E, 69°16'58'48"S; then north along the base of the Flatnes Ice Tongue ice cliffs, to a point at the terminus of the Flatnes Ice Tongue, 76°46'41.07'E, 69°14'44.37"S; then a straight line in a north-easterly direction connecting with the originating point at 76°53'54.48"E, 69°13'25.77"S (Map B).

Emperor penguins

During winter the emperor penguin colony is located on the fast ice in the south-west corner of Amanda Bay. Throughout the breeding season and especially once the chicks are mobile, various small groups form to the north, south and west of the wintering area. The islands are also occupied during spring and summer. Strong circular currents in Prydz Bay render the sea ice unstable for most of the year, thus providing the emperor penguins with good access to open water for feeding. The colony has occupied a number of sites within Amanda Bay since its discovery in 1957.

Other biota

South polar skuas (*Catharacta maccormicki*) and Wilson's storm petrels (*Oceanites oceanicus*) are known to breed on the islands of Amanda Bay, however the size of their breeding populations are currently unknown. More than 20 juvenile south polar skuas also occupy these islands in summer. Adélie penguins (*Pygoscelis adeliae*) frequently visit the Area and use these islands during their annual moult. Dozens of Weddell seals (*Leptonychotes weddelli*) regularly haul out in the Area, particularly in the southern area where the sea ice remains for most of the summer.

Climate

Amanda Bay is almost completely filled by fast ice (even during summer months) making it an important and rare habitat for both emperor penguins and Weddell seals.

Limited meteorological data exists for the immediate region. The nearest areas with a substantial record of meteorological data are the Vestfold Hills (Davis station), 75 km to the north-east, and the Larsemann Hills (Zhongshan, Progress and Bharati stations), 22 km to the south-west.

The prevailing wind within Amanda Bay appears to be highly variable but comes mainly from the east-south-east. The prevailing winds at Davis are northeast to east and of moderate strength. The mean annual wind speed is 18 km/hr. On average the windiest month is November and the least windy month is April. In the Larsemann Hills, violent southerly winds are often encountered. Persistent and strong katabatic winds also blow off the plateau from the northeast on most summer days.

From December to February daytime air temperatures in the Larsemann Hills frequently exceed 4°C and can exceed 10°C, and the mean monthly temperature is a little above 0°C. Mean monthly winter temperatures are between 15°C and -18°C. Precipitation occurs as snow and is unlikely to exceed 250 mm water equivalent annually. Davis experiences a mean monthly temperature range from +1°C in January to -18°C in July. Snowfall is very light and most snow accumulation is the result of drift snow blown from the plateau between March and October.

Geology

Rock outcrops in southern Prydz Bay – the Svenner Islands, the Brattstrand Cliffs, Amanda Bay, the Larsemann Hills, Bolingen Islands, Søstrene Island, the Munro Kerr Mountains and Landing Bluff – consist of interleaved paragneiss and orthogneiss with high temperature mineral assemblages and structures about 500 Ma in age (Pan African). The paragneiss preserves no conclusive evidence of earlier metamorphism, however the orthogneiss has local relics of high-grade metamorphism at 1000 Ma. The Pan-African event involved crustal thickening and burial of the paragneiss followed by exhumation. There are also a number of igneous intrusions that post-date peak metamorphism, including granitoid plutons and widespread pegmatic dykes which cross-cut the gneiss and plutons. One such granitoid pluton is found at Amanda Bay. This is K-feldspar rich and post-dates early foliations in the country gneiss. The pluton exhibits a biotite foliation, contains garnet, spinel and apatite and is thought to be syntectonic, intruded during the later stages of metamorphism.

6(ii)   Access to the Area

The Area may be accessed via helicopter or ground vehicle in accordance with the conditions presented in section 7(ii) of this plan.

6(iii)   Location of structures within and adjacent to the Area

Two automated cameras are temporarily located on the large island in the south eastern corner of Amanda Bay – for the purposes of monitoring the colony and ice conditions.

6(iv)   Location of other Protected Areas in the vicinity

The Larsemann Hills, Antarctic Specially Managed Area No 6 is located approximately 22 km to the south-west (69°30'S 76°19'58"E) of Amanda Bay. The other closest protected areas are Marine Plain, ASPA No 143 (68°36'S, 78°07'E) and Hawker Island, ASPA No 167 (68°35'S, 77°50'E), approximately 75 km north-east in the Vestfold Hills.

6(v)   Special zones within the Area

There are no special zones within the area.

7. Terms and conditions for entry permits

7(i)   General permit conditions

Entry into the Area is prohibited except in accordance with a permit issued by an appropriate national authority. Conditions for issuing a permit to enter the Area are that:

- the permit is issued only for compelling scientific reasons that cannot be served elsewhere, in particular for the scientific study of the avifauna and ecosystem of the Area, or for essential management purposes consistent with the objectives of this management plan, such as inspection, management or review;
- the actions permitted will not jeopardise the values of the Area or other permitted activities;
- the actions permitted are in accordance with this Management Plan;
- the permit, or an authorised copy, shall be carried within the Area;
- a visit report will be supplied to the authority that approved the permit, as soon as practicable after the visit to the ASPA has been completed, but no later than six months after the visit has occurred;
- permits shall be issued for a finite period;
- permit holders shall notify the appropriate authority of any activities or measures undertaken that were not authorised by the permit; and
- all census and GPS data shall be made available to the permitting authority and to the Parties responsible for the development of the management plan.

7(ii)   Access to, and movement within or over, the Area

Disturbance of the colony should be minimised at all times noting that environmental conditions and the location of the colony vary between and during seasons.

The coastline is partially comprised of a very large ice wall. This ice wall prevents direct land access from the west, south and east.

There are no marked pedestrian routes within the Area. Unless disturbance is authorised by a permit, pedestrians should keep at least 50 m from any penguin or concentrations of penguins.

Vehicle access should be overland from the south or from sea ice to the north, avoiding crossing between the colony and the sea. Vehicles should be kept at least 500 m from any penguin or concentrations of penguins.

As the emperor penguin colony does not remain in one fixed location it is not possible to designate helicopter landing sites and flight paths that will prevent disturbance at all times. Appropriate flight paths and a viable landing site (VLS) need to be assessed on a visit-by-visit basis, and caution exercised in accordance with the provisions of this management plan. When approaching and departing a VLS, the topography should be used to shield concentrations of penguins from direct noise.

The following conditions apply to the use of aircraft:

- aircraft shall not be operated over the Area between 01 May and 01 October each year;
- fixed wing aircraft shall not be landed in the Area;
- aircraft shall not be refuelled within the Area;
- helicopters may only land at a VLS, identified on each visit by making an initial assessment flight around the outer perimeter of the Area to determine penguin distribution and concentrations in relation to the topography;
- for twin-engine helicopters, the VLS must be located at least 1000 m from concentrations of penguins;
- for single-engine helicopters, the VLS must be a distance of 1000 m from concentrations of penguins, or where the topography (icebergs, islands etc) will shield concentrations of penguins from direct noise. (Note: A VLS *may* be present on the inner side of the eastern coastal edge of the large island in the south east corner of Amanda Bay at 69°16'21.2"S, 76°50"52.6"E).

7(iii)   Activities which may be conducted in the Area

The following activities may be conducted in the Area:

- compelling scientific research, which cannot be undertaken elsewhere and which will not jeopardise the avifauna or the ecosystem of the Area;
- essential management activities, including monitoring; and
- sampling, which should be the minimum required for the approved research programs.

As the emperor penguins are particularly sensitive to disturbance during the following periods:

- from mid-May to late July when they are incubating eggs;
- from late July to late September when adults are brooding chicks;
- from late November to late December when the chicks moult and fledge; and
- in late summer during the adults' moult

visitors should exercise particular care not to unduly disturb or interfere with the emperor penguins during these periods.

7(iv)   Installation, modification, or removal of structures

Permanent structures and installations are prohibited in the Area. Temporary structures and installations may only be established in the Area for compelling scientific or management reasons as specified in a permit.

Any temporary structure established in the Area must be:

- clearly identified by country, name of the principal agency, date of installation and date of expected removal;
- first cleaned of organisms, propagules (e.g. seeds, eggs) and non-sterile soil;
- made of materials that can withstand Antarctic conditions and pose minimal contamination risk to the Area; and
- removed when they are no longer required, or before the expiry of the permit, whichever is earlier.

7(v)   Location of field camps

Camping may only be undertaken within the Area if:

- it facilitates compelling scientific research or management operations;
- it is temporary only; and
- every effort is made to locate and keep the camp at least 500 m from penguin concentrations.

7(vi)   Restrictions on materials and organisms which may be brought into the Area

The following restrictions apply:

- no poultry products, including dried food containing egg powder, are to be taken into the Area;
- no depots of food or other supplies are to be left within the Area beyond the time period for which they are required;
- no living animals, plant materials, microorganisms or non-sterile soils are to be deliberately introduced into the Area. Precautions must be taken to prevent the accidental introduction of living animals, plant materials, microorganisms or non-sterile soils into the Area;
- no herbicides or pesticides are to be taken into the Area. Any other chemicals (including radionuclides or stable isotopes which may be introduced for scientific or management purposes specified in a permit) will be removed from the Area at or before the conclusion of the activity for which the permit was granted;
- fuel must not to be stored in the Area unless it is required for essential purposes connected with the activity for which the permit has been granted. All such fuel must be removed from the Area at or before the conclusion of the permitted activity. Permanent or semi-permanent fuel depots are not permitted; and
- all material introduced to the Area shall be for a stated time period only and if left unattended, labelled with a country identifier. All material introduced to the Area will be removed at or before the conclusion of that stated time period, and will be stored and handled in a manner that will minimise the risk of environment impacts.

7(vii)   Taking of, or harmful interference with, native flora and fauna

Taking of or harmful interference with native flora and fauna is prohibited except in accordance with a permit. Where taking or harmful interference with animals is involved this should, as a minimum standard, be in accordance with the *SCAR Code of Conduct for the Use of Animals for Scientific Purposes in Antarctica.*

Ornithological research on the breeding birds present within the Area shall be limited to activities that are non-invasive and non-disruptive. If the capture of individuals is required, capture should occur outside the Area if at all possible to reduce disturbance to the colony.

7(viii)   Collection or removal of materials not brought into the Area by the permit holder

Material may only be collected or removed from the Area in accordance with a permit and should be limited to the minimum quantity necessary to meet scientific or management needs.

Material of human origin likely to compromise the values of the Area, and which was not brought into the Area by the permit holder or otherwise authorised, may be removed unless the impact of the removal is likely to be greater than leaving the material *in situ*. If this is the case, the appropriate national authority must be notified and approval obtained.

7(ix) Disposal of waste

All wastes, including human wastes, shall be removed from the Area.

7(x) Measures that may be necessary to ensure that the aims and objectives of the management plan can continue to be met

Permits may be granted to allow biological monitoring and Area management and inspection activities which may involve:

- the collection of samples for analysis or review;
- the establishment or maintenance of scientific equipment, structures and signposts; and
- other protective measures.

Any specific sites of long-term monitoring shall be appropriately marked and GPS coordinates obtained for lodgement with the Antarctic Data Directory System through the appropriate national authority.

Ornithological research shall be limited to activities that, where practicable, are non-invasive and non-disruptive to the breeding birds present within the Area. Invasive and/or disruptive research activities shall only be authorised if they will have no effect or only a temporary and transient effect on the population.

Visitors shall take special precautions against the introduction of alien organisms into the Area. Of particular concern are pathogenic, microbial or vegetation introductions sourced from soils, flora or fauna at other Antarctic sites (including research stations). To minimise the risk of introductions, before entering the Area all visitors shall thoroughly clean their footwear, sampling equipment, markers etc.

7(xi) Requirements for reports

Parties shall ensure that the principal permit holder for each permit issued submits, to the appropriate national authority, a report on activities undertaken.

Such reports shall include, as appropriate, the information identified in the visit report form contained in Appendix 4 of the *Guide to the Preparation of Management Plans for Antarctic Specially Protected Areas* appended to Resolution 2 (1998).

Parties shall maintain a record of such activities.

In the Annual Exchange of Information, Parties shall provide summary descriptions of activities conducted by persons subject to their jurisdiction, in sufficient detail to allow an evaluation of the effectiveness of the management plan.

Parties shall, wherever possible, deposit original reports or copies of such in a publicly accessible archive to maintain a record of usage for the benefit of a review of the management plan and the organisation of science in the Area.

A copy of the report shall be forwarded to the Party responsible for the development of the management plan.

Additionally, visit reports shall provide detailed information on census data, locations of any new colonies or nests not previously recorded, a brief summary of research findings, and copies of photographs taken in the Area.

8. Supporting documentation

Some or all of the data used within this paper were obtained from the Australian Antarctic Data Centre (IDN Node AMD/AU), a part of the Australian Antarctic Division (Commonwealth of Australia).

Budd, G.M. (1961). The biotopes of emperor penguin rookeries. *Emu* 61:171-189.

Budd, G.M. (1962). Population studies in rookeries of the emperor penguin *Aptenodytes forsteri*. *Proceedings of the Zoological Society, London* 139:365-388.

Cracknell, G.S. (1986). Population counts and observations at the emperor penguin *Aptenodytes forsteri* colony at Amanda Bay, Antarctica. *Emu* 86(2):113-117.

Crohn, P.W. (1959). A contribution to the geology and glaciology of the western part of the Australian Antarctic Territory. *Bulletin of the Bureau of Mineral Resources, Geology and Geophysics Australia* No 32.

Easther, R. (1986). Winter journey to the Amanda Bay emperor penguin rookery. *ANARE News* September 1986. P. 14.

Fitzsimons, I. (1988). Amanda Bay region geology studies fill important information gap. *ANARE News*, March 1988. P. 5.

Fitzsimons, I. (1997). The Brattstrand Paragneiss and the Søstrene Orthogneiss: A Review of Pan-African Metamorphism and Grevillian Relics in Southern Prydz Bay. In *The Antarctic Region: Geological Processes*. Pp. 121-130.

Fretwell, P.T., LaRue, M. A., Morin, P., Kooyman, G.L., Wienecke, B., Ratcliffe, N., Fox, A.J., Fleming, A.H.

Porter, C. and Trathan, P. (2012). An emperor penguin population estimate: the first global, synoptic survey of a species from space. *PLoS ONE* 7(4): e33751. doi:10.1371/journal.pone.0033751

Gales, N.J., Klages, N.T.W., Williams, R. and Woehler, E.J. (1990). The diet of the emperor penguin, *Aptenodytes forsteri*, in Amanda Bay, Princess Elizabeth Land, Antarctica. *Antarctic Science* 2(1):23-28.

Giese, M. and Riddle, M. (1999). Disturbance of emperor penguin *Aptenodytes forsteri* chicks by helicopters. *Polar Biology* 22(6):366-371.

Horne, R.S.C. (1983). The distribution of penguin breeding colonies on the Australian Antarctic Territory, Heard Island, the McDonald Islands and Macquarie Island. *ANARE Research Notes* No 9.

Johnstone, G.W., Lugg, D.J. and Brown, D.A. (1973). The biology of the Vestfold Hills, Antarctica. Melbourne. Department of Science, Antarctic Division, *ANARE Scientific Reports, Series B (1) Zoology* No 123.

Kirkwood, R. and Robertson, G. (1997). Seasonal change in the foraging ecology of emperor penguins on the Mawson Coast, Antarctica. *Marine Ecology Progress Series* 156:205-223.

Kirkwood, R. and Robertson, G. (1997). The energy assimilation efficiency of emperor penguins, *Aptenodytes forsteri*, fed a diet of Antarctic krill, *Euphausia superba. Physiological Zoology* 70:27-32.

Kirkwood, R. and Robertson, G. (1997). The foraging ecology of female emperor penguins in winter. *Ecological Monographs* 67:155-176.

Kirkwood, R. and Robertson, G. (1999). The occurrence and purpose of huddling by Emperor penguins during foraging trips. *Emu* 99:40-45.

Korotkevich, E.S. (1964). Observations on birds during the first wintering of the Soviet Antarctic Expedition in 1956-1957. *Soviet Antarctic Expedition Information Bulletin*, Elsevier Publishing Company, Amsterdam. Pp. 149-152.

Lewis, D. (1984). Icebound in Antarctica. *National Geographic* 166(5):634-663.

Lewis, D. (1987). *Icebound in Antarctica.* William Heinemann Australia, Richmond, Victoria.

Lewis, D. and George, M., eds. (1984). The Initial Reports of the Mawson Anniversary and Frozen Sea Expeditions, nos. 4 and 11. *Oceanic Research Foundation Occasional Publication* 1.

Robertson, G. (1990). Huddles. *Australian Geographic* 20:76-94.

Robertson, G. (1992). Population size and breeding success of Emperor penguins *Aptenodytes forsteri* at the Auster and Amanda Glacier Colonies, Mawson Coast, Antarctica. *Emu* 92:62-71.

Robertson, G. and Newgrain, K. (1992). Efficacy of the tritiated water and 22Na turnover methods in estimating food and energy intake by Emperor penguins *Aptenodytes forsteri. Physiological Zoology*. 65:933-951.

Robertson, G. (1994). *The Foraging Ecology of Emperor Penguins* (Aptenodytes forsteri) *at two Mawson Coast Colonies, Antarctica*. PhD Thesis, University of Tasmania.

Robertson, G., Williams, R., Green, K. and Robertson, L. (1994). Diet composition of Emperor penguin chicks *Aptenodytes forsteri* at two Mawson Coast colonies, Antarctica. *Ibis* 136:19-31.

Robertson, G. (1995). The foraging ecology of Emperor penguins *Aptenodytes forsteri* at two Mawson Coast colonies, Antarctica. *ANARE Reports* No 138.

Schwerdtfeger, W. (1970). The climate of the Antarctic. In: Orvig, S. (Ed). *Climates of the Polar Regions.* Pp. 253-355.

Schwerdtfeger, W. (1984). Weather and climate of the Antarctic. In: Orvig, S. (Ed). *Climates of the Polar Regions.* P. 261.

Todd, F.S., Splettstosser, J.F., Ledingham, R. and Gavrilo, M. (1999). Observations in some emperor penguin *Aptenodytes forsteri* colonies in East Antarctica. *Emu* 99:142-145.

Trathan, P.N., Fretwell, P.T. and Stonehouse, B. (2011). First recorded loss of an emperor penguin colony in the recent period of Antarctic regional warming: implications for other colonies. *PLoS ONE* 6(2): e14738. doi:10.1371/journal.pone.0014738.

Wienecke, B.C. and Pedersen, P. (2009). Population estimates of emperor penguins at Amanda Bay, Ingrid Christensen Coast, Antarctica. *Polar Record* 45:207-214.

Wienecke, B., Kirkwood, R. and Robertson, G. (2004). Pre-moult foraging trips and moult locations of Emperor penguins at the Mawson Coast. *Polar Biology* 27:83-91.

Wienecke, B.C. and Robertson, G. (1997). Foraging space of emperor penguins *Aptenodytes forsteri* in Antarctic shelf waters in winter. *Marine Ecology Progress* Series 159:249-263.

Willing, R.L. (1958). Feeding habits of emperor penguins. *Nature* 182:194-195.

Willing, R.L. (1958). Australian discoveries of emperor penguin rookeries in Antarctica during 1954-57. *Nature*, London 182:1393-1394.

Woehler, E.J. [compiler], Poncet, S. and International Council of Scientific Unions. Scientific Committee on Antarctic Research. Bird Biology Subcommittee, Scott Polar Research Institute. (1993). *The distribution and abundance of Antarctic and subantarctic penguins.* Scientific Committee on Antarctic Research (SCAR), Cambridge.

Woehler, E.J. *et. al.* and International Council of Scientific Unions. Scientific Committee on Antarctic Research, Bird Biology Subcommittee, Commission for the Conservation of Antarctic Marine Living Resources, National Science Foundation [U.S.]. (2001). *A statistical assessment of the status and trends of Antarctic and sub-Antarctic seabirds.* Scientific Committee on Antarctic Research (SCAR).

Woehler, E.J. and Johnstone, G.W. (1991). Status and conservation of the seabirds of the Australian Antarctic Territory Islands. In: *Seabird - status and conservation: a supplement.* International Council for Bird Preservation, Cambridge. Pp. 279-297.

Appendix 1. History of emperor penguin population observations at Amanda Bay 1956-1997

Date	Estimated number of penguins present in colony	Comments	Reference
1956/57	5000 birds along Ingrid Christensen Coast	General reference, no systematic census	Korotkevich (1964)
September 1957	1000-2000 birds	No systematic count, no distinction between adults and chicks	Willing (1958)
1961	1500 adults	Unspecified reference, no date given, no systematic count conducted	ANARE in Horne (1983)
29-30 September 1983	2339 ± 69 chicks, 2448 ± 23 adults	Adults: en masse count after Budd (1961), chicks: combined en masse count group I and indirect count of group II (see Budd 1961)	Cracknell (1986)
1987	9000?	Unspecified reference, no date, no specification of unit, no systematic census	ANARE in Woehler and Johnstone (1991)
13 December 1992	5500 – 6000 chicks	Chicks in five groups, estimate based on grid counts	Todd (1999)
21 December 1996	1000 – 5000 total birds	Rough estimate from over flight	Todd (1999)
November 1997	8000 chicks	No systematic count, rough estimate	J. Gallagher, pers. comm., in Giese and Riddle (1999)

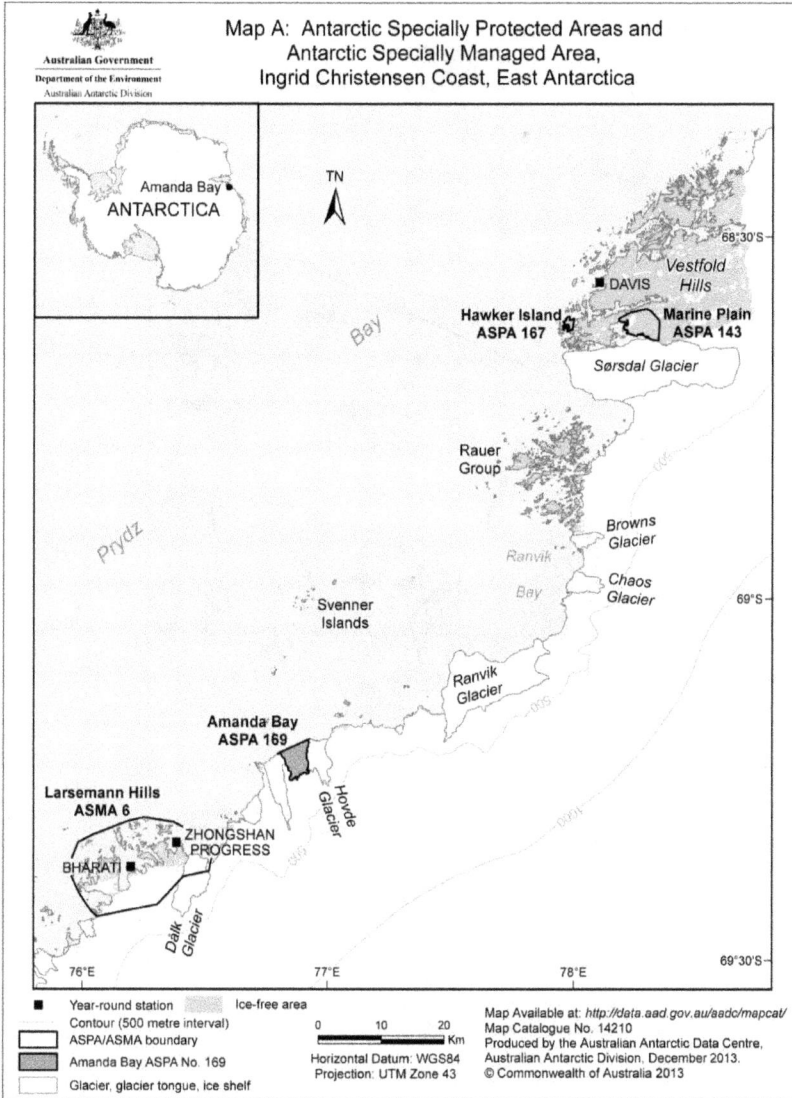

Map A: Antarctic Specially Protected Areas and Antarctic Specially Managed Area, Ingrid Christensen Coast, East Antarctica

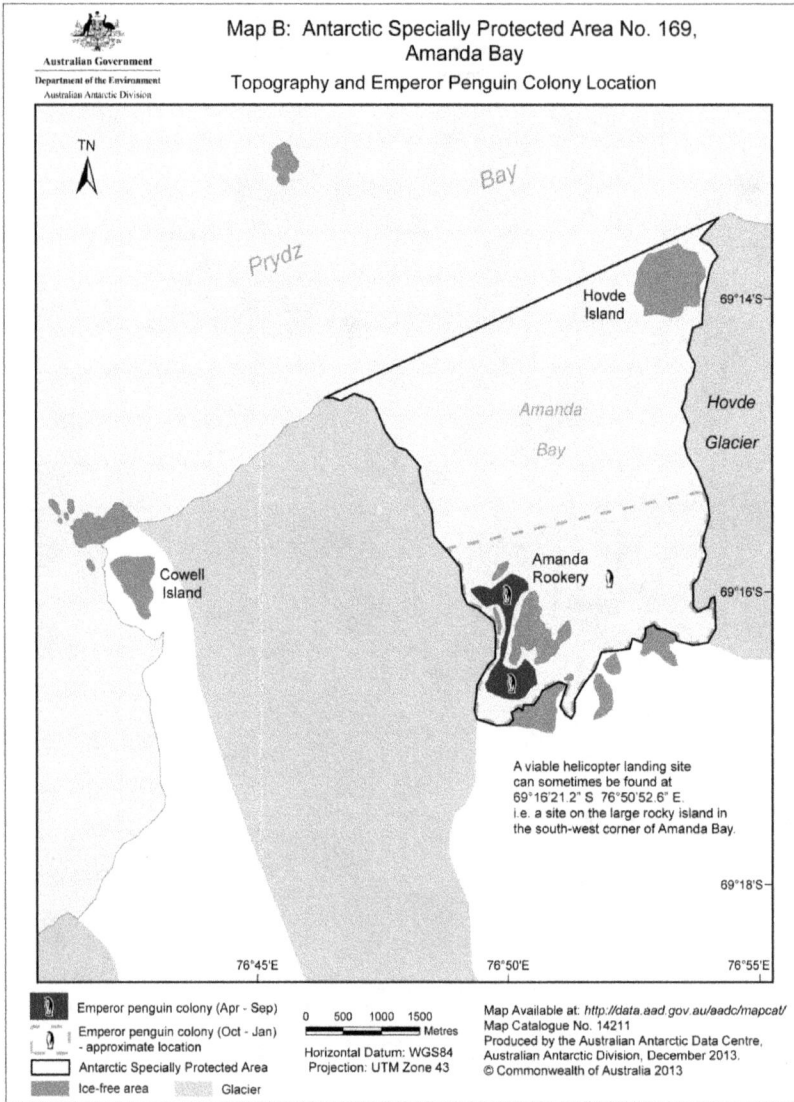

Map B: Antarctic Specially Protected Area No. 169, Amanda Bay
Topography and Emperor Penguin Colony Location

Management Plan for
Antarctic Specially Protected Area No. 171

NARĘBSKI POINT, BARTON PENINSULA,
KING GEORGE ISLAND

Introduction

Narębski Point is located on the southeast coast of Barton Peninsula, King George Island. The Area is delimited as latitude 62° 13' 40"S - 62° 14' 23"S and longitude 58° 45' 25"W - 58° 47' 00"W, and easily distinguished by mountain peaks on the north and the east boundaries and coastline on the southwest boundary.

The unique topography of the Area gives the outstanding aesthetic beauty with panoramic views, and the Area provides exceptional opportunities for scientific studies of terrestrial biological communities with high diversity and complexity of ecosystem. In particular, the coverage of mosses and lichens is very extensive. The most conspicuous vegetal communities are the associations of lichens and the moss turf dominated by *Usnea-Himantormia*. The present flora includes one Antarctic flowering plant species (only two flowering plant species were found as yet in the Antarctica), 51 lichen species, 29 moss species, six liverwort species, and one algae species.

Another noticeable feature in the Area is that over 3,000 pairs of Chinstrap Penguins (*Pygoscelis antarcticus*) – the largest number in King George Island – and over 2,300 pairs of Gentoo Penguins (*Pygoscelis papua*) inhabit in the Area (MOE 2013). There are also 16 other bird species. Among them, eight breeding birds include the Brown Skua (*Stercorarius antarcticus lonnbergi*), South Polar Skua (*Stercorarius maccormicki*), Kelp Gull (*Larus dominicanus*), Antarctic Tern (*Sterna vittata*), Wilson's Storm Petrel (*Oceanites oceanicus*), Black-bellied Storm Petrel (*Fregetta tropica*), Snowy Sheathbill (*Chionis albus*), and the Southern Giant Petrel (*Macronectes giganteus*).

The Area also includes water-shed systems, such as lakes and creeks, where dense microbial and algal mats with complex species assemblages are frequently found. These fresh water resources are essential to the diverse life forms in this Area. The high biodiversity of terrestrial vegetation with complexity of habitats enhance the potential values of the Area to be protected.

Through the Korea Antarctic Research Program, scientists have visited the Area regularly since 1980s in order to study its fauna and flora and geology. In recent years, however, Narębski Point has been frequented by visitors from the nearby stations with purposes other than scientific research, particularly during the reproductive season, and vulnerability to human interference has been increasing. Some studies note that King George Island has the potential for tourism development (ASOC, 2007 & 2008; Peter *et al.*, 2005) and visitors to the King Sejong Station have increased from less than 20 people a year in the late 1980s to over 110 in recent years.

The primary reason for designation of the Area as an Antarctic Specially Protected Area is to protect its ecological, scientific, and aesthetic values from human interference. Long-term protection and monitoring of diverse range of species and assemblages at Narębski Point will contribute to the development of appropriate regional and global conservation strategies for the species and will provide information for comparisons with elsewhere.

1. Description of Values to be Protected

The Narębski Point area is designated as an Antarctic Specially Protected Area to protect its outstanding environmental values and to facilitate ongoing and planned scientific research.

The Area provides exceptional opportunities for scientific studies of terrestrial biological communities. Scientific research, including the monitoring of penguin colonies, has been carried out by several countries since the early 1980s. Outcomes of the research revealed the potential value of the Area as a reference site, particularly in relation to global warming and the impacts from human activities.

The unique topography of the Area, together with the abundance and diversity of fauna and flora, gives the Area an exceptional aesthetic value. Among others, the mountain peaks and the southernmost peaks provide breathtaking panoramic views.

For above reasons, the Area should be protected and subject to minimal disturbance by human activities with the exception of occasional monitoring studies including vegetation, bird populations, geological and geomorphologic studies.

2. Aims and Objectives

Management of Narębski Point aims to:

- Avoid degradation of or substantial risk to the values of the Area by preventing unnecessary human disturbance to the Area;
- Allow scientific research that cannot be carried out elsewhere, as well as the continuity of ongoing long term biological studies established in the Area;
- Protect the Area's aesthetic and scientific values.

3. Management Activities

The following management activities are to be undertaken to protect the values of the Area:

- Personnel accessing the site shall be specifically instructed, by their national program (or competent authority) as to the content of the Management Plan;
- Signs illustrating the location and boundaries, with clear statements of entry restrictions, shall be placed at appropriate locations at the boundaries of the Area;
- All signs as well as scientific equipments and markers erected in the Area will be secured and maintained in proper conditions;
- The biological condition of the Area will be adequately monitored, including census on penguins and other birds populations;
- Visits shall be made as necessary (no less than once every five years) to assess whether the Area continues to serve the purposes for which it was designated and to ensure that maintenance and management measures are adequate;
- National Antarctic Programs operating in the region are encouraged to consult with each other and exchange information to ensure that activities in the Area are undertaken in a manner consistent with the aims and objectives of this Management Plan.

4. Period of Designation

Designated for an indefinite period.

5. Maps

Maps 1 to 6 are attached at the end of this management plan as Annex II.

- Map 1: Location of Narębski Point in relation to the King George Island
    and the existing protected areas (ASMA, ASPAs, and HSMs)
- Map 2: Boundary of the ASPA No. 171
- Map 3: Distribution of bird colonies and seal haul-out sites within the ASPA No. 171
- Map 4: Distribution of the plant communities in the ASPA No. 171

- Map 5: Geomorphologic details of the ASPA No. 171
- Map 6: Access routes to the ASPA No. 171

6. Description of the Area

6(i) Geographical co-ordinates, boundary markers, and natural features

Narębski Point is located on the southeast coast of Barton Peninsula, King George Island, and the Area is delimited as latitude 62° 13' 40"S - 62° 14' 23"S and longitude 58° 45' 25" W - 58° 47' 00" W. Boundaries are delimited by mountain peaks on the north and the east and coastline on the southwest. The southwest boundary can be easily recognized due to its distinguished geomorphology. The Area includes only the terrestrial area, excluding the intertidal zone. The total size of the Area is approximately 1 km².

The Area is rich in flora and fauna, of which the abundance of some species is exceptional. The cover of mosses and lichens is very extensive. There are large numbers of Chinstrap and Gentoo Penguins and the breeding areas of eight other birds including the nests of the Southern Giant Petrel. The high diversity in relief and coastal forms, due to the presence of different geologies and a prominent system of fractures, in addition to an extensive and varied vegetation cover, provides unusual scenic diversity in the Antarctic environment.

Climate

Meteorological data for the Area are confined entirely to observations at the King Sejong Station (1998-2013), about 2 km northwest of Narębski point. The climate is humid and relatively mild because of a strong maritime effect. The Area has an annual average temperature of -1.8 °C (maximum 9.8°C, minimum -23.1°C), relative humidity of 89%, total precipitation of 597.2 mm, and cloud cover of 6.8 Octas. The mean wind velocity is 7.1 m/s (37.6 m/s at the greatest), predominantly from the northwest and east throughout the year. The occurrence of blizzards from 2007 to 2013 was 30.7 (average total duration time 332 hours).

Geology

The lowermost lithostratigraphic unit in Barton peninsula is the Sejong formation (Yoo *et al.*, 2001), formally regarded as a lower volcanic member. The Sejong formation is distributed in the southern and southeastern cliffs of Barton Peninsula (Lee *et al.*, 2002). It is largely composed of volcaniclastic constituents gently dipping to the south and southwest. Mafic to intermediated volcanic lavas overlying the Sejong formation are widespread in Barton Peninsula, including the Area. They are mostly plagioclase-phyric or plagioclase- and clinopyroxene-phyric basaltic andesite to andesite with rare massive andesite. Some thick-bedded lapilli tuffs are intercalated with the lava flows. Mafic dikes, Narębski Point being one of them, cut the Sejong formation along the southern coast of the peninsula. Soils of the peninsula are subdivided into four suites based on bedrock type, namely those on granodiorite, basaltic andesite, lapilli tuff, and the Sejong formation (Lee *et al.*, 2004). Soils are generally poor in organic materials and nutrients, except for those near seabird colonies.

Penguins

Breeding colonies of Chinstrap Penguins (*Pygoscelis antarcticus*) and Gentoo Penguins (*Pygoscelis papua*) are distributed on rocky inclines and hill crests of Narębski Point.

The Chinstrap Penguin is the most abundant breeding species at the site, with a total of 3,157 pairs observed in 2013/14. Chinstrap Penguins begin to lay eggs in early November and incubate for 32-43 days, and the peak seasons of laying and hatching are estimated to be mid-November and mid-December, respectively (Kim, 2002). The maximum number of breeding Chinstrap Penguins was estimated at 3,332 pairs in 2012/13 (MOE, 2013. Since 1989/90, breeding pairs of Chinstrap Penguins have gradually increased and maintained its population between 2,600 and 3,000 pairs from 1994/95 to 2013/14 (see Figure 1).

Breeding pairs of Gentoo Penguins have increased steadily from 500 pairs, since1984/85. A total of 2,378 pairs of Gentoo Penguins were counted in 2013/14 (see Figure 1). Gentoo Penguins start to lay eggs during

169

mid-October, with the peak season occurring in late October. They incubate for 33-40 days and hatch in early December (Kim, 2002).

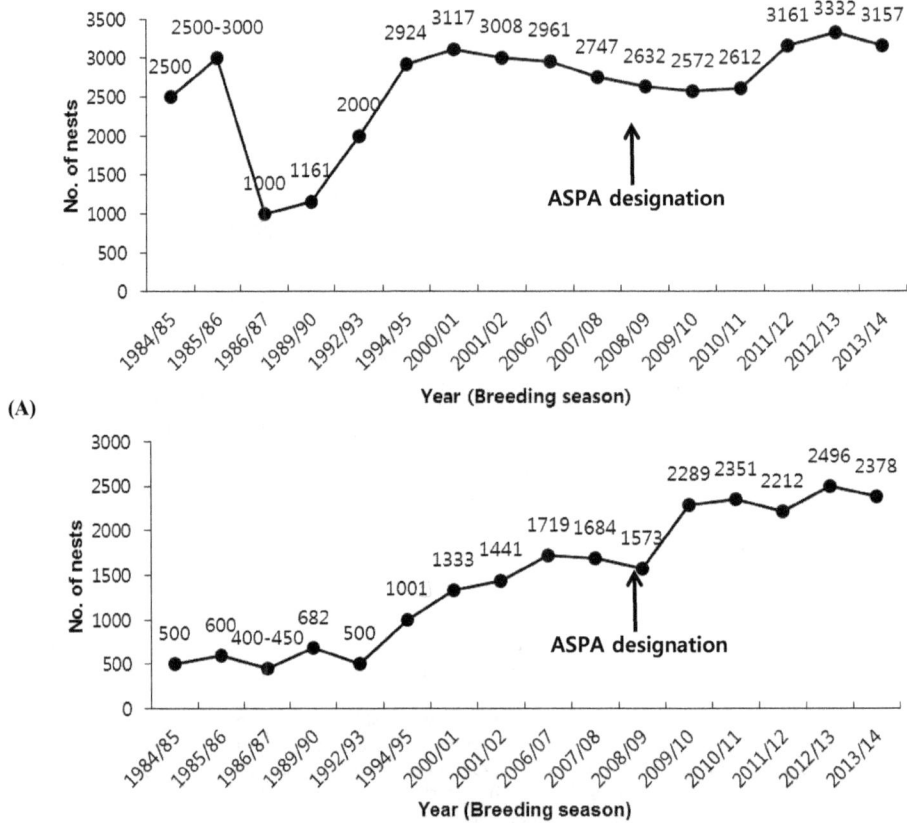

(A)

(B)

Figure 1. Breeding populations of (A) Chinstrap Penguins and (B) Gentoo Penguins at the Narębski Point (Peter *et al.*, 1986; Rauschert *et al.*, 1987; Mönke & Bick, 1988; Yoon, 1990; MOST, 1993; MAF, 1997; Kim, 2002; MOE, 2007; MOE, 2011; MOE, 2012; MOE, 2013)

Other birds

There are eight more nesting bird species in the Area along with two penguin species: the Brown Skua (*Stercorarius antarcticus lonnbergi*), South Polar Skua (*Stercorarius maccormicki*), Kelp Gull (*Larus dominicanus*), Antarctic Tern (*Sterna vittata*), Southern Giant Petrel (*Macronectes giganteus*), Wilson's Storm Petrel (*Oceanites oceanicus*), Black-bellied Storm Petrel (*Fregetta tropica*), and Snowy Sheathbill (*Chionis albus*). In addition, eight non-breeding bird species have been recorded in the Area, including the Adelie Penguin (*Pygoscelis adelie*), Macaroni Penguin (*Eudyptes chrysolophus*), Antarctic Shag (*Leucocarbo bransfieldensis*), Arctic Tern (*Sterna paradisaea*), Cape Petrel (*Daption capense*), Antarctic Petrel

(*Thalassoica antarctica*), Snow Petrel (*Pagodroma nivea*), and Southern Fulmar (*Fulmarus glacialoides*). A summary of the estimated number of nests by species is presented in Table 1.

Brown Skuas and South Polar Skuas prey on penguin eggs and chicks, and some pairs of skuas occupy penguin sub-colonies as feeding territory during breeding season (Trivelpiece *et al.*, 1980; Hagelin and Miller, 1997; Pezzo *et al.*, 2001; Hahn and Peter, 2003). South Polar Skuas nesting in the Area do not depend on penguin eggs and chicks for their chick-rearing. On the contrary, during the 2006/07 season, all Brown Skua pairs (4 pairs) breeding in this Area were observed to occupy their own feeding territory in penguin sub-colonies and defend them.

Two pairs of the Snowy Sheathbill bred near penguin rookery in Narębski Point (in 2006/07 and 2013/14). Snowy Sheathbills are omnivores and forage for food around the breeding colonies of seabirds. They feed on penguin faeces, eggs, and dead chicks, and also steal krill from penguins at the site.

Table 1. Estimated number of nests, by species (2006/07 and 2013/14)

Species		Number of nests	
		2006/2007	2013/2014
Gentoo Penguin	*Pygoscelis papua*	1719	2378
Chinstrap Penguin	*Pygoscelis antarcticus*	2961	3157
Brown Skua	*Stercorarius antarcticus lonnbergi*	4	7
South Polar Skua	*Stercorarius maccormicki*	27	-
Kelp Gull	*Larus dominicanus*	6	-
Antarctic Tern	*Sterna vittata*	41	-
Southern Giant Petrel	*Macronectes giganteus*	9	5
Wilson's Storm Petrel	*Oceanites oceanicus*	19	>10
Snowy Sheathbill	*Chionis albus*	2	2

Vegetation

Most of the ice-free areas of Barton Peninsula are covered by relatively rich vegetation, dominated by cryptogamic species. The cover of mosses and lichens is very extensive within the Area. The most conspicuous vegetal communities are the associations of dominant lichens *Usnea-Himantormia* and the moss turf dominated by *Sanionia-Chorisodontium*. The algal community is dominated by the green fresh water alga *Prasiola crispa*, which is established around penguin colonies. The present flora includes one Antarctic flowering plant species, 51 lichen species, 29 moss species, six liverwort species, and one algae species. In the case of algae, only the species forming macroscopically detectable stands were recorded. No information on cyanobacteria and mycobiota occurring in this Area is available, as studies have not been undertaken. The detailed vegetation list is shown in Annex I.

6(ii) Access to the area

Access to the Area is possible on foot along the coast or by small boat without anchoring. The access routes and the landing site are shown in Map 6. Vehicle traffic of any type is not permitted inside the Area. Access restrictions apply within the Area, the specific conditions for which are set out in Section 7(ii) below.

6(iii) Location of structures within and adjacent to the Area

Only one refuge facility is located at the southeastern coast in the Area. The King Sejong Station (Republic of Korea), which is located 2 km to the northwest of Narębski Point, is the closest major facility.

6(iv) Location of other protected areas in the vicinity

• ASMA No. 1, Admiralty Bay, King George Island, South Shetland islands lies about 8 km northeast.

- ASPA No. 125, Fildes Peninsula, King George Island, South Shetland islands lies about 11 km west.

- ASPA No. 128, Western Shore of Admiralty Bay, King George Island, South Shetland islands lies about 17 km east.

- ASPA No. 132, Potter Peninsula, King George Island, South Shetland islands lies about 5 km east.

- ASPA No. 133, Harmony Point, Nelson Island, South Shetland islands lies about 25 km southwest.

- ASPA No. 150, Ardley Island, King George Island, South Shetland islands lies about 9 km to the west.

- ASPA No. 151, Lions Rump, King George Island, South Shetland islands lies about 35km northeast.

- HSM No. 36, Replica of a metal plaque erected by Eduard Dallmann at Potter Cove, King George Island, lies about 5 km east.

- HSM No. 50, Plaque to commemorate the research vessel Professor Siedlecki which landed in February 1976, Fildes Peninsula, King George Island lies about 10 km west.

- HSM No. 51, Grave of W. Puchalski, an artist and a producer of documentary films, who died on 19 January 1979, lies about 18 km northeast.

- HSM No. 52, Monolith erected to commemorate the establishment on 20 February 1985 of Great Wall Station (China), Fildes Peninsula, King George Island lies about 10 km west.

- HSM No. 82, Plaque at the foot of the monument commemorating the Signatories to the Antarctic Treaty and successive IPYs, lies about 12 km west.

6(v) Special zones within the Area

There are no special zones within the Area.

7. Terms and conditions for entry permits

7(i) General permit conditions

Entry into the Area is prohibited except in accordance with a permit issued by appropriate national authorities as designated under Article 7 of Annex V of the Protocol on Environmental Protection to the Antarctic Treaty.

Conditions for issuing a permit to enter the Area are that:

- It is issued only for scientific purposes that cannot be met elsewhere;

- The actions permitted will not jeopardize the natural ecological system of the Area;

- The actions permitted are in accordance with this Management Plan;

- Any management activities are in support of the objectives of the Management Plan;

- The permit, or an authorized copy, must be carried within the Area;

- Permits shall be valid for a stated period and identify the competent authority;

- A report regarding the visit shall be submitted to the competent national authority named in the permit.

7(ii) Access to, and movements within or over, the Area

- Access to the Area is possible on foot along the coast or by small boat without anchoring. The access routes and the landing site are shown in Map 6.

- Pedestrian movements should be kept with caution so as to minimize disturbance to flora and fauna, and should walk on snow or rocky terrain if practical, but taking care not to damage lichens.

- Vehicle traffic of any type is not permitted inside the Area.

- The operation of aircraft over the Area will be carried out, as a minimum requirement, in compliance with Resolution 2 (2004), "Guidelines for the Operation of Aircraft near Concentrations of Birds" . As a general rule, no aircraft should fly over the ASPA at less than 610 meters, except in cases of emergency or aircraft security. Over flights, however, should be avoided.

7(iii) Activities which may be conducted within the Area Scientific research activities that cannot be conducted elsewhere and that do not jeopardize the ecosystem of the Area;

- Essential management activities, including monitoring;
- Constraints may be placed on the use of motor-driven tools and any activity likely to generate noise and thereby cause disturbances to nesting birds during the breeding period (from October 1 to March 31).

7(iv) Installation, modification, or removal of structures

- No structures will be built and no equipment installed within the Area, with the exception of scientific or management activities, as specified in the permit.
- Any scientific equipment installed in the Area should be approved by a permit and clearly identify the permitting country, name of the principal investigator, and the year of installation and date of expected removal. All the equipment should pose a minimum risk of pollution to the Area or a minimum risk of causing disturbances to the flora or to the fauna.
- Signs of investigation should not remain after the permit expires. If a specific project cannot be finished within the allowed time period, an extension should be sought that authorizes the continued presence of any object in the Area.

7(v) Location of field camps

- Camping is prohibited within the Area except in an emergency, but if necessary, the use of the refuge facility located on the shore near the eastern boundary of the Area is strongly encouraged (see Map 2).

7(vi) Restriction on material and organisms which may be brought into the Area

- No living animals or plant material shall be deliberately introduced into the Area.
- No uncooked poultry products or fresh fruit and vegetables are to be taken into the Area.
- To minimize the risk of microbial or vegetation introductions from soils at other Antarctic sites, including the station, or from regions outside Antarctica, footwear and any equipment (particularly sampling equipment and markers) to be used in the Area shall be thoroughly cleaned before entering the Area (any terrestrial activity should be consistent with the 'Environmental code of conduct for terrestrial scientific field research in Antarctica').
- No herbicides or pesticides shall be introduced into the Area. Any other chemical product, which shall be introduced with the corresponding permit, shall be removed from the Area upon conclusion of the activity for which the permit was granted. The use and type of chemical products should be documented, as clearly as possible, for the knowledge of other researchers.
- Fuel, food, and other material are not to be stored in the Area, unless required for essential purposes connected with the activity for which the permit has been granted, provided it is securely stored so that wildlife cannot have access to it.

7(vii) Taking of, or harmful interference with, native flora and fauna

- Any taking or harmful interference, except in accordance with a permit, is prohibited and should be consistent with the *SCAR Code of Conduct for the use of Animals for Scientific Purposes* in Antarctica as a minimum requirement.
- Information on taking or harmful interference will be exchanged through the System of Information Exchange of the Antarctic Treaty.

7(viii) The collection or removal of materials not brought into the Area by the permit holder

- Collection or removal of materials not brought into the Area by the permit holder shall only be in accordance with a permit and should be limited to the minimum necessary to meet scientific or management needs.

- Anything of human origin likely to compromise the values of the Area, which were not brought into the Area by the permit holder or otherwise authorized, may be removed unless the impact of removal is likely to be greater than leaving the material *in situ*: if this is the case, the appropriate authority should be notified.

7(ix) Disposal of waste

- All wastes, including all human wastes, shall be removed from the Area. Human waste may be disposed of into the sea in accordance with Article 5 of Annex III of the Protocol on Environmental Protection to the Antarctic Treaty.

7(x) Measures that may be necessary to continue to meet the aims and objectives of the Management Plan

- Permits may be granted to enter the Area to carry out biological monitoring and site inspection activities, which may involve the collection of a small number of samples for scientific analysis, to erect or maintain signboards, or to carry out protective measures.

7(xi) Requirements for reports

The principal permit holder for each issued permit shall submit a report of activities undertaken in the Area. Such reports should include the information identified in the Visit Report form suggested by SCAR. This report shall be submitted to the authority named in the permit as soon as practicable, but not later than 6 months after the visit has taken place. Records of such reports should be stored indefinitely and made accessible to any interested Party, SCAR, CCAMLR, and COMNAP if requested, so as to provide necessary information of human activities in the Area to ensure adequate management of the Area.

8. Supporting documentation

Aguirre, C.A. & Acero, J.M. (1995) Distribution and abundance of birds in the Errera Channel, Antarctic Peninsula during the 1992/93 breeding season. Mar. Ornithol. 23, 129-134.

ASOC (2007) Implementing the Madrid Protpcol: A case study of Fildes Peninsula, King George Island, XXX ATCM/IP136.

ASOC (2008) Some land-based facilities used to support/manage Antarctic tourism in King George Island, XXXI ATCM/IP41.

Bednarek-Ochyra, H., Vana, R. & Lewis-Smith, R.I. (2000) The liverwort flora of Antarctica. Polish Academy of Sciences, Institute of Botany, Cracow.

Chang, S.K. (2004) Preliminary report on the ecology of the penguins observed in the cold years and a less cold year in the vicinity of King Sejong Station, King George Island off the Antarctic Peninsula. In: Annual report of environmental monitoring on human impacts at the King Sejong Station, Antarctica. KORDI, ECPP 03 102.

Esponda, C.M.G. Coria, N.R. & Montalti, D. (2000) Breeding birds at Halfmoon Island, South Shetland Islands, Antarctica, 1995/96. Mar. Ornithol. 28, 59-62.

Hagelin, J.C., and Miller, G.D. (1997) Nest-site selection in South polar skuas: Balancing nest safty and access to recources. Auk 114, 638-546.

Hahn, S., Peter, H-U., Quillfeldt, P. & Reinhardt, K. (1998) The birds of the Potter Peninsula, King George Island, South Shetland, Antarctica, 1965–1998, Mar. Ornithol. 26, 1-6.

Jablonski, B. (1984) Distribution and number of penguins in the region of King George Island, South Shetland Islands in the breeding season 1980/81. Polish Polar Research 5, 17-30.

Kim, D. (2002) Effect of variation in food supply on reproduction in Gentoo (*Pygoscelis papua*) and Chinstrap penguins (*P. antarctica*). p.195-222. In: Annual report of environmental monitoring on human impacts at the King Sejong Station, Antarctica. KORDI EC PP 01 001-B2.

Kim, J.H. Ahn, I.Y., Lee , K.S., Chung, H. & Choi, H.-G. (2007) Vegetation of Barton Peninsula in the neighbourhood of King Sejong Station (King George Island, Maritime Antarctic). Polar Biol. 30, 903-916.

Kim J.H., Chung, H., Kim, J.H., Yoo, J.C. & Ahn, I.Y. (2005) Nest distribution of skuas on Barton and Weaver peninsulas of the King George Island, the Antarctic. Ocean and Polar Research 27(4), 443-450.

KORDI (1998-2007) Annual Weather Report at King Sejong Station.

Lee, J.I., Hur, S.D., Yoo, C.M., Ueo, J.P., Kim, H., Hwang J., Choe, M.Y., Nam, S.H., Kim. Y., Park, B-K., Zheng X. & López- Martínez, J. (2002) Explanatory text of the geological map of Barton and Weaver Peninsulas, King George Island, Antarctica. Korea Ocean Research and Development Institute.

Lee YI, Lim HS & Yoon HI (2004) Geochemistry of soils of King George Island, South Shetland Islands, West Antarctica: implication for pedogenesis in cold polar regions. Geochim Cosmochim Acta 68, 4319–4333.

Lewis-Smith, R.I. and Poncet, S. (1985) New southernmost record for Antarctic flowering plants. Polar Record 22, 425-427.

López- Martínez, J., Serrano, E. & Lee, J.I. (2002) Geomorphological map of Barton and Weaver Peninsulas, King George Island, Antarctica. Korea Ocean Research and Development Institute.

Lumper, P., and Weidinger, K. (2000) Distribution, numbers and breeding of birds at the Northern Ice-free areas of Nelson Island, South Shetland Islands, 1990–1992. Mar. Ornithol. 28, 41-56.

Ministry of Environment (MOE) (2007) The fundamental study for designation of Antarctic Specially Protected Area. BSPN07030-71-3.

Ministry of Environment (MOE) (2011) Management of and monitoring on Antarctic Specially Protected Area . Ministry of Environment.

Ministry of Environment (MOE) (2012) Management of and monitoring on Antarctic Specially Protected Area (II). Ministry of Environment.

Ministry of Environment (MOE) (2013) Management of and monitoring on Antarctic Specially Protected Area (III). Ministry of Environment.

Ministry of Maritime Affairs and Fisheries (MAF) (1997) Overwintering Report of the 8th Korea Antarctic Research Program at King Sejong Station (November 1994-December 1995). BSE 520001-982-7.

Ministry of Science and Technology (MOST) (1989) A study on Natural Environment in the area around the Korea Antarctic Station, King George Island (II). BSPG00081-246-7.

Ministry of Science and Technology (MOST) (1992) The Research on Natural Environments and Resources of Antarctica. BSPG 00169-5-485-7.

Ministry of Science and Technology (MOST) (1993) Overwintering Report of the 4th Korea Antarctic Research Program at King Sejong Station (December 1991-December 1992). BSPN 00221-1-678-7.

Mönke, R. & Bick, A. (1988) Fachlicher Bericht über die Teilnahme der DDRBiologengruppe an der 31. Sowjetischen Antarktisexpedition (SAE), Station "Bellingshausen", King-George-Island (Südshetland Inseln/Antarktis), Berlin, Potsdam.

Ochyra, R. (1998) The moss flora of King George Island Antarctica. Polish Academy of Sciences, W. Szafer Institute of Botany, Cracow.

Øvstedal, D.O. & Lewis-Smith. R.I. (2001) Lichens of Antarctica and South Georgia: a guide to their identification and ecology. Cambridge University Press, Cambridge, P. 411.

Peter, H.-U., Kaiser, M. & Gebauer, A. (1986) Reisebericht - Teil 2, Wissenschaftliche Ergebnisse der Teilnahme an der 29. Sowjetischen Antarktisexpedition Überwinterungsgruppe, Station Bellingshausen 21.11.1983-18.05.1985, Berlin, Potsdam.

Peter, H.-U., Busser, C., Mustafa, O & Pfeiffer, S. (2005) Preliminary Results of the Research Project "Risk assessment for the Fildes Peninsula and Ardley Island and the development management plans for designation as ASMA (unpublished survey results presented at the Fildes meeting at INACH).

Pezzo, F.,Olmastroni, S., Corsolini, S., & Focardi, S. (2001) Factors affecting the breeding success of the south polar skua *Catharacta maccormicki* at Edmonson Point, Victoria Land, Antarctica. Polar Biol 24, 389-393.

Rauschert, M., Zippel, D. & Gruner, M. (1987) Reisebericht Teil 2. Fachlicher Bericht über die Teilnahme der Biologengruppe der DDR an der 30. Sowjetischen Antarktisexpedition (SAE), Station "Bellingshausen", King George Island (Südshetlandinseln/Antarktis), unveröffentl. Ber. Berlin, Potsdam.

Schroeter, B., Kappen, L. Green, T.G.A. & Seppelt, R.D. (1997) Lichens and the Antarctic environment: effect of temperature and water availability on phytosynthetisis. In Ecosystem processes in Antarctic ice-free landscapes, ed. W.B. Lyons, C. Howard-Williams & I. Hawes, pp. 103-117. Rotterdam, Balkema.

Shuford, W.D. & Spear, L.B. (1988) Survey of Breeding Penguins and other seabirds in the South Shetland Islands, Antarctica, January-February 1987. NOAA Technical Memorandum NMFS-F/NEC-59.

Takahashi, A., Kokubun N., Mori, Y. & Shin, H-C. (2008) Krill-feeding behaviour of gentoo penguins as shown by animal-borne camera loggers. Polar Biol. 31, 1291-1294.

Trivelpiece, W, Butler, R.G. & Volkman, N.J. (1980) Feeding territoties of brown skuas (*Catharacta lonnbergi*). Auk 97, 669-676.

Trivelpiece, W.Z., Trivelpiece, S.G. & Volkman, N.J. (1987) Ecological segregation of adelie, gentoo, Chinstrap penguins at King George Island, Antarctica. Ecology 68, 351-361.

Yoon, M.B. (1990) Observation of birds around King Sejong Station during 1989/90 austral summer. In A study on Natural Environment in the Area Around the Korean Antarctic Station, King George Island (III). pp.433-459. MOST BSPG-00111-317-7.

Yoo, C.M., Choe, M.Y., Jo, H.R., Kim, Y. & Kim, K.H. (2001) Vocaniclastic sedimentation of the Sejong Formation (Late Paleocene-Eocene), Barton Peninsula, King George Island, Antarctica. Ocean and Polar Research, 23, 97-107.

Vaughan, D.G., Marshall, G.J., Connolley, W.M., King, J.C. & Mulvaney, R. (2001) Devil in the detail. Science 293, 1777-1779.

ANNEX I. List of flora in the Site

Taxa

Lichens
Acrospora austroshetlandica (C.W. Dodge) Øvstedal
Bryoria sp.
Buellia anisomera Vain.
Buellia russa (Hue)Darb.
Caloplaca lucens (Nyl.) Zahlbr.
Caloplaca sublobulata (Nyl.) Zahlbr.
Cetraria aculeata (Schreb.) Fr.
Cladonia borealis S. Stenroos
Cladonia chlorophaea (Flörke ex Sommerf.) Spreng.
Cladonia furcata (Huds.) Schaer.
Cladonia gracilis (L.) Willd.
Cladonia merochlorophaea var *novochlorophaea* Sipman
Cladonia pleurota (Flörke) Schaer.
Cladonia pyxidata (L.) Hoffm.
Cladonia scabriuscula (Delise) Nyl.
Haematomma erythromma (Nyl.) Zahlbr
Himantormia lugubris (Hue.) I. M. Lamb
Huea coralligera (Hue) C. W. Dodge & G. E. Baker
Lecania brialmontii (Vain.) Zahlbr.
Lecania gerlachei (Vain.) Darb.
Lecanora polytropa (Hoffm.) Rabenh.
Lecidea cancriformis C.W. Dodge and G.E. Baker
Lecidella carpathica Körb.
Massalongia carnosa (Dicks.) Körb.
Ochlorechia frigida (Sw.) Lynge
Pannaria austro-orcadensis Øvstedal
Pertusaria excudens Nyl.
Physcia caesia (Hoffm.) Fürnr.
Physcia dubia (Hoffm.) Lettau
Physconia muscigena (Ach.) Poelt
Placopsis contourtuplicata I. M. Lamb
Porpidia austrosheltandica Hertel
Pseudophebe pubescens (L.) M. Choisy
Psoroma cinnamomeum Malme
Psoroma hypnorum (Vahl) Gray
Ramalina terebrata Hook f, & Taylor
Rhizocarpon geographicum (L.) DC.
Rhizoplaca aspidophora (Vain.) Redón
Rhizoplaca melanophthalma (Ram.) Leuckert & Poelt
Rinodina olivaceobrunnea C.W. Dodge & G. B. Baker
Sphaerophorus globosus (Huds.) Vain.
Stereocaulon alpinum Laurer
Tephromela atra (Huds.) Hafellmer ex Kalb
Tremolecia atrata (Ach.) Hertel
Turgidosculum complicatulum (Nyl.) J. Kohlm. & E. Kohlm
Umbilicaria antarctica Frey & I. M. Lamb
Umbilicaria decussata (Vill.) Zahlbr.
Usnea antarctica Du Rietz
Usnea aurantiaco-atra (Jacq.) Bory

Xanthoria candelaria (L.) Th. Fr.
Xanthoria elegans (Link) Th. Fr.

Mosses
Andreaea depressinervis Cardot
Andreaea gainii Cardot
Andreaea regularis Müll. Hal.
Bartramia patens Brid.
Bryum argenteum Hedw.
Bryum orbiculatifolium Cardot & Broth.
Bryum pseudotriquetrum (Hedw.) C.F. Gaertn. et al.
Ceratodon purpureus (Hedw.) Brid.
Chorisodontium aciphyllum (Hook. f. & Wils.)
Dicranoweisia brevipes (Müll. Hal.) Cardot
Dicranoweisia crispula (Hedw.) Lindb. Ex Milde
Ditrichum hyalinum (Mitt.) Kuntze
Ditrichum lewis-smithii Ochyra
Encalypta rhaptocarpa Schwägr.
Hennediella antarctica (Ångstr.) Ochyra & Matteri
Notoligotrichum trichodon (Hook. f. Wils.) G. L. Sm.
Pohlia drummondii (Müll. Hal.) A. K. Andrews
Pohlia nutans (Hedw.) Lindb.
Pohlia wahlenbergii (Web. & Mohr) A. L. Andrews
Polytrichastrum alpinum (Hedw.) G. L. Sm.
Polytrichum strictum Brid.
Racomitrium sudeticum (Funck) Bruch & Schimp.
Sanionia georgico-uncinata (Müll. Hal.) Ochyra & Hedenäs
Sanionia uncinata (Hedw.) Loeske
Schistidium antarctici (Card.) L. I. Savicz & Smirnova
Syntrichia filaris (Müll. Hal.) Zand.
Syntrichia princeps (De Not.) Mitt.
Syntrichia saxicola (Card.) Zand.
Warnstorfia sarmentosa (Wahlenb.) Hedenäs

Liverworts
Barbilophozia hatcheri (A. Evans) Loeske
Cephalozia badia (Gottsche) Steph.
Cephaloziella varians (Gottsche) Steph.
Herzogobryum teres (Carrington & Pearson) Grolle
Lophozia excisa (Dicks.) Dumort.
Pachyglossa disstifidolia Herzog & Grolle

Algae
Prasiola crispa (Ligtf.) Menegh.

Flowering plant
Deschampsia antarctica Desv.

ANNEX II. Maps

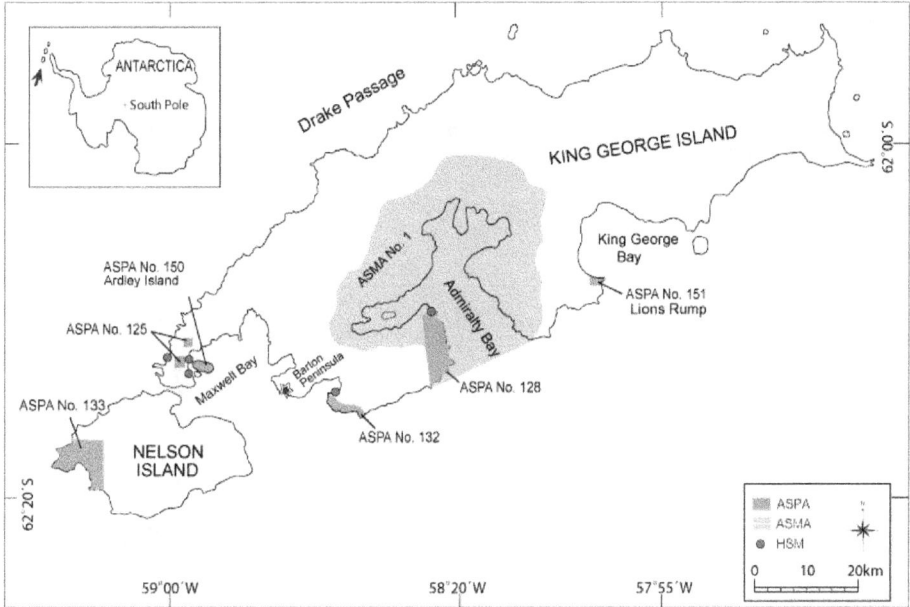

Map 1. Location of Narębski Point (✷) in relation to King George Island and the existing protected areas (ASMA, ASPAs, and HSMs)

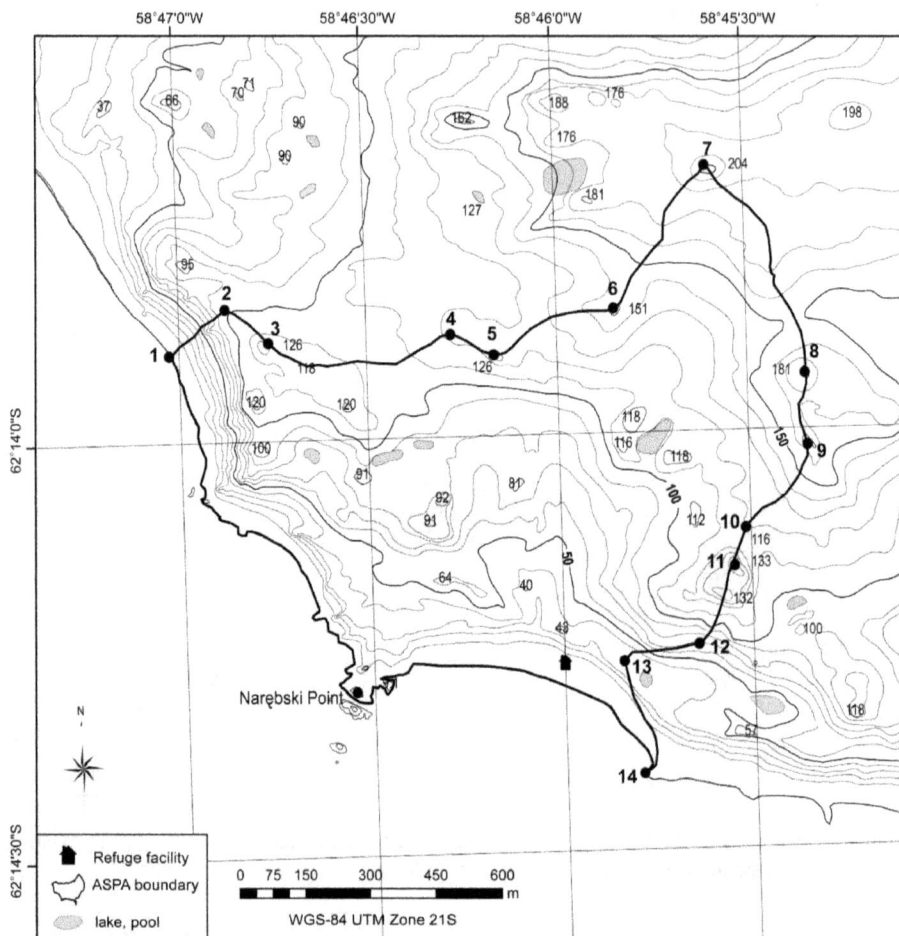

	Latitude	Longitude		Latitude	Longitude
1	62°13′53.69″S	58°47′01.31″W	9	62°14′00.86″S	58°45′20.85″W
2	62°13′50.48″S	58°46′52.37″W	10	62°14′06.96″S	58°45′30.62″W
3	62°13′52.85″S	58°46′45.84″W	11	62°14′09.73″S	58°45′33.08″W
4	62°13′52.53″S	58°46′16.62″W	12	62°14′15.30″S	58°45′38.87″W
5	62°13′54.18″S	58°46′09.53″W	13	62°14′16.43″S	58°45′50.37″W
6	62°13′51.11″S	58°45′50.64″W	14	62°14′24.55″S	58°45′48.00″W
7	62°13′40.97″S	58°45′35.60″W	NP	62°14′18.17″S	58°46′32.99″W
8	62°13′55.95″S	58°45′20.71″W			

Map 2. Boundary of the ASPA No. 171

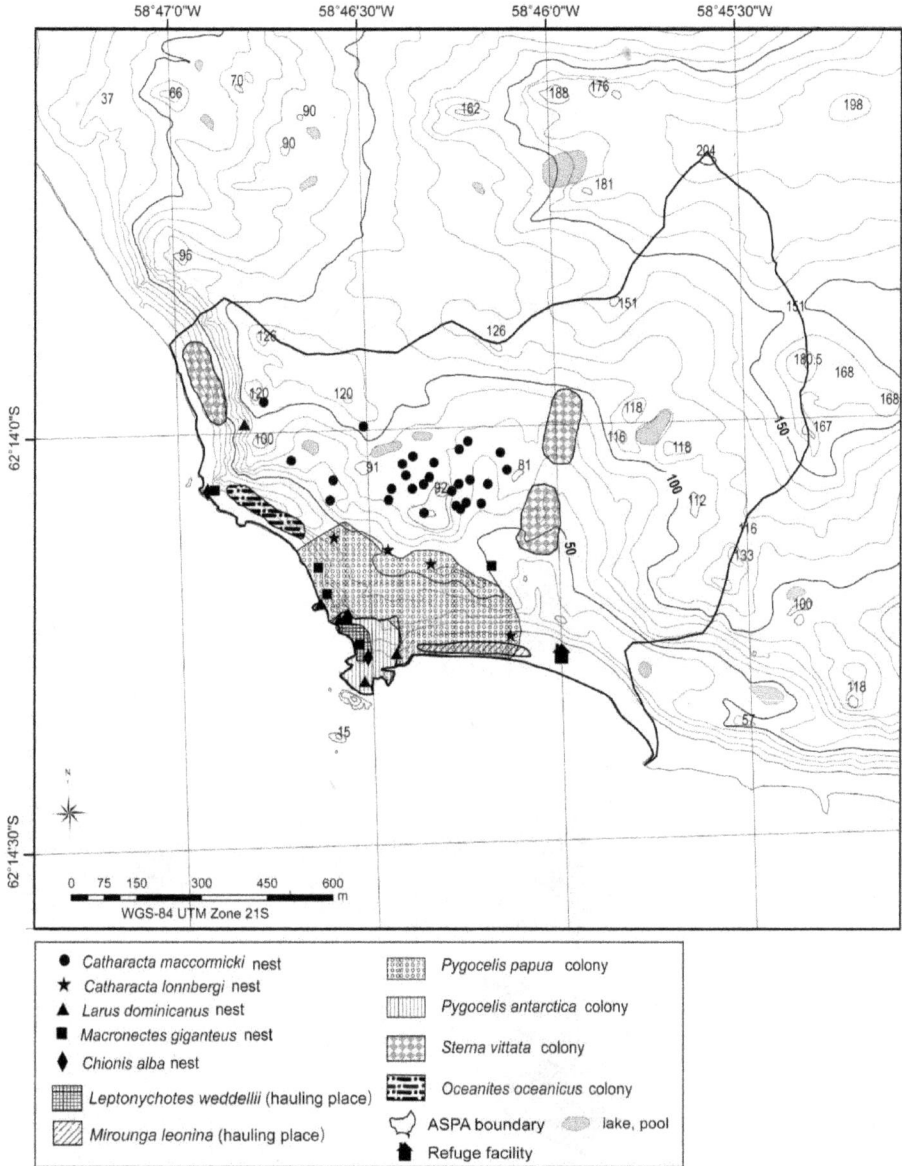

Map 3. Distribution of bird colonies and seal haul-out sites within the ASPA No. 171

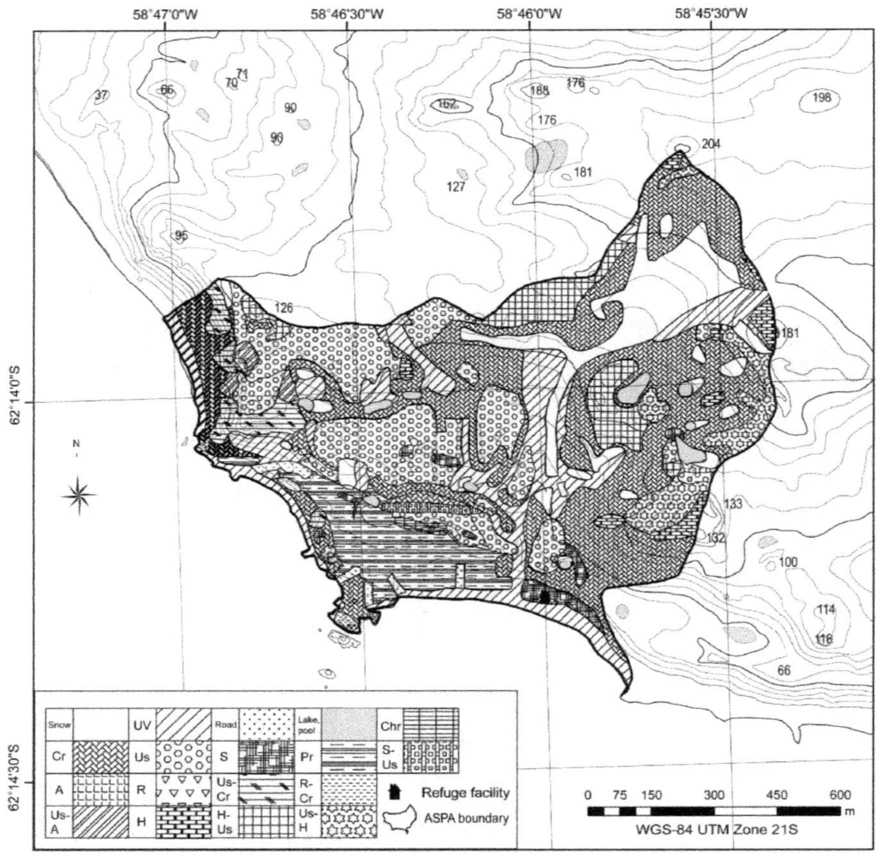

Community abbreviations

UV: unvegetated area
Cr: Crustose lichens
S: *Sanionia* spp., Pr: *Prasiola*
Chr: *Chorisodontium aciphyllum*
A: *Andreaea*, Us: *Usnea* spp.
R: *Ramalina terebrata*
Us-Cr: *Usnea-Crustose* lichens
R-Cr: *Ramalina-Crustose* lichens
S-Us: *Sanionia-Usnea* spp.
Us-A: *Usnea-Andreaea*
H: *Himantormia lugubris*
H-Us: *Himantormia-Usnea*
Us-H: *Usnea-Himantormia*

**Total coverage of each
community (%)**

Cr: 75.2	S: 99.9	Pr: 86.8
Chr: 100	A: 93.8	Us: 95.4
R: 100		Us-Cr: 93.1
R-Cr: 100		S-Us: 98.2
Us-A: 98		H: 100
H-Us: 99.6		Us-H: 98.8

WGS-84 UTM Zone 21S

0 75 150 300 450 600 m

Map 4. Distribution of plant communities in the ASPA No. 171

182

58°47'0"W 58°46'30"W 58°46'0"W 58°45'30"W

62°14'0"S

62°14'30"S

37 66 70 71 90 90 162 188 176 176 198
127 181 204
95 126 181
120 118 150
116
133
132
100
100
43
14
12 118
15 57

N

0 75 150 300 450 600 m

WGS-84 UTM Zone 21S

Legend

- Contours on rock
- Scarp
- Over-deepened basin
- Rock bar, riegel
- Roches moutonnees, abraded & plucked surfaces
- Lake, pool
- Seasonal streams
- Gorge
- Nivation niche
- Patterned ground
- Present-day beach & Holocene raised beaches
- Middle platforms and scarps
- Upper platforms and scarps
- Highest marine deposits
- Till, glacial deposit
- Stone stripes
- Gelifluction lobes
- Debris slope
- Stone stream
- Refuge facility
- ASPA boundary

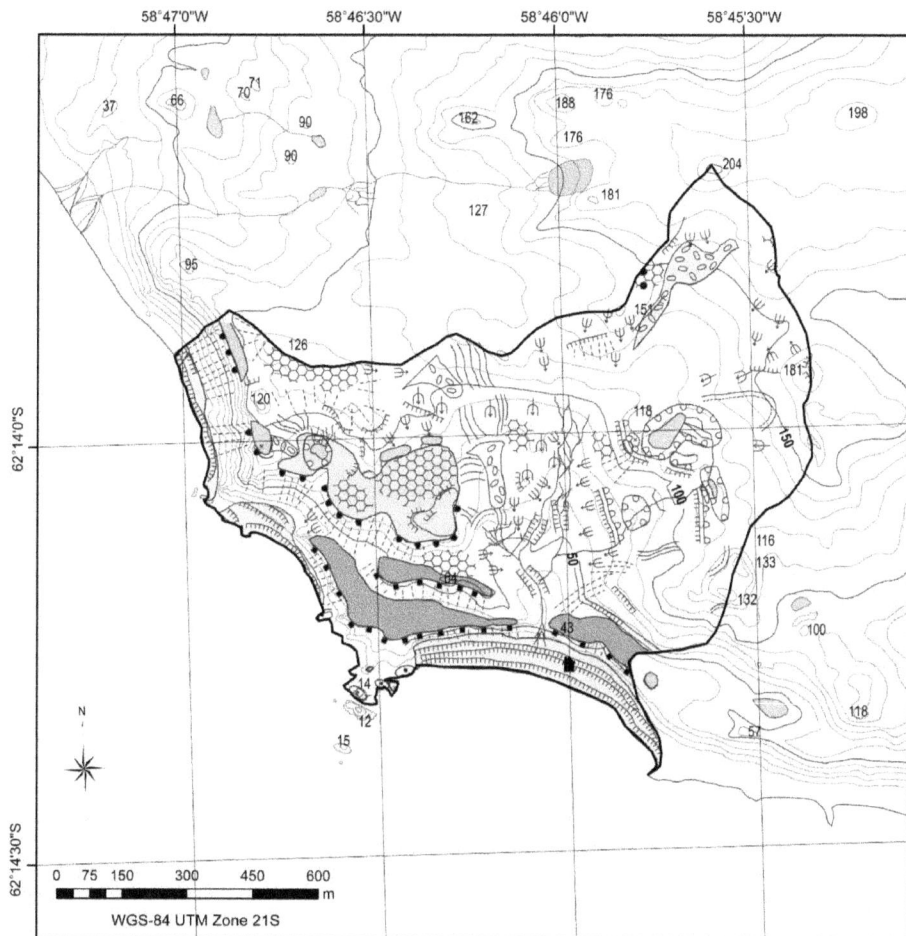

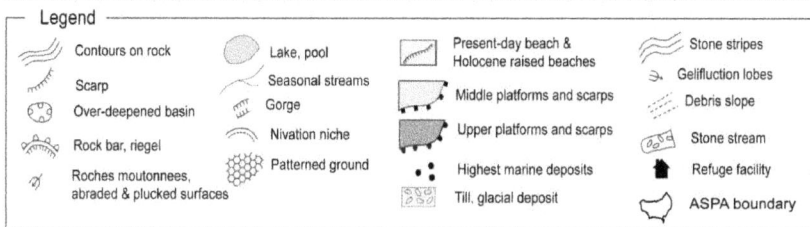

Map 5. Geomorphologic details of the ASPA No. 171

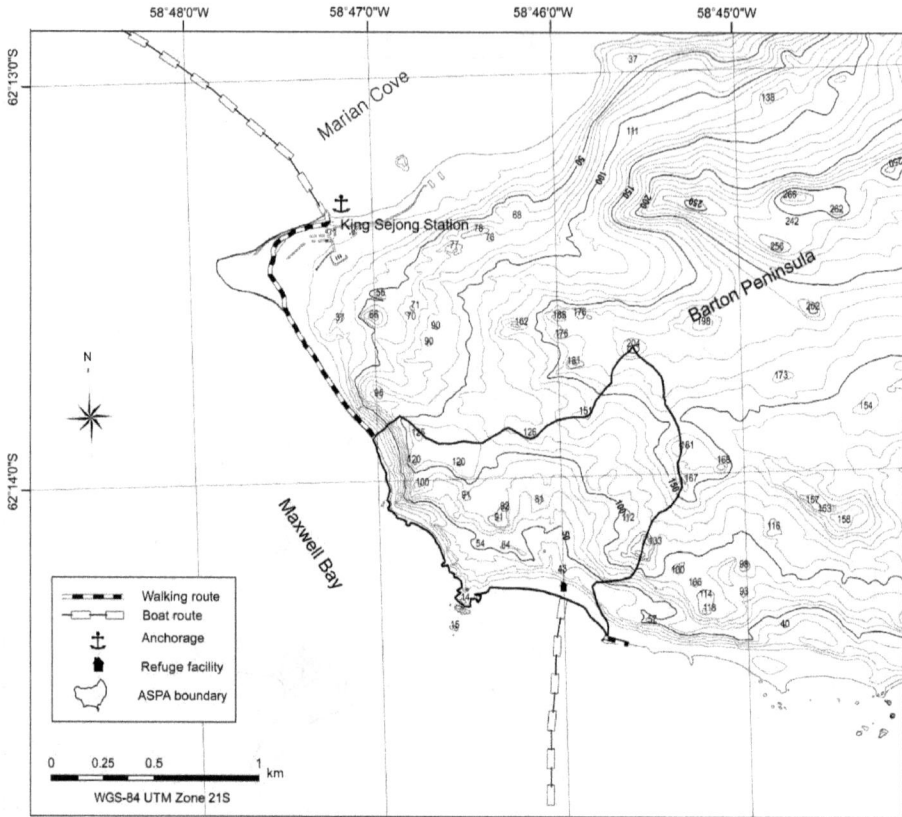

Map 6. Access routes to the ASPA No. 171

Management Plan for
Antarctic Specially Protected Area No. 174

STORNES, LARSEMANN HILLS, PRINCESS ELIZABETH LAND

Introduction

Stornes (69°25'S, 76°6'E) is the largest peninsula in the Larsemann Hills, on the south-eastern coast of Prydz Bay, Princess Elizabeth Land, East Antarctica. Stornes is located within Antarctic Specially Managed Area (ASMA) No. 6 Larsemann Hills, which was designated under Measure 2 (2007). In the original Larsemann Hills ASMA Management Plan, Stornes was designated a restricted zone.

Stornes appears to be geologically unique in the development of the borosilicate minerals boralsilite, prismatine and grandidierite, and of the phosphate mineral wagnerite. These mineral assemblages are considered highly significant in both their variety and areal extent, and the richness of extremely rare granulite-facies borosilicate and phosphate mineralogy is notable. The ASPA is primarily designated to protect the outstanding geological features of this area, specifically the rare mineral occurrences and the highly unusual host rocks in which they occur. Such protection will also maintain the overall geological integrity and context of these rare mineral occurrences for future study, and for preserving the possibility of discovery of new mineral species and occurrences.

Stornes is also one of only two locations on the East Antarctic margin where fossiliferous sediments contain evidence of the palaeoenvironment at a time of reduced ice volume some 4 million years ago.

The Area is located in relatively close proximity to continually-occupied stations and its geological values are therefore susceptible to damage from over-sampling or unauthorised removals; and disturbance from field research and logistical activities, including the use of vehicles and the establishment of infrastructure. ASPA designation assists in ensuring that this geologically significant location is protected for future studies of the palaeoenvironment of Antarctica.

Designation of Stornes as an ASPA also recognises the desirability of protecting this infrequently visited and relatively minimally impacted peninsula as a reference site for future comparison with other parts of the Larsemann Hills where several research stations are located.

Description of values to be protected

Geological values

Stornes is unique on account of the presence of a diverse suite of borosilicate minerals (five species) and phosphate minerals (nine species). The relatively rare borosilicates prismatine and grandidierite are found abundantly in spectacular crystals and segregations over a wide area, while the ferromagnesian fluorphosphate wagnerite forms spectacular nodules locally and microscopic grains regionally.

Stornes is the discovery (or type) locality for three new mineral species: the boron mineral boralsilite and the phosphate minerals stornesite-(yttrium) and tassieite. In addition, wagnerite occurs as two different polytypes (that is, having the same chemical formula but different crystal structure); indeed the first discovery of wagnerite showing polytypism was in specimens from the Larsemann Hills. Furthermore, the boron minerals grandidierite, prismatine and dumortierite, as well as wagnerite, are present in unusual abundance or as large crystals in the Larsemann Hills; few localities elsewhere in the world can compare. It is the spectacular development of these minerals and boralsilite, one of the few recently described minerals to be readily visible to the naked eye, which makes these rare minerals vulnerable to damage.

Scientific values

The borosilicate and phosphate assemblages at Stornes are considered scientifically significant both in their variety and origin. A major question being addressed in ongoing research is what geologic processes concentrated boron and phosphorus to such an extent.

Sediments on north-eastern Stornes (at approximately 69°25'S 76°0'E) contain abundant well preserved foraminifera, diatoms and fragmentary molluscs which allow determination of age and palaeoenvironment at a time (4 Ma) when Antarctic ice volume was reduced. This location represents one of only two recorded sites in East Antarctica displaying sediment from this time interval. The sediments are thin and friable and thus require protection from human disturbance which may jeopardise future scientific investigations.

The ice sheet on Stornes has almost no connection with the Antarctic plateau. Its size (about 2 km in diameter), position and isolation make it an accessible and interesting object for glaciological research in the Larsemann Hills. Modern surveying techniques allow observations of this kind. As a comparatively small body of ice, the glacier does not have much inertia and as such it will rapidly respond to and indicate climate change. Studies of this site combined with glaciological monitoring observations undertaken in other oases, will generate new knowledge in the region.

Stornes has been infrequently visited and is minimally impacted by human activities. ASPA protection also serves to establish a reference site for possible future comparison with other peninsulas within the Larsemann Hills which have been subject to notable alteration as a result of the establishment and operation of research stations. To this end, the ASPA encompasses as large an area of the peninsula as possible while accommodating the logistics that may be needed to service the research stations that were established before the ASPA and ASMA were designated.

1. Aims and objectives

Management of the ASPA aims to:

- avoid degradation of, or substantial risk to, the values of the Area by preventing unnecessary or inadvertent human disturbance through uncontrolled access and inappropriate collections of geological material;
- allow scientific research in the Area provided it is for compelling reasons which cannot be served elsewhere;
- preserve the Area as a reference area for future comparative studies, in particular with station areas in the Larsemann Hills; and
- allow visits for management purposes in support of the aims of the Management Plan.

2. Management activities

To protect the values of the Area:

- information about the ASPA, including copies of this Management Plan, shall be made available on vessels and at facilities operating in the region;
- personnel in the vicinity of, accessing or flying over the Area shall be specifically instructed, by their national program, as to the provisions and contents of the Management Plan;
- markers or signs erected within the Area for scientific or management purposes shall be secured and maintained in good condition and removed when no longer required;
- abandoned equipment or materials shall be removed to the maximum extent possible provided that doing so does not adversely impact on the values of the Area;
- national Antarctic programs operating in the Area shall work together to ensure the above aims are supported; and
- the Management Plan shall be reviewed no less than once every five years, and jointly updated by the Parties active in the Larsemann Hills (i.e. those participating in the ASMA Management Group).

3. Period of designation

Designated for an indefinite period.

4. Maps

Map A: Antarctic Specially Protected Area No. 174, Larsemann Hills, Princess Elizabeth Land.

Map B: Antarctic Specially Protected Area No. 174, Stornes, Larsemann Hills, Geology.

All map specifications: Horizontal Datum: WGS84; Projection: UTM Zone 43

5. Description of the Area

5(i) Geographical co-ordinates, boundary markers and natural features

General description

Stornes (69°25'S, 76°6'E) lies within the Larsemann Hills, a coastal ice-free area in southern Prydz Bay, East Antarctica. Stornes is located between Thala Fjord and Wilcock Bay and is 21.13 km² in area. The ASPA comprises the majority of Stornes, plus small unnamed promontories to the south-west (see Map B). The Area does not have a marine component.

Boundary coordinates for the Area are provided at Appendix 1.The Area boundary comprises the coastline (following the low tide mark) between a point on the western side of Thala Fjord at 76°8'29"E, 69°25'29"S (boundary point 1) to a point to the south of McCarthy Point at 76°3'22"E, 69°28'40"S (boundary point 25). The remainder of the boundary largely follows the southern limit of rock outcrops between the aforementioned points. An indentation from the coast on the eastern side of the peninsula accommodates the potential need for vehicle landings and access to the inland and Broknes when ice conditions do not allow the use of preferred landings and routes elsewhere in the Larsemann Hills.

Where possible the boundary uses natural features (e.g. coastline, contours and rock outcrops) for ease of on-ground navigation.

Geology

The Larsemann Hills area contains sedimentary and volcanic rocks that were laid down between 900 and 550 million years ago. Stornes is underlain by Proterozoic metasediments, deformed felsic orthogneisses, and early Palaeozoic granites and post-tectonic pegmatites. Proterozoic metasediments, collectively termed the Brattstrand Paragneiss, are exposed along a north-east trending corridor across central Stornes and an area to the south and east of Allison Ice Dome. The metasediments comprise a heterogeneous package of pelitic, psammatic and possible volcanogenic rocks that are characterised by unusual enrichment in boron (B) and phosphorous (P) and which host the rare B and P-bearing minerals found on Stornes. Precursor Brattstrand Paragneiss sediments were deposited (probably at ca. 950-1000 Ma) onto Mesoproterozoic crystalline 'basement' represented by the Søstrene Orthogneiss (ca. 1125 Ma), a layered felsic-mafic orthogneiss and which is best exposed on islands to the north and northeast of Stornes (e.g. McLeod Island, see Carson and Grew 2007). During an early Palaeozoic (ca. 530-515 Ma) high-grade tectonometamorphic event, the Brattstrand Paragneisses were tectonically transposed and interleaved with the felsic Blundell Orthogneiss (emplaced ca. 970 Ma), a widespread unit exposed on northern and southern Stornes. A number of granite bodies (e.g. Progress Granite) were also emplaced during the early Palaeozoic (ca. 520 Ma) high-grade tectonometamorphic event followed by the emplacement of minor planar post-tectonic felsic pegmatites.

In the north-east of the Area, the basement rocks are overlain by a patchy discontinuous layer of redeposited loose marine sediment with abundant fragmentary molluscs, well-preserved benthic foraminifera (Quilty *et al.*1990) and diatoms (McMinn and Harwood 1995) which provide the basis for the determination of age and palaeoenvironment. The fossils continue to provide data on past water temperature and age.

Glaciology

The peninsula includes a small glacier (approximately 2 km in diameter) that is separated from and has almost no connection with the Antarctic plateau. Its position, isolation and size make it a readily accessible and interesting object for glaciological research in the Larsemann Hills.

Vegetation

The terrestrial macroflora of the Larsemann Hills consists of at least 31 lichens, 6 mosses and 1 liverwort. No systematic studies have been undertaken on the terrestrial and lacustrine algae and cyanobacteria. However, in many areas of seasonal snow melt, extensive blackened areas can be seen where cyanobacteria and microscopic algae predominate. The availability of shelter from wind and wind-borne abrasives (snow, sand), and the local topographic features play a significant role in determining the distribution and abundance of the indigenous cryptogamic flora. In scattered moister sites, small moss beds occur. Sub-fossil moss (*Bryum pseudotriquetrum*) predating the last glacial maximum has been recovered from lacustrine deposits. The dominant lichen vegetation is found primarily on rocky slopes and outcrops but is nowhere particularly abundant. Floristically, the Larsemann Hills region is thought to be similar to many other outcroppings of the Ingrid Christensen Coast south from the Vestfold Hills and Rauer Islands.

Climate

A major feature of the climate of the Larsemann Hills area is the existence of persistent, strong katabatic winds that blow from the north-east most summer days. Day time air temperatures from December to February frequently exceed 4°C and can exceed 10°C, with the mean monthly temperature a little above 0°C. Mean monthly winter temperatures are between −15°C and −18°C. Pack ice is extensive inshore throughout summer, and the fjords and bays are rarely ice-free. Precipitation occurs as snow and is unlikely to exceed 250 mm water equivalent annually. Snow cover is generally deeper and more persistent on Stornes than it is on Broknes to its east. This is due to north-easterly prevailing winds and the perennial sea ice held in by the islands offshore from Stornes.

Seals

Weddell seals (*Leptonychotes weddelli*) are numerous on the Larsemann Hills coast. Pupping has been observed from October onwards on the sea ice adjacent to small islands north-east of eastern Broknes, and in late December groups of moulting seals have been observed hauled out near the Broknes shore adjacent to the stations and in tide cracks in the fjords to the west. Aerial surveys during the moulting period have observed greater than 1000 seals, with multiple large groups (50–100 seals) hauled out in Thala Fjord and on rafted ice immediately to the west of Stornes, and numerous smaller groups amongst offshore islands and ice to the northeast of Broknes. Crabeater seals (*Lobodon carcinophagus*) and leopard seals (*Hydrurga leptonyx*) are also occasional visitors to the region.

Seabirds

Three species of seabird breed within the Larsemann Hills area (south polar skuas, snow petrels and Wilson's storm petrels). Approximate numbers and locations of breeding pairs are documented for Broknes, and particularly eastern Broknes, but their distribution throughout the remainder of the area, including Stornes, is uncertain.

South polar skuas (*Catharacta maccormicki*) are present in the Larsemann Hills between mid-late October and early April, with approximately 17 breeding pairs nesting on Broknes and similar numbers of non-breeding birds present.

Snow petrel (*Pagodroma nivea*) and Wilson's storm petrel (*Oceanites oceanicus*) nests are found in sheltered bedrock fragments, crevices, boulder slopes and rock falls, and are generally occupied from October until February. Approximately 850–900 pairs of snow petrels and 40–50 pairs of Wilson's storm petrels are found on Broknes, with concentrations of snow petrels at Base Ridge and on rocky outcrops adjacent to the Dålk Glacier in the east and the plateau in the south.

Despite the apparent suitable exposed nesting habitat, no Adelie penguin (*Pygoscelis adeliae)* breeding colonies are found at Stornes, possibly due to the persistence of sea ice past the hatching period. Birds from colonies on nearby island groups (between the Svenner and Bolingen Islands) visit during summer to moult.

Environmental domains and biogeographic regions

Stornes is one of very few ASPAs designated primarily for the protection of geological values (i.e. ASPA 125 Fildes Peninsula, ASPA 147 Ablation Point, ASPA 148 Mount Flora and ASPA 168 Mount Harding), and the only ASPA designated primarily to protect mineral occurrences. Based on the Environmental Domains Analysis for Antarctica (Resolution 3 (2008)) Stornes is located within Environment D - East Antarctic coastal geologic. With reference to the Antarctic Conservation Biogeographic Regions identified in Resolution 6 (2012), Stornes is located within the East Antarctica Biogeographic Region.

5(ii) Access to the Area

A section of the eastern boundary of the ASPA approximates a route to the plateau that may be taken by vehicles landed near boundary point 1 (see Map B and coordinates at Appendix 1) on the western side of Thala Fjord. Vehicles travelling to the plateau along this boundary may, between boundary points 3 and 12, deviate to the west if essential to avoid hazards to navigation. Any such deviations will not extend beyond 200 m of the boundary line and must be restricted to crossings of snow or ice. Vehicles may not enter the Area for any other reason.

There are no specified helicopter or boat landing sites or access points, and no marked walking routes within the Area. Landings and overflights are permitted and where possible are to avoid routes over the lakes.

5(iii) Location of structures within and adjacent to the Area

There are no permanent structures within the Area.

The Area is approximately 1.6 km to the south-west of Bharati station (India) and approximately 9.3 km to the south-west of Eastern Broknes, on which Zhongshan station (China), Progress station (Russian Federation) and Law-Racovita-Negoita (Australia and Romania) are located.

A Russian hut is sited at 69°25'27"S, 76°08'25"E on the Thala Fjord side of Stornes, outside the ASPA (see Map B).

5(iv) Location of other protected areas in the vicinity

The Area is contained entirely within ASMA 6, Larsemann Hills, East Antarctica (69°30'S, 76°19'58"E).

ASPA 169, Amanda Bay, Ingrid Christensen Coast, Princess Elizabeth Land, East Antarctica (69°15'S, 76°49'59.9"E.) is located approximately 27 km to the north-east.

5(v) Special zones within the Area

There are no special zones within the Area.

6. Terms and conditions for entry permits

6(i) General permit conditions

Entry into the Area is prohibited except in accordance with a permit issued by an appropriate national authority. Conditions for issuing a permit to enter the Area are that:

- it is issued for compelling scientific reasons which cannot be served elsewhere, or for reasons essential to the management of the Area;
- the actions permitted are in accordance with this Management Plan;
- the activities permitted will give due consideration via the environmental impact assessment process to the continued protection of the scientific values of the Area;
- the permit shall be issued for a finite period; and
- the permit shall be carried when in the Area.

6(ii) Access to, and movement within or over, the Area

Vehicles are prohibited within the Area other than as described at Section 6(ii); all movement within the Area should be on foot.

Pedestrian traffic should be kept to the minimum necessary to undertake permitted activities and every reasonable effort should be made to minimise disturbance to sediments, vegetation, outcrops and other features of scientific and environmental value.

All landings and aircraft movements in the vicinity of the Area should avoid disturbance to any concentrations of wildlife. The operation of aircraft over the Area should be carried out, as a minimum requirement, in compliance with the 'Guidelines for the Operation of Aircraft near Concentrations of Birds' contained in Resolution 2 (2004). Landings in the area should be minimised.

6(iii) Activities which are, or may be conducted within the Area, including restrictions on time and place

Activities which may be conducted in the Area include:

- scientific research which cannot be undertaken elsewhere and that will not jeopardise the values for which the Area has been designated, or the ecosystems of the Area;
- glaciological monitoring and
- essential management activities, including monitoring.

Where geological sampling is involved this should, as a minimum standard, be in accordance with the following principles:

- Sampling should be done with the minimum disturbance practical.
- Sampling should be kept to the minimum necessary to achieve the research.
- Enough material/specimens should be left to allow future workers to understand the context of the material.
- Sample site should be left free of markings (paint, labels etc).
- Specimens should be retained in a recognised repository after the project finishes.
- Details of the GPS location of collection sites, volume/weight and type of material collected, and where the removed material will be housed, should be detailed in permit reports. A copy of these details should also be provided to the ASMA 6 Larsemann Hills Management Group to facilitate the review of the management plan and to enable the Management Group to provide advice to other Parties regarding the existence of materials in geological repositories, with a view to minimising unnecessary new or additional sampling.

6(iv) Installation, modification, or removal of structures

No structures are to be erected within the Area, or scientific equipment installed, except for compelling scientific or Area management reasons. Installations/structures may only be retained for a pre-established period, as specified in a permit.

All markers, structures or scientific equipment installed in the Area must be clearly identified by country, name of the principal investigator or agency, year of installation and date of expected removal.

All such items should be free of organisms, propagules (e.g. seeds, insect eggs) and non-sterile soil, and be made of materials that can withstand the environmental conditions and pose minimal risk of contamination of the Area.

Installation (including site selection), maintenance, modification or removal of structures and equipment shall be undertaken in a manner that minimises disturbance to the values of the Area.

Any new installations/structures are not to duplicate any existing installations/structures.

Permanent structures or installations are prohibited with the exception of survey markers.

6(v) Location of field camps

To minimise impacts associated with human activity, camping in the ASPA should be avoided. If camping is unavoidable, existing campsites should be used where possible. Sites previously used include northern central Stornes (at 69°24'13.1"S, 76°6'10.6"E) where there is a flat apron of alluvium between two small freshwater lakes, and on Priddy Promontory (at 69°25'39.9"S, 76°1'56.2"E) where there is a narrow beach adjacent to a tidal pool.

6(vi) Restrictions on materials and organisms that may be brought into the Area

The deliberate introduction of animals, plant material, micro-organisms and non-sterile soil into the Area shall not be permitted.

Precautions shall be taken to prevent the accidental introduction of animals, plant material, micro-organisms and non-sterile soil from other biologically distinct regions (within or beyond the Antarctic Treaty area); the biosecurity provisions for ASMA 6 Larsemann Hills apply to the ASPA.

Fuel or other chemicals shall not be stored in the Area unless specifically authorised by permit condition. They shall be stored and handled in a way that minimises the risk of their accidental introduction into the environment.

Materials introduced into the Area shall be for a stated period only and shall be removed by the end of that stated period.

6(vii) Taking of, or harmful interference with, native flora and fauna

Taking of, or harmful interference with, native flora and fauna is prohibited except in accordance with a permit issued in accordance with Annex II to the Protocol on Environmental Protection to the Antarctic Treaty. Where taking or harmful interference with animals is involved this should, as a minimum standard, be in accordance with the *SCAR Code of Conduct for the Use of Animals for Scientific Purposes in Antarctica.*

6(viii) Collection or removal of anything not brought into the Area by the permit holder

Material may only be collected or removed from the Area as authorised in a permit and should be limited to the minimum necessary to meet scientific or management needs. Upon completion of their study, all geological samples shall be housed in an appropriate educational facility or national geological survey to allow access by others, thus minimising the quantity of samples taken from the Area. Records of samples and sampling sites are to be maintained by the appropriate national authority.

Material of human origin likely to compromise the values of the Area, which was not brought into the Area by the permit holder or otherwise authorised, may be removed unless the impact of the removal is likely to be greater than leaving the material *in situ.* If such material is found the appropriate national authority must be notified.

6(ix) Disposal of waste

All wastes, including all human wastes, shall be removed from the Area.

6(x) Measures that may be necessary to continue to meet the aims of the management plan

Permits may be granted to enter the Area to:

- carry out monitoring and Area inspection activities, which may involve the collection of samples or data essential for analysis or review;
- erect or maintain signposts, structures or scientific equipment; and
- carry out protective measures.

Any specific sites of long-term monitoring shall be appropriately marked on site and on maps of the Area. A GPS position should be obtained for lodgement with the Antarctic Data Directory System through the appropriate national authority.

To help maintain the ecological and scientific values of the Area visitors shall take special precautions against introductions. Of particular concern are microbial, animal or vegetation introductions sourced from soils from other Antarctic sites, including stations, or from regions outside Antarctica. To the maximum extent practicable, visitors shall ensure that footwear, clothing and equipment – particularly any camping and sampling equipment – is thoroughly cleaned before entering the Area.

6(xi) Requirement for reports

The principal permit holder for each visit to the Area shall submit a report to the appropriate national authority as soon as practicable, and no later than six months after the visit has been completed.

Such reports should include, as appropriate, the information identified in the visit report form contained in the *Guide to the Preparation of Management Plans for Antarctic Specially Protected Areas*. If appropriate, the national authority should also forward a copy of the visit report to the Parties that proposed the Management Plan, to assist in managing the Area and reviewing the Management Plan.

Parties should, wherever possible, deposit originals or copies of such original visit reports in a publicly accessible archive to maintain a record of usage, for the purpose of any review of the Management Plan and in organising the scientific use of the Area.

7. Supporting documentation

Andreev, M.P. (1990). Lichens of oazis of the East Antarctic. *Novosti Sistematiki Nizshikh Rastenii* **27**:93-95.

Andreev, M.P. (2006). Lichens of the Prydz Bay area (Eastern Antarctica). *Novosti Sistematiki Nizshikh Rastenii* **39**:188-198.

Andreev, M.P. (2006). Lichens from Prince Charles Mountains (Radok Lake area, Mac. Robertson Land). SCAR XXIX/COMNAP XVIII Hobart Tasmania. SCAR Open Science Conference 12-14 July. Scalop Symposium 13 July. Abstract volume. Hobart, Tasmania. P. 421.

Andreev, M.P. (2006). The lichen flora of oases of continental Antarctic, and the ecological adaptations of Antarctic lichens. *KSM Newsletter* **18**(s):24-28.

Andreev, M.P. (2006). The lichen flora of oases of continental Antarctic, and the ecological adaptations of Antarctic lichens. 2006 International Meeting of the Federation of Korean Microbiological Societies, October 19-20, 2006, Seoul, Korea. Abstracts. Seoul. Pp. 77-80.

Andreev, M.P. (2008). Lichens from Prince Charles Mountains (Radok Lake area), Mac. Robertson Land. Polar research – Arctic and Antarctic perspectives in the International Polar Year. SCAR/IASC IPY Open Science Conference. St. Petersburg, Russia, July 8–11. 2008. Abstract Volume. P. 205.

Carson, C.J. and Grew, E.S. (2007). *Geology of the Larsemann Hills Region, Antarctica.* First Edition (1:25 000 scale map). Geoscience Australia, Canberra.

Carson, C.J., Hand, M. and Dirks, P.H.G.M. (1995). Stable coexistence of grandidierite and kornerupine during medium pressure granulite facies metamorphism. *Mineral Magazine* **59**:327-339.

Grew, E.S. and Carson, C.J. (2007). A treasure trove of minerals discovered in the Larsemann Hills. *Australian Antarctic Magazine* **13**:18-19.

Grew, E.S., McGee, J.J., Yates, M.G., Peacor, D.R., Rouse, R.C, Huijsmans, J.P.P., Shearer, C.K., Wiedenbeck, M., Thost, D.E., and Su, S.-C. (1998). Boralsilite ($Al_{16}B_6Si_2O_{37}$): A new mineral related to sillimanite from pegmatites in granulite-facies rocks. *American Mineralogist* **83**:638-651.

Grew, E.S, Armbruster, T., Medenbach, O., Yates, M.G., Carson, C.J. (2006). Stornesite-(Y), (Y, Ca)$_2$Na$_6$(Ca,Na)$_8$(Mg,Fe)$_{43}$(PO$_4$)$_{36}$, the first terrestrial Mg-dominant member of the fillowite group, from granulite-facies paragneiss in the Larsemann Hills, Prydz Bay, East Antarctica. *American Mineralogist* **91**:1412-1424.

Grew, E.S, Armbruster, T., Medenbach, O., Yates, M.G., Carson, C.J. (2007). Chopinite, [(Mg,Fe)$_3$](PO$_4$)$_2$, a new mineral isostructural with sarcopside, from a fluorapatite segregation in granulite-facies paragneiss, Larsemann Hills, Prydz Bay, East Antarctica. *European Journal of Mineralogy* **19**:229-245.

Grew, E.S, Armbruster, T., Medenbach, O., Yates, M.G., Carson, C.J. (2007). Tassieite, (Na,)Ca$_2$(Mg,Fe^{2+},Fe^{3+})$_2$(Fe^{3+},Mg)$_2$(Fe^{2+},Mg)$_2$(PO$_4$)$_6$(H$_2$O)$_2$, a new hydrothermal wicksite-group mineral in fluorapatite nodules from granulite-facies paragneiss in the Larsemann Hills, Prydz Bay, East Antarctica. *The Canadian Mineralogist* **45**:293-305.

Grew, E.S. and Carson, C.J. (2007) A treasure trove of minerals discovered in the Larsemann Hills. *Australian Antarctic Magazine* **13**:18-19.

Grew, E.S., Carson, C.J. Christy, A.G. and Boger, S.D. (in press). Boron- and phosphate-rich rocks in the Larsemann Hills, Prydz Bay, East Antarctica: Tectonic Implications. *Geological Society of London, Special Publications, Antarctic Thematic Set 2012, Volume I. Antarctica and Supercontinent Evolution.*

Grew, E.S., Christy, A.G. and Carson, C.J. (2006) A boron-enriched province in granulite-facies rocks, Larsemann Hills, Prydz Bay, Antarctica. *Geochimica et Cosmochimica Acta* **70**(18) Supplement, A217 [abstract].

Grew, E.S., Graetsch, H., Pöter, B., Yates, M.G., Buick, I., Bernhardt, H.-J., Schreyer, W., Werding, G., Carson, C.J. and Clarke, G.L. (2008). Boralsilite, $Al_{16}B_6Si_2O_{37}$, and "boron-mullite": compositional variations and associated phases in experiment and nature. *American Mineralogist* **93**:283-299.

McMinn, A. and Harwood, D. (1995). Biostratigraphy and palaeoecology of early Pliocene diatom assemblages from the Larsemann Hills, Eastern Antarctica. *Antarctic Science* **7**:115-116.

Peacor, D.R., Rouse, R.C. and Grew, E.S. (1999). Crystal structure of boralsilite and its relation to a family of boroaluminosilicates, sillimanite and andalusite. *American Mineralogist* **84**:1152-1161.

Quilty, P.G., Gillieson, D., Burgess, J., Gardiner, G., Spate, A., and Pidgeon, D. (1990). *Ammoelphidiella* and associated benthic foraminifera, Larsemann Hills, East Antarctica.
Journal of Foraminiferal Research **20**:1-7.

Ren, L., Grew, E.S., Xiong, M., and Ma, Z. (2003). Wagnerite-*Ma5bc*, a new polytype of $Mg_2(PO_4)(F,OH)$, from granulite-facies paragneiss, Larsemann Hills, Prydz Bay, East Antarctica. *Canadian Mineralogist* **41**:393-411.

Ren, L., Zhao, Y, Liu X, Chen, T. (1992). Re-examination of the metamorphic evolution of the Larsemann Hills, East Antarctica. In: Y. Yoshida, K. Kaminuma and K. Shiraishi (Eds). *Recent Progress in Antarctic Earth Science*. Pp. 145-153. Terra Scientific Publishing Co., Tokyo.

Ren, L., Grew, E.S., Xiong, M. and Wang, Y. (2005). Petrological implication of wagnerite-*Ma5bc* in the quartzofeldspathic gneiss, Larsemann Hills, East Antarctica. *Progress in Natural Science* **15**:523-529.

Wadoski, E.R., Grew, E.S. and Yates, M.G. (2011). Compositional evolution of tourmaline-supergroup minerals from granitic pegmatites in the Larsemann Hills, East Antarctica. *The Canadian Mineralogist* **49**(1):381-405.

Wang, Y., Liu, D., Chung, S.L., Tong, L. and Ren, L. (2008). SHRIMP zircon age constraints from the Larsemann Hills region, Prydz Bay, for a late Mesoproterozoic to early Neoproterozoic tectono-thermal event in East Antarctica. *American Journal of Science* **308**:573–617.

Zhao, Y., Song, B., Wang, Y., Ren, L., Li, J. and Chen, T. (1992). Geochronology of the late granite in the Larsemann Hills, East Antarctica. In: Yoshida, Y., Kaminuma, K. and Shiraishi, K. (Eds). *Recent Progress in Antarctic Earth Science*. Pp.155-161. Terra Scientific Publishing Co., Tokyo.

Zhao, Y., Liu, X, Song, B., Zhang, Z., Li, J., Yao, Y. and Wang, Y. (1995). Constraints on the stratigraphic age of metasedimentary rocks from the Larsemann Hills, East Antarctica: possible implications for Neoproterozoic tectonics. *Precambrian Research* **75**:175-188.

Appendix 1: Stornes, Antarctic Specially Protected Area No 174, boundary coordinates

Boundary Point	Longitude	Latitude	Boundary Point	Longitude	Latitude
1	76°8'29"E	69°25'29"S	15	76°8'25"E	69°26'39"S
2	76°8'6"E	69°25'29"S	16	76°8'28"E	69°26'42"S
3	76°7'45"E	69°25'34"S	17	76°8'30"E	69°26'47"S
4	76°5'60"E	69°26'1"S	18	76°8'29"E	69°26'51"S
5	76°5'52"E	69°26'4"S	19	76°8'26"E	69°26'55"S
6	76°5'44"E	69°26'8"S	20	76°8'22"E	69°26'60"S
7	76°5'38"E	69°26'11"S	21	76°8'18"E	69°27'3"S
8	76°5'37"E	69°26'15"S	22	76°8'14"E	69°27'6"S
9	76°5'38"E	69°26'19"S	23	76°8'8"E	69°27'10"S
10	76°5'44"E	69°26'22"S	24	76°3'36"E	69°28'39"S
11	76°5'51"E	69°26'24"S	25	76°3'22"E	69°28'40"S
12	76°6'1"E	69°26'26"S			
13	76°8'12"E	69°26'36"S	Then north-east following the coast line at the low tide mark to boundary point 1 (76°8'29"E, 69°25'29"S).		
14	76°8'21"E	69°26'38"S			

ATCM XXXVII Final Report

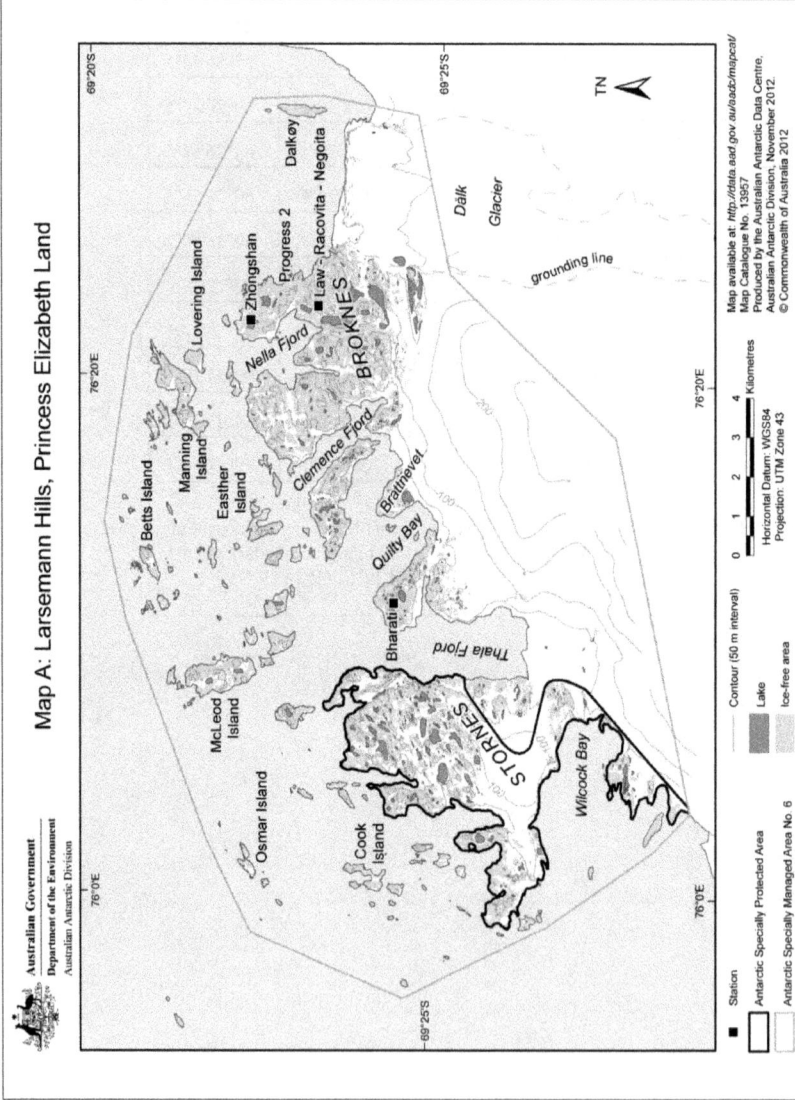

Map A: Larsemann Hills, Princess Elizabeth Land

196

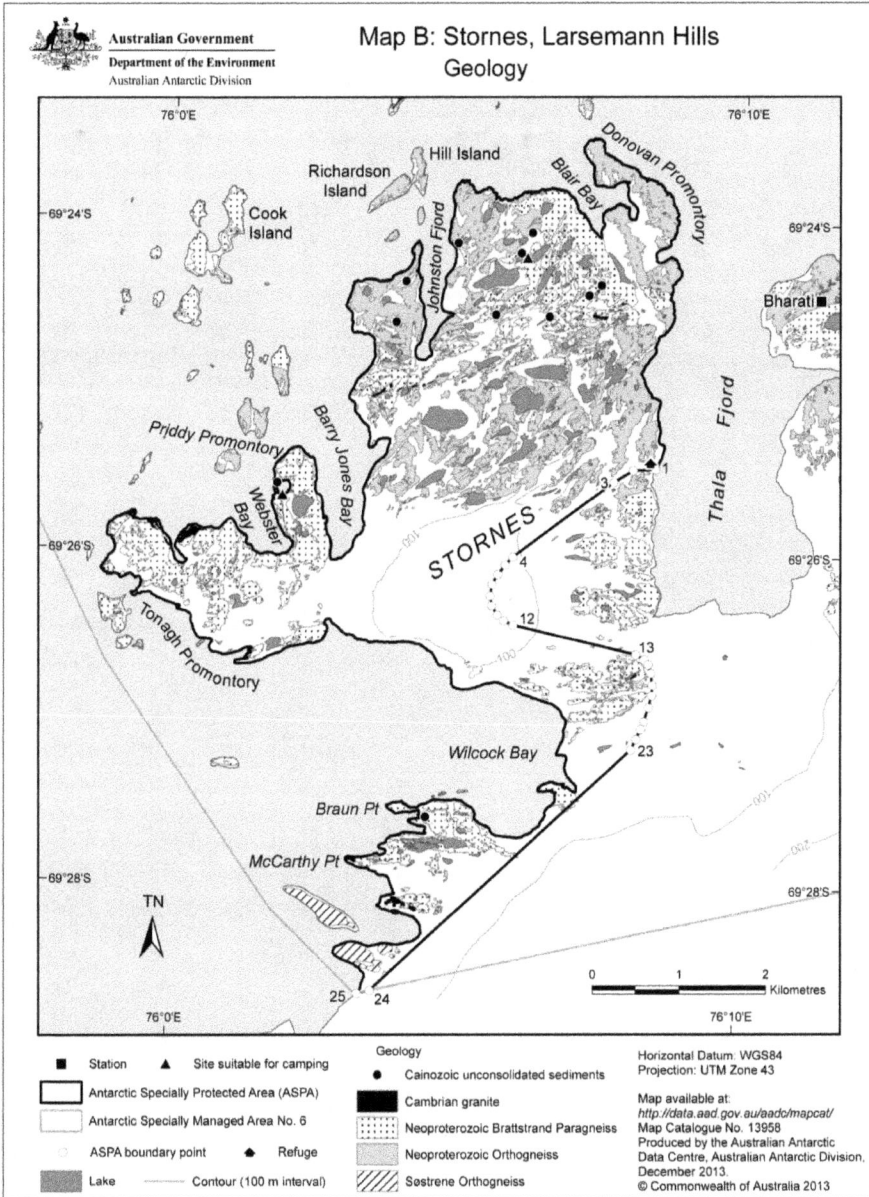

Australian Government
Department of the Environment
Australian Antarctic Division

Map B: Stornes, Larsemann Hills
Geology

Geology

■ Station   ▲ Site suitable for camping

□ Antarctic Specially Protected Area (ASPA)

□ Antarctic Specially Managed Area No. 6

◌ ASPA boundary point   ◆ Refuge

▨ Lake   —— Contour (100 m interval)

● Cainozoic unconsolidated sediments

■ Cambrian granite

▥ Neoproterozoic Brattstrand Paragneiss

▨ Neoproterozoic Orthogneiss

▨ Søstrene Orthogneiss

Horizontal Datum: WGS84
Projection: UTM Zone 43

Map available at:
http://data.aad.gov.au/aadc/mapcat/
Map Catalogue No. 13958
Produced by the Australian Antarctic
Data Centre, Australian Antarctic Division,
December 2013.
© Commonwealth of Australia 2013

Management Plan For
Antarctic Specially Protected Area No. 175

HIGH ALTITUDE GEOTHERMAL SITES OF THE ROSS SEA REGION
(including parts of the summits of Mount Erebus, Ross Island and Mount Melbourne and Mount Rittmann, northern Victoria Land)

Introduction:

There exist a few isolated sites in Antarctica where the ground surface is warmed by geothermal activity above the ambient air temperature. Steam emissions from fumaroles (openings at the Earth's surface that emit steam and gases) condense forming a regular supply of water which, coupled with warm soil temperatures, provides an environment that selects for a unique and diverse assemblage of organisms. Geothermal sites are rare and small in extent covering no more than a few hectares on the Antarctic continent and circumpolar islands (or maritime sites). The biological communities that occur at continental geothermal sites are at high altitude and differ markedly to those communities that occur at maritime geothermal sites due to the differences in the abiotic environment.

There are three high altitude geothermal sites in the Ross Sea region, known to have unique biological communities. These are the summits of Mount Erebus, on Ross Island, and Mount Melbourne and Mount Rittmann, both in northern Victoria Land. The only other known high altitude site in Antarctica where evidence of fumarolic activity has been seen is at Mount Berlin in Marie Byrd Land, West Antarctica, although no biological research has been conducted at this site.

High altitude geothermal sites are vulnerable to the introduction of new species, particularly from human vectors, as they present an environment where organisms typical of more temperate regions can survive. These once isolated sites are now more frequently visited by humans for science and recreation, both of which require logistical support. Species from sites within Antarctica, and locally non-native to geothermal sites, or from regions away from Antarctica, may inadvertently be introduced to the Area through human activity. High altitude geothermal sites are also vulnerable to physical damage to the substrate from trampling and over sampling because changes in the soil structure can affect the location and rate of steam emissions in which biological communities occur. The limited extent and fragility of these biological communities highlights the need for protection.

The primary reason for the designation of high altitude geothermal sites in the Ross Sea region as an Antarctic Specially Protected Area is to protect the outstanding ecological values, specifically the unique biological communities that occur in an environment where the selective factors are unique resulting in an assemblage of organisms not found anywhere else in the world. The biological communities are extremely vulnerable to the introduction of non-native species of plants, animals, microorganisms and non-sterile soils from biologically distinct regions within Antarctica and from regions outside Antarctica and to physical disturbance from trampling and oversampling through human activity. While high altitude geothermal sites are protected primarily for their outstanding ecological values (specifically the biological communities), they are also protected for their other scientific values such as microbiology, botany, terrestrial biology, geomorphology and geology.

The Area comprises three high altitude geothermal sites; Tramway Ridge on the summit of Mount Erebus (77° 31'S; 167° 06'E), three locations of geothermal activity on the summit of Mount Melbourne (74° 21'S; 164° 42'E), and the summit of Mount Rittmann (73° 28'S; 165° 37'E) (Map A).

Tramway Ridge, Mount Erebus was originally designated in Recommendation XIII-8 (1985) as a Site of Special Scientific Interest (SSSI) No. 11 after a proposal by New Zealand on the grounds that the Area supports an unusual ecosystem of exceptional scientific value to botanists and microbiologists. The

Management Plan was revised and adopted in Measure 2 (1995) and Measure 3 (1997). The site was re-designated Antarctic Specially Protected Area (ASPA) No. 130 in Decision 1 (2002). The Management Plan was revised and adopted in Measure 1 (2002). It was reviewed and endorsed without changes at CEP X (2007).

The summit of Mount Melbourne was originally designated in Recommendation XVI-5 (1987) as SSSI No. 24, after proposals by New Zealand and Italy, on the grounds that the Area contains geothermal soils that support a unique and diverse biological community. An area enclosed in SSSI No. 24, Cryptogam Ridge, was designated as Special Protected Area (SPA) No. 22 in Recommendation XVI-8 (1991). SSSI No. 24 and SPA No. 22 were re-designated as ASPA No. 118a and 118b respectively in Decision 1 (2002). A merged Management Plan designating both Areas as ASPA 118 was adopted in Measure 2 (2003), with Prohibited and Restricted Zones providing for more stringent access conditions within the former SPA No.22. A Revised Management Plan was adopted in Measure 5 (2008).

Mount Rittmann was discovered during the 4th Italian Expedition in the 1988/89 field season. During the 6th Italian Expedition in the 1991/92 field season, fumaroles and ground heated by geothermal activity were discovered in a small volcanic crater. This site has not been designated previously for protection.

Both Mount Erebus and Mount Melbourne are visited annually by scientists from a wide range of disciplines and for management reasons (e.g. survey marks, radio repeaters and field huts). Mount Rittmann has had an increased number of visitors since its discovery.

Tramway Ridge, Mount Erebus is situated in Environment S – McMurdo – South Victoria Land Geologic based on the Environmental Domains Analysis for Antarctica (Resolution 3 (2008)) and in Region 9 – South Victoria Land based on the Antarctic Conservation Biogeographic Regions (Resolution 6 (2012)). Other protected areas within Environment S includes ASPAs 105, 116, 121, 122, 123, 124, 131, 137, 138, 154, 155, 156, 157, 158, 161 and 172 and ASMA 2.

Both Mount Melbourne and Mount Rittmann are situated in Environment U – North Victoria Land Geologic based on the Environmental Domains Analysis for Antarctica and in Region 8 – North Victoria Land based on the Antarctic Conservation Biogeographic Regions. Other protected areas within Environment U include ASPAs 106, 165 and 173.

This is the only ASPA or ASMA in the Ross Sea region designated to protect geothermal environments. There is only one other ASPA within the protected area system that protects a geothermal environment, ASPA 140 Parts of Deception Island, South Shetland Islands. However, ASPA 140 protects biological communities of maritime Antarctica which significantly differ from high altitude biological communities.

The designation of these sites as a protected area complements the Antarctic protected areas system because the Area: (i) contains the known locations of Antarctic high altitude geothermally heated ground, which, due to the Area's physical and chemical characteristics, supports biological communities that are both regionally and globally unique, and (ii) is vulnerable to human interference, particularly the potential for the introduction of non-native species from biologically distinct regions within Antarctica and from regions outside Antarctica but also between geothermal locations at a specific site, and damage from trampling and over sampling. The Area is considered to be of sufficient size at each site to provide adequate protection of the values identified.

1. Description of values to be protected

The Ross Sea region has considerable areas of late Neogene and Quaternary volcanism. However, only three sites, Mounts Erebus, Melbourne and Rittmann, have been confirmed to show signs of present day geothermal activity. Fumaroles (opening in the ground emitting steam) and steaming warm ground are the surface manifestation of geothermal activity at these sites. Hollow ice towers or ice pinnacles (chimneys) can form around fumaroles up to many metres in diameter and height, formed by the condensation and freezing of water vapour. Ice and snow hummocks are also present over geothermally heated ground. Other areas of heated ground are commonly ice free during summer and maintain surface temperatures greater than ambient air temperatures.

Most areas of fumaroles and warm ground are on or adjacent to the summit calderas of each volcano, however areas of surface activity do extend down slope on the northwest side of Mount Melbourne. Although these areas in the Ross Sea region are isolated to the high altitude summits of volcanoes, the environment provides resident biological communities with a regular supply of free water (from condensed steam and melting of snow), temperatures suitable for growth and physical protection or shelter from extreme weather (under ice and snow hummocks). Because of the considerable isolation and unusual set of evolutionary selection pressures, some researchers believe that these habitats may host some of the earliest forms of life on the planet, many of which have still not been described.

The vegetation communities at high altitude continental geothermal sites differ markedly from other maritime geothermal sites in Antarctica and the sub-Antarctic. The communities in the Ross Sea region are dominated by algae with a low diversity of species present compared with maritime Antarctic sites. The latter are dominated by bryophytes and have high species diversity across several groups. In the Ross Sea region geothermally heated sites, diatoms are absent and only one possible lichen has been found, this being an unidentified black crust reported from Mount Melbourne. Twelve species of bryophytes, algae and protozoa that occur at one or more of these sites have no other known Antarctic record (Annex 1, Table 1). Although these areas are located within the same geographic region, the vegetation communities at each of the three sites differ from one another, with five of the twelve species of bryophytes, algae and protozoa, which have no other Antarctic record, reported from only a single geothermal site in the Ross Sea region (Annex 1, Table 1).

The microorganisms in these communities have been poorly characterised, or in some cases remain uncharacterised. However recent studies are beginning to reveal the unique and diverse microbial communities present. Studies on extremophiles (organisms that thrive in physically or geochemically extreme environments) are recognised as useful for understanding the evolution of life as the first inhabitants of Earth possibly evolved in extreme habitats. Not all microorganisms identified from these sites are thermophiles (organisms that have their optimum growth rates at high temperatures typically between 45° and 122°C). Some grow optimally at mesophilic temperatures (moderate temperatures typically between 20°C and 45°C) some distance away from the fumaroles (Annex 1, Table 2). This highlights the vulnerability of these biological communities to physical disturbance of the substrate from trampling or sampling.

While the environmental conditions (i.e. regular supply of free water, temperatures suitable for growth and physical protection or shelter from extreme weather) at the three isolated high altitude geothermal sites in the Ross Sea region superficially appear similar, the biological communities differ between the sites. A possible explanation is that the physico-chemical differences of the soils (e.g. pH, nutrient availability, substrate grain size, moisture content) select for a unique assemblage of species at each site. An alternative hypothesis suggests these environments may have been occasionally colonised by viable propagules carried by wind from other sites in Antarctica or from circumpolar islands or other continents. Dispersal may be rare events resulting in the colonization of the soil by viable propagules of the few species that are deposited at each site. For example, several of the isolated strains of *B. fumarioli* from Mount Rittmann showed remarkable similarity with strains identified from the Candlemas Islands, South Sandwich archipelago even though the two sites are over 5,600 km apart. Colonization from a common source and more likely aerial dispersal of free spores or potential human contamination has been proposed. More simply, the differences could be due to stochastic factors.

An increase in human activity at the Area's three sites emphasises the need for adequate protective measures in order to reduce the possibility of the introduction of new organisms by a human vector.

The highly unusual biological communities at all three sites are of outstanding scientific value. These sites provide insights into biogeography and dispersal as well as physiology of Antarctic organisms operating under unusual conditions. The limited geographical extent of the Area's ecosystems, the vulnerability of the sites to the introduction of non-native species from biologically distinct regions within Antarctica and from regions outside Antarctica but also between geothermal locations at a specific site and ground disturbance is such that appropriate management of these sites is necessary to ensure their long term protection.

2. Aims and objectives

The management of high altitude geothermal sites of the Ross Sea region aims to:

- avoid degradation of, or substantial risk to, the values of the Area by preventing unnecessary human disturbance to the Area;
- prevent or minimise the introduction to the Area of non-native plants, animals, microorganisms and non-sterile soils from biologically distinct regions within Antarctica and from regions outside of Antarctica and between geothermal locations at a specific site;
- preserve a part of the natural ecosystem of each of the Area's three sites, which are declared Prohibited Zones, as reference areas for future scientific studies;
- allow scientific research in the Area provided it is for compelling reasons which cannot be served elsewhere and which will not jeopardize the natural ecological system, specifically the biological communities and geology in the Area's three sites;
- ensure that the biological communities and geology are not adversely affected by excessive sampling or ground disturbance within the Area;
- allow visits for management purposes in support of the aims of the Management Plan.

3. Management Activities

The following management activities shall be undertaken to protect the values of the Area:

- Information on the location of the Area's three sites, stating special restrictions that apply, shall be displayed prominently, and a copy of this Management Plan shall be made available, at National Antarctic Programme stations, and research, management or field huts close to the Area's three sites.
- Signs and/or boundary markers illustrating the locations of the Area's three sites, with clear statements of entry restrictions, shall be placed at appropriate locations on the boundary of the individual sites [and Prohibited Zones] to help avoid inadvertent entry.
- Markers, signs or other structures erected within the Area for scientific, management or essential communication purposes shall be secured and maintained in good condition and removed when no longer required.
- The Area shall be visited as necessary, and no less than once every five years, to assess whether it continues to serve the purposes for which it was designated and to ensure that management activities are adequate.
- National Antarctic Programmes operating in the Area shall consult together with a view to ensuring the above management activities are implemented. In particular, National Antarctic Programmes are encouraged to consult with one another to prevent excessive sampling of soil and biological material within the Area. Also, National Antarctic Programmes are encouraged to consider joint implementation of guidelines intended to minimize the introduction and dispersal of non-native species within the Area and between the Area's three sites.

4. Period of designation

Designated for an indefinite period.

5. Maps

Map A: High altitude geothermal sites of the Ross Sea region location map. Horizontal Datum: WGS84, Antarctica Polar Stereographic Projection. Data Source: Base Vector Data, Antarctic Digital Database Version 6.

Map A1: ASPA 175 Tramway Ridge, Mount Erebus topographical map. Horizontal Datum: WGS72, Camp Area Projection. Vertical Datum: Mean Sea Level. Data Sources – Survey Data: Department of Survey and Land Information (DOSLI) Survey Plan 37/142 (Plan sourced from Land Information New Zealand (LINZ)); Contours and geothermally heated area: Data supplied by the University of Canterbury; Main map and inset overview diagram imagery: Digital Globe World View-2 Satellite (0.5 m resolution). Imagery date 23 January 2011. Imagery provided by the Polar Geospatial Centre, Department of Earth Sciences, University of Minnesota; Inset site photograph: Terrestrial photograph of Tramway Ridge geothermally heated ground looking north upslope. Image taken 26 November, 2010. Image provided by University of Waikato.

Map A2: ASPA 175 Cryptogam Ridge and Geothermal Slope, Mount Melbourne topographical map. Horizontal Datum: WGS84, UTM Zone 58S Projection. Vertical Datum: WGS84. Data Sources – Contours and protected areas derived from data collected during field survey undertaken 17 November, 2012 by LINZ; Main map and inset overview diagram imagery: DigitalGlobe GeoEye satellite imagery (0.5 m resolution). Imagery date 14 November, 2011. Imagery provided by the Polar Geospatial Centre, Department of Earth Sciences, University of Minnesota; Inset site photograph: Terrestrial photograph taken looking northeast with Cryptogam Ridge in the foreground. Image taken 17 November, 2012. Image provided by Antarctica New Zealand.

Map A2/1: ASPA 175 Northwest slope, Mount Melbourne topographical map. Horizontal Datum: WGS84, UTM Zone 58 Projection. Vertical Datum: WGS84. Data Sources - Main map and inset overview diagram imagery: Digital Globe World View-2 Satellite (0.5 m resolution). Imagery date 14 November, 2011. Imagery provided by the Polar Geospatial Centre, Department of Earth Sciences, University of Minnesota; Inset site photograph: Terrestrial photograph of northwest slope geothermally heated ground looking east. Image taken in 2002. Image provided by R. Bargagli and the PNRA (the Italian National Programme for Antarctic Research).

Map A3: ASPA 175 Mount Rittmann topographical map. Horizontal Datum: WGS72, UTM Zone 58S Projection. Vertical Datum: WGS84 Vertical Datum. Data Sources – Contours and protected areas derived from data collected during field survey undertaken 16 November, 2012 by LINZ; Main map: DigitalGlobe World View-1 satellite imagery (0.5 m resolution). Imagery date 3 March, 2009. Imagery provided by the Polar Geospatial Centre, Department of Earth Sciences, University of Minnesota; Inset site photograph: Terrestrial photograph taken looking north toward Mount Rittmann remnant caldera. Image taken 16 November, 2012. Image provided by Antarctica New Zealand.

6. Description of the Area

6(i) Geographical co-ordinates, boundary markers and natural features

This ASPA consists of three sites including Tramway Ridge on the summit of Mount Erebus, three locations on the summit of Mount Melbourne and the summit of Mount Rittmann.

Tramway Ridge, Mount Erebus
Site Description:
Mount Erebus, (77° 31'S, 167° 06'E) is the largest and most active volcano in Antarctica and it is located on Ross Island (Map A). It rises to an altitude of 3,794 metres above sea level. It is a unique stratovolcano with a convecting anorthoclase phonolite lava lake in the main crater. The predominant rock type, and the only one which crops out near the summit, is anorthoclase phonolite.

The steep slopes of the main crater flatten out to an extensive plateau at an altitude of about 3,200 – 3,500 metres above sea level except on the south east slopes where the outer slope continues to drop steeply. Tramway Ridge is a ridge that rises to approximately 3,450 metres above sea level on the northwest slope of the main crater (Map A1; Inset 1). The site is located along this ridge approximately 1.5 kilometres from the main crater. It is the most extensive area of geothermally heated ground on the summit of Mount Erebus, though locations of geothermally heated ground are widespread at the summit.

The site is, in general, on a gentle slope of about 5°, with much of the ice-free ground in the form of terraces which have a typical vertical height of about 0.5 metres and steeper sides of up to 30° in slope. The steep sides of the terraces are colonised by the majority of visible vegetation, and it is from these sides that visible steam emissions occur. Visible vegetation covers about 16% of the site. Low ice hummocks, up to approximately one metre in height and formed where steam has frozen, are distributed over the site. Ground temperatures of up to about 75°C have been recorded at 4 centimetres depth.

Boundaries: The boundary of the designated site is defined as a rectangle of 200 metres by 200.8 metres which encompasses most of the geothermally heated ground of lower Tramway Ridge. The western boundary of the site at the NW boundary corner extends from the coordinates 77° 31' 01.853" S; 167° 06' 21.251"E (Point A) south to the SW boundary corner at 77° 31' 08.327" S; 167° 06' 20.686"E (Point E). The boundary then extends east to the SE boundary corner at 77° 31' 08.448" S; 167° 06' 50.521"E (Point D). The boundary then extends north to the NE boundary corner at 77° 31' 01.976" S; 167° 06' 51.074"E (Point B) (Map A1).

The site is divided into two parts of almost equal size, the northern half being a Prohibited Zone (Map A1). The boundaries of the Prohibited Zone are described in Section 6(v).

The boundaries of the site (marked by boundary markers at each corner), the Prohibited Zone and prominent features are shown on Map A1. The boundary points of the Area and Prohibited Zone are marked by a boundary marker (Map A1; Point A-F) with a further boundary marker (Point H) located partway along the southern boundary of the Prohibited Zone. Two boundary markers (G and H) have been offset to better facilitate people working within the ASPA to identify the southern boundary of the Prohibited Zone and avoid entering the area (Map A1; ASPA Boundary Table of Coordinates).When bamboo flags are inserted in each boundary marker, the boundaries of the site and Prohibited Zone are visible when working in the ASPA.

Mount Melbourne
Site Description: Mount Melbourne (74° 21'S 164° 42'E) is a stratovolcano located in northern Victoria Land, between Wood Bay and Terra Nova Bay, on the western side of the Ross Sea, and about 10 kilometres east of Campbell Glacier (Map A). It rises to an altitude of 2,733 metres above sea level.

Mount Melbourne is part of the McMurdo Volcanic Group, which is a line of dormant and extinct volcanoes running along the coast of Victoria Land. The Mount Melbourne region is thought to be late Quaternary in age and the most recent eruption may have been as little as 150 years ago. The volcanic rocks have been described as trachyte to trachyandesite on the mountain itself, with basalt at its base.

Mount Melbourne is an almost perfect low-angle volcanic cone with locations of geothermally heated ground, fumaroles, and ice towers scattered around the summit crater and on some upper parts of the mountain. The summit caldera is about one kilometre in diameter and forms the névé for a westward flowing glacier. Several smaller basaltic cones and mounds occur near the base and on the flanks of the mountain. Geothermally heated ground is generally marked by snow-free, steaming ground or fumaroles and ice towers or pinnacles up to one metre in height. Surface soil temperatures have been recorded up to 50 °C at depths of a few centimetres.

Boundaries: The site consists of three separate locations, two on the main summit crater (Map A2) and a third on the northwest slope of the mountain (Map A2/1). On the south-eastern rim of the main summit crater of Mount Melbourne, there are two adjacent designated locations.

The first location, Cryptogam Ridge, is a distinct crescent shaped ridge and consists of areas of snow-covered unheated ground, snow-free geothermally-heated ground and ice-hummocks covering steam emissions that extends c. 40 metres in all directions from the ridge line.

The western boundary of the site from the NW boundary corner extends from the coordinates 74° 21' 20.389" S; 164° 41' 31.652" E (Point 1A) south approximately 50 metres to the SW boundary corner at 74° 21' 22.096" S; 164° 41' 32.551" E (Point 1N). The boundary then extends east following the crescent shape of Cryptogam Ridge to unmarked points at 74° 21' 21.383" S; 164° 41' 38.254" E (Point 1M); 74° 21' 20.840" S; 164° 41' 45.230" E (Point 1L); 74° 21' 21.220" S; 164° 41' 49.934" E (Point 1K); 74° 21' 21.815" S; 164° 41' 54.574" E (Point 1J); 74° 21' 22.588" S; 164° 41' 58.044" E (Point 1I) to the SE boundary corner at 74° 21' 24.103" S; 164° 42' 00.579" E (Point 1H). The boundary then extends north to the NE boundary corner at 74° 21' 23.355" S; 164° 42' 07.010" E (Point 1G). The northern boundary extends west following the crescent shape of Cryptogam Ridge to unmarked points at 74° 21' 21.523" S; 164° 42' 03.989" E (Point 1F); 74° 21' 20.117" S; 164° 41' 57.869" E (Point 1E); 74° 21' 19.307" S; 164° 41' 51.137" E (Point 1D); 74° 21' 19.153" S; 164° 41' 45.329" E (Point 1C); 74° 21' 19.650" S; 164° 41' 37.695" E (Point 1B) to the NE boundary corner (Point 1A) (Map A2). Both the northern and southern boundaries are situated below the ice free ridge.

Cryptogam Ridge is divided into two parts with the western portion designated as a Prohibited Zone (Map A2). The boundaries of the Prohibited Zone are described in Section 6(v).

The second location (Geothermal Slope) on the south-eastern rim of the main summit crater of Mount Melbourne is adjacent to Cryptogam Ridge on a slope leading up the eastern rim of the summit crater (Map A2; Inset 2). Geothermal activity is evident on the hill slope as crevasses and ice towers extending up the steep caldera rim, approximately 50 metres wide (Map A2). The northern boundary of the site from the NW boundary corner extends from the coordinates 74° 21' 13.740" S; 164° 42' 01.816" E (Point 2A) south approximately 50 metres to the SW boundary corner at 74° 21' 15.620" S; 164° 42' 03.474" E (Point 2D). The boundary then extends east up the slope to the SE boundary corner at 74° 21' 14.567" S; 164° 42' 12.729" E (Point 2C), then north to the NE boundary corner at 74° 21' 12.865" S; 164° 42' 08.972" E (Point 2B) (Map. A2).

The third location (Northwest Slope) is on the northwest slopes of the volcano (Map A2/1) approximately 1.5 kilometres northwest of from Cryptogam Ridge. Geothermal activity is evident as a northwest to southeast trending line of ice towers and small patches of bare ground along the edge of a steep cliff. The boundaries for the location were not surveyed in the field but obtained via inference from satellite imagery. The northern boundary of the site from the NW boundary corner extends from the coordinates 74° 21' 00" S; 164° 39' 02" E (Point 3A) south downslope to the SW boundary corner at 74° 21' 11" S; 164° 39' 02" E (Point 3D). The boundary then extends east to the SE boundary corner at 74° 21' 11" S; 164° 42' 05" E (Point 3C), then north up slope to the NE boundary corner at 74° 21' 00" S; 164° 40' 05" E (Point 3B) (Map A2/1).

Mount Rittmann
Site Description: Mount Rittmann (73° 28'S, 165° 37'E) is located in the Mountaineer Range on the south side of the Aviator Glacier, between the Pilot Glacier and the head of the Icebreaker Glacier in northern Victoria Land (Map A3). It rises to an altitude of 2,600 metres above sea level and is approximately 103 kilometres north of Mount Melbourne and approximately 50 kilometres inland from the coast.

Fumaroles and geothermally heated ground occur within a single outcrop at the summit of Mount Rittmann in a minor caldera rim at approximately 2,000 metres above sea level. The entire site is surrounded by glacial ice (Map A3; Inset). The site consists of a rough and unstable steep slope approximately 300 metres wide and 80 metres high (Map A3). The ground consists of pyroclastic rocks and volcanic debris in a sandy matrix.

Two adjacent ice-free areas are situated at the centre of the site. Ice free geothermally heated ground and fumaroles dominate the areas with ice hummocks and ice towers generally situated around the edges of the ice-free areas and along the rim of the caldera structure. Around the fumaroles the ground is covered by a whitish efflorescence and patches of moss are visible on the surface of these areas. Surface soil temperatures of between 50 and 63°C have been recorded at 10 centimetres depth. The western side of the site is covered in ice, but geothermal activity is visible along the caldera rim as ice towers or steaming ground.

Boundaries: The site encompasses the entire exposed caldera of Mount Rittmann. The western most boundary corner is located at the western edge of the caldera rim at 73° 28' 18.797"S; 165° 36' 43.851"E (Point A). The boundary follows the caldera rim east to unmarked points at 73° 28' 16.818" S; 165° 36' 54.698" E (Point B); 73° 28' 16.290" S; 165° 37' 00.144" E (Point C); 73° 28' 16.405" S; 165° 37' 04.438" E (Point D); 73° 28' 17.655" S; 165° 37' 12.235" E (Point E); 73° 28' 18.024" S; 165° 37' 14.468" E (Point F); 73° 28' 19.823" S; 165° 37' 16.943" E (Point G); 73° 28' 20.628" S; 165° 37' 20.089" E (Point H); 73° 28' 21.530" S; 165° 37' 21.567" E (Point I) to the easternmost boundary corner at 73° 28' 22.015" S; 165° 37' 23.817" E (Point J).

The boundary then extends south (downslope) to the SE boundary corner at 73° 28' 23.436" S; 165° 37' 20.540" E (Point K).The boundary then follows the bottom of the steep slope below the caldera rim and ice free areas to unmarked points at 73° 28' 22.414" S; 165° 37' 17.302" E (Point L); 73° 28' 20.945" S; 165° 37' 13.936" E (Point M); 73° 28' 19.430" S; 165° 37' 08.865" E (Point N); 73° 28' 18.558" S; 165° 37' 03.457" E (Point O); 73° 28' 18.722" S; 165° 37' 56.296" E (Point P); 73° 28' 19.778" S; 165° 36' 50.065" E (Point Q), then upslope to the westernmost boundary corner (Point A).

The eastern ice free area is designated as a Prohibited Zone (Map A3). The boundaries of the Prohibited Zone are described in Section 6(v).

6(ii) Access to the Area

Access conditions applicable to all sites are listed in Section 7(ii). Site specific conditions for accessing each site are listed below.

Tramway Ridge, Mount Erebus
- Due to the high altitude of Tramway Ridge, helicopters should not be heavily loaded.
- There is a designated helicopter landing site approximately 250 metres northwest of the site at 77° 31' 00" S; 167° 05' 48" E or the helicopter may land near the United States Antarctic Programme (USAP) Upper (77° 30' 37.857"S; 167° 08' 48.5736"E) or Lower (77° 31' 32.6172"S; 167° 08' 12.8688"E) Erebus huts (Map A1; Inset 1).
- When travelling between Upper and Lower Erebus huts, it is strongly encouraged to keep to the preferred snowmobile route, and wherever practical, stay at least 200 metres away from the site boundary (Map A1; Inset 1).
- Access to the site should primarily be from Boundary Marker D (Map A1; Inset 2).

Mount Melbourne
- There is a designated helicopter landing site approximately 40 metres from Cryptogam Ridge at 74° 21' 24.6" S; 164° 41' 56.0" E or at the alternative landing site at the summit of Mount Melbourne at 74° 20' 57.7"S; 164° 41' 28.9"E (Map A2 and A2/1; Inset 1).

Mount Rittmann
- The site is a steep unstable slope surrounded by glacial ice. Helicopters shall only land, where it is safe to do so, on glacial ice. When landing a helicopter in front of the slope, to the maximum extent practical (and that is safe), helicopters should not land within 100 metres of the sites boundary. When landing a helicopter above the slope, to the maximum extent practical (and that is safe), helicopters should not land within 25 metres of the site boundary (caldera rim) (Map A3).

6(iii) Location of structures within and adjacent to the Area

Tramway Ridge, Mount Erebus
- There are seven boundary markers indicating the boundary corner points and the southern boundary of the Prohibited Zone (Map A1; ASPA Boundary Table of Coordinates). A marker flag, attached to a pole, may be fixed to the boundary markers to define the Area and avoid inadvertent entry to the Area or the Prohibited Zone.
- There are three survey marks adjacent to the site (Map A1; Survey Mark Table of Coordinates).
- The Upper and Lower Erebus huts are located approximately 1 kilometre to the northeast (3,400 metres above sea level) and southeast (3,612 metres above sea level) of the site, respectively (Map A1; Inset).

Mount Melbourne
- There are two survey marks. MM01 is adjacent to Location 2 and is a metal mark set into a rock. MM02 is adjacent to Location 1 and consists of a metal tube set into a concrete base (Survey Mark Table of Coordinates; Map A2).
- National programmes operating in the area maintain a number of installations (weather stations, radio repeater and science experiments) on the highest summit of Mount Melbourne (Map A2; Inset 1).

Mount Rittmann
- There are two survey marks along the northeast boundary edge above the caldera rim (Map A3; Survey Mark Table of Coordinates). Both survey marks are a metal mark set into a rock.

6(iv) Location of other protected areas in the vicinity

Tramway Ridge, Mount Erebus
The nearest protected areas to Tramway Ridge, Mount Erebus are on Ross Island (Map A).

- ASPA 116: New College Valley, Caughley Beach, Cape Bird is 37 km to the north north-west.
- ASPA 156: Lewis Bay, Mount Erebus, Ross Island is 14 km to the north.
- ASPA 124: Cape Crozier, Ross Island is 54 km to the east.
- ASPA 122: Arrival Heights, Hut Point Peninsula, Ross Island and ASPA 158: Hut Point, Ross Island are 35 km and 38 km to the south, respectively.
- ASPA 155: Cape Evans, Ross Island is 21 km to the southwest.
- ASPA 121: Cape Royds, Ross Island and ASPA 157: Backdoor Bay, Cape Royds, Ross Island are 23 km to the west.

Mount Melbourne
The nearest protected areas to Mount Melbourne are in Terra Nova Bay (Map A).

- ASPA 161: Terra Nova Bay, Ross Sea is 45 km to the southeast.
- ASPA 165: Edmonson Point, Wood Bay, Ross Sea is 22 km to the east.
- ASPA 173: Cape Washington and Silverfish Bay, northern Terra Nova Bay, Ross Sea is 34 km to the south.

Mount Rittmann
Mount Rittmann is 103 km to the north of Mount Melbourne. There are no protected areas within a 100 km radius of Mount Rittmann (Map A).

6(v) Special zones within the Area

Access to the Prohibited Zone at each of the Area's three sites is strictly prohibited until such time that it is agreed, during a management plan review, that access should be allowed.

Tramway Ridge, Mount Erebus
The northern half of the site (Map A1) is designated a Prohibited Zone in order to preserve part of the site as a reference area for future scientific studies, while the southern half of the site (which is similar in biology, features and character) is available for scientific research.

The southern boundary of the Prohibited Zone is defined by a line from 77° 31' 05.103"S; 167° 06' 20.968"E (Point F) to 77° 31' 05.224"S; 167° 06' 50.792"E (Point C) that bisects the Area. The other three boundaries of the Prohibited Zone are defined by the boundaries of the Area with Point C (77° 31' 05.224"S; 167° 06' 50.792"E "E) to Point B (77° 31' 01.967"S; 167° 06' 51.074"E) making up the eastern boundary; Point B to Point A (77° 31' 01.853"S; 167° 06' 21.251"E) making up the northern boundary; and Point A to Point F making up the western boundary.

The southern boundary of the Prohibited Zone may be identified, approximately, on the ground as an extension westwards of the south ridge line of lower Tramway Ridge. When standing in the Area, the boundary markers (G, H and C) allow the bisecting line to be clearly visible.

Summit of Mount Melbourne
The westernmost 100 metres of Cryptogam Ridge (Location 1; Map A2) is designated a Prohibited Zone, in order to protect the most extensive stand of vegetation and preserve a part of the site as a reference area for future scientific studies, while the remainder of Cryptogam Ridge and Location 2 and 3 are available for scientific research.

The western boundary of the site from the NW boundary corner extends from the coordinates 74° 21' 20.389" S; 164° 41' 31.652" E (Point 1A) south approximately 50 metres to the SW boundary corner at 74° 21' 22.096" S; 164° 41' 32.551" E (Point 1N). The boundary then extends east following the crescent shape of Cryptogam ridge to unmarked points at 74° 21' 20.840" S; 164° 41' 45.230" E (Point 1L), then north to the NE boundary corner at 74° 21' 19.153" S; 164° 41' 45.329" E (Point 1C) (Map A2).

The Prohibited Zone is identified by the distinct change in slope of the ridge as it starts to decrease in elevation.

Mount Rittmann
Of the three geothermally heated areas identified at the site (Map A3), the eastern most area is designated a Prohibited Zone in order to preserve part of the site as a reference area for future scientific studies, while the remainder of the site (which is similar in biology, features and character) is available for scientific research.

The western boundary of the site from the NW boundary corner extends from the caldera rim at 73° 28' 17.655" S; 165° 37' 12.235" E (Point E) south down the steep slope approximately 80 metres to the SW boundary corner at 73° 28' 19.430" S; 165° 37' 08.865" E (Point N). The boundary then extends east following the bottom of the slope to the SE corner at 73° 28' 20.945" S; 165° 37' 13.936" E (Point M). The boundary then extends upslope north to the NE boundary corner at 73° 28' 19.823" S; 165° 37' 16.943" E (Point G) (Map A3).

7. Terms and conditions for entry permits

ALL PROVISIONS FOR ENTRY PERMITS APPLY TO THE AREA'S THREE SITES

7(i) General permit conditions
Entry into any of the Area's three sites is prohibited except in accordance with a Permit issued by an appropriate national authority. Conditions for issuing a Permit to enter the Area are that:

- it is issued for compelling scientific reasons which cannot be served elsewhere, or for reasons essential to the management of the Area;

- the actions permitted will not jeopardise the biological communities, ecological or scientific values of the Area;
- the actions permitted are in accordance with this Management Plan;
- access to the Prohibited Zones shall be prohibited;
- any management activities are in support of the objectives of the Management Plan;
- a Permit, or a copy, shall be carried within the Area, including a copy of all relevant maps from the Management Plan.

7(ii) Access to, and movement within or over, the Area
- Access to the summit of each volcano is generally by helicopter.
- Landing of helicopters within the Area's three sites is strictly prohibited.
- Helicopters should land at designated landing sites outside of the Area's three sites (refer to Section 6(ii) or Maps A1, A2 and A3).
- Helicopters should only land away from the designated landing sites in the event of an emergency.
- Helicopter overflights or hovering over any ice-free area of the Area's three sites should be avoided, except for essential scientific or management purposes when helicopters shall in no instance fly lower than 50 metres above the ground surface.
- The use of helicopter smoke grenades within the Area's three sites is prohibited.
- Vehicles (e.g. skidoos) are prohibited within the Area's three sites.
- Only those persons specifically authorised by Permit are allowed to enter the Area.
- All movement within the Area's three sites should be on foot.
- Permit holders should be aware that walking in the Area can compact soil, alter temperature gradients (which may change rates of steam release), and break thin ice crusts which may form over geothermally heated ground, with resulting damage to soil and biota below. The presence of snow or ice surfaces is not a guaranteed indication of a suitable pathway: therefore every reasonable effort should be made to minimise the effects of walking activity. Pedestrian traffic should be kept to the absolute minimum necessary consistent with the objectives of any permitted activities.
- Permit holders should also avoid walking on areas of visible vegetation or moist soil both on ice-free ground and among ice hummocks and, as far as practicable, areas of geothermally heated ground.
- Permit holders are strongly encouraged to collect GPS data for all movements within the Area and submit this data to the appropriate national authority with the visit report (see Section 7(x)).
- Permit holders shall not interfere (drill, sample, damage) with any ice structures unless specified in a Permit.

7(iii) Activities which may be conducted within the Area
Activities which may be conducted within the Area include:
- compelling scientific research which cannot be undertaken elsewhere and which will not jeopardise the biological communities, ecological or scientific values of the Area;
- essential management activities, including monitoring and inspection.

7(iv) Installation, modification, or removal of structures
- No new structures (i.e. signs or boundary markers) are to be erected within the Area, or scientific equipment installed, except for compelling scientific or management reasons and for pre-established periods, as specified in a Permit.
- All markers, structures or scientific equipment installed in the Area must be clearly identified by country, name of the principal investigator or agency, year of installation and date of expected removal.
- All such items should be sterilised prior to installation to ensure, that to the maximum extent possible, they are free of organisms, propagules and non-sterile soil, and be made of materials that can withstand the environmental conditions and pose minimal risk of contamination to the Area.
- Removal of specific structures or equipment for which the Permit has expired shall be the responsibility of the authority which granted the original Permit and shall be a condition of the Permit.

7(v) Location of field camps
- Camping is prohibited within the Area.
- Camping required for work at Tramway Ridge, Mount Erebus should be near the existing Upper (77° 30' 37.857"S; 167° 08' 48.5736"E) or Lower (77° 31' 32.6172"S; 167° 08' 12.8688"E) Erebus huts (Map A1; Inset 1).
- Camping is discouraged anywhere within 100 metres of the three locations on Mount Melbourne and Mount Rittmann.
- Camping should be on ice-covered ground only.

7(vi) Restrictions on materials and organisms which may be brought into the Area
To avoid compromising the ecological values, specifically the unique biological communities, for which the Area is protected, the following restrictions apply to all activities in the Area:
- The deliberate introduction of plants, animals, microorganisms and non-sterile soil into the Area shall not be permitted.
- To ensure that the ecological values of the Area are maintained, special precautions shall be taken against accidentally introducing plants, animals, microorganism or non-sterile soil from other Antarctic sites, including other sites or locations within the Area, stations, or from regions outside Antarctica, to any of the Area's three sites or between the Area's three sites by following the measures outlined in Section 7(x).
- All sampling equipment or markers brought into the Area shall be cleaned or sterilized.
- To the maximum extent practicable, footwear and other equipment used or brought into the Area (including bags or backpacks) shall be thoroughly cleaned before entering the Area.
- Visitors moving between the Area's three sites shall take extra care to ensure that all materials and equipment used at one site are cleaned or sterilized before moving to another site to avoid transferring species between these biologically distinct, but physically and climatically similar sites. In addition, because microbial diversity can differ over short distances, visitors moving between geothermal locations within a site shall take the same precautions.
- Neither fuel nor food is to be brought into the Area.
- Equipment or other materials are not to be stored in the Area.
- Chemicals, including radio-nuclides or stable isotopes, which may be brought into the Area for scientific or management purposes specified in the Permit, shall not be released into the environment and be removed from the Area at or before the conclusion of the activity for which the Permit was granted.
- Materials introduced into the Area shall be for a stated period only and shall be removed by the end of that stated period.
- Further guidance for reducing the risk of transfer of non-native species can be found in the CEP Non-native Species Manual (Edition 2011) and COMNAP/SCAR Checklists for supply chain managers of National Antarctic Programmes.

7(vii) Taking of, or harmful interference with, native flora and fauna
- Taking of, or harmful interference with, native flora and fauna and biological communities (specifically the microbiology) at these sites is prohibited, except in accordance with a permit issued in accordance with Annex II of the Protocol on Environmental Protection to the Antarctic Treaty.

7(viii) The collection or removal of materials not brought into the Area by the permit holder
- Material may be collected or removed from the Area only in accordance with a Permit and should be limited to the minimum necessary to meet scientific or management needs. Permits shall not be granted if there is reasonable concern that the sampling proposed would take, remove or damage such quantities of soil, sediment, microbiota, flora or fauna that their distribution or abundance within the Area would be significantly affected.
- Material of human origin likely to compromise the values of the Areas, which was not brought into the Area by the Permit Holder or otherwise authorised, may be removed from the Area, unless the impact of removal is likely to be greater than leaving the material *in situ*; if this is the case the appropriate authority should be notified.

7(ix) Disposal of waste
- All wastes, including all human wastes, shall be removed from the Area.

7(x) Measures that may be necessary to continue to meet the aims of the Management Plan
Permits may be granted to enter the Area to:
- carry out monitoring and Area inspection activities, which may involve the collection of samples or data for analysis or review;
- erect or maintain signposts, structures or scientific equipment; or
- carry out management activities.

To help maintain the ecological and scientific values derived from the isolation and relatively low level of human impact of the Area, visitors shall take special precautions against introductions, especially when visiting more than one of the Area's three sites in a season. Of particular concern are introductions sourced from:

- geothermal areas, both Antarctic and non-Antarctic;
- geothermal areas located at the same high altitude site which are not included within the Area;
- moving between any of the Area's three sites;
- soils from any other Antarctic site, including those near stations; and
- soils from regions outside Antarctica.

To this end, visitors shall take the following measures to minimise the risk of introductions:

- Any sampling equipment or markers brought into the Area shall be sterilised and maintained in a sterile condition before being used within the Area. To the maximum extent practicable, footwear and other equipment used or brought into the Area (including backpacks or carrybags) shall be thoroughly cleaned or sterilised and maintained in this condition before entering the Area;
- Sterilisation should be by an acceptable method, such as by UV light, autoclave, or by washing surfaces in 70% ethanol solution in water.
- Sterile protective over-clothing shall be worn. The over-clothing shall be suitable for working at temperatures of -20°C or below and comprise, at a minimum, sterile overalls to cover arms, legs and body and sterile gloves suitable for placing over the top of cold-weather gloves. Disposable sterile/protective foot coverings are not suitable for the scoria surface and should not be used. Instead, all footwear should be thoroughly brushed to remove soil particles and wiped with 70% ethanol solution.
- Both the interior and exterior of helicopters should be cleaned, as far as practicable, before moving to and from the Area, or between the Area's three sites.

7(xi) Requirements for reports
The principal permit holder for each visit to the Area shall submit a report to the appropriate national authority as soon as practicable, and no later than six months after the visit has been completed. Such visit reports should include, as applicable, the information identified in the recommended visit report form, contained in Appendix 2 of the Revised Guide to the Preparation of Management Plans for Antarctic Specially Protected Areas appended to Resolution 2 (2011), available from the website of the Secretariat of the Antarctic Treaty (www.ats.aq), and where possible, GPS data for all movements within the Area. The report shall take into account and identify which of the Area's three sites was visited.

If appropriate, the national authority should forward a copy of the visit report to the Party that proposed the Management Plan, to assist in managing the Area and reviewing the Management Plan.

8. Supporting documentation

Allan, R.N., Lebbe, L., Heyrman, J., De Vos, P., Buchanan, C.J. and Logan, N.A. 2005. *Brevibacillus levickii* sp. nov. and *Aneurinibacillus terranovensis* sp. nov., two new thermoacidophiles isolated from geothermal soils of northern Victoria Land, Antarctica. International Journal of Systematics and Evolutionary Microbiology 55: 1039-1050.

Armienti, P. And Tripodo, A. 1991. Petrography and chemistry of lavas and comagmatic xenoliths of Mount Rittmann, a volcano discovered during the IV Italian expedition in northern Victoria Land (Antarctica). Memorie della Societa Geologica Italiana 46: 427-451.

Bargagli, R., Broady, P.A. and Walton, D.W.H. 1996. Preliminary investigation of the thermal biosystem of Mount Rittmann fumaroles (northern Victoria Land, Antarctica). Antarctic Science 8(2): 121-126.

Bargagli, R., Skotnicki, M.L., Marri, L., Pepi, M., Mackenzie, A. and Agnorelli, C. 2004. New record of moss and thermophilic bacteria species and physicochemical properties of geothermal soils on the north-west slope of Mt. Melbourne (Antarctica). Polar Biology 27: 423-431.

Bonaccorso, A., Maione, M., Pertusati, P.C., Privitera, E. and Ricci, C.A. 1991. Fumarolic activity at Mount Rittmann volcano (northern Victoria Land, Antarctica). Memorie della Societa Geologica Italiana 46: 453-456.

Broady, P.A. 1984. Taxonomic and ecological investigations of algae on steam-warmed soil on Mt. Erebus, Ross Island, Antarctica. Phycologia 23: 257-271.

Broady, P.A. 1993. Soils heated by volcanism. Pages 413-432 in E.I. Friedmann (ed.), Antarctic microbiology. New York, Wiley-Liss.

Broady, P.A., Given, D., Greenfield, L.G. and Thompson, K. 1987. The biota and environment of fumaroles on Mt. Melbourne, northern Victoria Land. Polar Biology 7: 97-113.

Greenfield, L.G. 1983. Thermophilic fungi and actinomycetes from Mt. Erebus and a fungus pathogenic to *Bryum antarcticum* at Cape Bird. New Zealand Antarctic Record 4(3): 10-11.

Hudson, J.A. and Daniel, R.M. 1988. Enumeration of thermophilic heterotrophs in geothermally heated soils from Mount Erebus, Ross Island, Antarctica. Applied and Environmental Microbiology 54: 622-624.

Hudson, J.A., Daniel, R.M. and Morgan, H.W. 1988. Isolation of a strain of *Bacillus schlegelii* from geothermally heated Antarctic soil. FEMS Microbiology 51(1): 57-60.

Hudson, J.A., Daniel, R.M. and Morgan, H.W. 1989. Acidophilic and thermophilic Bacillus strains from geothermally heated Antarctic soil. FEMS Microbiology Letters 60: 279-282.

Imperio, T., Viti, C. And Marri, L. 2008. *Alicyclobacillus pohliae* sp. Nov., a Thermophilic, endospore forming bacterium isolated from geothermal soil of the north west slope of Mount Melbourne (Antarctica). International Journal of Systematic and Evolutionary Microbiology 58: 221-225.

Janetschek, H. 1963. On the terrestrial fauna of the Ross Sea area, Antarctica. Pacific Insects 5: 305-311.

LeMasurier, W.E. and Wade, F.A. 1968. Fumarolic activity in Marie Byrd Land, Antarctica. Science 162: 352.

Lesser, M.O., Barry, T.M and Banaszak, A.T. 2002. Effects of UV radiation on a chlorophyte alga (*Scenedesmus* sp.) isolated from the fumarole fields of Mt. Erebus, Antarctica. Journal of Phycology 38: 473-481.

Logan, N.A., Lebbe, L., Hoste, B., Goris, J., Forsyth, G., Heyndrickx, M., Murray, B.L., Syme, N., Wynn-Williams, D.D. and De Vos, P. 2000. Aerobic endospore-forming bacteria from geothermal environments in northern Victoria Land, Antarctica, and Candlemas Island, South Sandwich archipelago, with the proposal of *Bacillus fumarioli* sp. nov. International Journal of Systematic and Evolutionary Microbiology 50: 1741-1753.

Logan, N. and Allan, R.N. 2008. Aerobic endospore forming bacteria from Antarctic geothermal soils. Pages 155-175. In: Dion, P. And Nautiyal, C.S. (Eds.). Microbiology of Extreme Soils. Springer Verlang Berlin Heidelberg.

Lyon, G.L. and Giggenbach, W.F. 1974. Geothermal activity in Victoria Land, Antarctica. New Zealand Journal of Geology and Geophysics 17(3): 511-521.

Melick, D., Broady, P.A. and Rowan, K.S. 1991. Morphological and physiological characteristics of a non-heterocystous strain of *Mastigocladus laminosus* Cohn from fumarolic soils on Mount Erebus, Antarctica. Polar Biology 11:81-89.

Nathan, S. And Schulte, F.J., 1967. Recent thermal and volcanic activity on Mount Melbourne, northern Victoria Land, Antarctica. New Zealand Journal of Geology and Geophysics 10: 422-430.

Nicolaus, B., Marsiglia, F., Esposito, E., Tricone, A., Lama, L., Sharp, R., Di Prisco, G. and Gambacarta, A. 1991. Isolation of five strains of thermophilic eubacteria in Antarctica. Polar Biology 11: 425-429.

Nicolaus, B., Lama, L., Esposito, E., Manca, M.C., Di Prisco, G. And Gambacorta, A. 1996. *Bacillus thermoantarcticus* sp. nov. from Mount Melbourne, Antarctica: a novel thermophilic species. Polar Biology 16: 101-104.

Nicolaus, B., Improta, R., Manca, M.C., Lama, L., Esposito, E. And Gambacorta, A. 1998. Alicyclobacilli from an unexplored geothermal soil in Antarctica: Mount Rittmann. Polar Biology 19: 133-141.

Nicolaus, B., Lama, L., Esposito, E., Bellitti, M.R., Improta, R., Panico, A. And Gambacorta, A. 2000. Extremophiles in Antarctica. Italian Journal of Zoology 1: 169-174.

Nicolaus, B., Manca, M.C., Lama, L., Esposito, E. And Gambacorta, A. 2001. Lipid modulation by environmental stresses in two models of extremophiles isolated from Antarctica. Polar Biology 24: 1-8.

Nicolaus, B., Lama, L. And Gambacorta, A. 2002. Thermophilic Bacillus isolates from Antarctic environments. Pages 47-63 in Berkeley, R., Heyndrickx, M., Logan, N. And De Vos, P. (eds.), Applications and systematic of Bacillus and relatives. Balckwell Publishing.

Pepi, M., Agnorelli, C. And Bargagli, R. 2005. Iron demand by Thermophilic and mesophilic bacteria isolated from an Antarctic geothermal soil. Biometals 18(5): 529-536.

Poli, A., Esposito, E., Lama, L., Orlando, P., Nicolaus, G., deAppolonia, F., Gambacorta, A. And Nicolaus, B. 2006. *Anoxybacillus amylolyticus* sp. nov., a thermophilic amylase producing bacterium isolated from Mount Rittmann (Antarctica). Systematics and Applied Microbiology 29: 300-307.

Skotnicki, M.L., Selkirk, P.M., Broady, P., Adam, K.D. and Ninham, J.A. 2001. Dispersal of the moss *Campylopus pyriformis* on geothermal ground near the summits of Mount Erebus and Mount Melbourne, Victoria Land, Antarctica. Antarctic Science 13(3): 280-285.

Skotnicki, M.L., Bargagli, R. And Ninham, J.A. 2002. Genetic diversity in the moss *Pohlia nutans* on geothermal ground of Mount Rittmann, Victoria Land, Antarctica. Polar Biology 25: 771-777.

Soo, R.M., Wood, S.A., Grzymski, J.J., McDonald, I.R. and Cary, S.C. 2009. Microbial biodiversity of thermophilic communities in hot mineral soils of Tramway Ridge, Mount Erebus, Antarctica. Environmental Microbiology 11(3): 715-728.

Smith, G.H. 1992. Distribution and ecology of the testate rhizopod fauna of the continental Antarctic zone. Polar Biology 12: 629-634.

Ugolini, F.A. and Starkey, R.L. 1966. Soils and micro-organism from Mt. Erebus, Antarctica. Nature 211: 440-441.

Vickers, C.J. 2012. Investigating the physiological and metabolic requirements of the Tramway Ridge microbial community, Mount Erebus, Antarctica. MSc thesis, University of Waikato, New Zealand.

ANNEX 1: Site specific description of biological communities at each geothermal site.

Tramway Ridge, Mount Erebus
Located 1.5 kilometres northwest of the main Mount Erebus crater is an ice-free, gently sloping geothermal area known as Tramway Ridge (Map A1). Soil temperatures have been recorded up to 75°C at 4 centimetres depth. The steam-warmed lithosols at the site provide an unusual habitat of limited extent. The geothermal heat, the acidic soils and the unusual regular supply of moisture by condensation of steam produce conditions that contrast markedly with most Antarctic soils.

The vegetation comprises a single bryophyte species and a diverse range of algae which differs from that found in other high altitude geothermal sites, as well as other Antarctic plant communities from low altitude areas (Table 1). A number of fungi have been identified but no detailed studies have taken place. The single moss species, *Campylopus pyriformis*, is unusual in that it has never been seen to produce leaves but persists in the protonematal stage (a thread like chain of cells). *C. pyriformis* is widely known from both northern and southern temperate regions of the world including Australia, New Zealand and South America. This species has not been recorded at any other continental location in Antarctica except at Mount Melbourne where it occurs as small cushions of mature leafy gametophytes up to about 4 cm^2 forming populations covering areas up to 200 cm^2 with up to 70% ground cover.

The vegetation occurs in zones related to surface temperature. The warmest ground, from about 35 to 60°C, is colonised by dark blue-green and reddish-brown mats of cyanobacteria, whereas cooler surfaces of about 10 to 30°C are dominated by green crusts of coccoid chlorophytes and moss protonema. Bare ground, lacking any macroscopic vegetation, has a temperature of between 0 and 20°C. The presence of a thermophilic cyanobacterium is especially noteworthy as it is an unusual variety of the hot spring cyanobacterium *Mastigocladus laminosus*, which is common elsewhere in the world. There is little evidence of the presence of micro-invertebrates in the soils. An early investigation reported the presence of a rhizopod protozoan and bdelloid rotifer although subsequent more detailed studies did not report these.

Early studies investigating bacterial communities on Tramway Ridge, using classical cultivation techniques, successfully cultured a limited number of novel thermophilic bacteria from the genera *Clostridia* and *Bacillus*. The three bacterial species found at Mount Erebus (*Bacillus schlegelii*, *Alicyclobacillus acidocaldarius* (previously *Bacillus acidocaldarius*) and *Thermoanaerobacter thermohydrosulfuricus* (previously *Clostridium thermohydrosulfuricum*)) have not been identified in samples collected from Mount Melbourne and Mount Rittmann (Table 2). Several halophilic (organisms that live in high salt concentrations) strains were also isolated from soil samples from Tramway Ridge and based on phenotypic characteristics assigned to *Micrococcus*.

New techniques (genetic based culture independent methods) have been employed at this site to characterize the microbial diversity. Analyses show a clear delineation in bacterial and cyanobacterial community structure between communities closest to fumaroles and communities away from the fumaroles. The soil temperature, pH, percentage carbon and moisture at the hottest temperature sites next to fumaroles were significantly different from sites away from the fumaroles, selecting for organisms with unique physiological traits. Phylogenetic analysis identified the presence and exceptionally deep branching of bacterial sequences which varied to known microbial strains suggesting the soils at Tramway Ridge provide an atypical and unique habitat for microbial life and contain several yet to be described bacterial groups. Diversity of Archaea diversity was found to be low with a high sequence homology with known distant deep subsurface Archaea strains, indicating the Tramway Ridge species are from ancient lineages.

Mount Melbourne:
Geothermal activity on Mount Melbourne is concentrated in two main areas; at the rim of the main summit crater and on the northwest slope of the mountain. On the main summit crater, there are two locations within the Area. On the southern rim of the main summit crater of Mount Melbourne is a distinct deglaciated, crescent shaped ridge known at Cryptogam Ridge (Location 1; Map A2). Here warm ground extends along approximately 110 metres of the ridge. The areas of geothermally heated ground are marked by snow free areas, ice and snow hummocks up to a metre in height. Adjacent to Cryptogam Ridge is a slope (referred to as

the geothermal slope) leading up to the eastern rim of the summit crater (Location 2; Map A2). The ground is marked by crevasses and ice towers extending up the steep caldera rim. On the northwest slopes of the volcano there is a northwest to southeast trending line of ice towers and small patches of bare ground that make up the third location at this site (Map A2/1).

Soil temperatures at these locations typically reach between 30 and 50°C at depths of a few centimetres. Survival of plant life is only possible through the occurrence of small water droplets, formed by the condensation of steam, which keep the soils moist and acts as a water source for the vegetation.

Mount Melbourne supports a unique biological assemblage with high biodiversity relative to the other two high altitude geothermal sites in the Ross Sea region (Table 1). Biota includes (i) algae (11 species) within crusts and mats that coat small substrata, (ii) bryophytes (two species of moss and one of liverwort), and (iii) a protozoan. Many of the species are not of a local provenance and are thought to have been dispersed to the site from outside Antarctica, probably by winds. A lichen association has been observed as a component of black crusts over small areas of warm soil. The warmest areas of ground on Cryptogam Ridge (Location 1) support yellowish-green patches of the moss *Campylopus pyriformis,* along with the liverwort *Cephaloziella varians* and brownish crusts of algae. The unusual occurrence of shallow peat is evidence of bryophyte growth over at least several decades. Sporophytes of *C. pyriformis* have not been observed at Mount Melbourne indicating it reproduces asexually by dispersal of vegetative propagules. Analysis of the population found genetic evidence that indicated a single colonisation event probably occurred followed by multiple mutations. A comparison with samples of *C. pyriformis* collected from Mount Erebus, 350 kilometres south of Mount Melbourne, found the two populations to be closely related providing evidence for dispersal between areas of heated ground. Only sporadic patches of moss have been observed on the geothermal slope (Location 2). The amoeboid protozoan *Corythion dubium* was observed as empty shells in both mineral substrates and amongst bryophytes. The species is not common in continental Antarctica, and only found at one other site in Victoria Land. A number of fungi have been identified but no detailed studies have taken place.

The description of biota on Mount Melbourne is generally focused on Cryptogam Ridge (Location 1). More recent investigations of the biota on the northwest slope (Location 3) found no significant difference among the algal flora which is generally less well developed than that of Cryptogam Ridge. However, a third bryophyte species *Pohlia nutans* was identified from this location, a species closely related to populations found at Mount Rittmann and absent from Cryptogam Ridge. Furthermore, different populations of bacteria were identified from the two separate areas of geothermal activity on Mount Melbourne, even though they are only separated by a few kilometres.

Early microbial investigations carried out on samples collected from Crytpogram Ridge (Location 1) isolated new species of thermophilic bacteria such as *Bacillus thermoantarcticus* (now *thermantarcticus*), *Bacillus* (now *Alicyclobacillus*) *acidocaldarius* and *Bacillus fumarioli.* Later investigations were concerned with the soils on the northwest slope (Location 3) and identified the thermophilic strains *Alicyclobacillus* sp. and three mesophilic bacteria, *Micrococcus* sp., *Paenibacillus validus* and *Paenibacillus apiaries.* A further two novel species were identified more recently from the northwest slope, *Alicyclobacillus pohliae* sp. nov and *Brevibacillus levickii,* both of which have not been found on Cryptogam Ridge, but during the same investigation a new species of *Aneurinibacillus* genus was isolated from Cryptogam Ridge, and not the northwest slope. The name *Aneurinibacillus terranovensis* sp. nov. was proposed (Table 2).

Due to the restriction of certain species to certain locations on Mount Melbourne, investigations focussed on the metabolism of the different species and the soil characteristics and considered that the physico-chemical features of the geothermally heated ground may affect the colonisation history and dispersal of microorganisms and mosses at this site.

Mount Rittmann:
Although several expeditions into northern Victoria Land recognised the general distribution of volcanic centres in the region, Mount Rittmann was discovered only in the late 1980s. Located to the east of the head of the Aviator Glacier, a minor crater structure of Mount Rittmann is visible as a crescent shaped outcrop of a

rough and unstable near vertical steep slope (approximately 300 metres wide and 80 metres high) surrounded by glacial ice (Map A3). Soil temperatures range from 50 to 63°C at 10 centimetres depth.

Like Tramway Ridge, Mount Erebus and the three locations on Mount Melbourne, the biota consists of bryophytes and a diverse range of algae and protozoa which differs from that found in other high altitude geothermal sites, as well as other Antarctic plant communities from low altitude areas (Table 1). A single bryophyte species, *Pohlia nutans* occurs as small loose colonies of short shoots only 1-2 mm in length with soil visible between the shoots. It is a cosmopolitan species known from Europe, Asia, Africa, Australasia and a number of locations around Antarctica including Mount Melbourne, although it is notably absent from Mount Erebus. Sporophytes have not been observed and it appears *P. nutans* reproduces asexually. Genetic analysis found the population at Mount Rittmann has low levels of genetic diversity and appears to be derived from a single immigration event followed by mutations, similar to the *C. pyriformis* on Mount Melbourne. A diverse range of algae has been cultured and identified, while direct microscopic examination of original samples only revealed occasional algae. While examining cultures for algae, two protozoa were found, one a small cyst forming naked rhizopod and the other a flagellate resembling *Bodo sp.*, neither of which were found on Mount Melbourne or Mount Erebus.

Microbial investigations carried out on samples collected from Mount Rittmann isolated thermophilic acidophilic (organisms that survive in acidic conditions) strains belonging to the genus *Alicyclobacillus* and the thermophilic genus *Anoxybacillus*. The genetic relatedness of the isolated strains of *Alicyclobacillus* suggested that the strains could be related to the species *A. acidocaldarius* or it could be distinct enough to be a new sub-species and the name *Alicyclobacillus acidocaldarius* subsp. *rittmannii* was proposed. The characteristics of the isolated strain of *Anoxybacillus* were found to represent a novel species and the name *Anoxybacillus amylolyticus* sp. nov. was proposed. Two species of bacteria, including *Aneurinibacillus terranovensis* and *Bacillus fumarioli,* were isolated from samples taken from Cryptogam Ridge on Mount Melbourne and Mount Rittmann but were unable to be isolated from the northwest slope on Mount Melbourne even though the two sites on Mount Melbourne are approximately 1.5 kilometres apart and Mount Melbourne and Mount Rittmann are approximately 103 kilometres apart (Table 2).

Table 1: Flora and fauna of fumarolic ground in high altitude geothermal areas of the Ross Sea region.

Taxon	Mount Erebus [a]	Mount Melbourne [b]	Mount Rittmann [c]
Bryophytes			
Campylopus pyriformis[†] (Moss)	+	+	
Pohlia nutans (Moss)		+	+
Cephaloziella exiliflora[‡] (Liverwort)		+	
Algae - Cyanobacteria			
Aphanocapsa elachista[†]	+	+	
Gloeocapsa magma[‡]		+	
Phormidium fragile	+	+	
cf. *Phormidium fragile*			+
Tolypothrix bouteillei[‡]		+	
Mastigocladus laminosus[†]	+	+	+
Non-heterocystous *M. laminosus*	+		
Stigonema ocellatum[†‡]		+	
Nostoc sp.			+
Algae - Chlorophyta			
Bracteacoccus cf. minor	+		
Chlorella emersonii[†]	+	+	
Chlorella protothecoides[†]	+		
Chlorella cf. protothecoides			+
Chlorella reisiglii	+		
Chlorella cf. reisiglii			+
Chlorella cf. reniformis[†]		+	+
Chlorella saccharophila[†‡]	+		
Coccomyxa curvata[‡]	+		
Coccomyxa gloeobotrydiformis	+	+	
Coccomyxa cf. gloeobotrydiformis			+
Coenocystis oleifera	+	+	
Coenocystis cf. oleifera			+
Oocystis minuta	+		
cf. *Oocystis minuta*			+
Pseudococcomyxa simplex	+	+	
cf. *Pseudococcomyxa simplex*			+
Scotiellopsis terrestris[†]	+		
Scotiellopsis cf. terrestris			+
cf. *Lyngbya sp.*[†‡]			+
Scenedesmus sp.[‡]	+		
Protozoa			
Corythion dubium[‡]		+	
Small cyst-forming naked rhizopod			+
Flagellate cf. *Bodo sp.*			+
Rhizopod protozoa	+		

218

Taxon	Mount Erebus [a]	Mount Melbourne [b]	Mount Rittmann [c]
Bdelloid rotifer	+		
Fungi			
Aspergillus sp.	+	+	
Chaetomium sp.		+	
Cryptococcus sp.		+	
Unidentified dematiacean sp.	+		
Malbranchea pulchella var. *sulfurea*		+	
Mucor sp.	+		
Myceliophthora thermophila		+	
Neurospora sp.	+		
Paecilomyces sp.		+	
Penicillium sp.	+		
Unidentified yeast	+		
Actinomycetes			
Streptomyces coelicolor[†]	+	+	
Thermoactinomyces vulgaris	+		
Thermomonospora sp.[†]	+	+	

[a] Broady, 1984; Ugolini and Starkey, 1966; Hudson and Daniel, 1988; Skotnicki et al., 2001; Janetschek, 1963
[b] Broady et al., 1987; Nicolaus et al., 1991; Lesser at al., 2002
[c] Skotnicki et al., 2002; Bargagli et al., 1996 (Species identification is tentative as isolates were not established for more detailed study).
[†] No other Antarctic record.
[‡] No other record from Victoria Land.

Table 2: Bacterial diversity of fumarolic ground in high altitude geothermal areas of the Ross Sea region.

Genus species	Mount Erebus	Mount Melbourne	Mount Rittman	Reference
Thermophilic Bacteria				
Bacillus				
- *Bacillus schlegelii*	+			Hudson and Daniel, 1988
- *Bacillus thermoantarcticus*		+		Hudson et al., 1988
- *Bacillus fumarioli*		+	+	Nicolaus et al., 1996 Logan et al., 2000
Alicyclobacillus				
- *Alicyclobacillus acidocaldarius* (previously *Bacillus acidocaldarius)*	+			Hudson and Daniel, 1988
- *Alicyclobacillus acidocaldarius* subsp. *rittmannii*			+	Nicolaus et al., 1998
- *Alicyclobacillus sp.*		+	+	Pepi et al., 2005 Bargagli et al., 2004 Nicolaus et al.. 1998
- *Alicyclobacillus pohliae*		+		Imperio et al., 2008
Aneurinibacillus				
- *Aneurinibacillus terranovensis*		+	+	Allan et al., 2005
Anoxybacillus				
- *Anoxybacillus amylolyticus*			+	Poli et al., 2006
Brevibacillus				
- *Brevibacillus levickii*		+		Allan et al., 2005
Themoanaerobacter				
- *Thermoanaerobacter thermohydrosulfuricus* (previously *Clostridium thermohydrosulfuricum*)	+			Hudson and Daniel, 1988
Mesophilic Bacteria				
- *Micrococcus sp.*	+	+		Nicolaus et al., 2000; Nicolaus et al., 2001
- *Paenibacillus validus*		+		Pepi et al., 2005 Bargagli et al., 2004
- *Paenibacillus apiarius*		+		Pepi et al., 2005 Bargagli et al., 2004

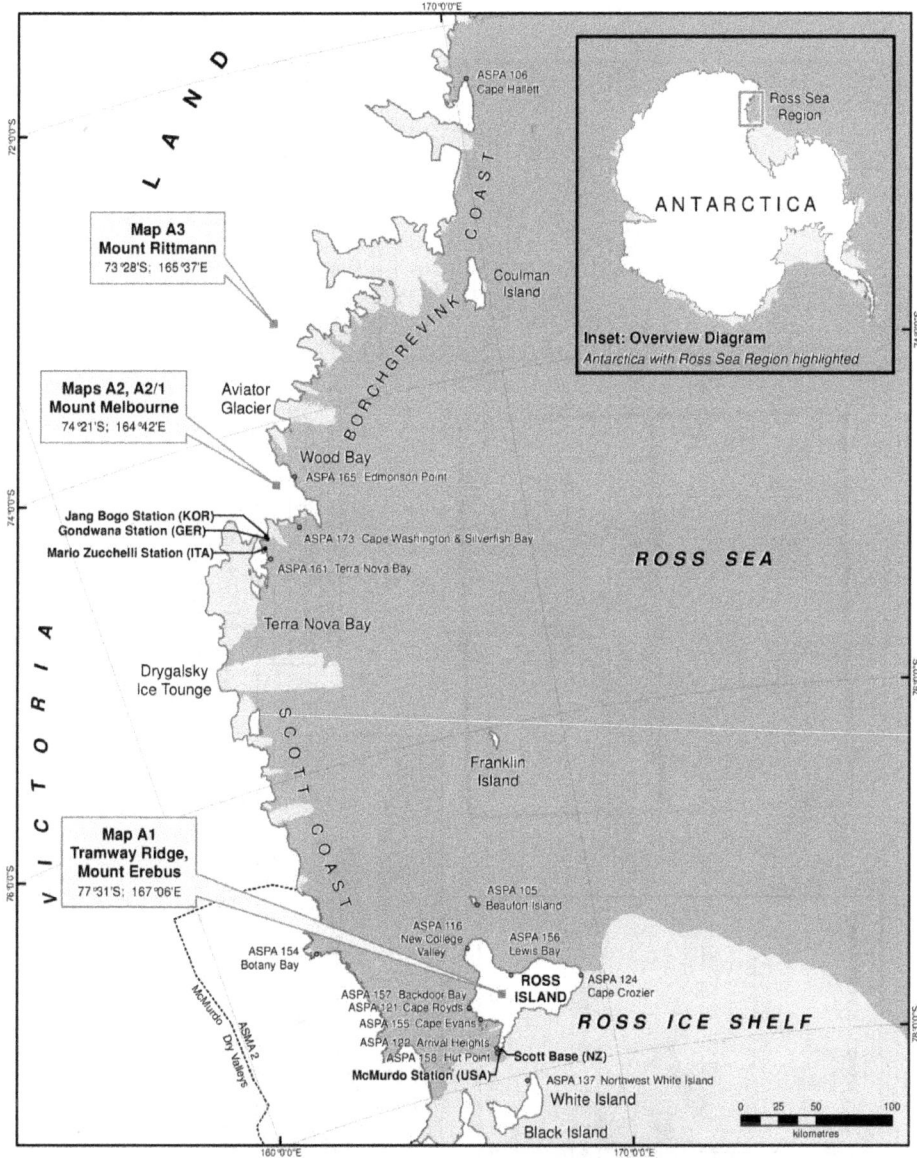

Map A - High Altitude Geothermal Sites of the Ross Sea Region
Location Diagram

Map Information:
Version 1.5 - 9 May 2014 (final).
Horizontal Datum: WGS84, Antarctica Polar Stereographic Projection.
True north is coincident with lines of longitude.

Data Sources:
Base Vector Data: Antarctic Digital Database Version 6.

Map A1 - ASPA 175: High Altitude Geothermal Sites of the Ross Sea Region
Tramway Ridge, Mount Erebus Topographical Map

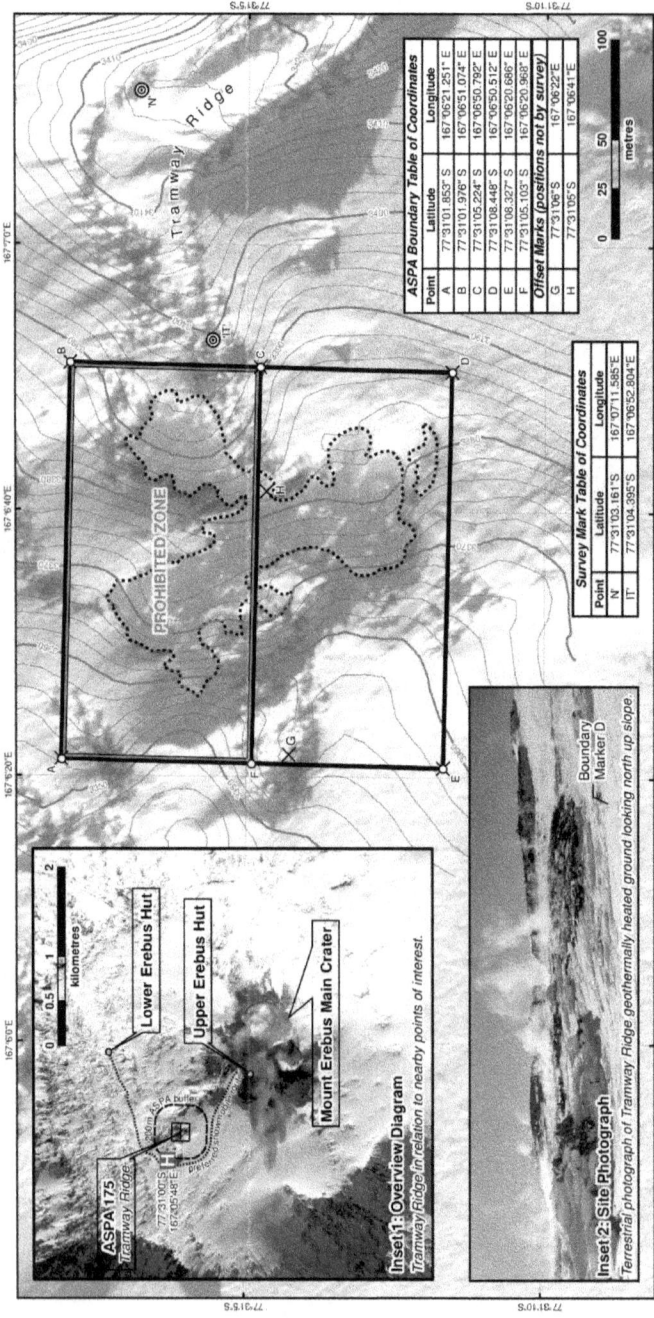

Inset 1: Overview Diagram
Tramway Ridge in relation to nearby points of interest.

Inset 2: Site Photograph
Terrestrial photograph of Tramway Ridge geothermally heated ground looking north up slope.

ASPA Boundary Table of Coordinates

Point	Latitude	Longitude
A	77°31'01.853" S	167°06'21.251" E
B	77°31'01.976" S	167°06'51.074" E
C	77°31'05.224" S	167°06'50.792" E
D	77°31'08.448" S	167°06'50.512" E
E	77°31'08.327" S	167°06'20.686" E
F	77°31'05.103" S	167°06'20.968" E

Offset Marks (positions not by survey)

| G | 77°31'06" S | 167°06'22" E |
| H | 77°31'05" S | 167°06'41" E |

Survey Mark Table of Coordinates

Point	Latitude	Longitude
N	77°31'03.161"S	167°07'11.585"E
TT	77°31'04.395"S	167°06'52.804"E

Map Information:
Version 1.7 - 9 May 2014 (final).
Horizontal Datum: WGS72, Camp Area Projection.
Vertical Datum: Mean Sea Level.
Satellite Imagery: orthorectified without ground-truthing.

Data Sources:
Survey Data: DOSLI Survey Plan 37/142.
Contours & Geothermally Heated Area: University of Canterbury.
Main Map & Overview Diagram Imagery: Digital Globe WorldView-2 Satellite (0.5 m resolution).
Site Photograph: University of Waikato.

222

Survey Mark Table of Coordinates

Point	Latitude	Longitude
MM01	74°21'13.880" S	164°42'13.557" E
MM02	74°21'26.428" S	164°42'01.776" E

ASPA Boundary Table of Coordinates

Point	Latitude	Longitude
1A	74°21'20.389" S	164°41'31.652" E
1B	74°21'19.650" S	164°41'37.695" E
1C	74°21'19.153" S	164°41'45.329" E
1D	74°21'19.307" S	164°41'51.137" E
1E	74°21'20.117" S	164°41'57.869" E
1F	74°21'21.523" S	164°42'03.969" E
1G	74°21'23.355" S	164°42'07.010" E
1H	74°21'22.588" S	164°41'58.044" E
1I	74°21'21.815" S	164°41'54.574" E
1J	74°21'21.200" S	164°41'49.934" E
1K	74°21'20.840" S	164°41'45.230" E
1L	74°21'21.383" S	164°41'38.551" E
1M	74°21'22.096" S	164°41'32.551" E

ASPA Boundary Table of Coordinates

Point	Latitude	Longitude
2A	74°21'13.740" S	164°42'01.816" E
2B	74°21'12.865" S	164°42'08.972" E
2C	74°21'14.567" S	164°42'12.729" E
2D	74°21'15.620" S	164°42'03.474" E

Location 2 — Geothermal Slope

Location 1 — Cryptogam Ridge

74°21'24.6"S 164°41'56.0"E

MM01

MM02

Inset 1: Overview Diagram
Locations in relation to nearby points of interest.

Mount Melbourne Summit
Science and communication equipment

74°20'57.7"S 164°41'28.9"E

Location 3
Northwest Slope
(refer to Map A2/1)

Location 2
Geothermal Slope

Location 1
Cryptogam Ridge

74°21'24.6"S 164°41'56.0"E

kilometres
0 0.25 0.5 1

Inset 2: Site Photograph
Terrestrial photograph taken looking northeast with Cryptogam Ridge in foreground.

Location 2 - Geothermal Slope

Location 1 - Cryptogam Ridge

Map A2 - ASPA 175: High Altitude Geothermal Sites of the Ross Sea Region
Cryptogam Ridge and Geothermal Slope, Mount Melbourne Topographical Map

Map Information:
Version 1.6 - 9 May 2014 (final).
Horizontal Datum: WGS84, UTM Zone 58 Projection.
Vertical Datum: WGS84.
Satellite Imagery: orthorectified without ground-truthing.

Data Sources:
Survey Data: Obtained by field survey 17 November 2012.
Main Map & Overview Diagram Imagery: Digital Globe GeoEye Satellite (0.5 m resolution).
Site Photograph: Antarctica New Zealand.

metres
0 50 100 200

◉ Survey Mark	〜2500〜 Contour – 10-metre interval
○ ASPA Boundary Point (unmarked)	〜〜 Contour – 2-metre interval
▮ ASPA Boundary	▣ Helicopter Landing Site
▢ Prohibited Zone Boundary	〜 Geothermally Heated Ground (approx. & subject to change)

N

223

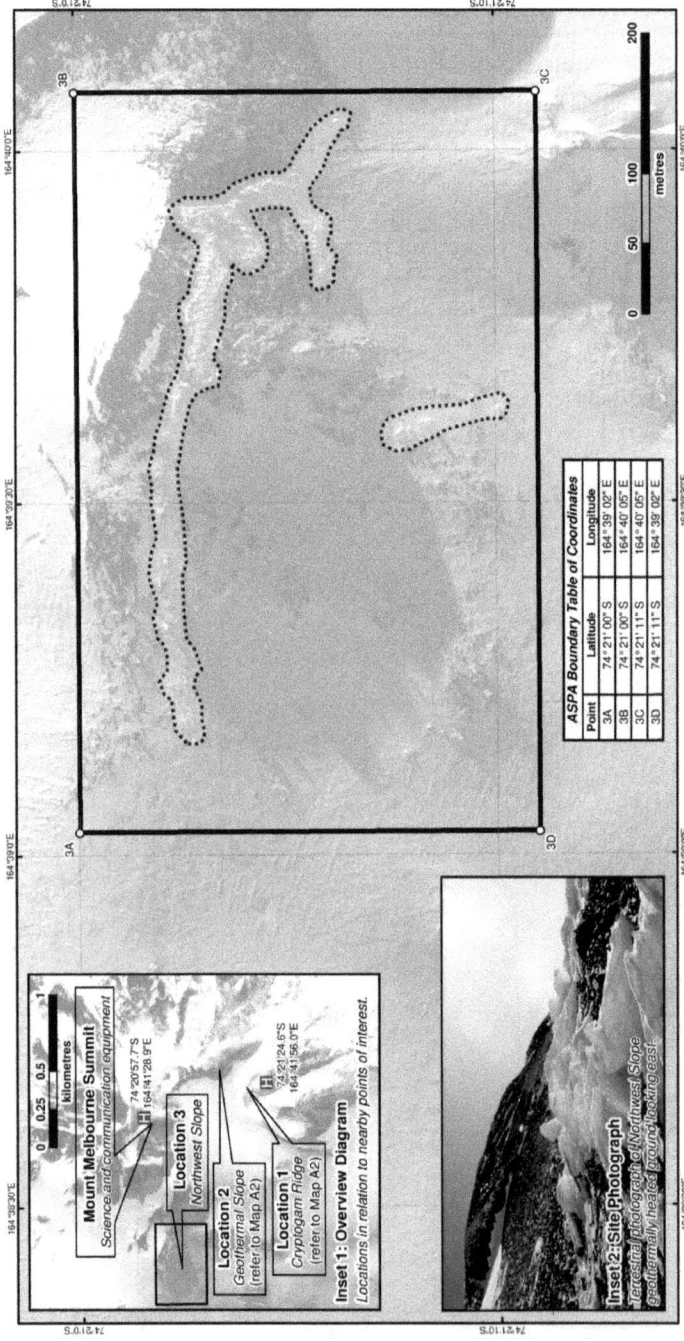

Map A2/1 - ASPA 175: High Altitude Geothermal Sites of the Ross Sea Region
Northwest Slope, Mount Melbourne Topographical Map

Map Information:

Version 1.4 - 9 May 2014 (final).
Horizontal Datum: WGS84, UTM Zone 58 Projection.
Vertical Datum: WGS84.
Satellite Imagery: orthorectified without ground-truthing.

Data Sources:

Survey Data: Data not by field survey. ASPA boundary obtained via inference from satellite imagery.
Main Map & Overview Diagram Imagery: Digital Globe GeoEye Satellite (0.5 m resolution).
Site Photograph: University of Siena.

ASPA Boundary Table of Coordinates

Point	Latitude	Longitude
3A	74° 21' 00" S	164° 39' 02" E
3B	74° 21' 00" S	164° 40' 05" E
3C	74° 21' 11" S	164° 40' 05" E
3D	74° 21' 11" S	164° 39' 02" E

○ ASPA Boundary Point (unmarked)

▭ ASPA Boundary

⬡ Helicopter Landing Site

⬠ Geothermally Heated Ground (approx. & subject to change)

N

0 50 100 200
metres

Inset 1: Overview Diagram

Mount Melbourne Summit
Science and communication equipment

Location 3
Northwest Slope

Location 2
Geothermal Slope
(refer to Map A2)

Location 1
Cryptogam Ridge
(refer to Map A2)

74° 20'57.7" S
164° 41'28.9" E

74° 21'24.6" S
164° 41'56.0" E

0 0.25 0.5 1
kilometres

Locations in relation to nearby points of interest.

Inset 2: Site Photograph

Terrestrial photograph of Northwest Slope geothermally heated ground, looking east.

Survey Mark Table of Coordinates		
Point	Latitude	Longitude
MR01	73° 28' 20.402" S	165° 37' 19.232" E
MR02	73° 28' 20.098" S	165° 37' 31.624" E

ASPA Boundary Table of Coordinates		
Point	Latitude	Longitude
A	73° 28' 18.797" S	165° 36' 43.851" E
B	73° 28' 16.818" S	165° 36' 54.698" E
C	73° 28' 16.290" S	165° 37' 00.144" E
D	73° 28' 16.405" S	165° 37' 04.438" E
E	73° 28' 17.655" S	165° 37' 12.235" E
F	73° 28' 18.024" S	165° 37' 14.468" E
G	73° 28' 19.823" S	165° 37' 16.943" E
H	73° 28' 20.628" S	165° 37' 20.089" E
J	73° 28' 21.530" S	165° 37' 21.567" E
J	73° 28' 22.015" S	165° 37' 23.817" E
K	73° 28' 23.436" S	165° 37' 20.540" E
L	73° 28' 22.414" S	165° 37' 17.302" E
M	73° 28' 20.945" S	165° 37' 13.936" E
N	73° 28' 19.430" S	165° 37' 08.865" E
O	73° 28' 18.556" S	165° 37' 03.457" E
P	73° 28' 18.722" S	165° 36' 56.296" E
Q	73° 28' 19.778" S	165° 36' 50.065" E

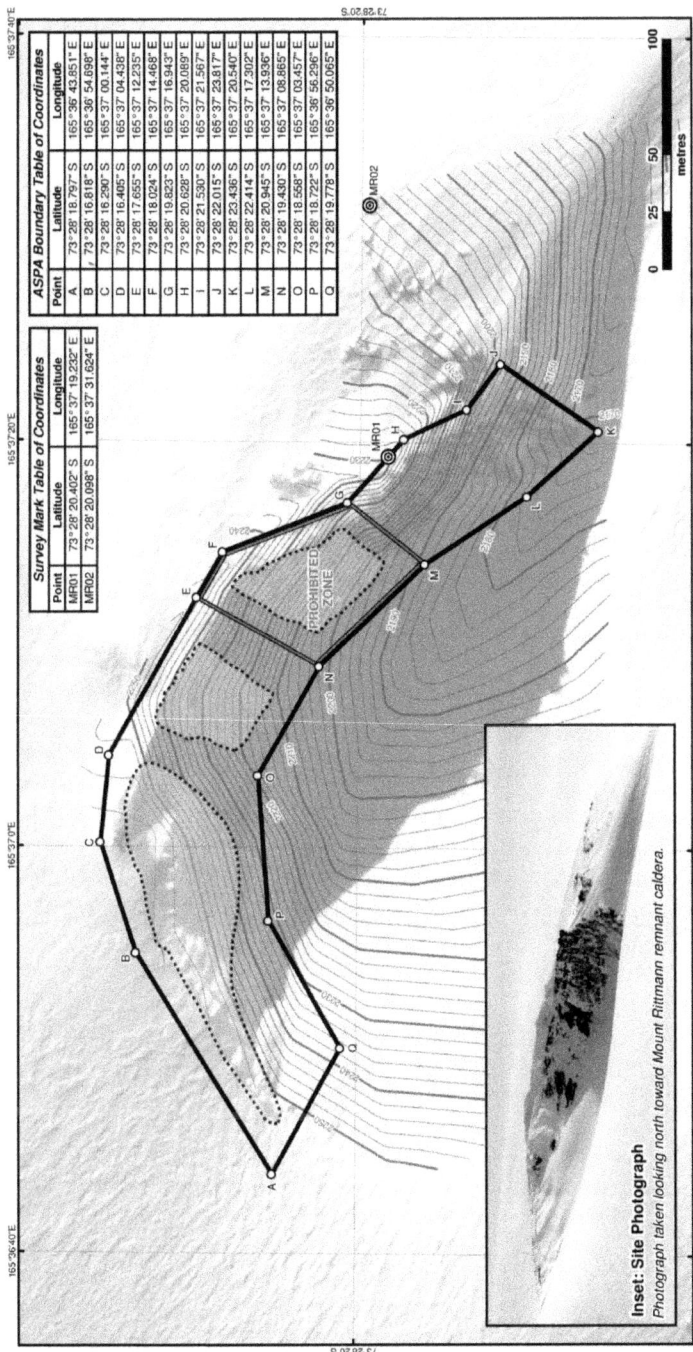

Map A3 - ASPA 175: High Altitude Geothermal Sites of the Ross Sea Region
Mount Rittmann Topographical Map

Inset: Site Photograph
Photograph taken looking north toward Mount Rittmann remnant caldera.

◉ Survey Mark

○ ASPA Boundary Point (unmarked)

◻ ASPA Boundary

◻ Prohibited Zone Boundary

〜ᴬᵂᵁ〜 Contour – 10-metre interval

〜〜〜 Contour – 2-metre interval

〔 〕 Geothermally Heated Ground (approx. & subject to change)

Map Information:
Version 1.5 - 9 May 2014 (final).
Horizontal Datum: WGS84, UTM Zone 58 Projection.
Vertical Datum: WGS84.
Satellite Imagery: orthorectified with limited ground-truthing.

Data Sources:
Survey Data: Obtained by field survey 16 November 2012.
Main Map & Overview Diagram Imagery: Digital Globe WorldView-1 Satellite (0.5 m resolution).
Site Photograph: Antarctica New Zealand.

225

Management Plan for
Antarctic Specially Managed Area No.1

ADMIRALTY BAY, KING GEORGE ISLAND

Introduction

Admiralty Bay is located on King George Island, South Shetland Islands, about 125 kilometers from the northern tip of Antarctic Peninsula (Fig. 1). The primary reason for its designation as an Antarctic Specially Managed Area (ASMA) is to protect its outstanding environmental, historical, scientific, and aesthetic values. Admiralty Bay was first visited by sealers and whalers in the 19th and early 20th centuries, and relics from these periods still remain. The area is characterized by magnificent glaciated mountainous landscape, varied geological features, rich sea-bird and mammal breeding grounds, diverse marine communities, and terrestrial plant habitats. For nearly four decades coordinated scientific research has been conducted in Admiralty Bay by five different countries. The studies on penguins have been undertaken continuously since 1976, and is the longest ever done in Antarctica. Admiralty Bay also has one of the longest historical series of meteorological data collected for the Antarctic Peninsula, considered as one of the most sensitive areas of the planet to climate change.

The Area comprises environments laying within three domains defined in the Environmental Domains Analysis for Antarctica: Environment A – Antarctic Peninsula northern geologic; Environment E – Antarctic Peninsula and Alexander Island main ice fields; and Environment G – Antarctic Peninsula offshore island geologic (Resolution 3 (2008)). Under the Antarctic Conservation Biogeographic Regions (ACBR) classification the Area lies within ACBR 3 – Northwest Antarctic Peninsula (Resolution 6 (2012)).

The Area, which includes all the marine and terrestrial areas within the glacial drainage basin of Admiralty Bay, is considered to be sufficiently large to provide adequate protection to the values described below.

Admiralty Bay has become a site of increasingly diverse human activities, which are continuously growing, becoming more complex and creating a situation of conflicting uses. During the last 30 years, more stations have settled, visitors increased in numbers per year, from a few hundreds to over 3000 and commercial krill fishing operations have been conducted in the Area in the season 2009/2010. Better planning and coordination of existing and future activities will help to avoid or to reduce the risk of mutual interference and minimize environmental impacts, thus providing more effective mechanisms for the conservation of the valuable features that characterize the Area.

Five Consultative Parties – Poland, Brazil, United States, Peru and Ecuador – have active research programs in the area. Poland and Brazil operate two all-year round stations (Poland: Henryk Arctowski Station at Thomas Point; and Brazil: Comandante Ferraz Antarctic Station at Keller Peninsula). Peru and the United States operate two summer stations (Peru: Machu Picchu Station at Crepin Point; USA: Copacabana Field Camp south of Llano Point). Ecuador has a refuge at Hennequin Point. There are several small permanent and semi-permanent installations elsewhere.

The Area includes one ASPA (ASPA No. 128 Western Shore of Admiralty Bay – former SSSI No. 8) and one Historic Site and Monument (HSM No. 51: Puchalski Grave) at Arctowski Station. Seven graves at Keller Peninsula are under special protection.

In addition to numerous scientists, supporting personnel and research expeditions, Admiralty Bay is visited by an increasing number of tourists, the latter mainly as organized tourist ship expeditions and private yachts.

A Management Plan for designating Admiralty Bay and its surroundings (herein called the Area) as an Antarctic Specially Managed Area (ASMA), under Annex V of the Protocol to the Antarctic Treaty on Environmental Protection (herein called Protocol), was jointly proposed by Brazil and Poland, in coordination with Ecuador and Peru and voluntarily adopted by the ATCPs at ATCM XX (Utrecht, 1996). In 2006, a revised version of the Management Plan was presented and approved at the Committee for Environmental Protection, which designated the Area as ASMA No 1 (Measure 2, CEP IX – ATCM XXIX, 2006, Edinburgh). This revised management plan was prepared with reference to the "Guide to the Preparation of Management Plans for Antarctic Specially Protected Areas" (Resolution 2, CEP XIV – ATCM XXXIV, 2011, Buenos Aires).

1. Description of values to be protected

i. Aesthetic values

Admiralty Bay has basic physiographic and aesthetic values as one of the most typical examples of bay/fjord settings in the South Shetland Islands. The ice-free areas within Admiralty Bay were formed by recent and raised pebble-cobble beaches, recent and sub-recent moraines, mountainous peninsulas, rocky islets, spurs and nunataks. The terrain is heavily shaped by glacial, nival and coastal marine processes. These, together with the geological features of the area, add to the great scenic beauty of the landscape.

ii. Environmental values

The area of Admiralty Bay is representative of the terrestrial, limnetic, coastal, near-shore, pelagic, and fjord bottom ecosystems of King George Island. Flora is mostly represented by more than 300 species of lichens, around 60 species of mosses and numerous algae, as well as two species of native vascular plants (*Deschampsia antarctica* and *Colobanthus quitensis*) (Appendix A). Plant associations are accompanied by a large diversity of soil microorganisms. Twenty-four species of birds and six species of pinnipeds have been registered for the Area, but only fourteen species of birds and three species of pinnipeds actually breed within the Area (Appendix C, Fig. 5 and 6). The marine ecosystem of the bay largely reflects the general environmental conditions prevailing in the South Shetland Islands. The Admiralty Bay shelf benthic community is characterized by high species richness and high assemblage diversity. Giant algae (specially *Himantothallus* sp.), with a very diverse associated fauna, are found near the coastal zone, between 15 and 30 m depth, in several sites of the bay (Appendix B). An unique site, Napier Rock, situated at the entrance of the bay, supports especially rich and highly diverse benthic invertebrate fauna. Fish are represented by fifteen species of Nototheniidae.

iii. Scientific values

Admiralty Bay is of outstanding scientific interest, especially for research in biology and geoscience. King George Island was discovered in 1908 year and since that time was visited occasionally by whalers, sailors and scientists. More important geological investigation was performed by British scientists from Base G on Keller Peninsula, Admiralty Bay between 1948 – 1960. Several scientific expeditions were carried out also later, However, diverse and continuous scientific activities have been undertaken in the Area since the 1970s supported by the Polish Henryk Arctowski Station, by the Brazilian Comandante Ferraz Station and by the US Antarctic Program at ASPA No. 128 Western Shore of Admiralty Bay. Research activities at the Peruvian Machu Picchu Station (at Crepin Point) and at the Ecuadorian refuge (at Hennequin Point) have occurred intermittently during the Antarctic summer seasons.

The main subjects for field and laboratory research at the Polish and Brazilian stations have been marine and terrestrial biology, including physiology and adaptation of Antarctic fish and krill; taxonomy and ecology of the benthic fauna; vascular plants; mosses and lichens; terrestrial and marine ecology; migration and dispersion of birds; microbiological studies. A long-term research project on the biology and dynamics of bird populations (mainly Pygoscelid penguins and *Catharacta* skuas) has been carried out by the US Antarctic Program since 1976. This study is relevant to the CCAMLR Ecosystem Monitoring Programme (CEMP). Since 1985 a research program monitoring non-native grass *Poa annua* around Arctowski Station and in ASPA No 128 has been conducted. Long term monitoring of atmospheric and air temperature records undertaken by Brazilian researchers has revealed an increase in the mean air temperature of 1.1°C from 1956 to 2000. This increase in temperature has been associated with a 12% frontal glacier retreat during the same period. In King George Island, a retreat of the valley-type tidewater glaciers front by 1 km has been observed since 1956. Retreat of glaciers in the middle and outer parts of Admiralty Bay has exposed new ice-free coastal areas suitable for breeding grounds of some species of seals. The ice-free areas have enlarged threefold during the last 20 years, creating conditions for inhabitation and succession. Phytosociological research and vegetation mapping of the areas successively freed by retreating glaciers are carried out.

Due to warmer temperatures, winter sea-ice duration in the region is shortening, impacting spawning and nursery areas of krill (*Euphausia superba*). The decrease in krill population has been found to coincide with an increase in salps (*Salpa thompsoni*). These changes among key species may have profound implications for the food web of the Area.

In the last 30 years the number of penguins has decreased in the Area - the Adelie (*Pygoscelis adeliae*) and chinstrap penguins (*Pygoscelis antarctica)* suffered an overall decline by roughly 57%, and the population of gentoo penguin (*Pygoscelis papua*) has increased by about 64% since the establishment of the ASMA. The numbers of fur seals change in multi-annual cycles. The abundance of elephant seals has kept stable, whereas those of Weddell and crabeater seals has declined.

Other studies conducted in the Area include geology and palaeontology, glaciology and palaeoclimatology of the King George Island ice cap; and glacio-marine sedimentation within Admiralty Bay. Paleogene and Neogene rocks of King George Island preserve evidences of globally important environmental and climatic transition from greenhouse to icehouse world, that culminated at the Eocene-Oligocene boundary. That best record of the first Cenozoic glaciation in the Southern Hemisphere is well documented in stratigraphical, lithological and paleontological investigations on King George Island, which were summarized in geological map done by Birkenmajker in 2002 year. The Eocene base of these rock formations build up the bedrock of ASMA 1 area and is continued eastward in younger rocks to the end of the island, proving Oligocene and Miocene glaciations.

Additional scientific values to note from the landscape viewpoint including geological and geomorphological attributes, are the following:

- The island display landforms in ice-free areas resulting from proglacial and aeolian erosion. Sea action led to formation of beach bands along shoreline, several of them raised up to 20 m a.s.l. due to galcio-izostatic uplift during the Holocene.

- Presence of early-middle Eocene fossiliferous sites of great scientific importance, at Ulmann and Hennequin Points, Keller Peninsula, Ezcurra Inlet, along the coastal area, behind Arctowski Station, on Błaszczyk moraine and at Read Hill. Fossilized wood of Araucaria, *Nothofagus* and leaf impressions of higher plants and pteridophytes, are common and well-preserved.

- Presence of well-preserved paleosols of ages dating back to 20 MA, with evidences of temperate to subtropical paleoclimates in their formation, with great scientific importance. These features can be found in Punta Plaza, Copacabana and Hennequin Point.

- Permafrost is generally present on northern slopes at altitudes higher than 30 meters, being absent or sporadic below that level. The Admiralty Bay is considered a key area for monitoring permafrost in the Shetlands Archipelago, and for being representative of the well-protected inner bay zones under Maritime Antarctic climate.

A year-round seismic and Earth-magnetism observatory, was functioning at Arctowski Station since 1978 until 1994, and in 2013 a research program aimed at monitoring the structure of Earth's electric field was begun at Arctowski Station. Studies on atmospheric chemistry, geomagnetism, the ionosphere and astrophysics have been conducted at Ferraz Station since 1984. A meteorological station has been operational at Arctowski since 1977 until 2000, and at Ferraz Station since 1984 to provide basic data and to support logistic operations. Research on upper atmosphere winds have been developed at Machu Picchu Station with the aid of a MST radar. Since 2006, a long-term research project on marine plankton, macrobenthos biodiversity and quality of the marine environment in Mackellar Inlet has been carried out. Also ozone layer decrease anomalies study has been developed.

Both Arctowski and Ferraz stations have hosted scientists from many countries (Argentina, Belgium, Chile, Germany, Russia, The Netherlands, New Zealand, North America, Uruguay, Spain, Italy, Czech Republic, Ukraine, Bulgaria, Peru and others) There is a strong tradition of co-operation between Polish and Brazilian scientists in matters related to Admiralty Bay and the South Shetland Islands as a whole. Both countries cooperated during the past International Polar Year (2007-2008) through the Census of Antarctic Marine Life and comprehensively gathered marine benthic data from the past 30 years.

A comprehensive study of the state of the environment in the Area is under way at Ferraz Station, since 2002, comprising the analysis of a series of biotic and abiotic parameters. Brazil created a National Institute of Science and Technology on Antarctic Environmental Research (INCT-APA, in Portuguese) in 2008, and this has ensured the continuity of a monitoring program and other environmental studies. An environmental and biological database has been set in place to support assessments of atmospheric, oceanic and terrestrial trends. This will contribute to the monitoring of human activities in the Area and for the implementation of environmental management strategies for the ASMA.

iv. Historic values

The presence of sheltered deep harbors and accessible beaches ensured an early start to activities in Admiralty Bay. The bay offered protection for ships in the area during the sealing and whaling periods in the 19th and early 20th centuries, and some remains related to the those periods still exist (e.g. old whaling boat on Keller Peninsula, collection of whaling harpoons at Arctowski Station). Whale bones cover the beaches and are part of the landscape, remaining as heritage of those periods.

The Area was visited by the second French Antarctic Expedition Pourquoi Pas?, under Dr J B Charcot (1908-10), and by D Ferguson (1913-14), a geologist who took part in a British whaling expedition. Reports on minerals and rocks collected during these expeditions, published between 1910 and 1921, are among the first earth-science publications on Admiralty Bay and the South Shetland Islands. The famous British Discovery voyages of 1934 and 1937 collected more rocks, as well as plants and animals from the Area. Results published from 1948 to 1964 constituted a substantial contribution to knowledge of the geology of Admiralty Bay. Argentina established a refuge hut at Keller Peninsula in 1948 (since dismantled) and the work of Argentinean geologists in Admiralty Bay in 1953 focused on fossil plants from the Tertiary age.

The UK Base "G", on Keller Peninsula, was established in 1947 as a center for meteorological observations, and glaciological and geological research in the Area. In 1961 it was closed and later on dismantled.

A small hut named Campo Bove was built in Ezcurra Inlet in 1975 by the Italian expedition led by Giacomo Bove. It was dismantled in March 1976.

v. Educational and touristic values

Admiralty Bay is a place of special attraction to tourists because of its accessibility, biological diversity and presence of several scientific stations. Therefore, its sites of ecological interest and scientific installations in the Area are frequently visited by tourists and participants in non-governmental expeditions, who have thus an opportunity to become familiar with the Antarctic environment and international scientific operations.

Education and outreach of Antarctic science should be widely encouraged in countries that develop scientific research in the Area. Penguins and krill are easily observed and are considered as iconic species of the Antarctic. The capture of images and videos provide a high level of educative potential. Promoting and facilitating the incorporation of Antarctic science at all levels of formal education, and informing the public and the media about the importance of studies in Antarctica are part of the strategy for Antarctic conservation (see Summary of SCAR's Strategic Plan 2011-2016 - http://www.scar.org/treaty/atcmxxxiv/ATCM34_ip054_e.pdf). Furthermore, as a region that distinctly shows the effects of climate change, the Area is considered an outdoor laboratory and represents a great opportunity to encourage interest and training of early career researchers (SCAR Strategy for Capacity building, Education and Training, Report 27, 2006).

2. Aims and Objectives

The aim of this Management Plan is to conserve and protect the unique and outstanding environment of Admiralty Bay by managing and coordinating human activities in the Area in such a way as to provide long-term protection to the values, avoid possible conflict of interest and promote cooperation.

The specific objectives of management in the Area are to:

- Safeguarding the long-term scientific research in the Area while maintaining stewardship of the environment;

- Protecting important physiographic features, and the outstanding biological, ecological, scientific, historical and aesthetic values of the Area;

- Managing potential or actual conflicts of interest between different activities, including science, logistics, commercial fishing and tourism;
- Assisting with the planning and coordination of human activities in the Area;
- Ensuring that any marine harvesting activities are coordinated with scientific research and other activities taking place within the Area and are based on the precautionary approach;
- Avoiding or minimizing the risk of mutual interference and cumulative impacts on the terrestrial and marine environments;
- Improving the level of mutual assistance and co-operation among Parties operating in the Area;
- Encouraging communication and cooperation between users of the Area through dissemination of information on the Area and the provisions that apply;
- Minimizing the possibility of non-native species introduction through human activities and management of any non-native species already established in the Area;
- Managing visitation to the Area and promoting an awareness, through education, of its ecological and scientific significance.

3. Management Activities

The following management activities should be undertaken to achieve the aims of this Management Plan:

- Parties that have active research programs within the Area shall establish an Admiralty Bay Management Group to:
  - review the functioning and implementation of the Management Plan;
  - monitor the Area to investigate possible sources of environmental impact including cumulative impacts;
  - provide forum for facilitating communication among those working or visiting the Area, and for resolving potential conflicts;
  - promote dissemination of information on this Management Plan to those working or visiting the Area;
  - promote and encourage coordination of activities among those working or visiting the Area with the aim of protecting important values of the Area;
  - promote and encourage cooperation among National Antarctic Programs conducting environmental monitoring of the Area with the aim of developing a joint environmental study of the Area;
  - maintain a record of activities taking place in the Area.
- Parties belonging to the Management Group should consult amongst themselves with a view to:
  - designate a person to coordinate the implementation of the Management Plan in the Area (ASMA Coordinator). Designation will be for a 5 year period on a rotational basis. Duties of the ASMA Coordinator are: (i) Coordinate information exchange by Parties about the activities undertaken in the ASMA and analyze them in order to identify possible overlaps and unconformities in relation to the objectives of this Management Plan. (ii) Report to the Parties and, as appropriate, to the CCAMLR Secretariat, any incident that may cause impact to environment or research activities in the Area.
- Parties belonging to the Management Group should convene on an annual basis or when necessary to discuss all matters concerning the management of the Area. Other Parties and organizations active in the Area may be invited to participate in the discussions.
- National Antarctic Programs operating within the Area, as well as all other visitors, should undertake activities in accordance with the General Code of Conduct contained in this Management Plan.
- Wherever feasible, markers delimiting boundaries of already existing protected areas and other zones of ecological or scientific interest identified in this Management Plan with warnings for visitors about their nature should be provided, and removed when no longer necessary.

- Tour operators and other organizations planning activities in the Area should coordinate them with National Antarctic Programs operating in the Area in advance to ensure that they do not pose risks to its important values.

- National Antarctic Programs that have active research programs in the Area should make arrangements with other Parties that have installations and/or structures now abandoned to consider their value for reuse. Conservation plans should be formulated if any of the installations are assessed to be of historical value. If not, plans should be formulated for their removal in accordance with the provisions of Annex III on Waste Disposal and Waste Management to the Protocol on Environmental Protection.

- Parties operating permanent/seasonal facilities in the Area are encouraged to consult and, as far as practicable, coordinate their contingency plans for oil spills and other possible accidents with the aim of developing a multi-operator plan encompassing the Area.

- National Antarctic Programs, tour operators and other organization active in the Area should seek to minimize to the maximum extent the risk of introduction of non-native species. Any non-native species present within the Area should be systematically monitored , and policies on its containment or/and eradication should be developed as a priority.

- National Antarctic Programs operating in the Area should ensure that their personnel have been briefed on the requirements of the Management Plan and, in particular, on the Code of Conduct for Visitors (Appendix E) and Scientific and Environmental Guidelines (Appendix F) that apply within the Area.

- Tour operators visiting the Area should ensure that their staff, crew and passengers are briefed on, and are aware of the requirements of this Management Plan and the Code of Conduct for Visitors (Appendix E).

- Copies of this management plan and supporting documentation, such as maps and appendices, should be kept in appropriate stations and refuges in the Area, and be made available to all persons in the Area.

- Visits to the Area should be made as necessary (no less than once every five years) to evaluate the effectiveness of the Management Plan, and to ensure that its requirements are being met.

4. Period of Designation

Designated for an indefinite period.

5. Maps

Figure 1: Location of ASMA No. 1 in King George Island, Antarctic Peninsula.

Figure 2: Admiralty Bay Antarctic Specially Managed Area – ASMA No. 1.

Figure 3: Location of Scientific Zones.

Figure 4: Permanent Environmental Monitoring Area (INCT-APA, Brazil).

Figure 5: Flora (colonized areas) and Birds (occurrence sites).

Figure 6: Main birds breeding sites.

Figure 7: Visitor Zone – Comandante Ferraz Station

Figure 8: Visitor Zone – Henryk Arctowski Station

Figure 9: Facilities Zones – Machu Picchu Station

6. Description of the Area

6(i) Geographical co-ordinates, boundary markers and natural features

General description

Admiralty Bay is a large fjord, in the southern coast of King George Island, the biggest island in the South Shetland Archipelago, off the north-west coast of the Antarctic Peninsula, separated from it by the Bransfield

232

Strait (Fig. 1). The bay is characterized by the extreme bottom heterogeneity. It is surrounded by different kinds of landscapes, such as coastlines with penguin rookeries and seal wallows, big glacier forelands, lichen heaths, swamps, grasslands or barren rocky lands. An area of approximately 360 km² comprising of Admiralty Bay and the surrounding area is designated as an Antarctic Specially Managed Area to manage human activities for the protection of scientific, environmental, historical and aesthetic values.

ASMA No. 1: Admiralty Bay, King George Island (62°01'21"S – 62°14'09"S/ 58° 15'05"W– 58°41'02"W) comprises the terrestrial and marine areas immediately within the glacial drainage basin of this bay (Fig. 2). In addition, it includes ASPA No. 128 Western Shore of Admiralty Bay, part of which is outside the drainage basin area. One Historic Site and Monument, HSM No 51 Puchalski Grave, is located within the Area.

The Area is bounded by a line extending from its southern margin at the Telefon Point (62°14' 09.3" S, 58° 28'00.5" W) to The Tower (58°28'48"W, 62°12'55"S), and then toward Jardine Peak (58°29'54"W, 62°10'03"S) intersecting the ice divide of the Warszawa ice-field, thence following this divide to the west of Ezucurra Inlet, north-eastward to enclose Mackellar and Martel inlets, and then southward through Ternyck Needle (62°04'52.6" S, 58°15'24.1" W) to Cape Syrezol (62°11'38.4" S, 58°16'29.6" W) on the eastern shore of Admiralty Bay. The waters of Admiralty Bay and a small part of Bransfield Strait, north of a straight line between Cape Syrezol and Telefon Point, are also included in the ASMA. There are no fixed survey points available at the Area boundaries, but markers indicating the ASMA will be fixed at appropriate arrival points on land.

The revised total area of ASMA No. 1 is 360 km², of which 194 km² are ice covered, including 138 km² of Admiralty Bay Waters and an adjoining 7 km2 of the Bransfield Strait (Admiralty Chart N° 6258, 1968, London; Polish Chart Admiralty Bay, King George Island, 1:50,000, Battke, S, Warszawa, 1990; ASPA No. 128: Western Shore of Admiralty Bay, King George Island, 1:12 500, ed. Department of Antarctic Biology, Polish Academy of Sciences, Pudełko R., 2002; Brazilian Chart No. 25121, Baía do Almirantado, 1:40,000, 1984, Rio de Janeiro; Braun *et al.* 2001a and b; Arigony-Neto, 2001). Approximately 90% of the land area within the proposed ASMA is ice-covered, the ice-free areas representing about 37 km².

Earth Science features

The glacial drainage basin is formed mainly by the main ice cap of King George Island which flows from north, east and west towards the trough of Admiralty Bay. At the head of the bay, the ice cap spills into three inlets: Ezcurra, Mackellar and Martel inlets. Heavily crevassed outlet glaciers descend towards the sea becoming tidewater glaciers or floating glaciers

Geomorphology of the area is dominated by glacial erosional and depositional landforms, fresh and old moraine ridges, flat basal moraines, rocky ice streams valleys and deposits of sand, pebble to cobble ~~covered~~ forming recent beaches and raised marine terraces. Assemblages of poor tundra vegetation were already described in the coastal area influenced by birds, seals and sea spray fertilization, and in inland ecosystems suffering nutrients poverty. Adequate soil units (in diversified taxonomic modes) were proposed for that ecosystems. However, ecological mapping of the area was not performed till now. Particularly rich and diversified terrestrial ecosystems have been developed around penguin rookeries. Paternal profiles of ornithogenic soils of maritime Antarctic formed in the result of the phosphatization considered as a soil forming process were described along coast in several sites. Igneous basaltic andesite rocks outcropping around Admiralty Bay intercalated with fossil plant bearing sedimentary, terrestrial and locally glacial deposits record, cryosphere formation and Cenozoic evolution of a volcanic island arc. Volcanic, pyroclastic and sedimentary rock sequences of Eocene provide evidence of environmental changes preceding Oligocene glaciation, first signs of coming cooling were found in tillite from Herve Cove (62°10'44.7" S, 58°32'00.6" W) interpreted as alpine Eocene glaciation.

Climate

The climate of the Area is typical of maritime Antarctica. Based on more than 25 years of data obtained at the Polish Arctowski Station and at the Brazilian Comandante Ferraz Station, the local microclimate is characterized by an average annual temperature of around -1.8°C (-2.1 ± 1.0°C, set from Deception Island data and measured at UK Base "G", Bellingshausen and Ferraz, from 1944 to 2010) and an average annual wind speed in the order of 6.5 m s-¹ (6.0 ± 1.2 ms⁻¹, measured at Base G, Bellingshausen and Ferraz Stations, from 1986 to 2010). Annual average precipitation is 508.5 mm, humidity is 82% and pressure is 991 hPa (991.6 ± 1.3 hPa, set from Deception Island's data, and measured at UK Base "G", Bellingshausen e Ferraz, from 1948 to 2010). The waters of Admiralty Bay have an average annual temperature range of -1.8° to +4°C, being well mixed by tides and strongly influenced by currents from the west of Bransfield Strait. Currently, reconstruction of climate fluctuation in the historical time is the subject of multi proxy investigation performed on the base of sediment cores extracted from Admiralty Bay.

Freshwater habitat

In the area of ASMA No 1 there are no significant lakes, although there are numerous small ponds and streams, situated mostly on the southern and south-western coast of Admiralty Bay. The streams support some mosses as well as a diverse algae and cyanobacteria. Freshwater fauna, found in small ponds, moss banks and streams consists of Protozoa, Rotifera, Nematoda, Tardigrada, Collembolla (*Cryptopygus antarcticus* e *Friesea grisea*) and only two species of Crustacea (*Branchinecta gainii* and *Pseudoboeckella poppei*).

Special attention have been lately paid to the laguna that has been forming at the front of retreating Ecology Glacier (62°11'00.0" S, 58°28'00.0" W) during last 30 years. The laguna permitted large spectrum of environments: from freshwater glacier stream to marine waters. Several similar lagunas has been developed along coast of Admiralty Bay during late Holocene during intense retreat of glaciers in the last time.

Flora

In the adjoining ice-free areas of Admiralty Bay, the distribution of plant communities is closely related to geoforms, and to the presence of birds and soil. Wherever edaphic conditions are favorable, mosses form strands which also contain lichen and fungi formations. The lichenized mycobiota is restricted to the rock fragments and rock outcrops, sometimes associated with bird colonies. The coastal areas are the most densely covered, with flora being represented mostly by moss carpet formations. Near the Brazilian Ferraz Station two of these areas occur, both of which are almost 300 m long. Hennequin Point has large moss carpet areas as well. As elevations rise, showing rocky outcrops, crustose lichens and mosses which grow directly on rock predominate. The green algae *Prasiola crispa* occupies high nutrient concentrated areas, near bird breeding locations, and it has a large associated fauna. The species are listed at Appendix A and B.

Birds

Within the Area, 14 species of birds breed. Three sympatrically breeding Pygoscelid penguins make up 91% of the number and up to 95% of the biomass of the breeding bird communities. Other seabirds breeding in the Area are: Southern giant petrel (*Macronectes giganteus*); Antarctic shag *(Phalacrocorax atriceps bransfieldensis)*; Brown skua and south polar skua (*Stercorarius antarcticus, Stercorarius maccormicki* and *Catharacta chilensis*); Wilson's storm petrel (*Oceanites oceanicus*); Black-bellied storm petrel (*Fregeta tropica)*; Cape petrel *(Daption capense);* Kelp gull (*Larus dominicanus);* Antarctic tern (*Sterna vittata)* and Pale-faced sheathbill (*Chionis albus*). The areas of ASPA No. 128 Western Shore of Admiralty Bay, Cape Vauréal, Chabrier Island, Shag Island and surroundings, are the most important bird breeding locations in Admiralty Bay. In Cape Vauréal are found 50% of giant petrel population of the Area, and in Shag Island are found all nests of Antarctic shag, which share territory with chinstrap penguins (*Pygoscelis antarcticus*). Hennequin Point and Keller Peninsula are the most important breeding location for *Stercorarius maccormicki*, where are found 90% of the breeding pairs. For *S. lonnbergi*, areas with high concentration of penguin, like ASPA No 128, are the most important. There is a register of a hybrid breeding pair of *C. chilensis* and *Stercorarius maccormicki* at Hennequin Point.

Two species that were classified as sporadic have become frequent: *Aptenodytes patagonicus* and *Eudyptes chrysocome. A. patagonicus* is being registered annually at Arctowski Station and there have been two sitings at Keller Peninsula. *E. chrysocome* has been found every year since 2004 at Chabrier Rock, always followed by an *Eudyptes chrysolophus* specimen. The species are listed at Appendix C.

Mammals

Six species of pinnipeds occur in the Area (Appendix C). The most frequent mammal during winter is the crabeater seal (*Lobodon carcinophagus*). During summer, elephant seals (*Mirounga leonina*) and fur seals (*Arctocephalus gazella*) are the most frequent and abundant species. In periods when the ice covered areas decreases, it is possible to find lots of crabeater seal in the Area, especially at Ezcurra region. Fur seals, once relatively rare, have increased in number in recent years. Elephant seals and Weddell seals (*Leptonychotes weddelli*) breed in the area. Leopard seals (*Hydrurga leptonyx*) are found throughout the year in varying numbers. Ross seals (*Ommatophoca rossi*) rarely occur in the Area. Humpback whale (*Megaptera novaeangliae*) is the most frequent cetacean during summer, though killer (*Orcinus orca*) and minke whales (*Balaenoptera bonaerensis*) have also occasionally been seen in the area.

Marine ecology

Seasonal fluctuation in the condition of marine ecosystem is driven by marine current, tidal currents, and seasonal biological changes. During last years attention was focused on unusually high early summer blooming (dominated by diatoms) followed melting of winter fast ice covering Admiralty Bay all the winter. (rare case because usually the bay is not perennially frozen during winter). Detailed environmental and phytoplankton investigation was performed in the frame of international ClicOPEN IPY and IMCOAST UE projects and results are synchronize for the whole region.
Usually, multicellular algae, predominantly Heterokontophyta, Chrophophyta and Rhodophyta, characterize the shallow water bottom community down to 50-60 m depth. With the exception of the limpet (*Nacella concinna*), epifauna is practically absent in the intertidal zone. The vagile benthos is abundant with a high variety and density of Amphipoda. Below 4-5 m, substrata are typically sandy and dominated by Isopoda, particularly the genus *Serolis*. With the increasing depth, vagile species such as *Sterechinus*, *Neobuccinum* and *Parborlasia* dominate. In deeper waters, on a muddy and more stable substrata, sessile forms include sponges, anemones, the bivalve *Laternula elliptica* and tunicates, besides high-density concentrations of echinoderms such as *Amphioplus acutus*, *Ophionotus victoriae* and *Odontaster validus*. Invertebrate scavengers include *Labidiaster annulatus*, *Gliptonotus antarcticus*, *Parborlasia corrugatus*, *Odontaster validus* and *Neobuccinum eatoni*. In total, almost 1300 benthic species, including diatoms (157), foraminiferans (135), macroalgae (55), invertebrates (>400 species) and demersal fish (30) have been recognized in Admiralty Bay. The species found in the area are largely the same as those observed on similar substrata at other sites in the region, indicating homogeneity in the benthic fauna of the Antarctic Peninsula and related areas. Fishes are represented by fifteen Nototheniidae, mainly *Notothenia rossii*, *N. neglecta*, *N. gibberifrons*, *N. coriiceps*, *Nototheniops nudifrons*, *Trematodus newnesi*, *T. borchgrewincki* and *Pleuragramma antarcticum*, two Channichthydae species, Hapagiferidae and Zoarcidae. The species are listed at Appendix B and D.

Human activities and impact

Since the establishment of the ASMA, human activities in the Area have been related to scientific research, science-related logistic activities and tourism. Krill fishing has taken place in the Area recently. Scientific and logistic support are received from ships belonging to or chartered by National Parties.

Base G, the first permanent station on King George Island, was constructed by Great Britain in 1947 at Keller Peninsula. In 1948, a refuge hut was set up by Argentina in the same area. Base G was closed in 1961 and later dismantled, as was also the case with Argentinian hut. In the summer 1975-1976 Italian alpinist expedition built a small hut (Campo Bove) on the shores of the Ezcurra Inlet at Italia Valley. The camp was dismantled in March 1976.

During the last ten years, number of tour ships has fluctuated between 13 and 25, and number of tourists between 3000 and 5700 per austral summer. Tourists typically land at Arctowski or Ferraz Stations for a tour of facilities, go for a walk along the coast, and sometimes make short cruises in Zodiac boats. In the last 5 years, private yachts began to visit Admiralty Bay (3-4 yachts per season).

One alien species of grass (*Poa annua*) was recorded in summer 1985-1986 at Arctowski Station. Since then, small populations were observed in several places around the station, and, in 2008/2009, on the deglaciated moraines of the Ecology Glacier (approximate location 62°10'7"S, 58°27'54"W). In 2009/2010 soil seed bank of *P. annua* was found near the Arctowski Station. High genetic variability suggests several separate immigration events from different sources including Europe and South America. In 2009 propagules and pollen of the non-native rush *Juncus bufonius* were found in one location on the north-west boundary of ASPA No 128. In 2007-2010 extensive research (part of the international "Aliens in Antarctica" project) was conducted on the Arctowski Station to assess pathways by which non-native species can reach the station.

All fin-fishing is currently prohibited in the western Antarctic Peninsula region (CCAMLR Statistical Subarea 48.1) under CCAMLR Conservation Measure 32-02 (CCAMLR 2012a). Krill fishing occurred within Admiralty Bay during the 2009-2010 season, when the reported total krill catch was 11,500 tonnes (CCAMLR 2012b). In 2013 CCAMLR decided that any proposal to undertake commercial harvesting within an ASMA should be submitted to CCAMLR for its consideration and that the activities outlined in that proposal should only be taken with the prior approval of CCAMLR (CCAMLR-XXXII, Hobart 2013, paragraph 5.83).

6(ii) Access to the Area

Access to the Area is generally by ship or yacht, or less frequently by helicopter. Specific conditions of access are in Section 7(i).

6(iii) Structures within the Area

There are currently two permanent year-round research stations (Henryk Arctowski Station and Comandante Ferraz Station), three seasonal research stations/facilities (Machu Picchu Station, Copacabana Field Camp and Hannequin Point Refuge) and several minor structures (historical remains, emergency refugees, permanent field camps) in the Area.

(a) Main permanent structures and field camps in the Area (Fig. 2):

- *Henryk Arctowski Station (Poland):* 62°09'34''S – 58°28'15''W

  The station was established at Thomas Point in 1977 as a facility for scientific research and associated logistic operations of the Polish Antarctic Programme, and has been in year-round operation since then. It has dormitories for 14 residents in winter and up to 25 in summer; biological, meteorological and geophysical laboratories; storage facilities; a small hospital unit; double-walled fuel tanks with total capacity of more than 1,000 tonnes; hangars for boats and land vehicles etc. The station is equipped with two helicopter pads.

- *Comandante Ferraz Station (Brazil):* 62°05'07" S – 58°23'32"W

  The station was established in 1984 on the eastern coast of Keller Peninsula as the base for scientific research and associated logistic operations conducted by the Brazilian Antarctic Programme. It started year-round operations in 1986. In the summer of 2012, an accident destroyed 70% of Ferraz Station. Currently there are available two refuges, some isolated laboratories, 10 fuel tanks (capacity for 300,000 liters of arctic diesel), two modules of freshwater capture, and the Antarctic Emergency Modules (MAE, in Portuguese) to give support for Brazilian operations and the construction of the new station. They are composed of 38 modules (capacity to accommodate about 60 people) that include laboratory, dormitories, Sewage Treatment, Solid Waste Storage, diesel generators, etc.

- *Machu Picchu Station (Perú):* 62°05'30" S – 58°28'30" W

  The station was built in 1988 at Crepin Point, Mackellar Inlet. At present, it is used for summer operations only. The station consists of eight metallic modules including 2 dormitories, 1 kitchen and canteen, 1 generator room, 1 scientific laboratory, 1 waste treatment building, 1 emergency and 1 maintenance room. The station is equipped with one portable helicopter pad.

- *Copacabana Field Camp (United States of America):* 62°10'45" S – 58°26'49" W

  The summer station, consisting of three wooden huts for 4-6 people, is located in the south of Llano Point. It has been used every summer since its construction in 1977 as a field base for the Seabird Research Program (USA), in close cooperation with Arctowski station.

- Refuge at Hennequin Point (Equador): 62° 07' 16" S – 58° 23' 42" W

  The refuge was built in 1989, and has occasionally been used since then during summer seasons. It is a very important logistical support point for researchers with activities is that region.

(b) Emergency refuges in the Area (Fig. 2)

- three Brazilian emergency refuges (Refuge I - 62°05'16" S, 58°23'43" W, Refuge II - 62°04'24" S, 58°25'10" W, Ipanema Refuge - 62°05'10" S, 58°25'3'' W), and Brazilian scientific module on Keller Peninsula (62°05'28'' S, 58°24'15'' W);
- Polish refuge at Demay Point functioning as summer field camp (62°13'2.9" S, 58°26'32.27" W);
- Polish refuge (an Apple type hut) at Italia Valley functioning as summer field camp (62°10'32.3" S, 58°0'49.0" W).

(c) Historical remains in the Area

- HSM No 51 Puchalski Grave near Arctowski Station (62°13'S 58°28'W) (Fig. 2)
- the remains of Italian hut Campo Bove at Italia Valley, Ezcurra Inlet (62°10'32.3" S, 58°30'49.0" W);
- the remains of an old whaling boat at Ferraz Station, on Keller Peninsula (62°05'1.0" S, 58°23'30.0" W);
- an assembled whale skeleton at Ferraz Station on Keller Peninsula (62°04'55.0" S, 58°23'32.0" W);
- wooden barrels from whaling period at Barrel Point (62°10'00.0" S, 58°35'00.0" W), Ezcurra Inlet;
- a collection of whaling harpoons assembled on the shores of Admiralty Bay, exhibited at Arctowski Station;
- a group of seven crosses and graves on Keller Peninsula above Ferraz Station. Four of them are British graves, with crosses erected in memory of members of British expeditions who perished at sea and on ice. Three crosses were erected in honor of deceased members of the Brazilian military, two of them in honor of the Brazilian military that have died in the fire of the Ferraz Station; and
- a wooden cross on top of Flagstaff Hill (62°04'52.8" S, 58°24'14.0" W) on Keller Peninsula.

6(iv) Restricted and managed zones within the Area

Three types of management zones (Facilities, Scientific, Visitor) are designated within the Area.

    a. Facilities Zones

Facilities Zones are established to ensure that permanent and semi-permanent facilities in the Area are concentrated in defined locations with the aim of minimizing human impact on the important values of the Area. The existing Facilities Zones in the Area are listed in 6(iii) Structures in the Area (Fig 2).

The designation of new Facilities Zones should be done sparingly and after careful consideration of scientific and/or logistical justification. New installations should, as far as practicable, be located inside existing Facilities Zones. Parties active in the Area are encouraged to practice the cooperative use of infrastructure.

    b. Scientific Zones

Scientific Zones are established to protect the important scientific and ecological values of the Area from human disturbance. They have considerable scientific/ecological interest as breeding sites and/or concentrations of birds and/or mammals, feeding sites for birds and marine mammals, sites of typical vegetation cover, and varied marine habitats. Some of these zones, such as Chabrier Rock - Vaureal Cape, on the eastern shore of Admiralty Bay are of great relevance, as the only breeding sites for the Antarctic blue-eyed shag, penguins and southern giant petrel outside ASPA 128 Western Shore of Admiralty Bay.

Activities in all these zones should be carried out with particular care to avoid or minimize disturbance of wildlife, trampling of vegetation and interference with on-going research.

Designated Scientific Zones in the Area (see Fig. 3, 5 and 6):

A - Fresh water lakes around Arctowski and Ferraz Station: example of freshwater environment;

B - Italia Valley (62°10'32.3" S, 58°30'49.0" W): concentration of seals;

C - Dufayel Island/Ezcurra inlet (62°09'59.4" S, 58°33'29.5" W): concentration of seals;

D - Machu Picchu Station (62°05'30'' S, 58°28'30'' W): breeding areas for Antarctic stern and skuas;

D - Crépin Point (62°05'28.6" S, 58°28'09.5" W): concentration of seals and breeding location of *Sterna vittata*;

E - Area north-west of Ferraz Station: concentration of seals;

F - Area west of Ferraz Station: concentration of seals;

G - Coastal area from Refuge No. 1 (Ferraz Station) to Plaza Point (southern tip of Keller Peninsula, 62°05'27.4" S, 58°24'18.9" W): concentration of seals and penguins, breeding location for *Larus dominicanus* ;

H - Ipanema, south-west coast of Keller Peninsula, approximate location (62°05'S, 58°26'W): breeding location for *Larus dominicanus*, presence of vegetation banks;

I - Coastal area up to 7 m in shore, north of Base "G" hill, above Ferraz Station: presence of vegetation banks;

J - Crosses Hill on northern flank of Ferraz Station, on Keller Peninsula (62°05'07" S, 58°23'32" W): concentrations of terns.

K - Ullman Spur (Martel Inlet) (62°04'39.4" S, 58°20'34.5" W): concentration of seals;

L - Hennequin Point (62°07'24.9" S, 58°23'52.3" W): concentration of seals and plant fossil localities;

M - Cape Vaureal (62°10'49" S, 58°17'19.5" W) - Chabrier Rock (62°11'00" S, 58°19'00" W): breeding area for penguins, southern giant petrels and blue-eyed shags.;

N- Shallow marine waters down to 100 m in front of: ASPA No. 128, Martel, Mackellar and Ezcurra Inlets; Napier Rock (62°10'00.9" S, 58°26'22.7" W) and Monsimet Cove (62°10'49.2" S, 58°33'07.8" W): diverse benthic communities and scientific experiments and concentrations of different species of adult and juvenile fish;

P - area between Arctowski Station and ASPA N° 128: presence of vegetation banks;

R - Costal area from Refuge N° 2 (south-west coast of Keller Peninsula, approximate location 62°04'20.0" S, 58°25'30.0" W) to south-east part of Domeyco Glacier (62°04'00.0" S, 58°25'00.0" W): the most important breeding location for *Larus dominicanus* at Keller Peninsula, concentration of *Sterna vittata*, presence of vegetation banks;

S – Long-term Environmental Monitoring (see Fig. 4) - Brazilian monitoring program active since 2002, using remote sampling equipment (mini-box-corer), ROV for imaging, and scuba diving. The sampling stations were chosen taking into account the area of potential impact from Ferraz, and other three or four stations as reference areas. Approximate coordinates:

62°05'03.78"S, 58°23'12.18"W (depth 20-30 m)

62°05'59.94"S, 58°23'34.93"W (depth 20-30 m)

62°05'09.00"S, 58°20'59.20"W (depth 20-30 m)

62°04'26.00"S, 58°25'24.70"W (depth 20-30 m)

62°05'44.76''S, 58°21'48.52''W (depth 100 m)

62°06'03.99''S, 58°25'92.33''W (depth 100 m)

62°06'63.11''S, 58°27'11.33''W (depth 100 m)

62°06'74.74''S, 58°26'21.06''W (depth 300 m)

62°07'69.40''S, 58°24'62.52''W (depth 300 m)

62°08'87.72''S, 58°23'30.66''W (depth 300 m)

62°09'53.22'S, 58°24'27.68''W (depth 500 m)

62°10'15.76''S, 58°23'03.80''W (depth 500 m)

62°10'74.74''S, 58°23'20.08''W (depth 500 m)

Specific guidelines for the conduct within the Scientific Zones are presented in Appendix F (Scientific and Environmental Guidelines)

    c. Visitor Zones

Visitor Zones are established to manage the activities of tourists, non-governmental expeditions and National Antarctic Programs' scientists and staff when undertaking recreational visits to the Area.

Existing tour routes for visitors in the vicinity of Arctowski and Ferraz are presented on Fig. 7 and 8. These routes give the opportunity to observe wildlife and the station installations, while minimizing disturbance to the station activities and the environment, and avoiding habitat degradation. In future, routes for tourists may be established at Machu Picchu Station (Fig. 9) and Ecuador field camp.

Visits to Arctowski and Ferraz Stations are possible with prior agreement of the appropriate Station Leader.

Isolated laboratory modules, refuges and the area behind Ferraz Station: visits should be only by small groups accompanied by station personnel.

Specific guidelines for the conduct within the Visitor Zones are presented in Appendix E (Code of Conduct for Visitors).

6(v)

Location of other protected areas within the Area

The following areas are currently designated within the proposed ASMA :

* *ASPA No. 128 (Western shore of Admiralty Bay):* 62°09′46′′S – 62°14′10′′S – 58°25′15′′W – 58°29′58′′W

    This area is the site of long-term studies on bird biology performed by the US Antarctic Program, as well as intensive biological research of the Polish Academy of Sciences. It is entirely contained within ASMA No 1. Part of the Area western boundary (from Telefon Point to Warszawa Icefield – 62°12'S, 58°29'W) is shared with ASPA No 128.

* *Historic Site No. 51, at Arctowski Station: 62° 10'S – 58° 28'W:*

    The grave of Wlodzimierz Puchalski, a photographer and a producer of documentary nature films, who died on 19 January 1979. Bronze cross is located on a hill to the south of Arctowski Station, near the last working place of the late photographer. The cross is in fact a monumental sculpture with artistic impression of fauna seen by the eye of photo camera. It has been done by the famous artist Bronislaw Chromy, close friend of Wlodzimierz Puchalski.

6(vi). Location of other protected areas in the vicinity of the Area

* ASPA No 125 Fildes Peninsula, King George Island (25 de Mayo) and ASPA No 150 Ardley Island, Maxwell Bay, King George Island (25 de Mayo) lie ~27 km west of the Area.
* ASPA No 132, Potter Peninsula, King George Island (25 de Mayo), lies ~15 km to the west.
* ASPA No 151, Lion's Rump, King George Island, lies ~20 km to the east of the Area (see Fig. 1).

7. General Code of Conduct

The General Code of Conduct is proposed as an instrument for the management of activities in the Area, and as a guide for ongoing and future research and logistic operations of the Parties, tour operators and other organizations active in the Area. A Code of Conduct for Visitors and Scientific and Environmental Guidelines are presented in Appendix E and F.

7(i) Access to and movement within or over the Area.

Access to the Area is generally by ship or yacht, or less frequently by helicopter. There are no landing sites for fixed-wing aircraft in the Area.

- There are no special restrictions on the transit of ships through the Area, but anchoring should avoid marine components of Scientific Zones, and areas of environmental monitoring (Fig. 3 and 4). If anchoring near Ferraz Station is unavoidable, it should be done in front of the station at 62°05.111 S, 58°22.565 S (depth 50-60 m) or between Botany Point and Ullman Spur at 62°05.735 S, 58°20.968 W (approximate location);

- There are no restrictions on small boats landing on any beaches outside ASPA No 128. During boat landings care should be taken to avoid disturbing birds and seals. Extreme caution should be exercised when attempting to land in places where submerged rocks occur. Recommended landing sites for those visiting the stations located in Admiralty Bay are shown in Fig 3;

- Overflight operations by fixed-wing aircraft and helicopters should be carried out in accordance with the "Guidelines for the Operation of Aircraft near Concentrations of Birds" contained in Resolution 2 (2004), as a minimum requirement. Overflight of wildlife colonies should be avoided throughout the Area. Specific airflight restrictions apply to ASPA 128, and are contained in the Management Plan.

- Recommended helicopter landing sites are: Arctowski Station (62°09′34′′S, 58°28′15′′W), Ferraz Station (62°05′07" S, 58°23'32"W), Machu Picchu Station (62°05'30" S, 58°28'30" W). Landing at Copacabana Field Camp which is located inside ASPA No 128 is prohibited except in emergency.

- Except in emergencies, or in the course of carrying out inspections under Article VII of the Antarctic Treaty, helicopters ferrying scientists and visitors to and from Arctowski, Ferraz and Machu Picchu Stations and the Ecuador field camp should notify the relevant station/camp leader well in advance of the estimated time of arrival. They should land only on helicopter pads/landing sites indicated at each of the stations. There are no refueling facilities at the stations;

- Movement on land within the Area should be preferably on foot, although land vehicles may be used for scientific or logistical purposes inside some Facilities Zones (Arctowski Station – from Thomas point to the Shag Point, Ferraz Station – from the main station compound to the refuges on Keller Peninsula, and to the isolated modular laboratories around the main compound, Machu Picchu Station – inside main station compound).

- Snowmobiles may be used for scientific and logistical purposes in the glaciated parts of the Area, and in winter throughout the whole Area.

- The use of land vehicles is regulated by Leaders of the Stations, and should be done in a manner minimizing disturbance to wildlife, soil and vegetated areas. As far as practicable existing tracks should be used.

- Movement inside Scientific Zones should be, as far as possible, restricted to those conducting scientific research and essential logistic support. All movement should be undertaken carefully to minimize disturbance to animals, soil and vegetated areas.

- Movement inside Visitor Zones by tourists and other visitors to Arctowski and Ferraz Stations should, whenever possible, follow routes shown in Figures 7 and 8. These routes allow the observation of fauna and flora, while minimizing environmental impacts.

- Special guidelines regulating access and movement inside Scientific Zones are contained in Appendix F. Guidelines regulating access to and movement inside ASPA No 128 are contained in the ASPA Management Plan.

7(ii) Activities which may be conducted in the Area, which will not jeopardize the values of the area, and which are consistent with the Code of Conduct:

- Scientific research, or the logistical support of scientific research which will not jeopardize the values of the Area

- Tourist or private expedition visits consistent with the provisions of this Management Plan, Scientific and Environmental Guidelines and Code of Conduct for Visitors;

- Management activities, including maintenance or removal of facilities, clean-up of abandoned sites and monitoring the implementation of this Management Plan;

- Media, arts, education or other official national program visitors.

- Commercial harvesting of marine living resources, which should be conducted in coordination with research and other activities taking place, and could include development of a plan and guidelines that will help to ensure that harvesting activities did not pose a significant risk to the other important values of the Area.

All activities in the Area should be conducted in such a manner so as to minimize environmental impacts. Specific guidelines on the conduct of activities within the Area, including within Scientific Zones, can be found in the Appendices E and F, and in the Management Plan of ASPA No 128 Western Shore of Admiralty Bay.

7(iii) Installation, modification or removal of structures

Installation of new stations/refuges and modifications, or removal of already existing installations or other facilities in the Area, should be done only after consultation with the Parties that have active research programs in the Area, and in conformity with provisions of Article 8 and Annex 1 of the Environment Protocol and this Management Plan; in a manner that does not compromise the values of the Area. Existing installations and installation sites should be re-used as far as possible, and sharing of installations among National Antarctic Programs is encouraged.

As far as possible, permanent or semi-permanent structures should not be installed outside Facilities Zones, unless they are small in size and pose no significant threats to the important values of the Area.

Scientific equipment installed in the Area should be clearly identified by country, name of principal investigator, contact details, and date of installation. All such items should be free of organisms, propagules (e.g. seeds, eggs) and non-sterile soil, and be made of materials that can withstand the environmental conditions, and pose minimal risk of contamination or damage to the values of the Area. All equipment and associated materials should be removed when no longer in use.

Before construction of new installations in the Area National Antarctic Programs should exchange information through the ASMA Coordinator with the aim of sharing existing installations and minimizing the erection of new ones.

7(iv) Location of field camps

Field camps should be located as far as possible on non-vegetated sites, such as on barren ash plains, slopes or beaches, or on thick snow or ice cover when practicable, and should also avoid concentrations and breeding location of mammals and birds. Previously occupied campsites should be re-used where appropriate.

The location of field camps should be recorded, and the information exchanged through the ASMA Coordinator.

7(v) Taking or harmful interference with native flora and fauna

Taking or harmful interference with native flora or fauna is prohibited, except by Permit issued under the provisions of Article 3 of Annex V to the Protocol on Environmental Protection to the Antarctic Treaty. Where taking or harmful interference with animals is involved, the *SCAR Code of Conduct for the Use of Animals for Scientific Purposes in Antarctica* should be used as a minimum standard.

Taking of marine organisms for scientific purposes should be limited to that restrictedly necessary to meet the purpose of the research. Invasive methods involving dredging, grabbing, trawling, etc. should be undertaken sparingly and with greatest care possible.

Seismic operations should be avoided, particularly with the use of explosives. Geological sampling of bottom sediments, particularly in shallow waters, should be carried out with extreme care so as to minimize adverse impact on the environment, or interference with other scientific research under way on benthic ecology.

The coordinates of sites where invasive methods were used should be recorded, and the information should be exchanged through the ASMA Coordinator.

Harvesting of marine living resources should be conducted in accordance with the provisions of this Management Plan and with due recognition of the important scientific and environmental values of the Area. All those planning to conduct marine commercial harvesting in the Area should first submit their proposal to CCAMLR. The activities outlined in the proposal should only be taken with the prior approval of CCAMLR.

7(vi) Restrictions on materials and organisms which can be brought into the Area

All activities in the Area should be planned in a way minimizing risk of introduction of non-native species, including the transfer among different localities in Antarctica.

No living animals, plant material or microorganisms shall be deliberately introduced into the Area, except by permit issued in accordance with Annex II to the Protocol on Environmental Protection to the Antarctic Treaty.

"Non-native Species Manual" (Resolution 6, 2011) should be used to minimize the risk of unintentional introductions.

National Antarctic Programs, tour operators and organizations active in the Area should educate all visitors (scientists, station personnel, ship crews, tour operators' staff, tourists etc.) about the risks of non-native species' accidental introduction, and the methods used to minimize the probability of such an introduction.

National Antarctic Programs, tour operators and organizations active in the Area should, as far as practicable, minimize the importation of untreated wood, sand, aggregate and gravel to the Area.

National Antarctic Programs, tour operators and organizations active in the Area should, as far as is practicable, monitor all cargo, food and equipment unloaded in the Area for the presence of non-native species and propagules. National Antarctic Programs should also undertake periodic inspections of their facilities in the Area.

Visitors to the Area shall take special precautions against non-native species introduction. To the maximum extent practicable, footwear, outer clothing, backpacks and other equipment, including scientific samplers or markers, used or brought into the Area shall be thoroughly cleaned before entering the Area. Special care should be taken by persons visiting locations where non-native grass *Poa anuua* is present.

Considering the high level of endemic marine benthos in Antarctica, National Antarctic Programs, tour operators and organizations active in the Area should, as far as is practicable, take precautions minimizing the possibility of the introduction of marine invertebrate larvae in ballast water. Practical Guidelines for Ballast Water (Resolution 3, 2006) should be used for guidance.

In view of the presence of numerous breeding bird colonies within the Area dressed poultry should be free of disease or infection before shipment to the Area, and if introduced to the Area for food, all parts and wastes of poultry shall be completely removed from the Area or incinerated or boiled long enough to kill potentially infective bacteria or viruses. Care should be taken to prevent food or food wastes being accessed by wildlife.

Potential non-native species spotted in the Area should be reported to the appropriate authorities, and the reports should be made available to the ASMA Coordinator and the ASMA Management Group.

ASMA Management Group and other Parties or organizations, as appropriate, should exchange information about the discovery and distribution of any non-native species in the Area, results of the monitoring programs, and methods applied to minimize the risk of their accidental introduction. Policies on containment or eradication of non-native species should be discussed and developed as soon as possible.

7(vii) The collection or removal of materials not imported into the Area

Materials should only be collected and removed from the Area for scientific, management or educational purposes, and should be limited to the minimum necessary for those needs.

Souvenirs, specifically rocks, minerals, fossils, eggs, flora and fauna, or any other material not brought into the area by the visitor, should not be collected in, or removed from the Area.

It may be permissible to remove from the site materials such as beach litter or abandoned relics and artifacts of no historic value from previous activities. Historical relics and artifacts should be removed only for a compelling scientific purpose. Dead or pathological fauna or flora should be removed only for scientific purpose, with specific permit, because they are used as food by mammals and birds.

7(viii) Disposal of waste

Disposal of waste generated by scientific research programs, tourism and all other governmental or nongovernmental activities in the ASMA should be carried out in compliance with the provisions of Annex III to the Protocol on Environmental Protection to the Antarctic Treaty.

All wastes, other than human and domestic liquid waste, should be removed from the Area. Human waste and domestic liquid waste may be removed from the Area or disposed into the sea.

7(ix) Requirements for Reports

Reports of activities within the Area, which are not already covered under existing reporting requirements, should be, to the maximum extent practicable, made available to the ASMA Coordinator. The ASMA Coordinator should maintain them, and made available to all interested Parties.

8. Advance exchange of information

Parties operating in the Area should, as far as practicable, exchange information on their activities through the ASMA Coordinator with the aim of enabling greater coordination between their research programs, enhanced cooperation and minimization of possible cumulative impacts.

Parties proposing to conduct, support, or authorize research or other activities in the Area are encouraged to inform the ASMA Coordinator, as far in advance as possible, of their planned activities. The Coordinator should make the information available to the Management Group and other interested Parties. Copies of the permits issued to authorize entry into a designated protected area within the ASMA shall also be provided to the ASMA Coordinator. The ASMA Coordinator shall maintain a record of notifications and provide information when requested.

All NGO and tourist expeditions planning to conduct activities with the Area (both IAATO members and those not affiliated with IAATO) should, as far as practicable, provide the ASMA Coordinator in advance with details of planned visits.

All those planning to conduct marine harvesting within the Area should, as far as practicable, notify the ASMA Coordinator in advance of their location, duration and character. The commercial harvesting specified in the proposal shall only be undertaken after following review procedures designated by CCAMLR.

9. Supporting Documentation and select bibliography

Non-Native Species Manual. Resolution 6 (2011) – ATCM XXXIV – CEP XIV, Buenos Aires (available at *http://www.ats.aq/documents/atcm34/ww/atcm34_ww004_e.pdf*)

Guidelines for the Operation of Aircrafts near Concentrations of Birds in Antarctica. Resolution 2 (2004) – ATCM XXVII - CEP VII, Cape Town (available at *http://www.ats.aq/documents/recatt/Att224_e.pdf*)

COMNAP/SCAR Checklists for supply chain managers of National Antarctic Programmes for the reduction in risk of transfer of non-native species – ATCM XXXIV/CEP XIV, Buenos Aires (available at https://www.comnap.aq/Shared%20Documents/checklistsbrochure.pdf)

Practical Guidelines for Ballast Water Exchange in the Antarctic Treaty Area. Resolution 3 (2006) – ATCM XXIX – CEP IX, Edinburgh (available at *http://www.ats.aq/documents/recatt%5Catt345 e.pdf*)

SCAR Code of Conduct for the Use of Animals for Scientific Purposes (available at *http://www.scar.org/treaty/atcmxxxiv/ATCM34_ip053_e.pdf*)

SCAR's Environmental Code Of Conduct For Terrestrial Scientific Field Research In Antarctica (avaible at *http://www.scar.org/researchgroups/lifescience/Code_of_Conduct_Jan09.pdf*

General Guidelines for Visitors to the Antarctic. Resolution 3 (2011) – ATCM XXXIV – CEP XIV, Buenos Aires (available at http://www.ats.aq/documents/recatt%5Catt483_e.pdf)

A proposal prepared by Brazil and Poland, in coordination with Ecuador and Peru, that Admiralty Bay, King George Island South Shetland Islands be designated as an Antarctic Specially Managed Area (ASMA) 1996. Agenda item 20a XX ATCM WP 15 (Rev).

Guide to the Preparation of Management Plans for Antarctic Specially Protected Areas, appended to Resolution 2 (1998) of Antarctic Treaty Consultative Meeting XXII.

Final Report of the Twelfth Antarctic Treaty Special Consultative Meeting. The Haque, 11-15 September 2000 Management Plan for Site of Special Scientific Interest N° 8 (ASPA 121), Western shore of Admiralty Bay, King George Island, South Shetland islands, 68-73.

Final Report of the Twelfth Antarctic Treaty Special Consultative Meeting. The Haque, 11-15 September 2000 Management Plan for Site of Special Scientific Interest No.34. (ASPA 151) Lions Rump, King George Island, South Shetland Islands, 95-102.

ALBUQUERQUE, M.P.; VICTORIA, F.C.; SCHUNEMANN, A.L.; PUTZKE, J.; GUNSKI, R.J.; SEIBERT, S.; PETRY, M.V.; PEREIRA, A.B. 2012. Plant Composition of Skuas Nests at Hennequin Point, King George Island, Antarctica. American Journal of Plant Sciences 3: 688-692.

ANGIEL, P.J.; KORCZAK M. 2008. Comparison Of Population Size of Penguins Concerning Present And Archive Data From ASPA 128 and ASPA 151 (King George Island). Scientific Committee on Antarctic Research (SCAR), International Arctic Science Committee (IASC), Polar Research. In St. Petersburg, Russia. July 8th – 11th 2008: SCAR/IASC IPY. Open Science Conference.

AUGUSTYNIAK-KRAM, A.; CHWEDORZEWSKA, K.J.; KORCZAK-ABSHIRE, M.; OLECH, M.; LITYŃSKA-ZAJĄC, M. 2013. An analysis of fungal propagules transported to the *Henryk Arctowski* Stadion. Polish Polar Research, 34, 269-278

AQUINO, F.E.; FERRON, F.A.; SIMÕES, J.C.; SETZER, A.W. 2001. Série temporal de temperatura média em superfície na Ilha Rei George. Revista do Departamento de Geografia/USP 14: 25-32.

BATTKE, Z.; MARSZ A.; PUDEŁKO, R. 2001. Procesy deglacjacji na obszarze SSSI No. 8 i ich uwarunkowania klimatyczne oraz hydrologiczne (zatoka Admiralicji, Wyspa Króla Jerzego, Szetlandy Południowe). Problemy Klimatologii Polarnej 11: 121–135.

BÍCEGO, M.C.; ZANARDI-LAMARDO, E.; WEBER, R.R. 2003. Four-year of dissolved/dispersed petroleum hydrocarbons on surface waters of Admiralty Bay, King George Island, Antarctica. Revista Brasileira de Oceanografia 51: 33-38.

BIRKENMAJER, K. 2001. Geological results of the Polish Antarctic Expeditions (part XIII). Studia Geologica Polonica 118.

BIRKENMAJER K. 2002 Retreat of Ecology Glacier, Admiralty Bay, King George Island (South Shetland Islands, West Antarctica), 1956-2001. Bulletin. of the Polish Academy of Sciences 50,1: 15-29.

BIRKENMAJER, K. 2003. Admiralty Bay King George Island, South Shetland Islands, West Antarctica. Geological Cross-sections and geological mao. Studia Geologica Polonica 120.

BIRKENMAJER, K. 2008. Geological results of the Polish Antarctic Expeditions (part XV). Studia Geologica Polonica 128.

BIRKENMAJER, K.; GAZDZICKI, A.; KRAJEWSKI, A.; PRZYBYCIN, A.; SOLECKI, A.; TATUR, A.; YOON IL. 2005. First Cenozoic glaciers in West Antarctica. Pol. Polar Res 26,1: 3-12.

BRANCO, J.O.; COSTA, E.S.; ARAUJO, J.; DURIGON, E., ALVES, M.A.S. 2009. Kelp gulls, *Larus dominicanus* (Aves: Laridae), breeding in Keller Peninsula, King George Island, Antarctic Peninsula. Zoologia (Curitiba, Impresso) 26: 562-566.

CAMPOS, L.S.; BARBOZA, C.A.M.; BASSOI, M.; BERNARDES, M.; BROMBERG, S.; CORBISIER, T.; FONTES, R.C.; GHELLER, P.F.; HAJDU, E.; KAWALL, H.G.; LANGE, P.K.; LANNA, A.M.; LAVRADO, H.P.; MONTEIRO, G.C.S.; MONTONE, R.; MORALES, T.; MOURA, R.B.; NAKAYAMA, C.R.; OACKES, T.; PARANHOS, R.; PASSOS, F.D.; PETTI, M.A.V.; PELLIZARI, V.H.; REZENDE, C.E.; RODRIGUES, M.; ROSA, L.H.; SECCHI, E.; TENENBAUM, D.R.; YONESHIGUE-VALENTIN, Y. 2013. Environmental processes, biodiversity and changes in Admiralty Bay, King George Island, Antarctica. In: VERDE, C.; DI PRISCO, G. (eds). Adaptation and evolution in marine environments - The impact of global change on biodiversity, Vol.2. Series "From Pole to Pole", Springer-Verlag Berlin Heidelberg: 127-156.

CAMPOS, L.S.; MONTONE, R.C.; MOURA, R.B.; YONESHIGUE-VALENTIN, Y.; KAWALL, H.G.; CONVEY, P. 2013. Anthropogenic impacts on sub-Antarctic and Antarctic islands and the adjacent marine environments In: VERDE, C.; DI PRISCO, G. (eds) Adaptation and evolution in marine environments - The impact of global change on biodiversity, Vol.2. Series "From Pole to Pole", Springer-Verlag Berlin Heidelberg: 177-203.

CCAMLR. 2012a. Schedule of Conservation Measures in force 2012/2013 season. CCAMLR, Hobart, Australia.

CCAMLR. 2012b. Statistical Bulletin Vol. 24 (2002-2011). CCAMLR, Hobart, Australia.

CHWEDORZEWSKA, K.J. 2008. *Poa annua* L. in Antarctic: searching for the source of introduction. Polar Biology 31: 263-268.

CHWEDORZEWSKA, K.; KORCZAK-ABSHIRE, M.; OLECH M.; LITYŃSKA-ZAJĄC, M.; AUGUSTYNIUK-KRAM, A. 2013. Alien invertebrates transported accidentally to the Polish Antarctic Station in cargo and on fresh food. Polish Polar Research, 34, 55-66

CIAPUTA, P.; SALWICKA, K. 1997. Tourism at Antarctic Arctowski Station 1991-1997. Policies for better management. Polish Polar Research 18(3-4): 227-239.

CIAPUTA, P.; SIERAKOWSKI K. 1999. Long-term population changes of Adelie, chinstrap, and gentoo penguins in the regions of SSSI No. 8 and SSSI No. 34, King George Island, Antarctica. Polish Polar Research 20 (4): 355–365.

CORBISIER, T.N.; PETTI, M.A.V.; SKOWRONSKI, R.S.P.; BRITO, T.A.S. 2004. Trophic relationships in the nearshore zone of Martel Inlet (King George Island, Antarctica): 13C stable isotope analysis. Polar Biology 27 (2): 75-82.

COSTA, E.S.; ALVES, M.A.S. 2008. The breeding birds of Hennequin Point: an ice-free area of Almiralt Bay (Antarctic Specially Managed Area), King George Island, Antarctic. Revista Brasileira de Ornitologia, 16: 137-141.

DANI, N.; SIMÕES, J.C.; ARIGONY NETO, J.; AHLERT, S.A. 2004. Geographical Information System applied to the Antarctic Specially Managed Area (ASMA) of Admiralty Bay. Terra Nostra 4: 349-350.

ECHEVERRÍA, C.A.; LAVRADO, H.P.; CAMPOS, L. S.; PAIVA, P.C. 2009. A new mini box corer for sampling muddy bottoms in Antarctic shallow waters. Brazilian Archives of Biology and Technology 52: 629-636.

FILGUEIRAS, V.L.; CAMPOS, L. S.; LAVRADO, H.P.; FRENSEL, R.; POLLERY, R. C. G. 2007. Vertical distribution of macrobenthic infauna from the shallow sublittoral zone of Admiralty Bay, King George Island, Antarctica. Polar Biology 11: 1439-1447.

FRASER, R.W.; HOFMANN, E.E. 2003. A predatoe's perspective on casual links between climate change, physical forcing and ecosystem response. Mar. Ecol. Prog. Series, 265: 1-15.

HARRIS, C.M. 1991. Environmental management on King George Island, South Shetland Islands, Antarctica. Polar Record 27, n 16: 1-24.

HEADLAND, R.K.; KEAGE, P.L. 1985. Activities on the King George Island Group, South Shetland Islands, Antarctica. Polar Record 22 (140): 475-484.

JAŻDŻEWSKI, K.; DE BROYER, C.; PUDLARZ, M.; ZIERLIŃSKI, D. 2001. Seasonal fluctuations of vagile benthos in the uppermost sublittoral of a maritime Antarctic fjord. Polar Biology 24: 910-917.

KEJNA, M. 1999. Air temperature on King George Island, South Shetlands, Antarctica. Polish Polar Research 20, 3: 183-201.

KITTEL, P. 2001. Inventory of whaling objects on the Admiralty Bay shores (King George Island, South Shetland Islands) in the years 1996-1998. Polish Polar Research: 45-70.

KORCZAK-ABSHIRE, M.; LEES, A.C.; JOJCZYK, A. 2011. First documented record of Barn Swallow Hirundo rustica in the Antarctic. Polish Polar Research 32 (4): 355-360.

KORCZAK-ABSHIRE, M.; CHWEDORZEWSKA, K.J.; WĄSOWICZ. P.; BENDAREK, P. 2012. Genetic structure of declining chinstrap penguin (Pygoscelis antarcticus) populations from South Shetland Islands (Antarctica). Polar Biology 35, Issue 11: 1681-1689.

KULESZ, J. 1999. Ichthyofauna of lagoons of the Admiralty Bay (King George Island, Antarctica) in 1997. Polish Archives of Hydrobiology 46, 2: 173-184.

LANGE, P.K.; TENENBAUM, D.R.; BRAGA, E.S.; CAMPOS, L. S. 2007. Microphytoplankton assemblages in shallow waters at Admiralty Bay (King George Island, Antarctica) during the summer 2002-2003. Polar Biology 30: 1483-1492.

LAPAG – Laboratório de Pesquisas Antárticas e Glaciológicas. 2003. CD-Room. Projeto Integração de dados ambientais da área AAEG da Baía do Almirantado. Porto Alegre.UFRGS.

LITYŃSKA-ZAJĄC M.; CHWEDORZEWSKA, K.; OLECH, M.; KORCZAK-ABSHIRE, M.; AUGUSTYNIUK-KRAM, A. 2012. Diaspores and phyto-remains accidentally transported to the Antarctic Station during three expeditions. Biodiversity and Conservation 21: 3411-3421.

LYNCH, H.J.; NAVEEN, R.; FAGAN, W.F. 2008. Censuses of penguin, blue-eyed shag, *Phalacrocorax atriceps*, and southern giant petrel, *Macronectes giganteus* populations on the Antarctic Peninsula, 2001-2007. Mar. Ornithology, 36: 83-97.

MAJEWSKI, W. 2005. Benthic foraminiferal distribution and ecology in Admiralty Bay, King George Island, West Antarctica. Polish Polar Research, vol. 26, no. 3, pp. 159–214, 2005.

MAJEWSKI, W.; LECROQ, B.; SINNIGER. F.; PAWŁOWSKI, J. 2007.Monothalamous foraminifera from Admiralty Bay, King George Island, West Antarctica. Polish Polar Research, 28, 187–210.

MAJEWSKI, W.; OLEMPSKA, E. 2005. Recent ostracods from Admiralty Bay, King George Island, West Antarctica. Polish Polar Research, 26,1 13-36, 187–210.

MAJEWSKI, W.; TATUR, A. 2009. *Criboelphdium webbi* sp. Nov.: A new Antarctic foraminifer species for detecting climate changes in sub Recent glacier – proximal sediments. Antarctic Science 21,5: 439-448

MARTINS, C.C.; VENKATESAN, M.I.; MONTONE, R.C. 2002. Sterols and linear alkyl benzenes in marine sediments from Admiralty Bay, Antarctica. Antarctic Science 14 (3): 244-252.

MARTINS, C.C.; BÍCEGO, M.C.; TANIGUCHI, S.; MONTONE, R.C. 2004. Aliphatic (Ahs) and Aromatic Hydrocarbons (PAHs) in surface sediments in Admiralty Bay, King George Island, Antarctica: A regional survey of organic contaminants resulting from human activity. Antarctic Science 16 (2): 117-122.

MONTONE, R.C.; TANIGUCHI, S.; WEBER, R.R. 2003. PCBs in the atmosphere of King George Island, Antarctica. The Science of the Total Environment 308: 167-173.

MONTONE, R.C.; MARTINS, C.C.; BÍCEGO, M.C.; TANIGUCHI, S.; SILVA, D.A.M.; CAMPOS, L.S.; WEBER, R.R. 2010. Distribution of sewage input in marine sediments around a maritime Antarctic research station indicated by molecular geochemical indicators. Science of the Total Environment 408: 4665–4671.

MONTONE, R.C.; ALVAREZ, C.E.; BÍCEGO, M.C.; BRAGA, E.S.; BRITO, T.A.S.; CAMPOS, L.S.; FONTES, R.F.C.; CASTRO, B.M.; CORBISIER, T. N.; EVANGELISTA, H.; FRANCELINO, M.; GOMES, V.; ITO, R.G.; LAVRADO, H.P.; LEME, N.P. ; MAHIQUES, M.M.; MARTINS, C. C.; NAKAYAMA, C. R.; NGAN, P.V.; PELLIZARI, V.H.; PEREIRA, A.B.; PETTI, M.A. V.; SANDER, M.; SCHAEFER, C.E.G.R.; WEBER, R.R. 2013. Chapter 9- Environmental Assessment of Admiralty Bay, King George Island, Antarctica. In: VERDE, C.; DI PRISCO, G. (Eds.). Adaptation and Evolution in Marine Environments 157, Vol. 2. From Pole to Pole. Springer-Verlag Berlin Heidelberg: 157-175.

MORGAN, F.; BARKER, G.; BRIGGS, C.; PRICE, R.; KEYS, H. 2007. Environmental Domains of Antarctica Version 2.0 Final Report, Manaaki Whenua Landcare Research New Zealand Ltd. 89 pp.

NAVEEN, R.; FORREST, S.C.; DAGIT R.G.; BLIGHT, L.K.; TRIVELPIECE, W.Z.; TRIVELPIECE, S.G. 2000. Census of penguin, blue-eyed shag, and southern giant petrel populations in the Antarctic Peninsula region, 1994-2000. Polar Record, 36: 323-334.

NONATO, E.F.; BRITO, T.A.S.; PAIVA, P.C.D.; PETTI, M.A.V.; CORBISIER, T. N. 2000. Benthic megafauna of the nearshore zone of Martel Inlet (King George Island, South Shetland Islands, Antarctica): depth zonation and underwater observations. Polar Biology 23: 580-588.

OLECH M. 1996. Human impact on terrestrial ecosystems in west Antarctic. Proceed. Of the NIPR Symp. Polar Biology 9: 299-306.

OLECH M.; CHWEDORZEWSKA, K.J. 2011. The first appearance and establishment of an alien vascular plant in natural habitats on the forefield of a retreating glacier in Antarctica. Antarctic Science 23: 153-154.

OLECH, M. 2002. Plant communities on King George Island. Geoecology of Antarctic Ice-Free Coastal Landscapes: 215-231.

OLECH, M,; MASSALSKI, M.. 2001. Plant colonization and community development on the Sphinx Glacier forefield. Geographia 25: 111–119.

OSYCZKA, P.; MLECZKO, P.; KARASIŃSKI, D.; CHLEBICKI, A. 2012. Timber transported to Antarctica: a potential and undesirable carrier for alien fungi and insects. Biological Invasions 14: 15-20.

PUDEŁKO, R. 2007. Orthophotomap Western Shore of Admiralty Bay, King George Island, South Shetland Islands. Warsaw, Poland: Dept. Antarctic Biology PAS.

PUTZKE, J.; PEREIRA, A.B. 1990. Mosses of King George Island, Antarctica. Pesquisa Antartica Brasileira 2 (1): 17-71.

PRESLER, P.; FIGIELSKA, E. 1997. New data on the Asteroidea of Admiralty Bay, King George Island, South Shetland Islands. Polish Polar Research 18 (2): 107-117.

PRUSZAK, Z. 1980. Currents circulation of water of Admiralty Bay (region of Arctowiski Station on King George Island). Polish Polar Research 1: 55-74.

RAKUSA-SUSZCZEWSKI, S. 1995. The hydrography of Admiralty Bay and its inlets, coves and lagoons (King George Island, Antarctica). Polish Polar Research 16: 61-70.

RAKUSA-SUSZCZEWSKI, S. 1996. Spatial and seasonal variability of temperature and salinity in Bransfield Strait and Admiralty Bay, Antarctica. Polish Polar Research 17: 29-42.

RAKUSA-SUSZCZEWSKI, S. 2002. King George Island – South Shetland Islands, Maritime Antarctic Ecological Studiem, vol. 154. Beyer, L.; Bolter, M. (eds.) Geoecology of Antarctic Ice-Free Coastal Landscapes. Sprinter-Verlag Berlin Heidelberg: 23-39.

ROBAKIEWICZ, M.; RAKUSA-SUSZCZEWSKI, S. 1999. Aplication of 3D Circulation Model on Admiralty Bay. Polish Polar Research 1.

SALWICKA, K.;SIERAKOWSKI, K.. 1998. Seasonal numbers of five species of seals in Admiralty Bay (South Shetland Islands, Antarctica). Polish Polar Research 3-4: 235–247.

SALWICKA, K.; RAKUSA-SUSZCZEWSKI, S. 2002. Long-term Monitoring of Antarctic pinnipeds in Admiralty Bay (south Shetlands, Antarctica). Acta Theriologica 47 (4): 443-457.

SANDER, M.; CARNEIRO, A.P.B.; MASCARELLO, N.E.; SANTOS, C.R.; COSTA, E.S.; BALBÃO, T.C. 2006. Distribution and status of the kelp gull, *Larus dominicanus* Lichtenstein (1823), at Admiralty Bay, King George Island, South Shetland, Antarctica. Polar Biology 29: 902-904.

SANDER, M.; COSTA, E.S.; SANTOS, C.R.; PEREIRA, A.B. 2004. Colônias de Aves e Comunidades Vegetais da Península Keller, Ilha Rei George, Antártica. In: V Simpósio Argentino y 1º Latino Americano sobre investigaciones Antárticas, Livro de resumos.

SANTOS, I.R.; SILVA FILHO, E.V.; SCHAEFER, C.G.R; ALBUQUERQUE FILHO, M. R.; CAMPOS, L. S. 2005. Heavy metals contamination in coastal sediments and soils near the Brazilian Antarctic Station, King George Island. Marine Pollution Bulletin 50: 185-194.

SCAR'S Summary of Strategic Plan 2011-2016. Disponível em: http://www.scar.org/strategicplan2011/SCAR_Strat_Plan_2011-16.pdf. Acesso em 07 de março de 2013.

SCAR strategy for capacity building. Education and training Report 27. 2006. Disponível em: http://www.scar.org/strategicplan2011/CBETplan.pdf. Acesso em 07 de março de 2013.

SCHAEFER, C.E.G.R.; FRANCELINO, M.R.; SIMAS, F.N.B.; ALBUQUERQUE FILHO, M.R. (eds) 2004. Ecossistemas Costeiros e Monitoramento Ambiental da Antártica Marinha. NEPUT, Viçosa, Minas Gerais, 192 pg.

SICIŃSKI, J.; JAŻDŻEWSKI, K.; DE BROYER, C.; PRESLER, P.; LIGOWSKI, R.; NONATO, E.F.; CORBISIER, T.N.; PETTI, M.A.V.; BRITO, T.A.S.; LAVRADO, H.P.; BŁAŻEWICZ-PASZKOWYCZ, M.; PABIS, K.; JAŻDŻEWSKA, A.; CAMPOS, L.S. 2011. Admiralty Bay Benthos Diversity - A census of a complex polar ecosystem. Deep Sea Research Part II: Topical Studies in Oceanography 58 (1-2): 30-48.

SIMÕES, J.C.; DANI, N.; BREMER, U.F.; AQUINO, F.E; ARIGONY NETO, J. 2004. Small cirque glaciers retreat on Keller Peninsula, Admiralty Bay, King George Island, Antarctica. Pesquisa Antártica Brasileira 4: 49-56.

TATUR, A. 2002 Ornithogenic Ecosystems in Maritime Antarctic – Formation, Development and Disintegration Ecological Studies Vol.154. Beyer, L.; Bolter, M. (eds). Geoecology of Antarctic Ice-Free Coastal Landscapes. Springer-Verlag Berlin Heidelber.

TERAUDS, A.; CHOWN, S.L.; MORGAN, F.; PEAT, H.J.; WATTS, D.J.; KEYS H.; CONVEY, P.; BERGSTROM D.M. 2012. Conservation biogeography of the Antarctic. Diversity Distrib., 18: 762-741.

WEBER, R.R.; MONTONE, R.C. 2006. Rede 2 - Gerenciamento ambiental na Baía do Almirantado, Ilha Rei George, Antártica. Technical Report, Universidade de São Paulo, 252 pp.

WHYTE, L.G.; SCHULTZ, A.; VAN BEILEN, J.B.; LUZ, A.P.; PELLIZARI, V.; LABBÉ, D.; GREER, C.W. 2002. Prevalence of Alkane Monooxygenase Genes in Arctic and Antarctic Hydrocarbon-Contaminated and Pristine Soils. FEMS Microbial Ecology 41(2): 141-5.

WÓDKIEWICZ, M.; GALERA, H., CHWEDORZEWSKA, K.J.; GIEŁWANOWSKA, I.; OLECH, M. 2013. Diaspores of the introduced species *Poa annua* L. in soil samples from King George Island (South Shetlands, Antarctica). Arctic, Antarctic and Alpine Research, 45, 415-419

YONESHIGUE-VALENTIN, Y.; DALTO, A.G.; LAVRADO, H.P. 2009. Annual Activity Report 2009. Annual Activity Report of National Institute for Science and Technology Antarctic Environmental Research. Instituto Nacional de Ciência e Tecnologia Antártico de Pesquisas Ambientais (INCT – APA). São Carlos: Editora Cubo.

YONESHIGUE-VALENTIN, Y.; DALTO, A.G., LAVRADO, H.P. 2010. Annual Activity Report 2010. Annual Activity Report of National Institute for Science and Technology Antarctic Environmental Research. Instituto Nacional de Ciência e Tecnologia Antártico de Pesquisas Ambientais (INCT – APA). São Carlos: Editora Cubo.

YONESHIGUE-VALENTIN, Y.; DALTO, A.G., LAVRADO, H.P. 2011. Annual Activity Report 2011. Annual Activity Report of National Institute for Science and Technology Antarctic Environmental Research. Instituto Nacional de Ciência e Tecnologia Antártico de Pesquisas Ambientais (INCT – APA). São Carlos: Editora Cubo.

YONESHIGUE-VALENTIN, Y.; DALTO, A.G., LAVRADO, H.P., 2012. Annual Activity Report 2011. Annual Activity Report of National Institute for Science and Technology Antarctic Environmental Research. Instituto Nacional de Ciência e Tecnologia Antártico de Pesquisas Ambientais (INCT – APA). São Carlos: Editora Cubo.

ZDANOWSKI, M.K.; WĘGLEŃSKI, P. 2001. Ecophysiology of soil bacteria in the vicinity of Henry Arctowski Station, King George Island, Antarctica. Soil Biology and Biochemistry 33: 819-829.

APPENDIX A
Preliminary plant checklist from adjacent ice-free areas to
Admiralty Bay, King George Island

ANGIOSPERMAE

POACEAE

Deschampsia antarctica Desv.

CARYOPHYLLACEAE

Colobanthus quitensis (Kunth) Bartl.

MOSSES

AMBLYSTEGIACEAE

Orthotheciella varia (Hedw.) Ochyra

Sanionia uncinata (Hedw.) Loeske

S. georgico-uncinata (Mull Hal..) Ochyra & Hedenas

Warnstorfia laculosa (Müll. Hal.) Ochyra & Matteri

Warnstorfia sarmentosa (Wahlenb.) Hedenäs

ANDREAEACEAE

Andreaea depressinervis Card.

Andreaea gainii Card.

Andreaea regularis Muell.

BARTRAMIACEAE

Bartramia patens Brid.

Conostomum magellanicum Sull.

BRACHYTHECIACEAE

Brachythecium austrosalebrosum (Müll. Hal.) Kindb.

Brachythecium glaciale B.S.G.

BRYACEAE

Bryum amblyodon Müll. Hal.

Bryum argenteum Hedw.

Bryum orbiculatifolium Card. et Broth.

Bryum pallescens Schleich. ex Schwaegr.

Bryum pseudotriquetrum (Hedw.) Schwaegr.

Pohlia cruda (Hedw.) Lindb.

Pohlia drummondii (Müll. Hal.) A. L. Andrews in Grout

Pohlia nutans (Hedw.) Lindb.

Pohlia wahlenbergii (Web. Et Mohr.) Andrews

DICRANACEAE

Anisothecium cardotii (R. Br. ter.) Ochyra

Chorisodontium aciphyllum (Hook. f. et. Wills.) Broth.

Kiaeria pumila (Mitt. in Hook. f.) Ochyra – very rare.

DITRICHACEAE

Ceratodon purpureus (Hedw.) Brid.

Distichum capillaceum (Hedw.) B.S.G.

Ditrichum hyalinum (Mitt.) Kuntze

Ditrichum lewis-smithii Ochyra

ENCALYPTACEAE

Encalypta rhaptocarpa Schwaegr.

GRIMMIACEAE

Grimmia reflexidens Müll. Hal.

Racomitrium sudeticum (Funck) Bruch & Schimp. in BSG.

Schistidium amblyophyllum (Müll. Hal.) Ochyra & Hertel

Schistidium antactici (Card.) L. I. Savicz & Smirnova

Schistidium cupulare (Müll. Hal.) Ochyra

Schistidium falcatum (Hook. f. at Wils.) B. Bremer

Schistidium halinae Ochyra

Schistidium occultum (Müll. Hal.) Ochyra & Matteri

Schistidium rivulare (Brid.) Pobp.

Schistidium steerei Ochyra

Schistidium urnulaceum (Müll. Hal.) B. G. Bell.

HYPNACEAE

Hypnum revolutum (Mitt.) Lindb.

Platydictya jungermannioides (Brid.) Crum

MEESIACEAE

Meesia uliginosa Hedw.

ORTHOTRICHACEAE
Muelleriella crassifolia (Hook. f. et Wils.) Dus.

POLYTRICHACEAE
Polytrichastrum alpinum (Hedw.) G. L. Smith
Polytrichum strictum Brid.
Polytrichum juniperinum Hedw.
Polytrichum piliferum Hedw.

POTTIACEAE
Dydimodon gelidus Card.
Hennediella antarctica (Angstr.) Ochyra & Matteri
Hennediella heimii (Hedw.) Zand.
Stegonia latifolia (Schwaegr. in Schult.) Vent in Broth.
Syntrichia filaris (Müll. Hal.) Zand.
Syntrichia princeps (De Not.) Mitt.
Syntrichia saxicola (Card.) Zand.

SELIGERACEAE
Dicranoweisia brevipes (Müll. Hal.) Card..
Dicranoweisia crispula (Hredw.) Milde
Dicranoweisia grimmiaceae (Müll. Hal.) Broth.

ALGAE
MACROSCOPIC CONTINENTAL ALGAE
Prasiola crispa (Lightfoot) Menegh

MICROSCOPIC CONTINENTAL ALGAE
Bacillariophyceae

Coscinodiscales
Orthoseira cf. *dendroteres* (Ehrenberg) Crawford

Naviculales
Amphora veneta Kützing
Achnanthes lanceolata (Brébisson) Grunow
Achnanthes marginulata Grunow
Caloneis cf. *silicula* (Ehrenberg) Cleve
Caloneis cf. *schumanniana* (Grunov) Cleve

Cocconeis sp.,

Fragilaria bidens Heiberg

Fragilaria capucina Desmazieres

Fragilaria construens f. *binodis* (Ehrenberg) Hustedt

Fragilaria pinnata Ehrenberg

Gomphonema parvulum (Kützing) Kützing

Hantzschia amphioxys (Ehrenberg) Grunow

Luticola muticopsis (Van Heurck) D. G. Mann

Luticola mutica var. *ventricosa* (Kützing) Cleve et Grunow

Navicula cf. *bryophila* Petersen

Navicula elginensis (Gregory) Ralfs

Navicula glaciei Van Heurck,

Navicula phyllepta Kützing

Nitzschia agnita Hustedt

Nitzschia cf. *fontifuga* Cholnoky

Nitzschia frustulum (Kützing) Grunow

Nitzschia gracilis Hantzsch

Nitzschia homburgiensis Lange-Bertalot

Nitzschia cf. *hybrida* Grunow

Nitzschia inconspicua Grunow

Nitzschia perminuta (Grunow) M. Pergallo

Opephora olsenii Moeller

Pinnularia borealis Ehrenberg

Pinnularia ignobilis (Krasske) Cleve-Euler

Pinnularia microstauron (Ehrenberg) Cleve

Stauroneis cf. *anceps* Ehrenberg

Stauroneis cf. *simulans* (Donkin) R. Ross.

MACROSCOPIC FUNGI

Omphalina antarctica Sing.

Galerina moelleri Bas.

LICHENS AND LICHENICOLOUS FUNGI

Acarospora macrocyclos Vain.

Alectoria minuscula – Lindsay

Arthopyrenia maritima Øvstedal

Arthrorhaphis citrinella (Ach.) Poelt

Austrolecia antarctica Hertel

Bacidia stipata Lamb

Biatorella antarctica Murray

Bryonora castanea (Hepp) Poelt

Bryoria chalybeiformis (L.) Brodo et D. Hawksw.

Buellia anisomera Vain.

Buellia augusta Vain.

Buellia cladocarpiza Lamb

Buellia coniops (Wahlenb. in Ach.) Th. Fr.

Buellia granulosa (Darb.) Dodge

Buellia latemarginata Darb.

Buellia papillata (Sommerf.) Tuck.

Buellia perlata (Hue) Darb.

Buellia pycnogonoides Darb.

Buellia russa (Hue) Darb.

Buellia subpedicillata (Hue) Darb.

Caloplaca amniospila

Caloplaca athallina Darb.

Caloplaca buelliae Olech & Søchting

Caloplaca cirrochrooides (Vain.) Zahlbr.

Caloplaca citrina (Hoffm.) Th. Fr.

Caloplaca iomma Olech & Søchting

Caloplaca millegrana

Caloplaca psoromatis Olech & Søchting

Caloplaca regalis (Vain.) Zahlbr.

Caloplaca siphonospora Olech & Søchting

Caloplaca sublobulata (Vain.) Zahlbr.

Caloplaca tetraspora (Nyl.) H. Oliv.

Caloplaca tiroliensis Zahlbr.

Candelaria murrayi (Dodge) Poelt

Candelariella hallettensis (Murray) Øvstedal

Candelariella vitellina (Hoffm.) Müll. Arg.

Carbonea vorticosa (Flörke) Hertel

Catapyrenium daedaleum (Kremp.) Stein

Catapyrenium lachneum (Ach.) R. Sant.

Catillaria corymbosa (Hue) Lamb

Cladonia cariosa (Ach.) Spreng.

Cladonia furcata (Huds.) Schrader

Cladonia phyllophora Ehrh. ex Hoffm.

Cladonia pyxidata (L.) Hoffm.

Coelocaulon aculeatum (Schreber) Link

Coelocaulon epiphorellum (Nyl. in Crombie) Kärnef.

Cystocoleus ebeneus (Dillwyn) Thwaites

Dermatocarpon intestiniforme (Körb.) Hasse

Haematomma erythroma (Nyl.) Zahlbr.

Himantormia lugubris (Hue) Lamb

Hypogymnia lugubris (Pers.) Krog

Hypogymnia lububris (Pers.) Krog f. *compactior* (Zahlbr.) D. C. Linds.

Japewia tornoensis (Nyl.) Tønsberg

Lecania brialmontii (Vain.) Zahlbr.

Lecania gerlachei (Vain.) Zahlbr.

Lecanora dispersa (Pers.) Sommerf.

Lecanora expectans Darb.

Lecanora physciella (Darb.) Hertel

Lecanora polytropa (Hoffm.) Rabenh.

Lecidea assimilata Nyl.

Lecidea atrobrunnea (Ramond ex Lam. et DC.) Schaer.

Lecidea lapicida (Ach.) Ach.

Lecidea sarcogynoides Körb.

Lecidea sciatrapha Hue

Lecidella aff. *carpathica* Körb.

Lecidella stigmatea (Ach.) Hertel and Leuckert

Lecidella wulfenii (Hepp) Körb.

Leptogium puberulum Hue

Massalongia carnosa (Dicks.) Körb.

Mastodia tesselata Auct.

Megaspora verrucosa (Ach.) Hafellner

Microglaena antarctica Lamb

Ochrolechia frigida (Sw.) Lynge

Ochrolechia parella (L.) A. Massal.

Pannaria hookeri (Borrer ex Sm.) Nyl.

Parmelia saxatilis (L.) Ach.

Physcia caesia (Hoffm.) Fürnr.

Physcia dubia (Hoffm.) Lettau

Physcia cf. *wainioi* Räs.

Physconia muscigena (Ach.) Poelt

Placopsis contortuplicata Lamb

Poeltidea perusta (Nyl.) Hertel et Hafellner

Polyblastia gothica Th. Fr.

Porpidia albocaerulescens (Wulfen) Hertel et Knoph

Porpidia crustulata (Ach.) Hertel et knoph

Pseudephebe minuscula (Nyl. ex Arnold) Brodo et D. Hawksw.

Pseudephebe pubescens (L.) Choisy

Pseudevernia pubescens

Psoroma hypnorum (Vahl) Gray

Ramalina terebrata Hook et Tayl.

Rhizocarpon geminatum Körb.

Rhizocarpon geographicum (L.) DC.

Rhizocarpon polycarpon (Hepp) Th. Fr.

Rhizoplaca aspidophora (Vain.) Redón

Rhizoplaca melanophthalma (DC. in Lam. et DC.) Leuck. et Poelt

Rinodina deceptionis Lamb

Rinodina mniaraea (Ach.) Körb.

Rinodina petermanii (Hue) Darb.

Rinodina turfacea (Wahlenb.) Körb.

Sphaeorophorus fragilis (L.) Pers.

Sphaeorophorus globosus (Hudson) Vain.

Sphaeorophorus cfr. *melanocarpus* (Sw.) DC.

Staurothele gelida (Hook & Tayl.) Lamb

Stereocaulon alpinum Laurer ex Funck

Stereocaulon glabrum (Müll. Arg.) Vain.

Tephromela atra (Hudson) Hafellner

Thelocarpon cyaneum Olech et Alstrup

Tremolecia atrata (Ach.) Hertel

Umbilicaria aprina Nyl.

Umbilicaria cfr. *cristata* Dodge et Baker

Umbilicaria decussata (Vill.) Zahlbr. –

Umbilicaria propagulifera (Vain.) Llano

Umbilicaria rufidula (Hue) Filson

Usnea acromelana Stirton

Usnea antarctica Du Rietz

Usnea aurantiaco-atra (Jacq.) Bory

Verrucaria ceuthocarpa Wahlenb.

Verrucaria cylindrophora Vain.

Verrucaria dispartita Vain.

Verrucaria elaeoplaca Vain.

Verrucaria psycrophila Lamb

Verrucaria tesselatula Nyl.

Xanthoria candelaria (L.) Th. Fr.

Xanthoria elegans (Link.) Th. Fr.

APPENDIX B

Macroalgae checklist from

Admiralty Bay, King George Island

RHODOPHYTA

Bangiales

Bangiaceae

Porphyra plocamiestris R.W. Ricker

Pyropia endiviifolia (A.Gepp & E.Gepp) H.G. Choi & M.S. Hwang

Hildenbrandiales

Hildenbrandiaceae

Hildenbrandia lecannellieri Hariot

Bonnemaisoniales

Bonnemaisoniaceae

Delisea pulchra (Greville) Montagne

Palmariales

Palmariaceae

Palmaria decipiens (Reinsch) R.W. Ricker

Palmaria georgica (Reinsch) R.W. Ricker

Ceramiales

Wrangeliaceae

Georgiella confluens (Reinsch) Kylin

Delesseriaceae

Delesseria lancifolia J. Agardh

Delesseria salicifolia Reisch

Microrhinus carnosus (Reinsch) Skottsberg

Myriogramme manginii (Gain) Skottsberg

Neuroglossum delesseriae (Reinsch) M.J. Wynne

Phycodrys antartica (Skottsberg) Skottsberg

Phycodrys austrogeorgica Skottsberg

Phycodrys quercifolia (Bory) Skottsberg

Rhodomelaceae

Picconiella plumosa (Kylin) J. De Toni

Gigartinales

Cystocloniaceae

Acanthococcus antarcticus J.D. Hooker et Harvey

Gigartinaceae

Gigartina skottsbergii Setchell & N.L. Gardner

Iridaea cordata (Turner) Bory de Saint-Vincent

Sarcothalia papillosa (Bory) Leister

Kallymeniaceae

Callophyllis atrosanguinea (J.D.Hooker & Harvey) Hario

Callophylis pinnata Setchell & Swezy

Phyllophoraceae

Gymnogongrus antarcticus Skottsberg

Gymnogongrus turquetii Hariot

Gracilariales

Gracilariaceae

Curdiea racovitzae Hariot

Halymeniales

Halymeniaceae

Pachymenia orbicularis (Zanardini) Setchell & N.L. Gardner

Plocamiales

Plocamiaceae

Plocamium cartilagineum (L) P.S. Dixon

Plocamium hookeri Harvey

Rhodymeniales

Rhodymeniaceae

Rhodymenia coccocarpa (Montagne) M.J.Wynne

CHLOROPHYTA

Chaetophorales

Chaetophoraceae

Endophyton atroviride O´Kelly

Ulotrichales

Gomontiaceae

Monostroma hariotii Gain

259

Ulotrichaceae

Protomonostroma undulatum (Wittrock) K.L.Vinogradova

Ulothrix australis Gain

Ulothrix flacca (Dillwyn) Thuret

Ulvales

Kornmanniaceae

Blidingia minima (Nägeli ex Kützing) Kylin

Ulvaceae

Ulva bulbosa (Suhr) Hariot

Ulva compressa Linnaeus

Ulva intestinalis Linnaeus

Prasiolales

Prasiolaceae

Prasiola crispa (Lightfoot) Kützing

Prasiola sp.

Acrosiphoniales

Acrosiphoniaceae

Acrosiphonia arcta (Dillwyn) J. Agardh

Urospora penicilliformis (Roth) Areschoug

Cladophorales

Cladophoraceae

Chaetomorpha sp

HETEROKONTHOPHYTA

Syringodermatales

Syringodermataceae

Syringoderma australe Levring

Fucales

Seirococcaceae

Cystosphaera jacquinotii (Montagne) Skottsberg

Ectocarpales

Chordariaceae

Haplogloia moniliformis Ricker

Haplogloia andersonii (Farlow) Levring

Elachista antarctica Skottsberg

Acinetosporaceae

Geminocarpus austrogeorgiae Skottsberg

Geminocarpus geminatus (Hooker & Harvey) Skottsberg

Pylaiella littoralis (L.) Kjellman

Adenocystaceae

Adenocystis utricularis (Bory) Skottsberg

Scytosiphonaceae

Petalonia fascia (O. F. Müller) Kuntze

Desmarestiales

Desmarestiaceae

Desmarestia anceps Montagne

Desmarestia antarctica R.L. Moe & P.C. Silva

Desmarestia confervoides (Bory) M.E. Ramírez & A.F. Peters

Desmarestia menziesii J Agardh

Himantothallus grandifolius (A and E Gepp) Zinova

Phaeurus antarcticus Skottsberg

Ascoseirales

Ascoseiraceae

Ascoseira mirabilis Skottsberg

APPENDIX C
Fauna recorded at Admiralty Bay, King George Island

Birds recorded at Admiralty Bay

Breeding species:

Pygoscelis adeliae

Pygoscelis papua

Pygoscelis antarctica

Macronectes giganteus

Daption capense

Oceanites oceanicus

Fregetta tropica

Phalacrocorax bransfieldensis

Chionis alba

Catharacta maccormicki

Catharacta lonnbergi

Catharacta chilensis

Larus dominicanus

Sterna vittata

Non-breeding

Frequent:

Aptenodytes patagonicus

Eudyptes chrysolophus

Edyptes chrysocome

Fulmarus glacialoides

Pagodroma nivea

Sterna paradisaea

Sporadic:

Aptenodytes forsteri

Spheniscus magellanicus

Talassarche melanophris

Phoebetria fusca

Phoebetria palpebrata

Thalassoica Antarctica

Halobaena caerulea

Pachyptila desolata
Bubulcus ibis
Cygnus melanocoryphus
Anas sibilatrix
Anas georgica
Calidris fuscicollis
Steganopus tricolor
Hirundo rustica

Pinnipeds recorded at Admiralty Bay:
Breeding species:
Mirounga leonina
Leptonychotes weddelli
Arctocephalus gazelle (only two cases)

Non-breeding
Frequent:
Arctocephalus gazella
Hydrurga leptonyx
Lobodon carcinophagus

Sporadic:
Ommatophoca rossi (two visits)

Cetacea recorded at Admiralty Bay:
Megaptera novaeangliae
Balaenoptera bonaerensis
Orcinus orca

APPENDIX D

Marine invertebrates, benthic marine foraminifers and ostracods recorded at Admiralty Bay, King George Island

An updated list of antarctic marine invertebrates can be found on the website ABBED —Admiralty Bay Benthos Diversity Database (www.abbed.uni.lodz.pl/). This database was created by Poland, Belgian and Brazil, in the International Polar Year (2007-2009).

The list of benthic marine foraminifers (Majewski 2005, Majewski et al. 2007, Majewski and Tatur 2009) and ostracods (Majewski and Olempska 2005) can be accessed on-line in the listed papers.

APPENDIX E

Code of Conduct for Visitors

This code of conduct has been produced for commercial tour operators (IAATO and non-IAATO affiliated), private expeditions and National Antarctic Programs scientists and staff when undertaking recreational visits to Admiralty Bay.

•All visitors should get acquainted with and follow the precepts of the General Guidelines for Visitors to the Antarctic (Resolution 3 (2011).

•Tour operator should provide their visit schedules to the ASMA Coordinator in advance of their visits to the Area. ASMA Management Group should circulate this information among National Antarctic Programs active in the Area.

•Visits to Arctowski and Ferraz Stations are possible with prior agreement of the appropriate Station Leader. Visits to isolated laboratory modules, refuges and the area behind Ferraz Station should be made only in small groups accompanied by station personnel with prior agreement of the Station Leader.

•Visits should be undertaken in line with Recommendation XVIII-1, Measure 15 (2009) "Landing of Persons from Passenger vessels", Resolution 7 (2009) "General Principles of Antarctic Tourism", Resolution 7 (2009) "General Principles of Antarctic Tourism" and Resolution 3 (2011) "General Guidelines for Visitors to Antarctic). Visitors should be informed about the principles of this Code of Conduct, as well as the ASMA Management Plan

•Tour operators are encouraged to exchange itineraries with National Antarctic Programs using support vessels in the Area in order to avoid two ships unintentionally converging on a site simultaneously.

• Commercial cruise operators are encouraged to take care that no more than 100 passengers are ashore at a site at any time, accompanied by a minimum of one member of the expedition staff for every 20 passengers..

• Members of non-governmental and tourist expeditions, as well as National Antarctic Program staff during recreational visits to Arctowski and Ferraz stations should use the routes shown in Fig. 7 and 8. These routes provide the opportunity to observe wildlife and the station installations, while minimizing disturbance to station activities and the environment, and avoiding habitat degradation.

• In order to avoid environmental impact, disturbance of wildlife and interference with on-going scientific research, landing at or entering Scientific Zones listed in Section 6(iv) (Fig. 3, 5 and 6) should not take place, except in emergencies.

• All movement on land should be undertaken carefully to minimize disturbance to animals, soil and vegetated areas, or disturb scientific equipment. The visitor should:

◦ avoid walking on vegetation such as moss or lichen.

◦ maintain an appropriate distance from birds or seals which is safe and does not cause them disturbance. As a general rule, maintain a distance of 5 metres. Where practicable, keep at least 15 meters away from fur seals.

◦ wash boots and clean clothes, bags, tripods and walking sticks before landing, in order to prevent biological introductions.

◦ not leave any litter.

◦ not take biological or geological souvenirs or disturb artefacts.

◦ not write or draw graffiti on any man-made structure or natural surface.

◦ not touch or disturb scientific instruments or markers.

◦ not touch or disturb field depots or other equipment stored by National Antarctic Programs.

APPENDIX F

Scientific and Environmental Guidelines

In the last 60 years Admiralty Bay and its coastal areas have become an important site for scientific research, with many research teams of different specialties working there every year. These guidelines suggest a code of conduct formulated with the aim to protect the environmental, scientific, historical and aesthetic values of the area for the future generations.

- All scientific and logistical activities in the Area should be planned with the aim to minimize human impact on the values of the Area;

- Scientific research which can potentially disturb breeding birds or sea mammals should be conducted with a special care and only for compelling scientific reasons; where taking of or harmful interference with animals is involved, the *SCAR Code of Conduct for Use of Animals for Scientific Purposes in Antarctica* should be used as a minimum standard.

- Collecting any specimen (e.g. stones, fossils, historical objects etc.) except for approved scientific or educational purposes with appropriate permits should be prohibited;

- Sample size of biological or non-biological material should be, as far as possible, limited to the minimum;

- Long-term monitoring or experimental sites should be, as far as practicable, clearly identified, and the information should be exchanged through the ASMA Coordinator;

- Stringent measures to avoid the introduction or spread of non-native species should be taken;

- Human traffic should be undertaken carefully to minimize disturbance to animals, soil and vegetated areas.; as far as possible existing tracks should be used;

- Use of helicopters and land vehicles should be kept to an absolute minimum, and never – except in emergency – in places where near birds or sea mammals breed or congregate;

- Field camps should be located as far as possible on non-vegetated sites, and should also avoid concentrations and breeding location of mammals and birds. Previously occupied campsites should be re-used where appropriate. The location of field camps should be recorded, and the information exchanged through the ASMA Coordinator.

- Scientific research in the Scientific Zones should be conducted with a special care, avoiding or minimizing environmental impact;

- Visits and activities conducted in the Scientific Zones should be recorded (especially type and quantity of all samples), and the information should be exchanged through the ASMA Coordinator;

- Access to Scientific Zones designated for the presence of breeding birds should be restricted between 1 October to 15 April to those conducting essential scientific research, monitoring or maintenance;

- Access to Scientific Zones designated for the presence of vegetation banks should be restricted during the summer season to those conducting essential scientific research, monitoring or maintenance;

- Access to Scientific Zone designated on Crosses Hill on northern flank of Ferraz Station because of concentration of terns should be restricted between 1 October to 31 December to those conducting scientific research, monitoring or essential station operations;

- Research in Scientific Zones designated in shallow marine waters should, as far as possible, avoid or minimize the use of invasive methods (dredging, grabbing, trawling etc.). The coordinates of sites where invasive methods were used should be recorded, and the information should be exchanged through the ASMA Coordinator.

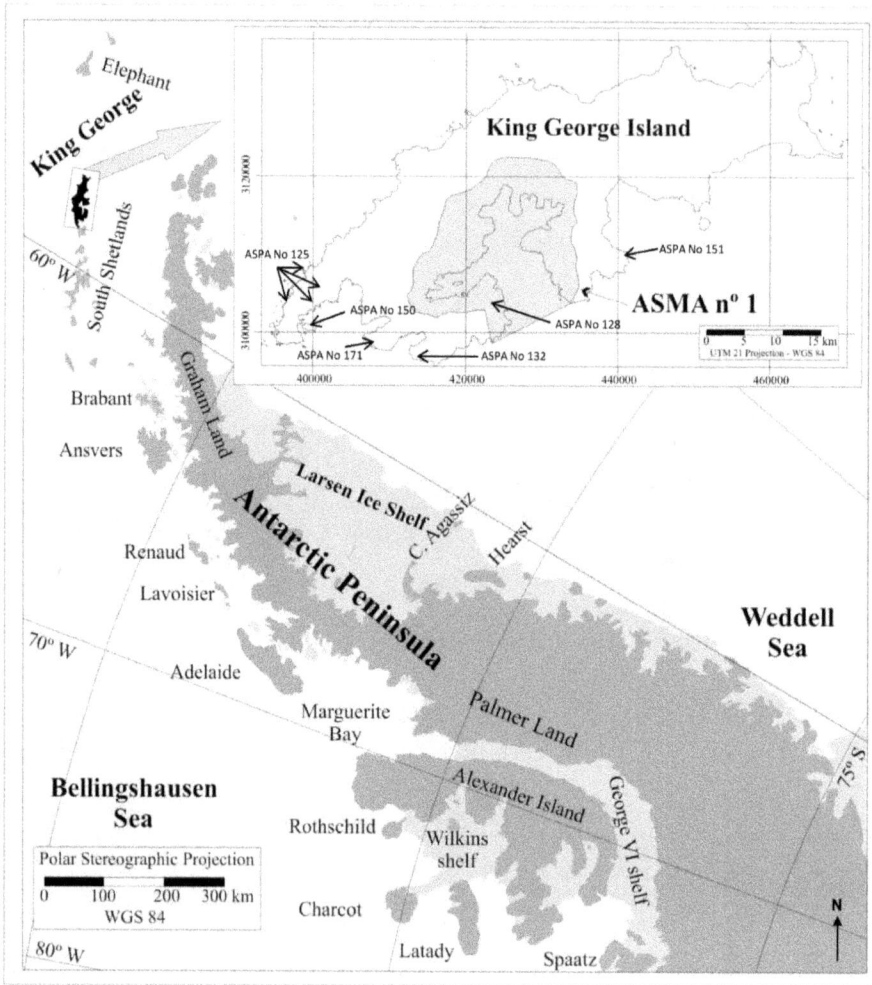

Fig. 1. Location of ASMA No 1 on King George Island, Antarctic Peninsula

Fig. 2. Admiralty Bay Antarctic Specially Protected Area – ASMA No 1

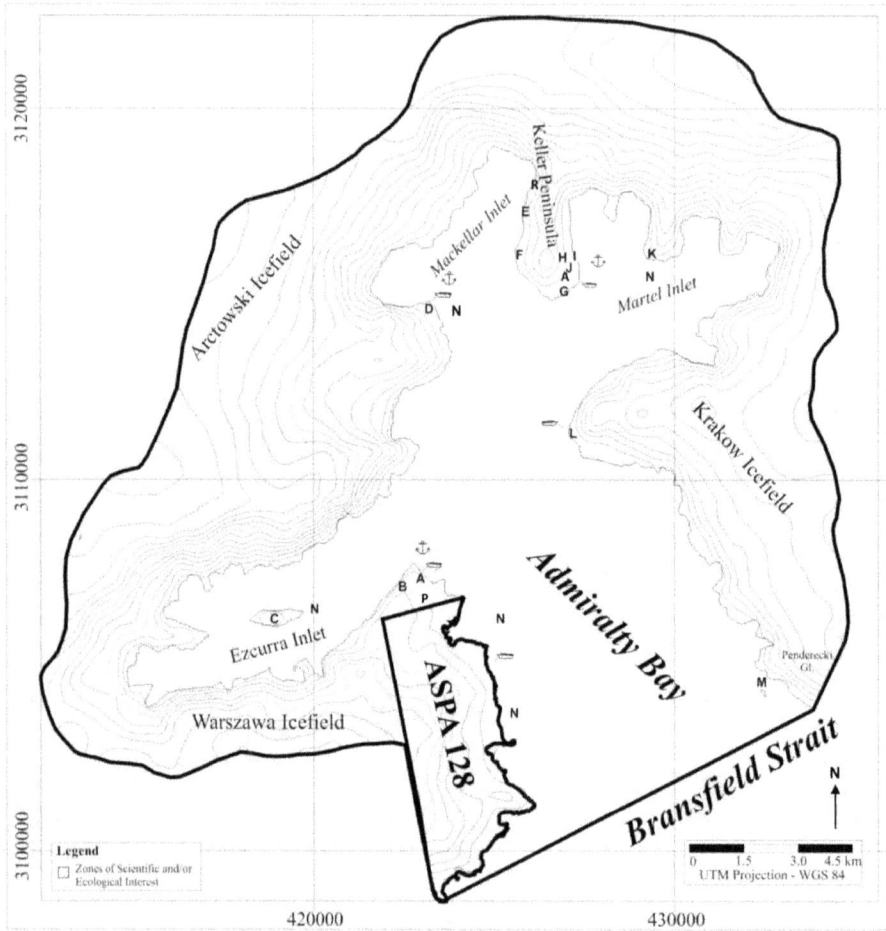

Fig. 3. Location of Scientific Zones (see 6(iv) Restricted and managed zones in the Area)

🛶 small boat landing site

⚓ anchorage

━━ ASMA boundary

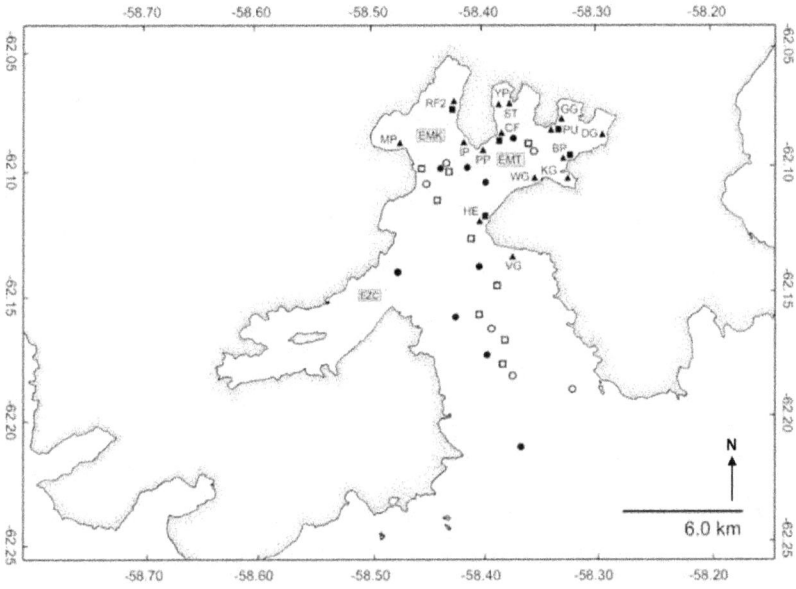

Fig. 4. Long-term Environmental Monitoring (INCT-APA, Brazil)

▲   Imaging stations

●   Stations sampled with a box-corer (2008-2009)

○   Stations sampled with a box-corer (2009-2010)

■   Stations sampled with dredge (2008-2009)

□   Stations sampled with dredge (2009-2010)

EFC – Ezcurra Inlet, EMK – Mackellar Inlet, EMT – Martel Inlet

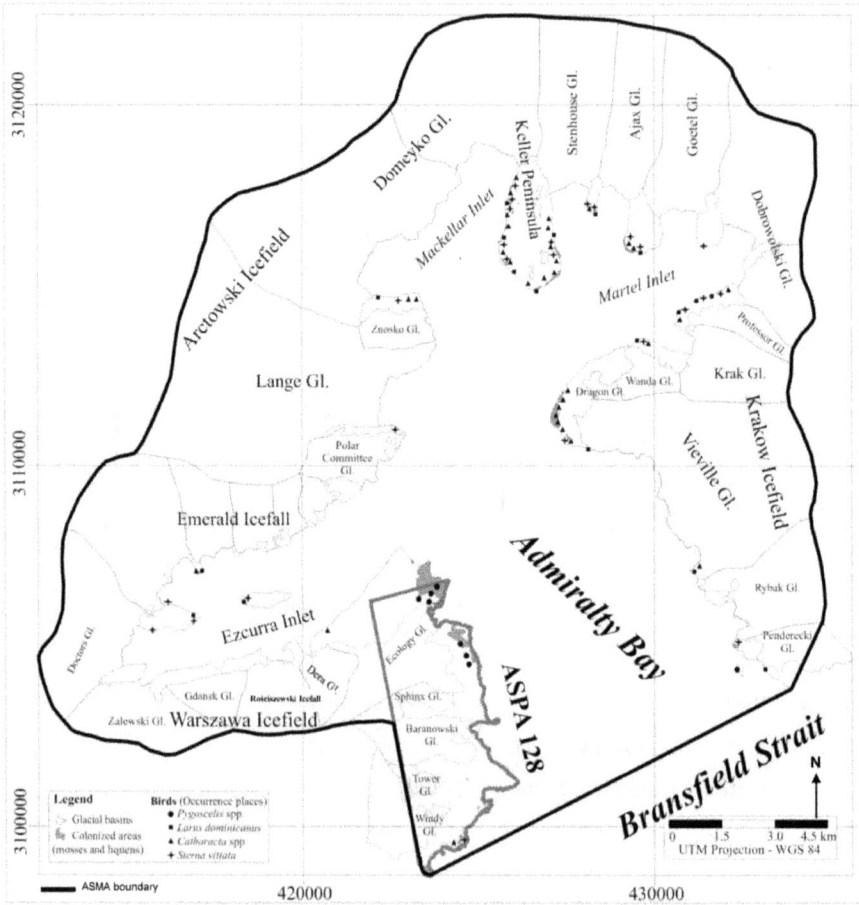

Fig. 5. Flora (colonized areas) and Birds (occurence sites)

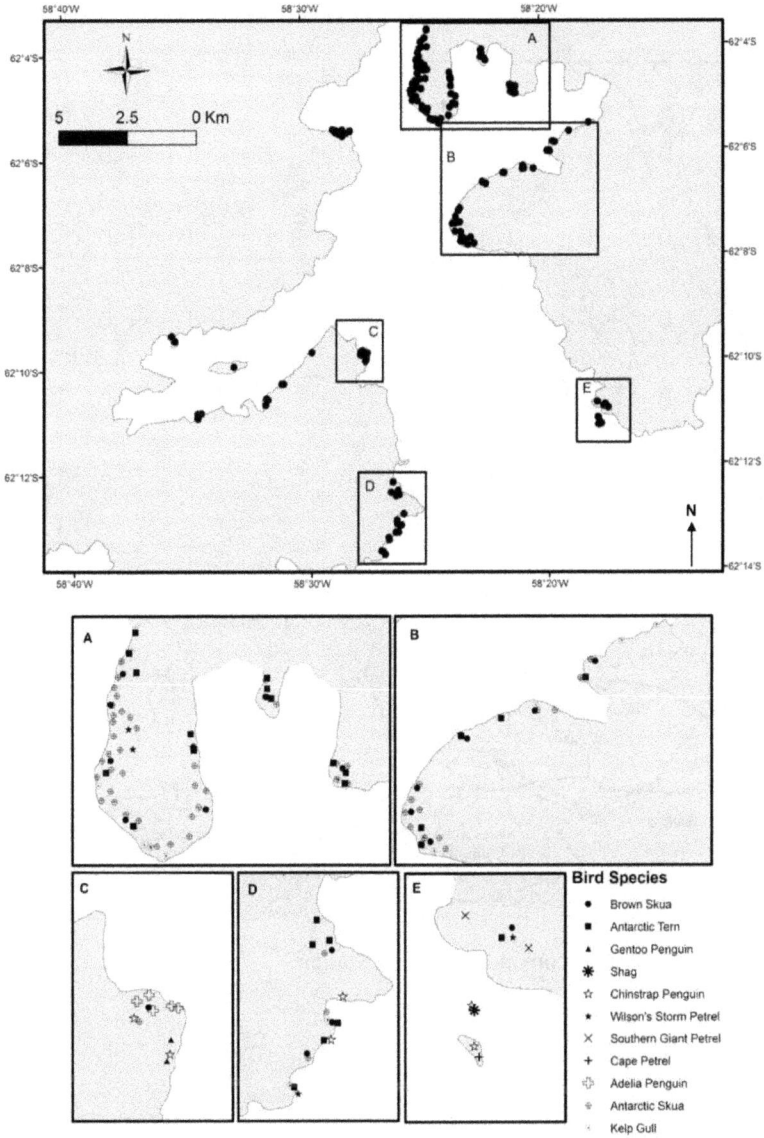

Fig. 6. Main birds breeding sites

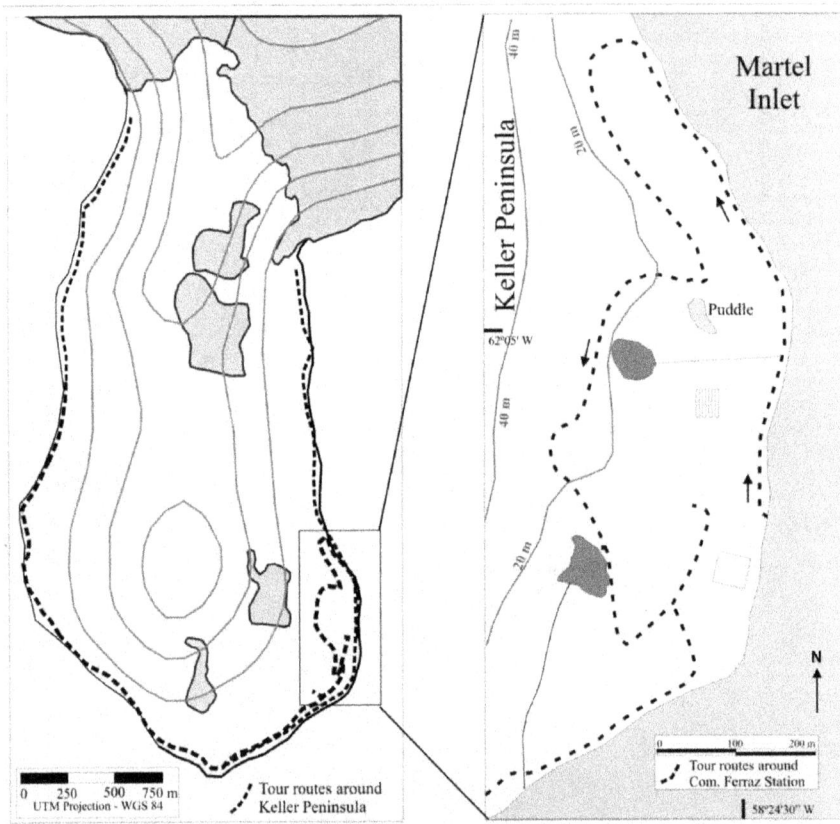

Fig. 7. Visitor Zone – Comandante Ferraz Station

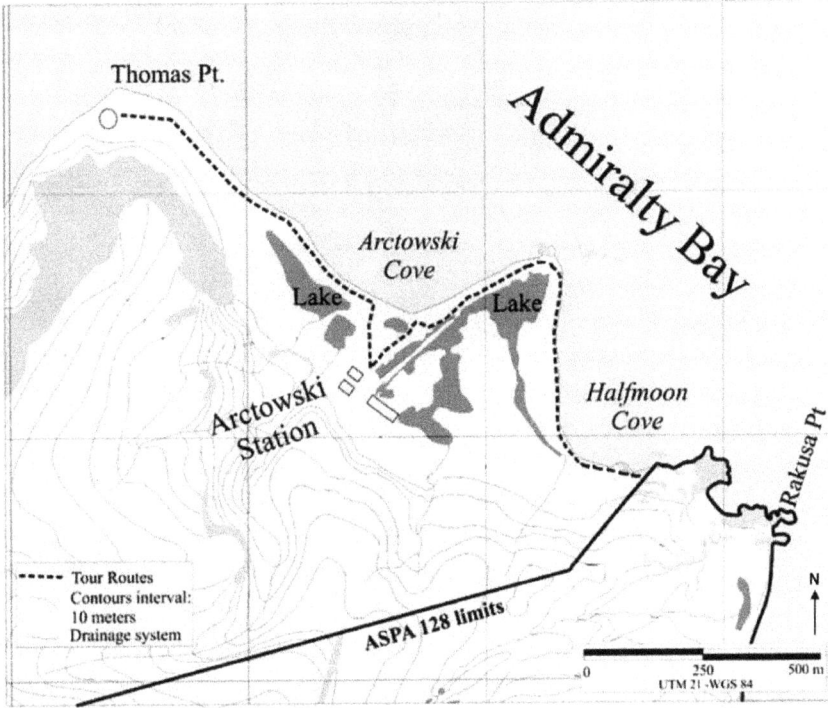

Fig. 8. Visitor Zone – Henryk Arctowski Station

1.Disembarkation point
2.Scientific Laboratory
3.Dining room/Kitchen
4.Generator room/ Maintenance room/Wate treatment building
5.Living quarters
6.Emergency refuge
7.Portable helicopter pad
8.Flag

Fig. 9. Facilities Zone – Machu Picchu Station

Larsemann Hills, East Antarctica
Antarctic Specially Managed Area
Management Plan

1. Introduction

The Larsemann Hills are an ice-free area of approximately 40 km² and the southernmost coastal 'oasis' in the Prydz Bay region of East Antarctica. Coastal ice-free areas are rare in Antarctica and as such the Larsemann Hills region is environmentally, scientifically and logistically significant.

In 2007 the Larsemann Hills were designated an Antarctic Specially Managed Area (ASMA) in response to a joint nomination by Australia, China, India, Romania and the Russian Federation. The primary reason for designation was to promote coordination and cooperation by Parties in the planning and conduct of activities in the region – with the view to achieving greater environmental protection outcomes.

The original management plan for Larsemann Hills ASMA No. 6 was adopted under Measure 2 (2007). The first review of the plan was completed in 2013.

1.1 Geography

The Larsemann Hills are located approximately halfway between the Vestfold Hills and the Amery Ice Shelf on the south-eastern coast of Prydz Bay, Princess Elizabeth Land, East Antarctica (69°30'S, 76°19'58"E) (Map A). The ice-free area consists of two major peninsulas (Stornes and Broknes), four minor peninsulas, and approximately 130 near-shore islands. The eastern-most peninsula, Broknes, is further divided into western and eastern components by Nella Fjord. The closest significant ice-free areas are the Bølingen Islands (69°31'58"S, 75°42'E) 25 km to the south-west and the Rauer Islands (68°50'59"S, 77°49'58"E) 60 km to the north-east.

1.2 Human presence

1.2.1 History of human visitation

The Larsemann Hills area was first charted in 1935 by a Norwegian expedition under Captain Klarius Mikkelsen. While brief visits were made by several nations during the following 50 years, human activity of a significant or sustained nature did not occur until the mid-1980s. The period 1986 to 1989 saw rapid infrastructure development in the area; an Australian summer research base (Law Base), a Chinese research station (Zhongshan) and two Russian research stations (at the time, identified as Progress I and Progress II) were established within approximately 3 km of each other on eastern Broknes. A 2000 m skiway was also operated by Russia on the ice plateau south of Broknes and used for over 100 intra-continental flights during this period. Law Base is currently seasonally operated as Law-Racovita-Negoita in conjunction with the Romanian Antarctic Foundation. Zhongshan and Progress (formerly Progress II) are operated year round, as is Bharati station which was established by India in 2012/13.

1.2.2 Science

Station-based research includes meteorology, seismology, geomagnetics, atmospheric chemistry, Global Positioning System (GPS) tracking, atmospheric and space physics, and human physiology. Field-based research in the Larsemann Hills has focused on geology, geomorphology, Quaternary science, glaciology, hydrology, limnology, ecology, geoecology, biology, and studies of biodiversity (including molecular), biotechnology and human impacts.

1.2.3 Tourist visits

Sporadic ship-based tourist visits have been made to the area since 1992. These have involved half-day trips, during which passengers have been transported ashore by helicopter to view station areas, lakes, bird colonies and other features around eastern Broknes by foot.

1.2.4 Future activities

Continuing human activity in the Larsemann Hills is promoted by the coastal location and ice-free landscape. Commitment to ongoing use by the Parties active in the area is evident both in the development and redevelopment of station facilities, and the staging of inland traverses from the area. For the next five years primary attention will be given to road improvements including the proposed levelling of the ridge on the road between Progress and the aerodrome.

1.3 Period of designation

The ASMA is designated for an indefinite period. The management plan is to be reviewed at least every 5 years.

2. Values of the Area

The Prydz Bay region contains a number of rock outcrops and offshore islands which represent a significant fraction of the ice-free component of the East Antarctic coastline. Comprising an ice-free area of approximately 40 km², the Larsemann Hills represent the southernmost coastal 'oasis' (69°30'S) in this geographic sector, and the second largest after the Vestfold Hills (~410 km²), 110 km to the north-east. Such coastal oases are particularly rare in Antarctica. As such, the Larsemann Hills represents a significant biogeographical location of environmental, scientific and logistical value.

2.1 Environmental and scientific values

Much of the scientific research in the Larsemann Hills depends on the natural environment being in a relatively undisturbed state, and for this reason the protection of scientific values will to a large extent contribute to the understanding and protection of the abundant environmental values of the area.

With their geology significantly different from that of other outcrops in the Prydz Bay region, the Larsemann Hills provide a significant geological window into the history of Antarctica. Widespread exposed geological and geomorphological features provide a valuable insight into landscape formation, and the history of the polar ice-sheet and sea level. Many of these features are highly vulnerable to physical disturbance.

Broknes peninsula is one of very few coastal areas of Antarctica that remained partially ice-free through the last glaciation, and sediments deposited there contain continuous biological and palaeoclimate records dating back some 130 000 years.

Stornes and Brattnevet peninsulas are unique in terms of their extensive development of diverse suites of borosilicate and phosphate mineral assemblages that are scientifically significant in their variety and origin. Ongoing research seeks to identify the geologic processes that have concentrated boron and phosphorus to such an extent. Stornes also has sediments containing abundant well-preserved foraminifera, diatoms and molluscs. The outstanding geological values of Stornes, and its value as a reference site for the more heavily impacted Broknes, are afforded protection within Antarctic Specially Protected Area (ASPA) No. [???].

The Larsemann Hills contain more than 150 lakes. Although some of the most scientifically important lakes are on eastern Broknes, the lakes of the Larsemann Hills are collectively recognised as the ASMA's most important ecological feature. The lakes are particularly valuable for their relatively simple natural ecosystems. As they are susceptible to physical, chemical and biological modification, a catchment-based approach to management of human activities is appropriate in protecting their scientific values. The snowfields on these catchments and streams are also important subjects for the measurement of natural hydrological processes and any expansion of human impacts.

The comparatively benign microclimate and the occurrence of fresh water in summer also support Antarctic life forms. Snow petrels, Wilson's storm petrels and south polar skuas breed in the area, and Weddell seals haul out close to shore to breed and moult. Mosses, lichens and cyanobacterial mats are widely distributed, and found in high concentrations in some locations. The comparative accessibility of these biological sites makes them a valuable and vulnerable characteristic of the area.

Due to the area's short, concentrated and well-documented history of human activity, the Larsemann Hills also presents an excellent opportunity to study and quantify the impacts of humans.

2.2 Logistical values

As the site of the year-round stations of three national Antarctic programs, the Larsemann Hills ASMA is an important logistical support base for access to the southern Prydz Bay region and the Antarctic interior including to Kunlun station at Dome A (China), Vostok (Russia) and the Groves Mountains region. Australia and China have conducted substantial inland traverses supported by facilities in the Larsemann Hills. In recent years Russia relocated its support base for the resupply of Vostok from Mirny to the Larsemann Hills.

2.3 Wilderness and aesthetic values

Stornes and the minor peninsulas and near shore islands show less evidence of human presence than elsewhere in the ASMA. The aesthetic value of the ASMA's rugged ice-free hills interspersed by lakes and fjords against the backdrops of the Dålk Glacier, near shore islands, icebergs and plateau is noteworthy and warrants protection.

3. Aims and objectives

The Larsemann Hills are designated as an ASMA in order to protect the environment by promoting coordination and cooperation by Parties in the planning and conduct of human activities in the Area.

Through the adoption of this Management Plan, Parties commit to:

- providing guidance on the appropriate conduct of activities to all visitors including personnel involved in national research programs, transitory national program visitors and participants in non-governmental activities;
- minimising cumulative and other environmental impacts by encouraging communication and a consistent, cooperative approach to environmental protection in the conduct of research and support activities;
- minimising physical disturbance, chemical contamination and biological impacts in the region, primarily through appropriately managing vehicle usage;
- preventing contamination of the environment through the implementation of comprehensive waste management practices and the appropriate handling and storage of harmful substances;
- implementing measures needed to protect the environment from the accidental introduction or release of non-native species;
- maintaining the wilderness and aesthetic values of the area;
- safeguarding the ability to conduct scientific research by not compromising the scientific values of the area; and
- improving understanding of natural processes in the area, including through the conduct of cooperative monitoring and recording programs.

4. Description of the Area

4.1 Geography and Area boundary

The ASMA comprises the ice-free area and near-shore islands collectively known as the Larsemann Hills (see Map A), and the adjacent plateau. The ASMA includes the land:

beginning at 69°23'20"S, 76°31'0"E east of the southern tip of Dalkoy and from there,

north to	69°22'20"S, 76°30'50"E north of Dalkoy
north-west to	69°20'40"S, 76°21'30"E north of Striped Island
north-west to	69°20'20"S, 76°14'20"E north-east of Betts Island
south-west to	69°20'40"S, 76°10'30"E north-west of Betts Island
south-west to	69°21'50"S, 76°2'10"E north-west of Osmar Island
south-west to	69°22'30"S, 75°58'30"E west of Osmar Island
south-west to	69°24'40"S, 75°56'0"E west of Mills Island
south-east to	69°26'40"S, 75°58'50"E south of Xiangsi Dao
south-east to	69°28'10"S, 76°1'50"E south-west of McCarthy Point
south-east to	coastline at 69°28'40"S, 76°3'20"E
north-east to	69°27'32"S, 76°17'55"E south of the Russian airstrip site
south-east to	69°25'10"S, 76°24'10"E on the western side of the Dålk Glacier
north-east to	69°24'40"S, 76°30'20"E on the eastern side of the Dålk Glacier, and
north-east returning to	69°23'20"S, 76°31'0"E.

The intention is however to manage, in accordance with this management plan, the conduct of all substantial human activity associated with the Larsemann Hills.

No artificial boundary markers are in place.

4.2 Climate

A major feature of the climate of the Larsemann Hills is the existence of persistent and strong katabatic winds that blow from the north-east on most summer days. Daytime air temperatures from December to February frequently exceed 4°C and can exceed 10°C, with the mean monthly temperature a little above 0°C. Mean monthly winter temperatures mostly range between –15°C and –18°C. Precipitation occurs as snow and is rarely exceeds 250 mm water equivalent annually. Snow cover is generally deeper and more persistent on Stornes than Broknes. The pack ice is extensive inshore throughout summer, and the fjords and bays are rarely ice-free.

4.3 Natural features

4.3.1 Geology

The Larsemann Hills (and neighbouring Bolingen Islands and Brattstrand Bluffs) differ from other parts of Prydz Bay, mainly due to the absence of mafic dykes and large charnockite bodies. Bedrock exposures in the Larsemann Hills are composed of supracrustal volcanogenic and sedimentary rocks metamorphosed under granulite facies conditions (800–860°C, 6–7 kbar at peak) during the early Palaeozoic 'Pan-African' event (~500-550 Ma). Peak metamorphic conditions were followed by decompression. The rocks were subjected to extensive melting and several deformational episodes, and have been intruded by several generations of pegmatites and granites. The supracrustal rocks are underlain by, and possibly derived from, a Proterozoic orthopyroxene-bearing orthogneiss basement.

4.3.2 Geomorphology

The elongated form of the large-scale topographic features of the Larsemann Hills results from compositional layering, folds and faults (lineaments) in the metamorphic bedrock. The landscape is dissected by large, structurally-controlled, steep-sided fjords and valleys rarely exceeding 100 m in depth on land; the longest is 3 km (Barry Jones Bay). The maximum elevation above mean sea level is 162 m (Blundell Peak).

The coastline is generally bedrock, and beaches occur only at the heads of fjords or in isolated sheltered bays. There are several sequences of ice-dammed lakes and associated gorges and alluvial fans. The offshore islands are likely to be roches moutonnees, isolated by the current sea level.

Landforms produced by wind are common, though ice and salt wedging clearly play a considerable role in grain detachment with wind primarily acting as a transporting agent. Periglacial landforms are also widespread, but not particularly abundant or well developed.

True soils are virtually absent due to a lack chemical and biological soil-forming processes. Surficial deposits are widespread but confined to lower areas and include snow patch gravels, wind-deposited materials, talus and fluvially deposited materials. Very thin soils (less than 10 cm) are also found in association with scattered moss beds and discontinuous lichen. A permafrost layer exists 20–70 cm below the surface in some areas.

On north-eastern Stornes at approximately 69°31'48"S, 76°07'E there is an outcrop of post-depositionally placed marine Pliocene (4.5–3.8 Ma) sediment up to 40 cm thick. These sediments occupy a narrow bench approximately 55 m above sea level and yield abundant well-preserved foraminifera and reasonably well-preserved diatoms and molluscs.

On Broknes, areas that have remained ice-free through the Last Glacial Maximum contain sediment deposits (in lakes) that record climate, biological and ecological changes spanning the last glacial cycle.

4.3.3 Lakes and snowfields

The Larsemann Hills contains more than 150 lakes ranging in salinity from fresh to slightly saline, and in size from shallow ponds to large ice-deepened basins, although most are small (5000–30 000 m²) and shallow (2–5 m). The surfaces of the lakes freeze during winter, and most thaw for up to 2 months in summer, allowing them to be well-mixed by the katabatic winds. Most lakes are fed by snow melt and some have entrance and exit streams that flow persistently during the summer and provide habitat for crustaceans, diatoms and rotifers. Such streams are particularly evident on Stornes.

Small catchment areas and the near pristine waters make the Larsemann Hills lakes particularly susceptible to impacts resulting from human activities. Research has shown that several lakes on eastern Broknes in the immediate vicinity of the station areas and their interlinking roads have experienced modified water chemistries and inputs of nutrients, melt water and sediment. Whilst these lakes clearly exhibit human impacts, the majority of the lakes on Broknes and elsewhere in the Area appear largely unmodified.

The lakes on east Broknes have the longest sediment record of any surface lakes in Antarctica. It appears that the ice sheet did not advance beyond Lake Nella and did not scour Progress Lake so these lakes and the lakes towards the north end of the peninsula are particularly valuable to the science community.

The surface area of the Larsemann Hills' snowfields has increased by an estimated 11% during the last 50 years. In the summer period, a temporal hydrographical net is forming from thawing water from snowfields and glaciers. Streams transport water, ions, suspended matter and pollutants on catchments areas and to the lakes and bays.

4.3.4 Lake and stream biota

Most of the phytoplankton comprises autotrophic nanoflagellates although dinoflagellates occur in many lakes, and a desmid belonging to the genus *Cosmarium* is a major component of at least one lake. Heterotrophic nanoflagellates are more common than autotrophic nanoflagellates, though exhibit low species diversity (only three or four species in most lakes). They are particularly abundant in shallow lakes; *Parphysomonas* is very common. Ciliates are found in low numbers, with *Strombidium* the most common species. A species of *Holyophyra* is also found in most lakes. Rotifers occur sporadically in a number of lakes, and the cladoceran *Daphniopsis studeri* is widespread but found in low numbers.

The most obvious biotic features observed in almost all the lakes are extensive blue-green cyanobacterial mats that have accumulated since ice retreat, in places being up to 130 000 years old. These mats are found to exceptional thicknesses – up to 1.5 m – and are not normally observed in other Antarctic freshwater systems. They are also widely distributed in streams and wet seepage areas. The mats contain cyanobacteria that are endemic to Antarctica and the Prydz Bay region, and diatom assemblages that are clearly differentiated from other regions of Antarctica. The oldest preserved mats on eastern Broknes contain diatom species that have not been found living elsewhere on the continent. Approximately 40% of the Larsemann Hills' freshwater and brackish diatom taxa are endemic to Prydz Bay or Antarctica.

4.3.5 Seabirds

South polar skuas (*Catharacta maccormicki*), snow petrels (*Pagodroma nivea*) and Wilson's storm petrels (*Oceanites oceanicus*) breed within the Larsemann Hills. While approximate numbers and locations of breeding pairs are documented for Broknes, and particularly eastern Broknes, their distribution throughout the remainder of the area is uncertain.

South polar skuas are present between mid-late October and early April, with approximately 17 breeding pairs nesting on Broknes, and similar numbers of non-breeding birds. Snow petrel and Wilson's storm petrel nests are found in sheltered bedrock fragments, crevices, boulder slopes and rock falls, and are generally occupied from October until February. Approximately 850–900 pairs of snow petrels and 40–50 pairs of Wilson's storm petrels are found on Broknes, with concentrations of snow petrels at Base Ridge and on rocky outcrops adjacent to the Dålk Glacier in the east and the plateau in the south.

Despite the apparent suitable exposed nesting habitat, no Adelie penguin (*Pygoscelis adeliae*) breeding colonies are found at the Larsemann Hills, possibly due to the persistence of sea ice past the hatching period. However birds from colonies on nearby island groups between the Svenner Islands and Bolingen Islands visit during summer to moult. Emperor penguins (*Aptenodytes forsteri*) also occasionally visit.

4.3.6 Seals

Weddell seals (*Leptonychotes weddelli*) are numerous on the Larsemann Hills coast, using the local sea ice to pup from October, and to moult from late December until March. Pupping has been observed on the sea ice adjacent to the small islands north-east of eastern Broknes, and groups of moulting seals have been observed hauled out near the Broknes shore adjacent to the stations and in tide cracks in the fjords to the west. Aerial surveys during the moulting period have noted more than 1000 seals, with multiple large groups (50–100 seals) hauled out in Thala Fjord and on rafted ice immediately to the west of Stornes, and numerous smaller groups amongst offshore islands and ice to the north-east of Broknes. Crabeater seals (*Lobodon carcinophagus*) and leopard seals (*Hydrurga leptonyx*) are also occasional visitors.

4.3.7 Micro fauna

Five genera of terrestrial tardigrade (*Hypsibius*, *Minibiotus*, *Diphascon*, *Milnesium* and *Pseudechiniscus*), which include six species, are known to be present in localities associated with vegetation. The lakes and streams provide a series of habitats that contain a rich and varied fauna. Seventeen species of rotifer, three tardigrades, two arthropods, protozoans, a platyhelminth and nematodes have been reported. The cladoceran *Daphniopsis studeri*, one of few species of freshwater crustacea known to occur in the lakes of continental Antarctica has been identified in most Larsemann Hills lakes, is the largest animal in these systems, and is currently restricted to the Prydz Bay region and the sub-Antarctic islands in the South Indian Ocean Province. It has been continuously present on eastern Broknes through the Last Glacial Maximum, providing evidence that Broknes has acted as an important glacial refuge for the Antarctic biota through one or more full glacial cycles.

4.3.8 Terrestrial vegetation

Sampling of the coastal areas from the Vestfold Hills to the Larsemann Hills indicates that the flora of the Ingrid Christensen Coast is relatively uniform, and restricted to a similar distribution of bryophytes, lichens and terrestrial algae. The nature of the basement rock and the prevailing wind direction in the greater Prydz Bay area likely contribute to the fact that less than 1% of the Larsemann Hills has vegetative cover.

Most terrestrial life, including mosses, lichens and accompanying invertebrates are found inland from the coast. Nevertheless, large moss beds are known to occur in sheltered sites on Stornes and on the larger islands (particularly Kolløy and Sigdøy) where they are associated with Adelie penguin moulting sites, and on nunataks in the southwest. There are seven positively identified moss species in the region: *Bryum pseudotriquetum* which is most abundant, *Grimmia antarctici, Grimmia lawiana, Ceratodon pupureus, Sarconeurum glaciale, Bryum algens* and *Bryum argentum.*

The bryophyte flora also comprises one species of liverwort (*Cephaloziella exiliflora*) found on an unnamed outcrop south of Stornes and known from only four other Antarctic localities. Lichen coverage is considerable on north-eastern Stornes and Law Ridge on Broknes; the lichen flora of the region comprises at least 25 positively identified species. Studies conducted in nearby locations on the Ingrid Christensen Coast suggest that it would not be unreasonable to expect the Larsemann Hills to exhibit close to 200 non-marine algal taxa and 100–120 fungal taxa.

4.4 Human impacts

Intensive human activity in the region since 1986 has resulted in notable localised alteration of the environment, concentrated on eastern Broknes and the peninsula between Thala Fjord and Quilty Bay. The construction of station buildings and associated facilities and roads has caused physical degradation of the ice-free surface. Breakdown of rocks and exposure of the permafrost layer through repeated vehicle use has caused surface erosion and altered drainage patterns. Chemical contamination of some lakes and soils has occurred through the collection of water, accidental spillage of hydrocarbons, and the local disposal of wastewater. Water withdrawals for station use have depleted lake water volumes on Broknes.

Introduced floral species have been detected (and removed), and there is historical evidence of ingestion of human-derived food by wildlife. Wind-blown litter and surface disturbance through repeated pedestrian access remains an issue.

Stornes, and the minor peninsulas and near shore islands, have been less frequently visited and are less disturbed. Maintaining this well-preserved state, and minimising impacts elsewhere, is a major priority for management of the Larsemann Hills.

4.5 Access to the Area

4.5.1 Land access

Fifteen kilometres of unsealed roads, formed from local material, have been established on eastern Broknes. They include a 6.7 km road linking each of the stations on Broknes and the continental plateau in the south. This road closely follows the most appropriate route with regard to avoiding lake catchments and steep slopes. There are four particularly steeps sections – a ridge approximately 0.5 km south of Zhongshan; a series of steep slopes between Progress and Law-Racovita-Negoita; a section traversing the slope to the west of Lake Sibthorpe; and the ascent to the plateau near the Dålk Glacier. The final kilometre of the route before entering the plateau proper is marked by canes at 50–100 m intervals. There are also vehicle routes within the immediate station areas of Zhongshan and Progress and a short access route connecting Law-Racovita-Negoita to the main road. Vehicle access over ice-free surfaces within the Area is restricted to these existing roads.

Sea ice usually persists in the fjords and between the shore and numerous near-shore islands until late in the summer season. Ice conditions are variable at the eastern and western margins of the ASMA due to the presence of glaciers. Sea ice travel must take account of these conditions. In winter, sea ice access to Zhonghan and Progress may be feasible via the beach west of Zhongshan (69°22'30"S, 76°21'33"E) and the beach adjacent to Progress (69°22'44"S, 76°23'36"E), depending on highly variable ice conditions. From the sea ice, it may then be possible to access the main road south of the steep section south of Progress via either the easternmost bay of Nella Fjord (69°22'58"S, 76°22'44"E) or via Seal Cove (69°23'6"S, 76°23'49"E).

The Larsemann Hills can be approached via the plateau from Davis in the north-east (approximately 330 km) and Mawson in the west following the Lambert Glacier traverse route (approximately 2200 km). This comprises a caned route which turns north from a marker at 69°55'23"S, 76°29'49"E and then follows series of canes and drum beacons north to connect with the major access route on eastern Broknes.

4.5.2 Sea access

No anchorages or barge landings are designated for the Area due to the variable sea ice conditions. Vessels usually anchor approximately 5 nm offshore, depending on ice conditions, however vessels chartered by India have reached as close as 50 m away from the site of Bharati. The main sites used are:

- the bay ~250 m NNE of Zhongshan at 69°22'12"S, 76°22'15"E which consists of a ~15 m opening between rock outcrops, and a large flat area on shore for vehicle operations;
- the beach adjacent to Progress (69°22'44"S, 76°23'53"E); and
- the beach west of Zhongshan opening into Nella Fjord (69°22'30"S, 76°21'25"E).

Access from ships to the eastern shore of Broknes by small boat is difficult and sometimes impossible due to ice debris up to hundreds of metres off shore, blown by the prevailing north-easterly winds. Helicopters are therefore the only reliable means by which persons and supplies can be transported ashore quickly.

4.5.3 Air access

Designated helicopter landing and refuelling sites are to be used preferentially for general helicopter operations.

There are two cement helicopter-landing sites (69°22'44"S, 76°21'32"E) at Zhongshan. The southerly pad is 15 m in diameter and displays a painted map of Antarctica. The other pad is about 25 m to its north and is 20 m in diameter. Usually heavy helicopters (e.g. Ka-32) land at the larger pad and lighter aircraft (Dolphins and Squirrels) land at the pad to the south. Landings are usually made from the western side of Zhongshan travelling towards the main building from the direction of the lake and descending gradually above the lake. Pilots should avoid reducing altitude on the southern side of the lake where there is a 58 m hill with radars used for upper atmospheric physics studies.

Progress has two helicopter-landing sites. The site near the fuel storage is a flat area (~20×20 m) of ground cleared of large rocks, and is adjacent to a large depot of 200 L fuel drums. The other landing site is concrete and north-west of the largest building in the station area (Map E).

Bharati has a concrete helicopter landing pad at 69°24.40' S, 76°11.59' E – west of the main station building at an elevation of 38.5 m.

The Law-Racovita-Negoita helicopter-landing site (69°23'20"S, 76°22'55"E) is approximately 60 m east of the base. Helicopters would normally land facing into the north-east prevailing winds.

Small ski/wheeled fixed-wing aircraft operations have previously been conducted infrequently in the region and may be possible on the sea ice adjacent to the stations, though ice conditions vary annually, and the proximity to wildlife colonies make operations on the plateau preferable. Landings have been conducted near the site of the previous Russian runway, and proposed compacted snow airstrip at 69°25'59"S, 76°10'25"E. Prevailing winds from the north-east and a slight rise in the surface suggest that landing and taking off towards the north-east is preferable.

4.5.4 Pedestrian access

Pedestrian access within the ASMA is not restricted, but is to be conducted in accordance with the Environmental Code of Conduct at Appendix 1. Established routes should be used to minimise physical disturbance of the land surface and to prevent further track formation. Where surface modification is not apparent, the most direct route between points should be taken, with consideration given to avoiding repetitive use of the same route and avoiding vegetation and other sensitive features such as the margins of lakes and wet seepage areas.

4.6 Location of structures in or near the Area

4.6.1 Zhongshan (People's Republic of China)

Zhongshan is located on the north-eastern tip of eastern Broknes at 69°22'24"S, 76°22'40"E and approximately 11 m above sea level. The station was established in the 1988/89 summer season and has since been operated continuously to facilitate the conduct of year-round scientific research activity by the Chinese Antarctic program. As noted earlier, Zhongshan also acts as the logistical support base for Kunlun station and for scientific research in other inland areas such as Grove Mountains and Amery Ice Shelf. As such, Zhongshan is an important supporting centre for China's inland research in Antarctica.

Station infrastructure

The station supports approximately 60 personnel in summer and 20–25 in winter, with a maximum capacity of 76. The station consists of seven main and several smaller buildings (Map D). Vehicle access to Zhongshan is via the main road from the plateau, and a network of routes link the main buildings within the station area. Two concrete helicopter-landing pads are located west of the main station building (see Section 4.5.3).

Power, fuel delivery and storage

Electrical power is provided by diesel generators. Fuel is transferred from the ship by barge or pipeline, depending on sea ice conditions, and stored in bulk tanks at the southern end of the station area. Between 200 and 300 m^3 of fuel are delivered to the station each year.

To avoid activities associated with oil storage and transport damaging the Antarctic environment, a new oil storage facility was built at Zhongshan in 2011. It is located on the eastern side of the station, on the border area with Progress. The facility can store about 500 t of fuel and also houses oil spill prevention equipment. The old oil storage system is routinely checked and maintained. It will be relocated to the new oil storage area to reducing crowding in the station and to improve the safety of its operation.

Water and waste water

Water for generator cooling and shower facilities is drawn from a large tarn immediately west of the station area. Gray water is used to flush toilets after treatment in the powerhouse. Black water is collected and treated in the sewage station and discharged to the ocean after passing through a series of gravity-driven settlement tanks.

Solid waste management

Combustible wastes are separated and burnt in a high temperature, diesel-fuelled incinerator. The quantity of combustible wastes produced requires an incinerator burn every three to four days on average. The ash is collected and stored for return to China. Non-combustible wastes are sorted into waste categories and stored south of the powerhouse for removal by ship.

Vehicles

Vehicles are used in the immediate station area and to transport materials to other sites on eastern Broknes. Maintenance of vehicles, generators and instruments is undertaken in the powerhouse or vehicle workshop. Waste oil is returned to China.

Resupply

Resupply is generally undertaken once a year in summer. Cargo is brought to shore using either barges or sleds towed behind traverse vehicles.

Communications

Verbal communication with China is largely by short-wave radio, INMARSAT and, increasingly, Broadband Global Area Network (BGAN). BGAN has become the main communication equipment for sending and receiving telephone calls, faxes, emails and scientific data. HF radio is used for communications in the Prydz Bay area and VHF radio is used for local communications. A radio-telephone link also provides contact with Davis (and via Davis to anywhere in the world), and this is used for conveying meteorological data on a daily basis. A Very Small Aperture Terminal (VSAT) satellite communication system has also been installed. It establishes 24-hour uninterrupted communication between the station and China and provides communication services in voice, words and data. Iridium communication is retained for emergencies.

Science

Science programs conducted from Zhongshan are largely of a station-based nature and include meteorology, ozone monitoring, upper atmosphere physics, auroral observations, geomagnetic observations (some in cooperation with the Australian Antarctic program), gravimetric observations, seismology, NOAA polar orbiting satellite image processing, atmospheric chemistry, remote sensing, GPS measurement and human physiology. Activities away from the immediate station area during seasons with summer research programs include environmental evaluation and monitoring of snow and ice, soil, seawater, freshwater, mosses, lichen, wildlife, geology, glaciology and sea ice ecosystems. Inland traverses have also been undertaken to conduct geological, geodetic, glaciological and meteorite studies.

4.6.2 Progress (Russia)

Progress is located on eastern Broknes, approximately 1 km south of Zhongshan, at 69°22'44"S, 76°23'13"E. The station was established in 1988 on a plateau 300 m from the western shoreline of Dålk Bay. The station was occupied sporadically and shut down during the 1993/94 summer and reopened in the 1997/98 summer season for operation as a year-round research facility. The station is suited to accommodating up to 100 personnel during summer.

Station infrastructure

The main station complex includes:

– an office/living three-storey building intended for accommodation of 50 people (25 people during winter when each person is provided with a single living room), five scientific laboratories (meteorological, 'wet' and dry oceanographic, and for satellite imagery, geophysical and hydrobiological studies), living rooms, a station office, radio-information hub, medical unit, galley, food supply storage, dining/mess room, gym, sauna, toilets and shower cubicles; and

– a radio-electronic observation unit for monitoring the satellite constellation orbits of the GLONASS navigation system and geodetic monitoring of the tectonic Earth's crust movements from GPS and GLONASS satellite systems, a geomagnetic pavilion, and radar for monitoring the state of coastal ice and icebergs and for air traffic control of helicopters and low-flying airplanes.

The station was recently rebuilt within the existing station boundaries, and the renovated buildings equipped with waste treatment facilities. Following completion of the rebuilding program the old buildings and facilities are to be demolished and removed from the Antarctic Treaty area. The existing routes will mostly be used to access the site.

Vehicle access to Progress is via the main road from the plateau and the network of routes linking the main buildings within the station area. There are two helicopter pads at Progress station, one of them is only for fuel delivery (see Section 4.5.3). The other helipad is equipped with lighting, navigation support and flight control.

Progress is also equipped with a GPS safety system to track movements of personnel and vehicles within 100 km of the station, displaying them on a monitor in the radio room.

Power, fuel delivery and storage

The station has a power supply complex consisting of a diesel-electric power station with a total capacity of 900 kW, a garage for the repair and maintenance of up to eight transporters, an automatic boiler for station heating that uses fuel-lubricant waste, a water treatment facility including water distillers and purifying and utilisation systems for all sewage water from station facilities, and repair shops.

Diesel and aviation fuel storage facilities include fifteen 75 m^3 double-walled tanks, a metal rack for storage of drummed fuel and lubricants, a dedicated helipad for fuel delivery, and a fuel pipeline to the power station.

Water supply

Drinking water is drawn from a small lake to the north-west of the station area in summer, and from Progress Lake near the plateau in winter. Water from either lake is transported to the station in a water tank, and stored in a large tank adjacent to the main building. In past years some fresh water has also been obtained by melting sea ice and small bergs near the station. Washing water is produced by a reverse osmosis desalination unit which utilises slightly brackish water from Stepped Lake.

Waste management

Small, non-combustible wastes are separated and compacted for removal. Kitchen wastes and combustibles are burnt in a high temperature incinerator. Sewage water from the main building is treated by a biological unit and discharged into the bay. The garage/workshop/power plant building is also equipped with a sewage treatment unit. The smaller, old buildings do not have sewage treatment units; human waste is drummed and returned to Russia.

Metal scrap is stockpiled on the beach adjacent to the station, for return to Russia.

Vehicles

Progress is the major transportation base for supporting inland traverses, including traverses to Vostok station. As many as twelve Kässbohrer Pisten Bully Polar 300 transporters are used for this purpose.

Other types of vehicles are also used in the proximity of the station for collecting water and transferring fuel and wastes, and transporting personnel and equipment to Progress I and the plateau. Some vehicles are stationed at Progress I, and some aerodrome vehicles are stationed at small outpost to the south. Several large unused vehicles are also stored west of the main Progress station area.

Resupply

Resupply is conducted using the RV *Akademik Fedorov* during summer (December – March). Heavy cargoes delivered by ship are transported over the fast ice to Progress 4, a landing area on Stornes, for later transportation to Progress. Other cargo is transferred by Kamov Ka-32 helicopters.

Communications

HF communications are used to contact other Russian stations. VHF communications are used for local aircraft, ship and field operations. INMARSAT B and C and Iridium systems are used to contact Russia and occasionally, other Russian stations.

Science

Progress is primarily intended as a support base for inland geological and glaciological operations. Meteorological, hydrological, geomagnetic observations and sea ice monitoring are also undertaken.

4.6.3 Bharati (India)

Bharati is located between Thala Fjord and Quilty Bay, east of Stornes, at 69°24.41' S, 76°11.72' E, approximately 35 m above sea level. The station was established in the 2012/13 summer to facilitate year-round scientific research activity by the Indian Antarctic program. It is accessible by ship through Quilty Bay but does not have direct access to the mainland by vehicle during summer. During winters the plateau can be accessed through fast ice passages.

Station infrastructure

Bharati consists of one multi-purpose building, a satellite camp and a number of smaller containerised modules. It can support 47 personnel in the main building. A network of routes links the buildings within the station area. A concrete helicopter-landing pad is located west of the main building (see Section 4.5.3).

Power, fuel delivery and storage

Electrical power is provided by three diesel-fired combined heat and power generating units that are housed within the main building. Fuel to the units is supplied from a day tank adjacent to the power station, which in turn draws fuel automatically from the fuel farm through leak resistant pipelines over a distance of about 300 m.

Jet-A1 fuel is supplied annually from the ship to the fuel farm using leak resistant reinforced rubber hose. The fuel farm comprises13 double-hulled tank containers each of 24 000 L capacity and is located by the shore at 69°24.31'S, 76°11.84' E, at an elevation of 20 m. It is equipped with oil spill sensors and prevention equipment.

Delivery of fuel to the heat and power generating units, and at the helipad for helicopters and vehicles, is through a network of pipelines, and is automatically controlled through a microprocessor-based centralised building management system. Bharati uses LPG for cooking which is supplied in 10 to 14 kg gas bottles.

Water and waste management

Seawater is drawn from Quilty Bay (east coast) at a depth of about 12 m using submersible pumps, and is lifted to the main building through a network of insulated pipeline over a distance of about 300 m. Seawater is fed into a reverse osmosis plant; the filtered water is re-mineralised and used for drinking, bathing etc.

Wastewater is recycled and used for flushing the toilets. Water from the kitchen is passed through oil traps, and along with the wastewater from the toilets, is filtered and biologically treated. Water of bathing quality as per European standards is put back in Quilty Bay about 100 m downstream of the water intake point. All liquid waste, including from the kitchen, is passed through an oil trap and a slush trap, the products of which are collected in 200 L drums.

Solid waste is separated into biodegradable and non-degradable and collected in 200 L drums for removal.

Logistics

Tracked vehicles – Pisten Bullies and snow scooters – are used for transportation of personnel and materials around the station. The maintenance of vehicles, generators and instruments is undertaken in the vehicle workshop. Waste oil is collected in drums and returned to India.

Resupply is generally undertaken once a year in summer. Until mid-December, cargo is transported ashore using Pisten Bullies and trailers over fast ice. Voyages after the melting of the fast ice use flat bottom barges for carrying cargo.

Communications

HF communications are used to contact neighbouring stations. VHF communications are used for local aircraft, ship and field operations. Iridium open port system provides connectivity to the rest of the world through phone and fax.

Science

Although the station first became operational in March 2012, scientific studies began in 2005 and include environmental evaluation, monitoring of snow and ice, soil, seawater, freshwater, mosses, lichen, wildlife, geology, glaciology and sea ice ecosystems. Geomagnetic/ GPS observations started in 2007.

4.6.4 Law-Racovita-Negoita (Australia – Romania)

Law-Racovita-Negoita is located towards the southern end of eastern Broknes, approximately 1 km south of Progress and 2 km south of Zhongshan at 69°23'16"S, 76°22'47"E. The Base was established in the 1986/87 summer season.

Station infrastructure

Law-Racovita-Negoita consists of a prefabricated multi-purpose building, five fibre-glass huts and a small shed for ablutions. All wastes generated are removed.

Power, fuel delivery and storage

A small petrol generator is used to provide electrical power and operated only when required to charge batteries etc. A small solar panel mounted on the roof of the main hut charges batteries to power the HF and VHF radios. Gas is used for cooking and heating the main hut.

Water

Drinking and washing water is generally obtained during summer by collecting and melting snow from a nearby snow bank. Drinking water is also sometimes collected from a small tarn adjacent to the section of road connecting Law-Racovita-Negoita with the main route between north-eastern Broknes and the plateau.

Logistics

Law-Racovita-Negoita is variously supported by helicopter from Davis, by stations in the immediate area and from ships resupplying any of these facilities. Quad bikes are occasionally stationed at Law-Racovita-Negoita. They are used on designated access routes to support summer science programs.

Communications

Law-Racovita-Negoita is equipped with HF and VHF radios.

Science

Summer research projects have included studies of the area's glacial history, geology, geomorphology, hydrology, limnology and biology, and studies of human impacts.

4.6.5 Compacted snow runway site and associated facilities (Russia)

The proposed site of a runway approximately 5 km south of Progress and running SW-NE at 69°25'43"S, 76°20'36"E to 69°26'51"S, 76°17'18"E is accessed by the ice-free plateau access route and the beginning of the inland traverse route.

A compacted snow runway 3000 m long and 60 m wide is suitable for heavy-wheeled aircraft. The runway complex includes four sledge-based container modules, namely a diesel electric power station; an air traffic control station, including meteorological, radio and Internet access facilities; living accommodate for six people; and, at the distant end, an automatic weather station.

4.6.6 Minor structures

Progress I (Russia) – 69°24'02"S, 76°24'07"E

A facility on the route from the station to the airfield, Progress I supported a wintering population of 16 in 1987 and 1988. It was partially dismantled and removed in 1991-92. Currently Progress I serves as a place for the formation of inland traverses. One functional building remains at the site which is also used to store Russian airstrip construction equipment and fuel drums. Chinese traverse sleds, traverse vans, and a depot of fuel drums for traverse vehicles are stored in the immediate vicinity. Australia also maintains a depot of aviation fuel in the area at 69°23'56"S, 76°24'37"E. A further Russian hut and airstrip construction vehicle storage area is located on the southernmost rock outcrop west of the caned vehicle route to the plateau, approximately 1 km past Progress I at 69°24'43"S, 76°24'35"E.

Progress II (Russia) – 69°23'01"S, 76°22'26"E

Progress II is a hut supporting seasonal oceanographic and hydrobiological studies in Nella Fjord.

Progress III (Russia) – 69°24'25"S, 76°24'14"E

Progress III is a field camp supporting airborne geophysical studies. The camp consists of a skiway used by Antonov An-2, and accommodation for aircrew and aviation and geophysical teams.

Progress IV (Russia) – 69°25'27"S, 76°08'25"E

Progress IV is a site on the eastern edge of the Stornes ASPA used for the staging of heavy cargo delivered ship-shore across the fast ice. There is an over-snow exit from this location to the plateau and airfield.

Monitoring site

A long-term monitoring site approximately 250 m north-east of Law-Racovita-Negoita, was established in 1990 to measure the rate of surface lowering caused by wind abrasion and salt weathering. The site is situated on exposed coarse-grained yellow gneiss, and consists of 24 micro-erosion sites marked by painted yellow rings. The site should not be crossed on foot as this will affect the measurements of natural erosion. (The practice of using paint or other such permanent means of marking sites is discouraged, and collection of GPS locations is preferable.)

Monuments

A rock cairn laid on 8 February 1958 to mark the first Australian National Antarctic Research Expeditions (ANARE) visit to the Larsemann Hills is located at the highest point on Knuckey Island (69°23'12"S, 76°3'55"E) approximately 1.1 km north-west of Stornes. The cairn contains a note listing the names of the landing party.

The grave of Skurihin Andrei, a Russian expeditioner who died 7 July 1998, is located on the hill overlooking the northern shore of Seal Cove at 69°22'58"S, 76°23'49"E. The site comprises a headstone and steel chest surrounded by a low metal railing.

A memorial to a vice president of the Chinese Arctic and Antarctic Administration is located on the northern side of the hill at the northernmost tip of the eastern Broknes coast, north of Zhongshan. The cement monument contains some of the vice president's ashes.

Cache

A very small emergency food cache is contained within a plastic box at the summit of Blundell Peak on Stornes (69°6'14"S, 76°6'14"E), the highest peak in the Larsemann Hills.

4.7 Location of other protected areas in the vicinity

Stornes ASPA [#?] is contained within the ASMA. Entry to the ASPA and activities within it require a permit and must be carried out in accordance with the ASPA management plan.

ASPA 169, Amanda Bay (69°15'S, 76°49'59.9"E), lies 22 km north-east of the Larsemann Hills. Similarly, entry to the ASPA and activities within it require a permit and must be carried out in accordance with the ASPA management plan.

5. Zones within the Area

All activities within the ASMA are to comply with the provisions of the Protocol on Environmental Protection to the Antarctic Treaty and the Environmental Code of Conduct appended to this management plan. In addition, two zones assist in meeting the objectives for managing the area.

5.1 Facilities Zone

The construction of station buildings and associated infrastructure has caused the greatest impact on the Larsemann Hills environment. However, these impacts have been mostly restricted to the immediate station areas and their connecting access routes. As the lakes are recognised as the most important ecological feature of the area, and are susceptible to the impact of human activities undertaken within their catchment limits, a catchment-based approach is the most appropriate means of managing activities in the ASMA. The stations on Broknes are relatively well clustered; most station infrastructure is located in drainage basins that discharge into the sea.

To ensure that this situation is maintained, a Facilities Zone is defined within the ASMA boundary (Map B), and encompasses most of eastern Broknes. The boundary of the Facilities Zone is defined by the Dålk Glacier in the east, the sea in the north, the coast or western margin of impacted catchments in the west, and the ice plateau including the airstrip and access route in the south. The installation of infrastructure within the ASMA will generally be restricted to already impacted areas in the Facilities Zone. The building of new infrastructure elsewhere may be considered based on adequate scientific and/or logistic justification.

5.2 Magnetic Quiet Zone

Several magnetometers are operated at Zhongshan. A circular zone of 80 m radius is defined surrounding the induction magnetometer sensors located in the gully north of the station at 69°22'12"S, 76°22'8"E. A further zone is defined to a radius of 80 m from the magnetometer array centred at 69°22'22"S, 76°21'46"E (Map D), west of the water supply lakes. All ferrous materials are to be excluded from these zones to avoid contamination of magnetic field measurements. Permission to enter must also be obtained. A magnetic quiet zone in Grovnes is planned by India.

6. Management activities

Communication between Parties, between on-ground personnel, and between on-ground personnel and national offices is needed to successfully implement the ASMA management plan. Accordingly, Parties with research programs in the area commit to ensuring appropriate communication at both a national program and on-ground level. Annual discussions to review the implementation of the management plan will be held in conjunction with the annual meetings of the Council of Managers of National Antarctic Programs.

The relevant station and field base leaders will also meet on an annual basis (logistics permitting) and maintain verbal communications throughout the year on issues relevant to the management of the Larsemann Hills region.

6.1 Logistics, including facilities

- Any further track and infrastructure development in ice-free areas will be restricted to that part of eastern Broknes already modified by human activities and delimited by the Facilities Zone (see Section 5.1), unless a location outside the Zone is justified for adequate scientific and/or logistical reasons. This restriction shall not apply to facilities to be set up for ensuring the safety of field workers.

- Environmental impact assessment will proceed as required by Article 8 of the Madrid Protocol before constructing or modifying structures. The Parties proposing to conduct such activities will inform other Parties with active research programs in the area.

- The cooperative use of infrastructure will be promoted in preference to the construction of new facilities.

- The potential impacts of man-made structures on wilderness and aesthetics values will be considered and minimised by restricting new structures to already impacted areas wherever possible, and by locating structures so as to minimise their visibility from surrounding areas. Research may be needed to assist in the full evaluation of such impacts prior to construction activities.

- New fuel storage areas will be bunded and located outside lake catchment boundaries wherever possible. The appropriateness of the current location of fuel storage areas will be examined prior to the plan's next scheduled review.

- Vehicle routes that do not serve the aims of this management plan will be closed and the impacted area rehabilitated wherever possible.

- Options for cooperation in the transfer of personnel, supplies and fuel will be explored.

- As a minimum, waste disposal and management activities will comply with the provisions laid down in Annex II to the Madrid Protocol.

- Wastes and disused equipment will be removed from the Antarctic Treaty Area at the earliest opportunity.

- The Parties with active research programs in the area will jointly develop contingency plans for incidents with the potential to adversely impact on the environment.

- Regular and opportunistic collection of wind-dispersed litter will be undertaken.

- All equipment left in the field will be periodically reviewed for potential removal and its interim protection from wind dispersal and the like will be assessed.

- The rehabilitation of modified and disused sites will be investigated and progressed as appropriate.

6.2 Introduced species

- Parties active in the Larsemann Hills will:
  - Educate program personnel, including contractors, about the potential risks to the environment through the introduction of non-native species.
  - Ensure that personnel entering the ASMA have clean footwear – through, for example, boot cleaning procedures (preferably before departure for Antarctica) or the issue of new footwear.
  - Avoid shipping untreated sand, aggregate and gravel to the ASMA.
  - Collect and incinerate or remove from the region any soil or other organic matter found on cargo.

- o Remove from the region or contain within station buildings, any non-sterile soil previously shipped to the ASMA.

- o Remind program personnel of the Madrid Protocol obligation not to take non-sterile soil to Antarctica, or grow new plants or import plants for decorative purposes.

- o Contain within station buildings, any plants grown for food.

- o Give priority to incinerating or repatriating food waste.

- o Prevent station food, and food waste, from access by wildlife.

- o Develop protocols to avoid the biological contamination, or cross-contamination, of the Area's lakes, in particular those outside the Facilities Zone.

- o Undertake surveillance for introduced species.

- o Share information on the finding of any non-native species introduced through program operations and persisting in the Area – in order to obtain scientific and operational advice, if required, on appropriate eradication or containment actions.

- o Jointly implement these measures, where appropriate.

6.3 Wildlife disturbance

- The need to maintain appropriate separation distances from wildlife will be taken into account in the planning and conduct of activities in the area.

6.4 Data management

- The Parties with active research programs in the area will jointly develop, and provide input to, a database for recording relevant management information and metadata records to assist the planning and coordination of activities. Such data sharing will include geographic information, and involve the addition of regional place names to the SCAR *Composite Gazetteer of Antarctica.*

- Efforts will be made to increase knowledge of the environmental values of the ASMA and the impacts of human activities upon those values, and to apply this knowledge to the environmental management of the ASMA.

6.5 Science

- Cooperation with, and coordination of, scientific research will be undertaken wherever possible.

6.6 Monitoring

- The Parties with active research programs in the area will jointly undertake monitoring activities to evaluate the effectiveness of this management plan.

6.7 Monuments

- Activities will be managed to ensure the preservation of existing monuments where such action is considered desirable.

- The placement of further cairns or monuments outside the Facilities Zone is prohibited.

6.8 Exchange of information

- To enhance cooperation and the coordination of activities in the ASMA, to avoid duplication of activities and to facilitate the consideration of cumulative impacts, Parties active in the area will:

    - distribute to other such Parties details of activities that may have a bearing on the operation of this management plan (that is, proposals to withdraw from or establish new research activities, proposals to construct new facilities, information obtained regarding non-governmental visits etc.); and

- provide reports to the Committee for Environmental Protection on significant developments in the implementation of this management plan.
- Other Parties proposing to conduct activities in the region, including non-governmental groups, will inform at least one of the Parties active in the ASMA of their intentions – in the spirit of the aims and objectives of this management plan.

Appendix 1. Environmental Code of Conduct

This Code of Conduct is intended to provide general guidelines to help minimise environmental impacts when in the Larsemann Hills, particularly for activities undertaken away from station areas.

General principles

- The Antarctic environment is highly susceptible to the impacts of human activities, and as a general rule has much less natural ability to recover from disturbance than the environments of other continents; consider this when undertaking activities in the field.

- Everything taken into the field must be removed. This includes human wastes and also means avoiding the use or dispersal of foreign materials that are difficult to collect and remove. Strip down excess packaging before going off-station.

- The collection or disturbance of any biological or geological specimen or man-made artefact may only be undertaken with prior approval and, if required, in accordance with a permit.

- Details of all field activities (such as sample sites, field camps, depots, oil spills, markers, equipment etc.) including the national program contact should be accurately recorded for transfer to a management database.

Travel

- Some biological communities and geological formations are especially fragile, even when concealed by snow. Be alert and avoid such features when travelling.

- Restrict your vehicle and helicopter usage to essential tasks to minimise atmospheric emissions; track formation and physical disturbance of the land surface; impacts on biological communities; wildlife disturbance; and the potential for fuel spills. Over-flying lakes should be avoided.

- Restrict your vehicle use to designated ice-free routes and to the sea ice and plateau ice. Only access facilities using existing routes.

- Plan and undertake vehicle use with reference to the wildlife distances identified in this Code.

- Fully refuel vehicles and other equipment on station before departure, to reduce the need for refuelling in the field.

- Plan activities to avoid the need to refuel or change oil in windy conditions or in areas that might direct accidental spillage into lakes and on vegetation and other sensitive areas. Use fuel cans with nozzles/funnels.

- When travelling on foot, use established tracks and designated crossing points wherever possible.

- Avoid making new tracks. Where established tracks do not exist, use the most direct route that avoids vegetated areas and delicate geological formations (such as screes, sediments, streambeds and lake margins).

Wildlife

- Do not feed wildlife.

- Maintain appropriate distances from wildlife (see table).

- When moving on foot around wildlife, keep quiet, move slowly, and stay low to the ground – increase your distance if disturbance is evident.

*Distances at which disturbance may be expected to occur
when approaching wildlife on foot*

Species	Distance (metres)
Giant petrels and albatrosses, breeding / nesting	100 m
Emperor penguins (in colonies, huddling, moulting, with eggs or with chicks)	50 m
All other penguins (in colonies, moulting, with eggs or chicks)	30 m
Prions, petrels, skuas, on nests Seals with pups and seal pups on their own	20 m
Non breeding penguins and adult seals	5 m

*Distance at which disturbance may be expected to occur
when approaching wildlife using small vehicles (e.g. quads and skidoos)*

All wildlife	150 m

*Distance at which disturbance may be expected to occur
when approaching wildlife using tracked vehicles*

All wildlife	250 m

*Distances at which disturbance may be expected to occur
when approaching wildlife using aircraft*

Birds	**Vertical** *Single-engine helicopters* 2500 ft (~ 750 m) *Twin-engine helicopters* 5000 ft (~1500 m) **Horizontal** ½ nm (~930 m)
Seals	**Vertical and horizontal** Single-engine helicopters 2500 ft (~ 750 m) Twin-engine helicopters 5000 ft (~1500 m) Twin-engine, fixed-wing aircraft

	2500 ft (~750 m)

Field camps

- Use existing accommodation where possible.
- Locate campsites as far away as practicable from lake shores, streambeds, vegetated sites and wildlife, to avoid contamination and/or disturbance.
- Ensure that equipment and stores are properly secured at all times to prevent foraging by wildlife and dispersion by high winds.
- Collect all wastes produced at field camps, including human wastes and grey water, for return to station and subsequent treatment or disposal.
- Where possible utilise solar or wind powered generators to minimise fuel usage.

Fieldwork

- Meticulously clean all clothing and equipment before bringing it to Antarctica and before moving between sampling locations, to prevent contamination, cross-contamination and the introduction and spread of foreign organisms.
- Do not build cairns, and minimise the use of other objects to mark sites. Remove markers on completion of the related task.
- When permitted to collect samples, adhere to the sample size specified in your permit and take samples from the least conspicuous location possible.
- Use a drop sheet when sampling soils and backfill soil pits to prevent wind erosion and dispersal of deeper sediments.
- Take great care when handling chemicals and fuels, and ensure you have appropriate materials with you to catch and absorb spills.
- Minimise the use of liquid water and chemicals that could contaminate the isotopic and chemical record within lake and glacier ice.
- Meticulously clean all water and sediment sampling equipment to avoid cross-contamination between lakes.
- Avoid reintroducing large volumes of water obtained from lower in the water column, to prevent lake contamination, or toxic effects on the biota at the surface. Excess water or sediment should be returned to station for appropriate disposal or treatment.
- Ensure that sampling equipment is securely tethered, and leave nothing frozen into the ice that may cause later contamination.
- Do not wash, swim or dive in lakes. These activities contaminate the water body and physically disturb the water column, delicate microbial communities and sediments.

Note: The guidelines laid down in this Environmental Code of Conduct need not apply in cases of emergency.

Appendix 2: National program contact details

Australia

Australian Antarctic Division

Channel Highway

Kingston

Tasmania 7050

Australia

Phone:	+61 (03) 6232 3209
Fax:	+61 (03) 6232 3357
E-mail:	Tony.Fleming@aad.gov.au
	Sandra.Potter@aad.gov.au

People's Republic of China

Chinese Arctic and Antarctic Administration

1 Fuxingmenwai Street

Beijing 100860

People's Republic of China

Phone:	+86 10 6803 6469
Fax:	+86 10 6801 2776
Email:	chinare@263.net.cn

India

National Centre for Antarctic & Ocean Research

Sada, Vasco-da-Gama

Goa 403 804

India

Phone:	+91 832 2525 501
Fax:	+91 832 2525 502
	+91 832 2520 877
Email :	director@ncaor.org

Russian Federation

Russian Antarctic Expedition

Arctic and Antarctic Research Institute

38 Bering Street

199397 St Petersburg

Russia

Phone:	+7 812 337 3205
Fax:	+7 812 337 3205
Email:	lukin@aari.ru
	pom@aari.ru

Appendix 3: Larsemann Hills references and select bibliography

Antony, R., Krishnan, K.P., Thomas, S., Abraham, W.P. *and* Thamban, M. (2009). Phenotypic and molecular identification of *Cellulosimicrobium cellulans* isolated from Antarctic snow. *Antonie van Leeuwenhoek International Journal of General and Molecular Microbiology* 96(4):627.

Antony, R., Mahalinganathan, K., Krishnan, K.P. *and* Thamban, M. (2011). Microbial preference for different size classes of organic carbon: A study from Antarctic snow. *Environmental Monitoring and Assessment* DOI 10.1007/s10661-011-2391-1.

Antony, R., Mahalinganathan, K., Thamban, M. *and* Nair, S. (2011). Organic carbon in Antarctic snow: spatial trends and possible sources. *Environmental Science and Technology* 45(23):9944–9950, DOI: 10.1021/es203512t.

Antony, R., Thamban, M., Krishnan, K.P. *and* Mahalinganathan, K. (2010). Is cloud seeding in coastal Antarctica linked to biogenic bromine and nitrate variability in snow? *Environmental Research Letters* 5:014009, doi:10.1088/1748-9326/5/1/014009.

Asthana, R., Shrivastava, P.K., Beg, M.J. *and* Jayapaul, D. (2013). Grain size analysis of lake sediments from Schirmacher Oasis (Priyadarshini) and Larsemann Hills, East Antarctica. *Twenty Fourth Indian Antarctic Expedition 2003-2005, Ministry of Earth Sciences Technical Publication* No. 22, pp. 175-185.

Beg, M.J. *and* Asthana, R. (2013). Geological studies in Larsemann Hills, Ingrid Christensen Coast, East Antarctica. *Twenty Fourth Indian Antarctic Expedition 2003-2005, Ministry of Earth Sciences Technical Publication* No. 22 pp. 363-367.

Bian, l., Lu, L. *and* Jia, P. (1996). Characteristics of ultraviolet radiation in 1993-1994 at the Larsemann Hills, Antarctica. *Antarctic Research (Chinese edition)* 8(3):29-35.

Burgess, J., Carson, C., Head, J. *and* Spate, A. (1997). Larsemann Hills – not heavily glaciated during the last glacial maximum. *The Antarctic Region: Geological Evolution and Processes.* Pp. 841-843.

Burgess, J. *and* Gillieson, D. (1988). On the thermal stratification of freshwater lakes in the Snowy Mountains, Australia, and the Larsemann Hills, Antarctica. *Search* 19(3):147-149.

Burgess, J. S. *and* Kaup, E. (1997). Some aspects of human impacts on lakes in the Larsemann Hills, Princess Elizabeth Land, Eastern Antarctica. In: Lyons, W., Howard-Williams, C. and Hawes, I. (Eds). *Ecosystem Process in Antarctic Ice-free Landscapes.* A.A. Balkema Publishers, Rotterdam. Pp. 259-264.

Burgess, J.S., Spate, A.P. *and* Norman, F.I. (1992). Environmental impacts of station development in the Larsemann Hills, Princess Elizabeth Land, Antarctica. *Journal of Environmental Management* 36:287-299.

Burgess, J.S., Spate, A.P. *and* Shevlin, J. (1994). The onset of deglaciation in the Larsemann Hills, East Antarctica. *Antarctic Science* 6(4):491-495.

Carson, C.J. *and* Grew, E.S. (2007). *Geology of the Larsemann Hills Region, Antarctica.* First Edition (1:25 000 scale map). Geoscience Australia, Canberra.

Carson, C.J., Dirks, P.G.H.M., Hand, M., Sims, J.P. *and* Wilson, C.J.L. (1995). Compressional and extensional tectonics in low-medium pressure granulites from the Larsemann Hills, East Antarctica. *Geological Magazine* 132(2):151-170.

Carson, C.J., Dirks, P.H. G.M. *and* Hand, M. (1995). Stable coexistence of grandidierite and kornerupine during medium pressure granulite facies metamorphism. *Mineralogical Magazine* 59:327-339.

Carson, C. J., Fanning, C.M. *and* Wilson, C.J. L. (1996). Timing of the Progress Granite, Larsemann Hills: additional evidence for Early Palaeozoic orogenisis within the east Antarctic Shield and implications for Gondwana assembly. *Australian Journal of Earth Sciences* 43:539-553.

China (1996). Oil spill contingency plan for Chinese Zhongshan Station in Antarctica. *Information Paper #87, ATCM XXI*, Christchurch, New Zealand.

Cromer, L., Gibson, J.A.E., Swadling, K.M. *and* Hodgson, D.A. (2006). Evidence for a lacustrine faunal refuge in the Larsemann Hills, East Antarctica, during the Last Glacial Maximum. *Journal of Biogeography* 33:1314-1323.

Dartnall, H.J.G. (1995). Rotifers and other aquatic invertebrates from the Larsemann Hills, Antarctica. *Papers and Proceedings of the Royal Society of Tasmania* 129:17-23.

Dirks, P.H.G.M., Carson, C.J. *and* Wilson, C.J.L. (1993). The deformational history of the Larsemann Hills, Prydz Bay: The importance of the Pan-African (500 Ma) in East Antarctica. *Antarctic Science* 5(2):179-192.

Ellis-Evans, J.C., Laybourn-Parry, J., Bayliss, P.R. *and* Perriss, S.J. (1998). Physical, chemical and microbial community characteristics of lakes of the Larsemann Hills, Continental Antarctica. *Archiv fur Hydrobiologia* 141(2):209-230.

Ellis-Evans, J.C., Laybourn-Parry, J., Bayliss, P.R. *and* Perriss, S.T. (1997). Human impact on an oligotrophic lake in the Larsemann Hills. In: Battaglia, B., Valencia, J. and Walton, D.W.H. (Eds). *Antarctic communities: Species, structure and survival*. Cambridge University Press, Cambridge, UK. Pp. 396-404.

Fedorova, I.V., Savatyugin, L.M., Anisimov, M.A. *and* Azarova, N.S. (2010). Change of the Schirmacher oasis hydrographic net (East Antarctic, Queen Maud Land) under deglaciation conditions. *Ice and Glacier* 3(111):63-70.

Fedorova, I.V., Verkulich, S.R., Potapova, T.M. *and* Chetverova, A.A. (2011). Postglacial estimation of the Schirmacher oasis lakes (East Antarctic) on the basis of hydrologo-geochemical and paleogeographical investigation. In: Kotlyakov, V.M. (Ed.). *Polar Cryosphere and Land Hydrology*. Pp. 242-251.

Gasparon, M. (2000). Human impacts in Antarctica: Trace element geochemistry of freshwater lakes in the Larsemann Hills, East Antarctica. *Environmental Geography* 39(9):963-976.

Gasparon, M., Lanyon, R., Burgess, J.S. *and* Sigurdsson, I.A. (2002). The freshwater lakes of the Larsemann Hills, East Antarctica: chemical characteristics of the water column. *ANARE Research Notes* 147: 1-28.

Gasparon, M. *and* Matschullat, J. (2006). Geogenic sources and sink trace metals in the Larsemann Hills, East Antarctica: Natural processes and human impact. *Applied Geochemistry* 21(2):318-334.

Gasparon, M. *and* Matschullat, J. (2006). Trace metals in Antarctic ecosystems: Results from the Larsemann Hills, East Antarctica. *Applied Geochemistry* 21(9):1593-1612.

Gibson, J.A.E. *and* Bayly, I.A.E. (2007). New insights into the origins of crustaceans of Antarctic lakes. *Antarctic Science* 19(2):157-164.

Gibson, J.A.E., Dartnall, H.J.G. *and* Swadling, K.M. (1998). On the occurrence of males and production of ephippial eggs in populations of *Daphniopsis studeri* (Cladocera) in lakes in the Vestfold and Larsemann Hills, East Antarctica. *Polar Biology* 19:148-150.

Gillieson, D. (1990). Diatom stratigraphy in Antarctic freshwater lakes. *Quaternary Research in Antarctica: Future Directions*, 6-7 December 1990. Pp. 55-67.

Gillieson, D. (1991). An environmental history of two freshwater lakes in the Larsemann Hills, Antarctica. *Hydrobiologia* 214:327-331.

Gillieson, D., Burgess, J., Spate, A. *and* Cochrane, A. (1990). An atlas of the lakes of the Larsemann Hills, Princess Elizabeth Land, Antarctica. *ANARE Research Notes* 74:1-73.

Goldsworthy, P.M., Canning, E.A. *and* Riddle, M.J. (2002). Contamination in the Larsemann Hills, East Antarctica: Is it a case of overlapping activities causing cumulative impacts? In: Snape, I. and Warren, R. (Eds). *Proceedings of the 3rd International Conference: Contaminants in Freezing Ground. Hobart, 14-18 April 2002*, pp. 60-61.

Goldsworthy, P.M., Canning, E.A. *and* Riddle, M.J. (2003). Soil and water contamination in the Larsemann Hills, East Antarctica. *Polar Record* 39(211):319-337.

Grew, E.S., McGee, J.J., Yates, M.G., Peacor, D.R., Rouse, R.C, Huijsmans, J.P.P., Shearer, C.K., Wiedenbeck, M., Thost, D.E. *and* Su, S.-C. (1998). Boralsilite ($Al_{16}B_6Si_2O_{37}$): A new mineral related to sillimanite from pegmatites in granulite-facies rocks. *American Mineralogist* 83:638-651.

Grew, E.S, Armbruster, T., Medenbach, O., Yates, M.G. *and* Carson, C.J. (2006). Stornesite-(Y), (Y, Ca)$\square_2$Na$_6$(Ca,Na)$_8$(Mg,Fe)$_{43}$(PO$_4$)$_{36}$, the first terrestrial Mg-dominant member of the fillowite group, from granulite-facies paragneiss in the Larsemann Hills, Prydz Bay, East Antarctica. *American Mineralogist* 91:1412-1424.

Grew, E.S, Armbruster, T., Medenbach, O., Yates, M.G. *and* Carson, C.J. (2007). Chopinite, [(Mg,Fe)$_3$$\square$](PO$_4$)$_2$, a new mineral isostructural with sarcopside, from a fluorapatite segregation in granulite-facies paragneiss, Larsemann Hills, Prydz Bay, East Antarctica. *European Journal of Mineralogy* 19:229-245.

Grew, E.S, Armbruster, T., Medenbach, O., Yates, M.G. *and* Carson, C.J. (2007). Tassieite, (Na,$\square$)Ca$_2$(Mg,Fe^{2+},Fe^{3+})$_2$(Fe^{3+},Mg)$_2$(Fe^{2+},Mg)$_2$(PO$_4$)$_6$(H$_2$O)$_2$, a new hydrothermal wicksite-group mineral in fluorapatite nodules from granulite-facies paragneiss in the Larsemann Hills, Prydz Bay, East Antarctica. *The Canadian Mineralogist* 45:293-305.

Grew, E.S., Graetsch, H., Pöter, B., Yates, M.G., Buick, I., Bernhardt, H.-J., Schreyer, W., Werding, G., Carson, C.J. *and* Clarke, G.L. (2008). Boralsilite, $Al_{16}B_6Si_2O_{37}$, and "boron-mullite": compositional variations and associated phases in experiment and nature. *American Mineralogist* 93:283-299.

He, J. *and* Chen, B. (1996). Vertical distribution and seasonal variation in ice algae biomass in coastal sea ice off Zhongshan Station, East Antarctica. *Antarctic Research (Chinese)* 7(2):150-163.

Hodgson, D.A., Noon, P.E., Vyvermann, W., Bryant, C.L., Gore, D.B., Appleby, P., Gilmour, M., Verleyen, E., Sabbe, K., Jones, V.J., Ellis-Evans, J.C. *and* Wood, P.B. (2001). Were the Larsemann Hills ice-free through the Last Glacial Maximum? *Antarctic Science* 13(4):440-454.

Hodgson, D.A., Verleyen, E., Sabbe. K., Squier, A.H., Keely, B.J., Leng, M.J., Saunders, K.M. *and* Vtyverman, W. (2005). Late Quaternary climate-driven environmental change in the Larsemann Hills, East Antarctica, multi-proxy evidence from a lake sediment core. *Quaternary Research* 64:83-99.

Jawak, S.D. *and* Luis, A.J. (2011). Applications of WorldView-2 satellite data for Extraction of Polar Spatial Information and DEM of Larsemann Hills, East Antarctica . International Conference on Fuzzy Systems and Neural Computing. Pp. 148-151

Kaup, E. *and* Burgess, J.S. (2002). Surface and subsurface flows of nutrients in natural and human impacted lake catchments on Broknes, Larsemann Hills, Antarctica. *Antarctic Science* 14(4):343-352.

Krishnan, K.P., Sinha, R.K., Kumar, K., Nair, S. *and* Singh, S.M. (2009). Microbially mediated redox transformation of manganese (II) along with some other trace elements: a case study from Antarctic lakes. *Polar Biology* 32:1765-1778.

Li, S. (1994). A preliminary study on aeolian landforms in the Larsemann Hills, East Antarctica. *Antarctic Research (Chinsese edition)* 6(4):23-31.

Mahalinganathan, K., Thamban, M. Laluraj, C.M. *and* Redkar, B.L. (2012). Relation between surface topography and sea-salt snow chemistry from Princess Elizabeth Land, East Antarctica. *The Cryosphere* 6:505-515.

Marchant, H. J., Bowman, J., Gibson, J., Laybourn-Parry, J. *and* McMinn, A. (2002). Aquatic microbiology: the ANARE perspective. In: Marchant, H.J., Lugg, D.J. and Quilty, P.G. (Eds). *Australian Antarctic Science: The first 50 years of ANARE*. Australian Antarctic Division, Hobart. Pp. 237-269.

McMinn, A. *and* Harwood, D. (1995). Biostratigraphy and palaeoecology of early Pliocene diatom assemblages from the Larsemann Hills, eastern Antarctica. *Antarctic Science* 7(1):115-116.

Miller, W.R., Heatwole, H., Pidgeon, R.W.J. *and* Gardiner, G.R. (1994). Tardigrades of the Australian Antarctic territories: the Larsemann Hills East Antarctica. *Transactions of the American Microscopical Society* 113(2):142-160.

Pahl, B.C., Terhune, J.M. *and* Burton, H.R. (1997). Repertoire and geographic variation in underwater vocalisations of Weddell Seals (*Leptonychotes weddellii*, Pinnipedia: Phocidae) at the Vestfold Hills, Antarctica. *Australian Journal of Zoology* 45:171-187.

Quilty, P.G. (1990). Significance of evidence for changes in the Antarctic marine environment over the last 5 million years. In: Kerry, K.R. and Hempel, G. (Eds). *Antarctic Ecosystems: Ecological change and conservation*. Springer-Verlag, Berlin. Pp. 3-8.

Quilty, P.G. (1993). Coastal East Antarctic Neogene sections and their contribution to the ice sheet evolution debate. In: Kennett, J.P. and Warnke, D. (Eds). *The Antarctic Paleo environment: A perspective on global change*. *Antarctic Research Series* 60:251-264.

Quilty, P.G., Gillieson, D., Burgess, J., Gardiner, G., Spate, A. *and* Pidgeon, R. (1990). *Ammophidiella* from the Pliocene of Larsemann Hill, East Antarctica. *Journal of Foraminiferal Research* 20(1):1-7.

Ren, L., Zhao, Y., Liu, X. *and* Chen, T. (1992). Re-examination of the metamorphic evolution of the Larsemann Hills, East Antarctica. In: Yoshida, Y., Kaminuma, K. and Shiraishi, K. (Eds). *Recent Progress in Antarctic Earth Science*. Terra Scientific Publishing, Tokyo, Japan. Pp.145-153.

Ren, L., Grew, E.S., Xiong, M. *and* Ma, Z. (2003). Wagnerite-*Ma5bc*, a new polytype of $Mg_2(PO_4)(F,OH)$, from granulite-facies paragneiss, Larsemann Hills, Prydz Bay, East Antarctica. *The Canadian Mineralogist* 41:393-411.

Riddle, M.J. (1997). The Larsemann Hills, at risk from cumulative impacts, a candidate for multi-nation management. *Proceedings of the IUCN Workshop on Cumulative Impacts in Antarctica*. Washington DC, USA. 18-21 September 1996. Pp. 82-86.

Russia (1999). Initial Environmental Evaluation Compacted Snow Runway at the Larsemann Hills. *Information Paper #79 Corr.2, ATCM XXIII*, Lima, Peru.

Sabbe, K., Verleyen, E., Hodgson, D.A. *and* Vyvermann, W. (2003). Benthic diatom flora of freshwater and saline lakes in the Larsemann Hills and Rauer Islands (East Antarctica). *Antarctic Science* 15:227-248.

Seppelt, R.D. (1986). Bryophytes of the Vestfold Hills. In: Pickard, J. (Ed.) *Antarctic Oasis: Terrestrial environments and history of the Vestfold Hills*. Academic Press, Sydney. Pp. 221-245.

Shrivastava, P.K., Asthana, R., Beg, M.J. and Singh, J. (2009). Climatic fluctuation imprinted in quartz grains of lake sediments from Schirmacher Oasis and Larsemann Hills area, East Antarctica. *Indian Journal of Geosciences* 63(1):81 – 87.

Shrivastava, P.K., Asthana, R., Beg, M.J. and Ravindra, R. (2011). Ionic characters of lake water of Bharati Promontory, Larsemann Hills, East Antarctica. *Journal of the Geological Society of India* 78(3):217-225.

Singh, A.K., Jayashree, B., Sinha, A.K., Rawat, R., Pathan, B.M. *and* Dhar, A. (2011). Observation of near conjugate high latitude substorm and their low latitude implications. *Current Science* 101(8):1073-1078.

Singh, A.K., Sinha, A.K., Rawat, R., Jayashree, B., Pathan, B.M. *and* Dhar, A. (2012). A broad climatology of very high latitude substorms. *Advances in Space Research* 50(11):1512-1523.

Singh, S.M., Nayaka, S. and Upreti, D.K. (2007). Lichen communities in Larsemann Hills, East Antarctica. *Current Science* 93(12):1670-1672.

Spate, A. P., Burgess, J. S. *and* Shevlin, J. (1995). Rates of rock surface lowering, Princess Elizabeth Land, Eastern Antarctica. *Earth Surface Processes and Landforms* 20:567-573.

Stuwe, K. *and* Powell, R. (1989). Low-pressure granulite facies metamorphism in the Larsemann Hills area, East Antarctica: Petrology and tectonic implications for the evolution of the Prydz Bay area. *Journal of Metamorphic Geology* 7(4):465-483.

Stuwe, K., Braun, H.M. *and* Peer, H. (1989). Geology and structure of the Larsemann Hills area, Prydz Bay, East Antarctica. *Australian Journal of Earth Sciences* 36:219-241.

Thamban, M. *and* Thakur, R.C. (2013). Trace metal concentrations of surface snow from Ingrid Christensen Coast, East Antarctica – Spatial variability and possible anthropogenic contributions. *Environmental Monitoring and Assessment* 184(4):2961-2975.

Thamban, M., Laluraj, C.M., Mahalinganathan, K., Redkar, B.L., Naik, S.S. *and* Shrivastava, P.K. (2010). Glacio-chemistry of surface snow from the Ingrid Christensen Coast, East Antarctica, and its environmental implications. *Antarctic Science* 22(4):435–441.

Wadoski, E.R., Grew, E.S. *and* Yates, M.G. (2011). Compositional evolution of tourmaline-supergroup minerals from granitic pegmatites in the Larsemann Hills, East Antarctica. *The Canadian Mineralogist* 49:381-405.

Walton, D. H., Vincent, W. F., Timperley, M.H., Hawes, I. *and* Howard-Williams, C. (1997). Synthesis: Polar deserts as indicators of change. In: Lyons, Howard-Williams and Hawes (Eds). *Ecosystem Processes in Antarctic Ice-free Landscapes*. Balkema, Rotterdam. Pp. 275-279.

Wang, Z. (1991). Ecology of *Catharacta maccormicki* near Zhongshan Station in Larsemann Hills, East Antarctica. *Antarctic Research (Chinese edition)* 3(3):45-55.

Wang, Z. *and* Norman, F.I. (1993). Foods of the south polar skua *Catharacta maccormicki* in the Larsemann Hills, East Antarctica. *Polar Biology* 13:255-262.

Wang, Z. *and* Norman, F.I. (1993). Timing of breeding, breeding success and chick growth in south polar skuas (*Catharacta maccormicki*) in the Eastern Larsemann Hills. *Notornis* 40(3):189-203.

Wang, Z., Norman, F.I., Burgess, J.S., Ward, S.J., Spate, A.P. *and* Carson, C.J. (1996). Human influences on breeding populations of south polar skuas in the eastern Larsemann Hills, Princess Elizabeth Land, East Antarctica. *Polar Record* 32(180):43-50.

Wang, Y., Liu, D., Chung, S.L., Tong, L. *and* Ren, L. (2008). SHRIMP zircon age constraints from the Larsmann Hills region, Prydz Bay, for a late Mesoproterozoic to early Neoproterozoic tectono-thermal event in East Antarctica. *American Journal of Science* 308:573–617.

Waterhouse, E.J. (1997). Implementing the protocol on ice free land: The New Zealand experience at Vanda Station. In: Lyons, Howard-Williams and Hawes (Eds.). *Ecosystem processes in Antarctic ice-free landscapes*. Balkema, Rotterdam. Pp. 265-274.

Whitehead, M.D. *and* Johnstone, G.W. (1990). The distribution and estimated abundance of Adelie penguins breeding in Prydz Bay, Antarctica. *Proceedings of the NIPR Symposium on Polar Biology* 3:91-98.

Woehler, E.J. *and* Johnstone, G.W. (1991). Status and conservation of the seabirds of the Australian Antarctic Territory. *ICBP Technical Publications* 11:279-308.

Zhao, Y., Liu, X, Song, B., Zhang, Z., Li, J., Yao, Y. *and* Wang, Y. (1995). Constraints on the stratigraphic age of metasedimentary rocks from the Larsemann Hills, East Antarctica: Possible implications for Neoproterozoic tectonics. *Precambrian Research* 75:175-188.

Zhao, Y., Song, B., Wang, Y., Ren, L., Li, J. *and* Chen, T. (1992). Geochronology of the late granite in the Larsemann Hills, East Antarctica. In: Yoshida, Y., Kaminuma, K. and Shiraishi, K. (Eds). *Recent Progress in Antarctic Earth Science*. Terra Scientific Publishing Co., Tokyo. Pp. 155-161.

Appendix 4: Larsemann Hills maps

Map A. Topography and physical features
Map B. Management zones and ice free areas
Map C. Detail of northern Broknes
Map D. Zhongshan station
Map E. Progress station

Detailed maps of the region are available via the Australian Antarctic Data Centre website at:
http://aadc-maps.aad.gov.au/aadc/mapcat/search_mapcat.cfm
(Map References # 13130 and 13135

Map A: Larsemann Hills Antarctic Specially Managed Area No.6, Ingrid Christensen Coast, East Antarctica
Topography and Physical Features

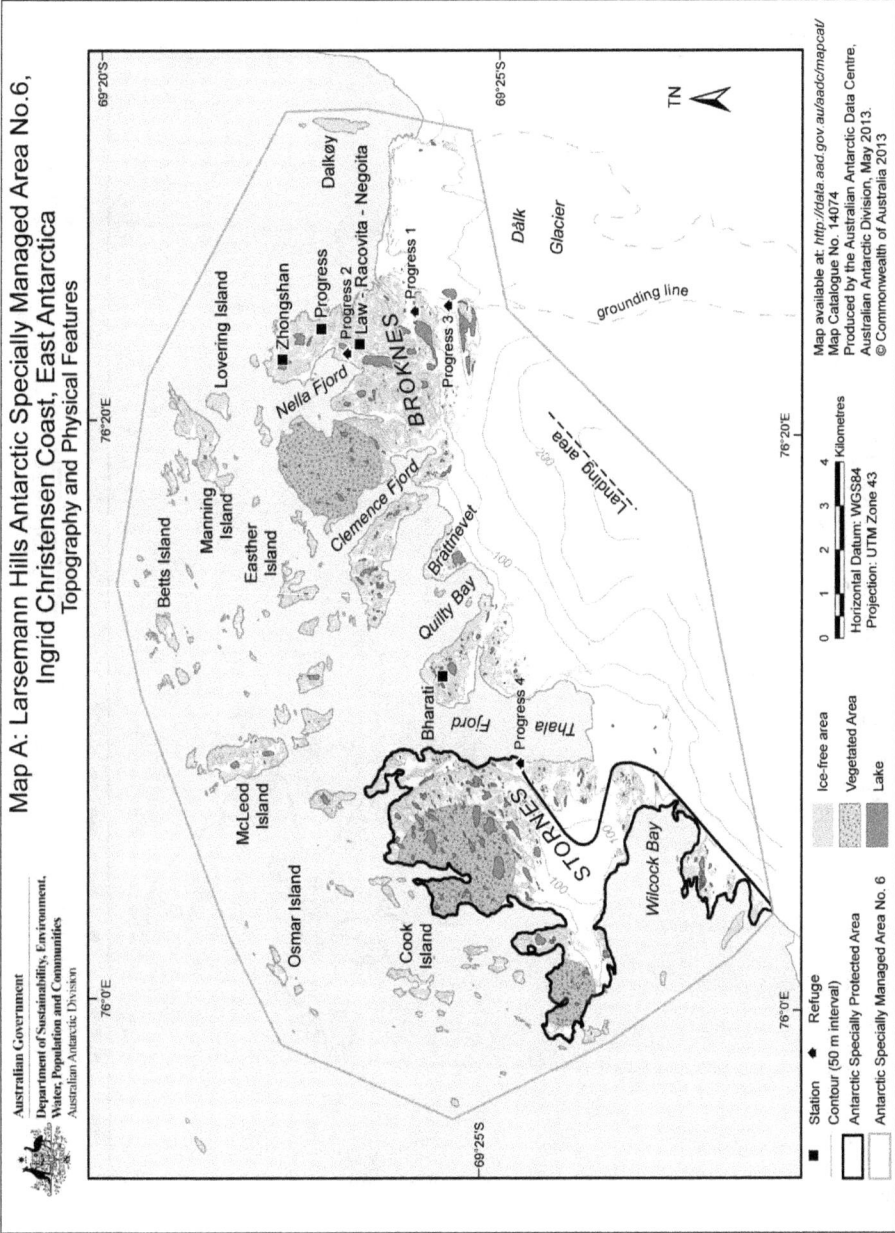

Australian Government

Department of Sustainability, Environment, Water, Population and Communities
Australian Antarctic Division

Station
Refuge
Contour (50 m interval)
Antarctic Specially Protected Area
Antarctic Specially Managed Area No. 6

Ice-free area
Vegetated Area
Lake

Horizontal Datum: WGS84
Projection: UTM Zone 43

Kilometres

Map available at: *http://data.aad.gov.au/aadc/mapcat/*
Map Catalogue No. 14074
Produced by the Australian Antarctic Data Centre,
Australian Antarctic Division, May 2013.
© Commonwealth of Australia 2013

305

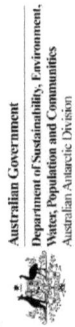

Map B: Larsemann Hills Antarctic Specially Managed Area No.6, Ingrid Christensen Coast, East Antarctica Management Zones

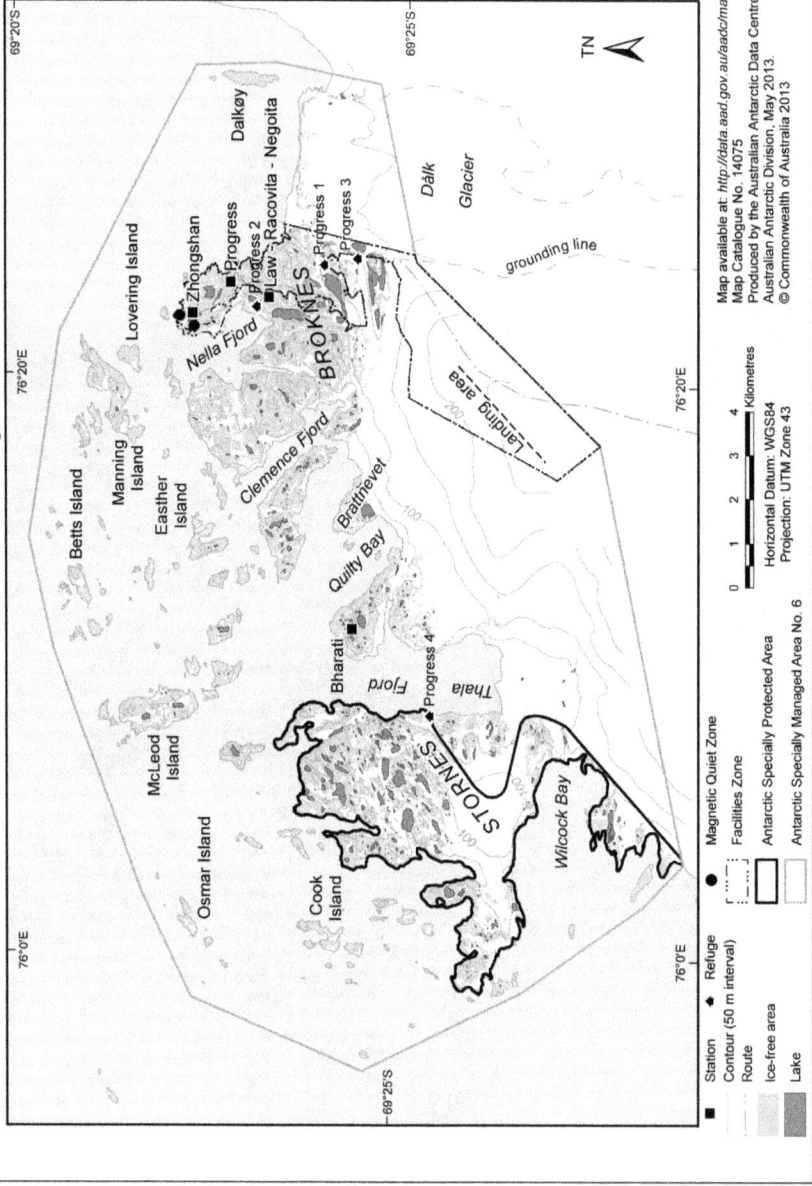

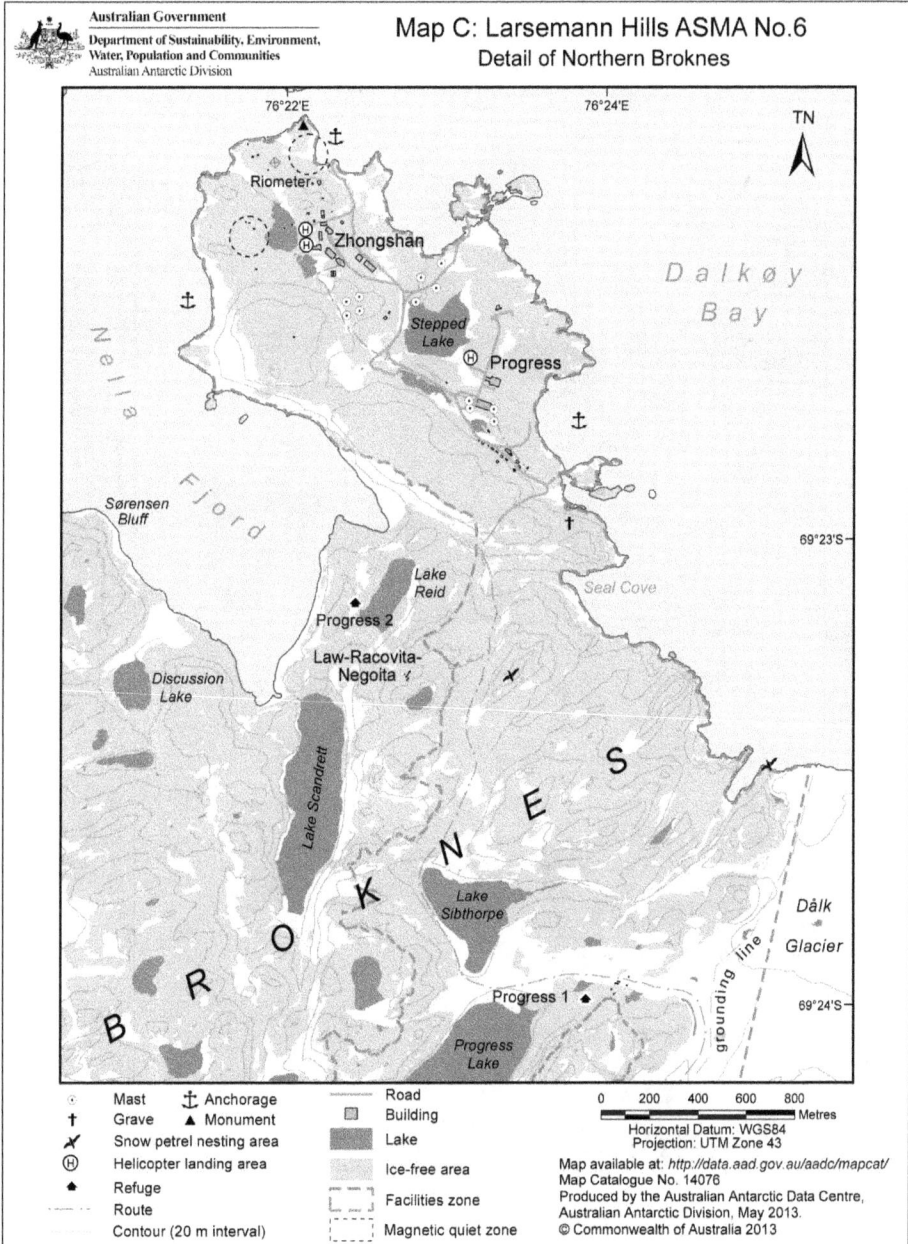

Australian Government
Department of Sustainability, Environment,
Water, Population and Communities
Australian Antarctic Division

Map C: Larsemann Hills ASMA No.6
Detail of Northern Broknes

76°22'E

76°24'E

TN

Riometer

Zhongshan

D a l k ø y
B a y

N
e
l
l
a

Stepped
Lake

Progress

F
j
o
r
d

Sørensen
Bluff

69°23'S

Seal Cove

Lake
Reid

Progress 2

Law-Racovita-
Negoita

Discussion
Lake

Lake Scandrett

B R O K N E S

Lake
Sibthorpe

Dålk
Glacier

Progress 1

grounding line

69°24'S

B

Progress
Lake

⊙	Mast	⌕	Anchorage
†	Grave	▲	Monument
✗	Snow petrel nesting area		
Ⓗ	Helicopter landing area		
◆	Refuge		
-----	Route		
	Contour (20 m interval)		

Road
Building
Lake
Ice-free area
Facilities zone
Magnetic quiet zone

0   200   400   600   800
Metres

Horizontal Datum: WGS84
Projection: UTM Zone 43
Map available at: *http://data.aad.gov.au/aadc/mapcat/*
Map Catalogue No. 14076
Produced by the Australian Antarctic Data Centre,
Australian Antarctic Division, May 2013.
© Commonwealth of Australia 2013

Australian Government

**Department of Sustainability, Environment,
Water, Population and Communities**

Australian Antarctic Division

Map D: Larsemann Hills Antarctic Specially Managed Area No. 6
Zhongshan Station

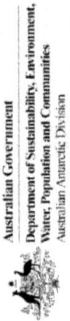

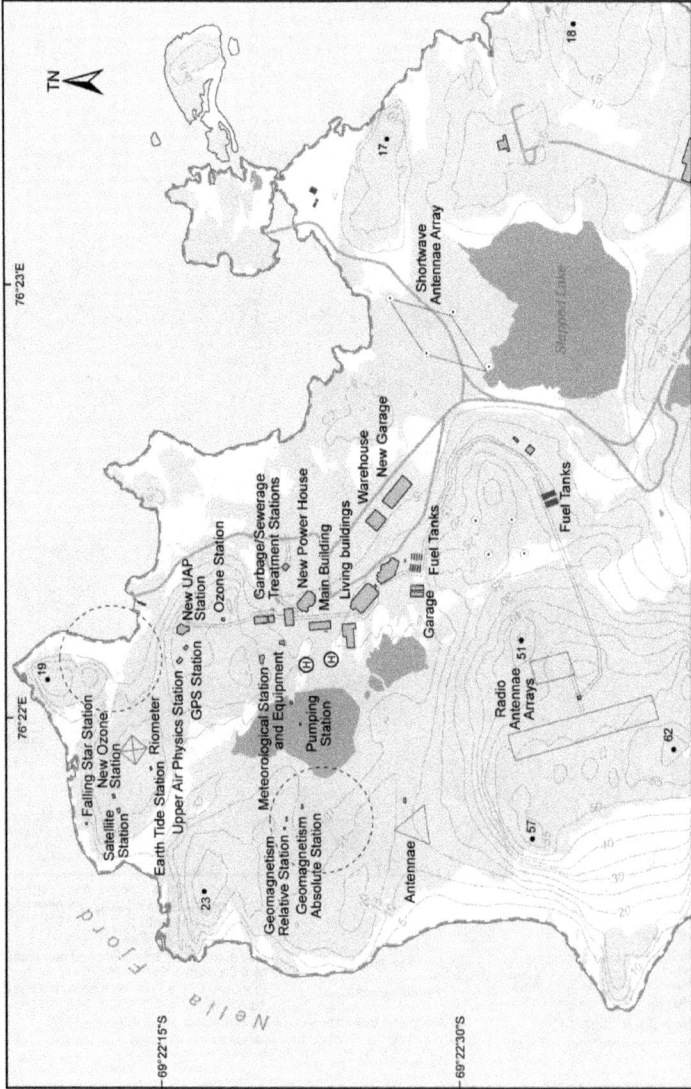

Spot elevation (metres)

Mast

Helicopter landing area

Contour (5 metre interval)

Road

Cable trays

Building

Lake

Ice-free area

Facilities zone

Magnetic quiet zone

Horizontal Datum: WGS84
Projection: UTM Zone 43

Map Available at: *http://data.aad.gov.au/aadc/mapcat/*
Map Catalogue No. 14077
Produced by the Australian Antarctic Data Centre,
Australian Antarctic Division, May 2013.
© Commonwealth of Australia 2013

308

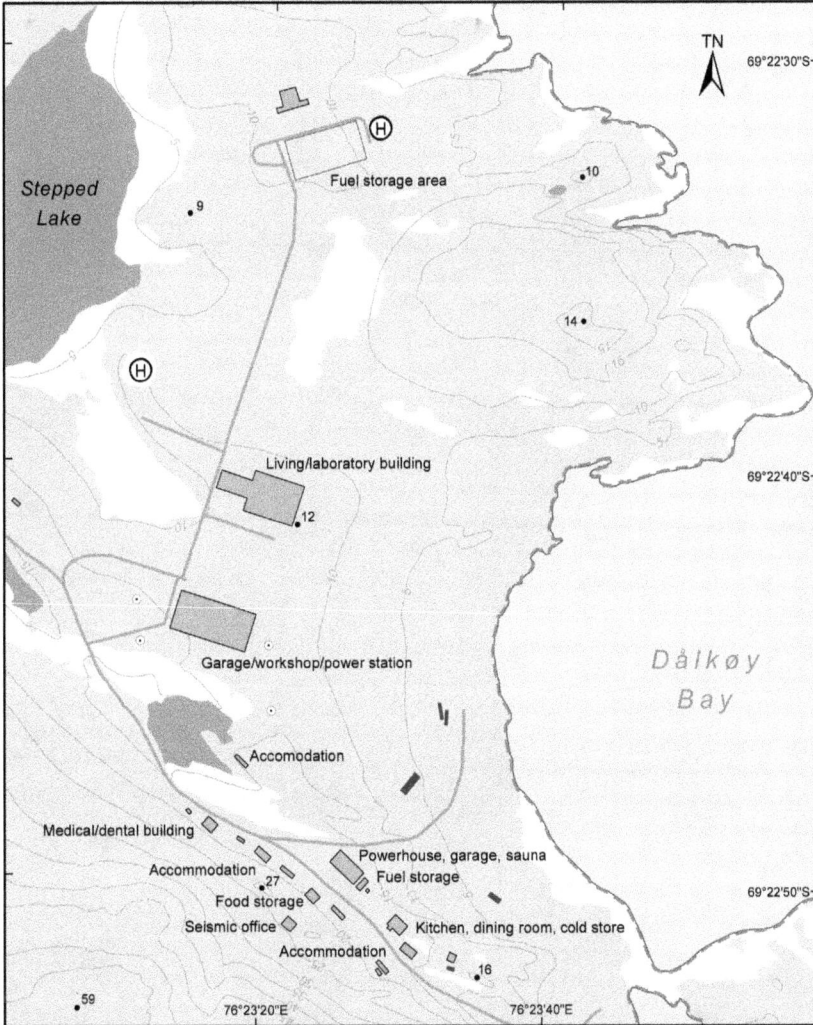

Map E: Larsemann Hills Antarctic Specially Managed Area No. 6 — Progress Station

PART III

Opening and Closing Addresses and Reports

1. Reports by Depositaries and Observers

Report of the Depositary Government of the Antarctic Treaty and its Protocol in accordance with Recommendation XIII-2

Information Paper submitted by the United States

This report covers events with respect to the Antarctic Treaty and the Protocol on Environmental Protection to the Antarctic Treaty.

In the past year, there have been no accessions to the Treaty or the Protocol. There are fifty (50) Parties to the Treaty and thirty-five (35) Parties to the Protocol.

The following countries have provided notification that they have designated the persons so noted as Arbitrators in accordance with Article 2(1) of the Schedule to the Protocol:

Bulgaria	Mrs. Guenka Beleva	30 July 2004
Chile	Amb. María Teresa Infante	June 2005
	Amb. Jorge Berguño	June 2005
	Dr. Francisco Orrego	June 2005
Finland	Amb. Holger Bertil Rotkirch	14 June 2006
India	Prof. Upendra Baxi	6 October 2004
	Mr. Ajai Saxena	6 October 2004
	Dr. N. Khare	6 October 2004
Japan	Judge Shunji Yanai	18 July 2008
Rep. of Korea	Prof. Park Ki Gab	21 October 2008
United States	Prof. Daniel Bodansky	1 May 2008
	Mr. David Colson	1 May 2008

Lists of Parties to the Treaty, to the Protocol, and of Recommendations/Measures and their approvals are attached.

Date of most recent action: March 1, 2012

The Antarctic Treaty

Done: Washington; December 1, 1959

Entry into force: June 23, 1961
                     In accordance with Article XIII, the Treaty was subject to ratification by the signatory
                     States and is open for accession by any State which is a Member of the United Nations,
                     or by any other State which may be invited to accede to the Treaty with the consent of
                     all the Contracting Parties whose representatives are entitled to participate in the
                     meetings provided for under Article IX of the Treaty; instruments of ratification and
                     instruments of accession shall be deposited with the Government of the United States of
                     America. Upon the deposit of instruments of ratification by all the signatory States, the
                     Treaty entered into force for those States and for States which had deposited instruments
                     of accession to the Treaty. Thereafter, the Treaty enters into force for any acceding
                     State upon deposit of its instrument of accession.

Legend: (no mark) = ratification; a = accession; d = succession; w = withdrawal or equivalent action

Participant	Signature	Consent to be bound		Other Action	Notes
Argentina	December 1, 1959	June 23, 1961			
Australia	December 1, 1959	June 23, 1961			
Austria		August 25, 1987	a		
Belarus		December 27, 2006	a		
Belgium	December 1, 1959	July 26, 1960			
Brazil		May 16, 1975	a		
Bulgaria		September 11, 1978	a		
Canada		May 4, 1988	a		
Chile	December 1, 1959	June 23, 1961			
China		June 8, 1983	a		
Colombia		January 31, 1989	a		
Cuba		August 16, 1984	a		
Czech Republic		January 1, 1993	d		i
Denmark		May 20, 1965	a		
Ecuador		September 15, 1987	a		
Estonia		May 17, 2001	a		
Finland		May 15, 1984	a		
France	December 1, 1959	September 16, 1960			
Germany		February 5, 1979	a		ii
Greece		January 8, 1987	a		
Guatemala		July 31, 1991	a		
Hungary		January 27, 1984	a		
India		August 19, 1983	a		
Italy		March 18, 1981	a		
Japan	December 1, 1959	August 4, 1960			
Korea (DPRK)		January 21, 1987	a		
Korea (ROK)		November 28, 1986	a		
Malaysia		October 31, 2011	a		
Monaco		May 31, 2008	a		

Netherlands		March 30, 1967	a		iii
New Zealand	December 1, 1959	November 1, 1960			
Norway	December 1, 1959	August 24, 1960			
Pakistan		March 1, 2012	a		
Papua New Guinea		March 16, 1981	d		iv
Peru		April 10, 1981	a		
Poland		June 8, 1961	a		
Portugal		January 29, 2010	a		
Romania		September 15, 1971	a		v
Russian Federation	December 1, 1959	November 2, 1960			vi
Slovak Republic		January 1, 1993	d		vii
South Africa	December 1, 1959	June 21, 1960			
Spain		March 31, 1982	a		
Sweden		April 24, 1984	a		
Switzerland		November 15, 1990	a		
Turkey		January 24, 1996	a		
Ukraine		October 28, 1992	a		
United Kingdom	December 1, 1959	May 31, 1960			
United States	December 1, 1959	August 18, 1960			
Uruguay		January 11, 1980	a		viii
Venezuela		March 24, 1999	a		

---

[i] Effective date of succession by the Czech Republic. Czechoslovakia deposited an instrument of accession to the Treaty on June 14, 1962. On December 31, 1992, at midnight, Czechoslovakia ceased to exist and was succeeded by two separate and independent states, the Czech Republic and the Slovak Republic.

[ii] The Embassy of the Federal Republic of Germany in Washington transmitted to the Department of State a diplomatic note, dated October 2, 1990, which reads as follows:

"The Embassy of the Federal Republic of Germany presents its compliments to the Department of State and has the honor to inform the Government of the United States of America as the depositary Government of the Antarctic Treaty that, t[h]rough the accession of the German Democratic Republic to the Federal Republic of Germany with effect from October 3, 1990, the two German states will unite to form one sovereign state which, as a contracting party to the Antarctic Treaty, will remain bound by the provisions of the Treaty and subject to those recommendations adopted at the 15 consultative meetings which the Federal Republic of Germany has approved. From the date of German unity, the Federal Republic of Germany will act under the designation of "Germany" within the framework of the [A]ntarctic system.
"The Embassy would be grateful if the Government of the United States of America could inform all contracting parties to the Antarctic Treaty of the contents of this note.
"The Embassy of the Federal Republic of Germany avails itself of this opportunity to renew to the Department of State the assurances of its highest consideration."

Prior to unification, on November 19, 1974, the German Democratic Republic deposited an instrument of accession to the Treaty, accompanied by a declaration, a Department of State English translation of which reads as follows:

"The German Democratic Republic takes the view that Article XIII, paragraph 1, of the Treaty is inconsistent with the principle that all States which are guided in their policies by the purposes and principles of the United Nations Charter have the right to become parties to treaties which affect the interest of all States."

Subsequently, on February 5, 1979, the Federal Republic of Germany deposited an instrument of accession to the Treaty accompanied by a statement, an English translation of which, provided by the Embassy of the Federal Republic of Germany, reads as follows:

"My dear Mr. Secretary,

"In connection with the deposit today of the instrument of accession to the Antarctic Treaty signed in Washington December 1, 1959, I have the honor to state on behalf of the Federal Republic of Germany that with effect from the day on which the treaty enters into force for the Federal Republic of Germany it will also apply to Berlin (West) subject to the rights and responsibilities of the French Republic, the United Kingdom of Great Britain and Northern Ireland and the United States of America including those relating to disarmament and demilitarization.

"Accept, Excellency, the expression of my highest consideration."

iii The instrument of accession to the Treaty by the Netherlands states that the accession is for the Kingdom in Europe, Suriname and the Netherlands Antilles.

Suriname became an independent state on November 25, 1975.

The Royal Netherlands Embassy in Washington transmitted to the Department of State a diplomatic note, dated January 9, 1986, which reads as follows:

"The Royal Netherlands Embassy presents its compliments to the Department of State and has the honor to request the Department's attention for the following with respect to the Department's capacity of depositary of [the Antarctic Treaty].

"Effective January 1, 1986 the island of Aruba – formerly part of the Netherlands Antilles – obtained internal autonomy as a country within the Kingdom of The Netherlands. Consequently the Kingdom of The Netherlands as of January 1, 1986 consists of three countries, to wit: the Netherlands proper, the Netherlands Antilles and Aruba.

"Since the abovementioned event concerns only a change in internal constitutional relations within the Kingdom of The Netherlands, and as the Kingdom as such, under international law, will remain the subject with which treaties are concluded, the aforementioned change will have no consequences in international law with regard to treaties concluded by the Kingdom, the application of which (treaties) were extended to the Netherlands Antilles, including Aruba.

"These treaties, thus, will remain applicable for Aruba in its new status as autonomous country within the Kingdom of The Netherlands effective January 1, 1986.

"Consequently the [Antarctic Treaty] to which the Kingdom of the Netherlands is a Party, and which [has] been extended to the Netherlands Antilles will as of January 1, 1986 apply to all three countries of the Kingdom of The Netherlands.

"The Embassy would appreciate if the other Parties concerned would be notified of the above.

"The Royal Netherlands Embassy avails itself of this opportunity to renew to the Department of State the assurance of its highest consideration."

The Royal Netherlands Embassy in Washington transmitted to the Department of State a diplomatic note, dated October 6, 2010, which reads in pertinent part as follows:

"The Kingdom of the Netherlands currently consists of three parts: the Netherlands, the Netherlands Antilles and Aruba. The Netherlands Antilles consists of the islands of Curaçao, Sint Maarten, Bonaire, Sint Eustatius and Saba. "With effect from 10 October 2010, the Netherlands Antilles will cease to exist as a part of the Kingdom of the Netherlands. From that date onwards, the Kingdom will consist of four parts: the Netherlands, Aruba, Curaçao and Sint Maarten. Curaçao and Sint Maarten will enjoy internal self-government within the Kingdom, as Aruba and, up to 10 October 2010, the Netherlands Antilles do.

"These changes constitute a modification of the internal constitutional relations within the Kingdom of the Netherlands. The Kingdom of the Netherlands will accordingly remain the subject of international law with which agreements are ded. The modification of the structure of the Kingdom will therefore not affect the validity of the international agreements ratified by the Kingdom for the Netherlands Antilles; these agreements will continue to apply to Curaçao and Sint Maarten.

"The other islands that have until now formed part of the Netherlands Antilles – Bonaire, Sint Eustatius and Saba – will become part of the Netherlands, thus constituting 'the Caribbean part of the Netherlands'. The agreements that now apply to the Netherlands Antilles will also continue to apply to these islands; however, the Government of the Netherlands will now be responsible for implementing these agreements."

[iv] Date of deposit of notification of succession by Papua New Guinea; effective September 16, 1975, the date of its independence.

[v] The instrument of accession to the Treaty by Romania was accompanied by a note of the Ambassador of the Socialist Republic of Romania to the United States of America, dated September 15, 1971, which reads as follows:
"Dear Mr. Secretary:
"Submitting the instrument of adhesion of the Socialist Republic of Romania to the Antarctic Treaty, signed at Washington on December 1, 1959, I have the honor to inform you of the following:
'The Council of State of the Socialist Republic of Romania states that the provisions of the first paragraph of the article XIII of the Antarctic Treaty are not in accordance with the principle according to which the multilateral treaties whose object and purposes are concerning the international community, as a whole, should be opened for universal participation.'
"I am kindly requesting you, Mr. Secretary, to forward to all parties concerned the text of the Romanian instrument of adhesion to the Antarctic Treaty, as well as the text of this letter containing the above mentioned statement of the Romanian Government.
"I avail myself of this opportunity to renew to you, Mr. Secretary, the assurances of my highest consideration."

Copies of the Ambassador's letter and the Romanian instrument of accession to the Treaty were transmitted to the Antarctic Treaty parties by the Secretary of State's circular note dated October 1, 1971.

[vi] The Treaty was signed and ratified by the former Union of Soviet Socialist Republics. By a note dated January 13, 1992, the Russian Federation informed the United States Government that it "continues to perform the rights and fulfil the obligations following from the international agreements signed by the Union of Soviet Socialist Republics."

[vii] Effective date of succession by the Slovak Republic. Czechoslovakia deposited an instrument of accession to the

Treaty on June 14, 1962. On December 31, 1992, at midnight, Czechoslovakia ceased to exist and was succeeded by two separate and independent states, the Czech Republic and the Slovak Republic.

[viii] The instrument of accession to the Treaty by Uruguay was accompanied by a declaration, a Department of State English translation of which reads as follows:
"The Government of the Oriental Republic of Uruguay considers that, through its accession to the Antarctic Treaty signed at Washington (United States of America) on December 1, 1959, it helps to affirm the principles of using Antarctica exclusively for peaceful purposes, of prohibiting any nuclear explosion or radioactive waste disposal in this area, of freedom of scientific research in Antarctica in the service of mankind, and of international cooperation to achieve these objectives, which are established in said Treaty.
"Within the context of these principles Uruguay proposes, through a procedure based on the principle of legal equality, the establishment of a general and definitive statute on Antarctica in which, respecting the rights of States as recognized in international law, the interests of all States involved and of the international community as a whole would be considered equitably.
"The decision of the Uruguayan Government to accede to the Antarctic Treaty is based not only on the interest which, like all members of the international community, Uruguay has in Antarctica, but also on a special, direct, and substantial interest which arises from its geographic location, from the fact that its Atlantic coastline faces the continent of Antarctica, from the resultant influence upon its climate, ecology, and marine biology, from the historic bonds which

date back to the first expeditions which ventured to explore that continent and its waters, and also from the obligations assumed in conformity with the Inter-American Treaty of Reciprocal Assistance which includes a portion of Antarctic territory in the zone described in Article 4, by virtue of which Uruguay shares the responsibility of defending the region. "In communicating its decision to accede to the Antarctic Treaty, the Government of the Oriental Republic of Uruguay declares that it reserves its rights in Antarctica in accordance with international law."

PROTOCOL ON ENVIRONMENTAL PROTECTION TO THE ANTARCTIC TREATY

Signed at Madrid on October 4, 1991*

State	Date of Signature	Date deposit of Ratification, Acceptance (A) or Approval (AA)	Date deposit of Accession	Date of entry into force	Date Acceptance ANNEX V**	Date of entry into force of Annex V
CONSULTATIVE PARTIES						
Argentina	Oct. 4, 1991	Oct. 28, 1993 [3]		Jan. 14, 1998	Sept. 8, 2000 (A)	May 24, 2002
					Aug. 4, 1995 (B)	
Australia	Oct. 4, 1991	Apr. 6, 1994		Jan. 14, 1998	Apr. 6, 1994 (A)	May 24, 2002
					June 7, 1995 (B)	
Belgium	Oct. 4, 1991	Apr. 26, 1996		Jan. 14, 1998	Apr. 26, 1996 (A)	May 24, 2002
					Oct. 23, 2000 (B)	
Brazil	Oct. 4, 1991	Aug. 15, 1995		Jan. 14, 1998	May 20, 1998 (B)	May 24, 2002
Bulgaria			April 21, 1998	May 21, 1998	May 5, 1999 (AB)	May 24, 2002
Chile	Oct. 4, 1991	Jan. 11, 1995		Jan. 14, 1998	Mar. 25, 1998 (B)	May 24, 2002
China	Oct. 4, 1991	Aug. 2, 1994		Jan. 14, 1998	Jan. 26, 1995 (AB)	May 24, 2002
Czech Rep. [1,2]	Jan. 1, 1993	Aug. 25, 2004 [4]		Sept. 24, 2004		
Ecuador	Oct. 4, 1991	Jan. 4, 1993		Jan. 14, 1998	May 11, 2001 (A)	May 24, 2002
					Nov. 15, 2001 (B)	
Finland	Oct. 4, 1991	Nov. 1, 1996 (A)		Jan. 14, 1998	Nov. 1, 1996 (A)	May 24, 2002
					Apr. 2, 1997 (B)	
France	Oct. 4, 1991	Feb. 5, 1993 (AA)		Jan. 14, 1998	Apr. 26, 1995 (B)	May 24, 2002
					Nov. 18, 1998 (A)	
Germany	Oct. 4, 1991	Nov. 25, 1994		Jan. 14, 1998	Nov. 25, 1994 (A)	May 24, 2002
					Sept. 1, 1998 (B)	
India	July 2, 1992	Apr. 26, 1996		Jan. 14, 1998	May 24, 2002 (B)	May 24, 2002
Italy	Oct. 4, 1991	Mar. 31, 1995		Jan. 14, 1998	May 31, 1995 (A)	May 24, 2002
					Feb. 11, 1998 (B)	
Japan	Sept. 29, 1992	Dec. 15, 1997 (A)		Jan. 14, 1998	Dec. 15, 1997 (AB)	May 24, 2002
Korea, Rep. of	July 2, 1992	Jan. 2, 1996		Jan. 14, 1998	June 5, 1996 (B)	May 24, 2002
Netherlands	Oct. 4, 1991	Apr. 14, 1994 (A) [6]		Jan. 14, 1998	Mar. 18, 1998 (B)	May 24, 2002
New Zealand	Oct. 4, 1991	Dec. 22, 1994		Jan. 14, 1998	Oct. 21, 1992 (B)	May 24, 2002
Norway	Oct. 4, 1991	June 16, 1993		Jan. 14, 1998	Oct. 13, 1993 (B)	May 24, 2002
Peru	Oct. 4, 1991	Mar. 8, 1993		Jan. 14, 1998	Mar. 8, 1993 (A)	May 24, 2002
					Mar. 17, 1999 (B)	
Poland	Oct. 4, 1991	Nov. 1, 1995		Jan. 14, 1998	Sept. 20, 1995 (B)	May 24, 2002
Russian Federation	Oct. 4, 1991	Aug. 6, 1997		Jan. 14, 1998	June 19, 2001 (B)	May 24, 2002
South Africa	Oct. 4, 1991	Aug. 3, 1995		Jan. 14, 1998	June 14, 1995 (B)	May 24, 2002
Spain	Oct. 4, 1991	July 1, 1992		Jan. 14, 1998	Dec. 8, 1993 (A)	May 24, 2002

322

1. Reports by Depositaries and Observers

					**	
Sweden	Oct. 4, 1991	Mar. 30, 1994		Jan. 14, 1998	Feb. 18, 2000 (B) Mar. 30, 1994 (A) Apr. 7, 1994 (B)	May 24, 2002
Ukraine	Oct. 4, 1991		May 25, 2001	June 24, 2001	May 25, 2001 (A)	May 24, 2002
United Kingdom	Oct. 4, 1991	Apr. 25, 1995 [5]		Jan. 14, 1998	May 21, 1996 (B)	May 24, 2002
United States	Oct. 4, 1991	Apr. 17, 1997		Jan. 14, 1998	Apr. 17, 1997 (A)	May 24, 2002
Uruguay	Oct. 4, 1991	Jan. 11, 1995		Jan. 14, 1998	May 6, 1998 (B) May 15, 1995 (B)	May 24, 2002

** The following denotes date relating either
to acceptance of Annex V or approval of Recommendation XVI-10
(A) Acceptance of Annex V   (B) Approval of Recommendation XVI-10

State	Date of Signature	Ratification Acceptance or Approval	Date deposit of Accession	Date of entry into force	Date Acceptance ANNEX V**	Date of entry into force of Annex V
NON-CONSULTATIVE PARTIES						
Austria	Oct. 4, 1991		July 16, 2008	Aug. 15, 2008		
Belarus						
Canada	Oct. 4, 1991	Nov. 13, 2003		Dec. 13, 2003		
Colombia	Oct. 4, 1991					
Cuba	July 2, 1992					
Denmark						
Estonia						
Greece	Oct. 4, 1991	May 23, 1995		Jan. 14, 1998		
Guatemala						
Hungary	Oct. 4, 1991					
Korea, DPR of	Oct. 4, 1991					
Malaysia						
Monaco			July 1, 2009	July 31, 2009		
Pakistan			Mar. 1, 2012	Mar. 31, 2012		
Papua New Guinea						
Portugal						
Romania	Oct. 4, 1991	Feb. 3, 2003		Mar. 5, 2003	Feb. 3, 2003	Mar. 5, 2003
Slovak Rep.[1,2]	Jan. 1, 1993					
Switzerland	Oct. 4, 1991					
Turkey						
Venezuela						

* Signed at Madrid on October 4, 1991; thereafter at Washington until October 3, 1992. The Protocol will enter into force initially on the thirtieth day following the date of deposit of instruments of ratification, acceptance, approval or accession by all States which were Antarctic Treaty Consultative Parties at the date on which this Protocol was adopted. (Article 23)

** Adopted at Bonn on October 17, 1991 at XVIth Antarctic Consultative Meeting.

1. Signed for Czech & Slovak Federal Republic on Oct. 2, 1992 - Czechoslovakia accepts the jurisdiction of the International Court of Justice and Arbitral Tribunal for the settlement of disputes according to Article 19, paragraph 1. On December 31, 1992, at midnight, Czechoslovakia ceased to exist and was succeeded by two separate and independent states, the Czech Republic and the Slovak Republic.

2. Effective date of succession in respect of signature by Czechoslovakia which is subject to ratification by the Czech Republic and the Slovak Republic.

324

3. Accompanied by declaration, with informal translation provided by the Embassy of Argentina, which reads as follows: "The Argentine Republic declares that in as much as the Protocol to the Antarctic Treaty on the Protection of the Environment is a Complementary Agreement of the Antarctic Treaty and that its Article 4 fully respects what has been stated in Article IV, Subsection 1, Paragraph A) of said Treaty, none of its stipulations should be interpreted or be applied as affecting its rights, based on legal titles, acts of possession, contiguity and geological continuity in the region South of parallel 60, in which it has proclaimed and maintained its sovereignty."

4. Accompanied by declaration, with informal translation provided by the Embassy of the *Czech Republic*, which reads as follows: "The Czech Republic accepts the jurisdiction of the International Court of Justice and of the Arbitral Tribunal under Article 19, paragraph 1, of the Protocol on Environmental Protection to the Antarctic Treaty, done at Madrid on October 4, 1991."

5. Ratification on behalf of the United Kingdom of Great Britain and Northern Ireland, the Bailiwick of Jersey, the Bailiwick of Guernsey, the Isle of Man, Anguilla, Bermuda, the British Antarctic Territory, Cayman Islands, Falkland Islands, Montserrat, St. Helena and Dependencies, South Georgia and the South Sandwich Islands, Turks and Caicos Islands and British Virgin Islands.

6. Acceptance is for the Kingdom in Europe. At the time of its acceptance, the Kingdom of the Netherlands stated that it chooses both means for the settlement of disputes mentioned in Article 19, paragraph 1 of the Protocol, i.e. the International Court of Justice and the Arbitral Tribunal.

On October 27, 2004, the Kingdom of the Netherlands deposited a declaration accepting the Protocol for the Netherlands Antilles with a statement confirming that it chooses both means for the settlement of disputes mentioned in Article 19, paragraph 1 of the Protocol.

The Royal Netherlands Embassy in Washington transmitted to the Department of State a diplomatic note, dated October 6, 2010, which reads in pertinent part as follows:

"The Kingdom of the Netherlands currently consists of three parts: the Netherlands, the Netherlands Antilles and Aruba. The Netherlands Antilles consists of the islands of Curaçao, Sint Maarten, Bonaire, Sint Eustatius and Saba.

"With effect from 10 October 2010, the Netherlands Antilles will cease to exist as a part of the Kingdom of the Netherlands. From that date onwards, the Kingdom will consist of four parts: the Netherlands, Aruba, Curaçao and Sint Maarten. Curaçao and Sint Maarten will enjoy internal self-government within the Kingdom, as Aruba and, up to 10 October 2010, the Netherlands Antilles do.

"These changes constitute a modification of the internal constitutional relations within the Kingdom of the Netherlands. The Kingdom of the Netherlands will accordingly remain the subject of international law with which agreements are concluded. The modification of the structure of the Kingdom will therefore not affect the validity of the international agreements ratified by the Kingdom for the Netherlands Antilles; these agreements will continue to apply to Curaçao and Sint Maarten.

"The other islands that have until now formed part of the Netherlands Antilles – Bonaire, Sint Eustatius and Saba – will become part of the Netherlands, thus constituting 'the Caribbean part of the Netherlands'. The agreements that now apply to the Netherlands Antilles will also continue to apply to these islands; however, the Government of the Netherlands will now be responsible for implementing these agreements."

Department of State,
  Washington, March 27, 2014.

ATCM XXXVII Final Report

Approval, as notified to the Government of the United States of America, of measures relating to the furtherance of the principles and objectives of the Antarctic Treaty

	16 Recommendations adopted at First Meeting (Canberra 1961) Approved	10 Recommendations adopted at Second Meeting (Buenos Aires 1962) Approved	11 Recommendations adopted at Third Meeting (Brussels 1964) Approved	28 Recommendations adopted at Fourth Meeting (Santiago 1966) Approved	9 Recommendations adopted at Fifth Meeting (Paris 1968) Approved	15 Recommendations adopted at Sixth Meeting (Tokyo 1970) Approved
Argentina	ALL	ALL	ALL	ALL	ALL	ALL
Australia	ALL	ALL	ALL	ALL	ALL	ALL
Belgium	ALL	ALL	ALL	ALL	ALL	ALL
Brazil (1983)+	ALL	ALL	ALL	ALL	ALL	ALL (except 10)
Bulgaria (1998)+						
Chile	ALL	ALL	ALL	ALL	ALL	ALL
China (1985)+	ALL	ALL	ALL	ALL	ALL	ALL (except 10)
Czech Rep. (2014)+						
Ecuador (1990)+						
Finland (1989)+						
France	ALL	ALL	ALL	ALL	ALL	ALL
Germany (1981)+	ALL	ALL	ALL (except 8)	ALL (except 16-19)	ALL (except 6)	ALL (except 9)
India (1983)+	ALL	ALL	ALL (except 8***)	ALL (except 18)	ALL	ALL (except 9 & 10)
Italy (1987)+	ALL	ALL	ALL	ALL	ALL	ALL
Japan	ALL	ALL	ALL	ALL	ALL	ALL
Korea, Rep. (1989)+	ALL (except 11 & 15)	ALL (except 3, 5, 8 & 10)	ALL (except 3, 4, 6 & 9)	ALL(except 20, 25, 26 & 28)	ALL (except 1, 8 & 9)	ALL (except 15)
Netherlands (1990)+	ALL	ALL	ALL	ALL	ALL	ALL
New Zealand	ALL	ALL	ALL	ALL	ALL	ALL
Norway	ALL	ALL	ALL	ALL	ALL	ALL
Peru (1989)+	ALL	ALL	ALL	ALL	ALL	ALL
Poland (1977)+	ALL	ALL	ALL	ALL	ALL	ALL
Russia	ALL	ALL	ALL	ALL	ALL	ALL
South Africa	ALL	ALL	ALL	ALL	ALL	ALL
Spain (1988)+	ALL	ALL	ALL	ALL	ALL	ALL
Sweden (1988)+						
U.K.	ALL	ALL	ALL	ALL	ALL	ALL
Uruguay (1985)+	ALL	ALL	ALL	ALL	ALL	ALL
U.S.A.	ALL	ALL	ALL	ALL	ALL	ALL

* IV-6, IV-10, IV-12, and V-5 terminated by VIII-2

*** Accepted as interim guideline

+ Year attained Consultative Status. Acceptance by that State required to bring into force Recommendations or Measures of meetings from that year forward.

Approval, as notified to the Government of the United States of America, of measures relating to the furtherance of the principles and objectives of the Antarctic Treaty

	9 Recommendations adopted at Seventh Meeting (Wellington 1972) Approved	14 Recommendations adopted at Eighth Meeting (Oslo 1975) Approved	6 Recommendations adopted at Ninth Meeting (London 1977) Approved	9 Recommendations adopted at Tenth Meeting (Washington 1979) Approved	3 Recommendations adopted at Eleventh Meeting (Buenos Aires 1981) Approved	8 Recommendations adopted at Twelfth Meeting (Canberra 1983) Approved
Argentina	ALL	ALL	ALL	ALL	ALL	ALL
Australia	ALL	ALL	ALL	ALL	ALL	ALL
Belgium	ALL	ALL	ALL	ALL	ALL	ALL
Brazil (1983)+	ALL (except 5)	ALL	ALL	ALL	ALL	ALL
Bulgaria (1998)+						
Chile	ALL	ALL	ALL	ALL	ALL	ALL
China (1985)+	ALL (except 5)	ALL	ALL	ALL	ALL	ALL
Czech Rep. (2014)+						
Ecuador (1990)+						
Finland (1989)+						
France	ALL	ALL	ALL	ALL	ALL	ALL
Germany (1981)+	ALL (except 5)	ALL (except 2 & 5)	ALL	ALL	ALL	ALL
India (1983)+	ALL	ALL	ALL	ALL (except 1 & 9)	ALL	ALL
Italy (1987)+	ALL (except 5)	ALL	ALL	ALL (except 1 & 9)	ALL	ALL
Japan	ALL	ALL	ALL	ALL	ALL	ALL
Korea, Rep. (1989)+	ALL	ALL	ALL	ALL	ALL	ALL
Netherlands (1990)+	ALL	ALL	ALL (except 3)	ALL (except 9)	ALL (except 2)	ALL
New Zealand	ALL	ALL	ALL	ALL	ALL	ALL
Norway	ALL	ALL	ALL	ALL	ALL	ALL
Peru (1989)+	ALL	ALL	ALL	ALL	ALL	ALL
Poland (1977)+	ALL	ALL	ALL	ALL	ALL	ALL
Russia	ALL	ALL	ALL	ALL	ALL	ALL
South Africa	ALL	ALL	ALL	ALL	ALL	ALL
Spain (1988)+	ALL	ALL	ALL	ALL (except 1 & 9)	ALL (except 1)	ALL
Sweden (1988)+	ALL	ALL	ALL	ALL	ALL	ALL
U.K.	ALL	ALL	ALL	ALL	ALL	ALL
Uruguay (1985)+	ALL	ALL	ALL	ALL	ALL	ALL
U.S.A.	ALL	ALL	ALL	ALL	ALL	ALL

* IV-6, IV-10, IV-12, and V-5 terminated by VIII-2

*** Accepted as interim guideline

+ Year attained Consultative Status. Acceptance by that State required to bring into force Recommendations or Measures of meetings from that year forward.

ATCM XXXVII Final Report

Approval, as notified to the Government of the United States of America, of measures relating to the furtherance of the principles and objectives of the Antarctic Treaty

	16 Recommendations adopted at Thirteenth Meeting (Brussels 1985) Approved	10 Recommendations adopted at Fourteenth Meeting (Rio de Janeiro 1987) Approved	22 Recommendations adopted at Fifteenth Meeting (Paris 1989) Approved	13 Recommendations adopted at Sixteenth Meeting (Bonn 1991) Approved	4 Recommendations adopted at Seventeenth Meeting (Venice 1992) Approved	1 Recommendation adopted at Eighteenth Meeting (Kyoto 1994) Approved
Argentina	ALL	ALL	ALL	ALL	ALL	ALL
Australia	ALL	ALL	ALL	ALL	ALL	ALL
Belgium	ALL	ALL	ALL	ALL	ALL	ALL
Brazil (1983)+	ALL	ALL	ALL	XVI-10	ALL	ALL
Bulgaria (1998)+						
Chile	ALL	ALL	ALL	ALL	ALL	ALL
China (1985)+	ALL	ALL	ALL	ALL	ALL	ALL
Czech Rep. (2014)+						
Ecuador (1990)+				XVI-10	ALL	ALL
Finland (1989)+			ALL	ALL	ALL	ALL
France	ALL	ALL	ALL (except 3,8,10,11&22)	ALL	ALL	ALL
Germany (1981)+	ALL	ALL	ALL	ALL	ALL	ALL
India (1983)+	ALL	ALL	ALL	ALL	ALL	ALL
Italy (1987)+	ALL	ALL	ALL	ALL	ALL	ALL
Japan	ALL	ALL	ALL (except 1-11, 16, 18, 19)	ALL (except 1, 3-9, 12&13)	ALL (except 1-2 & 4)	ALL
Korea, Rep. (1989)+	ALL	ALL	ALL	ALL (except 12)	ALL (except 1)	ALL
Netherlands (1990)+	ALL	ALL (except 9)	ALL (except 22)	ALL	ALL	ALL
New Zealand	ALL	ALL	ALL	ALL	ALL	ALL
Norway	ALL	ALL	ALL	ALL	ALL	ALL
Peru (1989)+	ALL	ALL	ALL (except 22)	ALL (except 13)	ALL	ALL
Poland (1977)+	ALL	ALL	ALL	ALL	ALL	ALL
Russia	ALL	ALL	ALL	ALL	ALL	ALL
South Africa	ALL	ALL	ALL	ALL	ALL	ALL
Spain (1988)+	ALL	ALL	ALL	ALL	ALL	ALL
Sweden (1988)+	ALL	ALL	ALL	ALL	ALL	ALL
U.K.	ALL	ALL (except 2)	ALL (except 3, 4, 8, 10, 11)	ALL (except 4, 6, 8, & 9)	ALL	ALL
Uruguay (1985)+	ALL	ALL	ALL (except 1-4, 10, 11)	ALL	ALL	ALL
U.S.A.	ALL	ALL	ALL	ALL	ALL	ALL

* IV-6, IV-10, IV-12, and V-5 terminated by VIII-2

*** Accepted as interim guideline

+ Year attained Consultative Status. Acceptance by that State required to bring into force Recommendations or Measures of meetings from that year forward.

Approval, as notified to the Government of the United States of America, of measures relating to the furtherance of the principles and objectives of the Antarctic Treaty

	5 Measures adopted at Nineteenth Meeting (Seoul 1995) Approved	2 Measures adopted at Twentieth Meeting (Utrecht 1996) Approved	5 Measures adopted at Twenty-First Meeting (Christchurch 1997) Approved	2 Measures adopted at Twenty-Second Meeting (Tromso 1998) Approved	1 Measure adopted at Twenty-Third Meeting (Lima 1999) Approved
Argentina	ALL	ALL	ALL	ALL	ALL
Australia	ALL	ALL	ALL	ALL	ALL
Belgium	ALL	ALL	ALL	ALL	ALL
Brazil (1983)+	ALL	ALL	ALL	ALL	ALL
Bulgaria (1998)+					
Chile	ALL	ALL	ALL	ALL	ALL
China (1985)+	ALL	ALL	ALL	ALL	ALL
Czech Rep. (2014)+					
Ecuador (1990)+					
Finland (1989)+	ALL	ALL	ALL	ALL	ALL
France	ALL	ALL	ALL	ALL	ALL
Germany (1981)+	ALL	ALL	ALL	ALL	ALL
India (1983)+	ALL	ALL	ALL	ALL	ALL
Italy (1987)+	ALL	ALL	ALL	ALL	ALL
Japan	ALL (except 2&5)	ALL (except 1)	All (except 1-2 & 5)	ALL	ALL
Korea, Rep. (1989)+	ALL	ALL	ALL	ALL	ALL
Netherlands (1990)+	ALL	ALL	ALL	ALL	ALL
New Zealand	ALL	ALL	ALL	ALL	ALL
Norway	ALL	ALL	ALL	ALL	ALL
Peru (1989)+	ALL	ALL	ALL	ALL	ALL
Poland (1977)+	ALL	ALL	ALL	ALL	ALL
Russia	ALL	ALL	ALL	ALL	ALL
South Africa	ALL	ALL	ALL	ALL	ALL
Spain (1988)+	ALL	ALL	ALL	ALL	ALL
Sweden (1988)+	ALL	ALL	ALL	ALL	ALL
U.K.	ALL	ALL	ALL	ALL	ALL
Uruguay (1985)+	ALL	ALL	ALL	ALL	ALL
U.S.A.	ALL	ALL	ALL	ALL	ALL

"+Year attained Consultative Status. Acceptance by that state required to bring into force Recommendations or Measures of meetings from that Year forward."

329

Approval, as notified to the Government of the United States of America, of measures relating to the furtherance of the principles and objectives of the Antarctic Treaty

	2 Measures — adopted at Twelfth Special Meeting (The Hague 2000) Approved	3 Measures — adopted at Twenty-Fourth Meeting (St. Petersburg 2001) Approved	1 Measure — adopted at Twenty-Fifth Meeting (Warsaw 2002) Approved	3 Measures — adopted at Twenty-Sixth Meeting (Madrid 2003) Approved	4 Measures — adopted at Twenty-Seventh Meeting (Cape Town 2004) Approved
Argentina	ALL	ALL	*	XXVI-1, XXVI-2 *, XXVI-3 **	XXVII-1 *, XXVII-2 *, XXVII-3 **
Australia	ALL	ALL	ALL	XXVI-1, XXVI-2 *, XXVI-3 **	XXVII-1 *, XXVII-2 *, XXVII-3 **
Belgium	ALL	ALL	ALL	ALL	ALL
Brazil (1983)+	ALL	ALL	*	ALL	XXVII-1, XXVII-2, XXVII-3
Bulgaria (1998)+				XXVI-1, XXVII-2 *, XXVI-3 **	XXVII-1 *, XXVII-2 *, XXVII-3 **
Chile	ALL	ALL	ALL	ALL	ALL
China (1985)+	ALL	ALL	ALL	ALL	XXVII-1 *, XXVII-2 *, XXVII-3 **
Czech Rep. (2014)+					
Ecuador (1990)+			*	XXVI-1, XXVI-2 *, XXVI-3 **	XXVII-1 *, XXVII-2 *, XXVII-3 **, XXVII-4
Finland (1989)+	ALL	ALL	*	XXVI-1, XXVI-2 *, XXVI-3 **	4
France	ALL (except SATCM XII-2)	ALL	*	XXVI-1, XXVI-2 *, XXVI-3 **	XXVII-1, XXVII-2 *, XXVII-3, XXVII-4
Germany (1981)+	ALL	ALL	ALL	ALL	XXVII-1 *, XXVII-2 *, XXVII-3 **
India (1983)+	ALL	ALL	ALL	ALL	XXVII-1 *, XXVII-2 *, XXVII-3 **
Italy (1987)+			*	XXVI-1, XXVI-2 *, XXVI-3 **	XXVII-1 *, XXVII-2 *, XXVII-3 **, XXVII-4
Japan	ALL	ALL		ALL	4
Korea, Rep. (1989)+	ALL	ALL	*	XXVI-1, XXVI-2 *, XXVI-3 **	XXVII-1 *, XXVII-2 *, XXVII-3 **
Netherlands (1990)+	ALL	ALL	ALL	ALL	ALL
New Zealand	ALL	ALL	ALL	ALL	XXVII-1 *, XXVII-2 *, XXVII-3 **, XXVII-4
Norway	ALL	ALL	*	XXVI-1, XXVI-2 *, XXVI-3 **	XXVII-1 *, XXVII-2 *, XXVII-3 **
Peru (1989)+	ALL	ALL	ALL	XXVI-1, XXVI-2 *, XXVI-3 **	XXVII-1 *, XXVII-2 *, XXVII-3 **
Poland (1977)+	ALL	ALL	ALL	ALL	ALL
Russia	ALL	ALL	ALL	XXVI-1, XXVI-2, XXVI-3 **	XXVII-1, XXVII-2, XXVII-3 **
South Africa	ALL	ALL	*	ALL	ALL
Spain (1988)+			ALL	XXVI-1, XXVI-2 *, XXVI-3 **	XXVII-1 *, XXVII-2 *, XXVII-3 **
Sweden (1988)+	ALL	ALL		ALL	XXVII-1 *, XXVII-2 *, XXVII-3 **
Ukraine (2004)+			ALL	ALL	XXVII-1 *, XXVII-2 *, XXVII-3 **
U.K.	ALL (except SATCM XII-2)	ALL (except XXIV-3)	ALL	ALL	XXVII-1 *, XXVII-2 *, XXVII-3 **, XXVII-4
Uruguay (1985)+	ALL	ALL	*	XXVI-1, XXVI-2 *, XXVI-3	4
U.S.A.	ALL	ALL	*	XXVI-1, XXVI-2 *, XXVI-3 **	XXVII-1 *, XXVII-2 *, XXVII-3 **

"+Year attained Consultative Status. Acceptance by that state required to bring into force Recommendations or Measures of meetings from that Year forward."

* Management Plans annexed to this Measure were deemed to have been approved in accordance with Article 6(1) of Annex V to the Protocol on Environmental Protection to the Antarctic Treaty and the Measure not specifying a different approval method.

** Revised and updated List of Historic Sites and Monuments annexed to this Measure was deemed to have been approved in accordance with Article 8(2) of Annex V to the Protocol on Environmental Protection to the Antarctic Treaty and the Measure not specifying a different approval method.

Approval, as notified to the Government of the United States of America, of measures relating to the furtherance of the principles and objectives of the Antarctic Treaty

	5 Measures adopted at Twenty-Eighth Meeting (Stockholm 2005) Approved	4 Measures adopted at Twenty-Ninth Meeting (Edinburgh 2006) Approved	3 Measures adopted at Thirtieth Meeting (New Delhi 2007) Approved	14 Measures adopted at Thirty-first Meeting (Kyiv 2008) Approved
Argentina	XXVIII-2 *, XXVIII-3 *, XXVIII-4 *, XXVIII-5 **	XXIX-1 *, XXIX-2 *, XXIX-3 **, XXIX-4 ***	XXX-1 *, XXX-2 *, XXX-3 **	XXXI-1 - XXXI-14 *
Australia	XXVIII-2 *, XXVIII-3 *, XXVIII-4 *, XXVIII-5 **	XXIX-1 *, XXIX-2 *, XXIX-3 **, XXIX-4 ***	XXX-1 *, XXX-2 *, XXX-3 **	XXXI-1 - XXXI-14 *
Belgium	ALL except Measure 1	ALL	ALL	XXXI-1 - XXXI-14 *
Brazil (1983)+	ALL except Measure 1	XXIX-1 *, XXIX-2 *, XXIX-3 **, XXIX-4 ***	XXX-1 *, XXX-2 *, XXX-3 **	XXXI-1 - XXXI-14 *
Bulgaria (1998)+	XXVIII-2 *, XXVIII-3 *, XXVIII-4 *, XXVIII-5 **	XXIX-1 *, XXIX-2 *, XXIX-3 **, XXIX-4 ***	XXX-1 *, XXX-2 *, XXX-3 **	XXXI-1 - XXXI-14 *
Chile	ALL except Measure 1	XXIX-1 *, XXIX-2 *, XXIX-3 **, XXIX-4 ***	XXX-1 *, XXX-2 *, XXX-3 **	XXXI-1 - XXXI-14 *
China (1985)+	XXVIII-2 *, XXVIII-3 *, XXVIII-4 *, XXVIII-5 **	XXIX-1 *, XXIX-2 *, XXIX-3 **, XXIX-4 ***	XXX-1 *, XXX-2 *, XXX-3 **	XXXI-1 - XXXI-14 *
Czech Rep. (2014)+				
Ecuador (1990)+	XXVIII-2 *, XXVIII-3 *, XXVIII-4 *, XXVIII-5 **	XXIX-1 *, XXIX-2 *, XXIX-3 **, XXIX-4 ***	XXX-1 *, XXX-2 *, XXX-3 **	XXXI-1 - XXXI-14 *
	XXVIII-1, XXVIII-2 *, XXVIII-3 *, XXVIII-4 *, XXVIII-5 **			
Finland (1989)+	XXVIII-2 *, XXVIII-3 *, XXVIII-4 *, XXVIII-5 **	XXIX-1 *, XXIX-2 *, XXIX-3 **, XXIX-4 ***	XXX-1 *, XXX-2 *, XXX-3 **	XXXI-1 - XXXI-14 *
France	XXVIII-2 *, XXVIII-3 *, XXVIII-4 *, XXVIII-5 **	XXIX-1 *, XXIX-2 *, XXIX-3 **, XXIX-4 ***	XXX-1 *, XXX-2 *, XXX-3 **	XXXI-1 - XXXI-14 *
Germany (1981)+	XXVIII-2 *, XXVIII-3 *, XXVIII-4 *, XXVIII-5 **	XXIX-1 *, XXIX-2 *, XXIX-3 **, XXIX-4 ***	XXX-1 *, XXX-2 *, XXX-3 **	XXXI-1 - XXXI-14 *
India (1983)+	XXVIII-2 *, XXVIII-3 *, XXVIII-4 *, XXVIII-5 **	XXIX-1 *, XXIX-2 *, XXIX-3 **, XXIX-4 ***	XXX-1 *, XXX-2 *, XXX-3 **	XXXI-1 - XXXI-14 *
Italy (1987)+	XXVIII-2 *, XXVIII-3 *, XXVIII-4 *, XXVIII-5 **	XXIX-1 *, XXIX-2 *, XXIX-3 **, XXIX-4 ***	XXX-1 *, XXX-2 *, XXX-3 **	XXXI-1 - XXXI-14 *
Japan	XXVIII-2 *, XXVIII-3 *, XXVIII-4 *, XXVIII-5 **	XXIX-1 *, XXIX-2 *, XXIX-3 **, XXIX-4 ***	XXX-1 *, XXX-2 *, XXX-3 **	XXXI-1 - XXXI-14 *
Korea, Rep. (1989)+	XXVIII-2 *, XXVIII-3 *, XXVIII-4 *, XXVIII-5 **	XXIX-1 *, XXIX-2 *, XXIX-3 **, XXIX-4 ***	XXX-1 *, XXX-2 *, XXX-3 **	XXXI-1 - XXXI-14 *
Netherlands (1990)+	ALL except Measure 1	ALL	ALL	ALL
	XXVIII-1, XXVIII-2 *, XXVIII-3 *, XXVIII-4 *, XXVIII-5 **			
New Zealand	XXVIII-1, XXVIII-2 *, XXVIII-3 *, XXVIII-4 *, XXVIII-5 **	XXIX-1 *, XXIX-2 *, XXIX-3 **, XXIX-4 ***	XXX-1 *, XXX-2 *, XXX-3 **	XXXI-1 - XXXI-14 *
Norway	XXVIII-1, XXVIII-2 *, XXVIII-3 *, XXVIII-4 *, XXVIII-5 **	XXIX-1 *, XXIX-2 *, XXIX-3 **, XXIX-4 ***	XXX-1 *, XXX-2 *, XXX-3 **	XXXI-1 - XXXI-14 *
Peru (1989)+	XXVIII-1, XXVIII-2 *, XXVIII-3 *, XXVIII-4 *, XXVIII-5 **	XXIX-1 *, XXIX-2 *, XXIX-3 **, XXIX-4 ***	XXX-1 *, XXX-2 *, XXX-3 **	XXXI-1 - XXXI-14 *
Poland (1977)+	ALL	ALL	ALL	XXXI-1 - XXXI-14 *
Russia	XXVIII-2 *, XXVIII-3 *, XXVIII-4 *, XXVIII-5 **	ALL	XXX-1 *, XXX-2 *, XXX-3 **	XXXI-1 - XXXI-14 *
South Africa	XXVIII-2 *, XXVIII-3 *, XXVIII-4 *, XXVIII-5 **	ALL	XXX-1 *, XXX-2 *, XXX-3 **	XXXI-1 - XXXI-14 *
Spain (1988)+	XXVIII-1, XXVIII-2 *, XXVIII-3 *, XXVIII-4 *, XXVIII-5 **	XXIX-1 *, XXIX-2 *, XXIX-3 **, XXIX-4 ***	XXX-1 *, XXX-2 *, XXX-3 **	XXXI-1 - XXXI-14 *
Sweden (1988)+	XXVIII-1, XXVIII-2 *, XXVIII-3 *, XXVIII-4 *, XXVIII-5 **	XXIX-1 *, XXIX-2 *, XXIX-3 **, XXIX-4 ***	XXX-1 *, XXX-2 *, XXX-3 **	XXXI-1 - XXXI-14 *
Ukraine (2004)+	XXVIII-1, XXVIII-2 *, XXVIII-3 *, XXVIII-4 *, XXVIII-5 **	XXIX-1 *, XXIX-2 *, XXIX-3 **, XXIX-4 ***	XXX-1 *, XXX-2 *, XXX-3 **	XXXI-1 - XXXI-14 *
	XXVIII-1, XXVIII-2 *, XXVIII-3 *, XXVIII-4 *, XXVIII-5 **			
U.K.	XXVIII-2 *, XXVIII-3 *, XXVIII-4 *, XXVIII-5 **	XXIX-1 *, XXIX-2 *, XXIX-3 **, XXIX-4 ***	XXX-1 *, XXX-2 *, XXX-3 **	XXXI-1 - XXXI-14 *
Uruguay (1985)+	XXVIII-2 *, XXVIII-3 *, XXVIII-4 *, XXVIII-5 **	XXIX-1 *, XXIX-2 *, XXIX-3 **, XXIX-4 ***	XXX-1 *, XXX-2 *, XXX-3 **	XXXI-1 - XXXI-14 *
U.S.A.	XXVIII-2 *, XXVIII-3 *, XXVIII-4 *, XXVIII-5 **	XXIX-1 *, XXIX-2 *, XXIX-3 **, XXIX-4 ***	XXX-1 *, XXX-2 *, XXX-3 **	XXXI-1 - XXXI-14 *

"+=Year attained Consultative Status. Acceptance by that state required to bring into force Recommendations or Measures of meetings from that Year forward."

* Management Plans annexed to this Measure deemed to have been approved in accordance with Article 6(1) of Annex V to the Protocol on Environmental Protection to the Antarctic Treaty and the Measure not specifying a different approval method.

** Revised and updated List of Historic Sites and Monuments annexed to this Measure deemed to have been approved in accordance with Article 8(2) of Annex V to the Protocol on Environmental Protection to the Antarctic Treaty and the Measure not specifying a different approval method.

*** Modification of Appendix A to Annex II to the Protocol on Environmental Protection to the Antarctic Treaty deemed to have been approved in accordance with Article 9(1) of Annex II to the Protocol on Environmental Protection to the Antarctic Treaty and the Measure not specifying a different approval method.

Approval, as notified to the Government of the United States of America, of measures relating to the furtherance of the principles and objectives of the Antarctic Treaty

	16 Measures adopted at Thirty-second Meeting (Baltimore 2009) Approved	15 Measures adopted at Thirty-third Meeting (Punta del Este 2010) Approved	12 Measures adopted at Thirty-fourth Meeting (Buenos Aires 2011) Approved	11 Measures adopted at Thirty-fifth Meeting (Hobart 2012) Approved	21 Measures adopted at Thirty-sixth Meeting (Brussels 2013) Approved
Argentina	XXXII-1 - XXXII-13* and XXXII-14**	XXXIII-1 - XXXIII-14* and XXXIII-15**	XXXIV-1 - XXXIV-10* and XXXIV-11 - XXXIV-12**	XXXV-1 - XXXV-10* and XXXV-11**	XXXVI-1 - XXXVI-17* and XXXVI-18 - XXXVI-21**
Australia	XXXII-1 - XXXII-13* and XXXII-14**	XXXIII-1 - XXXIII-14* and XXXIII-15**	XXXIV-1 - XXXIV-10* and XXXIV-11 - XXXIV-12**	XXXV-1 - XXXV-10* and XXXV-11**	XXXVI-1 - XXXVI-17* and XXXVI-18 - XXXVI-21**
Belgium	XXXII-1 - XXXII-13* and XXXII-14**	XXXIII-1 - XXXIII-14* and XXXIII-15**	XXXIV-1 - XXXIV-10* and XXXIV-11 - XXXIV-12**	XXXV-1 - XXXV-10* and XXXV-11**	XXXVI-1 - XXXVI-17* and XXXVI-18 - XXXVI-21**
Brazil (1983)+	XXXII-1 - XXXII-13* and XXXII-14**	XXXIII-1 - XXXIII-14* and XXXIII-15**	XXXIV-1 - XXXIV-10* and XXXIV-11 - XXXIV-12**	XXXV-1 - XXXV-10* and XXXV-11**	XXXVI-1 - XXXVI-17* and XXXVI-18 - XXXVI-21**
Bulgaria (1998)+	XXXII-1 - XXXII-13* and XXXII-14**	XXXIII-1 - XXXIII-14* and XXXIII-15**	XXXIV-1 - XXXIV-10* and XXXIV-11 - XXXIV-12**	XXXV-1 - XXXV-10* and XXXV-11**	XXXVI-1 - XXXVI-17* and XXXVI-18 - XXXVI-21**
Chile	XXXII-1 - XXXII-13* and XXXII-14**	XXXIII-1 - XXXIII-14* and XXXIII-15**	XXXIV-1 - XXXIV-10* and XXXIV-11 - XXXIV-12**	XXXV-1 - XXXV-10* and XXXV-11**	XXXVI-1 - XXXVI-17* and XXXVI-18 - XXXVI-21**
China (1985)+ Czech Rep. (2014)+	XXXII-1 - XXXII-13* and XXXII-14**	XXXIII-1 - XXXIII-14* and XXXIII-15**	XXXIV-1 - XXXIV-10* and XXXIV-11 - XXXIV-12**	XXXV-1 - XXXV-10* and XXXV-11**	XXXVI-1 - XXXVI-17* and XXXVI-18 - XXXVI-21**
Ecuador (1990)+	XXXII-1 - XXXII-13* and XXXII-14**	XXXIII-1 - XXXIII-14* and XXXIII-15**	XXXIV-1 - XXXIV-10* and XXXIV-11 - XXXIV-12**	XXXV-1 - XXXV-10* and XXXV-11**	XXXVI-1 - XXXVI-17* and XXXVI-18 - XXXVI-21**
Finland (1989)+	XXXII-1 - XXXII-13* and XXXII-14**; XXXII-16	XXXIII-1 - XXXIII-14* and XXXIII-15**	XXXIV-1 - XXXIV-10* and XXXIV-11 - XXXIV-12**	XXXV-1 - XXXV-10* and XXXV-11**	XXXVI-1 - XXXVI-17* and XXXVI-18 - XXXVI-21**
France	XXXII-1 - XXXII-13* and XXXII-14**; XXXII-15	XXXIII-1 - XXXIII-14* and XXXIII-15**	XXXIV-1 - XXXIV-10* and XXXIV-11 - XXXIV-12**	XXXV-1 - XXXV-10* and XXXV-11**	XXXVI-1 - XXXVI-17* and XXXVI-18 - XXXVI-21**
Germany (1981)+	XXXII-1 - XXXII-13* and XXXII-14**	XXXIII-1 - XXXIII-14* and XXXIII-15**	XXXIV-1 - XXXIV-10* and XXXIV-11 - XXXIV-12**	XXXV-1 - XXXV-10* and XXXV-11**	XXXVI-1 - XXXVI-17* and XXXVI-18 - XXXVI-21**
India (1983)+	XXXII-1 - XXXII-13* and XXXII-14**	XXXIII-1 - XXXIII-14* and XXXIII-15**	XXXIV-1 - XXXIV-10* and XXXIV-11 - XXXIV-12**	XXXV-1 - XXXV-10* and XXXV-11**	XXXVI-1 - XXXVI-17* and XXXVI-18 - XXXVI-21**
Italy (1987)+	XXXII-1 - XXXII-13* and XXXII-14**	XXXIII-1 - XXXIII-14* and XXXIII-15**	XXXIV-1 - XXXIV-10* and XXXIV-11 - XXXIV-12**	XXXV-1 - XXXV-10* and XXXV-11**	XXXVI-1 - XXXVI-17* and XXXVI-18 - XXXVI-21**
Japan	XXXII-1 - XXXII-13* and XXXII-14**; XXXII-15	XXXIII-1 - XXXIII-14* and XXXIII-15**	XXXIV-1 - XXXIV-10* and XXXIV-11 - XXXIV-12**	XXXV-1 - XXXV-10* and XXXV-11**	XXXVI-1 - XXXVI-17* and XXXVI-18 - XXXVI-21**
Korea, Rep. (1989)+	XXXII-1 - XXXII-13* and XXXII-14**	XXXIII-1 - XXXIII-14* and XXXIII-15**	XXXIV-1 - XXXIV-10* and XXXIV-11 - XXXIV-12**	XXXV-1 - XXXV-10* and XXXV-11**	XXXVI-1 - XXXVI-17* and XXXVI-18 - XXXVI-21**
Netherlands (1990)+	XXXII-1 - XXXII-13 and XXXII-14	ALL	XXXIV-1 - XXXIV-10* and XXXIV-11 - XXXIV-12**	ALL	XXXVI-1 - XXXVI-17* and XXXVI-18 - XXXVI-21**
New Zealand	XXXII-1 - XXXII-13* and XXXII-14**	XXXIII-1 - XXXIII-14* and XXXIII-15**	XXXIV-1 - XXXIV-10* and XXXIV-11 - XXXIV-12**	XXXV-1 - XXXV-10* and XXXV-11**	XXXVI-1 - XXXVI-17* and XXXVI-18 - XXXVI-21**
Norway	XXXII-1 - XXXII-13* and XXXII-14**	XXXIII-1 - XXXIII-14* and XXXIII-15**	XXXIV-1 - XXXIV-10* and XXXIV-11 - XXXIV-12**	XXXV-1 - XXXV-10* and XXXV-11**	XXXVI-1 - XXXVI-17* and XXXVI-18 - XXXVI-21**
Peru (1989)+	XXXII-1 - XXXII-13* and XXXII-14**	XXXIII-1 - XXXIII-14* and XXXIII-15**	XXXIV-1 - XXXIV-10* and XXXIV-11 - XXXIV-12**	XXXV-1 - XXXV-10* and XXXV-11**	XXXVI-1 - XXXVI-17* and XXXVI-18 - XXXVI-21**
Poland (1977)+	XXXII-1 - XXXII-13* and XXXII-14**	XXXIII-1 - XXXIII-14* and XXXIII-15**	XXXIV-1 - XXXIV-10* and XXXIV-11 - XXXIV-12**	XXXV-1 - XXXV-10* and XXXV-11**	XXXVI-1 - XXXVI-17* and XXXVI-18 - XXXVI-21**

1. Reports by Depositaries and Observers

Russia	XXXII-1 - XXXII-13* and XXXII-14**	XXXIII-1 - XXXIII-14* and XXXIII-15**	XXXIV-1 - XXXIV-10* and XXXIV-11 - XXXIV-12**	XXXV-1 - XXXV-10* and XXXV-11**	XXXVI-1 - XXXVI-17* and XXXVI-18 - XXXVI-21**
South Africa	XXXII-1 - XXXII-13* and XXXII-14**	XXXIII-1 - XXXIII-14* and XXXIII-15**	XXXIV-1 - XXXIV-10* and XXXIV-11 - XXXIV-12**	XXXV-1 - XXXV-10* and XXXV-11**	XXXVI-1 - XXXVI-17* and XXXVI-18 - XXXVI-21**
Spain (1988)+	XXXII-1 - XXXII-13* and XXXII-14**	XXXIII-1 - XXXIII-14* and XXXIII-15**	XXXIV-1 - XXXIV-10* and XXXIV-11 - XXXIV-12**	XXXV-1 - XXXV-10* and XXXV-11**	XXXVI-1 - XXXVI-17* and XXXVI-18 - XXXVI-21**
Sweden (1988)+	XXXII-1 - XXXII-13* and XXXII-14**	XXXIII-1 - XXXIII-14* and XXXIII-15**	XXXIV-1 - XXXIV-10* and XXXIV-11 - XXXIV-12**	XXXV-1 - XXXV-10* and XXXV-11**	XXXVI-1 - XXXVI-17* and XXXVI-18 - XXXVI-21**
Ukraine (2004)+	XXXII-1 - XXXII-13* and XXXII-14**; XXXII-15 - XXXII-16	XXXIII-1 - XXXIII-14* and XXXIII-15**	XXXIV-1 - XXXIV-10* and XXXIV-11 - XXXIV-12**	XXXV-1 - XXXV-10* and XXXV-11**	XXXVI-1 - XXXVI-17* and XXXVI-18 - XXXVI-21**
U.K.	XXXII-1 - XXXII-13* and XXXII-14**	XXXIII-1 - XXXIII-14* and XXXIII-15**	XXXIV-1 - XXXIV-10* and XXXIV-11 - XXXIV-12**	XXXV-1 - XXXV-10* and XXXV-11**	XXXVI-1 - XXXVI-17* and XXXVI-18 - XXXVI-21**
Uruguay (1985)+	XXXII-1 - XXXII-13* and XXXII-14**; XXXII-15	XXXIII-1 - XXXIII-14* and XXXIII-15**	XXXIV-1 - XXXIV-10* and XXXIV-11 - XXXIV-12**	XXXV-1 - XXXV-10* and XXXV-11**	XXXVI-1 - XXXVI-17* and XXXVI-18 - XXXVI-21**
U.S.A.	XXXII-1 - XXXII-13* and XXXII-14**	XXXIII-1 - XXXIII-14* and XXXIII-15**	XXXIV-1 - XXXIV-10* and XXXIV-11 - XXXIV-12**	XXXV-1 - XXXV-10* and XXXV-11**	XXXVI-1 - XXXVI-17* and XXXVI-18 - XXXVI-21**

"+Year attained Consultative Status. Acceptance by that state required to bring into force Recommendations or Measures of meetings from that Year forward."

* Management Plans annexed to these Measures deemed to have been approved in accordance with Article 6(1) of Annex V to the Protocol on Environmental Protection to the Antarctic Treaty and the Measure not specifying a different approval method.

** Modifications and/or additions to List of Historic Sites and Monuments deemed to have been approved in accordance with Article 8(2) of Annex V to the Protocol on Environmental Protection to the Antarctic Treaty and the Measure not specifying a different approval method.

Office of the Assistant Legal Adviser for Treaty Affairs
Department of State
Washington, March 27, 2014.

Report of the Depositary Government for the Convention on the Conservation of Antarctic Marine Living Resources (CCAMLR)

Information paper submitted by Australia

Abstract

A report is provided by Australia as Depositary of the Convention on the Conservation of Antarctic Marine Living Resources 1980.

Background

Australia, as Depositary of the *Convention on the Conservation of Antarctic Marine Living Resources* 1980 ('the Convention') is pleased to report to the Thirty-seventh Antarctic Treaty Consultative Meeting (ATCM XXXVII) on the status of the Convention.

Australia advises Antarctic Treaty Parties that, since the Thirty-sixth Antarctic Treaty Consultative Meeting (ATCM XXXVI), there has been no depository activity.

A copy of the status list for the Convention is available via the internet on the Australian Treaties Database at the following address:

http://www.austlii.edu.au/au/other/dfat/treaty_list/depository/CCAMLR.html

The status list is also available on request to the Treaties Secretariat of the Australian Government Department of Foreign Affairs and Trade. Requests can be conveyed through Australian diplomatic missions.

Report by the Depositary Government for the Convention for the Conservation of Antarctic Seals in Accordance with Recommendation XIII-2, Paragraph 2(D)

Report submitted by the United Kingdom

New Accessions to CCAS

No requests to accede to CCAS have been received since the previous Report; ATCM XXXVI /IP013.

Following a request from Spain in 2012, all Contracting Parties confirmed consent, in accordance with the provisions of Article 12 of the Convention, for the Spanish Government to be formally invited to deposit an instrument of accession. The UK communicated this to the Spanish Government on 25th March 2013. However, to date no instrument of accession from Spain has been received by the UK. Spain would formally accede to the Convention 30 days after such an instrument of accession was received by the UK.

The full list of countries which were original signatories to the Convention, and countries which have subsequently acceded is attached to this report (Annex A).

CCAS Annual Return 2012/2013

Annex B lists all capturing and killing of Antarctic seals by Contracting Parties to CCAS for the reporting year 1 March 2012 to 28 February 2013. All reported captures were for scientific research.

Next CCAS Annual Return

Contracting Parties to CCAS are again reminded that the Exchange of Information, referred to in Paragraph 6(a) in the Annex to the Convention, for the reporting period of 1 March 2013 to 28 February 2014 is due by **30 June 2014**. CCAS Parties should submit their returns, including nil returns, to both the United Kingdom and to SCAR. The UK would like to encourage all Contracting Parties to CCAS to submit their returns on time.

The CCAS report for the reporting period 2013/2014 will be submitted to ATCM XXXVIII, once the June 2014 deadline for exchange of information has passed.

ANNEX A

PARTIES TO THE CONVENTION FOR THE CONSERVATION OF ANTARCTIC SEALS (CCAS)

London, 1 June – 31 December 1972
(The Convention entered into force on 11 March 1978)

State	Date of Signature	Date of deposit (Ratification or Acceptance)
Argentina[1]	9 June 1972	7 March 1978
Australia	5 October 1972	1 July 1987
Belgium	9 June 1972	9 February 1978
Chile[1]	28 December 1972	7 February 1980
France[2]	19 December 1972	19 February 1975
Japan	28 December 1972	28 August 1980
Norway	9 June 1972	10 December 1973
Russia[1,2,4]	9 June 1972	8 February 1978
South Africa	9 June 1972	15 August 1972
United Kingdom[2]	9 June 1972	10 September 1974[3]
United States of America[2]	28 June 1972	19 January 1977

ACCESSIONS

State	Date of deposit of Instrument of Accession
Brazil	11 February 1991
Canada	4 October 1990
Germany[1]	30 September 1987
Italy	2 April 1992
Poland	15 August 1980
Pakistan	25 March 2013

[1] Declaration or Reservation
[2] Objection
[3] The instrument of ratification included the Channel Islands and the Isle of Man
[4] Former USSR

ANNUAL CCAS REPORT 2012/2013

Synopsis of reporting in accordance with Article 5 and the Annex of the Convention: Capturing and killing of seals during the period 1 March 2012 to 28 February 2013.

Contracting Party	Antarctic Seals Captured	Antarctic Seals Killed
Argentina	317 (a)	0
Australia	0	0
Belgium	0	0
Brazil	0	0
Canada	0	0
Chile	73 (b)	0
France	53 (c)	0
Germany	0	0
Italy	0	0
Japan	0	0
Norway	0	0
Poland	0	0
Russia	Information not yet received	
South Africa	0	0
United Kingdom	0	0
United States of America	1575 (d)	2 (e)

(a) **6** male adult Elephant Seals, **44** unknown gender adults and juvenile Elephant Seals.
197 Southern Elephant Seal pups, **16** recaptured juvenile and adult Southern Elephant Seals, **6** Leopard Seals, **48** Unspecified Seals (combination of Leopard, Weddell and Crabeater Seals).

(b) **24** female Antarctic Fur Seals, **15** Southern Elephant Seals, **16** Weddell Seals, **15** Leopard Seals, **3** Crabeater Seals.

(c) **8** adult or sub-adult Weddell Seals and **45** juvenile Weddell Seals.

(d) **228** female adult Weddell Seals, **122** male adult Weddell Seals, **14** undisclosed adult Weddell Seals, **1** female juvenile Weddell Seal, **2** male juvenile Weddell Seals, **4** unknown juvenile Weddell Seals, **314** Weddell Seals pups, **278** male Weddell Seal pups, **33** unknown Weddell Seal pups **29** undisclosed age and gender Weddell Seals, **41** adult Antarctic Fur Seals, **9** juvenile Antarctic fur seals, **442** Antarctic Fur Seals pups, **21** adult Leopard Seals, **1** juvenile Antarctic Fur Seal, **11** adult Southern Elephant Seals and **25** Southern Elephant Seal pups.

(e) **1** male Weddell Seal pup mortality, handled in reporting year (and included within the captured figure) and **1** female Weddell Seal adult mortality, not handled in reporting year (and not reported within the 2011-2012 CCAS return). Both fatalities were apparently due to natural causes which occurred well after capture.

All reported capturing was for scientific research.

Report of the Depositary Government for the Agreement on the Conservation of Albatrosses and Petrels (ACAP)

Information paper submitted by Australia

Abstract

A report is provided by Australia as Depositary of the *Agreement on the Conservation of Albatrosses and Petrels* 2001.

Background

Australia, as Depositary of the *Agreement on the Conservation of Albatrosses and Petrels* 2001 ('the Agreement') is pleased to report to the Thirty-seventh Antarctic Treaty Consultative Meeting (ATCM XXXVII) on the status of the Agreement.

Australia advises Antarctic Treaty Parties that, since the Thirty-sixth Antarctic Treaty Consultative Meeting (ATCM XXXVI), no States have acceded to the Agreement.

A copy of the status list for the Agreement is available via the internet on the Australian Treaties Database at the following address:

http://www.austlii.edu.au/au/other/dfat/treaty_list/depository/consalbnpet.html

The status list is also available on request to the Treaties Secretariat of the Australian Government Department of Foreign Affairs and Trade. Requests can be conveyed through Australian diplomatic missions.

Report by the CCAMLR Observer to the Thirty-seventh Antarctic Treaty Consultative Meeting

Summary of the Report of the Thirty-second Meeting of the Commission[1]

Hobart, Australia
23 October to 1 November 2013

1.   The Thirty-second Annual Meeting of the Commission for the Conservation of Antarctic Marine Living Resources (CCAMLR-XXXII) was chaired by Mr Leszek Dybiec (Poland). 25 Members, The Netherlands, Vanuatu and representatives of NGOs and industry participated. A copy of the Report of CCAMR-XXXII is available at http://www.ccamlr.org/en/ccamlr-xxxii

STATUS OF THE CONVENTION

2.   Australia, the Depository for the Convention, advised that the Republic of Panama had acceded to the Convention on 20 March 2013. The Convention entered into force for Panama on 19 April 2013. The Membership of the Commission is unchanged.

IMPLEMENTATION AND COMPLIANCE

3.   The Commission approved a review of its Catch Documentation Scheme and agreed to call for tenders for a new vessel monitoring system. It successfully implemented a Compliance Evaluation Procedure for the first time and approved a Non-Contracting Party-IUU Vessel List (http://www.ccamlr.org/en/compliance/illegal-unreported-and-unregulated-iuu-fishing).

FINANCE AND ADMINISTRATION

4.   The Commission endorsed on-going efforts to develop a sustainable financing strategy. It requested that the Secretariat review its current Strategic Plan (2012-2014) and revise it, as appropriate, to serve the period 2015 to 2017 for consideration at CCAMLR-XXXIII.

SCIENTIFIC COMMITTEE

Krill resources

5.   In 2012/13, five Members harvested 217 000 tonnes of krill from Subareas 48.1 (154 000 tonnes), 48.2 (31 000 tonnes) and 48.3 (32 000 tonnes)[2]. In comparison, the total reported catch of krill in 2011/12 was 161 000 tonnes taken from Subareas 48.1 (76 000 tonnes), 48.2 (29 000 tonnes) and 48.3 (56 000 tonnes) (SC-CAMLR-XXXII, Table 2).

---

[1] Prepared by the CCAMLR Secretariat
[2] The catch figures for all fisheries have been updated since the conclusion of CCAMLR-XXXII to reflect preliminary, end-of-season figures (30 November 2013)

6.   Notifications for krill fishing in 2013/14 were received from six Members and 19 vessels all in Area 48 (SC-CAMLR-XXXII, paragraph 3.3); there were no notifications for exploratory krill fisheries.

7.   The Commission noted the Scientific Committee's re-evaluation of the work plan and timescale of implementation of a feedback management process for management of the krill fishery. It welcomed the establishment of new CEMP sites by Poland and the Ukraine and the collaboration with krill fishing industry regarding the collection of acoustic data and ecological research on commercial vessels.

Finfish resources

8.   In 2012/13, 11 Members fished for toothfish (*Dissostichus eleginoides* and/or *D. mawsoni*) in Subareas 48.3, 48.4, 48.6, 58.6, 58.7, 88.1 and 88.2 and Divisions 58.4.1, 58.4.2, 58.4.3a, 58.5.1 and 58.5.2; Members also conducted research fishing for *Dissostichus* spp. in Subarea 48.5 and Division 58.4.4b. The reported total catch of *Dissostichus* spp. was 12 900. In comparison, the total reported catch of toothfish in 2011/12 was 14 702 tonnes (SC-CAMLR-XXXII, Table 2). The Commission noted that during 2013 the Secretariat had closed toothfish fisheries in Subareas 48.4N, 88.1 and 88.2 as catch limits were reached.

9.   The Commission noted the occurrence of catches of *D. eleginoides* from outside the Convention Area, including regions outside EEZs, reported by Members through the CDS, (SC-CAMLR-XXXII, Table 3).

10.   In 2012/13, two Members targeted icefish (*Champsocephalus gunnari*) in Subarea 48.3 and one Member targeted icefish in Division 58.5.2; this species was also reported as by-catch in the krill fishery. The reported total catch of *C. gunnari* was 2 000 tonnes; in comparison, the total reported catch of icefish in 2011/12 was 1 011 tonnes (SC-CAMLR-XXXII, Table 1).

Exploratory fisheries

11.   Seven Members submitted notifications for exploratory fisheries in Divisions 58.4.1, 58.4.2 and 58.4.3a and Subareas 48.6, 88.1 and 88.2 (SC-CAMLR-XXXII, paragraph 3.145). Four Members submitted notifications to conduct research fishing for the closed areas in Divisions 58.4.4a and 58.4.4b, and Subareas 48.2 and 48.5. No new fisheries were notified for 2013/14. These notifications were endorsed by the Commission, with revised catch limits set out in the Conservation Measures adopted at CCAMLR-XXXII (http://www.ccamlr.org/en/document/publications/schedule-conservation-measures-force-2013/14)

Fish and invertebrate by-catch

11.   The Scientific Committee's recommendations in relation to by-catch issues included the need to examine finfish by-catch across the krill fishing fleet for vessels using all trawl gears and the development of a risk-based sustainable management approach for the impact of toothfish fisheries on skates.

Assessment and avoidance of incidental mortality

12.   The Commission noted the Scientific Committee's general advice on incidental mortality of seabirds and marine mammals (SC-CAMLR-XXXII, paragraphs 4.1 and 4.4), in particular the total extrapolated mortalities of seabirds within the Convention Area which totalled 141 (the lowest reported to date).

Bottom fishing and vulnerable marine ecosystems

13.   The Commission noted that:

(i)   no VMEs were added to the VME registry during 2013. There are currently forty-six VMEs in the registry: Subareas 48.1 (22 VMEs), 48.2 (13 VMEs) and 88.1 (9 VMEs), and Division 58.4.1 (2 VMEs). These VMEs were observed using *in situ* photography and benthic sampling.

(ii)   there were five notifications of encounters with potential VMEs during exploratory bottom fisheries in 2012/13 with one new VME risk-area declared in Subarea 88.1 in 2013 (SC-CAMLR-XXXII, Annex 6, paragraph 7.13; CCAMLR-XXXII/BG/06 Rev. 1), and a total of 64 VME risk-areas closed to fishing since the introduction of this conservation measure in 2008/09.

Marine Protected Areas

14.   The Commission noted the progress towards a representative system of MPAs within the Convention Area in relation to Domain 1 (Western Antarctic Peninsula–South Scotia Arc), preparatory work in Domains 3 (Weddell Sea) and the southern part of Domain 4 (Bouvet–Maud) up to 20°E. The Commission welcomed the proposal for an international workshop in April 2014 in Bremerhaven, Germany, to progress the scientific work on a Weddell Sea MPA. The Commission also noted that Norway has undertaken preliminary discussions about the potential for an MPA planning process around Bouvet Island (southern part of Domain 4.

15.   The Commission noted the consideration by the Scientific Committee of Antarctic specially managed areas (ASMAs) and Antarctic specially protected areas (ASPAs) in the Convention Area and agreed that the provision of advice from CCAMLR to the ATCM, in order that such advice could be included in decision-making, was consistent with the spirit of cooperation and harmonisation between CCAMLR and the ATCM.

Climate change

16.   The Commission requested that it be prioritised in the agenda of next year's meeting.

Administrative matters

17.   Dr Anna Panasiuk-Chodnicka, from the University of Gdańsk, Poland, was selected to receive a CCAMLR Scholarship in 2013. She is the fourth recipient of the Scholarship. The previous recipients are from Chile, Argentina and China.

SCHEME OF INTERNATIONAL SCIENTIFIC OBSERVATION

18.   The Commission noted that SISO was reviewed in 2013 and that detailed consideration of the outcomes of the review would be considered intersessionally and reported to its meeting in 2014.

CONSERVATION MEASURES

Proposals for MPAs and special areas

19.   Building on discussions that occurred at the Special Meeting of the Commission at Bremerhaven, Germany, 11-16 July 2013, Australia, France and the EU introduced a revised proposal to establish a representative system of MPAs in the East Antarctica Planning Domain (EARSMPA; CCAMLR-XXXII/34 Rev. 1) and New Zealand and the USA introduced a revised proposal for the establishment of a Ross Sea Region MPA (CCAMLR-XXXII/27). CCAMLR-XXXII considered a broad range of issues associated with both proposals including:
*   Pre-ambular text

- Boundaries and area
- Duration and review periods
- Provisions for fishing and other activities
- Research and monitoring arrangements, and
- Relationship to the General Framework for the establishment of CCAMLR MPAs.

20.   The Commission was unable to reach consensus for the implementation of either of the two MPA proposals.

Licensing and inspection obligations of Contracting Parties

21.   The Commission endorsed SCIC's advice to revise CM 10-02 to improve the licensing and inspection obligations of Contracting Parties with regard to their vessels operating in the Convention Area and agreed that IMO numbers should be mandatory for all vessels operating in the Convention Area.

22.   Following discussions that occurred in the Search and Rescue Working Group established by ATCM-XXXV, the Commission agreed to require the provision of vessel communication details to facilitate the use of CCAMLR's VMS in support of search and rescue operations in the Convention Area and for a MoU to be developed between CCAMLR and Maritime Rescue Coordination Centres to facilitate these efforts.

Port inspection of fishing vessels

23.   The Commission endorsed SCIC's advice to amend CM 10-03 to require the mandatory provision of port inspection reports to the Flag State of the vessel inspected.

General fishery matters

Notifications

25.   The Commission revised the requirements for the notification of krill fisheries to provide more detailed information on krill processing and the configuration of nets and mammal exclusion devices used on board vessels (Annex 21-03/A) and further strengthened the reporting requirement for the estimation of the green weight of krill caught (Annex 21-03/B). The requirements for notification were also extended to include information on the collection of acoustic data (SC-CAMLR-XXX, paragraph 2.10).

26.   The Commission adopted conservation measures concerning fishing seasons, closed areas, prohibition of fishing, by-catch limits, catch limits, research requirements in relation to data poor exploratory fisheries and managing fishing activity in the event inaccessibility due to ice cover for CCAMLR-managed fisheries for Patagonian toothfish *(D. eleginoides),* Antarctic toothfish *(D. mawsoni)* and icefish *(Champsocephalus gunnari).*

27.   Conservation measures and resolutions adopted at CCAMLR-XXXII have been published in the *Schedule of Conservation Measures in Force 2013/14* http://www.ccamlr.org/en/conservation-and-management/conservation-measures

IMPLEMENTATION OF CONVENTION OBJECTIVES

Follow-up to the 2008 CCAMLR Performance Review

28.   The Commission agreed to start a process to evaluate the potential scope of a second Performance Review of CCAMLR.

COOPERATION WITH THE ANTARCTIC TREATY SYSTEM AND INTERNATIONAL ORGANISATIONS

Cooperation with SCAR

29.   The Commission noted the advice of the Scientific Committee on the benefits of a more strategic approach to the relationship between CCAMLR and SCAR and, in particular, the outcomes of an Action Group meeting between SCAR and CCAMLR in Brussels, Belgium, associated with ATCM XXXVI.

OTHER BUSINESS

Date and location of the next meeting

30.   The Thirty-third Meeting will be held at the CCAMLR Headquarters, Hobart from 20 to 31 October 2014. The Thirty-third Meeting of the Scientific Committee will be held in Hobart from 20 to 24 October 2014.

The Scientific Committee on Antarctic Research (SCAR) Annual Report 2013/14

1. Background

The Scientific Committee on Antarctic Research (SCAR) is a non-governmental, Interdisciplinary Scientific Body of the International Council for Science (ICSU), and Observer to the Antarctic Treaty and the UNFCCC.

SCAR's Mission is (i) to be the leading, independent, non-governmental facilitator, coordinator, and advocate of excellence in Antarctic and Southern Ocean science and research and (ii) to provide independent, sound, scientifically-based advice to the Antarctic Treaty System and other policy makers including the use of science to identify emerging trends and bring these issues to the attention of policy makers.

2. Introduction

SCAR's scientific research adds value to national efforts by enabling national researchers to collaborate on large-scale scientific programmes to accomplish objectives not easily obtainable by any single country. SCAR's Members currently include 37 nations and 9 ICSU scientific Unions.

SCAR's success depends on the quality and timeliness of its scientific outputs. Descriptions of SCAR's research programmes and scientific outputs are available at: www.scar.org. This paper should be read in conjunction with a separate Background Paper that highlights recent science papers published since the last Treaty meeting.

SCAR produces an electronic quarterly Newsletter highlighting relevant science and other SCAR related issues. Please email: info@scar.org if you wish to be added to the mailing list. As well as the web (www.scar.org), SCAR is also available on Facebook, LinkedIn, Google+ and Twitter.

3. SCAR Highlights (2013/14)

In this paper we highlight examples of SCAR activities that we believe to be of particular interest to Treaty Parties. For further details see www.scar.org.

State of the Antarctic Ecosystem (AntEco) *www.scar.org/srp/anteco*

The Scientific Research Programme (SRP) AntEco focuses on patterns of biodiversity across terrestrial, limnological, glacial and marine environments within the Antarctic, sub-Antarctic and Southern Ocean regions, and will provide scientific knowledge on biodiversity that can be also used for conservation and management. A primary product of this programme will be recommendations concerning Antarctica's management and conservation.

Antarctic Thresholds - Ecosystem Resilience and Adaptation (AnT-ERA) *www.scar.org/srp/ant-era*

The AnT-ERA SRP examines the current biological processes in Antarctic ecosystems, to define their thresholds and thereby determine resistance and resilience to change. Polar ecosystem processes are key to informing wider ecological debate about the nature of stability and change in ecosystems. The programme will attempt to determine the likelihood of cataclysmic shifts or "tipping points" in Antarctic ecosystems.

Antarctic Climate Change in the 21st Century (AntClim[21]) *www.scar.org/srp/antclim21*

The goals of the SRP AntClim[21] are to deliver improved regional predictions of key elements of the Antarctic atmosphere, ocean and cryosphere for the next 20 to 200 years and to understand the responses of the physical and biological systems to natural and anthropogenic forcing factors. Palaeo-reconstructions of selected time periods, recognised as past analogues for future climate predictions, will be used to validate model performances for the Antarctic region.

Southern Ocean Acidification *www.scar.org/ssg/physical-sciences/acidification*

SCAR will synthesise the scientific understanding of Southern Ocean acidification. The Action Group tasked with this consists of an international cross-disciplinary team of ocean acidification experts representing the fields of marine carbonate chemistry, global and regional modelling, marine ecology, ecotoxicology/physiology and paleoceanography. The final report will be published in August 2014 and copies made available to Treaty Parties.

Geoheritage Values *www.scar.org/ssg/geosciences/geoheritage*

A new Action Group on Geoheritage values, conservation and management has been formed by SCAR. In this context, Geological "values" will examine aspects such as unique mineral or fossil localities and landforms or outcrops of special significance. The outcomes of discussions held at the Treaty will be considered when the Terms of Reference and future work plan of this group are discussed during the SCAR Business meetings in August 2014.

Antarctic Biodiversity Informatics *www.scar.org/ssg/life-sciences/abi*

Biodiversity Informatics is the application of informatics techniques to biodiversity information for improved management, presentation, discovery, exploration and analysis. This Expert Group will coordinate biodiversity informatics activities across SCAR for research, management, conservation and monitoring purposes and promote free and open access.

Environmental Contamination in Antarctica *www.scar.org/ssg/life-sciences/eca*

The main aims of the Environmental Contamination in Antarctica Action Group are the analysis and comparison of national research projects, the coordination of studies on environmental contamination in Polar Regions and to identify new research on the subject.

Ice Sheet Mass Balance and Sea Level *www.scar.org/ssg/physical-sciences/ismass*

The SCAR/IASC/CliC Expert Group on Ice Sheet Mass Balance and Sea Level aims to improve estimation of the mass balance of ice sheets and their contribution to sea level, to facilitate coordination of the different international efforts focused on this field of research, to propose directions for future research in this area, to integrate the observations and modelling efforts, as well as the distribution and archiving of the corresponding data, and to attract a new generation of scientists into this field of research.

Operational Meteorology in the Antarctic *www.scar.org/ssg/physical-sciences/opmet*

This Expert Group focuses on establishing links between groups working in the same area of operational meteorology in Antarctica, in particular the WMO EC-PORS (Panel of Experts on Polar Observations, Research and Services) group.

Remote Sensing *www.scar.org/ssg/life-sciences/remotesensing*

The SCAR Action Group on Remote Sensing has been established with the full name "Development of a satellite-based, Antarctic-wide, remote sensing approach to monitor bird and animal populations", with the aim to address the topic of "Animal monitoring via remote sensing".

The Southern Ocean Observing System *www.soos.aq*

The SCAR/SCOR Southern Ocean Observing System (SOOS) has the mission *to establish a multidisciplinary observing system to deliver the sustained observations of the Southern Ocean*. A SOOS International Project Office, established in Australia and supported by the Institute for Marine and Antarctic Studies at the University of Tasmania in Hobart and Antarctica New Zealand, supports implementation of the SOOS.

The Antarctic Climate Change and the Environment *www.scar.org/othergroups/acce*

The climatic, physical and biological properties of Antarctica and the Southern Ocean are closely coupled to other parts of the global environment by the oceans and the atmosphere. In 2009 SCAR published the landmark Antarctic Climate Change and the Environment Report and since then has provided annual updates. See the separate IP on the ACCE.

The SCAR Science Horizon Scan *www.scar.org/horizonscanning/*

Following the crowdsourcing of over 850 unique scientific questions and the nomination of almost 500 leading scientist by the SCAR community, the 1st SCAR Antarctic and Southern Ocean Science Horizon Scan assembled more than 70 of the world's leading Antarctic scientists, policy makers and visionaries (including many early career scientists) in Queenstown, NZ, in April this year. Their remit was to identify the most important scientific questions, that will or should be addressed by research in and from the southern polar regions over the next two decades. The Scan outcomes will assist in aligning international programmes, projects and resources to effectively facilitate Antarctic and Southern Ocean science in the coming years. A full report will be submitted to the 2015 Treaty Meeting.

Antarctic Conservation in the 21st Century www.scar.org/antarctic-treaty-system/scats

SCAR, in collaboration with several partners, are developing a strategy entitled 'Antarctic Conservation for the 21st Century'. The activity will encourage participation from all stakeholders in the region. The approach will be structured to align with both the Protocol on Environmental Protection to the Antarctic Treaty and the Five Year Work Plan of the Committee for Environmental Protection. The Antarctic Conservation Strategy links closely with the Antarctic Environments Portal. See also the COMNAP-SCAR WP entitled 'Antarctic Conservation Strategy: Scoping Workshop on Practical Solutions'. Note that a conservation 'flipped symposium' will be held during the SCAR Open Science Conference in August 2014 as part of this process.

Antarctic Data Management www.scar.org/data-products

SCAR promotes free and unrestricted access to Antarctic data and information by promoting open and accessible archiving practices, through its Standing Committees on Antarctic Data Management (SCADM) and Antarctic Geographic Information (SCAGI). SCAR also has several Products of use to the Antarctic Community.

4. SCAR Fellowships and Prizes

In order to expand capacity in all its Members, SCAR runs several Fellowship and Prize Schemes (www.scar.awards):

- *SCAR/COMNAP Fellowships* are focussed on early career scientists and engineers in Antarctic scientific research, to build new connections and further strengthen international capacity and cooperation in Antarctic research. The fellowships are being launched in tandem with the CCAMLR Scholarships.
- *Martha T Muse Prize for Science and Policy in Antarctica,* sponsored by the Tinker Foundation, is a US$ 100,000 unrestricted award presented to an individual in the fields of Antarctic science or policy. See: www.museprize.org.
- *SCAR Visiting Professor Scheme* provides mid to late career scientists the opportunity to undertake short-term visits to a facility in or operated by SCAR Member countries, to provide training and mentoring.

5. SCAR wins 2013 Prix Biodiversité of the Prince Albert II of Monaco Foundation

SCAR was awarded the Prince Albert II of Monaco Foundation's 2013 Prix Biodiversité was in recognition of its contribution to science and its work to improve our understanding of the environment.

6. Future SCAR Meetings

There are several major SCAR Meetings coming up (www.scar.org/events/), including:

- *XXXIII SCAR Meetings and Open Science Conference.* 22 August - 3 September 2014, Auckland, New Zealand. The SCAR Open Science Conference will be held on 25-29 August. See: http://www.scar2014.com.
- *XII International Symposium on Antarctic Earth Sciences (ISAES) 2015.* 13-17th July 2015, Goa, India. http://www.ncaor.gov.in/files/ISAES-2015Flyer1.pdf

Annual Report for 2013 of the Council of Managers of National Antarctic Programs (COMNAP)

COMNAP is the organisation of National Antarctic Programs which brings together, in particular, the managers of those programs, that is, the national officials responsible for planning, conducting and managing support to science in Antarctica on behalf of their respective governments, all Antarctic Treaty Consultative Parties.

COMNAP was established in September 1988, and so, 2013 marked the 25th anniversary of our association. In celebration, COMNAP published *A Story of Antarctic Cooperation: 25 Years of the Council of Managers of National Antarctic Programs*. Copies have been freely distributed to COMNAP Members, to libraries and one copy has been placed in each ATCM delegation box. Further copies are available upon request.

In 2013, the Czech Republic National Antarctic Program was granted COMNAP membership. Thus, COMNAP has grown into an international association whose Members are the 29 National Antarctic Programs from the Consultative Parties of Argentina, Australia, Belgium, Brazil, Bulgaria, Chile, China, Czech Republic, Ecuador, Finland, France, Germany, India, Italy, Japan, Republic of Korea, Netherlands, New Zealand, Norway, Peru, Poland, Russian Federation, South Africa, Spain, Sweden, United Kingdom, Ukraine, Uruguay and USA. Presently, the National Antarctic Program of the Republic of Belarus is a COMNAP observer organisation.

COMNAP's Constitution asserts its purpose: to develop and promote best practice in managing the support of scientific research in the Antarctic. As an organisation, COMNAP acts to add value to National Antarctic Program's efforts by serving as a forum to develop practices that improve effectiveness of activities in an environmentally responsible manner, by facilitating and promoting international partnerships, and by providing opportunities and systems for information exchange.

COMNAP strives to provide the Antarctic Treaty System with objective, practical, technical and non-political advice drawn from the National Antarctic Programs' extensive pool of expertise and their first-hand Antarctic knowledge. A full list of COMNAP's papers can be found in ATCM XXXIV IP007 *Review of COMNAP Working Papers and Information Papers presented to the ATCM 1988 - 2011*.

Antarctic sea ice is thickening in some coastal Antarctic areas. While in other areas warming is bringing changes to areas and associated infrastructure. These changing conditions are challenging National Antarctic Programs in their delivery of supplies and personnel to stations and therefore threatening timely delivery of Antarctic science and results. Such challenges necessitate the need for cooperation. Such cooperation takes place each year under planned circumstances through long established MOUs or through short-term requirements of operations and science. Sometimes, cooperation is required in order to address an unplanned situation or eventuality. The COMNAP survey on international cooperation clearly demonstrates that there is a high level of international cooperation taking place amongst National Antarctic Programs.

COMNAP attended meetings in the past twelve months as an invited observer and wishes to thank CCAMLR, FARO, HCA and IAATO for that opportunity. The COMNAP Chair and the Executive Secretary also participated in the SCAR Horizon Scan Retreat as did several of the National Antarctic Program managers. COMNAP was pleased to contribute sponsorship to SCAR to support the Horizon Scan process.

The COMNAP Annual General Meeting was held in July 2013 in Seoul, Republic of Korea, hosted by the KOPRI. Heinrich Miller (AWI) continues as COMNAP Chair and Michelle Rogan-Finnemore continues as Executive Secretary.

COMNAP Highlights and Achievements for 2013

COMNAP Book

To mark the COMNAP 25th anniversary, COMNAP published *A Story of Antarctic Cooperation: 25 Years of the Council of Managers of National Antarctic Programs* (ISBN 978-0-473-24776-8). The book documents the rich contribution that the organisation has made to the Antarctic community. The author, former COMNAP Chair, Gillian Wratt, wrote the book to serve as a reference to the work that COMNAP has achieved in its relatively short history.

Antarctic Conservation Challenges Scoping Workshop

John Shears (BAS) and Kevin Hughes (BAS) convened, on behalf of COMNAP and SCAR, this workshop in Cambridge (24-25 September 2013) to identify practical National Antarctic Program-led responses to Antarctic conservation challenges (see Chown et al., 2012). The workshop outcomes were to inform the drafting by SCAR of an Antarctic Conservation Strategy. The workshop final report can be found in the joint COMNAP-SCAR Information Paper to this ATCM. An open Conservation Challenges workshop will be held at the SCAR OSC on 26 August 2014 in Auckland, New Zealand.

Icebreaker Workshop

Heinrich Miller (COMNAP Chair) convened the COMNAP Icebreaker Workshop on 21–23 October 2013 in Capetown, South Africa. The open workshop was held aboard the new research and survey vessel *S.A. Agulhus II* and was made possible due to with generous organisational support from the SANAP. The workshop provided an opportunity for National Antarctic Programs to discuss requirements and plans for new icebreakers. More information can be found in the COMNAP Information Paper *Icebreaker Workshop* presented to this meeting.

Southern Ocean Observing System (SOOS) Workshop

Rob Wooding (AAD) convened the COMNAP SOOS Workshop on 7 July 2013, on the margins of the COMNAP AGM in Seoul, Republic of Korea, with support from Louise Newman (SOOS Project Office). Keynote speakers included Oscar Schofield (USA), Andrew Constable (Australia) and Anna Wahlin (Sweden). In addition, National Antarctic Programs gave insightful presentations on their marine science priorities, shipping schedules and vessel capacities. Presentations available at www.comnap.aq/Publications/SitePages/Home.aspx. As a result of the workshop and after discussions at the COMNAP AGM, COMNAP established a "SOOS Think Tank" for National Antarctic Programs to exchange information that might be useful in support of the SOOS project.

COMNAP Antarctic Research Fellowship

COMNAP established the Antarctic Research Fellowship in 2011. For the 2013 round, COMNAP was able to offer a full Fellowship to Charlotte Havermans (Belgium) to undertake research at the AWI on the impact of environmental changes on the amphipod Themisto gaudichaudii. COMNAP and SCAR each offered a half Fellowship to Luis Rodriguez (Spain) to work at the AAD on niche modelling as a tool for invasive risk assessment of Antarctic vascular plants. COMNAP and SCAR have agreed to once again offer the Fellowships for 2014. Both organisations are also working with CCAMLR to promote their scholarships. Applications for all three schemes are now open and the 2014 COMNAP Antarctic Research Fellow will be announced in August 2014 as part of the COMNAP AGM in Christchurch, New Zealand. For COMNAP Fellowship recipients reports see www.comnap.aq/SitePages/fellowships.aspx.

COMNAP Products and Tools

Search and Rescue (SAR) webpage

As a result of ATCM Resolution 4 (2013) adopted as a result of discussion at the ATCM SAR-WG, COMNAP has established a SAR webpage in consultation with RCCs at www.comnap.aq/membersonly/SitePages/SAR.aspx. See also the COMNAP Information Paper to this meeting entitled *COMNAP SAR Website Update*.

Accident, Incident and Near-Miss Reporting (AINMR)

Information on problems encountered in Antarctica has always been exchanged. The very first ATCM agreed in Recommendation I-VII Exchange *of Information on Logistics Problems* that this should be so (effective 30 April 1962). COMNAP Annual General Meetings offer an opportunity for Members to exchange such information and also an on-line, comprehensive AINMR System is in place and is running on the members-only area of the COMNAP website. The AINMR's primary objective is: to capture information about events that had, or could have had, serious consequences; and/or reveal lessons to be learned; and/or are novel, very unusual events. Full reports on accidents can also be posted on the site and can be discussed and reviewed. So that National Antarctic Programs can learn from each other to reduce the risk of serious consequences occurring in the course of their Antarctic activities. www.comnap.aq/membersonly/AINMR/SitePages/Home.aspx.

COMNAP Ship Position Reporting System (SPRS)

The SPRS (www.comnap.aq/sprs) is an optional, voluntary system for exchange of information about National Antarctic Program ship operations. Its primary purpose is to facilitate collaboration. It can also, however, make a very useful contribution to safety with all SPRS information made available to the RCCs as an additional source of information complementing all other national and international systems in place. Position information is delivered via email and can be graphically displayed in Google Earth. There was an average of 21 vessels regularly reporting during their Antarctic voyages this season.

The Antarctic Flight Information Manual (AFIM)

AFIM is a handbook of aeronautical information published by COMNAP as a tool towards safe air operations in Antarctica as recommended by the ATCM Recommendation XV-20 and updated as Resolution 1 (2013). COMNAP has entered the trial phase of an electronic AFIM. The AFIM will continue to be updated via information from National Antarctic Programs. The most recent AFIM paper revision set was produced and distributed to AFIM holders on 21 February 2014.

Antarctic Telecommunications Operators Manual (ATOM)

ATOM is an evolution of the handbook of telecommunications practices to which ATCM Recommendation X-3 *Improvement of Telecommunications in Antarctica and the Collection and Distribution of Antarctic Meteorological Data* refers. COMNAP Members and SAR authorities have access to the latest version (Feb 2014) via the COMNAP website.

_____

For more information see www.comnap.aq or email info@comnap.aq.
Also, see Appendix 1 and Appendix 2 to this Annual Report.

Appendix 1. COMNAP officers, projects and expert groups

Executive Committee (EXCOM)

The COMNAP Chair and Vice-Chairs are elected officers of COMNAP. The elected officers plus the Executive Secretary, compose the COMNAP Executive Committee as follows:

Position	Officer	Term expires
Chair	Heinrich Miller (AWI) heinrich.miller@awi.de	AGM 2014
Vice-Chairs	Hyoung Chul Shin (KOPRI) hcshin@kopri.re.kr	AGM 2016
	John Hall (BAS) jhal@bas.ac.uk	AGM 2016
	Juan Jose Dañobeitia (CSIC) jjdanobeitia@cmima.csic.es	AGM 2014
	Brian Stone (USAP/NSF) bstone@nsf.gov	AGM 2014
	Jose Olmedo (INAE) jolmedo@midena.gob.ec	AGM 2015
Executive Secretary	Michelle Rogan-Finnemore michelle.finnemore@comnap.aq	

Table 1 – COMNAP Executive Committee.

Projects

Project	Project Manager	EXCOM officer (oversight)
Antarctic Flight Information Manual (AFIM) – Implementation of new format	Paul Morin	Brian Stone
Antarctic Glossary	Valery Lukin	John Hall
Antarctic Peninsula Advanced Science Information (APASI)	Jose Retamales	Heinrich Miller
Conservation Challenges	John Hall	Heinrich Miller
Fuel Tank Automated Warning System	Oleksandr Kuzko	Brian Stone
Hydroponics Survey (Update)	Sandra Potter	Hyoung Chul Shin
SAR Webpage Development	Michelle Rogan-Finnemore	Heinrich Miller
Suppliers Database	David Blake	Juan Jose Dañobeitia
Symposium "Success through International Cooperation"	John Hall	Heinrich Miller
Telemedicine Workshop	Jeff Ayton	John Hall
Waste Water Workshop	Sandra Potter/Jose Retamales	Hyoung Chul Shin

Table 2 – COMNAP Projects currently in progress.

Expert Groups

Expert Group (topic)	Expert Group leader	EXCOM officer (oversight)
Air	Giuseppe De Rossi	Brian Stone
Energy & Technology	David Blake	Juan Jose Dañobeitia
Environment	Sandra Potter	Hyoung Chul Shin
Medical	Jeff Ayton	John Hall
Outreach	Eva Gronlund	EXCOM All
Safety	Henrik Tornberg	Jose Olmedo
Science	Jose Retamales	Heinrich Miller
Shipping	Miguel Ojeda	Juan Jose Dañobeitia
Training	Veronica Vlasich	Brian Stone

Table 3 – COMNAP Expert Groups.

Appendix 2. Meetings

Previous 12 months

7 July 2013, COMNAP SOOS Workshop (jointly convened with SCAR), Seoul, Republic of Korea.

8–10 July 2013, COMNAP Annual General Meeting (COMNAP XXV), hosted by KOPRI, Seoul, Republic of Korea.

25–26 September 2013, Antarctic Conservation Challenges Scoping Workshop (jointly convened with SCAR), Cambridge, UK.

24 and 27 September 2013, COMNAP EXCOM Meeting, BAS, Cambridge, UK.

21–23 October 2013, COMNAP Icebreaker Workshop, (onboard) SA Agulhas II, Capetown, South Africa.

Upcoming 12 months

24 August, COMNAP SCAR joint Executive Meeting, Auckland, New Zealand.

25 August 2014, COMNAP Symposium "Success through International Co-operation", Auckland, New Zealand.

26 August 2014, Antarctic Conservation Challenges Symposium (jointly with SCAR), Auckland, New Zealand.

27–29 August 2014, COMNAP Annual General Meeting (COMNAP XXVI), hosted by Antarctica New Zealand, Christchurch, New Zealand (includes a Safety Workshop and Waste Water Workshop on 28 August 2014).

2. Reports by Experts

Report of the Antarctic and Southern Ocean Coalition

1.   Introduction

ASOC is pleased to be in Brasilia for the XXXVII Antarctic Treaty Consultative Meeting. This report briefly describes ASOC's work over the past year, and outlines some key issues for this ATCM.

ASOC's Secretariat is in Washington DC, USA and its website is http://www.asoc.org. ASOC has 24 full member groups in 10 countries and supporting groups in those and several other countries. ASOC campaigns are carried out by teams of experts in Argentina, Australia, China, France, Germany, Japan, The Netherlands, New Zealand, Norway, South Africa, South Korea, Spain, Russia, Ukraine, UK and USA.

2.   Intersessional activities

Since XXXVI ATCM ASOC and its member groups' representatives participated actively in intersessional discussions in the ATCM and CEP fora, including ICGs on promoting broader Antarctic cooperation (moderated by Chile); the exercise of jurisdiction in the Antarctic Treaty Area (moderated by France); discussions on draft CEEs for two new proposed stations (moderated each by Australia and USA); climate change (moderated by the United Kingdom and Norway); informal discussions on tourism and the risk of introducing non-native organisms (moderated by Germany); and informal discussions on monitoring ASPAs wildlife values for reviewed Management Plans (moderated by the Russian Federation). ASOC also monitored remaining ICGs.

In addition, ASOC and member group representatives attended a range of meetings relevant to Antarctic environmental protection including the intersessional CCAMLR meeting in Bremerhaven, the XXXII CCAMLR Meeting, the Subsidiary Bodies in Bonn and 19th Conference of Parties in Warsaw of the UN Framework Convention on Climate Change (UNFCCC), the tenth World Wilderness Congress, and a number of International Maritime Organization meetings relating to the Polar Code. ASOC also participated in SCAR's horizon scan, to which ASOC experts contributed with research questions on key issues.

3.   Papers for XXXVII ATCM

ASOC has introduced 7 Information Papers. These papers address key environmental issues, and contain recommendations for the ATCM and CEP that will help achieve more effective environmental protection and conservation of Antarctica.

Antarctic Climate Change Report Card 2014 (IP 68) - ASOC has summarised some research findings related to climate change that have been published in the intersessional period. These findings add to the considerable existing evidence that climate change is having a major impact on Antarctica already, and is going to continue to do so. Although climate change is a global problem, Antarctic Treaty Consultative Parties have a unique ability to raise Antarctic issues in other fora where climate change is discussed, in addition to taking steps within the Antarctic Treaty System, such as funding more research.

Antarctic Resolution at the 10th World Wilderness Congress (IP 69) - In October 2013, the Tenth World Wilderness Congress was convened in Salamanca, Spain. Dedicated professionals from national, regional, and local governments, national and international non-governmental indigenous people, students, and researchers met to share how their communities and programs are protecting wilderness. WILD10 delegates passed a resolution regarding the Antarctic. Congress members reaffirmed their commitments to take actions to protect the entire Antarctic Treaty Area as wilderness, by 2016, the 25th anniversary of the signing of the Protocol and they agreed to adopt concrete measures to prevent the further increase of the human footprint in Antarctica. We urge the Parties to take practical steps to put this resolution into practice.

Management of Vessels in the Antarctic Treaty Area (IP 70) - In this paper, ASOC reflects on three recent vessel incidents in the Southern Ocean and the relevance of these incidents to ASOC's previous recommendations on the importance of comprehensive reporting on vessel incidents to inform the development of new policy and regulations. The paper also highlights the importance of extending hydrographic surveys in the region, and limiting access to areas with limited survey data until such time as up to date hydrographic data is available. The paper goes on to consider aspects of the Polar Code, and urges further attention and strengthening of the Code before it is adopted later in 2014.

Managing Human Footprint, Protecting Wilderness: A Way Forward (IP 71) - The Antarctic environment is subject to a diverse range of human impacts. In recognition of this, the CEP has committed to work that would assist in managing the human footprint and protecting wilderness values and thus the unique characteristics of the continent. Over the past several years, Parties have done considerable work on these issues and presented substantive papers to the CEP. The CEP has illustrated the importance of addressing these issues in a timely manner by including relevant elements in its workplan. In this paper, we review this work and recommend next steps for immediate action so the CEP can make timely progress on these issues in advance of celebrations for the 25th anniversary of the Protocol in 2016.

Near-term Antarctic Impacts of Black Carbon and Short-lived Climate Pollutant Mitigation (IP 72) - Previous modelling studies of the impact of short-lived climate pollutants have not included Antarctica, largely because of the region's remoteness from larger anthropogenic black carbon sources. A recent report co-published by the World Bank and ASOC member organisation the International Cryosphere Climate Institute (ICCI) in November 2013 showed a surprising degree of Antarctic climate benefits from black carbon and methane reductions, equal to about two-thirds those in the Arctic. ASOC urges ATCPs to begin conducting emissions inventories of black carbon sources in the Antarctic, following the Arctic Council model, as well as to work to reduce black carbon and other short-lived climate pollutants from other Southern Hemisphere sources.

New Antarctic stations: Are they justified? (IP 73) - Building on various assessments in the peer-reviewed literature, this Information Paper contrasts the scientific research output of Antarctic Treaty Consultative Parties 1980-2004 with the infrastructure that existed in 2004. In practice, there appears to be no substantive relationship between the number of Antarctic stations operated by a particular Party, and that Party's scientific research output. Official inspection reports 2004-2014 seem to corroborate this assessment. In this context, ASOC also makes several practical suggestions to enhance international cooperation, the quantity and quality of science, and reduce environmental impacts, and recommends that all alternatives to building a new station should be carefully considered beforehand.

The West Antarctic Ice Sheet in the Fifth Assessment Report of the Intergovernmental Panel on Climate Change (IPCC): a key threat, a key uncertainty (IP 74) - This information paper focuses on one of the most uncertain and most globally relevant IPCC assessment topics: sea level rise, particularly the contribution of ice sheets and especially the unstable West Antarctic Ice Sheet. In light of the information in the report, including a higher projection for sea level rise, ASOC encourages all ATCPs to stop rehashing "debates" about climate change and start implementing proactive and practical mitigation management strategies in the Antarctic. Furthermore, Antarctic research programs support some of the most important climate research being carried out. ASOC encourages support climate research at current or stronger levels.

4.   *Other Important Issues for XXXVII ATCM*

Tourism - The development of a long-term strategy for managing tourism remains critically important. ASOC urges Parties to focus on the larger picture of tourism in addition to addressing new issues such as the use of UAVs. Given the dynamic nature of commercial tourism, the ATCM cannot rely solely on initiating discussions about particular aspects of tourism after new modalities of tourism have becomes established (including *inter alia* as a result of new activities, new means of transport, or new locations). Rather, strategic discussions need to take place ahead of new developments.

Marine protection in the Antarctic Treaty Area - Many of the issues discussed here have a marine dimension that requires attention from the ATCM, in accordance with Protocol requirements, and as a complement of the work carried out in parallel by CCAMLR, including through the development of a network of Marine Protected Areas. Further harmonisation of the work of these two bodies (as well as the CEP and SC-CAMLR) will become increasingly important in years to come as a result of growing local, regional and global pressures on the marine environment.

Bioprospecting - In ASOC's view it is essential that ATCPs develop a better understanding of the extent of biological prospecting activities in Antarctica, and their impact on scientific research and cooperation as well as on the environment.

Multi-year strategic workplan - To address the current and emerging issues facing the Antarctic, ATCPs need to take a pro-active, strategic approach. A multi-year strategic workplan needs to be developed as early as possible, and implemented effectively.

5.   *Concluding Remarks*

Now is a critical time for Antarctica, and an opportune time for the ATCM to address current and emerging issues strategically. ASOC urges ATCPs to take swift, decisive action on all issues relevant to the protection of the Antarctic environment to ensure that the world's last great wilderness is fully protected.

Report by the International Hydrographic Organization

Status of Hydrographic Surveying and Charting in Antarctic Waters

Introduction

The International Hydrographic Organization (IHO) is an intergovernmental consultative and technical organization. It comprises 82 Member States. Each State is normally represented by its national Hydrographer.

The IHO coordinates on a worldwide basis the setting of standards for hydrographic data and the provision of hydrographic services in support of safety of navigation and the protection and sustainable use of the marine environment. The principal aim of the IHO is to ensure that all the world's seas, oceans and navigable waters are surveyed and charted.

What is Hydrography?

Hydrography is the branch of applied sciences which deals with the measurement and description of the physical features of oceans, seas, coastal areas, lakes and rivers, as well as with the prediction of their change over time, for the primary purpose of safety of navigation and in support of all other marine activities, including economic development, security and defence, scientific research, and environmental protection.

Importance of Hydrography in Antarctica

Hydrographic information is a fundamental pre-requisite for the development of successful and environmentally sustainable human activities in the seas and oceans. Unfortunately, there is little or no hydrographic information for a number of parts of the world, especially in Antarctica.

Status of Hydrography and Charting in Antarctica

Over 90% of Antarctic waters are unsurveyed. Large areas are uncharted and where charts do exist, they have limited utility because of the lack of reliable depth information. The grounding of vessels operating outside previously navigated routes in Antarctica is not uncommon.

Hydrographic surveying in Antarctic waters is expensive and problematic. This is because of hostile and unpredictable sea conditions, short seasons for surveying and the long logistic train involved in supporting ships and equipment. There is no indication of significant improvements in the level of hydrographic surveying being conducted in Antarctica. Indeed, reports to the IHO indicate that government-sponsored surveying activity in Antarctica is actually declining because of financial pressures and competing priorities in home waters.

> **The fact that over 90% of Antarctic waters are unsurveyed should be a cause of particular concern to the ATCM.**

IHO Hydrographic Commission on Antarctica

The IHO Hydrographic Commission on Antarctica (IHO HCA) is dedicated to improving the quality, coverage and availability of nautical charting and other hydrographic information and services covering the region. The HCA comprises 23 IHO Member States (Argentina, Australia, Brazil, Chile, China, Ecuador,

France, Germany, Greece, India, Italy, Japan, Republic of Korea, New Zealand, Norway, Peru, Russian Federation, South Africa, Spain, United Kingdom, Uruguay, USA, Venezuela), all of which have acceded to the Antarctic Treaty and are therefore also directly represented in the ATCM.

The IHO HCA works closely with stakeholder organizations. The following participate in the IHO HCA and its activities: ATS, COMNAP, IAATO, SCAR, IMO, IOC.

The 13th annual meeting of the IHO HCA took place in Spain in December 2013. The HCA reviewed the progress of charting and surveying and updated its plans for the coordinated production of nautical charts and associated publications.

Status Report on Surveys in Antarctica

Most Antarctic waters remain unsurveyed. Few systematic surveys have been conducted. Surveys are mostly centred on some of the Antarctic bases and around the Antarctic Peninsula.

Status Report on Nautical Charts of Antarctica

Paper Charts. 71 of an anticipated 111 paper charts in the IHO INT Chart schema have been published. Another 18 charts are planned to be published over the next two years.

Electronic Navigational Charts (ENCs). According to international (SOLAS) requirements, ENCs are now required for navigation in all passenger vessels and an increasing number of vessels of other types. So far, only 87 ENCs have been published for Antarctica out of an anticipated requirement of about 170 ENCs.

The production of ENCs for Antarctica is severely hampered by the lack of data, the poor state of the corresponding paper charts and the production and financial priorities of those States that have volunteered to make the ENCs.

Realistic Options for Improving Hydrography and Nautical Charting in Antarctica

In view of the serious shortfall in depth data available to make reliable and authoritative nautical charts of Antarctic waters, the IHO, through its HCA, considers that a multi-party, multi-disciplinary approach to obtaining suitable depth data is necessary to augment traditional, systematic and fully regulated survey operations.

Traditional High-Resolution Surveys Using Specialist Hydrographic Survey Ships and Aircraft

Specialist hydrographic survey ships and aircraft provide the highest quality and most reliable depth data for charting and other specialist purposes, but they are inherently expensive to deploy. For this reason, it is best if specialist ships, boats or aircraft are deployed in designated high priority areas that have already undergone some form of assessment to confirm their potential as shipping routes or for other special purposes.

Commercial Contract Support

An increasing number of the world's national Hydrographic Offices are using commercial contractor support to supplement their own efforts. These contractors collect high-quality depth data on behalf of governments using hydrographic ships and aircraft fitted with laser-airborne (Lidar) systems. Lidar is being used successfully in the Arctic region.

In 2013 the IHO HCA adopted a Declaration that recognises and encourages mutually beneficial cooperation between commercial hydrographic support providers and governments.

The employment of contractors using airborne bathymetric survey sensors offers an attractive and cost-effective option in regions such as Antarctica, especially if supported by the existing assets of participating ATCM Member States.

Crowd-Sourced Bathymetry

Depth data collected by so-called *ships of opportunity* is known as *crowd-sourced bathymetry*. Depending on its quality and reliability, crowd-sourced bathymetry can be used to confirm existing charted data, determine new surveying priorities or sometimes to improve the chart itself directly. Limited amounts of crowd-sourced bathymetry have been collected, mostly around the Antarctic Peninsula where the majority of commercial vessels including cruise ships operate. This has been done in cooperation with several governmental, industry and individual partners, including IAATO.

Additionally, there are various commercial crowd-sourcing initiatives in operation, particularly in the fishing sector. The data from these commercial programmes needs to be made available to improve nautical charts.

The IHO considers that the crowd-sourced collection of depth data should be extended to all parts of the world. The IHO proposes to broaden the global IHO-IOC GEBCO ocean mapping programme by enabling the IHO Data Centre for Digital Bathymetry (DCDB) to accept open-source (non-commercial) crowd-sourced bathymetry. This will facilitate the collection of crowd-sourced data and enable Hydrographic Offices to access the data for chart improvement purposes. The IHO has already identified minimal-cost equipment for ships to do this.

> **ATCM may wish to consider ways to encourage or require that all professionally crewed and managed ships operating in Antarctica collect passage soundings at minimal cost to help improve nautical charts.**

In addition,

> **ATCM may wish to consider ways to encourage the concept of multi-purpose, multi-disciplinary environmental data gathering using common observing platforms.**

Satellite Derived Bathymetry

In clear water, it is possible to determine depth and other parameters in the water column down to about 20 metres by analysing imagery from multi-spectral satellite sensors. The IHO is encouraging further development of the technique which is much less expensive than traditional surveying and, when applicable, is an economical option to identify non navigable areas. However, it is unlikely to be able to replace depth measurements taken from a ship or an aircraft or those required for safety of navigation (for example, in restricted or pilotage waters) where water depths are critical for navigational safety.

Data Mining

Over the years, significant amounts of depth data has been collected as part of broader scientific studies in Antarctica but the existence of the data is not known or has not been made available to the relevant Hydrographic Office for use in improving nautical charts. Campaigns are required to locate and access this potentially useful data.

> **ATCM may wish to consider ways for facilitating access to existing depth data obtained as part of scientific activities in Antarctica, regardless of the nationality of the ship or the scientific party.**

Conclusion

The state of hydrographic surveying and nautical charting in Antarctica poses serious risks for the safety of navigation as well as impeding the conduct of most activities taking place in the surrounding seas and oceans.

A number of IHO Member States, through their national Hydrographic Offices, are attempting to improve the situation. However, resources are limited and there does not appear to be much prospect of significant improvements in the near future unless new policy action is taken by governments and by ATCM.

There are a number of ATCM **Recommendations** on Operational Matters that relate directly to hydrography and nautical charting (see ATCM XXVII WP1 *Review of ATCM Recommendations on Operational Matters*). The options for improvements being proposed by the IHO are all in harmony with those Recommendations.

The IHO would like to see ATCM and its member governments acting positively upon its own Recommendations on Operational Matters, and in particular, to consider practical measures related to:

- vessels' obligations to conduct passage sounding and to render observed depth data to the relevant charting authority,

- the promotion of initiatives that include commercial hydrographic support to extend national, ATCM and IHO-HCA survey programs,

- the concept of multi-purpose, multi-disciplinary data gathering using common observing platforms, and

- access by Hydrographic Offices to all depth data already gathered as part of scientific activities conducted in Antarctica.

Report of the International Association of Antarctica Tour Operators 2013-14

Under Article III (2) of the Antarctic Treaty

Introduction

The International Association of Antarctica Tour Operators (IAATO) is pleased to report its activities to ATCM XXXVII, under Article III (2) of the Antarctic Treaty.

IAATO continues to focus activities in support of its mission statement to advocate, promote and practice safe and environmentally responsible private sector travel to Antarctica by ensuring:
- Effective day-to-day management of Member activities in Antarctica;
- Educational outreach, including scientific collaboration; and
- Development and promotion of Antarctic tourism best practices.

A detailed description of IAATO, its mission statement, primary activities and recent developments can be found in the *2014-15 Fact Sheet*, and on the IAATO website: www.iaato.org.

IAATO Membership and Member Activity

IAATO comprises 118 Members, Associates and Affiliates. Member offices are located worldwide, representing 61% of the Antarctic Treaty Consultative Party countries, and carrying nationals from nearly all Treaty Parties annually to Antarctica.

Due to the timing of ATCM XXXVII, it has not been possible to compile or analyse the statistical data from the Post Visit Reports for the just-concluded 2013-2014 season. However, preliminary numbers indicate that the general picture is similar to that forecast in ATCM XXXVI IP103 *IAATO Overview of Antarctic Tourism 2012-13 Antarctic Season and Preliminary Estimates for 2013-14 Seaso*n.

It is expected that the detailed 2013-14 season information, including details on landing site use, will be available in June 2014. It will be posted on the IAATO website (www.iaato.org) under Guidelines and Resources, Tourism Statistics.

Details on anticipated tourism statistics for 2014-15 season can be found in ATCM XXXVII IP45 *IAATO Overview of Antarctic Tourism: Preliminary Estimates for 2014-15*. These numbers reflect only those travelling with IAATO member companies. The Membership Directory and additional statistics on IAATO member activities can be found at *www.iaato.org*.

Recent Work and Activities

A number of initiatives were undertaken during the year, including:

- Strengthening of the Association's corporate governance and institutional robustness. This includes a review of anti-trust and liability policies, creation of a new Operations and Communications Assistant role within the Secretariat and relocating the office from Providence to Newport, Rhode Island.

- In February 2014, two IAATO operators conducted a Search and Rescue Communications exercise in partnership with MRCC Ushuaia and IAATO. Details of the exercise can be found in ATCM XXXVII IP79 *SAR Communication Exercise: Argentina - IAATO* (Argentina and IAATO)

- The Dockside Observer program for IAATO yachts, a new component in the association's enhanced observer scheme, was trialled successfully. This is the first time that actual observations of IAATO yacht operations has taken place.

- The Field Staff Online Assessment and Certification Program continues to evolve, incorporating feedback from a survey of field staff. A total of 383 staff have now passed at least one of the assessments, with more than 243 successful participants this past season. This reflects an increased participation of 17% and 13% respectively. Additionally, the IAATO Field Staff Newsletter, with news and updates from around the Continent, continues to build a forum for field staff to consider mutual issues, challenges and opportunities, including sharing best practice and discussions on situational leadership and risk assessments.

- A full review of the wildlife guidelines and boot-washing and decontamination guidelines was undertaken, including seeking expert independent advice on management techniques.

- The IAATO information sheet, *Understanding Climate Change in Antarctica*, which is available to all members for distribution to their clients, was updated to take into account the latest information from SCAR's ACCE report. Additionally, a list of actions that IAATO members may undertake to minimise their carbon footprint was circulated to all operators.

- Improving hydrographic information on a trial and opportunistic basis by a number of IAATO vessel operators has continued. The initiatives included:

  1. Crowd Sourcing project in conjunction with Hydrographic Offices and private service providers; and

  2. A collaborative effort between an IAATO Member and the French Hydrographic Office (SHOM), which surveyed, processed and subsequently produced seven charts of previously poorly surveyed channels and anchorages in the Peninsula.

- IAATO's Marine, Accreditation and Executive Committees all met during the year to progress work on initiatives such as the enhanced observer scheme and incident review processes.

- Collaborations with IAATO's northern counterpart, Association Arctic Expedition Cruise Operators (AECO), on issues of mutual concern, including field staff training, safety and environmental issues.

IAATO Meeting and Participation at Other Meetings during 2013-14

IAATO Secretariat staff and member representatives participated in internal and external meetings, liaising with National Antarctic Programs, governmental, scientific, environmental and industry organisations.

- Representation at COMNAP XXV in Seoul, Korea (July 2013). IAATO places great merit in good cooperation and collaboration between its Membership and National Antarctic Programs.

- IAATO welcomed the opportunity to take part in Chile's CIMAR Ice Navigator Training course in Valparaiso, Chile October 2013.

- An IAATO representative attended the 13th International Hydrographic Organization / Hydrographic Commission on Antarctica (IHO/HCA) Meeting in Cadiz, Spain (December 2013). IAATO remains a strong supporter of the on-going work of the HCA, and will continue to work with HOs and HCA in the development of a crowd-sourcing hydrographic data collection scheme.

- As an advisor to Cruise Lines International Association (CLIA), IAATO continues to be active in the development of the International Maritime Organization's (IMO) mandatory Polar Code, participating in various IMO MSC and MEPC committee and sub-committee meetings and working groups.

- Looking forward, the IAATO 25th Meeting will take place May 27-29, 2014, in Providence, Rhode Island, USA. In addition to the above-mentioned initiatives, the meeting will also consider:

- Development of an incident, accident and near miss database, potentially in conjunction with AECO.;
- Guidelines for the use of remotely operated drones or quadcopters for aerial photography; and
- A dedicated session on tourism growth management.

Immediately following the IAATO 25th Meeting, there will be a half-day Adventure tourism workshop, considering both deep field and additional or new activities that are taking place from traditional ship- or yacht-based platforms. The workshop will include a panel discussion, comprising a mix of operators and Treaty Party representatives, and breakout groups to consider specific case studies from the perspective of risk management and environmental considerations.

As in previous years, Treaty Party representatives are invited to join any of the open sessions during the IAATO Meeting and subsequent workshop. Additional information can be found at http://iaato.org/iaato-25th-annual-meeting.

Environmental Monitoring

IAATO continues to provide ATCM and CEP with detailed information on member activities in Antarctica. As noted above, statistical data for the 2013-14 season will be available in June 2014 and accessible via the IAATO website.

IAATO continues to work collaboratively with scientific institutions particularly on environmental monitoring and educational outreach. This includes working with Antarctic Site Inventory, the Lynch Lab at Stoney Brook University and the Zoological Society of London/Oxford University. Additionally, IAATO operators note sightings of fishing vessels for subsequent reporting to CCAMLR in support of the work against IUU fishing.

IAATO welcomes opportunities for collaboration with other organisations.

Tourism Incidents 2013-14

IAATO continues to follow a policy of disclosing incidents to ensure risks are understood and appropriate lessons are learned for all Antarctic operators. To date, incidents involving IAATO Operators that have been reported during the 2013-14 season included:

- In November a series of three medevacs via Maxwell Bay involved additional support from National Antarctic Programs, two through Bellingshausen Base (RAE) and one through Great Wall Station (CHINARE). IAATO and the Member operators involved are grateful for the assistance provided. Following these events, a reminder was sent to all field staff regarding the importance of self-sufficiency. Subsequent medevacs were conducted without any assistance from National Antarctic Programs.

- During a South Pole traverse ski expedition, practices outlined in a Waste Management Permit were not followed. The IAATO operator supporting the expedition has had discussions with the US-NSF and the expedition participants and a clean up of waste was made by a subsequent expedition. The incident will be discussed at IAATO 25 with the intention of developing tighter practices.

- On February 20th, MV *Orion* had a technical issue with its engine cooling system. The vessel used auxiliary systems until the issue was rectified some hours later. There was no threat to life or the environment.

Scientific and Conservation Support

During the 2013-14 season, IAATO Members cost-effectively or on *pro bono* basis transported over 125 scientific, support and conservation staff, and their equipment and supplies between stations, field sites and gateway ports. This included:

- Transfers of scientists between stations;
- Non-urgent medical evacuations;
- Collection of scientific samples and other data collection for research programs (all permitted);
- Transport of scientific equipment to/from stations.

Initial reports indicate that IAATO operators and their passengers also contributed more than US$400,000 to scientific and conservation organisations active in Antarctica and the sub-Antarctic (e.g. Save the Albatross, Antarctic Heritage Trust, Last Ocean, Mawson's Huts Foundation, Oceanites and World Wildlife Fund).

Over the past nine years, these donations have totalled approximately US$3.5 million in cash donations.

With Thanks

IAATO appreciates the opportunity to work cooperatively with Antarctic Treaty Parties, COMNAP, SCAR, CCAMLR, IHO/HCA, ASOC and others toward the long-term protection of Antarctica.

PART IV

Additional Documents from ATCM XXXVII

1. Additional documents

SCAR Lecture: "Back to the Future: Past Antarctic Climates, Ice Sheet History & Their Relevance for Understanding Future Trends"

C. Escutia, Spanish Research Council, Granada, Spain
& the SCAR PAIS Steering Committee

Polar ice is an important component of the modern climate system, affecting global sea level, ocean circulation, heat transport, marine productivity, and planetary albedo. Antarctica became glaciated ~34 million years ago whereas full scale, permanent Northern Hemisphere continental ice only began forming ~3 million years ago. The study of ice cores retrieved from the Antarctic ice cap has afforded major breakthroughs in understanding natural climate variability over the last 800,000 years, and offers insight into the future response of the Earth to anthropogenic forcing. However, the correlations between (i) the records of temperature, CO_2, and ice sheet volume (and equivalent sea level), and (ii) the mechanisms responsible for glacial-interglacial cycles (i.e., role of atmospheric CO_2) have not been yet fully elucidated.

With current rising atmospheric greenhouse gases resulting in rapidly increasing global temperatures (IPCC, 2013), studies of polar climates and ice sheet dynamics and stability are prominent on the research agenda. The lower values of forecasted atmospheric CO_2 and temperatures in the IPCC AR5 report (2013) for the end of this century have not been experienced on our Planet for over 5 million years (i.e. before the Arctic ice sheets formed), and the higher forecasted values since before the ice sheets in Antarctica formed. Antarctica and its margins are therefore the only place to retrieve the long-term records needed for a detailed understanding of how ice sheets responded to past climate forcings and how they might respond in the future.

The overarching goal of the SCAR PAIS (Past Antarctic Ice Sheet Dynamics) Scientific Research Programme is to improve confidence in predictions of ice sheet and sea level response to future climate change and ocean warming. For this, PAIS aims to improve understanding of the sensitivity of East, West, and Antarctic Peninsula Ice Sheets to a broad range of climatic and oceanic conditions. Study intervals span a range of timescales, including past "greenhouse" climates warmer than today, and times of more recent warming and ice sheet retreat during glacial terminations. The PAIS research is based on data-model integration and intercomparison, and the development of "ice-to-abyss" data transects, extending from the ice sheet interior to the deep sea. The data-transect concept will link ice core, ice sheet-proximal, offshore, and far-field records of past ice sheet behaviour and sea level, yielding an unprecedented view of past changes in ice sheet geometry, volume, and ice sheet-ocean interactions.

2. List of Documents

2. List of Documents

Working Papers								
Number	Ag. Items	Title	Submitted By	E	F	R	S	Attachments
WP001	CEP 3	CEP Five-Year Work Plan adopted at the XVIth CEP Meeting in Brussels	France					CEP Five-year Workplan
WP002	ATCM 12	Key Thematic Recommendations from 10 years of Antarctic Treaty Inspection Reports	United Kingdom Australia France Germany Netherlands Russian Federation South Africa Spain Sweden					
WP003	CEP 9a	Revised Management Plan for Antarctic Specially Protected Area No.139 Biscoe Point, Anvers Island, Palmer Archipelago	United States					ASPA 139 Map 1 ASPA 139 Map 2 ASPA 139 Map 3 ASPA 139 Revised Management Plan
WP004	ATCM 11 CEP 10a	Report on the informal discussion on tourism and the risk of introducing non-native organisms	Germany					
WP005	CEP 8b	UAVs and their possible environmental impacts	Germany Poland					
WP006	CEP 9a	Revised Management Plan for Antarctic Specially Protected Area No. 113 Litchfield Island, Arthur Harbor Anvers Island, Palmer Archipelago	United States					ASPA 113 Map 1 ASPA 113 Map 2 ASPA 113 Revised Management Plan
WP007	CEP 9a	Revised Management Plan for Antarctic Specially Protected Area No. 121 Cape Royds, Ross Island	United States					ASPA 121 Map 1 ASPA 121 Map 2 ASPA 121 Revised Management Plan
WP008	CEP 7	Report from ICG on Climate Change	Norway United Kingdom					Climate Change Matrix (CCM) ICG on Climate Change: Review of progress against ATME Recommendations
WP009	ATCM 15 CEP 13	Education and Outreach activities associated with Antarctic Treaty Consultative Meetings (ATCM)	Brazil Belgium Bulgaria Portugal United Kingdom					
WP010	CEP 3	Antarctic Environments Portal: Progress Report	New Zealand Australia Belgium Norway SCAR					
WP011	CEP 9a	Review of Antarctic Specially Protected Area (ASPA) No. 142 - Svarthamaren	Norway					ASPA 142 Revised Management Plan
WP012	ATCM 17	Assessing Bioprospecting in Antarctica	Belgium					
WP013	ATCM	Coastal Camping Activities	United					Attachment A - Questions.

Working Papers

Number	Ag. Items	Title	Submitted By	E	F	R	S	Attachments
	11 CEP 8b	Conducted by Non-Governmental Organizations	States Norway					Attachment B - Summary of Responses
WP014	CEP 11	Advances in creating digital elevation models for Antarctic Specially Managed and Protected Areas	United States	▣	▣	▣	▣	Annex – Supporting Figure (High resolution)
WP015	CEP 9a	Report of the Informal Discussions on the Proposal for a new Antarctic Specially Managed Area at Chinese Antarctic Kunlun Station, Dome A	China	▣	▣	▣	▣	
WP016	CEP 8a	The Draft Comprehensive Environmental Evaluation for the construction and operation of the New Chinese Research Station, Victoria Land, Antarctica	China	▣	▣	▣	▣	Draft CEE New Chinese Research Station. Non-technical summary
WP017	CEP 11	Advancing Recommendations of the CEP Tourism Study	Australia New Zealand Norway United Kingdom United States	▣	▣	▣	▣	
WP018	CEP 9a	Revision of the Management Plan for Antarctic Specially Protected Area (ASPA) No. 169 Amanda Bay, Ingrid Christensen Coast, Princess Elizabeth Land, East Antarctica	Australia China	▣	▣	▣	▣	ASPA 169 Map A ASPA 169 Map B ASPA 169 Revised Management Plan
WP019	CEP 9a	Revision of the Management Plan for Antarctic Specially Protected Area (ASPA) No. 136 Clark Peninsula, Budd Coast, Wilkes Land, East Antarctica	Australia	▣	▣	▣	▣	ASPA 136 Map A ASPA 136 Map B ASPA 136 Map C ASPA 136 Map D ASPA 136 Revised Management Plan
WP020	ATCM 5	Marine Protected Areas in the Antarctic Treaty System	Russian Federation	▣	▣	▣	▣	
WP021	CEP 9a	Revision of the Management Plan for Antarctic Specially Managed Area (ASMA) No. 6 Larsemann Hills, East Antarctica	Australia China India Russian Federation	▣	▣	▣	▣	ASMA 6 Map A ASMA 6 Map B ASMA 6 Map C ASMA 6 Map D ASMA 6 Map E ASMA 6 Revised Management Plan
WP022	CEP 8a	Construction and Operation of Belarusian Antarctic Research Station at Mount Vechernyaya, Enderby Land. Draft Comprehensive Environmental Evaluation	Belarus	▣	▣	▣	▣	Draft Comprehensive Environmental Evaluation Non-Technical Summary
WP023	CEP 9c	Horseshoe Island Visitor Site Guidelines: Proposed Revision	United Kingdom	▣	▣	▣	▣	Horseshoe Island Visitor Site Guideline – proposed revisions
WP024	CEP	Improvements to the	United	▣	▣	▣	▣	

Working Papers

Number	Ag. Items	Title	Submitted By	E	F	R	S	Attachments
	8b	Antarctic Environmental Impact Assessment process	Kingdom					
WP025	CEP 9a	The status of Antarctic Specially Protected Area No. 114 Northern Coronation Island, South Orkney Islands	United Kingdom	📄	📄	📄	📄	
WP026	CEP 9a	Revised Management Plan for Antarctic Specially Protected Area No. 124 Cape Crozier, Ross Island	United States	📄	📄	📄	📄	ASPA 124 Map 1 ASPA 124 Map 2 ASPA 124 Revised Management Plan
WP027	CEP 8a	Report of the intersessional open-ended contact group established to consider the draft CEE for the "Construction and operation of Belarusian Antarctic Research Station at Mount Vechernyaya, Enderby Land"	Australia	📄	📄	📄	📄	
WP028	CEP 6	Antarctic clean-up activities: checklist for preliminary site assessment	Australia	📄	📄	📄	📄	Checklist for preliminary site assessment
WP029	CEP 8b	Review of the Guidelines for Environmental Impact Assessment in Antarctica	Australia	📄	📄	📄	📄	
WP030	CEP 9a CEP 9c	Proposal to modify the management arrangements for Mawson's Huts and Cape Denison	Australia	📄	📄	📄	📄	ASPA 162 Map A ASPA 162 Map B ASPA 162 Map C ASPA 162 Revised Management Plan Revised Visitor Site Guide for Mawson's Huts and Cape Denison Revised Visitor Site Guide for Mawson's Huts and Cape Denison - Hut's interior Revised Visitor Site Guide for Mawson's Huts and Cape Denison - Hut's picture Revised Visitor Site Guide for Mawson's Huts and Cape Denison - Map 2 Revised Visitor Site Guide for Mawson's Huts and Cape Denison - Revised Map 1 Revised Visitor Site Guide for Mawson's Huts and Cape Denison - Texts for maps
WP031	CEP 9a	Subsidiary Group on Management Plans – Report on 2013/14 Intersessional Work	Norway	📄	📄	📄	📄	ASPA 175 Ross Sea Geothermal Map A2-1 ASPA 175 Ross Sea Geothermal Management Plan ASPA 175 Ross Sea Geothermal Map A1 ASPA 175 Ross Sea Geothermal Map A2 ASPA 175 Ross Sea Geothermal Map A3 Attachment A - ASPA 141 Map 1 Attachment A - ASPA 141 Map 2 Attachment A - ASPA 141 Map 3

Working Papers

Number	Ag. Items	Title	Submitted By	E	F	R	S	Attachments
								Attachment A - ASPA 141 Revised Management Plan
Attachment B - ASPA Stornes Draft Management Plan
Attachment B - ASPA Stornes Draft Map A
Attachment B - ASPA Stornes Draft Map B
Attachment C - ASPA 128 Map 1
Attachment C - ASPA 128 Map 2
Attachment C - ASPA 128 Revised Management Plan
Attachment E - ASMA 1 Figure 1
Attachment E - ASMA 1 Figure 2
Attachment E - ASMA 1 Figure 3
Attachment E - ASMA 1 Figure 4
Attachment E - ASMA 1 Figure 5
Attachment E - ASMA 1 Figure 6
Attachment E - ASMA 1 Figure 7
Attachment E - ASMA 1 Figure 8
Attachment E - ASMA 1 Figure 9
Attachment E - ASMA 1 Revised Management Plan
WP032	ATCM 11	Framework for future discussions on experiences and challenges identified by competent authorities with regard to diverse types of tourism and nongovernmental activities	Norway	🗎	🗎	🗎	🗎	
WP033	CEP 9f	Background and initial thoughts and questions: Need for and development of procedures concerning ASPA and ASMA designation	Norway	🗎	🗎	🗎	🗎	
WP034	CEP 8b	IEE or CEE: which one to choose?	France Belgium	🗎	🗎	🗎	🗎	
WP035	CEP 9f	The Antarctic Protected Area system: protection of outstanding geological features	United Kingdom Argentina Australia Spain	🗎	🗎	🗎	🗎	
WP036	CEP 9f	Monitoring vegetation cover in Antarctic Specially Protected Areas using satellite remote sensing: a pilot study	United Kingdom	🗎	🗎	🗎	🗎	
WP037	ATCM 5	Final Report of the Intersessional Contact Group on the exercise of jurisdiction in the Antarctic Treaty Area	France	🗎	🗎	🗎	🗎	

Working Papers								
Number	**Ag. Items**	**Title**	**Submitted By**	**E**	**F**	**R**	**S**	**Attachments**
WP038	ATCM 6	Final Report of the Intersessional Contact Group on the Development of a Glossary of Terms and Expressions used by the ATCM	France					Draft Glossary
WP039	CEP 9e	The concept of "outstanding values" in the marine environment under Annex V of the Protocol	Belgium France					
WP040	ATCM 14 CEP 7	Fostering Coordinated Antarctic Climate Change Monitoring	United States Norway United Kingdom					
WP041	ATCM 13	Strategic Scientific Priorities for Antarctic Research of the Netherlands	Netherlands					
WP042	ATCM 10	Supporting the Continued Development of the Polar Code	United States					
WP043	CEP 8a	Report of the Intersessional Open-ended Contact Group Established to Consider the Draft CEE for the "Proposed Construction and Operation of a New Chinese Research Station, Victoria Land, Antarctica"	United States					
WP044	ATCM 11	Toward a Risk-based Assessment of Tourist Activities	United States					Appendix – "Assessing Risks and Abating Hazards"
WP045	ATCM 10	Operational Matters ICG: Strengthening Cooperation in Hydrographic Surveying and Charting of Antarctic Waters	United States					
WP046	CEP 7	Antarctic trial of WWF's Rapid Assessment of Circum-Arctic Ecosystem Resilience (RACER) Conservation Planning Tool	United Kingdom Germany Norway Spain					
WP047 rev.1	CEP 3	Outreach Activities on occasion of the 25th Anniversary of the signing of the Protocol on Environment Protection to the Antarctic Treaty	Argentina Chile					
WP048	ATCM 11	Entry into force of Measure 4 (2004)	France United Kingdom Chile Finland Netherlands New Zealand South Africa					
WP049	ATCM 11 ATCM 16	On the Issue of Commercial Tour Vessels navigating under a Third-party Flag in the Antarctic	France					

Working Papers								
Number	**Ag. Items**	**Title**	**Submitted By**	**E**	**F**	**R**	**S**	**Attachments**
		Treaty Area						
WP050	ATCM 11	Continuation of the Intersessional Contact Group on Marathons and Large-Scale Sporting Events held in Antarctica	Chile					
WP051	ATCM 10 CEP 8b	Considerations for the use of unmanned aircraft systems (UAS) for research, monitoring, and observation in Antarctica	United States					
WP052	CEP 9a	Revision of Management Plan for Antarctic Specially Protected Area (ASPA) No. 150, Ardley Island (Ardley Peninsula), Maxwell Bay, King George Island	Chile					ASPA 150 Revised Management Plan
WP053	ATCM 10	Antarctic Search and Rescue. Understanding Planning Assumptions	United States					
WP054	CEP 9a	Revision of Management Plan for Antarctic Specially Protected Area (ASPA) No. 125, Fildes Peninsula, King George Island	Chile					ASPA 125 Revised Management Plan
WP055	ATCM 16	Reviewing information exchange requirements	Australia					
WP056	ATCM 5	Intersessional Contact Group Report on Cooperation in Antarctica	Chile					
WP057	CEP 9f	Contributions to the Protection of Fossils in Antarctica	Argentina					
WP058 rev.1	CEP 9a	Revised Management Plan for Antarctic Specially Protected Area No. 171, Narębski Point, Barton Peninsula, King George Island	Korea (ROK)					ASPA 171 Revised Management Plan
WP059	CEP 9f	Informal intersessional discussion on the need of ASPA values monitoring in connection with ASPA Management Plan reviews	Russian Federation					

Information Papers

Number	Ag. Items	Title	Submitted By	E	F	R	S	Attachments
IP001	ATCM 10	Joint SANAP / MRCC SAR Exercise	South Africa	▭				
IP002	ATCM 15	The mission and objectives of the recently established Polar Educators International (PEI)	Portugal Belgium Brazil Bulgaria	▭				
IP003	ATCM 4 CEP 5	The Annual Report for 2013 of the Council of Managers of National Antarctic Programs (COMNAP)	COMNAP	▭	▭	▭	▭	
IP004 rev.1	ATCM 4	Report Submitted to Antarctic Treaty Consultative Meeting XXXVII by the Depositary Government for the Convention for the Conservation of Antarctic Seals in Accordance with Recommendation XIII-2, Paragraph 2(D)	United Kingdom	▭	▭	▭	▭	
IP005	ATCM 10	XXXVII Antarctic Operation (OPERANTAR XXXII)	Brazil	▭				
IP006	ATCM 13	Reconstruction Project of the Brazilian Antarctic Station	Brazil	▭				
IP007	CEP 6	Remediation Plan for the Brazilian Antarctic Station area	Brazil	▭				
IP008	CEP 11	Persistent organic pollutants (POPs) in Admiralty Bay - Antarctic Specially Managed Area (ASMA 1): Bioaccumulation and temporal trend	Brazil	▭				
IP009	ATCM 13	An action plan for the Brazilian Antarctic science over the next 10 years	Brazil	▭				
IP010	CEP 5	Report by the SC-CAMLR Observer to the Seventeenth Meeting of the Committee for Environmental Protection	CCAMLR	▭	▭	▭	▭	
IP011	ATCM 13 CEP 10c	Antarctic Conservation Strategy: Scoping Workshop on Practical Solutions	COMNAP SCAR	▭				Antarctic Conservation for the 21st Century: Scoping Workshop on Practical Solutions Final Report (ver 13 January 2014).
IP012	CEP 11	Developing a New Methodology to Analyse Site Sensitivities	Australia New Zealand Norway United Kingdom United States	▭				
IP013	ATCM 4 CEP 5	The Scientific Committee on Antarctic Research (SCAR) Annual Report for 2013/14	SCAR	▭	▭	▭	▭	

Information Papers

Number	Ag. Items	Title	Submitted By	E	F	R	S	Attachments
IP014	ATCM 13 CEP 11	Report on the 2013-2014 activities of the Southern Ocean Observing System (SOOS)	SCAR	📄				
IP015	ATCM 10 ATCM 4	Report by the International Hydrographic Organization. Status of Hydrographic Surveying and Charting in Antarctic Waters	IHO	📄	📄	📄	📄	
IP016	ATCM 11 ATCM 16 CEP 9b	Judgment of the Regional Court of Paris dated 6 February 2014 regarding the carrying out of undeclared and unauthorised non-governmental activities in the area of the Treaty and the Damage caused to the Wordie House Hut (HSM no 62)	France	📄	📄	📄	📄	
IP017	ATCM 4	Report by the CCAMLR Observer to the Thirty-seventh Antarctic Treaty Consultative Meeting	CCAMLR	📄	📄	📄	📄	
IP018	CEP 9c	Site Guidelines: mapping update	United Kingdom United States Argentina Australia	📄				Map of Brown Bluff Map of Orne harbour
IP019	CEP 10c	Use of hydroponics by national Antarctic programs	COMNAP	📄				
IP020	ATCM 10	COMNAP Icebreaker Workshop	COMNAP	📄				Icebreaker Workshop Participants List; Icebreaker Workshop Schedule.
IP021	ATCM 10	Transfer of Parodi and Huneeus Stations to Union Glacier	Chile	📄	📄	📄	📄	
IP022	CEP 9f	Antarctic Specially Protected Areas protecting geological features: a review	United Kingdom	📄				
IP023	CEP 10a	Colonisation status of known non-native species in the Antarctic terrestrial environment (updated 2014)	United Kingdom	📄				
IP024	CEP 9f	Antarctic Specially Protected Areas: compatible management of conservation and scientific research goals	United Kingdom Spain	📄				Area protection in Antarctica: How can conservation and scientific research goals be managed compatibly? Hughes et al.
IP025	CEP 9b	The 1912 Ascent of Mount Erebus by members of the Terra Nova Expedition: the location of additional campsites and further information on HSM 89	United Kingdom New Zealand United States	📄				
IP026	CEP 10c	Remote sensing: emperor penguins breeding on ice shelves	United Kingdom United States	📄				

Information Papers

Number	Ag. Items	Title	Submitted By	E	F	R	S	Attachments
IP027 rev.1	ATCM 11 CEP 9c	Antarctic Site Inventory: 1994-2014	United States	📄				
IP028	CEP 11	Informe de monitoreo ambiental en Base O'Higgins Temporada 2013	Chile				📄	
IP029	ATCM 4 CEP 7	WMO-led developments in Meteorological (and related) Polar Observations, Research and Services	WMO	📄				
IP030	ATCM 5	On the need for alignment in the Use and Provision of Polar Meteorological (and related) Observations, Research and Services	WMO	📄				
IP031	ATCM 10	Antarctic Flight Information Manual (AFIM) - An update on the status of the reformatting	COMNAP	📄				Proposed new page lay-out of the AFIM
IP032	ATCM 10	Update on Search and Rescue (SAR) Website	COMNAP	📄				
IP033	ATCM 13	Australia's Antarctic Strategic Science Priorities	Australia	📄				Executive summary of the Australian Antarctic Science Strategic Plan 2011-12 to 2020-21
IP034	ATCM 13	Japan's Antarctic Research Highlights 2013–14	Japan	📄				
IP035	CEP 13	COMNAP Waste Water Management Workshop Information	COMNAP	📄				
IP036	CEP 8b	Establishment and Beginning of Pilot Operation of the 2nd Korean Antarctic Research Station "Jang Bogo" at Terra Nova Bay	Korea (ROK)	📄				
IP037	CEP 8a	The Draft Comprehensive Environmental Evaluation for the construction and operation of the New Chinese Research Station, Victoria Land, Antarctica	China	📄				Full Draft CEE of the new Chinese station in Antarctica (19 MB)
IP038	CEP 11	Proposed Long-Term Environmental Monitoring at Bharati Station (LTEM-BS)	India	📄				
IP039	ATCM 14 CEP 7	SCAR engagement with the United Nations Framework Convention on Climate Change (UNFCCC)	SCAR	📄				
IP040	ATCM 4	Report of the Depositary Government of the Antarctic Treaty and its Protocol in accordance with Recommendation XIII-2	United States	📄	📄	📄	📄	Antarctic Treaty Status Table List of Recommendations/Measures and their approvals Protocol Status Table
IP041	ATCM 15	Joint Chile and United States Antarctic Educational Expedition for High School	United States Chile	📄			📄	Figure 1 in high resolution Figure 2 in high resolution

Information Papers

Number	Ag. Items	Title	Submitted By	E	F	R	S	Attachments
		Students and Teachers: a Pilot Program						
IP042	CEP 10c	Developing general guidelines for operating in geothermal environments	New Zealand SCAR United Kingdom United States	▣				
IP043	CEP 9f	McMurdo Dry Valleys ASMA Management Group Report	New Zealand United States	▣				ASMA No. 2 Map 1: Overview ASMA No.2 McMurdo Dry Valleys: boundary and zones Attachment 2: ASMA No. 2 Map 2: Overview Central Dry Valleys Attachment 3: ASMA No. 2 Map 8: Lake Bonney, Taylor Valley Attachment 4: ASMA No. 2 Map 17: Mount Feather – Beacon Valley Attachment 5: ASMA No. 2 Map 18: Don Juan Pond, Wright Valley Attachment 6: ASMA No. 2 Management Group Work Plan
IP044	ATCM 4	Report of the International Association of Antarctica Tour Operators 2013-14	IAATO	▣	▣	▣	▣	
IP045 rev.1	ATCM 11	IAATO Overview of Antarctic Tourism: 2013-14 Season and Preliminary Estimates for 2014-15 Season	IAATO	▣				
IP046	ATCM 15 CEP 13	COMNAP Practical Training Modules: Module 1 – Environmental Protocol	COMNAP	▣				COMNAP Training Module 1 – Environmental Protocol (ver 1)
IP047	ATCM 13 CEP 13	International Scientific and Logistic Collaboration in Antarctica	COMNAP	▣				
IP048	ATCM 11	The SV "Infinity", Ross Sea February 2014	New Zealand	▣				
IP049	ATCM 5 CEP 9e	The role of the Antarctic Treaty Consultative Meeting in protecting the marine environment through marine spatial protection	Netherlands	▣				
IP050	ATCM 10	Operational Ice Information around Antarctica	Germany	▣				
IP051	ATCM 4	Report of the Depositary Government for the Agreement on the Conservation of Albatrosses and Petrels (ACAP)	Australia	▣	▣	▣	▣	
IP052	ATCM 4	Report of the Depositary Government for the Convention on the Conservation of Antarctic Marine Living Resources (CCAMLR)	Australia	▣	▣	▣	▣	

Information Papers

Number	Ag. Items	Title	Submitted By	E	F	R	S	Attachments
IP053	ATCM 9	Implementation of Annex VI of the Protocol on Environmental Protection to the Antarctic Treaty: A South African update	South Africa					
IP054	CEP 8a	The Initial Responses to the Comments on the Draft CEE for the construction and operation of the New Chinese Research Station, Victoria Land, Antarctica	China					Annex 1: Responses to the Comments on China´s draft CEE Annex 2: A list of main research fields of Chinese new station on the Victoria Land Antarctica Annex 3: CFD simulation - risk analysis of wind resistance and snow accumulation on the form of the buildings Annex 4: introduction of Magnetic Pyrolysis Furnace
IP055	ATCM 11	Data Collection and Reporting on Yachting Activity in Antarctica in 2013-14	United Kingdom IAATO					
IP056	CEP 8b	Initial Environmental Evaluation for the realization of a new access road to Enigma Lake Twin Otter Runway at Mario Zucchelli Station, Terra Nova Bay, Ross Sea, Antarctica	Italy					
IP057	CEP 8b	Towards the realization of a gravel runway in Terra Nova Bay: results of the 2013-2014 survey campaign	Italy					
IP058	CEP 9f	Proposal to afford greater protection to an extremely restricted endemic plant on Caliente Hill (ASPA 140 – sub-site C), Deception Island	Spain					
IP059	ATCM 11 CEP 9c	National Antarctic Programme use of locations with Visitor Site Guidelines in 2013-14	United Kingdom Argentina Australia United States					
IP060	ATCM 14 CEP 7	Antarctic Climate Change and the Environment – 2014 Update	SCAR					
IP061	ATCM 10	Status report on the development of the International Code for ships operating in Polar Waters (Polar Code)	IMO					
IP062	ATCM 5	Strengthening Support for the Protocol on Environmental Protection to the Antarctic Treaty	Australia France Spain					
IP063	CEP 8b	Results of drilling operations for the study of the lower part of the glacier in deep borehole at Vostok station in the season 2013-2014	Russian Federation					
IP064	CEP 8b	Study of the water column of the Subglacial Lake Vostok	Russian Federation					Study of the water column of the subglasial Lake Vostok. Initial Environmental Evaluation

Information Papers

Number	Ag. Items	Title	Submitted By	E	F	R	S	Attachments
IP065	ATCM 10	Ice incident with the Russian vessel "Akademik Shokalsky" in the season 2013-2014	Russian Federation	📄		📄		
IP066	ATCM 10	On rendering urgent medical aid by doctors of Russian Antarctic stations to personnel of foreign Antarctic expeditions and ship crews	Russian Federation	📄		📄		
IP067	CEP 9f	Report of the Antarctic Specially Managed Area No. 6 Larsemann Hills Management Group	Australia China India Russian Federation	📄				
IP068	ATCM 14 CEP 7	Antarctic Climate Change Report Card 2014	ASOC	📄				
IP069	CEP 9d	Antarctic Resolution at the 10th World Wilderness Congress	ASOC	📄				Antarctic Resolution
IP070	ATCM 10	Management of Vessels in the Antarctic Treaty Area	ASOC	📄				
IP071 rev.1	CEP 9d	Managing Human Footprint, Protecting Wilderness: A Way Forward	ASOC	📄				
IP072	ATCM 14 CEP 7	Near-term Antarctic Impacts of Black Carbon and Short-lived Climate Pollutant Mitigation	ASOC	📄				
IP073	ATCM 13 CEP 8b	New Antarctic stations: Are they justified?	ASOC	📄				
IP074	ATCM 14 CEP 7	The West Antarctic Ice Sheet in the Fifth Assessment Report of the Intergovernmental Panel on Climate Change (IPCC): a key threat, a key uncertainty	ASOC	📄				
IP075	ATCM 10 CEP 13	Amery Ice Shelf helicopter incident	Australia	📄				
IP076	ATCM 13 ATCM 4	Malaysia's Activities and Achievements in Antarctic Research and Diplomacy	Malaysia	📄				
IP077	ATCM 11	Management of tourism in Antarctica – an IAATO perspective	IAATO	📄				
IP078	ATCM 11	Adventure Tourism: Activities undertaken by IAATO Members	IAATO	📄				
IP079	ATCM 10	SAR Communication Exercise: Argentina - IAATO	Argentina IAATO	📄			📄	

Information Papers

Number	Ag. Items	Title	Submitted By	E	F	R	S	Attachments
IP080	ATCM 5	The Exercise of National Jurisdiction on Assets in Antarctica	Belgium	▤	▤	▤	▤	
IP081	ATCM 13	Norwegian Antarctic research	Norway	▤				
IP082	CEP 11	Site Sensitivity Analysis approach utilized in the Svalbard context	Norway	▤				
IP083	CEP 10a	Record of two species of non-native birds at 25 de Mayo island, South Shetland Islands	Argentina	▤			▤	
IP084	ATCM 11	Preliminary report on Antarctic tourist flows and cruise ships operating in Ushuaia during the 2013/2014 Austral summer season	Argentina	▤			▤	
IP085	CEP 10c	Estimation of the breeding population of Emperor Penguin, Aptenodytes forsteri, at Snow Hill Island (Isla Cerro Nevado), northeast of the Antarctic Peninsula	Argentina	▤			▤	
IP086	CEP 9c	Tourism Management Policy for Carlini Scientific Station	Argentina	▤	▤		▤	Tourism Management Policy for Carlini Scientific Station
IP087	ATCM 11	Areas of tourist interest in the Antarctic Peninsula and South Orkney Islands (Islas Orcadas del Sur) region. 2013/2014 Austral summer season	Argentina	▤			▤	
IP088	ATCM 11	Non-commercial pleasure and/or sport vessels which travelled to Antarctica through Ushuaia during the 2013/2014 season	Argentina	▤			▤	
IP089	ATCM 11	An account of optional activities offered by the Antarctic tour operators that operated through Ushuaia during the 2013-2014 Austral summer season	Argentina	▤			▤	
IP090	ATCM 13	Scientific activities in Terra Nova Bay: a brief overview of the Italian National Antarctic Program	Italy	▤				
IP091	ATCM 10	An update on the Antarctic Polar View sea ice information service	United Kingdom	▤				
IP092	ATCM 10	Search and Rescue cases in the Antarctic Peninsula Area. Season 2013 / 2014. MRCC Chile	Chile	▤			▤	
IP093	ATCM	Proyecto A: Residencias	Chile				▤	

387

Information Papers

Number	Ag. Items	Title	Submitted By	E	F	R	S	Attachments
	15	artísticas en la Antártica						
IP094 rev.1	CEP 7	Antarctic trial of WWF's Rapid Assessment of Circum-Arctic Ecosystem Resilience (RACER) Conservation Planning Tool – methodology and trial outcomes	United Kingdom	📄				RACER Trial Report: Annexes 1 - 7. RACER Trial Report: Appendix 1
IP095	ATCM 10	Akademik Shokalskiy incident	Australia	📄				
IP096	ATCM 13	Overview of Czech Research Activites in Antarctica in 2013-2014	Czech Republic	📄				
IP097	CEP 4	CEP XVII – Work done during the intersession period	France	📄				
IP098	CEP 9f	Romanian Activities Associated with the Antarctic Specially Managed Area No.6 Larsemann Hills Management Group	Romania	📄				
IP099	ATCM 10	Contribution of the Joint Antarctic Naval Patrol to the maritime and environmental protection operations in the Antarctic area	Chile Argentina	📄			📄	
IP100	ATCM 4	Report of the Antarctic and Southern Ocean Coalition	ASOC	📄	📄	📄	📄	

Secretariat Papers

Number	Ag. Items	Title	Submitted By	E	F	R	S	Attachments
SP001 rev.4	ATCM 3 CEP 2	ATCM XXXVII and CEP XVII Agenda and Schedule	ATS					Multi-Year Strategic Work Plan - Decision 5 (2013) Annex
SP002	ATCM 6	Secretariat Report 2013/14	ATS					Appendix 1: Audited Financial Report 2012/2013 Appendix 2: Provisional Financial Report 2013/14 Appendix 3: Contributions Received 2013/2014
SP003 rev.1	ATCM 6	Secretariat Programme 2014/15	ATS					Appendix 1: Provisional Report 2013/14, Budget 2014/15 and Forecast Budget 2015/16 Appendix 2: Contribution Scale 2015/16 Appendix 3: Salary Scale 2014/15
SP004	ATCM 6	Five Years Forward Budget Profile 2014 - 2018	ATS					Five Years Forward Budget Profile 2014 - 2018
SP005	CEP 8b	Annual list of Initial Environmental Evaluations (IEE) and Comprehensive Environmental Evaluations (CEE) prepared between April 1st 2013 and March 31st 2014	ATS					
SP007	ATCM 16 ATCM 7 CEP 4	ATCM Multi-Year Strategic Work Plan: Report of the Secretariat on Information Exchange Requirements and the Electronic Information Exchange System	ATS					
SP008	ATCM 10	ATCM Multi-Year Strategic Work Plan: Compilation of existing ATCM recommendations on safety issues	ATS					
SP009	ATCM 11	ATCM Multi-Year Strategic Work Plan: Summary of the ATCM discussions and decisions on land-based and adventure tourism	ATS					
SP010	ATCM 6	Report on Demarches for an Alternative Salary and Remuneration System	ATS					
SP011	ATCM 9	Reissue WP27 CEP XVI: Repair or Remediation of Environmental Damage: Report of the CEP intersessional contact group	ATS					
SP013	CEP 2	CEP XVII Summary of Papers	ATS					
SP014 rev.2	ATCM 16 ATCM 17 ATCM 5 ATCM	WG on Legal and Institutional Matters - Summary of papers	ATS					

Secretariat Papers

Number	Ag. Items	Title	Submitted By	E	F	R	S	Attachments
	6 ATCM 7 ATCM 9							
SP015 rev.2	ATCM 10 ATCM 12 ATCM 13 ATCM 14 ATCM 15	WG on Operational Matters - Summary of Papers	ATS	📄				
SP016	ATCM 11	WG on Tourism and Non-governmental Activities - Chairman's Proposed Agenda and Summary of Papers	ATS	📄				
SP017 rev.1	ATCM 1	List of Registered Delegates	ATS	📄				

Background Papers

Number	Ag. Items	Title	Submitted By	E	F	R	S	Attachments
BP001	ATCM 13	Brazilian automatic remote modules in the West Antarctic Ice Sheet	Brazil	📄				
BP002	ATCM 13	Scientific advances of the Brazilian oceanographic research in the Southern Ocean and its vicinity	Brazil	📄				
BP003	ATCM 13	The geological record of the transition from greenhouse to icehouse (Eocene to Oligocene) in Western Antarctica	Brazil	📄				
BP004	ATCM 13	National Institute of Science and Technology of the Cryosphere	Brazil	📄				
BP005	ATCM 13	National Institute for Science and Technology – Antarctic Environmental Research (INCT-APA): Five-Year Highlights	Brazil	📄				
BP006	ATCM 13	SCAR Lecture: "Back to the Future: Past Antarctic Climates, Ice Sheet History & Their Relevance for Understanding Future Trends"	SCAR	📄	📄	📄	📄	
BP007 rev.1	CEP 9f	Monitoring and Management Report of Narębski Point (ASPA No. 171) during the past 5 years (2009-2014)	Korea (ROK)	📄				
BP008	ATCM 13	Scientific & Science-related Collaborations with Other Parties During 2013-2014	Korea (ROK)	📄				
BP009	ATCM 4 CEP 5	The Scientific Committee on Antarctic Research (SCAR). Selected Science Highlights for 2013/14	SCAR	📄				
BP010	CEP 12	Recommendations of the Inspection Teams to Maitri Station and their Implementation	India	📄				
BP011	CEP 9a	Initiation of a review of ASPA 104: Sabrina Island, Northern Ross Sea, Antarctica	New Zealand	📄				
BP012	ATCM 13	New Zealand Antarctic and Southern Ocean Science: Directions and Priorities 2010 - 2020	New Zealand	📄				New Zealand Antarctic & Southern Ocean Science: Directions and Priorities 2010 - 2020
BP013	CEP 13	Progress on the development of a new waste water treatment facility at Australia's Davis station	Australia	📄				
BP014	CEP 5	Antarctica New Zealand Membership of the International Union for Conservation of Nature (IUCN)	New Zealand	📄				
BP015	ATCM 13	Digital upgrade of SuperDARN radar at SANAE	South Africa	📄				

Background Papers								
Number	Ag. Items	Title	Submitted By	E	F	R	S	Attachments
		IV 2013/2014						
BP016	ATCM 10 ATCM 13	Compilación de la producción cartográfica antártica española	Spain					
BP017	CEP 11	Remote sensing of environmental changes on King George Island (South Shetland Islands): establishing a new monitoring program	Poland					
BP018	CEP 6	Tareas de Gestión Ambiental en la Base Belgrano II	Argentina					
BP019	ATCM 13	Vigésimo Segunda Expedición Científica del Perú a la Antártida (ANTAR XXII)	Peru					
BP020	ATCM 13	Agenda Nacional de Investigación Científica Antártica 2014 – 2016 (ANTARPERU)	Peru					

3. List of Participants

3. List of Participants

PARTICIPANTS: CONSULTATIVE PARTIES				
PARTY	NAME	POSITION	ARRIVAL DATE	DEP.DATE
Argentina	Adad, Gabriel Carlos	Advisor	28/04/2014	08/05/2014
Argentina	Conde Garrido, Rodrigo	Delegate	28/04/2014	07/05/2014
Argentina	Coria, Nestor	Delegate	26/04/2014	08/05/2014
Argentina	Giudici, Tomás Martín	Delegate	26/04/2014	08/05/2014
Argentina	López Crozet, Fausto	Head of Delegation	26/04/2014	08/05/2014
Argentina	Memolli, Mariano A.	CEP Representative	26/04/2014	08/05/2014
Argentina	Ortúzar, Patricia	Delegate	26/04/2014	08/05/2014
Argentina	Rodríguez Lamas, Ezequiel	Delegate	26/04/2014	08/05/2014
Argentina	Vereda, Marisol	Advisor	28/04/2014	08/05/2014
Argentina	Vlasich, Verónica	Delegate	26/04/2014	08/05/2014
Australia	Compton, Peta	Delegate	27/04/2014	07/05/2014
Australia	Cooper, Katrina	Head of Delegation	25/04/2014	08/05/2014
Australia	Devlin, Quinton	Delegate	27/04/2014	07/05/2014
Australia	Fleming, Tony	Alternate	25/04/2014	04/05/2014
Australia	Goldsworthy, Lyn	Advisor	25/04/2014	06/05/2014
Australia	Lawless, Patrick	Delegate	27/04/2014	07/05/2014
Australia	Lendels, Lizzie	Delegate	27/04/2014	07/05/2014
Australia	McIvor, Ewan	CEP Representative	25/04/2014	08/05/2014
Australia	Mundy, Jason	Delegate	25/04/2014	08/05/2014
Australia	Press, Tony	Advisor	25/04/2014	09/05/2014
Australia	Scott-Kemmis, Cary	Delegate	25/04/2014	08/05/2014
Australia	Tracey, Phillip	Delegate	25/04/2014	08/05/2014
Australia	Trousselot, Chrissie	Advisor	26/04/2014	08/05/2014
Belgium	Chemay, Frédéric	CEP Representative	26/04/2014	08/05/2014
Belgium	Hottat, Sophie	Advisor	29/04/2014	07/05/2014
Belgium	Touzani, Rachid	Delegate	28/04/2014	05/05/2014
Belgium	Vancauwenberghe, Maaike	Delegate	27/04/2014	03/05/2014
Belgium	Vanden Bilcke, Christian	Head of Delegation	26/04/2014	08/05/2014
Belgium	Wilmotte, Annick	Delegate	27/04/2014	04/05/2014
Brazil	Abdenur, Adriana Erthal	Advisor	28/04/2014	07/05/2014
Brazil	Azeredo, Raphael	Head of Delegation	28/04/2014	07/05/2014
Brazil	Bello Chimos, Cinthya	Delegate	28/04/2014	07/05/2014
Brazil	Boechat de Almeida, Barbara	Delegate	28/04/2014	07/05/2014
Brazil	Brandão Cavalcanti, Roberto	Advisor	27/04/2014	07/05/2014
Brazil	Brasil, Paula Rassi	Delegate	28/04/2014	07/05/2014
Brazil	Buss de Souza, Ronald	Advisor	28/04/2014	07/05/2014
Brazil	Câmara, Paulo	Advisor	28/04/2014	07/05/2014
Brazil	Cardia Simões, Jefferson	Advisor	28/04/2014	07/05/2014
Brazil	Chaim Mattos, Bianca	Delegate	28/04/2014	07/05/2014
Brazil	Costa, Siddhartha	Delegate	28/04/2014	07/05/2014
Brazil	Cruz-Kaled, Andrea	Delegate	28/04/2014	07/05/2014
Brazil	Delduque de Medeiros, Marcos F.	Delegate	21/04/2014	07/05/2014
Brazil	Duleba, Wânia	Advisor	28/04/2014	07/05/2014
Brazil	Faria de Mattos, Leonardo	Delegate	28/04/2014	07/05/2014
Brazil	Faria Oliveira., Áthila	Delegate	21/04/2014	07/05/2014
Brazil	Fontes Faria, Maria Rita	Alternate	28/04/2014	07/05/2014
Brazil	Gonçalves, Paulo Rogério	Advisor	28/04/2014	07/05/2014
Brazil	Ibañez de Novion, Henry-Philippe	Delegate	28/04/2014	07/05/2014
Brazil	Legracie Júnior, José Renato	Delegate	28/04/2014	07/05/2014
Brazil	Leite, Marcio Renato	Delegate	21/04/2014	07/05/2014
Brazil	Lemmertz, Heloisa	Advisor	28/04/2014	07/05/2014
Brazil	Luna, Vera	Advisor	30/04/2014	07/05/2014
Brazil	Machado Calaço, Rachel	Delegate	28/04/2014	07/05/2014
Brazil	Madeira, Acir	Advisor	28/04/2014	07/05/2014

PARTICIPANTS: CONSULTATIVE PARTIES				
PARTY	NAME	POSITION	ARRIVAL DATE	DEP.DATE
Brazil	Madruga, Jaqueline Leal	Delegate	28/04/2014	07/05/2014
Brazil	Marcondes de Carvalho, José Antonio	ATCM Chairman	27/04/2014	07/05/2014
Brazil	Montone, Rosalinda	Advisor	28/04/2014	07/05/2014
Brazil	Moraes, Osvaldo	Delegate	28/04/2014	07/05/2014
Brazil	Morais Paranaguá, Marcus Henrique	Advisor	28/04/2014	07/05/2014
Brazil	Moreira Sales de Menezes, Mariana	Delegate	28/04/2014	07/05/2014
Brazil	Nobre, Carlos	Delegate	28/04/2014	07/05/2014
Brazil	Oliveira Caldas, Anderson	Delegate	21/04/2014	07/05/2014
Brazil	Oliveira Costalunga, Ana Lucia	Delegate	28/04/2014	07/05/2014
Brazil	Palazzi, Giovanna	Advisor	28/04/2014	07/05/2014
Brazil	Pellizari, Vivian	Advisor	29/04/2014	07/05/2014
Brazil	Penna Firme Horna, Luciane	Delegate	28/04/2014	07/05/2014
Brazil	Portella Sampaio, Daniela	Advisor	28/04/2014	07/05/2014
Brazil	Quitéria Souza dos Santos Gouvea, Ludmila	Delegate	28/04/2014	07/05/2014
Brazil	Ramos de Alencar da Costa, Felipe Augusto	Delegate	28/04/2014	07/05/2014
Brazil	Resende de Assis, Luis Guilherme	Advisor	05/05/2014	07/05/2014
Brazil	Rocha-Campos, Antonio Carlos	Advisor	28/04/2014	07/05/2014
Brazil	Rodrigues, Marcos Silva	Delegate	21/04/2014	07/05/2014
Brazil	Sodré Polejack, Andrei de Abreu	Delegate	28/04/2014	07/05/2014
Brazil	Sousa Picolo, Kenia Dias	Delegate	28/04/2014	07/05/2014
Brazil	Souza Della Nina, Clarissa	Delegate	28/04/2014	07/05/2014
Brazil	Suarez Sampaio, Carlos Hugo	Advisor	28/04/2014	07/05/2014
Brazil	Teixeira, Antonio José	Delegate	21/04/2014	07/05/2014
Brazil	Trotte-Duhá , Janice Romaguera	Delegate	28/04/2014	07/05/2014
Brazil	Valentin, yocie	Advisor	28/04/2014	07/05/2014
Brazil	Vieira Carneiro, José Eduardo	Delegate	21/04/2014	07/05/2014
Bulgaria	Jivkov, Christo	Alternate	24/04/2014	08/05/2014
Bulgaria	Kuchev, Yuriy	Delegate	24/04/2014	08/05/2014
Bulgaria	Mateev, Dragomir	Delegate	24/04/2014	08/05/2014
Bulgaria	Petrova, Elena	Delegate	24/04/2014	08/05/2014
Bulgaria	Pimpirev, Christo	CEP Representative	24/04/2014	08/05/2014
Bulgaria	Popova, Anna	Delegate	24/04/2014	29/04/2014
Bulgaria	Raytchev, Rayko	Head of Delegation	24/04/2014	08/05/2014
Bulgaria	Romanska, Tsvety	Delegate	24/04/2014	08/05/2014
Bulgaria	Yotov, Valeri	Alternate	24/04/2014	08/05/2014
Canada	Taillefer, David	Head of Delegation	27/04/2014	03/05/2014
Chile	Barticevic, Elías	Advisor	28/04/2014	07/05/2014
Chile	Berguño, Francisco	Head of Delegation	26/04/2014	07/05/2014
Chile	Berguño, Fernando	Delegate	28/04/2014	07/05/2014
Chile	Cariceo, Yanko	Advisor	28/04/2014	07/05/2014
Chile	Casiccia, Claudio	Advisor	28/04/2014	07/05/2014
Chile	Chomali, Jaime	Delegate	28/04/2014	07/05/2014
Chile	Durand, Jorge	Advisor	28/04/2014	07/05/2014
Chile	Espinoza, Patricio	Advisor	28/04/2014	07/05/2014
Chile	Ferrada, Luis Valentín	Advisor	28/04/2014	07/05/2014
Chile	Figueroa, Miguel	Advisor	28/04/2014	07/05/2014
Chile	Foxon, Javier	HCS Staff	21/04/2014	07/05/2014
Chile	Gamboa, César	Delegate	27/04/2014	07/05/2014
Chile	Iturriaga, Javier	Advisor	28/04/2014	07/05/2014
Chile	Madrid, Santiago	Advisor	28/04/2014	07/05/2014
Chile	Mayorga, Pedro	Advisor	28/04/2014	07/05/2014

3. List of Participants

PARTICIPANTS: CONSULTATIVE PARTIES				
PARTY	NAME	POSITION	ARRIVAL DATE	DEP.DATE
Chile	Mella, Leopoldo	Advisor	28/04/2014	07/05/2014
Chile	Pizarro, Cristián	Advisor	28/04/2014	07/05/2014
Chile	Retamales, José	Alternate	28/04/2014	07/05/2014
Chile	Vallejos, Verónica	CEP Representative	28/04/2014	03/05/2014
Chile	Velásquez, Ricardo	Advisor	28/04/2014	07/05/2014
China	Gao, Feng	Head of Delegation	26/04/2014	08/05/2014
China	Han, Zixuan	Delegate	26/04/2014	08/05/2014
China	Lu, Zhibo	CEP Representative	26/04/2014	08/05/2014
China	Qu, Tanzhou	Delegate	26/04/2014	08/05/2014
China	Sun, Bo	Advisor	26/04/2014	08/05/2014
China	Wei, Long	Delegate	26/04/2014	08/05/2014
China	Wu, Chenqi	Delegate	26/04/2014	08/05/2014
China	Zhang, Tijun	Advisor	26/04/2014	08/05/2014
China	Zhuo, Li	Delegate	26/04/2014	08/05/2014
Czech Republic	Havlik, Jiri	Head of Delegation	28/04/2014	07/05/2014
Czech Republic	Kapler, Pavel	Delegate	26/04/2014	02/05/2014
Czech Republic	Nyvlt, Daniel	CEP Representative	26/04/2014	02/05/2014
Czech Republic	Smuclerova, Martina	Alternate	27/04/2014	07/05/2014
Czech Republic	Venera, Zdenek	CEP Representative	27/04/2014	07/05/2014
Ecuador	Bonifaz Arboleda, Pablo A.	Advisor	05/05/2014	07/05/2014
Ecuador	Córdova Montero, Maria Soledad	Head of Delegation	05/05/2014	07/05/2014
Ecuador	Olmedo Morán, José	Alternate	27/04/2014	30/05/2014
Ecuador	Ruiz Xomchuk, Veronica	Advisor	28/04/2014	07/05/2014
Ecuador	Valenzuela, María José	Delegate	05/05/2014	07/05/2014
Finland	Mähönen, Outi	CEP Representative	26/04/2014	03/05/2014
Finland	Valjento, Liisa	Head of Delegation	25/04/2014	08/05/2014
France	Belna, Stéphanie	CEP Representative	27/04/2014	05/05/2014
France	Bolot, Pascal	Delegate	29/04/2014	02/05/2014
France	Choquet, Anne	Advisor	30/04/2014	07/05/2014
France	Frenot, Yves	CEP Representative	25/04/2014	07/05/2014
France	Guyomard, Ann-Isabelle	Delegate	27/04/2014	06/05/2014
France	Guyonvarch, Olivier	Head of Delegation	26/04/2014	08/05/2014
France	Jagour, Mathieu	Delegate	28/04/2014	07/05/2014
France	Lebouvier, Marc	CEP Representative	25/04/2014	07/05/2014
France	Mayet, Laurent	Delegate	27/04/2014	07/05/2014
France	Rocard, Michel	Delegate	27/04/2014	30/04/2014
France	Runyo, Fabienne	Alternate	27/04/2014	07/05/2014
Germany	Gaedicke, Christoph	Delegate	27/04/2014	02/05/2014
Germany	Hain, Stefan	Delegate	27/04/2014	07/05/2014
Germany	Herata, Heike	CEP Representative	26/04/2014	07/05/2014
Germany	Heyn, Andrea	Delegate	27/04/2014	07/05/2014
Germany	Kuhbier, Bernd	Delegate	27/04/2014	08/05/2014
Germany	Läufer, Andreas	Delegate	27/04/2014	02/05/2014
Germany	Liebschner, Alexander	Delegate	28/04/2014	02/05/2014
Germany	Lindemann, Christian	Delegate	26/04/2014	04/05/2014
Germany	Miller, Heinrich	Delegate	27/04/2014	06/05/2014
Germany	Ney, Martin	Head of Delegation	27/04/2014	30/04/2014
Germany	Nixdorf, Uwe	Delegate	27/04/2014	02/05/2014
Germany	Schueller, Dirk Gerhard	Delegate	27/04/2014	08/05/2014
Germany	Schulz, Christian	Alternate	27/04/2014	08/05/2014
India	Chaturvedi, Sanjay	Delegate	02/05/2014	08/05/2014
India	Mohan, Rahul	Delegate	02/05/2014	08/05/2014
India	Rajan, Sivaramakrishnan	Head of Delegation	26/04/2014	08/05/2014
India	Rao, Koteswara	Delegate	26/04/2014	07/05/2014
India	Sharma, R K	Delegate	02/05/2014	08/05/2014
India	Tiwari, Anoop	Delegate	26/04/2014	08/05/2014

PARTICIPANTS: CONSULTATIVE PARTIES				
PARTY	NAME	POSITION	ARRIVAL DATE	DEP.DATE
Italy	Mecozzi, Roberta	Delegate	28/04/2014	07/05/2014
Italy	Sgrò, Eugenio	Head of Delegation	28/04/2014	08/05/2014
Italy	Tomaselli, Maria Stefania	Delegate	28/04/2014	07/05/2014
Italy	Torcini, Sandro	CEP Representative	28/04/2014	07/05/2014
Japan	Hirano, Jun	Delegate	27/04/2014	07/05/2014
Japan	Shiraishi, Kazuyuki	Delegate	29/04/2014	05/05/2014
Japan	Takahashi, Kazuhiro	Head of Delegation	27/04/2014	07/05/2014
Japan	Takeda, Sayako	Delegate	28/04/2014	07/05/2014
Japan	Tanaka, Kenichiro	Delegate	27/04/2014	08/05/2014
Japan	Teramura, Satoshi	Delegate	27/04/2014	07/05/2014
Japan	Watanabe, Kentaro	Delegate	26/04/2014	08/05/2014
Korea (ROK)	Ahn, In-Young	CEP Representative	27/04/2014	03/05/2014
Korea (ROK)	Chung, Rae-kwang	Delegate	26/04/2014	03/05/2014
Korea (ROK)	Chung, Hosung	Delegate	27/04/2014	03/05/2014
Korea (ROK)	Kim, Yeadong	Delegate	26/04/2014	01/05/2014
Korea (ROK)	Kim, Ji Hee	Delegate	27/04/2014	03/05/2014
Korea (ROK)	Rhee, Zha-hyoung	Head of Delegation	26/04/2014	03/05/2014
Korea (ROK)	Seo, Young-min	Delegate	26/04/2014	07/05/2014
Korea (ROK)	Shin, Hyoung Chul	Delegate	27/04/2014	06/05/2014
Korea (ROK)	Son, Eun-jung	Delegate	26/04/2014	02/05/2014
Netherlands	Bastmeijer, Kees	Advisor	28/04/2014	07/05/2014
Netherlands	Elstgeest, Marlynda	Advisor	27/04/2014	07/05/2014
Netherlands	Hernaus, Reginald	CEP Representative	28/04/2014	06/05/2014
Netherlands	Lefeber, René J.M.	Head of Delegation	26/04/2014	07/05/2014
Netherlands	Peijs, Martijn	Advisor	28/04/2014	07/05/2014
New Zealand	Beggs, Peter	Delegate	26/04/2014	08/05/2014
New Zealand	Dempster, Jillian	Head of Delegation	26/04/2014	08/05/2014
New Zealand	Gilbert, Neil	CEP Representative	26/04/2014	08/05/2014
New Zealand	Kendall, Rachel	Delegate	26/04/2014	08/05/2014
New Zealand	MacKay, Don	Advisor	29/04/2014	08/05/2014
New Zealand	Morgan, Fraser	Advisor	26/04/2014	03/05/2014
New Zealand	Poirot, Ceisha	Delegate	26/04/2014	08/05/2014
New Zealand	Smithyman, Alex	Delegate	27/04/2014	07/05/2014
New Zealand	Stent, Danica	Delegate	26/04/2014	08/05/2014
New Zealand	Weeber, Barry	Advisor	27/04/2014	08/05/2014
Norway	Askjer, Angela Lahelle-Ekholdt	Delegate	29/04/2014	07/05/2014
Norway	Eikeland, Else Berit	Head of Delegation	29/04/2014	07/05/2014
Norway	Gaalaas, Siv Christin	Delegate	29/04/2014	06/05/2014
Norway	Halvorsen, Svein Tore	Delegate	27/04/2014	03/05/2014
Norway	Hodne Steen, Sissel	Delegate	28/04/2014	07/05/2014
Norway	Korsvoll, Marie Helene	Delegate	30/04/2014	07/05/2014
Norway	Njaastad, Birgit	CEP Representative	26/04/2014	07/05/2014
Norway	Strengehagen, Mette	Alternate	27/04/2014	02/05/2014
Norway	Wiig, Aud Marit	Delegate	28/04/2014	07/05/2014
Norway	Winther, Jan-Gunnar	Delegate	28/04/2014	02/05/2014
Peru	Bayona Medina, Jorge	Head of Delegation	28/04/2014	07/05/2014
Peru	Espino Sanchez, Marco Antonio	Delegate	28/04/2014	07/05/2014
Peru	Menezes, Raul	Delegate	28/04/2014	07/05/2014
Peru	Palacios, Carlos	Delegate	28/04/2014	07/05/2014
Peru	Rios, Carlos	Delegate	28/04/2014	07/05/2014
Poland	Kidawa, Anna	Delegate	28/04/2014	03/05/2014
Poland	Marciniak, Konrad	Alternate	28/04/2014	02/05/2014
Poland	Misztal, Andrzej	Head of Delegation	02/05/2014	07/05/2014
Poland	Tatur, Andrzej	Delegate	28/04/2014	07/05/2014
Russian Federation	Alexey, Egoskin	Advisor	28/04/2014	07/05/2014
Russian Federation	Chernysheva, Larisa	Delegate	26/04/2014	08/05/2014

PARTICIPANTS: CONSULTATIVE PARTIES				
PARTY	NAME	POSITION	ARRIVAL DATE	DEP.DATE
Russian Federation	Gonchar, Dmitry	Head of Delegation	26/04/2014	08/05/2014
Russian Federation	Konyashkina, Natalia	Delegate	26/04/2014	08/05/2014
Russian Federation	Lukin, Valery	CEP Representative	26/04/2014	10/05/2014
Russian Federation	Pomelov, Victor	Delegate	25/04/2014	09/05/2014
Russian Federation	Voevodin, Andrey	Delegate	25/04/2014	09/05/2014
South Africa	Dwarika, Yolande	Delegate	26/04/2014	08/05/2014
South Africa	Jacobs, Carol	CEP Representative	26/04/2014	04/05/2014
South Africa	Malefane, Nthabiseng	Alternate	27/04/2014	08/05/2014
South Africa	Mbete, Mphakama Nyangweni	Head of Delegation	07/05/2014	07/05/2014
South Africa	Mphepya, Jonas	Delegate	27/04/2014	08/05/2014
South Africa	Siko, Gilbert	Advisor	28/04/2014	07/05/2014
South Africa	Skinner, Richard	Delegate	27/04/2014	08/05/2014
South Africa	Solomons, Millicent	Delegate	26/04/2014	04/05/2014
South Africa	Valentine, Henry	Delegate	27/04/2014	08/05/2014
Spain	Catalan, Manuel	CEP Representative	26/04/2014	08/05/2014
Spain	Muñoz de Laborde Bardin, Juan Luis	Head of Delegation	26/04/2014	08/05/2014
Spain	Puig Marco, Roser	Advisor	25/04/2014	07/05/2014
Spain	Ramos, Sonia	Delegate	26/04/2014	08/05/2014
Sweden	Euren Hoglund, Lisa	Head of Delegation	27/04/2014	07/05/2014
Sweden	Josefsson Lazo, Pernilla	Delegate	28/04/2014	07/05/2014
Sweden	Linquist, Johanna	Delegate	28/04/2014	07/05/2014
Sweden	Selberg, Cecilia	CEP Representative	28/04/2014	07/05/2014
Ukraine	Liashenko , Oleksii	Advisor	25/04/2014	10/05/2014
Ukraine	Tronenko, Rostyslav	Head of Delegation	25/04/2014	10/05/2014
United Kingdom	Burgess, Henry	CEP Representative	26/04/2014	09/05/2014
United Kingdom	Clarke, Rachel	Delegate	27/04/2014	03/05/2014
United Kingdom	Cowan, Caroline	Delegate	27/04/2014	08/05/2014
United Kingdom	Downie, Rod	Advisor	28/04/2014	02/05/2014
United Kingdom	Ford, Andrew	Delegate	27/04/2014	08/05/2014
United Kingdom	Francis, Jane	Delegate	26/04/2014	05/05/2014
United Kingdom	Hughes, Kevin	Delegate	27/04/2014	03/05/2014
United Kingdom	Khan, Akbar	Delegate	26/04/2014	09/05/2014
United Kingdom	Nogueira, Thais	Delegate	27/04/2014	08/05/2014
United Kingdom	Rumble, Jane	Head of Delegation	26/04/2014	09/05/2014
United Kingdom	Shears, John	Delegate	27/04/2014	09/05/2014
United States	Bloom, Evan T.	Head of Delegation	26/04/2014	07/05/2014
United States	Edwards, David	Advisor	29/04/2014	07/05/2014
United States	Falkner, Kelly	Advisor	27/04/2014	02/05/2014
United States	Hahs, Ona	Advisor	27/04/2014	07/05/2014
United States	Hamady, Li Ling	Advisor	27/04/2014	07/05/2014
United States	Jones, Christopher	Delegate	28/04/2014	07/05/2014
United States	Karentz, Deneb	Advisor	27/04/2014	03/05/2014
United States	McGinn, Nature	Advisor	27/04/2014	07/05/2014
United States	Naveen, Ron	Advisor	27/04/2014	06/05/2014
United States	O'Reilly, Jessica	Advisor	27/04/2014	07/05/2014
United States	Penhale, Polly A.	CEP Representative	26/04/2014	07/05/2014
United States	Rudolph, Lawrence	Advisor	27/04/2014	07/05/2014
United States	Schandlbauer, Alfred	Alternate	26/04/2014	07/05/2014
United States	Stone, Brian	Advisor	27/04/2014	07/05/2014
United States	Toschik, Pamela	Advisor	27/04/2014	08/05/2014
United States	Trice, Jessica	Advisor	27/04/2014	07/05/2014
United States	Watters, George	Advisor	27/04/2014	07/05/2014
United States	Wheatley, Victoria	Advisor	27/04/2014	08/05/2014
Uruguay	Blanco, Marcelo	Delegate	27/04/2014	07/05/2014
Uruguay	Abdala, Juan	CEP Representative	27/04/2014	06/05/2014

PARTICIPANTS: CONSULTATIVE PARTIES

PARTY	NAME	POSITION	ARRIVAL DATE	DEP.DATE
Uruguay	Fajardo, Alberto	Alternate	26/04/2014	08/05/2014
Uruguay	Gorosito Pereira, Pablo Ricardo	Delegate	27/04/2014	07/05/2014
Uruguay	Lluberas, Albert	Delegate	26/04/2014	08/05/2014
Uruguay	Romano, Claudio	Head of Delegation	26/04/2014	08/05/2014
Uruguay	Vignali, Daniel	Advisor	27/04/2014	08/05/2014

PARTICIPANTS: NON-CONSULTATIVE PARTIES

PARTY	NAME	POSITION	ARRIVAL DATE	DEP.DATE
Belarus	Kakareka, Sergey	Delegate	28/04/2014	07/05/2014
Colombia	Cedeño, Alvaro	Delegate	28/04/2014	07/05/2014
Colombia	Fernández Restrepo, Luis Ricardo	Delegate	28/04/2014	07/05/2014
Colombia	García, Miriam	Delegate	27/04/2014	10/05/2014
Colombia	Kecan, Diana	Delegate	28/04/2014	07/05/2014
Colombia	Mikan, Sandra Lucía	Delegate	04/05/2014	10/05/2014
Colombia	Molano, Mauricio	Delegate	27/04/2014	08/05/2014
Colombia	Montenegro Coral, Ricardo	Head of Delegation	05/05/2014	07/05/2014
Greece	Kalaitzakis, Dimitris	Advisor	28/04/2014	07/05/2014
Greece	Panagiotidis, Georgios	Advisor	28/04/2014	07/05/2014
Malaysia	Abd Rahman, Mohd Nasaruddin	Delegate	27/04/2014	08/05/2014
Malaysia	Jayaseelan, Sumitra	Delegate	27/04/2014	01/05/2014
Malaysia	K.R Vasudevan, Sudha Devi	Delegate	27/04/2014	08/05/2014
Malaysia	Mansor, Ahmad Salman	Delegate	27/04/2014	08/05/2014
Malaysia	Mohd Nor, Salleh	Delegate	27/04/2014	08/05/2014
Malaysia	Mohd Shah, Rohani	Delegate	27/04/2014	08/05/2014
Malaysia	Shamsuddin, Shamsul Nizam	Delegate	27/04/2014	08/05/2014
Malaysia	Yahaya, Mohd Azhar	Head of Delegation	27/04/2014	01/05/2014
Monaco	Van Klaveren, Céline	CEP Representative	27/04/2014	02/05/2014
Portugal	Ferraz de Lima Sanchez da Motta, Goncalo	Delegate	27/04/2014	07/05/2014
Portugal	Xavier, José Carlos Caetano	Head of Delegation	27/04/2014	09/05/2014
Romania	Ocneriu, Veronica	Alternate	28/04/2014	07/05/2014
Romania	Radu, Diana Anca	Head of Delegation	28/04/2014	07/05/2014
Slovak Republic	Cigan, Milan	Head of Delegation	29/04/2014	07/05/2014
Switzerland	Reto Andreas, Durler	Head of Delegation	28/04/2014	07/05/2014
Turkey	Atasoy, Osman	Advisor	28/04/2014	07/05/2014
Turkey	Dirioz, Huseyin	Advisor	28/04/2014	07/05/2014
Turkey	Karasu, Sibel	Advisor	28/04/2014	07/05/2014
Turkey	Ozdemir , Leyla	Advisor	28/04/2014	07/05/2014
Turkey	Ozturk, Bayram	Advisor	28/04/2014	07/05/2014
Turkey	Polat, Orhan Dede	Delegate	25/04/2014	08/05/2014
Turkey	Tabak, Haluk	Delegate	25/04/2014	09/05/2014
Turkey	Türkel, Ebuzer	Delegate	25/04/2014	09/05/2014
Turkey	Türkel, Mehmet Ali	Head of Delegation	25/04/2014	09/05/2014
Venezuela	Alfonso, Juan A.	Head of Delegation	27/04/2014	08/05/2014
Venezuela	Carlos , Castellanos	Delegate	26/04/2014	08/05/2014
Venezuela	Gilberto, Jaimes	Delegate	28/04/2014	07/05/2014
Venezuela	Ronaldo, Sosa	Delegate	26/04/2014	08/05/2014
Venezuela	Vera, Jonny	Delegate	26/04/2014	08/05/2014

PARTICIPANTS: OBSERVERS

PARTY	NAME	POSITION	ARRIVAL DATE	DEP.DATE
CCAMLR	Jones, Christopher	Delegate	28/04/2014	07/05/2014
CCAMLR	Reid, Keith	Advisor	27/04/2014	06/05/2014

PARTICIPANTS: OBSERVERS

PARTY	NAME	POSITION	ARRIVAL DATE	DEP.DATE
CCAMLR	Wright, Andrew	Head of Delegation	27/04/2014	07/05/2014
COMNAP	Rogan-Finnemore, Michelle	Head of Delegation	26/04/2014	09/05/2014
SCAR	Chown, Steven L.	Delegate	27/04/2014	04/05/2014
SCAR	Escutia, Carlota	Delegate	27/04/2014	01/05/2014
SCAR	HANS , NELSON	Advisor	30/04/2014	07/05/2014
SCAR	López-Martínez, Jerónimo	Head of Delegation	27/04/2014	08/05/2014
SCAR	Sparrow, Mike	Delegate	27/04/2014	05/05/2014

PARTICIPANTS: EXPERTS

PARTY	NAME	POSITION	ARRIVAL DATE	DEP.DATE
ASOC	Barroso, Mario	Delegate	28/04/2014	07/05/2014
ASOC	Campbell, Steve	Delegate	27/04/2014	03/05/2014
ASOC	Christian, Claire	Delegate	26/04/2014	08/05/2014
ASOC	Epstein, Mark S.	Head of Delegation	27/04/2014	08/05/2014
ASOC	Janovsky, Julie	Delegate	26/04/2014	03/05/2014
ASOC	Kavanagh, Andrea	Delegate	26/04/2014	03/05/2014
ASOC	Lucci, Juan	Delegate	27/04/2014	07/05/2014
ASOC	Lynch, Heather	Delegate	27/04/2014	03/05/2014
ASOC	Pearson, Pam	Delegate	28/04/2014	03/05/2014
ASOC	Roura, Ricardo	CEP Representative	26/04/2014	08/05/2014
ASOC	Tsidulko, Grigory	Delegate	26/04/2014	03/05/2014
ASOC	Werner Kinkelin, Rodolfo	Delegate	27/04/2014	03/05/2014
ASOC	Zuur, Bob	Delegate	26/04/2014	07/05/2014
IAATO	Crosbie, Kim	Head of Delegation	26/04/2014	08/05/2014
IAATO	Hohn-Bowen, Ute	Delegate	29/04/2014	07/05/2014
IAATO	Holgate, Claudia	Alternate	26/04/2014	08/05/2014
IAATO	Lynnes, Amanda	Delegate	27/04/2014	07/05/2014
IAATO	Machado D'Olivera, Suzana	Delegate	27/04/2014	07/05/2014
IAATO	Schillat, Monika	Delegate	27/04/2014	08/05/2014
IAATO	Sharp, Mike	Delegate	29/04/2014	06/05/2014
IHO	Ward, Robert	Head of Delegation	27/04/2014	02/05/2014
UNEP	Gross, Tony	Advisor	27/04/2014	07/05/2014
UNEP	Hamú Marcos de la Penha, Denise	Delegate	27/04/2014	07/05/2014
UNEP	Mrema, Elizabeth Maruma	Head of Delegation	27/04/2014	03/05/2014
WMO	Ondras, Miroslav	Head of Delegation	26/04/2014	10/05/2014
WMO	Pendlebury, Steve	Advisor	26/04/2014	10/05/2014

PARTICIPANTS: SECRETARIATS

PARTY	NAME	POSITION	ARRIVAL DATE	DEP.DATE
AT Secretariat	Acero, José Maria	Alternate	23/04/2014	09/05/2014
AT Secretariat	Agraz, José Luis	Staff	21/04/2014	09/05/2014
AT Secretariat	Balok, Anna	Staff	23/04/2014	09/05/2014
AT Secretariat	Davies, Paul	Staff	23/04/2014	08/05/2014
AT Secretariat	Guretskaya, Anastasia	Staff	26/04/2014	07/05/2014
AT Secretariat	Phillips, Andrew	Staff	21/04/2014	08/05/2014
AT Secretariat	Reinke, Manfred	Head of Delegation	21/04/2014	09/05/2014
AT Secretariat	Wainschenker, Pablo	Staff	21/04/2014	09/05/2014
AT Secretariat	Walton, David W H	Staff	22/04/2014	08/05/2014
AT Secretariat	Wydler, Diego	Staff	21/04/2014	09/05/2014
HC Secretariat	A Magalhães Ferreira, Gustavo	HCS Staff	21/04/2014	07/05/2014
HC Secretariat	Almeida de Sousa, Frank	HCS Staff	21/04/2014	07/05/2014
HC Secretariat	Alves Bezerra, Manoel	HCS Staff	21/04/2014	07/05/2014

PARTICIPANTS: SECRETARIATS				
PARTY	NAME	POSITION	ARRIVAL DATE	DEP.DATE
HC Secretariat	Batista da Silva Moura, Maria Aparecida	HCS Staff	21/04/2014	07/05/2014
HC Secretariat	Bezerra, Ricardo	HCS Staff	21/04/2014	07/05/2014
HC Secretariat	Bezerra Vitor Ramos, Carlota de Azevedo	HCS Staff	21/04/2014	07/05/2014
HC Secretariat	Costa Messias, Alvina	HCS Staff	21/04/2014	07/05/2014
HC Secretariat	das Chagas Ribeiro, Josilda	HCS Staff	21/04/2014	07/05/2014
HC Secretariat	de Araujo Bianchi, Vânia Magda	HCS Staff	21/04/2014	07/05/2014
HC Secretariat	de Castro Salvio, José Claudio	HCS Staff	28/04/2014	07/05/2014
HC Secretariat	de Freitas, José Silvério	HCS Staff	28/04/2014	07/05/2014
HC Secretariat	de Santana, Thássio Felipe	HCS Staff	21/04/2014	07/05/2014
HC Secretariat	de Souza, Aline	HCS Staff	28/04/2014	07/05/2014
HC Secretariat	Fonseca de Carvalho Gonçalves, Luiz Eduardo	HCS Staff	28/04/2014	07/05/2014
HC Secretariat	Freire, Evaldo	HCS Staff	21/04/2014	07/05/2014
HC Secretariat	Gomes Pereira, Manoel	HCS Staff	21/04/2014	07/05/2014
HC Secretariat	Gonçalves de Oliveira, Ana Christina	HCS Staff	21/04/2014	07/05/2014
HC Secretariat	Grinits, Erick	HCS Staff	21/04/2014	07/05/2014
HC Secretariat	Lima, Daniel	HCS Staff	21/04/2014	07/05/2014
HC Secretariat	Nascimento, Hugo	HCS Staff	21/04/2014	07/05/2014
HC Secretariat	Pereira, Adriana	HCS Staff	21/04/2014	07/05/2014
HC Secretariat	Pinho, Bruno	HCS Staff	21/04/2014	07/05/2014
HC Secretariat	Ponce de León Bezerra, Áurea Cristina	HCS Staff	21/04/2014	07/05/2014
HC Secretariat	Rypl, André João	HCS Staff	28/04/2014	07/05/2014
HC Secretariat	Sacchi Guadagnin, Luis Henrique	HCS Staff	21/04/2014	07/05/2014
HC Secretariat	Sensi, Dario André	HCS Staff	21/04/2014	07/05/2014
HC Secretariat	Silva, Silas	HCS Staff	21/04/2014	07/05/2014
T&I Services	Alal, Cecilia	Alternate	28/04/2014	07/05/2014
T&I Services	Boury, Marjorie	Staff	28/04/2014	07/05/2014
T&I Services	Cook, Elena	Staff	28/04/2014	07/05/2014
T&I Services	Coussaert, Joelle	Staff	28/04/2014	07/05/2014
T&I Services	Escorihuela, Romina	Staff	28/04/2014	07/05/2014
T&I Services	Fernandez, Jimena	Staff	28/04/2014	07/05/2014
T&I Services	Garteiser, Claire	Staff	28/04/2014	07/05/2014
T&I Services	Gouchtchina, Galina	Staff	28/04/2014	07/05/2014
T&I Services	Lacey, Roslyn	Staff	28/04/2014	07/05/2014
T&I Services	Liapina, Ekaterina	Staff	28/04/2014	07/05/2014
T&I Services	Liegio, Paulo	Staff	28/04/2014	07/05/2014
T&I Services	Mullova, Ludmila	Staff	28/04/2014	07/05/2014
T&I Services	Noble, Ross	Staff	28/04/2014	07/05/2014
T&I Services	Oeyen, Camila	Staff	28/04/2014	07/05/2014
T&I Services	Orlando, Marc	Staff	28/04/2014	07/05/2014
T&I Services	Piccione Thomas, Georgina	Staff	28/04/2014	07/05/2014
T&I Services	Radetskaya, Maria	Staff	28/04/2014	07/05/2014
T&I Services	Rosenbrand, Irina	Staff	28/04/2014	07/05/2014
T&I Services	Speziali, Maria Laura	Staff	28/04/2014	07/05/2014
T&I Services	Tanguy, Philippe	Staff	28/04/2014	07/05/2014

www.ingramcontent.com/pod-product-compliance
Lightning Source LLC
Chambersburg PA
CBHW082058210326
41521CB00033B/2579